Deprivation and School Progress

Schools Council Research and Development Project
in Compensatory Education

Studies of Infant School Children

1. DEPRIVATION AND SCHOOL PROGRESS

Maurice Chazan
Alice Laing
Theo Cox
Susan Jackson
Gwyneth Lloyd

Basil Blackwell·Oxford

SB 3739 £30 · 6·77

Set by Preface Ltd, Salisbury
and printed in Great Britain
by Lowe & Brydone Ltd, Thetford

Contents

List of Tables

List of Figures

Preface

In November, 1967, the Schools Council gave its financial support to a Research and Development project in Compensatory Education, based in the Department of Education of the University College of Swansea. The project, which is concerned with children of infant school age in selected areas in England and Wales, has three main aims:

1. to provide screening techniques so that children in need of compensatory education may be identified as soon as possible after school entry;
2. to make longitudinal studies of infant school children in 'deprived areas', with particular reference to their response to schooling and their emotional development;
3. to develop language materials which may be used to help culturally deprived children at the infant school stage.

This volume is the first of a series of three, all related to the second of the above aims. It presents the results of a broad survey of over 700 infant school children in urban areas, a study of a sample of children in a rural area, and investigations into the views of both teachers and parents on approaches to teaching in the infant school, home-school contact, and the use of services. The second volume — 'Deprivation and Development' — presents two investigations in depth of sub-samples from the main sample surveyed here; and third book, entitled 'Deprivation and the Bilingual Child', is concerned with the effects of material and cultural deprivation upon the linguistic development (in both Welsh and English), adjustment to the school situation and educational attainments of Welsh-speaking infant school children.

The research team would like to acknowledge the help received from the following and to express its thanks to them:

The Schools Council for their financial support of the project and the officers of the Council for their help and co-operation throughout the whole period of the study.

The Directors of Education of the Local Education Authorities involved in the project for their co-operation with it and their permission to work in selected schools, and members of their staffs for help in the selection of the sample.

The School Medical Officers and their staff for allowing access to the school medical records, and for their active co-operation in the process of obtaining the relevant medical data.

The headteachers and classteachers of the project schools who gave their time and effort to provide a large amount of information on the children and the schools, who were most helpful and co-operative over arrangements for the testing of children in schools and who, in many cases, provided the use of their schools as a base during the periods of the home visiting.

The headteachers of those Swansea infant schools outside the research project who allowed access to their children for the purpose of trying out tests for inclusion in the final attainment survey and co-operated fully in the necessary arrangements.

The parents selected for interview who gave up considerable time for the interviews and who made the collection of home background information both possible and pleasant.

The children in the project for their active co-operation in the administration of the test programme.

The late Professor F. W. Warburton, of the Department of Education, Manchester University, and Mr. J. Valentine, Lecturer in the Department of Psychology, Bedford College, University of London, who acted as Statistical Consultants to the project.

Dr. K. Holt, of the University of London Institute of Child Health, who acted as Medical Consultant to the project.

Mrs. M. Stacey, Senior Lecturer in Sociology, University College of Swansea, who acted as Sociological Consultant to the project.

The late Aneurin Williams for his help in the construction and administering of some of the research instruments, and Mrs. P. Davies for her help in the preparation and analysis of the data.

The secretarial staff of the Schools Council project, Mrs. E. Wimmers, Miss C. Emmanuel, Mrs. D. James, Mrs. S. Williams, Mrs. J. Corte, Miss S. Hay, Mrs. M. Morgan, Mrs. E. Graham, Mrs. J. Kalton and Miss S. Bramwich who carried out the considerable amount of clerical work involved in constructing, analysing and presenting these studies.

The staff of the Department of Computation Services, University College of Swansea, for their help in the preparation for, and computer analysis of the data; in particular, Mrs. M. Viner and Mrs. P. Evans for writing the necessary computer programmes.

Mrs. P. J. Syrett and Mrs. T. Brissenden, and the students in the Diploma in Educational Psychology and the Diploma in Special Education courses at the University College of Swansea, during the year 1970–1971 (in particular, Mrs. L. Harris), for their assistance in administering and scoring the final attainment and ability tests in the research programme.

The National Foundation for Educational Research, for making available its experimental Basic Mathematics Test.

PART ONE — BACKGROUND

1 Introduction

During the past two decades a variety of official reports and research studies, particularly in the United States of America but also in other countries, have testified to the growing concern for children whose educational progress is impeded by environmental handicaps such as poverty, membership of a minority group, or a background offering little security or stimulation. On the premise that the handicaps of these children, usually referred to as 'culturally deprived' or 'socially disadvantaged', can be removed or remedied by social and educational action, compensatory programmes on a wide scale have been put into operation in the United States of America, designed to improve education from the pre-school to the high-school level (Passow, 1972).

There has been an awareness, too, in Great Britain of the needs of deprived children. Research studies such as those carried out by Floud, Halsey and Martin (1957), Fraser (1959), Wiseman (1964) and Douglas (1964) have not only established that children from the lower social classes tend to make much less progress at school than children from 'middle-class' homes, but have thrown light also on the specific environmental variables which are of importance in school achievement. The series of educational reports, too, published mainly by the Central Advisory Council for Education since the early 1950s (Early Leaving Report, 1954; Crowther Report, 1959 and 1960; Robbins Report, 1963 and 1964) has also highlighted the effects of home background on a child's school career. It was, however, particularly the Newsom Report (1963), dealing with the education of pupils aged 13 to 16 years of average and less than average ability, and the Plowden Report (1967), on primary education, which focussed attention on the more seriously deprived children who are handicapped by a combination of adverse environmental circumstances. The Plowden Report strongly recommended that schools in grossly deprived areas (termed 'educational priority areas' in the Report) should be given special help and extra resources so that they could supply an environment to compensate for the deprivation suffered by the pupils in these schools.

Action on a limited scale has followed the challenge set up by these reports and by the American example. Money has been allocated by the government for improving old and inadequate school buildings and for giving an extra allowance to teachers in schools designated as facing exceptional difficulties. In addition to local authorities' own efforts, there has been a national Urban Aid programme, concentrating on the provision of new nursery classes and schools and on improving the social services in areas of greatest need. In a number of areas, Community Development programmes, which include among their aims help for the deprived section of the community, have been started.

It has also been acknowledged that, in spite of the voluminous American literature, much more needs to be known about the effects of deprivation on children in the context of social conditions in this country, and consequently a number of research projects have been established in recent years to study more precisely how deprivation affects children's development and school progress and to suggest possible remedies. At the pre-school level, an action-research project was started in 1968 by the National Foundation for Educational Research, with the aim of introducing and evaluating a compensatory programme for language and perceptual stimulation for disadvantaged children attending nursery schools. In the same year, a wide-ranging Educational Priority Areas Project was set up by the Social Science Research Council in conjunction with the Department of Education and Science, to experiment with various forms of action to help deprived children and to make recommendations for appropriate educational and social policy (Halsey, 1972). In November 1967, the Schools Council, which had previously set up a working party to consider the problems of secondary school children suffering from social handicaps (Schools Council, 1970), established a Research and Development Project in Compensatory Education in the Department of Education of the University College of Swansea, which had the main aims of devising techniques to identify disadvantaged children at the infant school stage, studying

3

the problems of deprived infant school children, and producing materials to help their language development.

The emphasis placed on the infant school age group by the Schools Council project at Swansea, the work of which will be discussed in this book and its companion publications, was not intended to detract from the importance which has been increasingly attached to the pre-school years, nor indeed to suggest that useful measures to help deprived children can be put into operation only at a particular stage of school life. There were three main reasons for choosing infant school children as the focus of the investigations carried out. First, as a research project of this kind has only a limited period within which to complete its work, it was thought more useful to concentrate on a narrow age-range than to deal with a wide age-span. Second, very little work has previously been carried out on the needs and problems of disadvantaged infant school children, and yet the educational and social progress made by children during their stay in the infant school seems crucial to their later progress and achievement: in present conditions, low attainments at the age of 7 years may well mean educational retardation throughout a child's school career (Morris, 1966). Third, samples of children at the infant school stage were much more accessible than younger children (most of whom would not have started school) and could be studied in the context of their school as well as their home environment.

ORGANIZATION AND SCOPE OF PROJECT

To carry out the three main aims previously mentioned, the project was organized into four units: (i) the Identification Techniques Unit; (ii) the Programme Development Unit; (iii) the Unit for the Study of Emotional Development and Response to Schooling; and (iv) the Welsh Language Unit.

The *Identification Techniques Unit* has been concerned to provide simple screening techniques facilitating early identification of children in need of special help at the infant school stage. The Unit is publishing, for the use of teachers, devices which will enable schools to assess as accurately as possible which children need to be compensated for the deficiencies in their environment (Swansea Evaluation Profiles: Infant Schools).

The *Programme Development Unit* was set up to devise materials which might be of use to teachers in their work with deprived children. In view of the evidence indicating that these children tend to show considerable deficits in their language development, the resources of the unit have been devoted to producing a handbook for teachers containing suggestions for fostering language development in the first year of the infant school. (Language Development and the Disadvantaged Child.)

The main aims of the *Unit for the Study of Emotional Development and Response to Schooling* were as follows:

(i) to examine the effects of material and cultural deprivation on the educational, social and emotional development of infant school children;

(ii) to study the aims, methods and facilities of, and problems facing, a sample of schools serving children from 'deprived' backgrounds, and to compare these problems with those met within schools serving children from 'settled working-class' and 'middle-class' backgrounds; and

(iii) to liaise with the Programme Development Unit in the development of compensatory language materials based on the information gained from these studies and from discussions with teachers.

The aims of the fourth unit, the *Welsh Language Unit*, were related to those of the Unit for the Study of Emotional Development and Response to Schooling, but were particularly concerned with the effects of material and cultural deprivation upon the linguistic development, adjustment to the school situation and educational attainments of Welsh-speaking infant school children. The work of this unit is fully reported in 'Studies of Infant School Children 3 – Deprivation and the Bilingual Child' (Lloyd, to be published).

Although the project was concerned with the infant school period it seemed of value, at the outset, to investigate what effect material and cultural deprivation might have had on the children who made up the project sample, before they entered the infant school. Accordingly, a selected sample of the children who were living in 'deprived areas' was compared with a control group of children who were living in relatively advantaged localities in regard to:

1. the extent to which the parents were providing experiences which might be considered as helpful to the children in their subsequent adjustment to school;
2. the extent to which the children were showing behavioural disturbance of different types in the view of the mothers, before going to the infant school.

The findings of this study have been reported in a separate publication (Chazan, Laing and Jackson, 1971).

LONGITUDINAL STUDIES

The present volume reports on (i) a broad survey of a sample of infant school children in urban areas over a three-year period; (ii) a more detailed study of a small rural sample; and (iii) investigations into the views of headteachers, class teachers and parents on approaches to teaching in the infant school, contact between home and school and the use of services. The main aim of these studies was to throw light on the association between 'deprivation' and children's progress and adjustment at various stages during the infant school period.

As will be shown in Chapter 2, the concept of 'deprivation' is a complex one, and there is no clear-cut, homogeneous category of children who can be picked out as 'deprived', or who have definite and specific characteristics which are invariably associated with deprivation. Thus it is important in research studies such as those described in this volume to use criteria for deprivation which are as precise as possible, and to seek information about the children's home, school and neighbourhood environments at first-hand, through personal visits, supported by data from other sources. It is also desirable, particularly in the case of children at the infant school stage, to assess their development by personal contact on an individual basis rather than through reports alone, however systematically these may be obtained. With limited resources, however, it is practicable to gather such detailed information only if fairly small samples are involved. The project team, therefore, decided to make two studies in depth of children living in deprived areas, which would involve them in close contact with the children, as well as with the parents and teachers. These studies are reported in full in the companion volume, 'Deprivation and Development' (Chazan et al., to be published), but an outline of their scope will be given here.

Since little work has been carried out to show the effects of different levels of cultural and material deprivation on children's development *within* deprived areas, both of the intensive studies were concerned with comparisons between groups of children all living in deprived urban areas. The first study compared two groups of children, matched for age, sex, school and non-verbal intelligence but differentiated on the basis of the quality of the home background, one group being rated as highly deprived culturally and materially, the other as relatively advantaged. These children were studied mainly but not solely from the point of view of their language and conceptual development, since research to date has indicated that it is in these aspects of development in particular that disadvantaged children show deficiencies or limitations compared with children from more advantageous home backgrounds.

Since social and emotional adjustment has a considerable bearing on educational achievement, the second study focussed on a group of children, who, in their teachers' estimate, presented marked problems of emotional and social adjustment during their first year. The main aims of this study were to ascertain the extent and persistence of such problems, their relationship with variables in the home background, and the nature of the help and guidance needed by these children and their families. The problems presented by this group were highlighted by comparison with a control group of children living in similar areas but picked out as being particularly well adjusted in school.

Although these studies in depth allowed the research team to control variables in a way which would be difficult to achieve in a large-scale survey, it was decided that, in spite of the difficulties, a broader survey would also be carried out. Although this meant adopting less clear-cut indices of deprivation, it was considered to be of practical importance to study schools as whole units and to investigate the particular problems of a sample of urban schools serving catchment areas generally acknowledged to be 'deprived'. The selection of the sample and the aims of this part of the investigation are discussed in Chapter 3. Considerable difficulty was experienced by the research team in deciding on criteria for considering an area to be 'deprived', particularly as the team was anxious to include not only decaying inner-city areas, but also areas with new housing estates where there was perhaps relatively little material deprivation, but where problems arising out of cultural deprivation were well-known to the schools. Initially an attempt was made to devise an area index of cultural and material deprivation which might help to quantify the criteria for such deprivation, but it was finally considered that to arrive at a total score for an area by adding up indicators relating to deprivation was not scientifically justifiable. As will be seen in Chapter 3, it was decided that the local authorities concerned, being very familiar with the social problems of their schools, should be asked to nominate schools as representative of those serving different types of catchment area.

As very little attention has been given to problems arising out of the isolation, and often out of the restricted school provision, of rural areas, and since the project was based in Wales, which has a high proportion of small rural schools, it was considered desirable to include a sample of rural schools in the general study. It was not possible, however, to select this sample on the same basis as the urban sample, and so this part of the enquiry is presented separately.

Particular importance was attached by the research team to obtaining the views of the headteachers, class teachers and parents on the problems arising out of deprivation, their own felt needs, the use which they made of existing social and allied services, and the action they thought desirable to help them to overcome their difficul-

ties. Had resources permitted, a more comprehensive investigation would have been made of the teachers' attitudes and expectations, but it was possible to carry out only a limited enquiry into teachers' aims, methods and views on questions concerning compensatory education through personal interviews and written questionnaires. Even though restricted in scope, this part of the investigation was considered very valuable, especially as the teachers responded positively to the interviews. It also proved possible to interview a sample of 120 parents, representing a cross-section of parents of children drawn from the main sample, concerning their use of services and links with schools.

PLAN OF VOLUME

After a general consideration of the concept of deprivation in Chapter 2, a report on the urban survey will follow in Part Two of this book (Chapters 3 to 6). In Part Three (Chapters 7 to 10), the findings of the investigation in a rural area will be discussed, and in Part Four (Chapters 11 to 13) the information and opinions on teaching approaches, home-school contact and the use of services, gathered through visits to the schools as well as the homes of some of the children, will be presented. Chapter 14 provides a summary of the whole enquiry covered in this volume, with some consideration of its implications for action. The findings of the studies reported in this volume and in Volume 2, have also, where relevant, been incorporated in the aims and content of the language programme developed by the Programme Development Unit.

2 The Concept of Deprivation

In this book and the accompanying volumes, the effect of deprivation on infant school children will be considered from a variety of points of view. Although relatively little is known about the relationship between deprivation and progress and adjustment in school at the infant school stage, a great deal has already been written about the effects of environmental factors on children which is relevant to the work of the project described here. Because of its complexity, it will not be possible to survey this literature comprehensively and in detail. However, in addition to the references which will be made to previous work of relevance throughout the series, it will be useful, as a background to the account of the investigations given in the three volumes, to examine what is meant by deprivation and to highlight the main sources of deprivation which affect children, particularly in relation to their progress and social adjustment in the infant school.

As already mentioned in Chapter 1, the concept of deprivation is complex and difficult to define. The term is often used as if it referred to a unitary syndrome, but there are many different *kinds* of deprivation, and, although these are often inter-related and found in combination, it is important to distinguish between them. There are also different *degrees* of deprivation: for example, a child may suffer little or not at all if only *mildly* deprived of certain kinds of experience, but be considerably affected if *grossly* deprived of stimulation. The dictionary definition of 'deprivation' emphasises the idea of 'loss', but, as generally applied in the literature, the term suggests not only 'loss' but also a 'lack' of what is essential for adequate development, or a failure to satisfy basic needs. The concept of deprivation, indeed, is a relative one, implying as it does that some individuals lack what others have, and since individuals vary greatly in their views of what constitutes deprivation for themselves, it is never easy to determine what essential or desirable needs must be satisfied if adverse consequences are not to follow from a lack of satisfaction of these needs. Townsend (1970), for example, looks at deprivation not only from the point of view of a family's income but also takes into account their inability to satisfy needs which, while they may not be considered to be essential, are held to be important by most people in the community, such as holding a birthday party for children, or having a summer holiday away from home.

It is important, therefore, to keep in mind the wide range of individual differences which exist, and not to lose sight of the fact that children from affluent homes can be deprived, for example, of adequate parental affection and interest, while children from poverty-stricken homes can be given much love and even a sense of security from parents who show a warm concern for their welfare. Within areas considered, on a number of counts, to be deprived, there are always homes where the development of the children gives little cause for concern (Ferguson et al., 1971).

The extent to which deprivation – whether material, cultural or emotional – will adversely affect children's development is also influenced by such factors as the child's age, sex and genetic endowment. While there is no conclusive evidence that, if specific skills are not acquired at the normal time, they cannot be acquired later just as well or even better, it may be argued that, if learning does not take place at an early stage of readiness, the child is disadvantaged in comparison with his contemporaries and incurs a learning deficit which limits both his current and his future rate of development (Ausubel, 1966, 1967). For this reason, as well as others, emphasis has been put by many on compensating for environmental deficits at as early an age as possible (Hess and Bear, 1968; Robison, 1972).

There is considerable evidence to indicate that boys and girls differ in their ability to withstand adverse circumstances, such as malnutrition or illness; girls are less easily thrown off their growth curves by deprivation than boys, and the control of their growth is better stabilized (Tanner, 1961). Although the reasons for the increased vulnerability of boys are not fully understood, more boys than girls develop problems of educational backwardness or show behaviour disorders of some kind. Already by the age of seven, about 17 per cent of boys are in need of special help at school, as compared with about 11 per cent of girls (Davie et al., 1972).

The work of Skeels (1942) and Kirk (1958), among others, has shown that early action may provide some compensation for environmental deficiencies even in the case of the mentally retarded, but there is ample evidence to support the hypothesis that a child's genetic endowment may make it impossible for him to progress other than slowly, whatever is done to try to accelerate his rate of development. The still controversial question of the relative contribution made to a child's development by heredity and environment has received much attention in the literature, but cannot be discussed in detail here (for a comprehensive discussion of the issues involved, see the Harvard Educational Review, 1969). On the practical level, as Telford and Sawrey (1967) conclude, it is often impossible to differentiate between those individuals who function inadequately mainly because of a deprived environment and those who fail to learn because of an inherent lack of capacity, particularly as many children who do badly at school are handicapped both by genetically-determined limitations and by a deprived background. Jensen (1967), who discusses the problem of distinguishing cultural retardation from primary retardation with an essentially biological causation, suggests that deprivation particularly affects children whose measured intelligence quotients lie in the below average range. Curry (1962) also suggests that children with superior intellectual endowment are in a better position to overcome the effects of a deprived home environment than children with limited ability. However, at all levels of intelligence, it is difficult to assess the interaction between innate endowment and the environment, particularly as low ability, low attainment, poverty and a lack of stimulation are often found in combination (Stein and Susser, 1960; Chazan, 1964). It would be naive to suggest that, if there were no depriving conditions, problems of educational backwardness and retardation would cease to exist, but, in the light of the evidence of the importance of environmental influences on attainment, it is probable that many slow learning children would make better school progress if there were an improvement in the conditions in which they live. It can be suggested, therefore,

that even if the view is accepted that limited genetic endowment may prevent some children from benefiting fully from compensatory help, there are many children who are clearly underfunctioning and will respond to appropriate measures.

In view of the complex nature of the concept of deprivation, it is as well to avoid sweeping generalisations about deprived children or to suggest, as Frank Riessman (1962) does, that a well-defined portrait can be drawn of them. Apart from the other considerations already discussed, emphases differ from country to country. For example, in the American literature, references to deprived children relate mainly to children of minority racial groups; in Israel, the focus is on deprivation and disadvantage arising from the waves of immigration from the Orient rather than the West; and in Britain, it is the deprivation suffered by children of indigenous lower working-class families that has aroused most concern. Nevertheless, in spite of differences in emphasis and definition, research studies have provided much evidence about the effects of various kinds of deprivation on children and, as previously stated, have shown that these often closely interact. Thus while it is desirable to specify in what particular ways children may be considered to be deprived, both at home and school, it is also justifiable to look at deprivation from the point of view of certain reasonably well-defined 'educational priority' areas, where the interaction between a combination of handicaps is most clearly seen (Plowden Report, 1967).

Deprivation will, therefore, be considered in terms of *material* conditions at home, particularly family poverty, overcrowding and inadequate care, and also in the sense of a lack of *cultural* (particularly sensory and linguistic) stimulation. Children may also be *emotionally* deprived through being starved of affection, particularly if living in an incomplete family and if handicapped by the permanent absence of a parent; even in an unbroken home, they may receive little encouragement from their parents, and they may suffer some disadvantage as a result of being members of a large family. The deficits in their home life may be reinforced by a failure, on the part of the school system, to meet their educational needs or to improve their self-image in any way; and home and school may be set in a decaying neighbourhood which has earned the label of a deprived or depressed area. Although there is a considerable overlap between these various aspects of deprivation, they will, for the sake of convenience, be discussed separately below under the following headings:

1. Deprivation arising out of home conditions
   A. Material
   B. Cultural
   C. Emotional
2. Deprivation arising out of school conditions
3. Deprivation arising out of neighbourhood conditions.

1. DEPRIVATION ARISING OUT OF HOME CONDITIONS

A. Material deprivation

Material deprivation in the home may be considered from three main aspects: (i) poverty, (ii) bad housing conditions, and (iii) inadequate care.

(i) Poverty: Poverty is a relative rather than an absolute concept, and, because of the difficulties of assessing family income in relation to need, it has proved difficult to make accurate estimates of the extent and effects of poverty. There is, however, sufficient evidence to establish that even in the welfare state of Great Britain a great deal of poverty still exists. Abel-Smith and Townsend (1965), regarding those families as poor whose incomes did not exceed 140 per cent of their social security entitlement, estimated that over 14 per cent of the population were living in poverty. A report by the Ministry of Social Security in 1967 indicated that approximately one-and-a-quarter million children were living in impoverished conditions, as measured by reference to supplementary benefit rates. In 1971 the Child Poverty Action Group estimated that over two million children (one in six of all children) were living on or below the poverty line, pointing out, as the previous reports had done, that much poverty was found even in working families, the number of which had doubled since 1966 (Times Educational Supplement, 29 January, 1971). It is also of concern that, as the Ministry of Social Security Report (1967) showed, low-income families do not make full use of the benefits and services

available to them (see also Chapter 13 of this volume). A number of families are most reluctant to ask for state aid even when they are in need of it, with the result that the children in these families are unnecessarily deprived, as they are when parents who have a reasonable income do not budget wisely or spend frivolously.

Poverty usually means bad housing conditions (discussed below), a lack of suitable and adequate nutrition, low standards of hygiene in the home, and also strain and stress in the family. The child living in conditions of poverty may well feel insecure and develop a marked sense of inferiority. Harrington (1966), writing about over forty million American citizens in poverty, considers that to be impoverished is to be an internal alien, to grow up in a culture that is radically different from the one which dominates the society. Banks (1968) has stressed that poverty can make parents less willing to keep children on at school and can make it difficult for them to provide books, playthings or expeditions which help children to learn; furthermore, even when the parents are no longer poor, but have suffered poverty in the past, their former experiences may continue to influence their attitudes, values and aspirations. Holman (1970) stresses that the fathers of low income families are more likely to work overtime and therefore to spend less time with their children in conversation and play.

(ii) Bad housing conditions: In addition to poverty, homelessness and bad housing conditions can be regarded as major factors in the break-up of families and the causation of ill-health, strain and disharmony within the family, with consequent adverse effects on children's progress and adjustment in school. Low-standard accommodation and overcrowding mean a lack of privacy for the child and unsatisfactory facilities for study at home, particularly disadvantageous in the case of older children with academic aspirations. The development of younger children will be especially affected by restrictions and frustrations enforced by inadequate space for play and free activity both within and outside the home (Hunt, 1966). Harmonious relationships between the different members of the family will not be helped by their having to live in the closest proximity, and fatigue may well result from the children having to share bedrooms or even the same bed.

Such bad housing conditions affect a considerable number of children. According to Greve (1970), as many as 40 per cent of the population of England and Wales live in inadequate housing, with approximately five-and-a-half million people in slums. Davie et al. (1972) estimated that about 15 per cent of 7-year-old children were living in overcrowded conditions at home, the incidence of overcrowding being particularly high in the North of England and Scotland.

(iii) Inadequate care: In recent years, the general standard of children's health and cleanliness has greatly improved, as evidenced by the faster rate of growth and by the reduction in the number of physical defects found at school medical inspections (Plowden Report, Appendix 2, Vol. 2, 1967). Nevertheless, there are still a considerable number of children whose nutrition is inadequate or who suffer from some other form of neglect or physical deprivation (Wilson, 1970).

Although the factors which control physiological growth are manifold and although children have considerable recuperative powers (Tanner, 1961), malnutrition and illness during childhood can have a delaying effect on the physical development of the child, perhaps with consequent educational retardation.

Physical deficiencies such as poor vision, impaired hearing and dental decay are particularly common in low-income families (Bloom et al., 1965). Phillips et al. (1972) found a much greater incidence of such conditions as impetigo, lice and scabies in children attending schools in the deprived inner areas of a large city in Britain than in schools serving mainly working-class families in the suburbs. They also found, in a study of 56 grossly socially handicapped families, that the boys (aged 6−7 and 10−11 years) in this sample had more physical disabilities than did boys in control groups with lesser degrees of social handicap: their weight was significantly lower, visual and auditory impairments were more common, and illnesses more frequent. Most of the children who needed spectacles did not wear them, and, as Asher (1967) has also established, it would seem that children in deprived areas are less likely than others to receive treatment for physical defects, even those of a serious nature.

B. Cultural deprivation

Although the term 'culturally deprived' is often used to refer to children living in materially disadvantaged homes, it is useful to make a distinction between material and cultural deprivation, since many children whose material needs are adequately catered for are deprived of sensory and linguistic stimulation. It is important, however, not to equate being 'culturally deprived' with being 'culturally different', and much confusion has arisen because of a failure to differentiate between these concepts. A child's home background, while being different in life-style from that of the dominant culture, may still have much to offer him; and degrees of cultural deprivation, in terms of sensory or linguistic stimulation, may be found in homes of different social levels.

Objections to using the concepts of 'cultural deprivation' and 'linguistic deprivation', as well as to that of 'compensatory education' to remedy such deprivation, have been raised by several writers (Bernstein, 1970; Wilkerson, 1970) in that these terms seem to emphasize deficits in the family and the child, and to direct attention away from the failure of the school system to meet the needs of children who should be regarded as culturally different rather than deprived. While it may be agreed that labelling children or their families is unsatisfactory even if sometimes unavoidable, and that radical changes need to be made in the school system, it does seem useful to highlight what is lacking, from the developmental view, in the child's home background as well as in school conditions, since the deficits are well documented and are usually remediable, at least to some extent, by appropriate social and educational action. This is not to imply any criticism of parents, or denigration of particular life-styles, but merely to stress that it is desirable to look at factors in the child's total environment − at home, at school, and in the neighbourhood − if appropriate action on a comprehensive scale is to be taken.

Cultural deprivation will be discussed below under the main headings of sensory deprivation, linguistic deprivation and lack of parental interest in the child's education. These three kinds of deprivation, which are often inter-linked, will be found most often in homes where the parents themselves have had a limited education, and will be exacerbated in large families, especially where conditions of material hardship exist.

Clearly the ability of the parents to provide stimulation at home for their children will be related to their own educational background, which will also affect their attitudes to the education of their children as well as their ability to understand what the schools are trying to achieve (Plowden Report, Vol. 2, Appendix 3, 1967). Both Douglas (1964) and Davie et al. (1972) found that the parents' education had an important effect on children's progress, especially in reading, even when allowance is made for other factors.

Membership of a large family, of course, brings its own joys and pleasures, but the evidence suggests that culturally deprived children who belong to large families are especially disadvantaged, cognitively and educationally. Independent of social class, a negative correlation has been found between family size and measured intelligence (Lenz, 1927; Robbins, 1948; Scottish Council for Research in Education, 1949); and Nisbet (1953) and Fraser (1959) have shown that children from large families tend to do less well in educational attainment. It has been suggested, in explanation, that children from larger families receive neither the quantity nor the quality of verbal stimulation from adults which members of smaller families get (Sarason and Gladwin, 1958; Telford and Sawrey, 1967).

Douglas (1964) confirms the association between family size and measured ability found in previous enquiries, and draws attention to the particular disadvantages of children in large families in the manual working classes. His results suggested that, whereas in the middle classes it is only the child from a family containing four or more children who is educationally handicapped, in the lower-income groups the children are progressively handicapped with every increase in family size. In lower working class families the mother tends to give less personal care to her children as her family grows larger; problems of overcrowding become more serious, with children having to share their beds with siblings or even adults; and the amount spent on food for each member of the family falls as families increase in size. As a result of inadequate care and nutrition, children in the larger families in the lower socio-economic groups are less well-developed physically than children from more advantageous backgrounds (Tanner, 1961). As previously stated, statistics relating to poverty show that a very high proportion of children are involved, and there is a direct relationship between size of family and risk of poverty (Coates and Silburn, 1967). Both the problem families studied by Wilson (1962) and those investigated by Philp (1963) contained a large number of children, the size of family exacerbating the hardship caused by very low incomes.

With specific relevance to infant school children, recent analyses by Davie et al. (1972) of the data obtained from a national survey have reinforced previous general findings: even when allowance has been made for other variables such as age and social class, the effect of family size upon reading attainment as well as social adjustment — and, to a lesser extent, on progress in number — is shown to be very marked at age seven.

(i) Sensory deprivation: From extensive work with the blind, the deaf and some groups of physically handicapped children, much is now known about the effects of being deprived of the use of the senses of sight, hearing or touch. More is also being discovered about the effects on non-handicapped children of being starved of varied sensory experience. The importance of adequate sense-organ stimulation *in the early years of life* has been emphasized by Hebb (1949; 1966), who suggests that 'the sensory stimulations of the early environment are necessary for the maintenance of some neural structures, which would otherwise degenerate, and for the occurrence of learning which is essential for normal adult behaviour' (1966, p. 147).

Harvey (1966) and Denenberg (1966) have hypothesized that *exposure to diversity of experience* in early childhood is extremely important, and that a lack of variation in stimulation may have adverse consequences in later life. A monotonous environment, which may be found in the homes of all socio-economic levels but is particularly prevalent in those of lower-income families, can be a form of sensory deprivation. Many children live in dull, unstimulating neighbourhoods (such as a considerable number of our new housing estates) where there is little beauty or variety in the environment, and also in homes where there is a dearth of toys, books and stimulating experiences, considered by Moore (1968) to be vital for the child's cognitive development even at the age of 2½ years.

It is probably as a result of this lack of adequate sensory stimulation that children from homes of low socio-economic status enter school with relatively less well developed visual and auditory discrimination abilities which may retard their learning to read (Jensen, 1966, 1967). For example, as Cynthia Deutsch (1964) points out, children brought up in very noisy environments with little sustained speech stimulation are likely to be deficient in the discrimination and recognition of speech sounds and to be relatively inattentive to auditory stimuli. Denenberg (1966) makes the interesting suggestion that intense or even stressful stimulation during infancy can have beneficial effects for the developing organism, and it is to be hoped that further work will throw more light on this. Much more research, indeed, needs to be carried out on the effects of sensory deprivation in the early years of childhood and on the types of stimulation most appropriate at this stage, but there is sufficient evidence to indicate that, as Hunt (1966) states, 'early experience may be even more important for the perceptual, cognitive and intellective functions than it is for the emotional and temperamental functions' (p. 250). Hunt further suggests that we should emphasize the *sensory* aspects of child development instead of giving so much attention to its *motor* aspects, and that it is important that very young children should have a variety of things to listen to and to look at.

(ii) Linguistic deprivation: As many writers have stressed, the development of language is central to the emergence of cognitive skills. Although a good deal of language is used without much thought and although a certain amount of thinking can take place without language (Vygotsky, 1939; Carroll, 1964) — deaf children, for example, are able to perform some intellectual tasks as well as hearing children without having acquired language — most thinking skills depend upon language, without which a child's past experience cannot be adequately conserved.

Many factors affect the growth of speech and language in the child, and it should be remembered that children in homes of all social levels can be deprived of adequate language experience because of such factors as lack of contact with the mother, poor speech models, an unsatisfactory emotional atmosphere in the home, or an over-close relationship with a twin. However, children from lower working-class families are particularly handicapped by their linguistic background, as Bernstein (1960, 1961, 1965) has shown in his studies of the relationship between social class and language structure. He suggests that children from extreme social groups in societies are exposed from an early age to distinct and separate patterns of learning before their formal education begins. These patterns become more and more reinforced as the child develops, though the environmental influences on the child become increasingly complex. Whereas the middle-class family typically exposes the child to a 'formal' or 'elaborate' mode of language, with a rich and varied structure and syntax, and considers verbal explanations to be important in controlling expressions of feeling, the speech patterns of the lower working class are characterized by the rigidity of the syntax and the limited and restricted nature of sentence organization. The lower working class child becomes sensitive only to this 'public' or 'restricted' code of language, and grows up in a family environment where action is more important than explanation.

According to Bernstein's thesis, there is no serious clash between the school and the middle class child, who is well prepared for the language structure used by his teachers and behaves appropriately in a wide range of social circumstances. In the case of the lower working class child, however, there may be a lack of communication between teacher and pupil, since each is using a different language, and with large classes effective education is impossible. More recent work by Bernstein and his colleagues has given further support to the hypothesis that different implicit theories of learning in the home may conflict with the theories of learning held by the school, and thus give rise to major sources of discontinuity between home and school (Bernstein and Henderson, 1969).

Other writers have also stressed the verbal impoverishment of many children from poor home backgrounds. Riessman (1962) has stated that deprived children use a great many words with some degree of precision, but these are not the words needed for school. Martin Deutsch (1963, 1964, 1965) stresses that the verbal deficiencies of the child from the culturally deprived family are most striking when he is faced with highly structured tasks, and has suggested verbal enrichment techniques which take advantage of the child's freer flow of language in more unstructured situations. He has found that deprived children are able to verbalize more freely when they are encouraged to talk about some *action* they have *seen*. Templin (1957) and Loban (1963, 1965) have found that from the pre-school years, culturally deprived children are relatively retarded in size of vocabulary, sentence length and use of grammatical structure, the gap widening as the child grows older (Deutsch, 1965). Bereiter and Engelmann (1966) go so far as to assert that there is justification for treating cultural deprivation as synonymous with language deprivation, and, even if this is an extreme view, there is sufficient evidence to suggest that language enrichment should be one of the main aims of any compensatory programme for culturally deprived children.

For a further discussion of linguistic deprivation see, in particular, Chapter 3 in Volume 2 of this series.

(iii) Lack of parental interest in child's education: Even in homes where there is no lack of emotional warmth, the child can suffer because of a lack of parental encouragement and interest in education. Douglas (1964) has shown how important this variable is in school achievement. He found, for example, that the highest average scores (on tests of intelligence, vocabulary and scholastic attainment) were made in the primary school by the children whose parents were the most interested in their education and the lowest scores by those whose parents were the least concerned. This was partly due to the social class effect, middle class parents taking more interest in their children's progress than manual working-class parents, but the relationship between test scores and parental attitude persisted within each social class. Even when the effects of such variables as standard of home , size of family and academic record of the school were removed statistically, the 'advantage of the child with interested parents is somewhat reduced but still considerable'. Lack of parental encouragement was particularly evident in the case of children from large families, especially those in the manual working classes.

The importance of parental attitudes was con-firmed by the studies carried out for the Plowden Committee (Vol. 2, 1967). The National Survey of Parental Attitudes and Circumstances found that fewer manual working-class parents took an active interest in their children's schooling than did parents of higher socio-economic groups, and that relatively few working-class fathers played a significant part in their children's education. However, in spite of this connection between parental attitudes and home circumstances, the survey suggested that parental attitudes were more important for school progress than parental circumstances and social class. In a recent study of the relationship between various environmental factors and school achievement in a sample of 489 pupils in top primary classes in Middlesex, Miller (1972) also found that parental interest was a more important factor than social class: children who gained most from their educational opportunities tended strongly to come from homes where the children's curiosity and academic aspirations were supported and encouraged by their parents, and where the children perceived harmony between the values of their home and those of the school.

C. Emotional deprivation

Although emotional deprivation can be experienced by children living in good material conditions, and, conversely, children living even in extreme poverty may receive a good deal of warmth and affection (Lewis, 1954; Wilson, 1962), there is a tendency for a higher incidence of emotional deprivation to be found in low-income families. For example, the National Child Development Study (Pringle et al., 1966) of 7-year-old children showed that there were many more children living in atypical family situations (that is, situations where children were not living with both natural parents) in the lower income groups than in the higher income group. In all, nearly 8 per cent of the national sample of children studied were not living with both natural parents at the age of seven years, by which time a marked association already existed between broken homes and reading attainment.

Emotional deprivation may take a variety of forms, but, in particular, children may be regarded as emotionally deprived when they lack a consistent mother-figure, when the family is fatherless, and when warmth and affection are missing in the family, even when both parents are present. Emotional deprivation may also be experienced, in some form, by the only child who has little companionship from other children at home, but attention will be focussed here on the effects of maternal and paternal deprivation, in the widest sense of these terms.

(i) Maternal deprivation: Bowlby's early work (1952) drew attention to the possible long-term effects of separation from the mother in early childhood, suggesting that such separation could lead to emotional maladjustment, delinquency, educational problems, and even psychopathic behaviour. Later studies, including those by Bowlby himself and his colleagues (Bowlby et al., 1956) have refined the concept of maternal deprivation. Ainsworth (1962) emphasized that distinctions should be maintained between (a) *insufficiency* of interaction implicit in deprivation; (b) *distortion* in the character of the interaction, without respect to its quantity; and (c) the *discontinuity* of relations brought about through separation. Even without separation, a child can be greatly affected by the mother's failure to accept him, or if she shows attitudes of hostility, over-indulgence, or repressive control. Rejection by the mother, which can be shown in a variety of ways, is a form of severe deprivation for the child, who is likely to react by showing emotional or behavioural disturbance.

With regard to *separation* as such from the mother, it would seem that this is not inevitably followed by adverse effects either of a short-term or a long-term nature, and important variables affecting the outcome of such separation include the age of the child, the quality of the mother-child relationship before the separation, and the nature and extent of the separation experience. There is a need to look at the child's other interpersonal relationships as well as his relationship with his mother. However, prolonged and traumatic separation can impair development. Ainsworth (1962), reviewing the evidence, concluded that damage to a child's personality was likely to occur when separation began before two years of age and continued for as long as three years. Rutter (1972) also accepts that, in addition to the short-term distress shown by many children separated from their mothers on admission to hospital or a residential nursery, long-term emotional effects

may sometimes follow from multiple separation experiences and institutional care in early childhood. Nevertheless, on the grounds that 'material deprivation' covers such a wide range of different experiences that it no longer serves a useful purpose, he advocates that the term should no longer be used. However, while it can be agreed that the concept needs to be considered in its many aspects, there seems to be insufficient reason for not continuing to use 'maternal deprivation' as a global concept which includes a variety of different forms of deprivation of the affection and care of the mother.

(ii) Absence of the father: The effects of the absence of the father from the home have not been studied as fully as the effects of maternal deprivation, but the importance of the role of the father in the child's development is being increasingly recognised. Both the status and the self-image of the child depend to a very large extent on the father's occupational and social status, and the child in the fatherless family can be considered as severely deprived, both in the sense of often lacking a masculine model with which to identify and in the sense of often living in conditions of severe long-term material hardship, insecurity and emotional strain (Wynn, 1964). In the Plowden National Survey (1967) 56 per cent of the fatherless families had an income of £12.10.0 or less compared with 7 per cent of the families with two parents. Wynn (1964) estimated that there were over half-a-million fatherless families in Great Britain, including 785,000 dependent children, and Davie et al. (1972) found that nearly 3 per cent of a national sample of approximately 14,000 seven-year-olds were living in households with no male head.

Marsden (1969) has also highlighted the hardships of unmarried, separated, divorced and widowed mothers and their children. He found that the majority of the children did badly at school, and that the children's lack of success was related not only to the lowering of aspirations on the part of both mothers and children, but to the children being marked off from their schoolmates in a host of small ways. These included not having clothes for parties, not being able to go to cinema matinees or the swimming bath, and not being able to join groups where a uniform was required. At school, financial demands could not be met: the children had problems in getting the full range of clothes for PE, sport and science. They could not go on school trips, and even cookery expenses created difficulties. The unmarried mother and her child were in particularly acute need. Crellin et al. (1971), who studied 679 illegitimate children in Britain, also found that, at seven years of age, they tended to be socially disadvantaged, doing badly at school, and showing a high incidence of maladjustment. As Wimperis (1960) and Davis (1964) have observed, not only does the fatherless illegitimate child suffer the psychological consequences of the lack of a father from birth, but he is also penalized by a stigma and by legal and social disabilities with further damage to his self-image.

Affectional deprivation can also be suffered by the child when the mother or father is absent from home for long periods because of the nature of their employment or because of hospitalization or imprisonment. To an extent, furthermore, there is emotional deprivation when the father, even though living at home, withdraws himself so completely from the family that for all practical purposes he can be regarded as absent.

The above discussion on maternal and paternal deprivation has shown that the atmosphere of the home greatly influences the child's development and school progress. Cervantes (1965) suggests that the emotional climate of the family is an important differentiating factor, within lower income groups, when children who respond to schooling well in spite of their disadvantages are compared with others from a similar socio-economic background who fail scholastically. He compared two matched groups, each of 150 youths from lower-class families, one group having dropped out of school early and the other being in the process of successfully completing their high school education, and found great differences between the 'graduates' and the 'dropouts' in respect of the harmony and happiness of the home. On this basis, he asserts that school success or failure can be reliably predicted, in the case of children of average ability, by an analysis of interpersonal relationship in the family. Miller (1972) also found that children who gain least from their education tend strongly to come from homes where the parents are punitive and autocratic, making their children feel inferior through unfavourable comparisons with others, and where parents are over-protective without encouraging their children to feel that they are readily accessible to them.

2. DEPRIVATION ARISING FROM SCHOOL CONDITIONS

Although the disadvantages of children who are materially and culturally deprived stem basically from the home background factors already discussed, school factors may also contribute to their poor response to schooling. Conditions at school which amount to deprivation for the child include inadequate school buildings and amenities, a failure to provide appropriate stimulation, a lack of continuity in the teaching, and a lack of satisfactory relationships with other children.

The effects of deprivation at school are not clearly established: the interaction between school and home influences is a complex one, and investigations to date do not show a clear or consistent picture of their interrelationship. The importance of good school conditions in school achievement and later success in life has been stressed by Himmelweit and Swift (1969) and Douglas (1970). However, in the U.S.A. the Coleman Report (1966) concluded that school factors were of relatively modest importance in educational achievement as compared with home factors; and in Britain, the Plowden Report (Appendices 3 and 4, Vol. 2, 1967) also considered factors in the home to be much more important in producing educational disadvantage than those in the neighbourhood or school (for a discussion of the role of the school in educational achievement, see, for example, Wiseman, 1968; Morrison and McIntyre, 1971; Kelsall and Kelsall, 1971).

(i) Inadequate buildings and amenities: Much good work is done even in schools with very poor buildings and amenities, but unsatisfactory working conditions in school tend to lead to a lowering of morale and of achievement among both teachers and pupils. Not all schools in deprived areas are old and sub-standard, but at the secondary level, the Newsom Report (1963) found that 79 per cent of the schools in slum areas surveyed by the Committee had buildings and amenities which were seriously inadequate. The conditions of some primary schools, especially those in 'educational priority areas', are graphically

described in the Plowden Report (Vol. 1, 1967), which draws attention to the grim buildings, the lack of green playing spaces, the discomfort of the classrooms, and the restrictions on activity which have to be suffered by many schools, particularly those in 'deprived areas'. That children with deprived home backgrounds also tend to go to schools with poor amenities has been affirmed, too, by Sexton (1961), who, investigating how the age of schools and their facilities were related to family income in different school catchment areas in Detroit, concluded that with few exceptions the schools serving upper-income families had much better facilities than others.

(ii) Lack of appropriate stimulation: Several writers have suggested that children from deprived home backgrounds are likely to settle into school less well than those from homes which have adequately prepared them for the demands of school. Inappropriateness both in the kinds of experiences offered in school and in teachers' attitudes may contribute to the unsettledness of these children. The culturally deprived child may well be ambivalent towards the culture of the school which is so different from his own, and there may often be discrimination, albeit unintentional, in the classroom against underprivileged children, whose potential is often underestimated (Riessman, 1962; Goodacre 1968).

The aims and methods of teaching culturally deprived children are still a matter for controversy, but it has to be acknowledged that, although the aims of teaching these children may not differ widely from general educational aims, the initial approaches to them may need to be different from those appropriate for children from more advantageous backgrounds. In addition to the provision of extra help, particularly in their language development, it is important that teachers start off from the basis of the children's own experience and make real contact with them through an understanding of the milieu in which they live. However, it is equally important, once the child has adjusted to the school situation, that his experience is not too narrowly restricted and that he is helped to gain an understanding of the wider world outside his own (for discussions of the problems involved in teaching disadvantaged children see, for example, Blank and Solomon, 1969 and Cox and Waite, 1970).

(iii) Lack of continuity in teaching: In view of the difficulties met with in teaching in schools having a large proportion of deprived children, it is not surprising that teachers are not attracted to posts in these schools and that, even if they do accept such posts, they do not stay for long. In addition, this lack of continuity in teaching in schools in deprived areas is exacerbated by the high rate of turnover of the pupils themselves in deprived areas (Phillips et al., 1972), although a high rate of mobility is not confined to lower class families (Pringle et al., 1966). Particularly at the secondary school stage, there is a higher rate of staying away from school for various reasons, including truancy, among children of unskilled workers than among those with fathers in professional occupations (Tyerman, 1968).

(iv) Lack of satisfactory relationships with other children: Although younger children, including those at the infant stage, derive much pleasure from contact with other children, it may be said that they are particularly dependent on adults for emotional satisfaction as well as intellectual stimulation. It is at the junior school stage that relationships with contemporaries outside the home become increasingly important to children, and at this period, and for the subsequent school years, the child who fails to find acceptance in the eyes of the class group — the 'isolate', 'neglectee' or 'rejectee' — will almost certainly be disturbed about this (Evans, 1962). Children who come from socially handicapped families may, as previously mentioned, find themselves isolated from the group because of a lack of cleanliness or because they are unable to find money to join in group activities.

3. DEPRIVATION ARISING FROM CONDITIONS IN THE NEIGHBOURHOOD

Inner urban areas: Socially disadvantaged families are widely distributed and are to be found in a variety of areas. Nevertheless, they tend to congregate in certain districts, which have become labelled as 'deprived' or 'depressed' areas. In particular, some inner areas of big cities have presented gross social problems, for example the Crown Street area of Liverpool (Mays, 1962), the Sparkbrook district in Birmingham (Rex and Moore,

1966) and the St. Ann's district in Nottingham (Coates and Silburn, 1967). The Plowden Report (1967) highlighted the educational and social problems of children living in such areas, and recommended a policy of 'positive discrimination' to bring special help to these children. Holman (1970), while not suggesting that socially deprived families are to be found only in the inner areas of certain conurbations, lists the physical and social characteristics of these areas as follows:

(i) location in the inner urban area – the 'twilight zone'
(ii) a relatively high number of immigrants
(iii) much old, decaying property with over-crowding and a lack of basic amenities
(iv) above-average proportion of unskilled and semi-skilled workers
(v) above-average proportion of families receiving State aid
(vi) comparatively large number of fatherless families
(vii) lack of play space and recreational facilities
(viii) poorer health than in general population
(ix) high incidence of child neglect, poor school attendance, truancy and delinquency
(x) inadequate social services.

Conditions such as these are not found equally in different regions of this country. Educational facilities and social services are generally better, for example, in the south of England than in the north (Taylor and Ayres, 1969; Blackstone, 1971).

Although the identification of social deprivation by area is a crude one, and although the Plowden idea of positive discrimination for certain areas has been criticized on the grounds that it does not provide an efficient policy for distributing resources equitably to those poor families living outside the educational priority areas, deprived areas are very much a social reality, and in undoubted need of extra help.

Housing estates: The decaying districts of the big city are not the only ones which can be considered deprived. New housing estates, too, may present their own kind of social problems. Some have been established with very few social amenities, and lack both recreational and cultural facilities as well as ready access to shops and services, difficulties exacerbated by the high cost of transport to town centres. Difficulties may also arise from living in blocks of flats, where young children are often severely restricted in their activities both indoors and out of doors (Yudkin, 1967; Chazan et al., 1971).

Nor, in spite of the generally good amenities of homes on council estates, can it be assumed that children enjoy satisfactory living conditions in these homes: Davie et al. (1972), for example, found that the children of council house tenants were living in conditions of overcrowding comparable with those living in privately rented accommodation.

Rural isolation: As mentioned in Chapter 1, the particular needs of children in rural areas have received relatively little attention; yet many families living in rural areas may be considered as deprived because of their isolation and perhaps also because of the lack of essential household amenities. The children from such families may go to very small schools where they meet and play with few children of their own age, and where facilities may be extremely limited (Gittins Report, 1967).

Not everyone who lives in an area generally considered deprived considers himself to be disadvantaged. In the deprived area of St. Ann's in Nottingham, for example, nearly one-half of 176 people interviewed were not dissatisfied with the area as a place to live in (Coates and Silburn, 1967), and it is well known that many families are not necessarily happier if moved to better housing conditions in a district which they find strange and lonely (Young and Willmott, 1957). However, children living in deprived areas are likely to be directly affected by the lack of recreational facilities and the inadequacy of the social services. There is little evidence to show that areas with the greatest need are adequately provided with, for example, pre-school play groups, adventure playgrounds, youth clubs or social workers (Holman, 1970), although the Urban Aid programme is helping to fill some gaps. Further, children in deprived areas are affected not only by the physical conditions which surround them but also by attitudes of mind and types of behaviour which stem from the patterns of living in the neighbourhood. As they grow older, the children's attitudes are shaped in many cases not so much by the home as by the outlook and values of their contemporaries in the neighbourhood and by the code of conduct and opinion accepted in the teenage club and coffee bar (Wiseman, 1964). In socially disadvantaged areas, where life at home may offer little scope, stimulation or satisfaction, the adolescent may become attracted to the delinquent or deviant groups which tend to flourish in these districts (Shaw and McKay, 1942; Morris, 1957; Miller, 1966).

SUMMARY (CONCEPT OF DEPRIVATION)

Children may be deprived in a variety of ways. At home, they may lack essentials because of poverty, bad housing conditions or parental neglect; they may not be given the stimulation and encouragement which is necessary for the development of potential to the full; and they may be without the warmth and affection which is requisite for emotional growth. In school, they may, because of inadequate amenities or unsuitable teaching, be denied opportunities for appropriate learning experiences. In the neighbourhood, they may be deprived of basic facilities for play, recreation and cultural stimulation.

In assessing the effects of deprivation on children, many variables have to be taken into account, and it is important to consider the different kinds and degrees of deprivation from which children can suffer. However, while deprivation cannot be thought of as a unitary concept, it is important, in view of the interaction between the different sources of deprivation, to look also at the effects of various kinds of deficit found in combination.

PART TWO — SCHOOL PROGRESS AND ADJUSTMENT IN URBAN AREAS

3 The Sample and its Background

A. SAMPLE

As stated in Chapter 1, two of the aims of the Response to Schooling and Emotional Development Units were as follows:

(i) to examine the effects of material and cultural deprivation on the educational, social and emotional development of infant school children;

(ii) to study the aims, methods and facilities of, and problems facing, schools serving children from 'deprived' backgrounds and to compare these problems with those found in schools serving children from more favourable backgrounds.

The present section will be mainly concerned with findings related to the first of the above aims. Findings concerning the second aim will be fully discussed in Part Four (Chapters 11 and 12).

As stated in the previous chapter, it was decided to carry out a general study of children in schools serving 'deprived' areas, the focus of which was to be on the school and its catchment area. A fairly broad interpretation of the concept of deprivation was adopted in which schools serving council housing estates, both pre-war and modern, characterized by social and educational problems, were to be included, as well as schools serving more obviously deprived inner city areas presenting adverse features such as a high incidence of low income families, poor housing and limited linguistic background.

To serve as controls to these 'deprived' area schools, other schools serving areas not considered deprived were selected. These comprised schools serving predominantly 'middle-class' catchment areas and those serving mainly 'settled working-class' areas. The latter schools were included because it was considered important to avoid comparing only the groups representing the two extremes on the social class continuum i.e. 'middle-class' and 'lower working-class' ('deprived' area) schools. Thus the main focus of this general study was intended to be on the comparison of the schools serving 'deprived' areas with those serving 'non-deprived' areas, but the structure of the control group enabled additional comparisons to be made where this was considered appropriate, i.e. between the 'deprived' area schools and the 'middle-class' and 'settled working-class' area schools considered separately, or between the two latter groups of schools themselves. (See the introductory note to Chapter 4, page 55.)

In designating schools as serving 'middle-class', 'settled working-class' or 'deprived' areas respectively, it was recognized that social class is a relatively crude, global index and that there is some overlap, particularly between adjacent social groupings, in terms of material and cultural factors associated with social class. For example, in a survey of parental attitudes to education carried out for the Plowden Committee (1967), it was found that such attitudes were not entirely correlated with the social class status of the parents. Significant proportions of parents with very positive attitudes toward their children's education and future were found at all social class levels. Only about one quarter of the variation in such parental attitudes was attributable to social class indices (parents' occupations, material circumstances and education).

In the light of the requirements outlined above the sample of children in this general study was drawn from schools in three urban areas, Swansea, Cardiff and London. In each of these areas the LEA involved (two in the case of London) was asked, initially, to select four non-denominational infant-only schools serving catchment areas which they regarded as 'deprived' (bearing in mind the broad interpretation of deprivation described above), and four schools serving predominantly 'middle-class' (MC) and 'settled working-class' (SWC) areas. Since the children from the latter schools were serving as controls to the children from the Deprived Area (DA) schools for purposes of comparison, these schools will be referred to as the Control Area (CA) schools. The LEAs were asked not to include schools containing relatively high percentages of immigrant children, since the intention was to focus on problems of deprivation as they affected an indigenous population of children. Thus, the sample was originally drawn from 24 urban schools, 8 in each area. It was subsequently decided to increase the number of children in the DA sample and this was achieved by bringing in two additional DA schools, one in Cardiff and one in London, making a total of 26 urban schools.

In one of the urban areas (London) it was not possible for the two LEAs concerned to provide infant-only schools exclusively, and the schools drawn from this area included three Junior Mixed and Infant schools (one MC and two SWC area schools) and six infant schools with nursery classes attached to them (one MC and five DA schools).

The sample comprised all of those children born between 1 September 1963 and 31 March 1964 who entered the above schools in September 1968 or shortly afterwards (except in one school with an intake of over 80 children, where pupils from only one of the two reception classes were included to ensure numbers more comparable with those in other schools). Thus, these children were in the 'rising five' age group at school entry and were to spend three full years in their infant schools. Letters were sent to the parents of all of

the children inviting their co-operation in the research project and, in response to these, only three parents refused to allow their child to be included in the sample. In January 1969, the total sample from the 26 schools consisted of 689 children distributed over the urban areas as shown in Table 1.

It will be seen from the table that Swansea contributed most children to the sample (approximately 39.9 per cent), followed by Cardiff (33.7 per cent) and London (26.4 per cent). The number of children in the CA schools (317) was roughly comparable with that in the DA schools (372).

B. PROCEDURE

As already stated, the general study of children in urban areas was designed to throw light on the association between deprivation and children's progress and adjustment. In addition, the educational setting in which the children developed was studied and, in this context, information was obtained on the amenities and material provision in the project schools, the aims, organization and staffing of the schools, and the extent and type of

Table 1

Distribution of total Urban sample of children
in January 1969

Urban area	School area type				Total
	Control area (CA) schools			Deprived area (DA) schools	
	MC	SWC	MC+SWC		
Cardiff	45	50	95	137	232
London	39	38	77	105	182
Swansea	59	86	145	130	275
Total	143	174	317	372	689

educational problems facing them. As this was a descriptive study rather than 'action research', no changes in the methods or organization of these schools were suggested, nor any special programmes introduced, but what was actually happening in the schools at the time was simply recorded.

The following information on the children and their schools was obtained.

(i) School areas

The project's social worker compiled census and other descriptive information for each school catchment area, designed to throw light on some important cultural and material features of the 'deprived' and 'control' areas and thus help to put the findings of the study in perspective. It should be remembered that the designation of a school area as 'deprived' was based on subjective judgements by the LEAs concerned. There is little doubt that the standards of judgement used varied from one authority to another, not only because they were relative to a given urban area (a school area considered to be 'deprived' in one city, for example, might not be regarded as such in another city), but also because they were probably based on different criteria. The use of relevant census data enabled the school areas from the three cities to be compared in terms of relatively objective criteria. These data are presented and discussed in Section C (i) of this chapter, but it can be mentioned here that, on the whole, the census data supported the designation of school area type by the LEAs concerned.

(ii) Schools' amenities

An Infant School Amenities Index, designed to provide an objective assessment of the school building, the school's general amenities and equipment and other educational provision, was devised and completed in respect of all of the sample schools (see Appendix III). It was completed by members of the research team on the basis of discussion with the headteacher and observation of the school itself. The index comprised 100 items which could be objectively assessed, each scored on a 1 or 0 point basis according to whether an adverse feature was present or not. The overall score was the total number of adverse pointers.

(iii) School organization and staffing

Factual information concerning the size, organization, staffing and other features of each school (e.g. pupil turnover and percentage free meals) was obtained by means of a questionnaire completed by the headteachers (see Headteachers' Questionnaire, Part One in Appendix III).

(iv) School aims, methods and problems

Separate questionnaires for the headteachers and class teachers were drawn up to give information about the teachers' aims and educational methods and materials, their contact with parents and the educational problems facing them (see Headteachers' Questionnaire, Part Two, and Class Teachers' Questionnaire, Part One in Appendix III). Both questionnaires were completed by a member of the research team in a personal interview with the teacher. The class teachers' questionnaire was completed in respect of teachers involved with the project children during their first school year. In addition, these class teachers were asked to complete a supplementary written questionnaire containing questions of a more factual type (see Class Teachers' Questionnaire, Part Two, Appendix III). The main presentation and discussion of the findings from these questionnaires will be found in Part Four of this report.

(v) The school progress and adjustment of the children

The study of the children's educational progress and social and emotional adjustment was carried out mainly on the basis of a series of specially designed questionnaires (School Schedules) completed by the teacher in respect of each child at selected stages in his infant school career. The first of these schedules was completed after the first ten days of the child's schooling and subsequent schedules were completed at the end of each term of the children's first school year (Schedules 2 to 4), and at the end of the second and third years of their infant school careers (Schedules 5 and 6). All of the schedules were prepared in consultation with headteachers and class teachers engaged on the project. With one or two exceptions, the items in the schedules were simply two, three or four point ratings, pre-coded for convenience in computer analysis, and were designed to be as objective as possible for a rating scale (see Appendix III for copies of each schedule).

In addition to the School Schedules, further information on the educational achievements of the project children was obtained by means of a battery of attainment and ability tests, both group and individually administered, most of which were standardized and published in this country. These were administered to the project sample (both urban and rural) during the children's final infant school term (i.e. summer term 1971). The purpose of giving these tests was to gather objective information on the children's school achievements which would complement the more subjective data derived from the teachers' ratings, and also to enable a comparison of the children's performance to be made with that of the wider populations of children on which the tests were standardized.

The tests used were as follows:

1. Burt Graded Word Reading Test (Re-arranged by Vernon)

Vernon's (1938) re-arrangement of Burt's original test comprises a series of single words, graded in reading difficulty, which the child reads aloud to the examiner until his ceiling level is reached. It assesses the child's ability to recognize and pronounce words rather than his understanding of them.

2. Neale Analysis of Reading Ability

This test devised by Neale (1958) was chosen as a complement to the Burt test because it assesses the child's reading ability in three respects, accuracy of reading (word recognition), comprehension, and rate of reading, using a series of illustrated stories, graded in reading difficulty. The child is, therefore, reading connected prose rather than single words and many would regard this as a more meaningful task than the word recognition type of test.

3. Daniels and Diack Graded Spelling Test

This test by Daniels and Diack (1958) comprises 40 words, mostly of regular phonic construction, graded in order of spelling difficulty. Each word is embedded in a sentence spoken by the examiner before it is written by the child. It was given in the present study as a group test.

4. NFER Basic Mathematics Test

This experimental test was devised by the NFER for the assessment of mathematical skills and concepts in top year infant school children (i.e. between 7 and 8 years of age). It tests basic concepts in the areas of shape, time, money, simple fractions and number in a series of problems, some of which require computational skill to answer. The test is very much geared to the approach to mathematics common in infants schools today, i.e. one based upon a wide range of activities such as measuring, counting, shopping, weighing, sorting, interpretation of simple graphs and solving 'real life' problems. Since the test has not been standardized, no norms are available. The test is orally administered by the examiner to a group of children and is untimed.

5. NFER Picture Test 'A' (undated)

Although it is not officially described as such, this test could be regarded as a measure of intelligence or reasoning, for it is composed of items typically used in paper and pencil intelligence tests. The test is based upon pictures of objects and has three sub-sections. In the first the child is required to identify the object which does not belong in a series of objects (e.g. a chair among cooking utensils). In the second section he must choose an object from a series of alternatives to complete a pattern of objects or a sequence of actions (e.g. posting a letter). The third section involves reasoning by analogy in which the child has to infer the relationship between two key objects and then find two other objects which are related in the same way (e.g. glove – hand and hat – head). Each section is preceded by a practice/ demonstration sequence presented by the examiner. The test is group administered, and each sub-section is strictly timed. The wording of test instructions was slightly modified in an attempt to ensure that they were fully understood by the children.

6. WISC Vocabulary Sub-Test

This sub-test forms part of the Wechsler Intelligence Scale for Children (Wechsler, 1949) which was designed for and standardized on children in the U.S.A. in the age range 5 to 15 years. It is designed to assess a child's vocabulary development in terms of how adequately he can define the meaning of each test word. Insofar as this test assesses both the child's knowledge of the meaning of a word and his ability to verbally express that meaning, it can usefully be described as an expressive vocabulary measure. The standard procedure for administering this test was followed, except that neutral supplementary questions (e.g. 'explain that a little more') were asked in all cases where the child's initial definition was inadequate.

(vi) Medical condition and health of the children

Selected information on the health and medical condition of the children was extracted from the standard school medical record cards. This information was not available for all of the children in the sample because it was not collected until late in the children's second school year, in order to allow time for school medical examinations to be carried out. By that time a number of children had transferred to other schools and their medical records had been forwarded to the receiving LEAs. There was also a very small number of children who had not attended for examination. Moreover, of the children on whom records were available (approximately 640), the information was not always complete.

C. BACKGROUND INFORMATION ON THE SAMPLE

(i) The school areas

Census data are available for quite small areas but these do not coincide with school catchment areas. Details of how this difficulty was resolved are given in Appendix I (p. 352), but it is important to stress at this point the limitations of the data thus obtained. The areas described in the tables of census data presented in this report are not, in most cases, school catchment areas but are areas larger than, but completely containing, the school catchment area. With two exceptions, figures are taken from data collected for the 1966 Census which surveyed only ten per cent of the population, which means that figures which represent only small percentages of the population are subject to fairly large errors. The only figure which could be given for the school catchment area itself is that for the average rateable value of private dwellings but this too is subject to inaccuracy (see

Appendix I, p. 352). Unfortunately, the catchment area of an infant school is too small for figures to be available for items such as unemployment and the number of families in receipt of supplementary benefits which could be regarded as indications of 'deprivation'.

Two tables were compiled on the basis of the 1966 Census data, the first covering population characteristics of the school areas or, more accurately, census areas containing the school areas and the second, housing and household amenities within the areas. These tables were too lengthy to be presented in this chapter but will be found in Appendix II (Tables A5 and A6). However, in order to give an overall picture of between-area differences in population or housing characteristics, Tables 2 and 3 following present the average figures for each of the three school area types (SWC, MC and DA) on each item. It must be stressed that these figures must be regarded very cautiously because the census areas on which they were based are not of equal size, although roughly comparable in this respect. Moreover, the figures for the individual school areas falling within each category of school area type sometimes show marked variation, which is masked by the process of taking averages. It would be advisable to consult the full tables in Appendix III in order to put into perspective generalizations about the school area types which are made in the following discussion.

The data in the above tables, crude though they may be, support the conclusion that, on the whole, the designation of these areas as 'middle-class', 'settled working-class' and 'deprived' seems satisfactory. The control school areas (MC + SWC) show a rather higher proportion of men in social classes I and II and a correspondingly lower proportion in social classes IV and V relative to the 'deprived areas'. They have a lower proportion of people with terminal education age less than 16, of people born outside the U.K. and of people moving *within* the local authority area, but a rather higher proportion of people moving into such areas. In terms of housing and amenities, the 'control areas' appear to enjoy certain advantages over the 'deprived areas', with a higher percentage of properties having exclusive use of all amenities, less overcrowding, less sharing of households, a higher proportion of owner occupiers and higher rateable values than in the 'deprived areas'. On the whole, a similar pattern obtains when the 'settled

Table 2

Population characteristics of the urban school areas:
average figures

	Control areas			Deprived areas
	MC (N=6)	SWC (N=6)	MC+SWC (N=12)	(N=14)
% people with terminal educational age less than 16	59.60	81.2	69.4	83.74
Age composition %				
0 - 4 years	6.7	7.7	7.1	10.6
0 - 14 years	13.3	16.9	15.1	18.2
65+	14.6	9.7	12.2	9.2
Number of children under 15 per household	0.61	0.83	0.72	0.96
% born outside U.K.	2.7	2.0	2.3	5.7
% moving within local authority in last year	4.1	4.5	4.3	10.5
% moving into local authority in last year	4.3	2.5	3.4	2.0
% economically active and retired men in social class				
I and II	35.7	14.5	25.1	9.0
III	50.1	60.1	55.1	52.1
IV and V	14.2	25.4	19.8	38.9

Note: The above figures are averages derived from the figures for the individual school areas.   See Appendix Table A5 for the full data for each school area.

working-class' areas alone are compared with the 'deprived areas', although the differences are less marked than in the former comparison.

The differences between the 'control' and 'deprived' school areas (and between the 'settled working-class' school areas and 'deprived areas') in terms of their mean levels on some of the above items were tested for statistical significance, but it should be stressed again that these means should be treated with some caution. These were items which, in particular, might be regarded as possible indications of relative cultural or material deprivation in an area and which showed a reasonably wide range of variation over the school areas. Table 4 shows the results of this analysis.

It will be seen from the table that on all but two of the 'adverse' items (terminal educational age less than 16 and percentage sharing households), the deprived school areas showed significantly higher mean percentages than the control school areas. In the comparison between the SWC school areas, considered separately, and the de-

Table 3

Housing characteristics of the urban school areas:
average figures

	Control areas			Deprived areas
	MC (N=6)	SWC (N=6)	MC+SWC (M=12)	(N=14)
% with exclusive use of all amenities	91.2	85.4	88.3	62.3
% 6+ households	6.0	9.3	7.6	10.8
% single person households	14.5	8.8	11.6	14.3
% owner occupied	72.5	46.6	59.6	22.2
% rented from council	12.6	41.7	27.1	52.2
Average number of people per room	0.53	0.62	0.58	0.70
% over $1\frac{1}{2}$ persons per room	0.15	0.87	0.51	3.5
1 to $1\frac{1}{2}$ persons per room	2.2	4.1	3.1	8.4
$\frac{1}{2}$ to 1 persons per room	56.8	67.1	62.0	64.1
less than 1 person per room	40.9	27.9	34.4	24.0
% sharing households	5.5	1.7	3.3	8.1
Average rateable value of private dwellings in pounds	98.8	72.0	85.4	60.9

N.B.   The above figures are averages derived from the figures for
the individual school areas.   See Appendix Table A6 for
the full data for each school area.

prived school areas, only two of the comparisons reached statistical significance (percentage males in social classes 4 and 5 and percentage homes without exclusive use of all amenities), although all of the differences were in the same direction (i.e. the deprived school areas had higher means).

Inspection of the full data (Tables A5 and A6 in Appendix II) indicates some qualifications to the above generalizations. In London the distinction between the 'middle-class area' and the

'settled working-class area' is not very clear from the point of view of either housing or population characteristics, although the difference between both of these and the 'deprived areas' is quite marked in almost every respect. In Cardiff and Swansea, the distinction between 'settled working-class' and 'deprived' areas is not always so clear, particularly in terms of housing characteristics. In the case of social class status, however, the 'deprived areas' have lower proportions of males in

Table 4

Significance tests of differences between control and deprived

school areas on selected items of census data

Item	CA vs DA school areas (N=26)		SWC vs DA school areas (N=20)	
	t	p (two-tail)	t	p (two-tail)
1. % males in 'lower working-class' (groups 4 and 5)	5.47	< 0.1%	3.22	<1.0%
2. % people with terminal educational age less than 16	1.86	N.S.	0.26	N.S.
3. % people moving within local authority area during last year	2.22	< 5.0%	1.51	N.S.
4. % homes without exclusive use of all amenities	3.52	< 1.0%	2.22	< 5.0%
5. % over-crowding (over $1\frac{1}{2}$ persons per room)	2.87	< 1.0%	1.77	N.S.
6. % sharing households	1.63	N.S.	1.80	N.S.

social classes I and II and, conversely, higher proportions in social clases IV and V. 'Deprived area' H, (Cardiff) appears to have comparable, and, in some cases, more favourable characteristics than the two 'settled working-class' areas in that city. It certainly seems true that this area is not as severely deprived as the other Cardiff 'deprived areas', but the census data for area H are somewhat distorted by the inclusion of an enumeration district only part of which is in the school area and whose characteristics are more favourable than those of the district which covers the majority of the school area. Swansea's 'deprived area' E also appears more like a 'settled working-class area'. Both of these atypical areas, while perhaps having little 'deprivation' as reflected by Census data, suffer from the more subtle difficulties of large, new housing estates, isolated from the town, where families are separated from relatives, friends and town amenities and there is often a lack of community feeling.

A description of the housing and general amenities which characterize each school area now follows and this is based upon direct observation of each area by the project's social worker.

Cardiff

'Control' school areas. Area A (MC) is a fairly old established area, almost entirely residential, but with some industry on the edge of the area. It contains most of the usual amenities including a clinic, library and parade of shops. There is a small park and a nursery about a mile from the school, which is itself about three and a half miles from the town centre.

Area B (MC) is partly older and partly modern residential area with a large open park with many recreational facilities. Shops and other facilities are a little way from the main residential area and there is no clinic or nursery within a mile of the school, which is two and a half miles from the town centre.

Area C (SWC) consists mainly of a well-established council estate towards the edge of the city. There is a park and some open space within the area and most amenities, though not a nursery.

Area D (SWC) is mainly an old established residential area but also contains part of a council estate. All the usual amenities are contained within the area, including a clinic, library and nursery. There is a park on the edge of the area, which is three miles from the town centre, but 'bus services are not very frequent.

'Deprived' school areas. Of the four 'deprived areas', three are mainly council estates, area H quite modern, area E established a little while and area F a mainly older estate. Area G contains some very early council housing but consists mainly of older, terraced houses. Area H is four and a half miles from the centre and many of the amenities of the area are at the far end of the estate. Area F is slightly nearer town and contains most amenities. Area G is one where there has been a large amount of demolition work in progress during the period of this research and it is bounded by industrial buildings. It has a good selection of shops, a park with a swimming pool just outside the area and is only one and a half miles from the town centre, with a frequent bus service. Area H, a new estate, has very few facilities, just a few shops and a public house. It is right on the edge of the city with open country nearby but has a very infrequent bus service into either the town or the nearest shopping centre. There is virtually no private building in the school area itself (census figures for this area include an enumeration district largely outside the school catchment area). There is no park or playspace on the estate, apart from that at the school, but there is a park on the edge of the area.

London

'Control' school areas. Areas A (MC) and B (MC) are both well-established residential areas of mostly private building. There are pleasant open spaces nearby, though much of the area is a little way from shops and other facilities. Only area A contains a nursery.

Areas C (SWC) and D (SWC) both contain a mixture of private and council housing and are again entirely residential areas with open spaces nearby. Apart from the slightly less expensive housing, they differ little from areas A and B. All four of these areas are in a borough well out from the centre of London with a train journey of about twenty minutes to the centre.

'Deprived' school areas. Areas E to I are all in what is often referred to as 'the East End'. Area E contains a fairly high proportion of council property, mainly tower blocks of flats or maisonettes, the remainder of the property being old, terraced houses, some waiting for demolition. Few houses have gardens and there is only one very small play area and very little open space. There is a parade of shops, a post office and a library, but the clinic and nearest underground station are both a little walk from the school.

Area F is a very 'colourful' area with narrow streets lined with shops displaying their merchandise, including much foreign food, on pavement stalls. There are many small tailoring firms and men can be seen pushing rails of dresses along the streets, which are often littered with scraps of coloured cloth. The housing is mainly large, tenement-type blocks of flats, looking dismal enough from the outside but often very well kept inside. This area has many of the most adverse ratings of housing in Table A6. There is a small park much used by mothers with toddlers.

Area G contains a mixture of council flats and maisonettes, large and small older terraced houses, tenement-type blocks of flats and buildings occupied by 'homeless families'. There are a few open spaces, some shops and a railway line running across the area.

Area H consists mainly of new council buildings: flats, maisonettes and a very few houses. There are also some older blocks of tenement flats and some terraced houses, a few of these bordering small park-like 'squares'. The area contains a main road parade of shops and most amenities.

Area I had much older large blocks of flats, some with stones inset labelling them 'mansions', but some of these have now been demolished. There are also large blocks of older council flats (some now being 'modernized') and some terraced houses opening straight onto busy streets. There is the inevitable railway line with small traders under the arches and also some larger industrial buildings. There are small shops within the area and a main shopping street with market stalls nearby. There is a small park on the edge of the area.

Gardens are very rare in any of these areas, and though some estates have play spaces for children, these are often monopolised by groups of older children and many open spaces bear notices warning 'no ball games'.

Swansea

'Control' school areas.   Areas A and B (MC) are on the popular western side of the city, both having easy access to large open spaces (park or beach). They are entirely well established residential areas, with shopping centres. Both areas have a wide variety of housing within their boundaries ranging from large houses standing in their own grounds (and often converted into flats) to small terraced houses or picturesque cottages. Area A is five miles from the town centre, Area B only two miles.

Areas C and D (SWC) are both old established areas with a good variety of shops and most amenities. Area C consists mainly of older, well-built terraced houses with a few council houses built on small sites that became available. It has few open spaces or large gardens. Area D has a variety of private houses of differing ages and types and an older council estate. Both are about two miles from the centre.

'Deprived' school areas.   Area E consists mainly of a large, fifteen to twenty year-old council estate with a fringe of private dwellings. It is on the edge of the town, over four miles from the centre and bordered by open country, from which wild ponies stray into the estate. It has a small parade of shops catering for immediate needs only.

Areas F and H are on the less popular eastern side of the city, both containing a mixture of older private dwellings and council houses. The council housing in area H includes some blocks of quite modern flats, while in area F it is mainly older terraced or semi-detached houses. There is a small park in area F and open hillside along the edge of both areas. There are only a few small shops in either area and few other facilities, particularly in area H. There is no nursery in either area, no doctor or dentist and the clinic is just outside area F. They are rather isolated areas, over 3 miles from

the town centre and separated from it by rather bleak open country and industrial sites.

The greater part of area G is one of the earliest developments of council housing in the city but there is also a small area of private property. It has commanding views of the sea, docks or industrial valley since it stands on hill overlooking the city. Originally this area had a high proportion of tenants from the slum clearance areas in the town centre, which has given it a reputation which it has still not quite shaken off fifty years later. There are parades of shops within and on the edge of the area, and it is not far from the town centre. There is a recreation ground on the estate and a nursery within half a mile.

Area I is again an old established area of mainly small terraced houses opening straight onto the street. It is on the edge of the industrial area and has a sprinkling of derelict houses, factories, railway arches, some poorly surfaced roads and patches of waste ground being used (unofficially) as tips. However, some of the houses have been modernized and brightly painted and council houses have been built on small empty sites. There are one or two magnificent chapels. On the edge of the area, higher up the hillside is a small private estate and a large park.

(ii) The schools

(a) Organization, staffing, and general information on the schools

Organization.   As already mentioned, the intention was to draw the sample exclusively from infants only schools but, in fact, three of the urban schools (one MC and two SWC area) were of the junior mixed and infants type. In the case of the latter schools, information for the present section was obtained which concerned their infant departments only.

All of the urban schools took in children at the beginning of the term in which they attained the age of five years or, in some cases, the term preceding that in which the children became five. Thus, the majority of infant starters in these schools were just five years old or 'rising five'. In some cases, schools allowed individual children to start school during the term in which they attained school age. Just under half of the schools (six CA and six DA) arranged for the new intake of children to start school on the same day and the remaining schools staggered the entry of the intake over periods ranging from a few days to three weeks in an attempt to maximize their resources to cope with the problem of settling young children into school. Ten of the schools (four CA and six DA) had more than one reception class for the intake of children and all but two of these allocated children to these classes in terms of their age. The two exceptions were a SWC area and a DA school which adopted a random method of allocation but with some consideration for children's family connections and friendships in the former school.

The majority of the schools (11 CA and 12 DA) allocated children to their infant classes on an age basis, either in onr or more year groups or in age groups spanning less than one year (e.g. by term of entry) or a combination of these groupings. One (DA) school had adopted a 'family' or 'vertical' grouping system of allocation and two schools (one SWC and one DA) combined this system with age grouping (e.g. by confining the 'family grouping' to the first two years of the infant school and putting the 'top year' infants together). It follows from this that the normal 'promotion' procedure (where applicable) for the schools in this sample was by age. One DA school headteacher, however, mentioned that if it were necessary to promote children to the 'top' infant class(es) in order to make room for new intakes, then this was done on the basis of school ability rather than age.

All of the CA schools and twelve of the DA schools allocated their teaching staff to the children on the basis of one teacher for each class who was responsible for all or most of its activities. Of these, 4 CA and 8 DA schools had some degree of teacher specialization in certain activities such as music and art. Of the two remaining DA schools, one was experimenting with the team teaching approach involving two classes. The other used an unusual system in which, with the exception of the reception class which had its own teacher, each teacher was responsible for a specific type of activity such as mathematics or house play and the children circulated around the various activity areas on a free choice basis (within certain limits). However, the school was divided into groups under the direction of a teacher for administrative purposes and also the teaching of reading was carried out on a systematic basis with children allocated to specified groups. The teachers took responsibility for each of the activity areas in turn.

Staffing: assistant teachers. The majority of assistant teachers were two year college trained but, in addition, there were thirteen graduates (one in a SWC and twelve in DA schools) of whom eight had received teacher training (two had full postgraduate teacher training, five had the ILEA induction course training and one had both forms of training), and the remainder had received no teacher training. Further, there were five unqualified and untrained teachers in the DA schools. In all, 13 out of the 70 trained teachers (18.6 per cent) in CA schools and 23 out of the 77 teachers (29.9 per cent) in DA schools had received no infant school training. Information obtained from an infant school amenities index specially devised for the present study and discussed in a later section in this chapter, showed that in ten of the DA schools as compared with three CA schools, the ratio of teachers in infant classes not infant trained was higher than one in four.

In general, the CA school teachers had longer total teaching experience than the DA school teachers, the mean length of such experience being approximately 13 years for the CA group (14.8 years in MC schools and 11.8 in SWC schools) and 9.2 years for the DA group. A similar difference emerged when the two groups of teachers were compared for mean length of infant school teaching experience, the figures being 10.7 years for the CA schools (12.2 years in MC schools and 8.9 years in SWC schools) and 7.2 years for the DA schools. Both of these differences were statistically significant (at the 5 per cent level) for the CA vs DA comparison but not the SWC vs DA comparison. In addition, three MC area, 2 SWC area teachers and 5 DA teachers had had nursery school teaching experience.

In addition to the full-time teachers, whose training and experience are described above, a number of full-time and part-time teachers (expressed in terms of equivalent number of full-time teachers) and included part-time non-class teacher training and experience. Also there were three pairs of part-time class teachers (two in CA schools and one in a DA school) who shared responsibility for an infant class, all but two of these teachers having teacher training.

Information was obtained on the teacher-pupil

Table 5

Average teacher-pupil ratio and average class size in CA and DA
schools during summer term 1969

	CA schools			DA schools
	MC	SWC	MC+SWC	
Average teacher-pupil ratio:	34.1	32.6	33.3	31.8
range of ratios	29.5 to 40.5	31.6 to 39.5	29.5 to 40.5	23 to 39.5
Average class size	36.8	34.9	35.8	33.6
range of class sizes	32 to 40.5	31.6 to 39.5	31.6 to 40.5	23 to 39.2

N.B.   Expressed in full, the above ratios should be prefixed by one
       i.e.   1:34.1 etc.

ratio on the first day of the summer term during the school year 1968/69. This was based on the number of full time and part time teachers (expressed in terms of equivalent number of full time teachers) and included part time non-class teachers, teachers joining the school for a new intake of children, and temporary staff. It did not include supply teachers, students awaiting entry to college or any other supernumary staff. The average size of each class on the same date was also calculated and this information, together with that on teacher-pupil ratio is presented in Table 5.

This table shows that the DA schools enjoyed a slightly more favourable pupil teacher ratio and average class size than the CA schools, at least during the school term in question ('t' tests carried out on the mean differences in average class size between the CA and DA schools and SWC and DA schools yielded non-significant results). According to a government report, Statistics of Education (DES, 1967a), the national average pupil-teacher ratio in infant classes, taking into account the full-time equivalent of part-time teachers, was 28.2.

On this basis, all 12 of the CA schools and 11 of the 14 DA schools had ratios above the national average. The same report quotes a national average of class size of 34 pupils. On this figure the mean class size in the CA schools was rather above the national average and that for the DA schools slightly below it.

Information on the turnover of teachers during each of the school years from September 1968 to July 1971 was obtained by expressing the number of teachers leaving each school during the school year as a percentage of the number on roll at the beginning of that year. It should be noticed that this figure does not take into account teachers who completed a school year before leaving. It may be, therefore, that the percentages underestimate the true turnover of teachers in some schools. The information is presented in Table 6.

It will be seen from this table that, on average, over the three year period under study there was a higher mean percentage teacher turnover in the DA schools than in the CA schools although the difference fell short of statistical significance. However, when the figures for the MC and SWC area schools are examined separately it will be seen that the average turnover in the MC schools is not far below that in the DA schools. Moreover, whilst the turnover in the DA schools is higher than that in the CA schools during the first two years studied, it is lower in the third year. It seems, therefore, that there is considerable fluctuation in teacher turnover in all three types of school from year to year. It may well be that the main reasons for teacher turnover differ according to the type of school area, and tentative supporting evidence for this view is presented in the following discussion.

In addition to the above information on staffing, which was obtained by means of a written questionnaire completed by the headteachers (Headteachers' Questionnaire, Part One), the headteachers were also asked to comment on any problems they had concerning staffing of assistant teachers during the personal interview with members of the project team carried out in order to complete the Headteachers' Questionnaire, Part Two. All but two of the CA school heads considered that they had no such problems and the problems mentioned by the remaining heads in that group concerned the need for an extra teacher during the summer term to help to cope with the new intake of children. The CA school heads tended to regard their teaching staffs as stable over time and well qualified. Quite often a substantial proportion of the teachers lived within the school area. The main reasons for staff leaving appeared to be promotion or retirement.

Five of the DA school heads considered that they had no teacher staffing problems but, in two cases, the school had only recently had its full quota of teachers so that the head's judgement was based on an improved staffing situation. The problems of staffing mentioned by the remaining DA school heads mainly concerned the supply,

Table 6

Average percentage teacher turnover in CA and DA schools, based on number of teachers leaving their schools during the school year

	CA schools						DA schools	
	MC		SWC		MC+SWC			
Number leaving	N	%	N	%	N	%	N	%
School year								
1968–69	1(36.5)	3	0(42)	0	1(78.5)	1	13(89.2)	15
1969–70	5(37.5)	13	2(43)	5	7(80.5)	9	14(86.9)	16
1970–71	6(42.0)	14	4(46)	9	10(88.0)	11	8(91.4)	9
Overall average 1968–71	12(116)	10	6(131)	5	18(247)	7	35(267.5)	13

Total numbers of teachers (full-time and part-time) on staff at beginning of school year shown in brackets.

The number of part-time teachers is expressed in terms of the equivalent number of full-time teachers.

33

turnover, training, background and experience of teachers. Five DA school heads mentioned the difficulty of attracting teachers to the area, mainly, in their view, because few staff wanted to live locally so that travel to school was costly and, in some cases, difficult as a result.

The problem of obtaining teachers for some of the DA schools was, in the opinion of the heads, reflected in the training and experience of the teachers appointed. Six DA schools had some staff who were not infant trained and only one of the heads concerned did not appear to regard this as a problem (2 CA schools also had such teachers on staff but the heads did not consider this to constitute a problem). In other DA schools difficulty arose from the proportions of teachers without full infant training. In one school, for example, there was a high proportion of teachers (often graduates) trained for infants school work by a short 'induction course' run by the ILEA. In three DA schools, Commonwealth teachers had been appointed and two of the heads felt that the different cultural and linguistic background of some of their teachers could create difficulties in the teaching situation.

The DA schools appear to find greater difficulty not only in appointing permanent members of staff but also in finding supply teachers. Three DA heads commented that supply teachers were either not available or were unsuitable in some respect, or would not stay for as long as they were needed. No CA school head commented on such difficulties.

Six of the DA school heads but only one CA head mentioned the difficulty of retaining staff, reflected in the relatively high turnover of teachers in the DA schools. The most rapid turnover appeared to be among the younger teachers and one DA school head in an LEA where there was, in general, a good supply of teachers, commented 'There is no waiting list of teachers for this school'. In such schools new appointments were often made of young teachers direct from colleges of education. However one DA school head whose staff comprised young, relatively inexperienced teachers did not regard this as a source of difficulty.

Two DA heads complained that they were never consulted about teaching staff appointments. One DA head considered that the LEA should be very careful to appoint suitable teachers

for 'deprived area' schools and that older infant school boys would benefit from having a male teacher because of their 'toughness' and their tendency to present behaviour problems.

Despite the above problems, the majority of the heads were satisfied with their teacher-pupil ratios which, in many cases, had recently improved. None of the DA heads regarded the number of their teachers as inadequate and it will be recalled that the mean pupil-teacher ratio was slightly lower in the DA than the CA schools.

In general, the judgements made by the head-teachers concerning problems related to staffing, seemed to be substantiated by the factual data, presented earlier in this section, obtained from the written questionnaire which they completed.

Staffing: headteachers. The majority of the urban school headteachers were two year trained and a small number had additional diplomas or certificates. Two of the DA heads were emergency trained. In terms of age range trained for there was little difference between the DA and CA heads, roughly three quarters in each case being trained for the infant or nursery/infant or infant/junior age range. On average, the CA heads were slightly more experienced as teachers, their mean years of teaching being 29.5 (29.2 for the MC heads and 29.8 for the SWC heads) as compared with 27.5 years for the DA heads, a negligible difference. However, the DA heads had, on average, slightly longer teaching experience in infant schools, the mean years of teaching experience being 19.4 years for the CA heads (17.5 years for the MC and 21.3 for the SWC heads) and 24.9 years for the DA heads (three of the DA heads had also had nursery school experience and this has been included).

On average, the DA heads had held their present posts for slightly longer than the CA heads with a mean of 7.2 years as compared with 6.3 years (5.9 years for MC heads and 6.7 years for SWC heads). This suggests that, in this sample of schools at least, the higher turnover of class teachers in the DA schools is not accompanied by a correspondingly higher turnover of headteachers (none of these differences reached statistical significance).

The headteachers were also asked to state whether they did any teaching in their present post and if so, how much. One head of a small DA school was also a full-time teacher and, of the remaining heads, only three did not teach at all. The majority of heads, therefore, engaged in some teaching, most of this with small groups of children (e.g. backward or, sometimes, more able readers), although most of the heads took over classes in the absence of staff members. The time spent by the heads in teaching varied greatly but, in terms of mean teaching time, there was virtually no difference between the two groups (6.8 hours weekly for the DA heads and approximately 6.6 hours for the CA heads).

Staffing: other school staff. The DA schools enjoyed a small advantage over the CA schools in the number of infant helpers attached to the school, either on a full or part-time basis (8.5 helpers in DA schools compared with 4.5 in CA schools), although these were found in only a minority of schools in either group. Such aides were available in only two of the three project urban areas. Information on the training of these helpers was not complete but it seemed that the majority had received no formal training for their work. In addition, all of those schools which had nursery classes attached (5 DA and 1 CA) had trained or untrained nursery assistants.

The Headteachers' Questionnaire, Part Two, completed by interview, contained a question concerning the functions of infant aides or helpers, where available, classified as follows:

(a) general care of children (e.g. dressing, toilet, etc.)
(b) general help in classroom (e.g. preparing materials)
(c) involvement in educational activities (e.g. listening to children reading).

All of the schools with infant helpers used them for the first two of the above functions. The use of helpers for the third function varied much more and tended to be rather limited and subject to certain reservations and qualifications. Three schools (two DA and one CA) apparently did not involve their helpers in educational activities at all (except that one head stated that she would allow an aide to help supervise children during school visits). In addition, two MC area heads stated specifically that aides would not be allowed to engage in any direct (formal) teaching of children and this was probably true of all schools. Of the

various possible educational functions of the infant helpers, the following were carried out in some of the DA schools: supervision and guidance of some group activities, particularly non-academic work such as art and craft, but also number activities (for example showing children how to use apparatus), telling stories to the children, making contact with parents, and, finally, simply talking to the children. In addition, in three DA schools aides were allowed to hear children read, although in one of these schools this only applied to the more fluent readers. In one MC area school the aide was allowed to hear children reading but only during 'free choice' activities.

The attitude of the heads who had infant helpers toward their role varied considerably, ranging from a fairly rigid insistence that they should have no involvement in the more directly educational activities, toward a more flexible view in which the boundary between teaching and ancillary roles was blurred. In one DA school, for example, the full-time aide, among other functions, heard children read, told them stories, played the piano for music and movement and directed their handwork. (In fact this particular aide was planning to go on to teacher training.) Some of the heads spoke very highly of the quality of the work done by their aides with children despite their frequent lack of formal training or qualifications.

Information obtained from the School Amenities Index showed that all of the schools, both CA and DA, in one of the urban areas had either full-time or part-time secretarial assistance but none of the schools in the other two areas had any such help.

General information. The Plowden Report (1967) suggested a list of possible criteria for identifying what it called 'educational priority areas', i.e. school areas of relative deprivation, where educational handicaps are reinforced by social handicaps. Data on some of these suggested criteria were presented earlier in this chapter in the section on census data, namely social class composition (proportion of semi-skilled and unskilled manual workers), overcrowding and sharing of dwellings, and family size. It will be recalled that, on these criteria, the areas served by the DA schools in the present sample appeared to be at a disadvantage in comparison with the CA school areas. In the case of social class composition (based on the father's occupation), information was available from school medical records concerning the children in the project sample and this is a useful complement to the census data for this characteristic.

Data on the occupation of fathers of the sample children were extracted from the school medical records. Unfortunately, however, complete data were not available for the whole sample, either because children had left by the time the records were consulted (during the children's second school year) and their records forwarded to the receiving LEA, or because information on the child's father's occupation was omitted from the record. Out of the 689 children in the urban sample at the end of the children's first term, this

information was available for 527 children. Difficulty was sometimes encountered in classifying the occupations in terms of the Registrar-General's (1966) ratings because of the inadequacy of the information recorded, so that the reliability of the data is in question. Because of the possible unreliability and the incompleteness of the data, no firm conclusions can be drawn from it, although it will serve to indicate approximately the likely distribution of the sample in terms of occupational status. The data are presented in Table 7.

The table shows that, subject to the reservations made above, approximately 40 per cent of the CA group fathers fall into the 'non-manual' category (social classes 1 and 2) and 20 per cent in the semi-skilled, unskilled (social classes 4 and 5)

Table 7

Occupational (Social Class) status of fathers of children
in CA and DA samples

Occupational grouping	CA Group						DA Group	
	MC		SWC		MC+SWC			
	N=92		N=135		N=227		N=300	
	n	%	n	%	n	%	n	%
1 and 2	36	40.4	11	8.5	47	21.5	10	3.6
3 non-manual	19	21.3	21	16.2	40	18.3	16	5.7
3 manual (and 4 non-manual)	26	29.2	60	46.2	86	39.3	145	51.8
4 and 5	8	9.0	35	26.9	43	19.6	86	30.7
Unemployed	0		3	2.3	3	1.4	23	8.2
* No father	(3)	–	(5)	–	(8)	–	(20)	–

χ^2 CA vs DA (4 d.f.) 72.72, p < 0.1% (two-tail)
    SWC vs DA (4 d.f.) 20.75, p < 0.1% (two-tail)

* Figures not included in percentages or χ^2 analysis.

36

and unemployed categories, as against approximately 9 per cent and 40 per cent respectively of the DA group fathers. The difference in the distributions between the SWC group fathers and the DA group fathers, particularly over the 'working-class' occupational range, although statistically highly significant, was not as marked as might have been predicted on the basis of the designation of the two types of area from which these fathers were drawn as 'settled working-class' and 'deprived'. A possible explanation of this lack of clear differentiation between the two groups may lie in the fact noted earlier in this chapter in the section on the census data that there were two 'deprived areas' in the DA sample which, in terms of population characteristics, including occupational status of the father, were virtually inter-changeable with the SWC areas in the same city. The inclusion of fathers from these two particular areas would, therefore, tend to blur the occupational distinction between the SWC and DA group fathers. The incompleteness of the data should be borne in mind here also, for it is possible that if data had been available for the whole sample the differentiation between the groups might have been clearer.

The table shows that within each group the occupations of the fathers were distributed over the entire range (except that no MC area fathers fell into the unemployed category). Thus, for example, approximately 29 per cent of the MC area fathers were classified as 3 manual or 4 non-manual. This wide spread of occupational levels suggests that the terms 'middle-class', 'settled working-class' and 'deprived' area should be regarded as only broadly applicable as far as fathers' occupations are concerned.

Information on another of the Plowden criteria of 'deprivation' (number of children), was also extracted from the school medical records and this is presented in Table 8. Again, however, data were not available for the whole sample.

The table shows that approximately 78 per cent

Table 8

Size of family (number of children) in the CA and DA samples

Family size	CA Group						DA Group	
	MC		SWC		MC+SWC			
	N=120		N=150		N=270		N=289	
	n	%	n	%	n	%	n	%
1 child	17	14.2	14	9.3	31	11.5	26	9.0
2 children	50	41.7	56	37.3	106	39.3	79	27.3
3 children	37	30.8	36	24.0	73	27.0	71	24.6
4 children	10	8.3	23	15.3	33	12.2	61	21.1
5+ children	6	5.0	21	14.1	27	10.0	52	18.0

χ^2 CA vs DA (1 d.f.) = 17.42, p < 0.1% (two-tail)
SWC vs DA (1 d.f.) = 3.55, N.S. (two-tail)

Note: For these analyses the first three categories and the last two categories respectively were combined.

of the CA children for whom data were available came from 'smaller' families of one to three children, and 22 per cent from 'larger' families of four children plus, whereas approximately 60 per cent of the DA children came from 'smaller' and 40 per cent from 'larger' families, this difference being statistically highly significant. However, the distribution of the SWC sub-group of the CA group was much closer to that of the DA group, the difference between them falling just short of significance. Insofar as there is a link between social class and family size, these results are in the expected direction. Further, to the extent that coming from a relatively large family can be regarded as an educational handicap, then the DA children suffered this disadvantage to a greater extent than the CA children. Evidence showing that families in the lower social class groups tend to be larger than those in higher social class groups and that children from larger families tend to be retarded in school attainment as compared with children from smaller families has come from several large scale research studies in this country, the most recent being the National Child Development Study (Davie et al., 1972).

An interesting adjunct to information about the size of a child's family is knowledge about his birth order position within that family. Research has shown that such position is a factor of educational and psychological importance. Later-born children within a family tend to be at a disadvantage educationally as compared with earlier born children. For example, the National Child Development Study (Davie et al., 1972) found, in a large scale survey of a national sample of seven-year-old children, that the difference between the first born and fourth or later born children in reading attainment is equivalent to sixteen months of reading age, this effect operating *in addition* to the effect of family size in terms of number of younger children in the family. The authors suggest that the birth order effect may be attributable in the main to the sharing of family resources (e.g. the amount of time spent by parents talking to or playing with children) which occurs with increasing numbers of siblings, although, other factors may operate, for example, the parents of larger families may tend to have a different set of attitudes and values from those of smaller families.

Table 9 shows the distribution of the CA and

DA samples in terms of the children's birth order. From this it will be seen that the proportion of first born children in the CA sample (39 per cent) is larger than that in the DA sample (approximately 29 per cent) and, conversely, the proportion of fourth or later born children is lower in the CA group (approximately 15 per cent) than in the DA group (approximately 24 per cent). However, the distinction between the SWC sub-group of the CA group and the DA group in this respect is much less marked. The difference between the two main groups in their distribution over the birth order scale was statistically significant, but that between the SWC sub-group and the DA group fell well short of significance. This result suggests that the DA group are at an educational disadvantage in terms of the birth order of the children.

A further criterion of 'deprivation' suggested by the Plowden Report was the receipt by families of supplements in cash or kind from the state, in particular, free school meals. Data on the percentages of children receiving free school meals during the first week in each term for each of the three school years under study were obtained in the Headteachers' Questionnaire, Part One, and are presented in Table 10.

The table shows that the DA schools have a considerably higher percentage of free school meal children consistently over each of the three school years, than the CA schools, which suggests that the areas served by the former schools are characterized by a higher proportion of needy families than the areas served by the CA schools. (The differences in means between the CA and DA, and SWC and DA schools were statistically significant.) According to a DES Report (1967a) the national average percentage of children eligible for free meals was 8.34. On this figure, the mean percentage of DA school children receiving free meals was over twice the national average during the weeks sampled in each school year, whereas that for the CA schools fell below this average during each year. However, it will be noticed that the SWC area schools had a mean percentage of free meal children above the national average in each school year.

By implication, the Plowden Report suggested that a relatively high turnover of pupils in a school was another possible indication of a deprived area. Information on pupil turnover was obtained for each of the three school years in question and the

Table 9

Position of child in family (birth order):

CA and DA samples

Child's position in family	CA group						DA group	
	MC		SWC		MC+SWC			
	N=129		N=156		N=285		N=316	
	n	%	n	%	n	%	n	%
First	59	45.7	52	33.3	111	39.0	93	29.5
Second	34	26.4	47	30.1	81	28.4	86	27.3
Third	27	20.9	22	14.1	49	17.2	61	19.4
Fourth	5	3.9	25	16.0	30	10.5	35	11.1
Fifth or later	4	3.1	10	6.5	14	4.9	41	12.7

χ^2 CA vs DA (1 d.f.) = 6.52, p < 2% (two-tail)

SWC vs DA (1 d.f.) = 0.08, N.S. (two-tail)

Note: For these analyses the first three and last two categories respectively were combined.

Table 10

Percentages of children in CA and DA samples receiving free school meals

School year		CA schools			DA schools
		MC	SWC	MC+SWC	
1968-69	mean	2.8	9.7	6.2	22.4
	range	0.0-6.2	3.1-23.5	0.0-23.5	9.3-37.3
1969-70	mean	2.9	11.2	7.0	21.7
	range	0.7-7.3	3.2-26.6	0.7-26.6	9.7-35.3
1970-71	mean	3.2	11.5	7.3	20.7
	range	0.7-6.0	1.9-26.8	0.7-26.8	8.8-36.9
1968-71 overall	mean	3.0	10.8	6.9	21.6
	range	0.0-7.3	1.9-26.8	0.0-26.8	8.8-37.3

Table 11

Percentage pupil turnover in CA and DA schools

School year	CA schools			DA schools
	MC	SWC	MC+SWC	
	%	%	%	%
1968-69 overall mean	3.8	7.2	5.5	9.3
range of school means	0.0-5.7	3.0-16.1	0.0-16.1	2.4-24.6
1969-70 overall mean	9.2	10.6	9.9	13.7 *
range of school means	2.3-11.5	6.3-18.6	2.3-18.6	7.2-67.3
1970-71 overall mean	9.0	8.2	8.6	13.6
range of school means	4.4-19.0	0.0-16.4	0.0-19.0	0.0-27.0
1968-71 Overall means	7.3	8.7	8.0	13.9
Range of school means	0.0-19.0	0.0-18.6	0.0-19.0	0.0-67.3

* Largely accounted for by one school where 67.3% of the pupils left due to slum clearance in the area.

mean percentages for this are presented in Table 11. These were obtained by expressing the number of pupils leaving during a school year as a percentage of the number of children on the school roll at the beginning of that year.

The table shows that pupil turnover in the DA schools is consistently higher than that in the CA schools, although not markedly so (the difference falling just short of statistical significance in the CA vs DA comparison and well below significance in the SWC vs DA comparison). The fact that the figures for the DA schools were not much higher is probably due to the nature of the sample, which by design, included a proportion of schools serving council housing estates as well as those serving deprived inner city areas, where movement due to rehousing would be more likely.

The higher turnover among DA pupils is reflected in the fact, reported later in this chapter (see page 53), that there is a proportionately higher loss of DA than CA children from the total urban sample over the infant school period. This suggests a relatively greater degree of family mobility in the DA sample although data from the 1966 census presented in Table 2 indicated that the greater mobility of the DA families was *within* the local authority boundaries rather than across them. The child's school record contains information on the number of addresses that the child has had to date and Table 12 presents this information. It will be seen that the DA children's families showed a higher mobility than those of the CA children, the proportion of families with two or more recorded addresses being nearly twice as great in the DA group as in the CA group, although it was not possible to say whether this was local mobility rather than movement over a wider area.

The outcome of the comparisons between the CA and DA schools on the above 'Plowden criterion' supports the conclusion, stated earlier in connection with the census data that, on the whole, the designation of the schools as serving 'control' (SWC and MC) and 'deprived' areas (DA) seems satisfactory. A similar conclusion could be

Table 12

Number of recorded addresses of CA and DA children

Number of addresses	CA group						DA group N=343	
	MC N=133		SWC N=162		MC+SWC N=295			
	n	%	n	%	n	%	n	%
1	111	83.5	148	91.4	259	87.8	265	77.3
2+	22	16.5	14	8.6	36	12.2	78	22.7

χ^2 CA vs DA (1 d.f.) = 11.29, p < 0.1% (two tail)

SWC vs DA (1 d.f.) = 13.75, p < 0.1% (two tail)

drawn from a study carried out by another unit of the present research project and reported by Ferguson et al. (1971). This study examined the distribution of various disadvantaging factors in the home background over a sample of infant school entrants, drawn from three types of school classified by the LEA's concerned as 'deprived', 'settled working-class' and 'advantaged' according to the nature of the catchment areas which they served. These factors were of the type suggested in the Plowden Report as characterizing educational priority areas. It was found that the three types of schools were broadly differentiated on these factors, in items of their incidence in the sample of children, although there were some anomalies. On the evidence from this and the present study it would seem that LEA's can, with a reasonable degree of accuracy, select schools serving 'deprived' areas i.e. those showing a relatively high proportion of children needing educational or other help because of disadvantaging home conditions.

(h) School buildings, amenities and equipment
As already mentioned, the amenities, facilities and some general conditions of each school were rated by means of a specially devised instrument, the Infant School Amenities Index. It will be recalled that this was scored on the basis of one point for each adverse pointer, so that the larger the score received by a school, the more unfavourable it was in respect of the features covered. The theoretical maximum score was 100 points but the highest score obtained in the present sample of schools was 57 points. Information on the total Index scores received by the CA and DA schools is presented in Table 13, which also shows the scores of each group on the various sub-sections of the index and the results of 't' tests of the significance of the differences between the pairs of means.

It will be seen from this table that, overall, the DA schools tended to have more adverse features than the CA schools, although the difference between the mean total scores fell short of statistical significance. Moreover, the DA schools also showed greater variability than the CA schools in their scores, as indicated by their wider score range and larger standard deviation. The same pattern of results applied to the comparison between the SWC area schools and the DA schools, the difference in mean, again, falling below significance. It is also interesting to note that, within the CA group of schools, the MC area schools were more adversely rated than the SWC schools and showed wider variation in their total scores.

The Index was divided into eight sections, each comprising a number of items (see Appendix III).

Table 13

Scores on the Infant School Amenities Index:
CA and DA samples

	CA schools			DA schools
	MC (N=6)	SWC (N=6)	MC+SWC (N=12)	(N=14)
A. School Building				
Range	0 – 2	0 – 3	0 – 3	0 – 5
Mean	1.00	1.50	1.25	1.71
s.d.	0.58	1.12	0.93	1.44
Value of 't' CA vs DA = 0.93, N.S.				
Value of 't' SWC vs DA = 0.31, N.S.				
B. Entrance and Circulation areas				
Range	0 – 2	0 – 2	0 – 2	0 – 5
Mean	1.50	0.83	1.16	2.29
s.d.	0.76	0.69	0.80	1.58
Value of 't' CA vs DA = 2.14, p < 5%				
Value of 't' SWC vs DA = 2.06, N.S.				
C. Provision of rooms				
Range	0 – 7	0 – 5	0 – 7	2 – 6
Mean	3.50	2.33	2.92	3.71
s.d.	2.22	1.89	2.14	1.39
Value of 't' CA vs DA = 1.10, N.S.				
Value of 't' SWC vs DA = 1.73, N.S.				
D. Toilets and Cloakrooms				
Range	0 – 5	0 – 6	0 – 6	0 – 6
Mean	2.50	2.00	2.25	2.93
s.d.	1.61	1.92	1.78	1.83
Value of 't' CA vs DA = 0.92, N.S.				
Value of 't' SWC vs DA = 0.97, N.S.				
E. Classroom Facilities				
Range	1 – 8	0 – 7	0 – 8	0 – 15
Mean	4.83	3.33	4.08	4.57
s.d.	2.67	2.69	2.78	4.45
Value of 't' CA vs DA = 0.32, N.S.				
Value of 't' SWC vs DA = 0.60, N.S.				
F. Provision of materials				
Range	1 – 4	0 – 2	0 – 4	0 – 7
Mean	2.33	1.17	1.75	3.36
s.d.	0.94	0.69	1.01	1.84
Value of 't' CA vs DA = 2.60, p < 2%				
Value of 't' SWC vs DA = 2.69, p < 2%				

Continued on next page

42

G. School surrounds				
Range	3 - 7	1 - 6	1 - 7	2 - 9
Mean	4.50	3.33	3.92	4.71
s.d.	1.50	1.70	1.71	1.79

Value of 't' CA vs DA = 1.11, N.S.
Value of 't' SWC vs DA = 1.52, N.S.

H. School conditions				
Range	2 - 8	4 - 6	2 - 8	3 -10
Mean	5.17	4.83	5.00	6.71
s.d.	1.86	0.90	1.47	1.75

Value of 't' CA vs DA = 2.57, p < 2%
Value of 't' SWC vs DA = 2.37, p < 5%

Total score on index				
Range	14-37	10-28	10-37	17-57
Mean	25.33	19.33	22.33	30.00
s.d.	8.18	6.80	8.10	11.75

Value of 't' CA vs DA = 1.73, N.S.
Value of 't' SWC vs DA = 1.89, N.S.

All probability levels in the table are two-tailed.

The table shows that on all of the sections, the DA school mean was higher i.e. more adverse, than that for the CA schools, significantly so in the case of section B (school entrance and circulation areas), section F (provision of school materials), and section H (general school conditions). Of the sectional comparisons between the SWC area schools only and the DA schools, two reached statistical significance (sections F and H) and one approached the 5 per cent significance level (section B).

With the exception of section C the range of variation of the sectional scores within the DA schools was greater than that within the CA schools. The same pattern as regards mean and range of variation in scores applied also to the comparison between the SWC area and DA schools. It will also be seen than, on all sections except section A, the MC school mean was higher than that of the SWC school mean but, in turn, the MC school means were lower than those of the DA schools (except for section E).

Inspection of the table shows that section E (classroom facilities), G (school surrounds) and H (school conditions) produced the highest mean scores for the groups of schools, so that the adverse conditions characterizing some of the schools were most pronounced in these particular aspects. For example, in terms of classroom conditions, six out of the twelve CA schools and six of the fourteen DA schools had no sink in the reception classroom(s), five CA and eight DA schools had no built-in storage space and six schools in each group lacked adequate play space in the reception classroom(s). Under the heading of school surrounds it was shown that six CA schools and eight DA schools had direct access to a busy road and relatively high proportions of the schools had no immediate access to a grassed area (4 CA and 7 DA schools), no covered play space (7 CA and 6 DA schools), and no climbing frame or slide (9 CA and 12 DA schools). Features of school conditions showing a relatively high incidence of adverse pointers included a pupil-teacher ratio above the national average (all twelve CA schools and 11 of the 14 DA schools), a ratio of teachers not infant trained greater than 1 in 4 (3 CA and 10 DA schools) and space in reception or 'top' infant classes less than the DES recommendation (5 CA and 7 DA schools).

In other sections of the Index, particular items stood out as showing relatively high proportions of schools with adverse pointers. For example, four out of the 12 CA schools were housed in pre-1914 buildings as compared with eight out of the 14 DA schools, 6 CA schools and 10 DA schools had no entrance hall, and 5 CA and 6 DA schools lacked a kitchen. A usable tape recorder was lacking in half of the CA schools and most (11) of the DA schools.

What emerged very clearly from inspection of the data was the reflection of LEA policy and priorities in the scores received by the schools on certain items of the Index. With one or two minor exceptions, all of the schools, both CA and DA, in one of the education authorities concerned had secretarial assistance and ancillary help (e.g. infant aides), a medical room and a capitation allowance above the national average. In contrast, all of the schools (again with one or two small exceptions) in the other LEAs lacked these facilities and services and had a capitation allowance below the national average.

In addition to the information obtained from the Index, the headteachers were asked, during the interview carried out in connection with the Headteachers' Questionnaire (Part Two), whether they had any problems concerning the school buildings and surrounds, the amenities, and the school equipment and materials. Of course, the fact that a head did not mention a problem in this context does not necessarily mean that one did not exist, for she may have referred to her most pressing difficulties only. This means that any strict comparison of the CA and DA groups in terms of number of problems mentioned would be very unreliable. The value of the headteacher's responses lay more in the light they threw on the kinds of problems they regarded as sufficiently serious to mention.

In general, there were no clear differences between the types of problem mentioned by the CA and DA heads, except that only DA heads reported vandalism on school premises and thefts of school equipment or materials. Two DA heads mentioned such acts of vandalism as removing tiles and lead piping from school buildings, removing lavatory fittings, breaking of windows, and leaving broken bottles in toilets. One DA head reported the theft of a tape recorder, record player and other equipment and materials from the school during a summer holiday.

Most of the problems mentioned were referred to by heads in both groups of schools. For example, two CA and five DA heads mentioned problems associated with outdoor toilets. A few heads in each group described such school building hazards as indoor stairs or outdoor hazards such as sloping playgrounds. Other problems mentioned included lack of storage space in school (2 CA and 2 DA), no sinks in classrooms (1 CA and 2 DA) and an inadequate capitation allowance (2 DA and 2 CA). One DA head expressed the need for extra allowances to be paid in 'deprived areas' in order to offset heavy wear and tear and also because so much has to be supplied to the children by way of books, musical equipment, constructional toys and table games (presumably to compensate them for lack of such provision in their homes).

(iii) The children

Background data on the children fell under the headings of general information, medical factors and parental co-operation.

General information

Age. As already stated, the children in the sample were chosen from within a fairly narrow age range, the seven month period from 1 September 1963 to 31 March 1964, so that the CA and DA samples were unlikely to differ very much in age. The children's ages in years and months were calculated on the basis of a fixed date, 1 June 1971 (in connection with the final school attainment survey) and the differences between the groups in age were tested for statistical significance. The results of this analysis are presented in Tables 14 and 15. It will be seen that the DA children were slightly older (approximately 0.40 months) than the CA children and this result was statistically significant, although from an educational or psychological viewpoint the age difference is negligible. The mean age difference between the SWC and DA children was in the same direction and slightly greater (0.66 months) but, again, for practical purposes this difference can be disregarded.

Sex. The composition of the sample in terms of sex is shown in Table 16. These figures were based on the sample as it stood on 1 January 1969 (total N = 689). It will be observed that in the CA schools, the boys slightly outnumber the girls due to the predominance of boys in the MC schools, whereas the reverse is true in the DA schools.

School attendance. Information was obtained on each child's school attendance during his first

Table 14

Age in months of CA and DA samples during the children's
final infant school term (1 June 1971)

CA Group N=265		DA Group N=277		difference between means (CA-DA)	standard error of difference	t	P (two-tail)
mean	s.d.	mean	s.d.				
89.82	1.76	90.21	1.54	-0.39	0.14	-2.77	<1%

Table 15

Age of SWC and DA samples during the children's final
infant school term (1 June 1971)

SWC Group N=143		DA Group N=277		difference between means (SWC-DA)	standard error of difference	t	P (two-tail)
mean	s.d.	mean	s.d.				
89.55	1.78	90.21	1.54	0.66	0.17	-3.91	<0.1%

Table 16

Composition of CA and DA samples in terms of sex

CA Group						DA Group		Total	
MC N=143		SWC N=174		MC+SWC N=317		N=372		N=689	
Girls	Boys	Girls	Boys	Girls	Boys	Girls	Boys	Girls	Boys
61	82	89	85	150	167	190	182	340	349

and third infant school years, and this is presented in Table 17, together with the results of a statistical analysis.

The table shows that for both school years the DA children had a poorer attendance record than the CA children, the difference being statistically significant in each case, but particularly the latter year. During the first school year the difference in mean attendance between the SWC component of the CA group and the DA group was very small and well below statistical significance but during the final year the difference in favour of the SWC group was more marked and statistically highly significant (p $<$ 0.1%). Thus, the CA children enjoyed the advantage of higher school attendance than the DA children during both their first and third school years, but this advantage, although statistically highly significant, does not seem very substantial in psychological or educational terms, and probably makes only a small contribution to the differences in school achievement subsequently found between the two samples which are reported in the following chapters.

It should be mentioned, in addition, that the DA children showed appreciably wider variation in their school attendance than the CA children during both school years, as indicated by the differences in the standard deviations shown in the table.

It is interesting to note, in passing, that, for each group in the whole sample, the mean attendance figures are consistently higher during the final year than the first year, a trend which may be explicable in terms of medical and psychological factors.

Medical factors. As already mentioned, medical data on the urban sample were incomplete, either because a child's medical record was no longer available (if the child had transferred to another school) or because a particular item on the record was not filled in. This means that any observations based upon these records must be regarded as rather tentative. The full sample comprised 689 children at the end of the first infant school term (317 CA and 372 DA children) and medical records were available for 643 of these (297 CA and 346 DA children), although for any given item on the medical record, the number of children with an appropriate entry might fall below this. Data were not available for children's height and weight

because some of the LEAs involved had discontinued the routine collection of this information. On the second school schedule, completed by the class teachers at the end of the children's first infant school term, there were several items relating to the child's health, physical condition, vision and hearing and these will be referred to in the present section since they supplement the data obtained from the medical records.

According to the available data, there were few substantial differences between the CA and DA children on medical and physical factors but those differences that did appear tended to favour the CA children, although not always. Moreover, the numbers of children in either group showing defects under the various headings were often very small. In view of this, it is not proposed to present the medical data in comprehensive detail but merely to select and comment on items of particular interest because of their educational importance, and those showing statistically significant differences between the groups. The data will be presented under the headings of *specific factors*, namely those related to the child's hearing and vision, and *more general factors* such as the child's health and overall physical condition. The percentage figures quoted are all approximate, and refer to the total numbers of children for whom data were available. For each specific item on the record the school medical officer is required to select one of several ratings according to the presence and severity of any defect found in the child on examination. For convenience of analysis in the present study these ratings were re-classified under the headings of 'no defect', 'defect requiring observation' and 'defect requiring treatment'. Since the numbers of the project children falling into the two latter categories were often rather small, the following discussion will refer only to the combined numbers, i.e. of children presenting either type of defect. The results of the between-groups comparisons were statistically non-significant unless otherwise stated. Because the numbers of children showing medical defects tended to be rather small, separate incidence figures for the SWC and MC sub-groups of the CA sample are not given.

Hearing and related factors. Only 12 CA children (4 per cent) and 12 DA children (3 per cent) were rated as showing defects of hearing on

Table 17

Percentage school attendance of the CA and DA children
during their first and third infant school years

	CA Group						DA Group		Diff bet. means	S.E. diff.	t [*]	p (two-tail)
	MC		SWC		MC+SWC							
	N=122		N+142		N=264		N=277					
	mean	s.d.	mean	s.d.	mean	s.d.	mean	s.d.	CA-DA			
First year	88.80	6.83	85.20	9.77	86.87	8.72	84.88	11.53	1.99	0.88	2.25	< 5.0%
Third year	92.11	5.83	91.45	6.11	91.76	5.99	88.14	9.52	3.62	0.70	5.23	< 0.1%

* t test for non-correlated samples

Note: The numbers for the SWC and DA groups were very slightly lower for the third year
than the first year due to missing data.

47

examination and none wore a hearing aid at the time that School Schedule 2 was completed (end of children's first term). Ten CA children (3 per cent) had otitis media as compared with 21 DA children (6 per cent). Only one CA child (0.3 per cent) but 11 DA children (3 per cent) were rated as showing other defects of hearing. Similarly, a higher proportion of DA than CA children showed nose and throat defects, the figures being 23 (8 per cent) CA children and 45 (13 per cent) DA children. According to the class teachers, 33 CA children (10 per cent) and 28 DA children (7 per cent) suffered from frequent heavy colds and catarrh. With some exceptions, therefore, the DA children tended to show a higher incidence of hearing and related defects than the CA children but the percentages were rather small. In the case of otitis media, 'other' defects of hearing and nose and throat defects the between-group differences in incidence reached statistical significance.

Vision. The DA group showed a slightly higher incidence of defects of vision than the CA group, the figures being 45 DA children (13 per cent) as compared with 34 CA children (11 per cent). Similarly, more DA than CA children had a squint (20 DA children, or 6 per cent and 7 CA children or 2 per cent). On the other hand, according to the second school schedule, 13 CA children (4 per cent) wore glasses as compared with only 6 DA children (2 per cent).

Other defects. No CA child and only 6 DA children (2 per cent) showed infestation of the head during the medical examination. Roughly twice as many DA as CA children showed defects of their teeth (45 DA children or 13 per cent as compared with 22 CA children or 7 per cent). A similar pattern emerged in the rating of the children's speech. Here 14 DA children (4 per cent) showed defects as compared with 7 CA children, 2 per cent.

General ratings. The school medical records carry details of the children's illnesses and this information is presented in Table 18. The records

Table 18

Total number of illnesses among CA and DA children

Number of illnesses	CA Group						DA Group	
	MC		SWC		MC+SWC			
	N=91		N=142		N=233		N=274	
	n	%	n	%	n	%	n	%
0	37	40.7	49	34.5	86	36.9	111	40.5
1	37	40.7	53	37.3	90	38.6	89	32.5
2	13	14.3	26	18.3	39	16.7	55	20.1
3+	4	4.4	14	9.9	18	7.7	19	6.9

χ^2 CA vs DA (3 d.f.) = 2.63, N.S. (two-tail)

SWC vs DA (3 d.f.) = 2.68, N.S. (two-tail)

showed that, for some illnesses (whooping cough, scarlet fever, and German measles), there was a lower incidence in the DA group than the CA group, but for others (measles, chicken pox, and polio) the situation was reversed. However, none of the differences was statistically significant, nor do they appear to show a meaningful pattern from the medical point of view. In terms of total number of illnesses, the DA group contained a slightly higher proportion of children than the CA group with no recorded illnesses, and also of those with two illnesses, whereas the CA group showed slightly higher proportions of children with one and three or more illnesses respectively. Again, however, this result was statistically non-significant.

The final rating in the school medical examination is an overall one concerning the child's general physical condition. Only 5 DA children (1 per cent) and no CA children were rated as being in unsatisfactory medical condition. On School Schedule 2, the teachers were asked to indicate which children suffered from poor general health. Slightly more CA children (22, or 6 per cent) were so rated compared with DA children (17, or 5 per cent).

Also on School Schedule 2 (completed at the end of the children's first school term) the teachers were asked to indicate those children whom they suspected of showing an uncorrected physical handicap or defect, or an intellectual handicap. Only 7 DA children (2 per cent) and 8 CA children (2 per cent) were rated as showing possible physical handicaps and the figures for suspected intellectual handicap were 9 DA children (2 per cent) and 1 CA child (0.3 per cent). The latter result was statistically significant but this means little with such low incidence figures as these.

On the whole, the above results suggest that the DA group show a higher incidence of medical defects and disabilities compared with the CA group, although not markedly so. This trend is in line with the findings of surveys and other research studies. For example, Phillips et al. (1972) reported that a small sample of socially disadvantaged six to seven-year-old boys showed a higher incidence of impairment of vision and hearing and other medical defects and disabilities than a control group of boys.

Finally, the proportions of parents in the CA and DA groups who attended their children's school medical examination were compared and the results of this comparison are presented in Table 19.

It will be seen that a significantly higher proportion of CA than DA group parents attended the medical examination and this result held good when the MC component of the CA group was removed. The implication of this outcome will be discussed in the following section of the present chapter.

Parental co-operation with the school

During the final term of the children's infant school careers, the headteachers were asked to assess the frequency of the parents' contact with the school in respect of each child in the sample. This information is presented in Table 20.

The table shows that both the mothers and the fathers of the CA children, but particularly the fathers, have more frequent contact with the school than the DA parents, the results being statistically significant in the case of fathers. When the SWC group of parents, taken on its own, was compared with the DA group, both the mothers and fathers made significantly more frequent school contact. Insofar as the frequency of parental contact with school can be regarded as an index of parental interest in the child's education, then the above results are in keeping with the findings of large scale research studies such as the survey of parental attitudes carried out for the Plowden Report (1967), and the survey by Douglas (1964), which show a clear association between parental interest and social class in favour of the higher social classes.

It will be noticed that the proportion of fathers making one or more contacts with the school (other than for admission) is much lower than that for mothers in both CA and DA groups and this may be due, at least in part, to the difficulty experienced by the fathers in getting time off from work for the purpose of visiting school. Approximately 96 per cent of CA mothers and 92 per cent of DA mothers made such contact as against 47 per cent of CA fathers and only 26 per cent of DA fathers. The fact that the between-group difference in parental contact is much more pronounced in the case of fathers than mothers, may reflect social class differences in the interest shown by fathers in their children's education. In the survey

Table 19

Parents' attendance at school medical examination:
CA and DA samples

	CA Group						DA Group	
	MC		SWC		MC+SWC			
	N=132		N=160		N=292*		N=340*	
	n	%	n	%	n	%	n	%
Parent attended	131	99.2	153	95.6	284	97.3	298	87.7
Parent did not attend	1	0.8	7	4.4	8	2.7	42	12.4

χ^2 CA vs DA (1 d.f.) = 18.63, p < 0.1% (two-tail)

SWC vs DA (1 d.f.) = 6.96, p < 1.0% (two-tail)

* In the case of 5 CA group children and 6 DA group children, information concerning the parents' attendance at the medical examination was lacking.

of parental attitudes carried out for the Plowden Report mentioned above, for example, there were particularly marked differences between the proportions of 'non-manual' working fathers and semi-skilled and unskilled working fathers in such indications of interest in the child's schooling as visiting the school or choosing a school. It is also possible, however, that semi or unskilled workers may have relatively greater difficulty in getting time off from work to visit school than skilled manual or non-manual workers.

However, for several reasons, it would not be wise to assume that frequency of parental contact with school is an infallible guide to parental interest. For example, as shown in Chapter 12, schools differ in the extent to which they encourage parental visits and the degree of formality associated with such visits. In order to obtain a more sensitive indicator of parental interest, therefore, the headteachers were asked to rate the degree of co-operation shown by the parents toward the school in terms of their apparent interest in their children's education. This rating

was obtained at the same time as the ratings of frequency of parental contact with school (i.e. the children's final infant school term) and the data obtained from it are presented in Table 21.

It will be seen from this table that few parents in either group were rated as 'over-keen' in interest, although rather more in the CA than the DA group, and even fewer were rated as actually hostile in their attitude toward the school. These parents and also those falling into the 'not sufficient contact to assess' category, were omitted from the statistical analysis which was carried out on the resulting ordered scale of parental interest ('keen', 'interested', and 'passive'). The table shows that both the CA group parents as a whole and the SWC sub-group parents considered separately, received higher ratings of interest in their children's schooling than the DA group parents, the results being statistically highly significant in both cases. It should be remembered, however, that there were small numbers of parents whom the teacher did not feel able to assess on this scale due to lack of contact and it is possible, though

Table 20

Parental contact with school: CA and DA samples

	CA Group						DA Group	
	MC N=122		SWC N=143		MC+SWC N=265		N=279	
	n	%	n	%	n	%	n	%
Frequency of mother's contact with school								
Several times	81	66.4	107	74.8	188	70.9	178	63.8
Once or twice	34	27.9	33	23.1	67	25.3	80	28.7
Never (except for admission)	7	5.7	3	2.1	10	3.8	21	7.5
*No mother/mother substitute	(0)	–	(0)	–	(0)	–	(0)	–

Value of z, CA vs DA = 1.90, N.S.
        SWC vs DA = 2.43, p < 5%

	CA Group						DA Group	
Frequency of father's contact with school								
Several times	15	13.0	24	17.8	39	15.6	18	7.1
Once or twice	52	45.2	40	29.6	92	36.8	48	18.9
Never (except for admission)	48	41.7	71	52.6	119	47.6	188	74.0
*No father/father substitute	(7)	–	(8)	–	(15)	–	(25)	–

Value of z, CA vs DA = 5.94, p < 0.1%
        SWC vs DA = 4.36, p < 0.1%

* Rating not included in percentage figures or Kendall's 'tau' analysis.
  Probability levels in the table are two-tailed.

Table 21

Headteachers' ratings of parents' level of co-operation with school: CA and DA samples

Rating	CA Group						DA Group	
	MC N=122		SWC N=143		MC+SWC N=265		N=279	
	n	%	n	%	n	%	n	%
1. Over-keen	8	6.8	5	3.9	13	5.3	3	1.2
2. Keen	50	42.4	64	50.0	114	46.3	78	30.9
3. Interested	31	26.3	30	23.4	61	24.8	79	31.3
4. Passive	28	23.7	29	22.7	57	23.2	90	35.7
5. Hostile	1	0.8	0	0.0	1	0.4	2	0.8
6. Not sufficient contact to assess*	4	–	15	–	19	–	27	–

Value of z, CA vs DA = 3.83, $p < 0.1\%$ (two-tail) based on ratings 1, 3, and 4 only
SWC vs DA = 3.57, $p < 0.1\%$ (two-tail) based on ratings 1, 3, and 4 only

* Figures not included in percentages or Kendall's 'tau' analysis.

unlikely, that their inclusion in this analysis might have altered the outcome. These results are in line with the findings of previous research into social class differences in parental interest in children's education referred to earlier. It is interesting to note, though, that even in the so-called 'deprived area' schools, the proportion of parents rated as interested or keenly interested in their children's education is as high as 60 per cent (approximately). This lends support to the conclusion reached in the Plowden Report (1967), based on the findings of a national survey of parental attitudes, that many manual workers and their wives encourage and support their children's efforts to learn.

Finally, it will be recalled from the preceding section in this chapter, that the proportion of parents attending the children's school medical examination was higher for the CA group, 97.3 per cent, than for the DA group (87.7 per cent). This result was statistically significant though the difference was not as pronounced as might have been expected. The attendance of a parent at a child's school medical examination, can be regarded as a pointer toward her interest in the child's welfare, although perhaps not a very reliable one, so that this result is in line with the evidence presented above suggesting the greater degree of parental interest and co-operation shown by the CA parents in comparison with the DA parents.

To summarize the background information on the sample presented in this chapter, it appears that, in general, the differences between the CA and DA groups (and to some extent those between the MC and SWC components of the CA sample and between the SWC and DA groups) are more marked in respect of factors in the children's home background than in factors relating specifically to the school.

Concerning home background variables, the CA and DA groups appeared to be well differentiated in terms of social class status, family size and the child's birth order and with regard to the degree of parent-school contact and interest shown by the parents in their children's schooling. (In addition, it will be shown in Chapter 4 that, in some respects, the CA children appeared to be better prepared by their parents for school entry.) On the material side, there was a higher proportion of needy families in the DA group as indexed by receipt of free meals and the census data indicated

that the 'deprived areas' tended to be less favoured than the control areas in terms of certain housing characteristics. Moreover, there was a higher incidence of particular medical defects in the DA than the CA group, although the proportion of children in either group showing such defects was usually small. However, it must be stressed that some of the data summarized above were not available for the whole urban sample and, moreover, for certain items (notably fathers' occupational status and the items of census information), the reliability of the data was open to question.

With regard to school factors, there were some features in which the DA schools appeared to be at a slight disadvantage in comparison to the CA schools, for example, in the proportions of trained teachers, mean length of teaching experience of staff, teacher and pupil turnover and in certain aspects of the school building, amenities and material provision. On the other hand, there were some respects, such as pupil-teacher ratio, mean class size and the amount of ancillary help available, in which the DA schools enjoyed a small advantage and there were no differences of any consequence in the training and experience of the headteachers. Moreover, whilst the CA children had a significantly better school attendance record than the DA children the difference did not seem to be very substantial from the educational point of view.

On balance, therefore, it would seem that in the present sample school area type (i.e. 'deprived' or 'control') reflects home background factors to a much greater extent than school factors, although both sets of factors are involved. The findings of the study which are presented in the following chapters in this section should be seen in this perspective.

Losses from the sample

As stated earlier in this chapter, the full urban sample comprised 689 children in December 1968, the end of the children's first school term. In the summer term of the children's final infant school careers, this number had dropped to 544, a loss of 145 children of approximately 21 per cent of the total urban sample. Of the children leaving, 53 came from the CA group (nearly 17 per cent of that group) and 95 from the DA group (approximately 25 per cent of that group). Thus an appreciably higher proportion of DA than CA children left their original schools during the three year period of the study. Such a difference was predictable for, as the Plowden Report (1967) indicates, many 'deprived area' schools are likely to be characterized by a relatively high turnover of pupils.

The question arises as to whether these leavers formed a representative selection from the CA and DA samples respectively, or whether, as seemed quite likely, they tended to be unrepresentative. It might be, for example, that the CA sample leavers came from families where the father was ambitious and tended to move in order to gain promotion. In contrast, the DA sample leavers might have come from rather rootless families where the father changed jobs frequently or was in and out of employment. The implication of such trends, if confirmed, would be that the CA sample leavers would tend to be among the brighter and academically higher achievers in their group whilst, conversely, the DA sample leavers would be relatively dull and of low academic achievement within their group. Ideally, these children should have been followed up in their new schools in order to check on these possibilities, but the resources of the research unit did not allow such follow up. It was hoped to compare the leavers with the full samples from which they were drawn, in terms of the social class status of their families but, unfortunately, the information on the fathers' occupations (obtained via the school medical record) on which such a comparison could be based, was incomplete. However, it is possible to compare the leavers with their respective samples on the basis of the teachers' assessments of their progress and adjustment obtained by means of the school schedules. For this purpose, the leavers were divided into three groups according to when they left the project schools, i.e. during the first, second or third infant school years. Each of these groups was then compared with the sample from which it was drawn (CA or DA) on selected items from the most recent school schedule completed by the teachers prior to the children's transfer to another school. Items were chosen which recurred over the series of schedules and which represented the main areas of school progress and adjustment. These items were as follows:

level reached on the basic reading scheme
power of oral expression
ability to match the written number symbol to the correct number of objects
the child's relationship with the class teacher.

The ratings on the above items received by the leavers were then compared with those received by the full CA or DA samples by means of Kendall's tau technique and the full results of this analysis are presented in Appendix Tables A1 to A4. The outcome of the comparison was that, in the case of the CA leavers, there was no clear overall tendency for them to be rated either better or worse than average for their group on the above items. The detailed pattern of results for the subgroups of CA leavers (divided according to time of leaving) was in fact rather variable for, even on the same item, the direction of the difference in level of ratings varied among the sub groups. Thus, for example, in reading scheme level, the CA children who left during the first school year received rather lower ratings than the CA sample as a whole, whereas, those who left during the second school year were rated higher than the full sample. However, none of the results either for the CA or DA samples reached statistical significance and it must be noted that the numbers of children in the three leavers sub-groups are rather small, particularly in the case of the CA children, so that not much weight can be put on these comparisons.

In the case of the DA leavers, the overall pattern of results from the comparisons with the full DA sample is much clearer for, in all but two comparisons, the leavers tended to receive lower ratings than the full sample. It seems reasonable to conclude from this that, as predicted, the DA leavers were rather unrepresentative of the sample from which they were drawn, tending to be (non-significantly) poorer in the aspects of progress and adjustment chosen, according to their teachers.

This outcome should be borne in mind in the following chapters, which present the results of the general study of urban children. The implication is that wherever a clear trend emerges for the gap between the CA and DA samples to decrease over a period of time, such a trend may, in part, reflect the loss of DA children who are rather unrepresentative of the full group in at least some aspects of progress and adjustment. Such trends should, as a result, be regarded with caution.

4 Adjustment to School

ANALYSIS AND PRESENTATION OF DATA

In the following analysis of the data the main focus is primarily on comparing the Control Area (CA) sample, i.e. comprising children from schools serving the 'middle-class' (MC) and 'settled working-class' (SWC) schools with the Deprived Area (DA) sample. However, since both the SWC and DA schools serve predominantly 'working-class areas' it is interesting to make direct comparison between these groups, in addition to the main comparison. For this reason, wherever possible, the tables will show the breakdown of the scores or ratings of the Control Area (CA) group into its 'middle-class' (MC) and 'settled working-class' (SWC) components, and also the results of the statistical analysis for the SWC vs DA group comparisons, as well as those for the CA vs DA group comparisons. However, where a series of results from several school schedules are presented in one table, space does not allow the breakdown of the CA group data to be presented. In such cases, the outcome of the statistical analyses of the data will be presented both for the main comparison between the CA and DA samples and for the subsidiary comparison between the SWC group and the DA sample.

It would have been interesting to have carried out additional analyses of the research data based upon all possible comparisons between the subgroups in the sample, MC, SWC and DA, but this would have made the report far too lengthy. Accordingly, as stated above, the data derived from the school schedules were analysed in terms of the CA vs DA and SWC vs DA comparisons only. This course was adopted because of the sheer volume of the data from these schedules. However, in the case of the data obtained from the tests used in the final attainment survey, all of the sample sub-groups were systematically compared with each other and the results are reported in Chapter 6.

Where ratings in an item follow an ordered sequence, such as 'good', 'average' and 'poor' the method of statistical analysis used was Kendall's 'tau' technique which uses the normal distribution (z values) for testing significance. Most of the items in the school schedules are of this ordered type and so the results from them were analysed by the tau method. In other cases, where the categories in an item were not of this ordered type, the 'chi square' technique was used. (See Appendix I for notes on the statistical techniques used.)

A. PREPARATION FOR AND SETTLING INTO SCHOOL

(i) Preparation for school entry

Information concerning the preparation of the child for school entry and his initial adjustment to school was obtained from the first school schedule completed by the class teachers for each child in the sample after he or she had attended school for ten consecutive school days, i.e. the equivalent of two school weeks. Some follow-up information regarding the child's early school adjustment was obtained in the second school schedule, completed by the class teacher at the end of the children's first school term.

The first section of School Schedule 1 mainly comprised items concerning the parents' and child's contact with the school prior to the child's admission. Table 22 shows the extent to which the children in the 'control' and 'deprived area' groups visited their school prior to school entry.

This table shows that, although a higher proportion of Control Area (CA) than Deprived Area (DA) children visited the school prior to admission on two or more occasions, a slightly higher percentage of them did not make such a visit at all and the overall result was statistically non-significant. It is interesting to note, however, that the 'settled working-class' (SWC) component of the Control Area group showed a significantly higher proportion of children making such visits than the Deprived Area group. The difference is masked in the overall comparison between the CA and DA groups, but the table shows that in the 'middle-class' (MC) component of the CA group a lower proportion of children visited the school before entry than in the DA group.

Table 22

Extent to which the CA and DA children visited their schools before admission

(with breakdown of CA sample)

Item	Ratings	CA Group								DA Group	
		MC		SWC		MC+SWC					
		N=146		N=176		N=322				N=348	
		n	%	n	%	n	%			n	%
Did child visit school before admission?	two + occasions	32	21.9	94	53.4	126	39.1			93	26.7
	once only	70	47.9	49	27.8	119	37.0			188	54.0
	not at all	44	30.1	33	18.7	77	23.9			67	19.2

Value of z CA vs DA = 1.54, N.S.
Value of z SWC vs DA = 4.37, p < 0.1%

Probabilities in this table are two-tailed (see page 351).

As a follow-up to the above item, information was obtained on the extent to which those children who did in fact visit the school before admission also visited their future classrooms or teachers. These data are shown in Table 23. It will be seen that a significantly higher proportion of the CA children made such visits. The table shows, however, that the percentage figures for the MC component of the CA group are very similar to those for the DA group and, once again, it is the SWC component which differs very sharply from the DA group.

It is possible to compare the figures in Tables 22 and 23 with figures obtained in the National Survey carried out for the Plowden Committee (1967). The latter were obtained from a sample of 255 infant starters which, in turn, was drawn from the main survey sample. This sub-sample was not fully representative of the general population in terms of the children's social background, being somewhat overloaded in social class 3 (white collar and manual). Nevertheless, it could probably be regarded as roughly representative for the purpose of the present comparison. Table 24 shows the percentages of the children in the CA and DA groups who visited their schools or classrooms before entry in comparison with those for the National Survey sub-sample.

It will be seen from this table that both the CA and the DA groups, but particularly the latter, had a higher proportion of children visiting their schools before entry than the National Survey sub-sample. However, of such children, a higher percentage of the CA group, but a lower percentage of the DA children, visited the classroom before entry as compared with the latter sub-sample. This comparison with the National Survey sub-sample underlines the suprisingly high proportion of DA children who visited their schools before admission. Information was not obtained on who accompanied the children during such visits so that it is not possible to explore this unexpected finding further. One possibility however is that some of the DA children visited their schools prior to entry in the company of children already attending those schools. (As indicated on page 59 a higher proportion of DA than CA children had siblings at the same school.)

Two questions in the first school schedule concerned the parents' contact with the school prior to the child's admission. These distinguished between such contact which was specifically for the purpose of registering the child and that which was for other reasons, such as informally introducing the child to the headteacher. Table 25 shows the data obtained from these two items. This table shows that there was a greater tendency for the CA than DA parents to make prior visits to the schools in order to register their children, this result being highly significant. Similarly, a significantly higher proportion of CA parents made prior visits to the school for other reasons. This pattern of results held when the SWC sub-group alone was compared with the DA sample.

These results may reflect the relatively greater concern of the CA parents to prepare their children for school entry, although this interpretation must be tentative because the schools in the sample probably vary in the degree to which they encourage pre-admission contact from parents. Moreover, some of the headteachers in the CA schools pointed out that, where there was heavy pressure on the places available at a school, then a parent's pre-admission visit to the school could be mainly due to her anxiety to secure a place for her child. This motive, in itself, cannot be regarded as reflecting parental concern for the child's education for, at worst, it could simply reflect a parent's wish to have the child off her hands for the day.

Table 26 shows that the proportions of children in the two groups who attended a nursery school or some other form of pre-infant school provision, were virtually identical. However, the breakdown of the CA group figures for the MC and SWC separately shows that, compared with the DA group, a lower proportion of the SWC group but a higher proportion of the MC group had attended a nursery school or similar provision. This discrepancy between the two component sections of the CA sample suggests that the availability of nursery schools or pre-school groups may be greater for both the 'middle-class' and 'deprived' area schools than for the SWC schools in this sample, although probably for different reasons. The proportion of DA children (approximately one third) who had had nursery school or similar experience seems rather low in view of the fact that the children were living in deprived areas.

Six of the London schools in the sample (one MC school and the five DA schools) had nursery classes attached to them, in most of which the

Table 23

Extent to which the CA and DA children visited their future classrooms/teachers before admission (with breakdown of CA sample)

| Item | Rating | CA Group | | | | | | DA Group | |
| | | MC N=146 | | SWC N=176 | | MC+SWC N=322 | | N=348 | |
		n	%	n	%	n	%	n	%
If child visited before admission did he visit present classroom/teacher?	two + occasions	17	16.7	48	33.6	65	26.5	49	17.4
	once only	33	32.3	76	53.1	109	44.5	95	33.8
	not at all	52	51.0	19	13.3	71	29.0	137	48.7

Value of z CA vs DA = 4.40, p < 0.1%

Value of z SWC vs DA = 6.70, p < 0.1%

Probabilities in this table are two-tailed (see page 351).

Table 24

Extent to which children in urban sample visited
their schools/classrooms before admission as
compared with 1964 National Survey sub-sample

Item	Rating	Present samples		National Survey sub-sample
		CA group	DA group	
		N=322	N=348	N=255
		%	%	%
1. Did child visit school before entry?	Yes	76	81	71
	No	24	19	29
2. If yes, did child visit classroom before entry?	Yes	71	51	64
	No	29	49	36

children attended for a morning or afternoon session daily. Fifteen of the CA children (4.7 per cent) had attended such a nursery class and fifty-seven DA children (15.3 per cent). The proportion of DA children attending such classes was much higher than that in the CA group, simply because of the better provision of these nursery classes in the DA schools in the present sample.

Those children who attended nursery classes attached to their infant schools should have enjoyed a considerable advantage over children starting infant school without experience of any nursery provision and over children whose nursery class experience was elsewhere. The former children would probably be familiar with the routines and layout of the infant school and with at least some of the infant school teachers. Moreover, since the infant school/department headmistress was also head of the nursery class, there would probably be continuity of educational approach from the nursery class to infant reception class. These factors would lead one to expect that children attending such classes would settle into their infant reception classes more quickly than other children.

It might well be thought that having a brother or sister at the same infant school or department would be a support to the new school entrant and help him to settle into school. Table 27 shows the numbers of children in the sample who enjoyed this apparent advantage. This table shows that a significantly higher proportion of DA than CA children had brothers or sisters in the same school/department. In most cases, of course, these would be older siblings since the project children were new school entrants. This difference in proportions almost certainly reflects the fact, discussed in Chapter 3, that the DA children tended to come from bigger families (in terms of number of children in family) than the CA children.

The first school schedule also contained questions about the children's accomplishments in some basic educational skills and the data yielded by these are presented in Table 28.

The table shows that only a very small number of children in either the CA or DA sample was judged by the teachers to be able to read from a book, although in both groups there was a substantial number of children falling into the 'not observed' category. The difference between the two

Table 25

Parental contact with school prior to child's admission: CA and DA samples

(with breakdown of CA sample)

Item	Rating	CA group						DA group	
		MC N=146		SWC N=176		MC+SWC N=322		N=348	
		n	%	n	%	n	%	n	%
1. Has either parent made contact with school prior to admission to register him?	Yes	138	94.5	149	84.7	287	89.1	201	57.8
	No	8	5.5	27	15.3	35	10.9	147	42.2

Value of z   CA vs DA = 9.03, p < 0.1%
Value of z   SWC vs DA = 6.07, p < 0.1%

Item	Rating	CA group						DA group	
2. Has either parent made contact with school prior to admission for any other reason?	Yes	20	13.7	52	29.5	72	22.4	28	8.0
	No	126	86.3	124	70.5	250	77.6	320	91.9

Value of z   CA vs DA = 5.08, p < 0.1%
Value of z   SWC vs DA = 6.33, p < 0.1%

Probability levels in the table are two-tailed (see page 351).

60

Table 26

Number of children attending nursery school or similar establishments:
CA and DA samples (with breakdown of CA sample)

Item	Rating	CA group						DA group	
		MC		SWC		MC+SWC		N=348	
		N=146		N=176		N=322			
		n	%	n	%	n	%	n	%
Has child previously attended nursery school, day nursery or playgroup?	Yes	69	47.3	37	21.0	106	32.9	113	32.5
	No	77	52.7	139	79.0	216	67.1	235	67.5

Value of z CA vs DA = 0.04, N.S.

Value of z SWC vs DA = 2.63, p < 1.0%

Probabilities in this table are two-tailed (see page 351).

Table 27

Number of children with siblings in same infant school/department:
CA and DA samples (with breakdown of CA sample)

Item	Rating	CA group						DA group	
		MC		SWC		MC+SWC		N=348	
		N=146		N=176		N=322			
		n	%	n	%	n	%	n	%
Has siblings attending same infant school/department	Yes	24	16.4	47	26.7	71	22.0	132	37.9
	No	122	83.6	129	73.3	251	78.0	216	62.1

Value of z CA vs DA = 4.38, p < 0.1%

Value of z SWC vs DA = 2.46, p < 5%

Probabilities in this table are two-tailed (see page 351).

Table 28

Teachers' ratings of children's educational skills at time of school entry: CA and DA samples (with breakdown of CA sample)

Item	Rating	CA group								DA group	
		MC		SWC		MC+SWC					
		N=146		N=176		N=322				N=348	
		n	%	n	%	n	%			n	%
1. On entry to school could child read from a book?	Yes	8	7.6	4	2.5	12	4.5			8	2.6
	No	97	92.4	158	97.5	255	95.5			303	97.4
	*Not observed	41		14		55				37	
2. On entry to school could child write his name legibly?	Yes	32	22.0	21	12.6	53	17.0			40	12.4
	No	113	77.9	146	87.4	259	83.0			282	87.6
	*Not observed	1		9		10				26	
3. On entry to school could child draw simple recognisable objects?	Yes	75	54.3	76	44.7	151	49.0			209	67.2
	No	63	45.6	94	55.3	157	51.0			102	32.8
	*Not observed	8		6		14				37	

Value of z CA vs DA = 1.02, N.S.
Value of z SWC vs DA = 0.24, N.S.

Value of z CA vs DA = 1.51, N.S.
Value of z SWC vs DA = 0.10, N.S.

Value of z CA vs DA = 4.50, p < 0.1% (two-tail)
Value of z SWC vs DA = 4.70, p < 0.1% (two-tail)

*Children in not observed category not included in percentage figures or 'tau' analysis.
Probability levels in the table are one-tailed unless otherwise stated.

groups was not significant and the number of 'readers' in either case was so small that an analysis of the results of the follow-up question about the reading proficiency of such children (question 26 on School Schedule 1) was not justified. It had been thought that, in some of the MC area schools at least, there would be a sprinkling of children with some degree of reading skill at the time of school entry. It is possible, of course, that a number of children did have such a skill but that there was little opportunity for the teachers to observe this during the first two weeks of the children's schooling, although such children would, presumably, have been placed in the 'not observed' column.

The table also shows that there was a slightly, but not significantly, higher proportion of CA children rated as being able to write their names legibly at the time of school entry. It will be seen from the figures, however, that whilst the SWC and DA children had nearly identical percentages of children rated as having such a skill, the MC sub-group had nearly twice the percentage of the former groups (approximately 22 per cent). It was rather unexpected to find that over 12 per cent of the DA group were judged to be able to write their names but this figure should be regarded with caution because of the relatively large number of children in this group falling into the 'not observed' category.

The most surprising result, however, emerges from the analysis of the data from the item concerning the children's ability to draw simple recognizable objects at the time of school entry. This shows that a very substantial and significantly higher proportion of DA than CA children were rated as showing such ability. A number of teachers in the DA schools had commented, when being interviewed, that many children from such areas came to school without any skill in the manipulation and use of pencils. Clearly, the judgement of what is a recognizable object is highly subjective and it may be that the DA school teachers were more generous in their judgements than the CA teachers, possibly because of lower expectations of the children.

Summary: preparation for school entry

The CA children could be regarded as having been better prepared for school entry than the DA children insofar as a higher proportion of the SWC area children had visited the reception classroom or teacher before entry and a higher percentage of the MC and SWC area children's parents had contacted the schools prior to the children's admission. As against this, however, there was no difference between the groups in the proportions who had experienced some form of nursery provision, although, of these children, a higher proportion of DA than CA children had attended nursery classes attached to infant schools. Also, a higher proportion of DA than CA children had siblings attending the same infant school/ department. In terms of simple 'basic skills' possessed by the children at school entry, the only significant difference to emerge between the two groups was that a substantially higher percentage of the DA children were judged to be able to draw recognizable objects at the time of school entry.

(ii) Settling into School

Information on the early adjustment of each child to school was obtained on the first and second schedules. (It will be remembered that these were completed by the teachers after the first ten days of the child's schooling, and at the end of the first term respectively.)

The teachers were asked to state whether the children showed signs of distress on leaving the mother, and if so, whether they were still showing such distress at the time of completion of the schedule. Table 29 presents the data from these two items for the first two schedules.

The table shows that, during the first few days of schooling, a slightly higher proportion of DA children than CA children showed such signs of distress, the difference being significant at the 5 per cent level. Inspection of the figures for the MC and SWC sub-groups shows that this difference is due to the lower incidence of signs of distress among the children in the MC schools, for the figures for the SWC and DA groups are almost identical.

Of the children who showed such signs at school entry, a similar percentage in both the CA and DA samples continued to show distress after the first ten days of schooling, but the actual numbers of such children were rather small (17 children in the CA group and 25 children in the DA group). Clearly, the majority of children in both groups who initially showed signs of distress ceased to do so within the first few days of schooling, due, no doubt, at least in part, to the careful and sympathetic handling of the situation by the headteacher or reception class teachers.

Table 29 also shows that the percentage of children showing signs of distress at the end of the first school term was nearly identical in both groups. Of these children, under half in the DA group and over half in the CA group had been showing such signs for a period of three weeks or more, a fact which suggests that in such cases, there may have been problems of emotional immaturity or over-dependence on the mother. It is interesting to note that, in both groups, but especially the CA group, the number of children showing signs of distress at the end of the term is higher than the number recorded as still showing distress at the end of the first ten days of schooling. Clearly, some children who did not initially show such distress did so later on during the school term, a point made by some of the teachers during the interviews. On the other hand, of the children rated as showing signs of distress at the end of the first ten days of schooling (17 in the CA group and 25 in the DA group), 9 CA children and 9 DA children were rated as still showing such signs at the time of completion of the second school schedule. These particular children's apparent difficulties in settling into school appeared to have persisted at least over the length of a school term.

Comparative data on the incidence of distress upon leaving the mother were obtained for the National Survey sub-sample of infant school starters already referred to (see p. 57), and Table 30 presents the comparison with figures for the present sample.

The table shows that a higher proportion of both CA and DA children initially showed signs of distress on leaving the mother as compared with the National Survey sub-sample. However, in the former groups, only a relatively small percentage of children showing such signs continued to show distress after the first two weeks of schooling (16 per cent and 19 per cent respectively). Strictly comparable data on the duration of distress signs were not available from the National Survey sub-sample but, as the table shows, half of the children initially showing distress continued to do so after one week. It is possible, of course, that this proportion might have dropped to one com-

parable with the present after a further week of schooling.

In addition to the above items concerning signs of distress on leaving the mother, the first two schedules contained questions regarding other behaviour which might be indicative of early adjustment difficulties in the children. One of these in Schedule 1 asked whether the children tended to cling to the teacher or an older sibling during play times. Table 31 shows that there was a higher proportion of children showing such behaviour in the DA group (roughly 20 per cent) compared with the CA group (approximately 8 per cent). However, it must be remembered that the former group also had a higher proportion of children with siblings in the same school/department (see Table 27) so that the higher incidence of clinging behaviour among the DA children probably reflected to some extent the greater availability of older brothers and sisters to cling to. This interpretation must be tentative though because the question does not distinguish clinging to an older sibling from clinging to teacher.

A second question in this section was concerned with unusual or difficult behaviour presented by the children. There was no significant difference between the two groups in the incidence of such behaviour on either Schedules 1 or 2. After the first ten days of schooling (Schedule 1), approximately 12 per cent of children in either group were rated as showing such behaviour and this dropped to approximately 6 per cent by the end of the first term (Schedule 2). Examples of the kind of behaviour rated by the teachers as unusual or difficult can be classified under the following headings:

(a) distress on leaving the mother or home: one child was reported to have had three days of screaming sessions shortly after starting school and this was followed by a period of clinging to a friend. One or two children were inclined to run home during school day. One child clung to the teacher during the first few days, asking to go home.

(b) over-dependence upon the mother: one child was described as unable to do anything for himself on entry to school. He could not wash or dress himself or use the toilet unaided.

Table 29

Teachers' rating of signs of distress shown by the children on leaving the mother: (CA and DA samples (with breakdown of CA sample)

Schedule	Item	Rating	CA group MC N=146 n	%	CA group SWC N=176 n	%	CA group MC+SWC N=322 n	%	DA group N=348 n	%
1 (first 10 days)	1. Did child show signs of distress at leaving mother on first few days?	Yes	36	24.7	67	38.1	103	32.0	135	38.8
		No	110	75.3	109	61.9	219	68.0	213	61.2
	Value of z CA vs DA = 1.76, p < 5% Value of z SWC vs DA = 0.07, N.S.									
	2. If yes, is child still showing signs of distress?	Yes	6	16.7	11	16.4	17	16.5	25	18.5
		No	30	83.3	56	83.6	86	83.5	110	81.5
	Value of z CA vs DA = 0.23, N.S. Value of z SWC vs DA = 0.17, N.S.									
2 (end of first term, excluding first ten days)	3. Does child show signs of distress leaving mother?	Yes	9	6.3	18	10.9	27	8.7	27	8.3
		No	134	93.7	147	89.1	281	91.2	299	91.7
	Value of z CA vs DA = 0.08, N.S. Value of z SWC vs DA = 0.79, N.S.									
	4. If yes, for how long?	few days only	3	33.3	2	11.1	5	18.5	8	29.6
		1 - 2 weeks	1	11.1	5	27.8	6	22.2	8	29.6
		3 weeks or more	5	55.6	11	61.1	16	59.3	11	40.7
	Value of z CA vs DA = 1.19, N.S. Value of z SWC vs DA = 1.36, N.S.									

Probability levels in the table are one-tailed

Table 30

Incidence of signs of distress on leaving the mother:
a comparison between the present samples and the
the National Survey sub-sample

Item	Rating	Control area group	Deprived area group	National Survey sub-sample
		N=322	N=348	N=255
		%	%	%
1. Did child show signs of distress on leaving the mother?	Yes No	32 68	39 61	25 75
2. If yes, is child still showing such signs*	Yes No	16 84	19 81	50 50

* After two weeks of schooling in the case of the present sample
but after one week in the National Survey sample.

Table 31

Incidence of clinging behaviour in the children after first ten days of schooling:

CA and DA samples (with breakdown of CA sample)

Item	Rating	CA group						DA group	
		MC		SWC		MC+SWC			
		N=146		N=176		N=322		N=348	
		n	%	n	%	n	%	n	%
Does child cling to teacher or older sibling at play times?	Yes	9	6.2	15	8.7	24	7.6	65	20.2
	No	135	93.7	157	91.3	292	92.4	267	80.4
	*Not observed	2		4		6		16	

Value of z CA vs DA = 4.31, p < 0.1%
Value of z SWC vs DA = 3.03, p < 0.5%

*Children in not observed category not included in percentage figures or 'tau' analysis.

(c) lack of concentration/inability to settle to activities: one child wandered about the school during the first few days, ignoring teacher's instructions.

(d) withdrawal/non-participation: one child refused to sit with other children or to speak to anyone and sat on her own, humming and rocking to and fro, this pattern of behaviour persisting at least over the first school term. Another child hid behind chairs or covered his face with his hands, in the apparent belief that he was thereby hidden, this pattern again persisting over the entire term.

(e) stubbornness/defiance/disobedience: one child was reported to argue back with anyone in authority.

(f) aggressiveness/spitefulness to other children: this could take either physical or verbal forms as, for example, in bullying or in the use of bad language.

(g) language problems: one child was described as being unable to utter even simple words correctly but would use very immature approximations such as 'le' for please and 'loi' for toilet.

On both Schedules 1 and 2 there were questions dealing with the incidence of wetting, soiling or being sick during the school day. The numbers of children in either group and on either schedule who did show such behaviour were very small and not significantly different as between the CA and DA groups. Rather surprisingly, however, these numbers showed a consistent increase from Schedules 1 to 2. In the CA group the number of children wetting rose from 14 soon after school entry (Schedule 1) to 23 at the end of the first term, the number soiling rose from nil to 4 and the number being sick rose from 2 to 4. In the DA group the number wetting rose from 13 to 32, the number soiling from 3 to 9 and the number being sick from 2 to 8. This trend was in the opposite direction to that of the figures for unusual/difficult behaviour noted above and for signs of distress on leaving the mother, discussed earlier.

As a follow-up to the questions concerning unusual or difficult behaviour in the children, Schedule 2 included ratings of the children on aggressiveness, fearfulness and restlessness and the data from these ratings are presented in Table 32.

It will be seen from this table that, on all three items, both groups have between roughly 20 and 30 per cent of the children showing some behavioural difficulties. However, none of the results of the comparisons between the CA and DA samples reaches statistical significance.

Rather surprisingly, there was no significant difference between the two groups in the incidence of restless/over-active behaviour. It might be expected that children from culturally deprived home backgrounds would show more restless behaviour in the school situation, since they would enter school with less well developed skills, concept and attitudes appropriate to the school situation, as compared with children from more favoured backgrounds. Even more unexpected was the finding that, as compared with the DA children, a significantly higher proportion of the SWC area children were rated as showing restless behaviour.

The above results were also unexpected in that they did not accord with the rankings by the headteachers of the frequency within the schools of various kinds of behavioural problems (see Chapter 11, (p. 270). The head teachers in the CA group schools judged that the most frequent problems were, in order, nervousness, shyness, restlessness, disruptiveness and 'anti-social' behaviour. The DA group headteachers, on the other hand, estimated that their most frequent problems were restlessness, aggressiveness, shyness and disruptiveness, 'anti-social' behaviour and, finally, nervousness. On the basis of this evidence, therefore, one might have expected the DA children to show a relatively higher incidence of restless and aggressive behaviour than the CA group children and a lower incidence of nervous behaviour.

On the other hand, when the class teachers responsible for the project sample during the children's first infant school year were asked to assess the frequency of the behavioural problems mentioned above, both DA and CA group school teachers put restlessness followed by aggressiveness as being the most frequent, and shyness and nervousness as relatively less frequent.

A series of questions in both schedules related to the children's initial adjustment to school and their attitudes to the class teachers and other children. Information from there is given in Table 33.

Table 32

Incidence of behavioural difficulties in children at end of first term: CA and DA samples (with breakdown of CA sample)

Item	Rating	CA group						DA group	
		MC		SWC		MC+SWC			
		N=143*		N=174*		N=317		N=372	
		n	%	n	%	n	%	n	%
1. Is child aggressive towards other children?	Not at all	119	83.2	134	77.0	253	79.8	286	76.9
	Sometimes	23	16.1	39	22.4	62	19.6	82	22.0
	Usually	1	0.7	1	0.6	2	0.6	4	0.1
Value of z CA vs DA = 0.89, N.S.									
Value of z SWC vs DA = 0.01, N.S.									
2. Is child nervous or fearful?	Not at all	103	72.0	128	73.6	231	72.9	241	64.8
	Sometimes	37	25.9	41	23.6	78	24.6	116	31.2
	Usually	3	2.1	5	2.9	8	2.5	15	4.0
Value of z CA vs DA = 2.27, N.S.									
Value of z SWC vs DA = 1.97, N.S.									
3. Is child restless or overactive?	Not at all	113	79.0	102	58.6	215	67.8	274	73.7
	Sometimes	23	16.1	62	35.6	85	26.8	83	22.3
	Usually	7	4.9	10	5.7	17	5.4	15	4.0
Value of z CA vs DA = 1.65, N.S.									
Value of z SWC vs DA = 3.40, $p < 0.1\%$									

Probabilities in the table are two-tailed (see page 82).

* These data were missing for some children

Table 33

Teachers' ratings of children's initial attitudes and adjustment to school:
CA and DA samples (with breakdown of CA sample)

Item	Rating	First ten days of schooling (Schedule 1)												
		CA group								DA group	
		MC		SWC		MC+SWC		DA	
		N=146		N=176		N=322		N=348	
		n	%	n	%	n	%	n	%
1. To what extent is child overtired by end of day?	No sign of tiredness	106	72.6	105	59.7	211	65.5	233	67.0
	Somewhat tired	37	25.3	62	35.2	99	30.7	108	31.0
	Definitely overtired	3	2.1	9	5.1	12	3.7	7	2.0
Value of z CA vs DA = 0.48, N.S.									
Value of z SWC vs DA = 1.77, N.S. (two-tail)									
2. How would you rate child's initial attitude to the class teacher?	Very positive	69	47.3	70	39.8	139	43.2	133	38.2
	Positive	68	46.6	86	48.7	154	47.8	151	43.4
	Uncertain/negative	9	6.2	20	11.4	29	9.0	64	18.4
Value of z CA vs DA = 2.35, p < 1%									
Value of z SWC vs DA = 1.08, N.S.									
3. How would you rate child's initial attitude to other children in class?	Very positive	48	32.9	55	31.2	103	32.0	118	33.9
	Positive on the whole	87	59.6	89	50.6	176	54.7	153	44.0
	Uncertain/negative	11	7.5	32	18.2	43	13.3	77	22.1
Value of z CA vs DA = 1.00, N.S.									
Value of z SWC vs DA = 0.05, N.S.									
4. How would you rate child's initial adjustment to school?	Very good	67	45.9	82	46.6	149	46.3	142	40.8
	Average	76	52.1	84	47.7	160	49.7	187	53.7
	Poor	3	2.0	10	5.7	13	4.0	19	5.5
Value of z CA vs DA = 1.47, N.S.									
Value of z SWC vs DA = 1.06, N.S.									

continued overleaf

End of first term (Schedule 2)

Item	Rating	CA group						DA group	
		MC N=143		SWC N=174		MC+SWC N=317		N=372	
		n	%	n	%	n	%	n	%
1. To what extent is child overtired by end of day?	No sign of tiredness	103	72.0	84	48.3	187	59.0	221	59.4
	Somewhat tired	39	27.3	88	50.6	127	40.1	143	38.4
	Definitely overtired	1	0.7	2	1.1	3	0.9	8	2.1
Value of z CA vs DA = 0.03, N.S. Value of z SWC vs DA = 2.22, p < 5% (two tail)									
2. Child's initial attitude to the class teacher	Very positive	96	67.1	75	43.1	171	53.9	170	45.7
	Positive	44	30.9	79	45.4	123	38.8	146	39.2
	Uncertain/negative	3	2.1	20	11.5	23	7.3	56	15.0
Value of z CA vs DA = 2.76, p < 0.5% Value of z SWC vs DA = 0.01, N.S.									
3. Child's initial attitude to other children in class	Very positive	62	43.4	58	33.3	120	37.8	118	31.7
	Positive on the whole	69	48.2	90	51.7	159	50.2	184	49.5
	Uncertain/negative	12	8.4	26	14.9	38	12.0	70	18.8
Value of z CA vs DA = 2.34, p < 1% Value of z SWC vs DA = 0.75, N.S.									
4. Child's initial adjustment to school	Very good	86	60.1	63	36.2	149	47.0	184	49.5
	Average	57	39.9	101	58.0	158	49.8	171	46.0
	Poor	0	0.0	10	5.7	10	3.2	17	4.6
Value of z CA vs DA = 0.36, N.S. Value of z SWC vs DA = 2.75, p < 1% (two-tail)									

Probability levels in the table are one-tailed unless otherwise stated.

70

This table shows that on neither schedule was there a significant difference between the two groups in respect of incidence of tiredness among the children and that, in both groups, the percentage of children showing signs of tiredness fell over the course of the first school term. One point of interest concerning these figures, however, is that on both schedules, the SWC sub-group of the CA sample a higher proportion of 'tired children' than the DA group sample (significantly so on the second schedule). This trend was counter-balanced by the relatively low incidence of tiredness in the MC sub-group of the CA sample.

Data on the incidence of tiredness among infant school starters, shortly after they started school, were available from the National Survey sub-sample already referred to and are presented in Table 34.

It should be pointed out, however, that in the National Survey, the questionnaire containing the above item (and the previous items mentioned earlier) was completed by the class teachers at some stage during the children's first school term, rather than at the beginning or end of the term, as in the case of Schedules 1 and 2. Nevertheless, the data from this survey should be roughly comparable with that from the schedules. Indeed, the table shows that the percentage incidence of tiredness in the National Survey sample is similar to that in both the CA and DA samples, especially on School Schedule 2.

Table 33 also shows that, on both schedules, the CA children were rated as significantly more positive in their attitude to their class teachers than the DA children. (There was no significant difference, however, between the DA children and the SWC area children.) In either group, only a relatively small percentage of children were rated as being uncertain or negative in such attitudes. On a further question in each schedule the teachers were asked to judge whether these particular children were shy, withdrawn, or hostile. The data

Table 34

Incidence of tiredness in the children: a comparison between the present samples and the National Survey sub-sample

Item	Rating	Present samples				National Survey sub-sample
		Control area group		Deprived area group		
		N=322		N=348		N=254
		%		%		%
		Schedule No.				
		1	2	1	2	
To what extent is child over-tired at end of school day?	1. No sign of tiredness	65	59	67	60	55
	2. Somewhat tired (average)	31	40	31	38	41
	3. Definitely over-tired (markedly tired)	4	1	2	2	4

Wording used in National Survey question shown in brackets.

from this question are not presented here but there was no significant difference between the two groups in the distributions of the ratings over these categories, and on both schedules the number of children rated as actually hostile to the teacher was very small (on Schedule 1, three CA and six DA children, and on Schedule 2, no CA and two DA children). Thus, the majority of the children rated as uncertain or negative in their attitude to the class teacher fell into the 'shy' or 'withdrawn' category.

Similar questions to the above were asked regarding the children's attitudes to their peers and the results are presented in Table 33 (item 3). This shows that, whilst there was no significant difference between the two groups on the first schedule, on the second schedule the CA children showed a significantly more positive attitude to their peers than the DA children (although the difference between the DA children and the SWC area children was not significant). As in the case of attitude to class teacher, there was no significant difference between the two groups in the distribution of the children classed as uncertain or negative in attitude to other children, over the categories 'shy', 'withdrawn', and 'hostile'. Again, the number of children showing actual hostility in their attitude was very small in either group (on Schedule 1, six children in each group and, on Schedule 2, four in the CA group and five in the DA group).

It will be seen from Table 33 that there was no significant difference between the two groups in terms of the children's overall adjustment to the school situation, either after the first ten days of schooling or after the first term, the percentage distribution in either group over the three ratings being very similar on the two occasions. On the the first occasion, however, the DA group received significantly higher ratings of such adjustment than the SWC component of the CA group. However, when the same question was repeated at the end of the first school year (Schedule 4) the SWC group received slightly (non-significantly) higher overall adjustment ratings than the DA group, as Table 35 shows. Taken as a whole the CA children were rated as significantly better adjusted to school at the end of their first year than the DA children.

As will be discussed in the next section on teachers' ratings of the children's overall person-

ality adjustment within the classroom (see Table 38) obtained at intervals over the three year infant school period, the CA children were rated as better adjusted than the DA children during each of the three school years (significantly so at the end of the third year).

On School Schedule 2, two open-ended questions concerning the aspects of school life to which the children had made the most and least successful adjustment were included (see Appendix III, Schedule 2, items B5 and 6). Hovever, there was considerable difficulty in coding the teachers' responses to these two questions so that a meaningful pattern might emerge. For example, some children were rated as having adjusted equally well or poorly to several, or even to all, aspects of school life. As a result no meaningful statistical analysis of the data from these questions could be made.

The attendance records of the children during the first ten days of schooling were obtained, since it was thought that these might reflect, to some extent, school adjustment difficulties experienced by the children over that period. The data were analysed in terms of whether children made full attendance or less than full attendance during the period. In both groups, approximately 80 per cent of the children made full attendance, the result of the analysis being non-significant.

Summary: settling into school
In some respects, therefore, the Control Area group appeared to make a more successful adjustment to school life during the first term than the Deprived Area group. A significantly higher proportion of the Deprived Area children showed signs of distress on leaving the mother during the first two weeks of schooling, and clinging behaviour in the playground. The Control Area children were related as significantly more positive in attitude toward their class teachers, both at the beginning and the end of the first school term, and more positive toward their classroom peers at the end of that term. On the other hand, there were no significant differences between the groups in the incidence of unusual or difficult behaviour, of wetting, soiling or being sick in school, of tiredness at the end of the school day or in school attendance during the first ten days. The two groups received a similar pattern of ratings of overall adjustment to school on both the first and

Table 35

Teachers' ratings of children's overall adjustment to school

at end of their first school year:

CA and DA samples (with breakdown of CA sample)

Item	Rating	CA group								DA group	
		MC		SWC		MC+SWC					
		N=140		N=168		N=308				N=347	
		n	%	n	%	n	%			n	%
Child's overall adjustment to school	very good	109	77.9	93	55.4	202	65.6			185	53.3
	quite good	31	22.1	73	43.3	104	33.8			153	44.1
	poor	0	0.0	2	1.2	2	0.6			9	2.6

Value of z CA vs DA   = 3.26, p < 0.1% (one-tail)
Value of z SWC vs DA = 0.49, N.S. (one-tail)

73

second schedules. It was noted, however, that there were marked differences in the ratings received by the MC and SWC components of the Control Area group on some items in these schedules.

It had been expected that, since the DA children were probably less well prepared for school by reason of more limited cultural experiences and, perhaps, the relatively less positive attitudes of their parents toward the school and its aims, more marked differences between the two groups in their early adjustment to school would have emerged. The fact that such marked and consistent differences did not appear may well reflect credit on the British infant school system which, on the whole, provides a welcoming and sympathetic environment for new entrants and an orientation toward their individual needs. Another factor which should be taken into account here, however, is that of the relativity of the teachers' judgements of their children, i.e. each teacher assesses her children according to her own standards and the range of behaviours presented by those children. Thus, for example, in absolute terms, the rating 'well adjusted' in the context of population of 'deprived area' children with a fair sprinkling of children from 'problem families' may not be strictly equivalent to a similar rating awarded by a teacher of a sample of children from highly conforming 'middle-class' children. This difficulty of interpretation applies to all of the teachers' ratings data but, as will be seen from the findings presented in subsequent sections of this chapter and in Chapter 5, highly significant differences between the Control Area and Deprived Area samples *do* appear on many of the teachers' ratings, including some rather subjective ones.

B. SOCIAL COMPETENCE AND SOCIAL AND EMOTIONAL ADJUSTMENT

(i) Social competence

Three items on School Schedule 2 (completed at the end of the children's first term) related to the children's social competence and the data yielded by them are presented in Table 36.

It will be seen from this table that there was no significant difference in the pattern of ratings received by the CA and DA groups on any of the three items although, on each one, the CA group had a higher proportion of children in the most favourable rating category. The difference between the two groups in competence in managing school/classroom routines (item 2) fell just short of the 5 per cent significance level. However, it is interesting to observe that, on all three items, the MC sub-group of the CA group had markedly higher ratings than the SWC sub-group and the ratings of the latter group were significantly poorer than those of the DA group on two items, self-dependence in dressing, and competence in managing school/classroom routines.

These results were unexpected insofar as one would expect children from relatively deprived home backgrounds to have greater difficulty than children from more favoured backgrounds in managing school routines such as looking after materials assigned to them or their own possessions and finding their way about the classroom or school. Similarly, it seemed likely that such children would show relatively less self-reliance in carrying out class activities since these would probably be less familiar to them than to children from homes providing relevant educational experiences. When they were compared with the children in the MC group, this, indeed, was the case, but it was surprising to find the DA children rated as socially more competent than the SWC area children. With regard to self-dependence in dressing, however, there seems less reason to expect children from deprived homes to be retarded. On the contrary, in some such homes at least, teachers reported that the children sometimes had to take on a good deal of self-responsibility for dressing themselves in the morning and even for preparing their own breakfasts and getting to school, due to the apparent indifference or fecklessness of the parents. Even so, the proportion of children in the MC sub-group rated as quite independent in dressing was over twice that of children similarly rated in the DA group. It would seem from these results, therefore, that the MC children were distinctly more self-reliant and competent in their social skills than the children in either the SWC or DA groups, due, perhaps, to a greater drive towards achievement and independence induced by the attitudes and rearing methods of their parents.

Table 36

Teachers' ratings of children's social competence during their first school term: CA and DA samples (with breakdown of CA sample)

Item	Rating	CA group						DA group	
		MC		SWC		MC+SWC			
		N=143		N=174		N=317		N=372	
		n	%	n	%	n	%	n	%
1. Child's self-dependence in dressing	Quite independent	65	45.2	22	12.6	87	27.4	78	21.0
	Needs some help	71	49.6	138	79.3	209	65.9	273	73.4
	Very dependent	7	4.9	14	8.0	21	6.6	21	5.6
Value of z CA vs DA = 1.44, N.S.									
Value of z SWC vs DA = 2.35, p< 1% (two-tail)									
2. Child's competence in school/class routines	Very competent and reliable	75	52.4	33	19.0	108	34.1	94	25.3
	Quite competent and reliable	61	42.7	105	60.3	166	52.4	234	62.9
	Not very competent and reliable	7	4.9	36	20.7	43	13.6	44	11.8
Value of z CA vs DA = 1.60, N.S.									
Value of z SWC vs DA = 2.58, p< 0.5% (two-tail)									
3. Child's general degree of self-reliance in class activities	Very self-reliant	58	40.6	48	27.6	106	33.4	108	29.0
	Fairly self-reliant	72	50.3	94	54.0	166	52.4	201	54.0
	Lacking in self-reliance	13	9.1	32	18.4	45	14.2	63	16.9
Value of z CA vs DA = 1.35, N.S.									
Value of z SWC vs DA = 0.40, N.S.									

Probability levels in the table are one-tailed unless otherwise stated.

(ii) Relationship with other children and with teachers

Ratings of the level of the child's co-operation with other children and of his relationship with the class teacher were obtained over a series of schedules and these are presented in Table 37.

With regard to the level of the child's co-operation with other children the CA group received consistently higher ratings than the DA group over the four relevant schedules, but these differences were not very marked, reaching only the 5 per cent significance level on Schedules 2 and 6 but falling below significance on the remaining schedules. (In no case was the result of the comparison between the SWC area sub-group of the CA sample and the DA sample significant.) It will be seen from the table that in neither group is there a steady trend in the distribution of ratings over the series of schedules, the majority of children in both groups being rated as fairly or very co-operative and only a small proportion (between three and six per cent) rated as unco-operative with their peers. It sems quite likely that, even in culturally and materially deprived homes, children will have ample experience of social interaction with other children in their age group in the play setting and will develop the ability to co-operate with them to a similar degree to that of children from more favoured backgrounds. The lack of very marked differences between the two groups on these ratings is, therefore, not surprising, although a steady increase in the proportion of children rated as very co-operative over the three years covered by the schedules might have been expected, since the development of social skills in the children is presumably a major aim of the infant school (see Chapter 11).

The ratings received by the two groups in respect of their relationship with the class teacher show the same lack of trend over the series of schedules as in the case of the ratings of the children's level of co-operation with others, discussed above. On each schedule, the CA group received higher ratings than the DA group but, whilst the differences between the groups were statistically significant on the second, fourth and fifth schedules (highly significant on the latter two schedules), the difference fell below significance on the final (sixth) schedule. (Comparison between the SWC sub-group of the CA group and the DA

group yielded a similar pattern, except that the difference between the groups on Schedule 2 was non-significant.) The percentage figures in the table show that, on Schedule 6, the CA group received poorer ratings on this item than on any previous occasion, whilst this was not the case with the DA group, whose ratings over the four schedules showed less variability. It seems unlikely that the quality of the teacher-child relationship among children in the CA group really would deteriorate from one year to the next so the probable explanation of the decline in the ratings received by this group on Schedule 6, as compared with Schedule 5, is that it reflects the varying standards of judgement of the teachers carrying out the assessments on the two occasions. The overall result from the schedules on this item, therefore, is that the CA group showed a significantly more positive attitude toward their class teachers than the DA group, a finding in accord with the view of writers such as Bernstein (1970), who stresses the socio-cultural gap between teachers and children from lower-working-class homes, as well as with the findings of many American studies of disadvantaged children (see Chapter 2).

Some support for the above conclusion comes from the results of the analysis of the follow-up question to the rating of the child's relationship with his teacher, which was concerned with those children rated on the latter item as uncertain or negative in their attitudes (see item 3 in Table 37). This analysis shows, that, whereas the pattern of allocation of the CA group over the categories 'shy', 'withdrawn' and 'hostile' showed some variability over the series of schedules ('improving' from Schedule 2 to 4, but 'declining' over Schedules 5 and 6), that for the DA group showed a steady trend in the unfavourable direction, i.e. an increasingly large proportion of the children were rated as 'withdrawn' or 'hostile'. However, none of the differences in pattern of distribution between the two groups (using a 'chi-square' analysis since the categories do not fall on a continuum) was statistically significant, although that on Schedule 5 approached the 5 per cent level. (On Schedules 2 and 4, the chi-square analysis was invalid because the proportion of cells with an expected frequency of less than 5 was greater than the suggested limit.) Two notes of caution must be mentioned, however; firstly that

Table 37

Teachers' ratings of the children's co-operation with others and
of their relationship with the class teachers: CA and DA samples

Item and Rating	End of first term (Schedule 2)				End of first year (Schedule 4)				End of second year (Schedule 5)				End of third year (Schedule 6)			
	CA		DA		CA		DA		CA		DA		CA		DA	
	N = 317		N = 372		N = 308		N = 347		N = 280		N = 309		N = 265		N = 279	
	n	%	n	%	n	%	n	%	n	%	n	%	n	%	n	%
1. Child's co-operation with other children																
very co-operative	129	40.7	110	29.6	144	46.7	151	43.5	112	40.0	117	37.9	133	50.2	121	43.4
fairly co-operative	177	55.8	243	65.3	155	50.3	175	50.4	158	56.4	171	55.3	125	47.2	142	50.9
unco-operative	11	3.5	19	5.1	9	2.9	21	6.0	10	3.6	21	6.8	7	2.6	16	5.7
Value of z CA vs DA	3.4, p< 0.5%				1.15, N.S.				0.89, N.S.				1.81, p< 5%			
Value of z SWC vs DA	0.02, N.S.				0.93, N.S.				0.70, N.S.				1.49, N.S.			
2. Child's relationship with class teacher																
very positive	171	53.9	170	45.7	193	62.7	171	49.3	143	51.1	128	41.4	122	46.0	114	40.9
positive on whole	123	38.8	146	39.2	104	33.8	133	39.3	121	43.2	134	43.4	118	44.5	130	46.6
uncertain/negative	23	7.3	56	15.1	11	3.6	43	12.4	16	5.7	47	15.2	25	9.4	35	12.5
Value of z CA vs DA	2.76, p< 0.5%				4.00, p< 0.1%				3.13, p< 0.1%				1.36, N.S.			
Value of z SWC vs DA	0.01, N.S.				1.74, p< 5%				2.30, p< 2.5%				1.47, N.S.			
***3. If uncertain or negative is child:**	N=23		N=70		N=11		N=43		N=16		N=47		N=25		N=35	
shy	13	57	48	69	8	73	24	56	11	69	16	35	15	60	13	37
withdrawn	10	43	17	24	3	27	15	35	4	25	23	49	7	28	12	34
hostile	0	0	5	7	0	0	4	9	1	6	8	17	3	12	10	29
Value of X^2(2 d.f.): CA vs DA	**				**				5.92, N.S.(2-tail)				3.66, N.S.(2-tail)			
SWC vs DA	**				**				**				**			

Notes: * Chi-square was used to analyse the data from this item because the categories are not ordered on a continuum.

    ** In these cases the Chi-square analysis was invalid because more than 20 per cent of the expected frequencies were below 5.

Where the sample size drops below 100 percentage figures have been rounded to the nearest whole number.

Probability levels in the table are one-tailed unless otherwise stated.

the numbers of children in either group were relatively small, and secondly, that these numbers fluctuated from one schedule to another so that firm statements about meaningful trends are not possible.

(iii) Behaviour and overall adjustment

Schedules 3, 5 and 6 included a rating of the child's overall personality adjustment within the classroom setting which was extracted from the Classroom Behaviour Inventory by E. S. Schaefer (unpublished to date, see Vol. 2 in this series for details). The data from these ratings are presented in Table 38.

It will be seen that the CA children consistently received more favourable ratings than the DA children over the period covered by the schedules, although the majority of children in both groups were judged to be well adjusted or to have no significant adjustment problems (categories one and two). In particular, the percentage of children rated 'somewhat' or 'very disturbed' (categories three and four) was higher in the DA than the CA groups, ranging from 15 to 20 per cent in the former group over the three schedules, as against approximately 8 to 14 per cent in the latter group. The results of a 'chi-square' analysis carried out on these data (combining categories one and two, and three and four) reached statistical significance only at the end of the third school year, although approaching significance at the end of the second year. Comparison between the ratings received by the SWC area children and the DA children yielded a similar pattern, except that none of the results reached statistical significance.

In addition to the above ratings of overall adjustment on Schedules 3 and 6, the teachers were asked to complete Stott's (1966) six pointers to possible behaviour problems in respect of the children and Table 39 presents the results obtained from these ratings.

It will be seen that, at the end of the children's second school term (Schedule 3) the differences between the two groups in the incidence of behavioural problems or unusual behaviour are very slight, except in the case of abnormal, restless and aggressive behaviour, where the DA children showed a rather higher percentage than the CA children, significantly so in the case of aggressiveness. By the end of the infant school period

however (Schedule 6), the differences between the groups were a little more marked on some items, in particular in the incidence of abnormal behaviour, where the difference reached statistical significance. On the other hand, the difference between the groups in the incidence of aggressive behaviour fell short of significance whereas previously it was significant. The analysis of the differences between the SWC area children and the DA children on these ratings yielded a very similar pattern of results to that described above, except that none of the differences reached statistical significance on either schedule. Not too much weight should be put on the comparison of the two sets of ratings, however, because over the period between the third and sixth schedule a fairly large number of children, particularly in the Deprived Area, left for other schools and dropped out of the sample and such children may not have been representative of the groups from which they were drawn. Indeed, it will be recalled from Chapter 3 that there was evidence that the DA 'leavers' tended to have (non-significantly) poorer ratings on a selection of school schedule items than the full DA sample. (See Appendix Table A4.)

As well as comparing the groups on the individual Stott pointers, it is useful to examine the data in terms of the total number of adverse ratings on the six pointers received by the children. Table 40 presents these data.

It will be seen that, at the end of the ~~first~~ second term see Table 4 school ~~year~~ (Schedule 3), the DA group had a rather lower proportion of children with no adverse pointers compared with the CA group (73 per cent as opposed to 78 per cent), and a higher proportion of children with three or more pointers (approximately 10 per cent as opposed to 6 per cent). The overall result, however, fell short of statistical significance.

By the end of the third year, the comparison of the two groups gives a rather mixed result with a similar proportion of children in both groups (over 70 per cent) showing no adverse pointers, 14 per cent of the DA children and approximately 23 per cent of the CA children showing one or two adverse pointers, but roughly twice as many DA children as CA children, proportionately, showing three or more adverse pointers (approximately 13 per cent as compared with 6 per cent). Comparison of the SWC sub-group with the DA sample

Table 38

Teachers' ratings of children's overall adjustment within the classroom setting: CA and DA samples

Item	Rating	End of 2nd term (Schedule 3)				End of 2nd year (Schedule 5)				End of 3rd year (Schedule 6)			
		CA N=309		DA N=355		CA N=280		DA N=309		CA N=265		DA N=279	
		n	%	n	%	n	%	n	%	n	%	n	%
Schaefer ratings	1 Well adjusted	114	36.9	115	32.4	86	30.7	92	29.8	104	39.2	107	38.3
	2 No significant problems	156	50.5	182	51.3	156	55.7	156	50.5	138	52.1	128	45.9
	3 Somewhat disturbed	36	11.6	54	15.2	38	13.6	54	17.5	22	8.3	34	12.2
	4 Very disturbed	3	1.0	4	1.1	0	0.0	7	2.3	1	0.4	10	3.6
Value of χ^2	CA vs DA (1 d.f.)	1.84, N.S.				3.57, N.S.				5.69, p < 2%			
	SWC vs DA (1 d.f.)	0.04, N.S.				2.06, N.S.				3.06, N.S.			

Notes:

1. The test of significance used for these adjustment items was chi-square as this was the test used in an earlier analysis of behaviour problems in the project sample reported by Chazan and Jackson (1971).

2. For the calculation of chi-square the first and second, and third and fourth ratings were combined.

3. **All** probabilities given in this table are two-tailed. (See page 82).

Table 39

Children's behaviour problems (Stott's six pointers) during the first and third school years: CA and DA samples

| Question | Answer | end of 2nd term (Schedule 3) | | | | end of 3rd year (Schedule 6) | | | |
| | | CA N=309 | | DA N=355 | | CA N=265 | | DA N=279 | |
		n	%	n	%	n	%	n	%
1. Is the child's behaviour such as you would expect of a normal alert child of his/her age?	Yes	283	91.6	314	88.4	245	92.4	236	84.6
	No	26	8.4	41	11.5	20	7.5	43	15.4
	Value of X^2 CA vs DA	1.49, N.S.				7.46, p < 1%			
	Value of X^2 SWC vs DA	0.002, N.S.				2.76, N.S.			
2. Is the child exceptionally quiet, timid or withdrawn?	Yes	29	9.4	34	9.6	35	13.2	33	11.8
	No	280	90.6	321	90.4	230	86.8	246	88.2
	Value of X^2 CA vs DA	0.001, N.S.				0.13, N.S.			
	Value of X^2 SWC vs DA	0.71, N.S.				3.30, N.S.			
3. Is the child restless in a way that seriously hinders his/her learning?	Yes	23	7.4	39	11.0	24	9.1	35	12.5
	No	186	92.6	316	89.0	241	90.9	244	87.5
	Value of X^2 CA vs DA	2.09, N.S.				1.37, N.S.			
	Value of X^2 SWC vs DA	1.05, N.S.				1.25, N.S.			

Continued on next page

4. Is the child very aggressive?	Yes	10	3.2	29	8.2	13	4.9	20	7.2
	No	299	96.8	326	91.8	252	95.1	259	92.8
	Value of X^2		CA vs DA = 6.46, p < 2%				0.86, N.S.		
	Value of X^2		SWC vs DA = 3.21, N.S.				1.68, N.S.		
5. Does the child get on well with other children?	Yes	294	95.1	331	93.2	255	96.2	258	92.5
	No	15	4.8	24	6.8	10	3.8	21	7.5
	Value of X^2		CA vs DA = 0.79, N.S.				2.90, N.S.		
	Value of X^2		SWC vs DA = 0.002, N.S.				1.24, N.S.		
6. Is there anything in the child's behaviour to make you think that he might be unstable or suffer from nervous trouble?	Yes	31	10.0	38	10.7	31	11.7	37	13.3
	No	278	90.0	317	89.3	234	88.3	242	86.7
	Value of X^2		CA vs DA =0.003, N.S.				0.18, N.S.		
	Value of X^2		SWC vs DA =0.40, N.S.				0.06, N.S.		

Notes: 1. The test of significance used for these adjustment items was chi-square as this was the test used in an earlier analysis of behaviour problems in the project sample reported by Chazan and Jackson (1971).

2. All probabilities given in this table are two-tailed (see page 82).

3. For each value of chi-square in this table there was one degree of freedom.

4. The wording of the Stott pointers has been somewhat modified for use in connection with infant school children.

yields a similar pattern of results to that of the main comparison, except that, on Schedule 3, the proportions of children in the two groups with three or more adverse pointers, were almost identical.

The above results are in agreement with those presented earlier in this section in regard to the teachers' rating of the children's overall adjustment insofar as they both indicate that the DA group has a higher proportion than the CA group of children rated by the teachers as showing definite behavioural disturbance.

The association between social class status and social and emotional adjustment is by no means clear, as Chazan and Jackson (1971) point out, although some studies cited by those authors have shown a higher incidence of behavioural disturbance among children in lower class families or in 'deprived areas'. Although there is some evidence to support an expectation of a difference between the present groups in favour of the CA group on the Stott or Schaefer ratings, it was decided that this evidence is not conclusive. Accordingly, since the direction of the difference between the CA and DA groups was not firmly predicted, the probabilities shown in Tables 32, 38, 39 and 40 are two-tailed, in distinction from those for most other items in this and subsequent chapters in this section, which are one-tailed (see also page 35.

It is interesting to note that the DA children showed a higher incidence of restlessness and aggressiveness than the CA children on both occasions, whilst the figures for the incidence of nervous and timid behaviour are relatively closer for the two groups. This pattern lends some support to the finding, discussed earlier in this chapter, that the DA headteachers and class teachers thought that restless and aggressive behaviour were the relatively most frequent types of behavioural problem in their schools, whereas the CA headteachers (but not the class teachers) considered nervousness and shyness to be relatively the most frequent problems.

As discussed in an earlier section of this chapter, it had been expected that marked differences between the two main groups would have emerged with regard to the incidence of restless behaviour, in particular. The lack of such differences on this item in Schedules 3 and 6 is in line with the pattern of results found on a similar item

on the second schedule completed at the end of the children's first term, reported in section A (ii) of this chapter. For a more complete analysis and discussion of the difference between the CA and DA and rural samples on the Stott and Schaefer ratings, see the article by Chazan and Jackson (1971) cited above.

Summary: social competence and social and emotional adjustment

Children in the DA sample were rated by their teachers as lower in social competence than those in the CA sample as a whole, although they received significantly higher ratings than the SWC sub-group on some items. In comparison with the CA children, they were also rated less favourably with regard to their co-operation with other children over the infant school period and their relationships with their class teachers. In terms of overall personality adjustment, the DA children received consistently (but not always significantly) lower ratings than the CA children during each school year, and, on the two administrations of Stott's 'six pointers', significantly more of the DA children showed aggressive behaviour on the first occasion and abnormal behaviour on the second. On both occasions more of the DA children showed distinct signs of behaviour disturbance (three or more adverse pointers) although a similar proportion of children in either group showed no behavioural problems. In general, the above pattern of between group differences was maintained, when the SWC area children, considered separately, were compared with the CA children, although these differences were sometimes less pronounced than in the main comparison.

C. CHILDREN'S INTERESTS AND ACTIVITIES

The first two schedules, completed at the beginning and end of the children's first term respectively, contained a question concerning the level of interest shown by the children in the materials and experiences provided in the school. Table 41 presents the data from this question and it will be seen that, on both occasions, the CA group are rated as showing a significantly more active interest in their school experiences than the DA group, a finding consistent with the view that the DA children were relatively less well prepared by their

Table 40

Total number of Stott pointers scored by children in the CA and DA samples

Number of adverse ratings	End of 2nd term (Schedule 3)								End of 3rd year (Schedule 6)							
	MC N=140		SWC N=169		CA (MC+SWC) N=309		DA N=355		MC N=122		SWC N=143		CA (MC+SWC) N=265		DA N=279	
	n	%	n	%	n	%	n	%	n	%	n	%	n	%	n	%
0	118	84.3	124	73.4	242	78.1	259	73.0	95	77.9	94	65.7	189	71.3	205	73.5
1	11	7.8	16	9.5	27	8.7	49	13.8	14	11.5	30	21.0	44	16.6	26	9.3
2	8	5.7	13	7.7	21	6.8	12	3.4	6	4.9	10	7.0	16	6.0	13	4.7
3	2	1.4	13	7.7	15	4.9	14	3.9	5	4.1	4	2.8	9	3.4	15	5.4
4	1	0.7	3	1.8	4	1.3	21	5.9	2	1.6	5	3.5	7	2.6	20	7.2

Value of X^2 CA vs DA (2 d.f.) = 3.69, N.S.   11.83, p < 0.1%

Value of X^2 SWC vs DA (2 d.f.) = 0.02, N.S.   14.23, p < 0.1%

Note: All probabilities in this table are two-tailed (see p 82).

For the chi-square tests, three categories were used: 0; 1 or 2; and 3+ adverse ratings.

Table 41

Level of interest in classroom activities/experiences shown by the CA and DA samples during the first school term (with breakdown of CA sample)

Schedule	Item	Rating	CA group						DA group	
			MC N=146		SWC N=176		MC+SWC N=322		DA N=348	
			n	%	n	%	n	%	n	%
1 first ten days	Does child show active interest in materials/ experiences provided in school?	Very active interest	59	40.4	65	36.9	124	38.5	111	31.9
		Quite active interest	78	53.4	92	52.3	170	52.8	192	55.2
		Little interest	9	6.2	19	10.8	28	8.7	45	12.9
	Value of z CA vs DA = 2.11, p <2.5% Value of z SWC vs DA = 1.15, N.S.									
2 end of first term	Does child show active interest in materials/ experiences provided in school?		N=143		N=174		N=317		N=372	
		Very active interest	63	44.1	58	33.3	121	38.2	103	27.7
		Quite active interest	75	52.4	96	55.2	171	53.9	232	62.4
		Little interest	5	3.5	20	11.5	25	7.9	37	9.9
	Value of z CA vs DA = 2.77, p < 0.5% Value of z SWC vs DA = 0.79, N.S.									

Probability levels in the table are one-tailed.

home background experiences to take advantage of the experiences and opportunities provided in school. However, there was no significant difference on either schedule between the SWC area children and the DA children.

It will also be noted that, within each group, the pattern of distribution of the ratings is very similar on the two occasions (although that for the DA group shows a slight downward trend). It might have been expected that, over the course of the first school term, the proportion of children rated as showing a very active interest in the classroom materials/experiences would increase but this was not the case. The absence of such an upward trend in the ratings over the period in question cannot be attributed to variations in teachers' standards of judgement because, in most cases, the same class teacher completed both schedules in respect of each child.

Schedule 2 also contained a rating by the class teacher of each child's most preferred activity from the whole range of activities provided in the classroom. It was thought possible that children in the DA group would tend to show a lower preference for the more academic or sedentary activities such as pre-reading work or painting, and a stronger interest in, for example, physical or manipulative play, or socio-dramatic play, on the grounds they would have had relatively limited experience of the former type of activities at home, in comparison with children from more advantaged homes. Table 42 presents the data from this item and it will be seen that, although, as expected, the DA group had a lower percentage of children showing a clear preference for pre-reading/number activities and painting/drawing/music, this group did not show a correspondingly larger proportion of children preferring the 'less academic' activities. However, a meaningful interpretation of this table is greatly complicated by the fact that approximately 10 per cent of the CA group and 28 per cent of the DA group were rated as showing preference for a combination of the activities listed. If these combined preferences were taken into account, of course, the pattern of preferences shown by the two groups might be considerably altered. Because of this difficulty in interpreting the results no statistical analysis of these data is presented. It is of interest, in this connection, that the patterns of preferences among basic infant school activities shown by the

Control and Deprived groups in the Intensive Study reported in Vol. 2 (Part One, Chapter 6) in this series were remarkably similar to each other, in each case the more structured or intellectual activities, reading, writing, and number work, being rated in the lower half of the preference scale.

Following the argument presented above, it could be predicted that the DA children would show a lower level of concentration in the more structured or 'academic' activities such as reading, writing and number work. There is a good deal of evidence, based on both research and the practical experience of teachers, that children from disadvantaged homes show greater difficulty in concentrating and sustaining effort on school tasks than children from more favoured homes (see Vol. 2, Chapter 6, in this series, for some reference to such evidence), although whether this stems from motivational problems rather than attentional disabilities is arguable. On the schedules completed at the end of each of the three infant school years, the teachers were asked to rate the children's level of concentration in the more structured activities and the data from these ratings are presented in Table 43, which also includes data from teachers' ratings of the children's use of play materials and the quality of their creative activities.

The table shows that whilst the CA group received higher ratings in concentration than the DA group consistently over the schedules, the difference reached statistical significance only on Schedule 4 (end of first year). Differences between the SWC area children and the DA children were in the same direction as in the main comparison but did not reach significance level on any occasion.

Table 43 also shows that both CA and DA groups showed an upward trend in the ratings received over the two years covered by the schedules, particularly so in the case of the latter group. Such an improvement is, of course, to be expected as the children gain in mental and emotional maturity. The finding that the between-group differences fall below significance after the first year suggests the possibility that the DA children made a relatively greater improvement in concentration than the CA children during the second and third years, and inspection of the percentage figures in the table (item 1) supports this. However, as mentioned earlier, the fact that

Table 42

Children's preferences for classroom activities at the end of their first term: CA and DA samples (with breakdown of CA sample)

Item	Rating	CA group						DA group	
		MC N=143		SWC N=174		MC+SWC N=317		N=372	
		n	%	n	%	n	%	n	%
What classroom activities does child show preference for?	1. Vigorous physical play	7	4.9	17	9.8	24	7.6	10	2.7
	2. Manipulative play	32	22.4	36	20.7	68	21.4	84	22.6
	3. Social/dramatic play	9	6.3	9	5.2	18	5.7	21	5.6
	4. Painting/drawing/music	19	13.3	29	16.7	48	15.1	22	5.9
	5. Pre-reading/number	11	7.7	19	10.9	30	9.5	13	3.5
	6. Other	0	0.0	1	0.6	1	0.3	3	0.8
	7. No particular preference	56	39.2	41	23.6	97	30.6	114	30.6
	8. Combination (1 to 6)	9	6.3	22	12.6	31	9.8	105	28.2

the sample size drops steadily over the period makes the interpretation of such trends rather uncertain, since it was found that the DA 'leavers' tended to have poorer ratings on selected school schedule items than the full DA sample (see pp. 53 to 54). The present finding that the CA group showed better concentration in some school activities than the DA group is supported by a similar finding in the intensive study comparing children from culturally deprived home backgrounds with a control group of children reported in Volume 2 (Part One), Neither study yielded for a decline in the level of concentration shown by disadvantaged children as they progressed through school such as has been described by some American writers.

A related question to that on concentration concerns the child's use of play materials in school in terns of how frequently such play leads to an end product or successful conclusion. To the extent that the child's play has such a definite outcome, it requires a degree of sustained concentration and this question can be regarded as an interesting complement to that on concentration since it is not tied to the more structured, or intellectual, school activities. Table 43 presents the data obtained from this question over a series of schedules and it will be seen that the CA children received significantly higher ratings on each schedule than the DA children. However, this result appears to be largely attributable to the marked superiority of the MC area children, for the differences between the SWC sub-group and the DA group were not statistically significant, except on Schedule 6. This contrasts with the finding, discussed above, that, on the rating of concentration, the differences between the CA and DA groups were significant only on the first of the series of schedules. Both the CA and DA groups show a steady improvement in the ratings on the use of play materials over the period covered by the schedules, in line with that observed for the ratings on concentration.

The finding of significant differences between the two groups in favour of the CA group on their use of play materials is supported by a similar finding from the intensive study of a sub-sample of culturally deprived children reported in Volume 2

Table 43

Level of concentration, use of play materials and quality of children's creative activities in the CA and DA samples

Item and Rating	End of first term (Schedule 2)				End of first year (Schedule 4)				End of second year (Schedule 5)				End of third year (Schedule 6)			
	CA (N = 317)		DA (N = 372)		CA (N = 308)		DA (N = 347)		CA (N = 280)		DA (N = 309)		CA (N = 265)		DA (N = 279)	
	n	%	n	%	n	%	n	%	n	%	n	%	n	%	n	%
1. Level of concentration																
concentrates well																
usually	120	37.9	112	30.1	104	33.8	76	21.9	102	36.4	94	30.4	106	40.0	104	37.3
varies	144	45.4	193	51.9	145	47.1	176	50.7	128	45.7	149	48.2	114	43.0	116	41.6
lacks concentration	53	16.7	67	18.0	59	19.2	95	27.4	50	17.9	66	21.4	45	17.0	59	21.1
Value of z CA vs DA	1.74, p< 5%				3.55, p< 0.1%				1.57, N.S.				0.98, N.S.			
Value of z SWC vs DA	1.36, N.S.				0.84, N.S.				0.86, N.S.				1.32, N.S.			
2. Does use of play material lead to end product?																
usually	82	25.9	57	15.3	152	49.3	134	38.6	–	–	–	–	164	61.9	140	50.2
sometimes	177	55.8	232	62.4	135	43.8	156	45.0	–	–	–	–	85	32.1	100	35.8
rarely/never	58	18.3	83	22.3	21	6.8	57	16.4	–	–	–	–	16	6.0	39	14.0
Value of z CA vs DA	2.92, p< 0.5%				3.56, p< 0.1%								3.14, p< 0.1%			
Value of z SWC vs DA	0.51, N.S.				0.07, N.S.								2.28, p< 2.5%			
3. Quality of child's creative activities: shows imagination																
often	–	–	–	–	–	–	–	–	71	25.4	79	25.6	83	31.3	93	33.3
sometimes	–	–	–	–	–	–	–	–	165	58.9	159	51.5	139	52.4	133	47.7
rarely/never	–	–	–	–	–	–	–	–	44	15.7	71	23.0	43	16.2	53	19.0
Value of z CA vs DA									1.16, N.S.				0.01, N.S.			
SWC vs DA									0.79, N.S.				0.12, N.S.			

Probability levels in the table are one-tailed.

(Part One) of this series. This difference occurred despite the fact that, according to information provided by the class teachers responsible for the project children during the first school year (see chapter 10), the DA teachers showed a greater readiness than the CA teachers to involve themselves actively in the children's play, for example, by talking to and questioning the children and making suggestions concerning their play activities. On the other hand, it may well be that the CA children, coming from culturally advantaged homes, do not need as much structuring of their play experiences as less fortunate children, since in many cases they will have developed the ability to play purposefully and constructively by the time they enter school.

The children were also rated on the imaginative quality of their creative activities and it will be seen from Table 43 that, although the CA children were rated as showing more imagination in such activities than the DA children on all the schedules, the difference between the groups was most marked on Schedule 2 (end of first term), where it was statistically highly significant, in contrast to the subsequent results which were non-significant. The SWC sub-group did not receive significantly higher ratings than the DA group on this item on any of the schedules. Again, there is an upward trend in the ratings received by the two groups over the series of schedules but this seems less marked than in the case of the other two items in the table. The fact that the most marked difference between the two main samples occurred not long after school entry, suggests the possibility that the reason for this difference lay in the nature and quality of the children's play experiences prior to starting school. It may be, that in the 'middle class' homes the kind of play materials provided gave more scope to imaginative play than those available to DA children. For example, they may have had greater experience with expressive media such as paint, plasticene and sand.

Summary: children's interests and activities

The CA group as a whole, but not the SWC component of it taken by itself, showed a significantly more active interest in the materials and experience provided in schools during the first term, according to the teachers. No clear differences emerged between the two main groups in their patterns of preference among the various infant school activities, as had been thought possible. Also contrary to expectation, the CA group did not show a significantly higher level of concentration than the DA group in the more structured school activities, except at the end of the first school year, and this might have been due to a relatively greater increase in concentration by the latter group over the last two years of their infant schooling. However, according to the teachers there was a significantly greater tendency for the play activities of the Control Area children (in particular those in the MC sub-group), to lead to a definite end product or successful conclusion. In addition, the Control Area group (and, again, the MC sub-group in particular) appeared to show more imaginativeness or originality in their creative activities than the Deprived Area group, but this difference was statistically significant only at the end of the children's first term.

5 Basic Skills

A. ORAL LANGUAGE

Oral language skills are of fundamental importance in the educational process, but especially in the infant school stage where oral, as opposed to written language is the main medium of teaching. Considerable interest, therefore, centres on the language performance of the CA and DA groups of the present sample. Most of the information on this came from teachers' ratings of language skills in the series of school schedules but, in addition, a vocabulary test was included in the attainment test battery given to the children during their final infant school term. Table 44 presents the data obtained from the teachers' ratings.

The table shows that the general pattern is one of the overall superiority of the CA children with regard to oral language skills but the differences between the groups are not always statistically significant.

Looking at the results in more detail, it will be seen that the CA children received significantly higher ratings of clarity of speech articulation than the DA children on each school schedule. However, the SWC component of the CA sample were rated as significantly better in this skill only at the end of the third year (Schedule 6), so that this result mainly reflects the superior speech articulation of the MC area children.

The finding that the DA children were rated as being relatively less clear in their speech, is certainly in line with previous research (see Vol. II, Chapter 4 of this series). Indeed, poor articulation tends to be one of the more obvious features of the speech of children from deprived backgrounds. In the interviews of teachers in the present sample (see Chapter 11) distinctly more DA than CA teachers reported language problems with their children, including poor speech articulation.

It will also be observed that both main groups show a slight upward trend in their ratings between Schedule 2 and Schedule 6. A more marked improvement might have been expected since the schools involved were probably concerned to a greater or lesser degree to improve the quality of the children's articulation, particularly,

one would think, in the more deprived areas, where parental speech models are probably poor in this respect. The lack of a marked upward trend in the ratings may reflect differing standards of judgements as between teachers making the early ratings and those making the later ratings, the latter group being perhaps relatively more severe in their standards. The steady loss of children from both samples over the period covered by the schedules is a further possible source of distortion in the trend of results, since these leavers might not be typical of their groups in respect of this or, indeed, any other skill rated. As stated in Chapter 3, the DA leavers tended to receive lower ratings than the full DA sample on selected school schedule items, although if such children also tended to be poorer in articulation this would be an additional reason for expecting a rise in the level of DA sample ratings on this item over time.

In the range of vocabulary shown by the children in their spoken language, as in the case of speech articulation, the CA children received consistently and very significantly higher ratings than the DA children over the period covered by the schedules. This was not just a 'middle-class' phenomenon, however, for the SWC sub-group of the Control sample were also rated as significantly superior to the DA group on this item on Schedules 2 and 5, although not on the final schedule. Again, there is no marked upward trend in the ratings received by either group over the series of schedules (although the DA children show a more consistent improvement than the CA children), perhaps for the reasons discussed above in connection with ratings of speech articulation.

This finding that the CA children were significantly superior to the DA children in their rated vocabulary range is supported by the result of the comparison of the two groups in their performance on the WISC vocabulary sub-test, given as part of the attainment survey in the children's final school term, which is presented in Table 45. It will be seen that the CA children obtained a very significantly higher mean score on this sub-test than the DA children. This difference was maintained, although at a lower level of statistical

Table 44

Teachers' ratings of children's oral language skills for the CA and DA samples

Item and Rating	End of first term (Schedule 2)				End of first year (Schedule 4)				End of second year (Schedule 5)				End of third year (Schedule 6)			
	CA		DA		CA		DA		CA		DA		CA		DA	
	N = 317		N = 372		N = 308		N = 347		N = 280		N = 309		N = 265		N = 279	
	n	%	n	%	n	%	n	%	n	%	n	%	n	%	n	%
Productive skills																
1. Speech articulation																
very clear and well articulated	167	52.7	143	38.4	–		–		137	48.9	109	35.3	156	58.9	108	38.7
quite clear on the whole	127	40.1	180	48.4	–		–		127	45.4	160	51.8	97	36.6	151	54.1
difficult to follow	23	7.3	49	13.2	–		–		16	5.7	40	12.9	12	4.5	20	7.2
Value of z CA vs DA	3.95, p < 0.1%								3.80, p <0.1%				4.55, p< 0.1%			
Value of z SWC vs DA	0.31, N.S.								1.47, N.S.				2.31, p< 2.5%			
2. Range of vocabulary																
wide	63	19.9	26	7.0	–		–		49	17.5	29	9.4	49	18.5	35	12.5
adequate	223	70.3	268	72.0	–		–		209	74.6	226	73.1	200	75.5	119	71.3
poor	31	9.8	78	21.0	–		–		22	7.9	54	17.5	16	6.0	45	16.1
Value of z CA vs DA	5.79, p < 0.1%								4.12, p <0.1%				3.51, p <0.1%			
Value of z SWC vs DA	3.55, p < 0.1%								1.74, p <5%				1.29, N.S.			

90

3. Power of oral expression

very fluent and articulate	83 — 26.2	51 — 13.7	77 — 25.0	50 — 14.4	59 — 21.1	66 — 21.4	76 — 28.7	58 — 20.8
can express self adequately	207 — 65.3	267 — 71.8	190 — 61.7	206 — 59.4	191 — 68.2	195 — 63.1	167 — 63.0	179 — 64.2
poor – cannot communicate adequately	27 — 8.5	54 — 14.5	41 — 13.3	91 — 26.2	30 — 10.7	48 — 15.5	22 — 8.3	42 — 15.0
Value of z CA vs DA	4.33, p < 0.1%		4.71, p < 0.1%		0.81, N.S.		2.78, p < 0.1%	
Value of z SWC vs DA	1.35, N.S.		2.34, p < 1%		0.45, N.S.		1.12, N.S.	

Receptive skills

4. Ability to follow oral instructions

very well	141 — 44.5	124 — 33.3	—	—	115 — 41.1	98 — 31.7	122 — 46.0	129 — 46.2
quite well	144 — 45.4	204 — 54.8	—	—	135 — 48.2	173 — 56.0	126 — 47.5	120 — 43.0
poorly	32 — 10.1	44 — 11.8	—	—	30 — 10.7	38 — 12.3	17 — 6.4	30 — 10.7
Value of z CA vs DA	2.70, p < 5%		—		2.11, p < 2.5%		0.42, N.S.	
Value of z SWC vs DA	0.42, N.S.		—		0.93, N.S.		0.99, N.S.	

5. Ability to understand stories heard

very well	—	—	163 — 54.9	119 — 36.3	120 — 45.1	141 — 46.8	137 — 53.3	122 — 47.5
quite well	—	—	126 — 42.4	153 — 46.6	133 — 50.0	129 — 42.9	111 — 43.2	117 — 45.5
poorly	—	—	8 — 2.7	56 — 17.1	13 — 4.9	31 — 10.3	9 — 3.5	18 — 7.0
* not observed	—	—	11	19	14	8	4	22
Value of z CA vs DA		—	5.82, p < 0.1%		0.24, N.S.		1.55, N.S.	
Value of z SWC vs DA		—	2.63, p < 0.5%		1.02, N.S.		0.56, N.S.	

* Children in not observed category not included in percentage figures or 'tau' analysis.

Probability levels in the table are one-tailed.

Table 45

Raw scores of CA and DA samples on WISC Vocabulary sub-test
during the children's final infant school term

CA group N=263		DA group N=272		difference between means (CA-DA)	standard error or difference	t	P (one-tail)
mean	s.d.	mean	s.d.				
22.27	6.04	19.23	5.10	3.04	0.48	6.30	< 0.1%

Table 46

Raw scores of SWC sub-sample and DA sample on WISC Vocabulary
sub-test during the children's final infant school term

SWC group N=141		DA group N=272		difference between means (SWC-DA)	standard error of difference	t	P (one-tail)
mean	s.d.	mean	s.d.				
20.42	5.81	19.23	5.10	1.19	0.56	2.14	<2.5%

significance, when the SWC sub-group of the CA sample was compared with the DA sample (Table 46). There is some disparity between the latter result and the finding, reported above, of no significant difference between the SWC area children and DA children in range of vocabulary rated by the teachers on School Schedule 6 (which was completed at approximately the same time as the attainment survey was carried out).

The above finding of a highly significant difference between the CA and DA samples is fully in line with the findings concerning social class differences in vocabulary development and the achievement of disadvantaged children in this aspect of language reported in Volume 2 Part One (Chapter 3). In the intensive study presented in that volume, highly significant differences between the sub-sample of children from culturally deprived home backgrounds and a control group were found, both on teachers' ratings of the children's vocabulary range and on some standardized vocabulary tests. It is of interest that, in the present study, the difference between the CA and DA samples is maintained even when the MC sub-group is removed from the CA sample (except in Schedule 6). This supports the conclusion, reported in Volume 2, that social class differences in language performance exist *within* the broad 'working-class' group as well as between 'middle' and 'working-class' children.

Table 47

Performance of the Control Area and Deprived Area samples
(with breakdown of CA sample) on the WISC vocabulary
sub-test, in terms of age equivalent scores

CA group						DA group	
MC		SWC		MC+SWC			
N=122		N=141		N=263		N=272	
mean	s.d.	mean	s.d.	mean	s.d.	mean	s.d.
y m	y m	y m	y m	y m	y m	y m	y m
8 2	1 6	7 2	7 6	7 7	1 6	6 10	1 3

Table 48

Difference between mean attainment age and chronological
age* on the WISC vocabulary sub-test: CA and DA samples
(with breakdown of CA sample)

	CA group			DA group
	MC	SWC	MC+SWC	
	y m	y m	y m	y m
Attainment age minus chronological age	+0 8	−0 4	+0 1	−0 8

*The mean chronological age for the samples was calculated
on the basis of a fixed date, the first day of the month
in which the test was administered. This means that it
is a slight underestimate of the true mean age of the
groups.

The children's raw scores on the WISC vocabulary sub-test were converted to equivalent test ages and the means and standard deviations of the two samples, based upon these ages, are presented in Table 47.

It will be seen from the table that the mean difference in vocabulary age between the CA and DA groups was 9 months, but that the difference between the SWC sub-group of the CA sample and the DA sample was only 4 months. The approximate mean chronological age of all the groups (based on a fixed date) was 7 years 6 months and comparison of the attainment and chronological ages for each group yields the differences shown in Table 48.

This table shows that the CA sample as a whole performed just above its age norm, whereas the DA sample obtained a mean attainment age 8 months below its chronological age. However, the MC and SWC components of the CA group fell above and below the age norm respectively.

Figure 1 shows the distribution of the vocabulary attainment ages for the CA and DA samples. (The patterns of distribution for the MC and SWC sub-groups were broadly similar, despite the difference in mean attainment age between these groups.) It will be seen that the distribution for both samples, but particularly the DA group, are skewed toward the low end of the score range.

Nearly twice the proportion of DA as compared with CA children (approximately 44 per cent and 24 per cent respectively) obtained attainment ages of 6 years 7 months (6.6 years) or less, i.e. about one year or more below the sample's mean chronological age of 7 years 6 months. The same pattern holds for the proportions of children in the two groups with vocabulary ages of below 6 years, i.e. 18 months below the mean chronological age (approximately 35 per cent for the DA group and 20 per cent for the CA group). It should also be borne in mind that, as indicated in Figure 1, a substantial number of children in both samples fell below the test norms altogether and were arbitrarily awarded the lowest vocabulary age of 5 years 2 months. Thus, a substantial proportion of children in both groups, but particularly the DA group could, according to these results, be regarded as retarded in this aspect of vocabulary development (i.e. retarded by 18 months or more).

The above data on vocabulary attainment ages must be treated with considerable reserve, however, for several reasons. Firstly, and most seriously, the age norms used are based upon the standardization sample of American children and are not really applicable to British children, although the WISC is widely used by psychologists in this country. Moreover, as explained in Chapter 3, the standard procedure for administering the vocabulary sub-test was modified in an attempt to draw out the best verbal responses possible from the children. This modification might have had the effect of boosting the children's attainment ages in some cases. In addition, the mean attainment ages of each group will be slightly inflated because, as stated above, children scoring below the test norms were arbitrarily awarded the minimum test age.

On the ratings of the children's power of oral expression presented in Table 44, the CA group obtained consistently higher ratings than the DA group over the series of schedules, the results being statistically significant on all of the schedules except the fifth. Comparison of the ratings received by the SWC sub-group of the CA sample and the DA sample yields much the same pattern, except that the superiority of the SWC group falls below significance on the fifth and sixth schedules.

Inspection of the percentage figures in Table 44 shows no clear trend in the ratings of either group over the series of schedules. In fact, the rating distributions tend to fluctuate, although the position of the two groups on the final schedule shows a slight improvement compared with that on Schedule 2. This fluctuation is probably due to variations in the standards of judgement adopted by the different teachers completing the successive schedules. This particular rating is rather global and subjective and, therefore, probably rather susceptible to such variation in standards.

It is possible to compare the results of the teachers' ratings of children's power of oral expression in the present study with those obtained from a similar item in the study of a sub-sample of infant school children during their first school term, carried out as part of the National Survey, and presented in the Plowden Report (1967). As mentioned in Chapter 4, this sub-sample of 255 children was not fully representative of the general population in terms of social class composition, but it provides a useful reference sample. The comparison between the ratings in the present study from School Schedule 2 (completed during the children's first term) and those from the National Survey is presented in Table 49.

It will be seen that the CA sample has lower percentages than the National Survey sample of children rated in the highest and lowest categories, and the DA sample has a similar percentage to the National Survey sample of children with the lowest rating but a much lower percentage of children with the highest rating. To put it another way, the ratings of the CA and DA samples showed a greater clustering in the 'average' category than those of the survey sample.

On School Schedule 6 the teachers were asked to rate the quality of the children's sentence construction in their written language. It is interesting to include the results obtained on this rating in the present context of discussion of the

Figure 1

Distributions of attainment ages on WISC Vocabulary sub-test: CA and DA samples

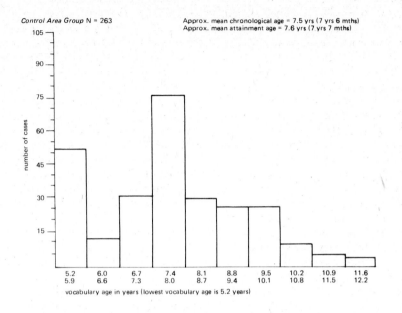

Note: First category includes 29 children falling below norms

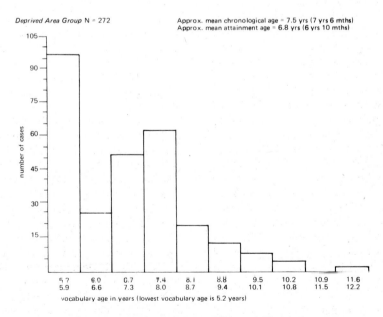

Note: First category includes 40 children falling below norms

Table 49

Comparison of CA and DA samples with 1964 National Survey
sub-sample in power of oral expression

Item	Rating	Present samples (Schedule 2, end of first term)		National Survey sub-sample
		Control area group	Deprived area group	
		N=322	N=348	N=254
		%	%	%
Power of oral expression:	Very fluent and articulate (good)	26.2	13.7	35.7
	Can express self adequately (average)	65.3	71.8	48.4
	Power of expression markedly poor (poor)	8.5	14.5	15.9

Note: ratings in brackets are those used in National Survey.

children's productive language and these are presented in Table 50.

It will be seen that both the CA sample as a whole and the SWC sub-group taken by itself obtained very significantly higher ratings on this item than the DA sample. The proportion of DA children rated in the lowest category on this item was approximately twice that of the CA children and vice versa in the case of the highest rating. These results are in accord with those yielded by the ratings of children's power of oral expression presented above, although, of course, it must be remembered that the children would be at a relatively early stage in the development of their written language skills at the time that the rating of their sentence construction was made.

Comparison of the two main groups on the ratings of the receptive skills of understanding stories and following oral instructions yields a broadly similar pattern of results in the two sets of assessments (Table 44 items 4 and 5). On both items, the CA sample obtained consistently higher ratings than the DA sample, but the differences between the groups fall below statistical significance on the final school schedule. Similarly, on both items, the DA children show a relatively greater improvement in their ratings between Schedules 2 and 6, which leads to the non-significant results on the final schedule. This apparent catching up of the CA children by the DA children seems quite feasible insofar as children coming from relatively deprived home backgrounds would tend, initially, to be poorer at understanding stories and following oral instructions, due to a comparative lack of experience of these in the home. However, during the course of their infant school careers, they would undoubtedly have had considerable experience of stories and oral instructions. The fact that a similar catching up process does not appear to occur in the case of

Table 50

Quality of the children's sentence construction
in their 'free writing' (at end of third year):
CA and DA samples (with breakdown of CA sample)

Item	Rating	CA group						DA group	
		MC		SWC		MC+SWC			
		N=122		N=143		N=265		N=279	
		n	%	n	%	n	%	n	%
Child's sentence construction in free writing	very well constructed	41	33.6	33	23.1	74	27.9	44	15.8
	adequately constructed	54	44.3	50	35.0	104	39.2	84	30.1
	correct but short	19	15.6	40	28.0	59	22.3	92	33.0
	very poorly constructed	8	6.6	20	14.0	28	10.6	59	21.1

Value of z CA vs DA = 5.15, p < 0.1% (one-tail)
Value of z SWC vs DA = 2.56, p < 1% (one-tail)

97

the productive language skills rated may be because children do not gain as much school experience, relatively speaking, in the latter skills, for example, experience of talking and discussing in one-to-one situations with the teacher or in small group situations. This is only a very tentative explanation of these findings, however, and it should be borne in mind, when interpreting the trends in the ratings of the receptive skills, that the numbers are not comparable from one shedule to another, and also, that, on the rating of the child's understanding of stories, a small number of children in each group were not rated (these numbers appear in brackets in the table). It should also be remembered that, as stated in Chapter 3, the DA children who transferred to other schools during the period under study tended to receive lower ratings than the full DA sample on selected school schedule items, including a rating of power of oral expression, and they may, therefore, have been relatively less able children. The loss of such children from the sample could partly explain the 'improvement' in the ratings received by the DA sample discussed above.

In the case of the rating of the children's understanding of stories, the pattern of results of the comparison between the SWC sub-group of the CA sample and the DA sample is similar to that of the comparison between the two main groups. However, this is not the case for the ratings of the children's ability to follow oral instructions, for here, none of the SWC versus DA sample comparisons are statistically significant. Indeed, on Schedules 2 and 6, the DA sample has a higher proportion of children with the highest rating on this item than the SWC sub-group. In the case of this item, therefore, the superiority of the CA sample seems largely attributable to the MC sub-group.

On School Schedule 2 (end of children's first term), a question was asked about the attentiveness of the children to stories told to them. This clearly relates to the understanding of stories although, of course, it is not synonymous with such understanding. It is interesting to see that there was a highly significant tendency for the CA group to show greater attentiveness to stories than the DA group, although this was largely because of the relatively high ratings received by the MC component of the CA sample. This finding supports the point made earlier in this discussion that

children from relatively deprived homes probably have less experience of hearing stories until they start school.

Summary: oral language skills
The CA sample showed clear and consistent superiority over the DA sample on the productive language ratings (speech articulation, range of spoken vocabulary and fluency in oral expression) throughout the period covered by the schedules in question. The CA children were also rated as significantly superior in the quality of their written sentence construction. On the whole, the differences between the SWC area children and the DA children followed the same pattern, although they tended to reach lower levels of significance and, in some cases, fell below significance. The finding of a significant difference between the groups in favour of the CA sample on rated vocabulary was supported by the result of the WISC vocabulary sub-test administered in the children's final infant school term as part of the attainment survey. The ratings on these items did not show the clear upward trend over time that might have been expected, possibly because of variation in teachers' standards of judgement and selective bias in losses from each sample. Nor did they indicate any clear tendency for the CA and DA groups to increasingly diverge from each other in their level of linguistic skills over the period under study.

In terms of age equivalent scores on the WISC vocabulary sub-test, the CA sample obtained a score in line with its mean chronological age (although the MC sub-group's mean vocabulary age was one year above that of the SWC sub-group), whilst the mean vocabulary age of the DA sample was over six months below its chronological age. The distributions of vocabulary ages for both samples showed a bias toward the lower end of the scale. However, these results should be regarded with caution mainly because of the lack of test standardization data for British children.

In the receptive language skills of understanding stories and following oral instructions the pattern of results deviate somewhat from that described above for, in both of these skills, the difference between the two groups fell below statistical significance at the end of the children's third year. It would appear that, in these skills, the DA children tended to make greater improvement relative to the CA children over the final year or so, although the interpretation of the trends in these ratings is complicated by the disparity in the sample size on the different schedules.

On the whole, the above findings are supported by the results of earlier research on social class differences in language performance, and research on the language deficits of disadvantaged children described in Volume 2 (Part One, Chapter 3), and also by the findings of the first intensive study reported in that volume, in which children from culturally and materially deprived home backgrounds were compared with a control group on various language and other measures, including those used in the present study. This study showed that the DA group were significantly poorer than the controls on both teachers' ratings and test measures of a whole range of language skills, both receptive and productive. The findings are also supported by the fact, reported in Chapter 12, that whilst the majority of CA schools had no real difficulties concerning the development of children's language skills, according to the teachers, the DA schools considered that they were faced with far more and serious problems, including children's poor speech articulation and listening skills, inability to express themselves, limited vocabulary and a poor background of stories and rhymes. It is also of interest in this connection that, whereas all of the CA class teachers interviewed considered that the children were getting sufficient practice for their needs in speaking and listening, about half of the DA teachers thought their children needed more practice.

B. READING AND RELATED SKILLS

(i) Reading and Spelling

Reading is one of the fundamental educational skills taught in the infant school, in the opinion of some the most important, and the child's level of accomplishment in reading at the end of the infant school stage, together with that in oral and written language skills may have far-reaching implications for his future success or failure in school and, possibly, beyond school. The information obtained on the performance in reading and related skills of the DA children in comparison with their controls is therefore of great interest and importance.

With the exception of the first schedule, all of the school schedules contained a comprehensive section on the reading skills of the children. Before the analysis of these ratings is presented, it is useful to examine the overall level of reading skill shown by the two samples at the end of the children's first term. It will be recalled from Chapter 4 that, according to the teachers' observations, only a tiny proportion of children in either the CA or the DA samples (4½ per cent and 2½ per cent respectively) were able to read from a book on school entry. At the end of the first term the status of the children, in terms of whether or not they had begun on the school's reading scheme, is indicated in Table 51.

It will be seen that the CA group were significantly more advanced in the development of reading skill than the DA group insofar as a higher percentage of them (approx 40 per cent as opposed to 29 per cent) had started upon the first book of the school's reading scheme. However, this result was due to the marked superiority of the MC area children in the CA group for the proportion of SWC area children on the first reading book or beyond was very close to that of DA children. It should be borne in mind that the decision about when to start a child on the reading scheme (assuming that one is used) is made by individual teachers and is likely to be based upon varying criteria related to the child's reading readiness. However, as reported in Chapter 11, interviews carried out on a sample of class teachers in charge of project children during the first school year revealed a high degree of uniformity in such criteria, the majority of the teachers considering a child ready to start on the reading scheme when he had built up a suitable basic sight vocabulary. In view of this relative lack of variability in the criteria used by teachers in the project sample for 'reading readiness', the finding, noted above, that, initially, similar proportions of DA children and SWC area children had started on a reading scheme was all the more surprising. However, as the following discussion will show, from the end of the children's second term to the end of the infant school period, the SWC children were rated as significantly more advanced than the DA children in terms of level reached on the reading scheme.

It will be observed from Table 51 that approximately 60 per cent of the CA children and approximately 71 per cent of the DA children were judged by the teachers to be at the 'pre-reading' stage, i.e. engaged wholly on pre-reading

Table 51

Overall reading level of children in the CA and DA samples
at end of first school term (with breakdown of CA sample)

Child's reading level	CA group						DA group	
	MC		SWC		MC+SWC			
	N=143		N=174		N=317		N=372	
	n	%	n	%	n	%	n	%
on first book of scheme or beyond	77	53.8	49	28.2	126	39.7	109	29.3
on pre-reading activities only	61	42.7	86	49.4	147	46.4	209	56.2
little interest in pre-reading activities	5	3.5	39	22.4	44	13.9	54	14.5

Value of z   CA vs DA   = 2.29, p < 2.5% (one-tail)
Value of z   SWC vs DA = 1.30, N.S. (one-tail)

activities such as picture or shape matching, and looking at picture books. (These percentages include those children rated as showing little interest in pre-reading activities.) It is interesting to look at the proportion of children still at the pre-reading stage at subsequent points in time and to compare the CA and DA children in this category in terms of their level of pre-reading skills. This information is given in Table 53 (item 1) on page 195. It will be seen that, as one would expect, the proportion of children in either group engaged wholly on pre-reading activities (i.e. not yet embarked on the reading scheme) drops very sharply from the end of the first term (Schedule 2) onwards and, by the end of the children's second school year (Schedule 5), no children in the CA sample and only 9 (2.9 per cent) in the DA sample were still at the pre-reading stage. The data available on the pre-reading skills of these children will, therefore, be selected only from Schedules 2 to 4 (end of first year) inclusive and are presented in Table 52. It should be borne in mind that the number of CA children in the pre-reading category at the end of the first school year (Schedule 4) is relatively small and the results of the statistical analysis in this case should be treated cautiously.

The overall pattern indicated in this table is one of the superiority of the CA children over the DA children in their level of reading readiness skills. However, the differences between the groups are statistically significant in only about half of the results, and in two cases (recognising single words or phrases, in Schedules 2 and 3) the DA children received (non-significantly) higher ratings. A similar pattern emerged from the comparison between the SWC area children and the DA children except that rather more of the results fell below statistical significance.

It will be seen that, over the period covered by these three schedules (the children's first school year), the proportional drop in the number of children still at the pre-reading stage is far greater in the CA than the DA group. Whereas the number of such children in the CA group drops from 191 to 17 at the end of the first year (a decrease of approximately 91 per cent), the number in the DA group drops from 263 to 84 (a decrease of approximately 66 per cent). Thus, among the CA children still at the pre-reading stage at the end of the first school term, 'promotion' to the reading scheme was much more rapid than among the DA

children. Because the numbers in both groups drop so rapidly over the period in question, there is little point in examining the results for any trend in the patterns of distribution over time.

Once a child had embarked on the school's reading scheme, the class teacher was asked to rate his level of performance on a range of aspects of reading skill. Table 53 shows the distributions of the CA and DA samples in terms of reading scheme level and teacher rated reading skills over a series of school schedules spanning all but the first term of the infant school period.

The overall picture indicated by the table is that the CA sample is consistently superior to the DA sample on both the reading scheme level reached and the aspects of reading skill rated by the teachers, in many cases the result of the between-group comparisons reaching a very high level of statistical significance. This pattern is preserved when the MC area children in the CA sample are removed and analyses carried out on the SWC area and DA children only.

These overall findings are fully supported by the results of the reading tests administered to the whole sample as part of the attainment survey carried out in the children's final infant school term. These results are presented in Tables 54 and 55. These tables show that both the CA group as a whole, and the SWC component of that group considered on its own, achieved significantly higher means scores on all of the reading tests and the spelling test. It will also be seen from Table 54 that, on the three Neale reading test measures, scores of the CA children showed a greater measure of variability than those of the DA children, as indicated by the relatively higher standard deviations. On the Burt test the two measures of variability were very close, whilst on the spelling test the scores of the DA children showed wider variation than those of the CA children. However, the interpretation of the standard deviations presented in the table is not straightforward as the raw score distributions for the two samples did not follow the pattern of the normal curve in all the tests. In the CA sample the raw score distributions for Neale Comprehension and Neale Accuracy were biased toward the lower end of the scale, whilst the score distributions of the DA sample on all of the reading and spelling measures showed a much more pronounced bias in the same direction.

Table 52

Reading readiness skills of children in the CA and DA samples still at pre-reading stage

Item	Rating	end of 1st term (Schedule 2) CA N=191		end of 1st term (Schedule 2) DA N=263		end of 2nd term (Schedule 3) CA N=39		end of 2nd term (Schedule 3) DA N=122		end of 1st year (Schedule 4) CA N=17		end of 1st year (Schedule 4) DA N=84	
		n	%	n	%	n	%	n	%	n	%	n	%
1. Matching shapes or pictures	easily and efficiently	86	45.0	104	39.5	9	23	22	18.0	2	12	22	26
	quite efficiently	83	43.5	134	50.9	26	67	65	53.3	12	71	38	45
	unable to do so	22	11.5	25	9.5	4	10	35	28.7	3	18	24	29
	Value of z CA vs DA	0.69, N.S.				1.83, p< 5%				0.03, N.S.			
	Value of z SWC vs DA	1.87, N.S.				1.22, N.S.				0.34, N.S.			
2. Can child recognize own name	Yes	-	-	-	-	33	85	72	59.0	16	94	55	65
	No	-	-	-	-	6	15	50	41.0	1	6	29	34
	Value of z CA vs DA					2.72, p< 0.5%				2.06, p< 2.5%			
	Value of z SWC vs DA					3.05, p< 0.5%				1.74, p< 5%			
3. Can child recognize single words/ phrases	7 plus words	24	12.6	62	23.6	0	0	7	5.7	0	0	7	8
	1 to 6 words	126	66.0	146	55.5	15	38	62	50.8	15	88	41	49
	none	41	21.5	55	20.9	24	61	53	43.4	2	12	36	43
	Value of z CA vs DA	1.82, N.S.				2.02, p< 5%				1.54, N.S.			
	Value of z SWC vs DA	2.10, p< 5%				1.80, N.S.				1.23, N.S.			

Continued on next page

102

4. Level of interest in looking at picture/story books

	n	%	n	%	n	%	n	%	n	%	n	%
very keen	57	29.8	36	13.7	2	5	4	3.3	1	6	2	2
quite keen	99	51.8	170	64.6	32	82	60	49.2	13	76	47	56
little/no interest	35	18.3	57	21.7	5	13	58	47.5	3	18	35	42

Value of z CA vs DA	3.14, p <0.1%	3.59, p< 0.1%	1.71, p <5%
Value of z SWC vs DA	0.68, N.S.	3.15, p< 0.1%	1.33, N.S.

5. Overall level of reading readiness

	n	%	n	%	n	%	n	%	n	%	n	%
ready for introductory reading	45	23.6	44	16.7	3	8	14	11.5	4	23	13	15
needs more pre-reading	92	48.2	145	55.1	26	67	47	38.5	10	59	39	46
unready	54	28.3	74	28.1	10	26	61	50.0	3	18	32	38

Value of z CA vs DA	0.69, N.S.	1.83, p <5%	0.03, N.S.
Value of z SWC vs DA	1.87, N.S.	1.22, N.S.	0.34, N.S.

Note: Where the sample size drops below 100 percentages have been rounded to the nearest whole number

Probabilities in the table are one-tailed.

Table 53

Children's level on reading scheme and teacher's ratings of their reading skills
over the infant school period: CA and DA samples

Item and Rating	End of second term (Schedule 3) CA N = 309		End of second term (Schedule 3) DA N = 355		End of first year (Schedule 4) CA N = 308		End of first year (Schedule 4) DA N = 347		End of second year (Schedule 5) CA N = 280		End of second year (Schedule 5) DA N = 309		End of third year (Schedule 6) CA N = 265		End of third year (Schedule 6) DA N = 279	
	n	%	n	%	n	%	n	%	n	%	n	%	n	%	n	%
1. Child's level of reading																
pre-reading	39	12.6	122	34.4	17	5.5	84	24.2	0	0.0	9	2.9	0	0.0	1	0.4
introductory book	85	25.7	108	30.4	45	14.6	90	25.9	1	0.4	22	7.1	0	0.0	14	5.0
Book 1	107	34.6	45	12.7	87	28.2	56	16.1	23	8.2	44	14.2	2	0.7	14	5.0
Book 2	51	16.5	43	12.1	97	31.5	53	15.3	60	21.4	60	19.4	13	4.9	28	10.0
Book 3	25	8.1	16	4.5	34	11.0	27	7.8	58	20.7	47	15.2	37	14.0	48	17.2
Book 4/beyond	2	0.6	21	5.9	28	9.1	37	10.7	121	43.2	113	36.6	140	52.8	104	37.3
beyond book scheme	0	0.0	0	0.0	0	0.0	0	0.0	17	6.1	14	4.5	73	27.5	70	25.1
Value of z CA vs DA	5.59, p< 0.1%				6.22, p< 0.1%				3.75, p< 0.5%				3.70, p< 0.1%			
Value of z SWC vs DA	2.71, p< 0.5%				3.93, p< 0.5%				2.34, p< 1%				1.73, p< 5%			
2. Range of sight vocabulary																
wide	39	14.4	26	11.2	60	20.6	33	12.5	82	29.3	74	24.8	109	41.1	85	30.6
adequate	123	45.6	129	55.4	166	57.0	141	53.6	138	49.3	183	44.3	108	40.7	114	41.0
poor	108	40.0	78	33.5	65	22.3	89	33.8	60	21.4	93	31.0	48	18.1	79	28.4
Value of z CA vs DA	0.71, N.S.				3.43, p< 0.1%				2.28, p< 2.5%				3.12, p< 0.1%			
Value of z SWC vs DA	0.71, N.S.				1.50, N.S.				0.99, N.S.				1.16, N.S.			

Continued on next page

104

	1	2	3	4	5	6	7	8
3. Interest in reading								
very keen	105 38.9	81 34.8	117 40.2	90 34.2	110 39.3	126 42.0	117 44.1	101 36.3
fairly keen	137 50.7	123 52.8	152 52.2	137 52.1	145 51.8	135 45.0	121 45.7	119 42.8
little interest	28 10.4	29 12.4	22 7.6	36 13.7	25 8.9	39 13.0	27 10.2	58 20.9
Value of z CA vs DA	1.00, N.S.		2.02, p< 2.5%		0.06, N.S.		2.79, p< 0.5%	
Value of z SWC vs DA	0.39, N.S.		1.09, N.S.		0.66, N.S.		2.47, p< 1%	
4. Reading comprehension								
good	–	–	–	–	107 38.2	108 36.0	129 48.7	96 34.5
good	–	–	–	–	141 50.4	142 47.3	107 40.4	130 46.8
poor	–	–	–	–	32 11.4	50 16.7	29 10.9	52 18.7
Value of z CA vs DA					1.13, N.S.		3.58, p< 0.1%	
Value of z SWC vs DA					0.18, N.S.		2.30, p< 2.5%	
5. Knowledge of letter sounds								
good	76 31.3		100 36.1	32 14.3	–	–	–	–
fairly good	110 45.3		111 40.1	86 38.4	–	–	–	–
poor	57 23.4		66 23.8	106 47.3	–	–	–	–
not observed	66		31	123	–	–	–	–
Value of z CA vs DA	7.70, p< 0.1%		6.43, p< 0.1%					
Value of z SWC vs DA	6.21, p< 0.1%		3.94, p< 0.1%					
6. Phonic word building								
very proficient	–	–	–	–	81 29.4	46 17.2	125 47.2	85 30.6
fairly proficient	–	–	–	–	125 45.4	110 41.2	117 44.1	125 45.0
little/no proficiency	–	–	–	–	69 25.0	111 41.6	23 8.7	68 24.5
not observed	–	–	–	–	5	43	0	0
Value of z CA vs DA					4.43, p< 0.1%		5.08, p< 0.1%	
Value of z SWC vs DA					2.87, p< 0.1%		3.64, p< 0.1%	

Notes:
1. Figures at the head of the columns apply to items one and five in the table only. Figures for the remaining items fall below these maxima for they concern only those children placed on the reading scheme.
2. Children in not observed category not included in percentage figures or 'tau' analysis.
3. Probability levels in the table are one-tailed.

Table 54

Raw scores of CA and DA samples in reading and spelling tests during the children's final infant school term

Test	N		CA group		DA group		difference between means (CA-DA)	standard error of difference	t	p (one-tail)
	CA*	DA*	mean	s.d.	mean	s.d.				
Burt Reading Test	247	247	39.10	16.94	26.24	16.81	12.86	1.52	8.45	< 0.1%
Neale Reading Test										
Accuracy	247	247	32.39	19.03	19.80	16.78	12.59	1.62	7.78	< 0.1%
Rate	247	247	45.40	22.63	36.76	20.76	8.64	1.96	4.41	< 0.1%
Comprehension	247	247	10.79	7.21	6.82	5.96	3.97	0.60	6.66	< 0.1%
Spelling Test	247	249	22.21	9.29	14.05	10.51	8.16	0.89	9.14	< 0.1%

* Children in the one Settled Working Class area and the one Deprived area school which used the 'i.t.a.' approach to teaching reading were not given the reading and spelling tests.

Table 55

Raw scores of SWC sub-sample and DA sample in reading and spelling tests during the children's final infant school term

| Test | * N | | SWC sub-group | | DA group | | difference between means (SWC-DA) | standard error of difference | t | p (one-tail) |
	SWC	DA	mean	s.d.	mean	s.d.				
Burt Reading Test	125	247	35.88	16.52	26.24	16.81	9.64	1.84	5.24	< 0.1%
Neale Reading Test Accuracy	125	247	28.43	17.78	19.80	16.78	8.63	1.88	4.58	< 0.1%
Rate	125	247	41.62	22.12	36.76	20.76	4.86	2.34	2.08	< 2.5%
Comprehension	125	247	9.34	6.65	6.82	5.96	2.52	0.68	3.70	< 0.1%
Spelling Test	125	249	20.04	9.71	14.05	10.51	5.99	1.13	5.32	< 0.1%

* Children in the one Settled Working Class area and the one Deprived area school which used the 'i.t.a.' approach to teaching reading were not given the reading and spelling tests.

Taken together, the results obtained from the tests and the teachers' ratings show very clearly that, from the first school term, the CA group advanced more rapidly in the development of their reading skills than the DA children and maintained this advance throughout the whole infant school period. This finding is fully in line with the prediction and with the considerable body of research evidence on social class differences in reading skills and the impairing effects of cultural deprivation on the development of such skills, some of which is summarized in Volume 2 (Part One) of this series. It is also supported by the finding of the intensive study reported in Part One of that volume that the sub-sample of culturally deprived children under study made poorer progress in reading skills throughout the infant school period than a control group, according to the teachers' judgement. On some of the final reading and spelling attainment tests however, the between-group differences in that study fell short of statistical significance.

Tables 54 and 55 show that the CA sample taken as a whole, and the SWC sub-group considered by itself, obtained very significantly higher mean scores on the Daniels and Diack Graded Spelling Test than the DA sample. This result is in line with the finding of the intensive study mentioned above that a sub-sample of children from deprived home backgrounds obtained (non-significantly) lower scores on the Daniels and Diack Spelling Test than a matched control group.

The major factors underlying the differences in reading and spelling progress and attainment between the CA and DA samples demonstrated in the present study are probably those relating to the children's home background. Parental interest and encouragement and attitudes toward the child's education have been shown by various research studies, such as that by Douglas 1964 and the National Child Development Study (Pringle et al. 1966), to have a very important influence on the development of children's educational skills. Although no direct information about the parental attitudes of the children in the present sample is available, in the estimation of the headteachers there was greater parental support of the child's reading development among CA parents than among DA parents. According to these estimates, on average, the proportion of CA parents showing interest in their children's reading progress was nearly twice that of DA parents (see Chapter 12). Indeed among the CA parents there appeared to be a competitiive spirit concerning the children's level of reading achievement, which probably transferred to some extent to the children.

Children from culturally deprived homes are also likely to be less well developed in respect of some of the skills and concepts which might be regarded as pre-requisites of reading ability, in particular oral language skills. The DA children in the present sample were significantly inferior in oral language skills to the CA children, as discussed in Section A of this chapter. Moreover, they also showed a (non-significantly) lower level of concentration in the more structured school activities, according to the teachers' judgements, and this would also tend to impede their reading progress (see Chapter 4, section C).

According to information given by the head-teachers and reported fully in Chapter 12 there were no major differences between the CA and DA schools in their approach to reading, although the CA schools appeared to introduce systematic phonic teaching earlier than the DA schools, a fact which might reflect the relatively faster growth of reading skills in the CA children. For example, the CA teachers showed a higher level of expectation of children's reading performance at the end of the first school year than the DA teachers, who appeared to face more difficulties in teaching reading than their CA colleagues, due to such problems as children's lack of concentration and interest in reading and limited language skills. Although the CA and DA headteachers seemed to have similar levels of expectation of children's reading performance at the end of their infant schooling, the DA teachers estimated that they had a higher proportion of children leaving school in need of special help in reading. In general, the view of the teachers concerning the problems they faced in teaching reading were supported by the results of the tests and ratings reported above.

There is a possibility, however, that the relatively poor performance of the DA children in reading (and in other basic educational skills) might have been partly due to lower levels of expectations of children's performance in the DA than the CA class teachers. As stated above the class teachers of the DA children during their first infant school year did, in fact, express a lower level of expectation regarding their children's reading performance at the end of that year than their CA counterparts (see also page 262 for fuller details). It may be that, in a similar fashion, the *class teachers* of the DA children in their subsequent years of infant schooling also showed a relatively lower expectation of reading performance despite the fact that the *head teachers* in both CA and DA schools showed similar levels of such expectation (see page 263 for details). If this were the case then the lower expectations of the DA teachers might have operated as a 'self-fulfilling prophecy' to depress the achievement of the DA children relative to their potential. Since the class teachers of the project children during their second and third infant school years were not interviewed, this hypothesis must remain speculative. However, there is some evidence from existing research suggesting that teachers' expectations can act in a self-fulfilling fashion (Rosenthal and Jacobson, 1966), and also that teachers of infant school children in 'lower working-class' areas tend to show relatively stereotyped attitudes toward their pupils and their backgrounds, regarding the children as, in general, intellectually as well as socially homogeneous (Goodacre, 1968).

The individual items presented in Table 53 will now be considered in a little more detail.

Item 1 in the table shows the progression of each group over the period of time covered by the schedules through the various levels of the basic reading schemes used. It will be seen that the difference between the CA and DA groups at the end of each school year was highly significant. There was no evidence here of any tendency for the difference between these groups to widen over the period under study. By the end of their infant school careers, approximately 80 per cent of the CA group and 62 per cent of the DA group are well advanced in their reading schemes (Book 4 or higher) or beyond the schemes altogether.

It should be borne in mind, of course, in interpreting these figures that the various reading schemes commonly used in infant schools are not strictly comparable in terms of their graded book levels. No common standard exists so that, for example, Book One on scheme 'A' can confidently be regarded as equivalent in difficulty to Book One on scheme 'B'. Moreover, the criteria adopted by different teachers for 'promoting' a child from a lower to a higher book in the series may vary considerably. Despite these limitations, however,

this reading primer criterion has been used in several large scale surveys of reading ability and can at least be regarded as a 'semi-objective' item. Moreover, Morris (1959) found, on the basis of questioning experienced teachers, that despite the variability in the level of difficulty in 'equivalent' books on different reading schemes, meaningful distinctions could be made between children reaching broadly different stages. The infant teachers in Morris' study regarded the first reading primer as dividing the poor and non-readers from the rest at age seven, and children who were on Books 2 or 3 at this age were considered to be at a stage of mainly mechanical reading and still in need of much skilled help and encouragement in order to progress further. Children reaching Book 4 or beyond, however, were regarded as having 'true reading ability' and to be relatively self sustaining in regard to future progress, given encouragement and suitable subsequent reading material.

The National Child Development Study (NCDS, Davie et al., 1972) made use of this reading primer criterion of children's reading progress in their study of over fifteen thousand seven-year-old infant school children, and it is interesting to compare the results from the present sample in this item with those from this large national survey of children in England, Scotland and Wales. The comparison is presented in Table 56.

This table shows that, in their final infant school term, the present sample as a whole appeared to be more advanced in terms of level reached on the basic reading scheme than the NCDS national sample and this finding applies to both the CA and DA samples taken separately. However, this comparison should be treated very cautiously because of important differences between the present and the NCDS samples. Perhaps the most important difference is in terms of the children's length of schooling. Because they were all March born children, the NCDS sample had had only 2 years or, at most, 2 years and one term in their infant schools, as opposed to the three years experienced by the present sample. It also seems possible that the NCDS children may have been assessed by the teachers at a slightly earlier stage in the final infant school term than the present sample, but the report does not indicate exactly when the assessments were made.

Table 56

Stages reached in basic reading scheme: comparison of present
CA and DA samples and National Child Development Study
sample (N.C.D.S.)

Stage on reading scheme	Present sample						N.C.D.S. sample
	CA group		DA group		Total sample		
	N=265		N=279		N=544		N=15496
	n	%	n	%	n	%	%
Book 4 or beyond	213	80.4	174	62.4	387	71.1	55.26
Books 2 or 3	50	18.9	76	27.2	126	23.2	34.59
Book 1 or below	2	0.7	29	10.4	31	5.7	10.15

Several studies reviewed by Pidgeon (1965) have shown that the younger children in a school intake age group are at a disadvantage educationally (e.g. a higher proportion of summer born than autumn born children tends to be found in lower streams and remedial groups), and the NCDS showed a significant association between length of schooling (with age controlled) and educational achievement in favour of children with longer schooling. Thus, the difference in length of schooling between the two samples, alone, may account for the apparent superiority in reading of the present sample. Another point to bear in mind is that the majority of the present sample (approximately 75 per cent) attended schools in Wales, whereas the NCDS sample was a national one, so that regional factors are involved in this comparison. However, the NCDS found that Welsh children tended to have a lower proportion of 'good' readers than children in England or Scotland, so that the result of the above comparison is contrary to this finding.

Finally, a number of schools in the NCDS sample probably used the 'Initial Teaching Alphabet' (i.t.a.) (Downing 1964) method of teaching reading and the associated reading schemes, which are not comparable in reading difficulty level to conventional schemes. Two schools in the present sample (one in each of the CA and DA samples) contributing 48 children (nearly 9 per cent) to the urban sample, definitely used such schemes, but Davie et al. (1972) do not give any comparable figures for the NCDS sample. The scheme used by both of the i.t.a. schools in the present sample contained approximately ten basic graded readers as opposed to the 4 or 5 in conventional reading schemes. It seems likely, therefore, that the inclusion of the i.t.a. children in the present sample would have the effect of inflating the overall figures shown in Table 56. The removal of these children from the present sample has the effect of bringing the overall reading performance of the present sample slightly more into line with that of the NCDS sample, but this revised comparison may be less valid than the original one in the absence of the knowledge of the proportion of 'i.t.a.' children in the NCDS sample. The possible bias in the results obtained for the present sample in terms of the reading scheme level reached (see

Table 53, item 1) due to the inclusion of the i.t.a. children is not serious from the point of view of comparing the CA and DA samples since each sample contains one of the 'i.t.a.' schools, so that any effect attributable to this approach should be balanced between the two samples (although there were rather more i.t.a. children in the DA than the CA sample).

With regard to the teachers' assessment of the children's range of sight vocabulary (item 2, Table 53), it will be seen that, from Schedule 4 (end of first year) onwards, the CA children received consistently and significantly higher ratings than the DA children. On the other hand, although the SWC sub-group of the CA sample obtained higher overall ratings than the DA sample, the difference between the groups did not reach statistical significance on any schedule. However, there is some discrepancy between the latter result and the finding that, on the Burt and Neale Accuracy reading tests, which can be thought of as measures of sight vocabulary, the differences between the groups in favour of the SWC sub-group were statistically highly significant (see Table 55). As in the case of reading scheme level, there is no indication in the results on this item of a widening gap in attainment between the CA and DA groups.

A rating of the children's level of reading comprehension was included on the final two schedules (5 and 6) only, and Table 53 shows that the CA sample received higher ratings than the DA sample on both occasions, significantly so in the second occasion (the children's final infant school term). The same pattern emerged in the comparison between the SWC area children and the DA children. The results obtained in Schedule 6 are supported by the finding of highly significant differences between the CA and DA samples (and also between the SWC sub-group and the DA sample) on the Neale Comprehension measure (see Tables 54 and 55). The fact that the difference between the groups was significant on the second but not the first occasion would suggest that the disparity between the CA and DA children in their level of reading comprehension increased over time. However the loss of numbers of children from both groups over the year in question prevents any firm statement on this question.

On the ratings of children's interest in reading activities (item 3, Table 53) the results obtained are rather variable, in that the difference between

the CA and DA samples in the distribution of ratings is statistically significant on Schedules 4 and 6 but not on Schedules 3 and 5, although always in favour of the CA sample. (For the SWC sub-group versus CA sample comparisons, only the final schedule yielded a significant difference.) Inspection of the figures in the table shows that, whilst the distribution of ratings received by the CA sample shows a slight but steady rise over the series of schedules, those for the DA sample fluctuate rather and the final schedule shows a higher proportion of children showing little interest in reading (approximately 21 per cent) than at any other time. It is difficult to know how much weight to put on the latter finding which may simply reflect differences in teachers' standards of judgement. One might have expected a more marked upward trend in the interest in reading shown by the two samples with the increase in the children's length of exposure to the reading oriented environment of the school.

Items 5 and 6 in Table 53 show that, in knowledge of letter sounds (Schedules 3 and 4) and phonic word building skills (Schedules 5 and 6), the CA children obtained significantly higher ratings than the DA children. The same pattern appeared when the SWC area children were compared with the DA children. These findings must be tentative since a substantial number of children fell into the 'not observed' category on the first three schedules in this series and, if these had been given ratings, their inclusion might have markedly altered the patterns of distribution shown. However, on the sixth schedule no children in either group fall into the 'not observed' category and the finding of a significant difference in distribution between the two samples here supports similar differences on the earlier schedules. In this connection it is interesting to note that, according to information provided by the headteachers (see Chapter 12), the CA schools tended to introduce the systematic teaching of phonics earlier than the DA schools.

These results are also supported by the finding of a highly significant difference between the CA and DA samples (and between the SWC sub-group and the DA sample) on the Daniels and Diack Spelling Test (see Tables 54 and 55). This test uses a selection of words graded in difficulty, many of them phonically regular in their spelling. One might well expect a strong measure of agreement between performance on this test, therefore, and teachers' ratings of children's phonic word building skills.

Comparison of the percentage figures in Table 53 (item 6) shows a marked upward trend in the rated phonic word building skill of the children in both main groups from the second year (Schedule 5) to the third year (Schedule 6). By the end of their infant school careers, nearly half of the CA sample (approx. 47 per cent) and one-third of the DA sample (approx. 31 per cent) were rated as very proficient in this skill, although nearly one-quarter (approx. 24 per cent) of the latter group were rated as showing little or no proficiency.

The children's raw scores on the reading tests were converted to attainment ages based on the test norms, and the mean and standard deviations of the two samples based upon these reading ages are presented in Table 57. On the three sub-tests of the Neale reading test, some children obtained scores which fell below the norms. Such children were arbitrarily awarded the lowest attainment age for that test. This means, of course, that the mean

attainment ages shown for the three Neale measures in the following tables are overestimates, the degree of inflation depending on the number of children falling below the norms in the group concerned. (See Figures 3 to 5, pages 116 to 118 for the numbers of such children in each group on each measure.)

It will be seen that the most marked differences between the CA and DA samples occur on the Burt and Neale Accuracy measures, both of which assess word recognition skills. On the Burt test the CA children are over one year ahead of the DA children and just under one year ahead on the Neale Accuracy measure. The differences between the two groups on the remaining Neale measures are smaller, although in the same direction, namely 5 months on Neale Rate, and 8 months on Neale Accuracy. The table also shows that, whilst the SWC component of the CA sample are between 3 and 12 months ahead of the DA sample on the various measures, the MC children in the CA sample are, roughly, 6 months ahead of the SWC children on the same measures.

It is interesting to compare the reading ages for

Table 57

Reading ages of the CA and DA samples (with breakdown of CA sample) on the reading and spelling tests

Test	CA group						DA group	
	MC		SWC		MC+SWC			
	N=122		N=125		N=247		N=247*	
	mean	s.d.	mean	s.d.	mean	s.d.	mean	s.d.
	y m	y m	y m	y m	y m	y m	y m	y m
Burt Reading Test	8 3	1 8	7 7	1 6	7 11	1 7	6 7	1 7
Neale Reading Test:								
Accuracy	8 6	1 3	8 0	1 0	8 3	1 1	7 5	1 1
Rate	8 4	1 5	7 11	1 1	8 1	1 3	7 8	1 1
Comprehension	8 3	1 5	7 8	1 5	8 0	1 3	7 4	1 0
Spelling Test	8 0	1 4	7 5	1 3	7 8	1 4	6 7	1 2

* N=249 in the Spelling test

Table 58

Differences between mean reading and spelling attainment
age and mean chronological age for the CA and DA samples
(with breakdown of the CA sample)

Test	CA group			DA group
	MC	SWC	MC+SWC	
	N=122	N=125	N=247	N=247
	y m	y m	y m	y m
Burt Reading Test	+0 9	+0 1	+0 5	-0 11
Neale Reading Test:				
Accuracy	+1 0	+0 6	+0 9	-0 1
Rate	+0 10	+0 5	+0 7	+0 2
Comprehension	+0 9	+0 2	+0 6	-0 2
Spelling Test	+0 6	-0 1	+0 2	-0 11

Note: The figures in this table were obtained by subtracting
each group's mean chronological age (7 years 6 months)
from its attainment age.

The mean chronological age for the sample was
calculated on the basis of a fixed date, the first
day of the month in which the tests were administered.
This means that it is a slight under-estimate of the
true mean age.

each group with the mean chronological age of the
sample (approximately 7 years 6 months) and
these comparisons are presented in Table 58.

This table shows that, on all of the tests, the
CA children obtained attainment ages above their
mean chronological age, the differences ranging
from 2 to 9 months. The same pattern applies for
the SWC area children except that, on spelling, this
group fell slightly below the age norm, and, on all
of the tests, their attainment ages were much
nearer to mean chronological age than those of the
MC sub-group. In contrast, on all of the measures
except Neale Rate, the DA children obtained
attainment ages below their chronological age, the
difference ranging from 1 to 11 months. The Neale
Rate measure, however, seems to be the least
satisfactory of the three yielded by this test as it is

subject to various distorting effects (see Volume 2,
Chapters 5 and 15 for a fuller discussion of this
point).

It will be noticed from Table 58 that the CA
sample obtained a mean spelling age only slightly
above its mean chronological age, whereas, on the
reading test measures, this group obtained mean
attainment ages well above the age norm. It was
noted in Chapter 11, that some of the sample
schools, at least, tended to de-emphasize the
systematic teaching of spelling, according to the
headteachers. However, such schools tended to be
in the DA rather than the CA group for three
quarters of the CA schools gave some informal
instruction in spelling, according to the headteachers. The explanation of the relatively poor
showing of the CA schools in spelling, as compared

with reading, does not, therefore, seem to lie in a de-emphasis of spelling although it was not possible to say how thorough and systematic the teaching of spelling was in those schools.

It is interesting to note that the DA children fall nearly one year below their age norms in mean score on the Burt reading test but only one month below such norms on the Neale Accuracy measure. Conversely, the mean score for the CA sample was further above the age norm in the case of Neale Accuracy than the Burt test. As already mentioned, these two test measures are probably highly overlapping in that they relate to word recognition skills, although in the different contexts of randomly chosen words (Burt) and story sequences (Neale). This contention is supported by the fact that the correlation between the two measures (raw scores) for the entire urban sample was as high as 0.97, a figure normally associated with test-retest reliability correlations (see Table 70). The implication of the discrepancy in outcome between the two test measures in terms of the attainment age/chronological age differences is that the Neale measure may be over-estimating, or the Burt test under-estimating the children's 'true' reading achievement. (The same discrepancy was found in the intensive study of a sub-sample of 'deprived' and 'control' children drawn from the present sample, reported in Volume 2, Chapter 5.) According to the corrected standards for the Burt reading test presented by the Ministry of Education (1950), in the score region covered by the CA and DA means (i.e. reading ages between 6½ and 8 years), the Burt test yields rather inflated scores in comparison with the Schonell and Vernon Graded Word Reading Tests. This would suggest that the Neal Accuracy measure is probably an overestimate of the reading achievement of the present sample, although more up-to-date information on the scoring standards of the two tests is badly needed.

In order to illustrate the relative performance, in terms of attainment ages, of the two samples on the reading and spelling tests, Figures 2 to 6 show the distributions of attainment ages for each sample on these tests. (The distribution patterns for the MC and SWC components of the CA sample were roughly similar and are not presented separately.) The overall picture shown by these histograms is that, for both samples, the attainment age distributions on the various measures are skewed towards the lower end of the score ranges, but that this tendency is far more pronounced in the case of the DA sample.

For the three Neale test measures the numbers of children falling below the test norms are indicated in the figures and it will be seen that, on the Rate measure, a substantial number of children in both groups are in this category. On the Accuracy measure the number in either group is negligible and, on the Comprehension measure, far more DA than CA children (28 as compared with 3) scored below the norms.

The percentage figures (not included in the histograms) show that, on the reading test measures, the proportions of DA children obtaining reading ages below approximately 7 years (the scoring intervals are not strictly comparable over the four scales) are roughly twice those of the CA children. On the Burt test, for example, approximately 64 per cent of the DA group and 34 per cent of the CA group obtained reading ages of 7 years or below. The difference between the two groups in the proportion of children with reading ages of 6 years or less (18 months below the mean chronological age) is even greater, approximately 38 per cent of the DA group as compared with 12 per cent for the CA group. The proportions in each group of children with relatively low reading ages on the Neale Accuracy measure are rather lower than in the case of the Burt test (approximately 43 per cent of DA children and 17 per cent of CA children had reading ages of just over 7 years or below) but, as discussed earlier, this test may tend to overestimate children's reading achievement. Even on the latter measure, however, just over 20 per cent of the DA children and 4 per cent of the CA children had reading ages of 6 years 5 months or less, i.e. over one year below the mean chronological age for the whole sample (7 years 6 months). On these two word recognition measures, therefore, a substantial proportion of the DA children can be regarded as retarded in this basic reading skill (at least one year below their age norms).

The Neale Rate and Accuracy measures show a similarly greater proportion of DA rather than CA children with reading ages in the region of 7 years and below, but both of these sub-tests have a higher basal reading age than the word recognition measures (6 years 6 months for Rate and 6 years 3 months for Comprehension). Consequently, they

Figure 2

Distributions of Attainment Ages on Burt Reading Test: CA and DA samples

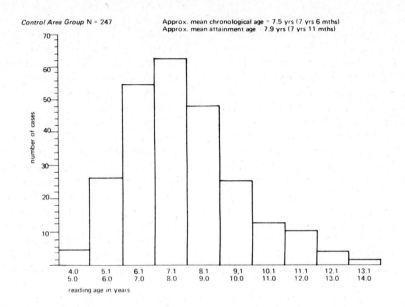

Control Area Group N = 247 Approx. mean chronological age = 7.5 yrs (7 yrs 6 mths)
Approx. mean attainment age   7.9 yrs (7 yrs 11 mths)

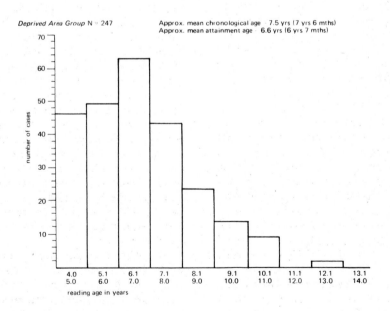

Deprived Area Group N = 247 Approx. mean chronological age   7.5 yrs (7 yrs 6 mths)
Approx. mean attainment age   6.6 yrs (6 yrs 7 mths)

115

Figure 3

Distributions of attainment ages on Neale Accuracy Test: CA and DA samples

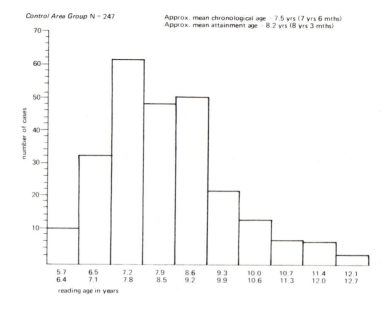

Note: First category includes one child falling below test norms

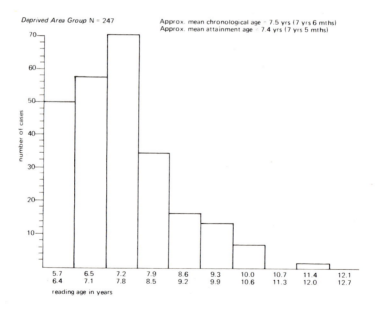

Note: First category includes 2 children falling below test norms

Figure 4

Distributions of attainment ages on Neale Rate Test: CA and DA sample

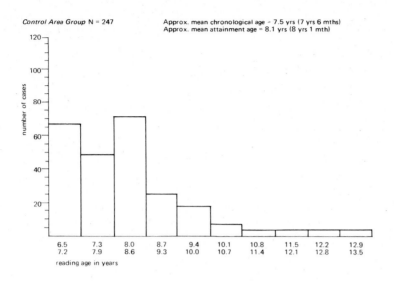

Note: First category includes 26 children falling below test norms

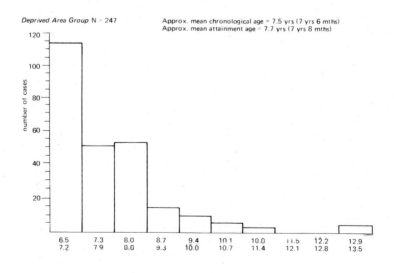

Note: First category includes 35 children falling below test norms

117

Figure 5

Distributions of attainment ages on Neale Comprehension Test: CA and DA samples

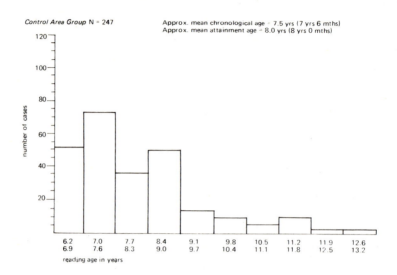

Note: First category includes 3 children falling below test norms

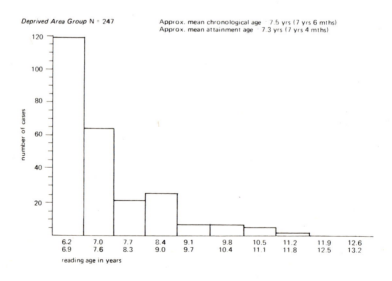

Note: First category includes 28 children falling below test norms

Figure 6

Distributions of attainment ages on Daniels and Diack Spelling Test: CA and DA samples

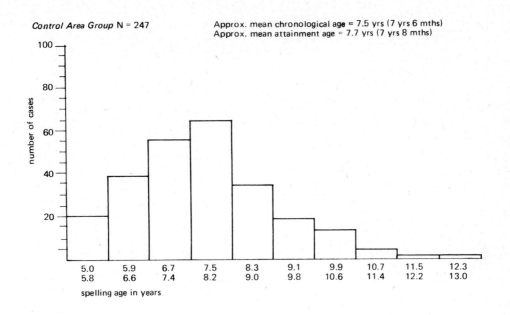

Control Area Group N = 247   Approx. mean chronological age = 7.5 yrs (7 yrs 6 mths)
Approx. mean attainment age = 7.7 yrs (7 yrs 8 mths)

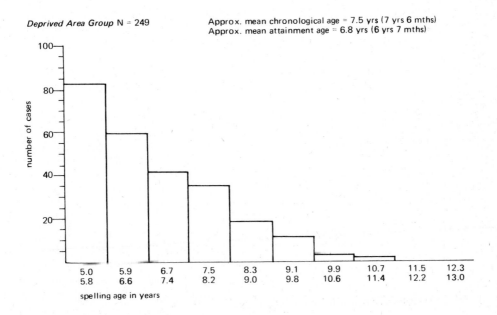

Deprived Area Group N = 249   Approx. mean chronological age = 7.5 yrs (7 yrs 6 mths)
Approx. mean attainment age = 6.8 yrs (6 yrs 7 mths)

discriminate less well among the poor readers in the sample, as shown by the number of children, particularly in the DA group, falling below the norms for these two sub-tests (see Figures 4 and 5).

On the spelling test approximately 57 per cent of the DA group and 23 per cent of the CA group obtained spelling ages of 6 years 7 months or below, i.e. approximately one year below the sample's mean chronological age. On a more stringent criterion of backwardness, a spelling age of 5 years 10 months or less, i.e. over 18 months below the mean chronological age, the proportions of retarded children in the DA and CA groups were approximately 33 per cent and 8 per cent respectively. The latter figures are fairly similar to those for the proportions, already quoted, of children obtaining a Burt reading age of 6 years or less. It is clear, therefore, that in spelling, as in reading, a substantial proportion of the DA children can be regarded as seriously retarded. It should be borne in mind that the figures for retardation in reading and spelling are likely to be conservative, firstly, because children failing to score, or falling below the test norms, were given an arbitrary reading age and, secondly, because the mean age of the sample (7 years 6 months) is a slight under-estimate, as already explained.

It will be noticed that the distribution patterns for the CA sample on the Burt and Neale Accuracy measures are much less negatively skewed than their score patterns on the Neale Rate and Comprehension measures. The fact mentioned earlier that the latter two measures have a higher basal or starting reading age than the word recognition measures may partly explain this difference but certainly does not wholly do so. As already discussed, the Neale Rate measure seems to be liable to distortion and may penalize the relatively good readers who proceed to the more difficult, time consuming story passages. The relative bias in the total sample's Neale Comprehension scores toward the lower end of the score range may indicate that the children tended to be relatively weak in this aspect of reading. (Table 58 showed them to be only 6 months above their chronological age on this measure, as opposed to 9 months on the Accuracy scores.) Alternatively, it may reflect a tendency for the children to concentrate on correct word recognition and, perhaps, good articulation rather than the understanding of

what is read. This particular reading comprehension measure is unusual in that the child is not allowed to refer back to the text in order to answer the questions, but must rely on his recall of the story after he has read it aloud. It is interesting to note that, whilst all of the reading test score distributions of the DA sample show a marked bias toward the low end of the scale, this tendency is especially pronounced on the Neale Rate and Comprehension measures just discussed. Thus, the factors discussed above may underlie the score patterns of both the CA and DA samples.

According to the NFER Picture Test A which can be regarded as a test of children's general intelligence, the majority of children in both the CA and DA samples obtained standardized scores within or above the broad average range (see Section D of this chapter for details). A direct comparison of these test scores with those obtained on the reading and spelling tests is not possible because the basis of the standardization is different between the picture test and the attainment tests. Nevertheless, the contrast, in both groups, between the roughly normal pattern of score distribution on Picture Test A and the markedly skewed distributions on the reading and spelling tests suggests the possibility that a substantial minority of children, especially in the DA sample, were 'under-functioning', i.e. performing educationally at a level well below that of their tested intelligence. However, it must be recognized that the whole concept of under-functioning is open to serious statistical and psychological objections (see, for example, Vernon 1960). Vernon (1960) has cautioned against using the results of a 'non-verbal' intelligence test to predict educational attainment, but, as discussed in the next chapter, it is not clear to what extent the picture test used in the present study is 'non-verbal' in content, and it seems reasonable to use the score obtained as a rough indication of a child's broad educational potential.

In this connection it is interesting to examine the picture test scores of the children who appeared to be backward in reading and spelling according to the attainment test results presented in Section B of this chapter. Table 59 shows the numbers and proportions of backward readers and spellers who obtained average or above, or below average standardized scores on the picture test (intelligence). In the case of the Burt reading test

Table 59 (A to D)

Picture test scores of children in the CA and DA samples who were backward in reading or spelling

A. Children with Burt reading test scores of 5 years 0 months or less

Standardized picture test score (mean=100)	CA group				DA group	
	MC	SWC	MC+SWC			
	n	n	n	%	n	%
90 or less	0	4	4	80	29	64
91+	0	1	1	20	16	36

B. Children with Burt reading test scores between 5 years 1 month and 6 years 0 months

	MC	SWC	MC+SWC	%	DA n	DA %
90 or less	3	8	11	42	23	48
91+	8	7	15	58	25	52

C. Children with Neale accuracy scores of 6 years 5 months or less

	MC	SWC	MC+SWC	%	DA n	DA %
90 or less	0	6	6	60	31	61
91+	0	4	4	40	20	39

D. Children with spelling test scores of 5 years 10 months or less

	MC	SWC	MC+SWC	%	DA n	DA %
90 or less	1	13	14	70	47	57
91+	2	4	6	30	35	43

two categories of backwardness are included, 'moderately' backward i.e. reading ages between 5 years and 6 years (1½ to 2½ years retardation), and seriously backward i.e. reading ages of 5 years or below (2½ years retardation or more). The criterion of backwardness chosen for the Neale Accuracy test, a reading age of 6 years 5 months or less represents a degree of retardation of approximately 13 months or more, and that for the spelling test, a spelling age of 5 years 10 months or less, represents a degree of retardation of approximately 20 months or more. All of these figures for retardation are based upon the mean average chronological age of the total urban sample (7 years 6 months) rather than the actual ages of the individual children and are, therefore, approximate, but they are unlikely to be seriously in error.

It will be seen that the numbers of CA children regarded as backward in reading or spelling, according to the criteria chosen, are rather small, and the proportion of children with average or above scores on the picture test varies from test to test, and, in the case of the Burt test, from the 'moderate' to the 'serious' degree of backwardness. With such small numbers percentages are rather meaningless. The numbers of DA children falling into the backward categories on the tests chosen are much more substantial and the tables show that the proportion of children of average intelligence or above ranges from approximately 36 per cent to 52 per cent on the attainment tests chosen. Perhaps the most striking result is that of the DA children with Burt reading ages of 5 years or less (i.e. approximately 2½ years retarded or more), over one third (36.6 per cent) appeared to be of average or above intelligence. Although caution must be observed in interpreting the results of the picture test (see discussion on page 120) it seems reasonable to conclude that, in the case of a substantial proportion of DA children, their retardation in reading and spelling does not appear to be due to low intelligence.

(ii) Mechanical writing ability

Several items on the school schedules were concerned with the development of the child's mechanical writing skill and information from these is presented in Table 60. Schedules 3 and 4, completed during the second and third terms of the children's first school year, contained questions on the child's ability to write his own name and to trace words written for him by the class teacher. It was found that, on both occasions, a significantly higher proportion of CA than DA children were judged to be able to write their names quite efficiently or efficiently (approximately 79 per cent of CA children and 60 per cent of DA children on Schedule 3, and 93 per cent of CA children and 68 per cent of DA children on Schedule 4). The significant difference was maintained when the SWC area children were compared with the DA children on the two occasions. Similarly, on both occasions, the CA children received significantly higher ratings than the DA children in their ability to trace words written by the teacher, an intermediate step in the development of writing skill. In this case, however, the difference was attributable to the marked superiority of the MC component of the CA sample, the differences between the SWC sub-group and the

CA sample falling well below significance on both schedules.

Table 60 also shows the teachers' ratings received by the two samples on their ability to copy words from a model and to write words unaided, regardless of spelling, in their 'free writing' (e.g. the writing of stories and news). It will be seen that, in regard to the copying of words from a model, the CA group received consistently higher ratings over the series of schedules, but, on the latest schedule (Number 5), the difference between the groups in their distributions fell below significance. Both samples show a steady rise in the ratings over the series of schedules but it would seem that, during the children's second school year (i.e. between Schedules 4 and 5), the DA group made relatively greater gains, although it must be remembered that the sample numbers are not comparable at the different points in time. The superiority of the CA sample in this skill was established early in their school careers because on a similar, but differently worded item on Schedule 2 (end of first term) the difference between the two groups was already highly significant ($z = 7.12$, $p < 0.1$ per cent). A similar pattern of results emerged from the comparison between the SWC element of the CA sample and the DA sample in their mechanical writing skills.

With regard to the more advanced skill of writing words unaided, rather than copying words, the picture is a little different in that the CA children maintain a statistically highly significant superiority over the DA children throughout the period under study, this pattern applying even when the MC component of the CA sample is removed. Both groups show a steady rise in the proportion of children able to write words efficiently, or quite efficiently, over the period covered by the schedules, although, by the end of the children's second year (Schedule 5), nearly half of the DA sample and one fifth of the CA sample were rated as unable to write words unaided, or to do so very poorly. No doubt, however, many of the children in this category would have improved their skill in writing during the final school year.

These findings on the children's mechanical writing skills were in the predicted direction and are supported by similar findings based upon comparison between a sub-sample of children from deprived home backgrounds and a control group,

Table 60

Teachers' ratings of children's mechanical writing skills:

CA and DA samples

Item	Rating	end of 2nd term (Schedule 3)				end of 1st year (Schedule 4)			
		CA N=309		DA N=355		CA N=308		DA N=347	
		n	%	n	%	n	%	n	%
1. Can child write his name?	easily and efficiently	144	46.6	70	19.7	197	64.0	109	31.4
	quite efficiently	99	32.0	145	40.8	90	29.2	128	36.9
	poorly/unable to do so	66	21.4	140	39.4	21	6.8	110	31.7
	Value of z CA vs DA	7.22, $p < 0.1\%$				9.36, $p < 0.1\%$			
	Value of z SWC vs DA	2.81, $p < 0.5\%$				5.91, $p < 0.1\%$			
2. Can child trace words written by teacher?	easily and efficiently	190	61.5	156	43.9	220	71.4	200	57.6
	quite efficiently	82	26.5	129	36.3	57	18.5	105	30.3
	poorly/unable to do so	37	12.0	70	19.7	31	10.1	42	12.1
	Value of z CA vs DA	4.47, $p < 0.1\%$				3.33, $p < 0.1\%$			
	Value of z SWC vs DA	0.32, N.S.				0.05, N.S.			

Continued overleaf

123

| Item | Rating | end of 2nd term (Schedule 3) | | | | end of 1st year (Schedule 4) | | | | end of 2nd year (Schedule 5) | | | |
| | | CA N=309 | | DA N=355 | | CA N=308 | | DA N=347 | | CA N=280 | | DA N=309 | |
		n	%	n	%	n	%	n	%	n	%	n	%
3. How well does child copy words?	easily and efficiently	156	50.5	108	30.4	197	54.0	151	43.5	164	58.6	186	60.2
	efficiently on whole	115	37.2	134	37.7	90	29.2	133	38.3	105	37.5	99	32.0
	poorly/unable to do so	38	12.3	113	31.8	21	6.8	63	18.2	11	3.9	24	7.8
	Value of z CA vs DA	6.44, p < 0.1%				5.64, p < 0.1%				0.05, N.S.			
	Value of z SWC vs DA	2.24, p < 2.5%				3.14, p < 0.1%				0.12, N.S.			
4. How well can child write words?	easily and efficiently	15	4.8	6	1.7	27	8.8	4	1.1	68	24.3	40	12.9
	efficiently on whole	45	14.6	39	11.0	100	32.5	70	20.2	152	54.3	118	38.2
	poorly/unable to do so	249	80.6	310	87.3	181	58.8	273	78.7	60	21.4	151	48.9
	Value of z CA vs DA	2.41, p < 1%				5.79, p < 0.1%				6.69, p < 0.1%			
	Value of z SWC vs DA	1.66, p < 5%				2.61, p < 0.5%				4.98, p < 0.1%			

Probability levels in the table are one-tailed.

both drawn from the present DA sample, reported in Volume 2 (Part One) in this series. That intensive study also found significant differences between the Control and Deprived groups, both in teachers' ratings of the children's motor co-ordination in fine manipulative skills such as writing and drawing, and in the children's performance on a simple pegboard test. No evidence is available on the motor co-ordination of the present sample unless one regards the results of the teachers' assessments of children's writing skills as indirect evidence. This would be very dubious evidence, though, since the poorer performance of the DA sample could be explained in terms of lower concentration in this field of activity. Jensen (1967) states that there is no firm evidence that culturally deprived children are retarded in motor-development or in any way deficient in motor skills.

Summary: reading and related skills

Teachers' ratings of children's reading skills were obtained from the end of the children's first school term and subsequently throughout the three infant school years under study. Over this period the CA children received consistently and often very significantly higher ratings of their reading skills than the DA children and made more rapid progress through the reading schemes used. This pattern of results was preserved when the SWC area children alone were compared with the DA children, although the between-group differences were sometimes less marked than in the main comparison. There was no firm evidence from the teachers' ratings for a widening gap in the level of reading skill of the CA and DA children over the period under study. The superiority of the CA children in reading skills was confirmed by the results of a battery of reading tests and a spelling test given to the children during their final infant school term. On these the CA group as a whole, and the SWC area children considered separately, achieved significantly higher mean scores. The results of the tests and the teachers' ratings showed that, from the first term, the CA children advanced more rapidly in their development of reading skills than the DA children and maintained this advance throughout the whole infant school period, a finding fully in accord with the results of earlier research into social class differences in reading skills, and also those of an intensive study of a sub-sample of children drawn from the present sample. It is possible that the relative inferiority of the DA children in basic reading attainments was partly a function of a lower level of teacher expectation in the DA schools relative to the CA schools but insufficient evidence was available from the present study to examine this hypothesis adequately.

The present CA and DA samples were compared with a very large national sample of children (National Child Development Study) in terms of level reached in the basic reading scheme and they appeared to be more advanced than the children in that sample. However, there were important differences between the two samples which may at least partly explain this result. The children's raw scores on the reading and spelling tests were converted to attainment ages based on the test norms and it was found that, in all of the tests, the CA children obtained mean attainment ages above their mean chronological age. (The mean attainment ages of the SWC area children, considered separately, were rather nearer to their chronological age and, in the case of spelling, fell slightly below it.) In contrast, in all of the reading and spelling test measures (except Neale Rate) the DA children fell below the age norms, particularly in the Burt reading test and the spelling test. On the word recognition measures and the spelling test the proportions of DA children retarded by one year or more were markedly greater than those of the CA children and the differences between these groups were even greater in the case of children retarded by eighteen months or more. A substantial proportion of the backward readers and spellers in the DA group appeared to be of average intelligence or above according to the picture test.

Comparison of the two groups in their development of mechanical writing skills showed a similar pattern of results to that described above i.e., the CA children were more advanced than the DA children in the early stages of such development, with the exception of one item (copying words), and maintained this superiority throughout the later stages, according to the teachers' judgement.

C. MATHEMATICAL SKILLS

The results of the teachers' ratings of children's mathematical skills over a series of the school schedules are presented in Tables 61 and 62. Two tables are necessary because the wording of some of the items was changed from Schedule 5 onwards in order to give a higher ceiling to the rating.

Inspection of these tables shows that whilst, in general, the CA children tend to receive higher ratings on most of the measures, the differences in patterns of distributions between the two samples falls below statistical significance in about half of the comparisons. A similar pattern of results emerges from a comparison between the SWC area children, considered separately, with the DA children, except that even fewer of the differences between the groups reach significance. In terms of trend in the pattern of results over the series of schedules the picture is rather variable, with some items showing a movement from non-significant to statistically significant differences and others showing a reverse trend. The superiority of the CA children in mathematical skills does not seem to be as marked or as clear cut as, for example, in the case of the teachers' ratings of the children's reading skills (see Table 53). Moreover, in three cases, item 6 (handling money) on Schedule 5, item 7 (use of counting aids) and item 8 (interest in mathematics) on Schedule 6, the DA children received non-significantly higher ratings than the CA children.

However, despite the somewhat variable pattern of results noted above, it is clear that, by the end of the infant school period (Schedule 6), according to the teachers, the CA children are markedly superior in computational ability (simple addition sums), and in their grasp of time and money concepts. They are not, however, rated as having a markedly better grasp of basic number concepts (although they are so rated in their ability to match the written number symbol with the corresponding number of objects). With the exception of the rating of the children's grasp of basic number concepts, these findings agree with the results of the Basic Mathematics Test given to the children in their final infant school term as part of the attainment survey. These results are presented in Tables 63 and 64 which show that the CA children obtained a very significantly higher mean score on this test than the DA children. Interestingly, however, the SWC sub-group of the CA sample obtained only a marginally higher mean score than the DA sample

(19.80 as compared with 19.38), this difference falling well below statistical significance. There is some discrepancy between the latter result and those yielded by the teachers' ratings of mathematical abilities on the last school schedule which was also completed in the final infant school term. On the basis of these ratings the SWC area children were significantly superior to the DA sample in matching number symbols to objects, simple computation (addition) and handling money, but, on the other hand, the differences between these two groups on ratings of grasp of basic numbers, concepts and ability to tell the time were non-significant.

One would expect a fairly good measure of agreement between the teachers' ratings of children's mathematical ability at the end of the infant school period (Schedule 6) and children's performance on the Basic Mathematics Test which, as discussed in Chapter 3, is geared to the approach to mathematics common in the modern infant school. As noted above, there is such agreement in the comparison between the CA sample as a whole and the DA sample, although rather less agreement in the SWC sub-group vs the DA sample comparison.

The results of the teachers' ratings, and the mathematical test, taken overall, are in agreement with previous findings into the relationship between social class and mathematical achievement, such as that of the National Child Development Study (Pringle et al., 1966) which showed significant differences in scores on a problem arithmetic test between higher and lower social class groups of children, in favour of the former. They are also supported by the finding of marked differences between the Deprived and Control intensive study sub-samples, both in teachers' ratings of the children's skills, and in their performance on the Basic Mathematics Test, reported in Volume 2 (Part One) in the present series. It may be that social class differences in skills are more marked in those aspects of mathematics in which verbal reasoning plays a major part, for example, in problem solving, as opposed to more mechanical arithmetical computations. However, it was not possible to differentiate between these aspects of mathematical skills in the present study. According to information obtained from the teachers during an interview (see Chapter 12), there appeared to be no major differences between the CA and DA

Table 61

Teachers' ratings of the mathematical skills of children in the CA and DA samples at the end of their first school year (with breakdown of CA sample)

| Item | Rating | CA group | | | | | | DA group | |
| | | MC N=140 | | SWC N=168 | | MC+SWC N=308 | | N=347 | |
		n	%	n	%	n	%	n	%
1. Can child count number of objects in a group?	Beyond 10	80	57.1	72	42.9	152	49.3	161	46.4
	6 - 10	54	38.6	59	35.1	113	36.7	112	32.3
	2 - 5	6	4.3	35	20.8	41	13.3	60	17.3
	Not at all	0	0.0	2	1.2	2	0.6	14	4.0

Value of z CA vs DA = 1.57, N.S.
Value of z SWC vs DA = 0.46, N.S.

Item	Rating	MC		SWC		MC+SWC		DA	
2. Can child match written number of symbols with corresponding number of objects?	Beyond 10	35	25.0	24	14.3	59	19.2	102	29.4
	6 - 10	98	70.0	92	54.8	190	61.7	129	37.2
	2 - 5	5	3.6	47	28.0	52	16.9	82	23.6
	Not at all	2	1.4	5	3.0	7	2.3	34	9.8

Value of z CA vs DA = 1.00, N.S.
Value of z SWC vs DA = 1.18, N.S.

Continued overleaf

3. Can child carry out simple addition sums?

Totalling 10 or more	31	22.1	30	27.0	61	24.3	95	32.2
Totalling up to 9	97	69.3	31	27.9	128	51.0	87	29.5
Unable to do so	12	8.6	50	45.0	62	24.7	113	38.3
*Not observed	0		57		57		52	

Value of z CA vs DA = 0.88, N.S.
Value of z SWC vs DA = 1.22, N.S.

4. Child's level of interest in mathematical

Very keen	56	40.0	35	20.8	91	29.5	55	15.8
Quite keen	76	54.3	110	65.5	186	60.4	187	53.9
Little/ no interest	8	5.7	23	13.7	31	10.1	105	30.3

Value of z CA vs DA = 6.52, $p < 0.1\%$
Value of z SWC vs DA = 3.54, $p < 0.1\%$

* Number in not observed category not included in percentage figures of 'tau' analysis.
  Probability levels in the table are one-tailed.

Table 62

Teachers' ratings of the mathematical skills of children in the CA and DA samples at the end of the second and third school years

Item	Rating	end of 2nd year (Schedule 5)				end of 3rd year (Schedule 6)			
		CA N=280		DA N=309		CA N=265		DA N=279	
		n	%	n	%	n	%	n	%
1. Can child count objects in a group presented to him?	beyond 20	206	73.6	173	56.0	–	–	–	–
	11-20	50	17.9	84	27.2	–	–	–	–
	2-10	24	8.6	45	14.6	–	–	–	–
	not at all	0	0.0	7	2.3	–	–	–	–
	Value of z CA vs DA	4.52, $p < 0.1\%$							
	Value of z SWC vs DA	0.75, N.S.							
2. Can child match written number symbol with corresponding number of objects?	beyond 20 objects	153	54.6	143	46.3	215	81.1	206	73.8
	11 to 20 objects	93	33.2	87	28.2	44	16.6	53	19.0
	2 to 10 objects	34	12.1	69	22.3	6	2.3	20	7.2
	not at all	0	0.0	10	3.2	0	0.0	0	0.0
	Value of z CA vs DA	3.13, $p < 0.1\%$				2.19, $p < 2.5\%$			
	Value of z SWC vs DA	0.32, N.S.				3.60, $p < 0.1\%$			
3. Can child carry out simple addition sums?	adds numbers totalling 20+	120	42.9	106	35.1	213	80.4	178	63.8
	adds numbers up to 20	86	30.7	90	29.8	46	17.4	63	22.6
	adds numbers up to 10	68	24.3	81	26.8	6	2.3	32	11.5
	unable to do so	6	2.1	25	8.3	0		6	2.1
	*not observed (Schedule 5 only)	0		7					
	Value of z CA vs DA	2.63, $p < 0.5\%$				4.69, $p < 0.1\%$			
	Value of z SWC vs DA	0.03, N.S.				5.15, $p < 0.1\%$			

Continued overleaf

129

		n	%	n	%	n	%	n	%
4. Child's grasp of basic number concepts	good	105	37.5	111	35.9	104	39.2	108	38.7
	adequate	141	50.4	140	45.3	138	50.1	126	45.2
	poor	34	12.1	58	18.8	23	8.7	45	16.1
	Value of z CA vs DA	1.21, N.S.				1.05, N.S.			
	Value of z SWC vs DA	C.07, N.S.				0.44, N.S.			
5. Can the child tell the time?	to within 5 minutes	59	21.1	26	8.4	142	53.6	97	34.8
	to within ¼ hour	86	30.7	36	11.6	59	22.3	52	18.6
	to within ½ hour	51	18.2	75	24.3	27	10.2	56	20.1
	knows hours only	64	22.9	104	33.7	30	11.3	51	18.3
	not at all	20	7.1	68	22.0	7	2.6	23	8.2
	Value of z CA vs DA	$7.94, p<0.1\%$				$5.30, p<0.1\%$			
	Value of z SWC vs DA	$5.61, p<0.1\%$				1.35, N.S.			
6. Child's ability to handle money in classroom shopping activities	*very proficient – handles amounts over 2/-	26	9.7	57	18.4	89	33.6	81	29.0
	fairly proficient	124	46.4	122	39.5	134	50.6	137	49.1
	can handle pence only	106	39.7	115	37.2	42	15.8	55	19.7
	no knowledge of money	11	4.1	15	4.8	0		6	2.1
	*not observed	13		0					
	Value of z CA vs DA	1.31, N.S.				$1.75, p<5\%$			
	Value of z SWC vs DA	1.84, N.S.				$1.85, p<5\%$			
7. Child's use of counting aids in computational work	no longer/occasionally uses	100	35.7	93	30.1	121	45.7	142	50.9
	needs/uses quite often	103	36.8	114	36.9	81	30.6	90	32.3
	nearly always needs/uses	77	27.5	102	33.0	63	23.8	47	16.8
	Value of z CA vs DA	1.64, N.S.				$1.65, p<5\%$			
	Value of z SWC vs DA	0.33, N.S.				$4.11, p<0.1\%$			
8. Child's level of interest in mathematical activities	very keen	73	26.1	69	22.3	53	20.0	76	27.2
	fairly keen	169	60.4	164	53.1	170	64.1	148	53.0
	little/no interest	38	13.6	76	24.6	42	15.8	55	19.7
	Value of z CA vs DA	$2.61, p<0.5\%$				0.62, N.S.			
	Value of z SWC vs DA	1.05, N.S.				1.38, N.S.			

* Number in not observed category not included in percentage figures on 'tau' analysis.

** Schedule 5 amounts over 2/-; Schedule 6 amounts over 50 n.p.

Probability levels in the table are one-tailed.

Table 63

Raw scores of CA and DA samples in the Basic Mathematics
Test during the children's final infant school term

CA group N=263		DA group N=275		difference between means (CA-DA)	standard error of difference	t	p (one-tail)
mean	s.d.	mean	s.d.				
22.83	8.21	19.38	7.90	3.45	0.70	4.97	< 0.1%

Table 64

Raw scores of SWC sub-sample and DA sample in the Basic Mathematics
Test during the children's final infant school term

SWC group N=142		DA group N=275		difference between means (SWC-DA)	standard error of difference	t	p (one-tail)
mean	s.d.	mean	s.d.				
19.80	7.49	19.38	7.90	0.42	0.80	0.53	N.S.

schools in their approach to mathematics, most schools using some variation of the 'Nuffield' scheme, except that some of the CA schools combined this with a 'traditional' approach. Neither group of schools reported any major problems concerning the teaching of mathematical skills to the children and, of the problems mentioned by the teachers, none seemed to be peculiar to, or predominantly associated with, the DA schools.

Looking at the results of the teachers' ratings shown in Tables 61 and 62 in more detail it will be seen that, in the case of the items concerning the child's ability to count, to match the number symbol to the corresponding number of objects and to do simple addition sums (the first three items in each table), the pattern is one of no significant difference between the groups at the end of the first school year (Schedule 4), but a significant difference in favour of the CA sample emerging during the second and third school years. Both groups show an upward trend in their ratings on these items over the period covered, as might be expected.

The finding of a non-significant difference between the samples in their grasp of basic number concepts as rated by the teachers (item 4 in Table 62) is rather surprising in view of the findings just discussed and the significant superiority of the CA sample in the mathematics test. One possible explanation lies in the rather subjective nature of this item which simply asks the teacher to rate the child as 'good', 'adequate', or 'poor' in his grasp of number concepts, whereas the other items concerning the child's mathematical achievements (excluding the rating of general interest in mathematical activities) are rather more objective and concrete in content. This means that, on this rating, the teachers will be judging each child relative to others in his class rather than in terms of some absolute standard of performance. In consequence, the child in the CA sample rated as poor in his grasp of number concepts may be appreciably better in this respect than a similarly rated child in the DA sample where the overall level of mathematics achievement appears to be lower. This relativity of teachers' judgements would, of course, operate to mask any underlying differences in levels of achievement between the CA and DA samples. The fact that there is no upward trend in the children's ratings on this item from Schedule 5 to Schedule 6, which one would expect, since children should improve in their understanding of number concepts as they progress through school, supports this explanation. It is interesting in this connection that, in the intensive study of sub-samples of children drawn from the present sample and reported in Volume 2 (Part One) in this series, there was a significant difference between the Deprived and Control groups of children on the teachers' ratings of the children's grasp of basic number concepts. The important point here is that these particular children were matched for school and in many cases the *same* teacher assessed both the deprived and control member of each pair so that, in general, the two groups would be assessed according to similar standards of judgement.

However, to put the above discussion about the problem of the relativity of teachers' judgements and its implications into perspective, it should be pointed out that the school schedules contained a number of rather subjective and generally worded items of a similar type to the rating of the child's grasp of numbers concepts and, in some cases, these have yielded significant differences between the CA and DA samples. (See, for example, the results of some of the ratings of reading skills in Table 53.)

In their ability to tell the time, as rated by the teachers, the CA children are significantly superior to the DA children at the end of the second and third school years (see item 5 Table 62). The same pattern obtains for the comparisons between the SWC area children and the DA children except that, on Schedule 6, the difference between the groups falls below significance. Both the CA and DA samples show a marked improvement in this skill during the final school year (from Schedule 5

to Schedule 6). By the end of their infant school careers, over half of the CA children and approximately one third of the DA children were judged to be able to tell the time to within five minutes, and only a very small proportion of children (approximately 3 per cent and 8 per cent respectively) appeared to be completely unable to tell the time.

It is interesting to note that, on the teachers' ratings of children's ability to handle money in classroom shopping activities, the DA children are (non-significantly) superior to the controls at the end of the second school year, although the situation is reversed by the end of the third school year (Schedule 6) when the CA children received significantly higher ratings than the DA children. During the interviews carried out as part of the study (see Chapter 12), a number of the teachers in the DA schools commented that, despite their educational deficiencies in other skills, children from culturally deprived home backgrounds often had a well developed ability to handle money, based on their experience of going on family shopping errands, a responsibility which may be less common among young children from more advantaged homes. However, it would seem that any early advantage which the DA children enjoyed in this respect was lost over the course of the final infant school year, as the CA children developed their skill in this area, although both groups showed a marked improvement in their ratings from the second to the third year.

Two rather general questions in this section of the school schedules, not directly reflecting the children's level of mathematical skills were asked, namely, the use made by the children of counting aids, and their general level of interest in mathematics (items 7 and 8 in Table 62). With regard to the former item, an interesting reversal of pattern in the results occurred during the children's final school year. On School Schedule 5 (end of second year), the CA children were rated as (non-significantly) less dependent upon counting aids in computational work than the DA children. However, by the end of the final school year (Schedule 6), it was the DA children who showed relatively less dependence on concrete aids, although both groups had shown a clear trend in the course of that year toward greater independence of such aids. In fact, there was a statistically highly significant difference between the SWC area children and the DA children in favour of the latter on the final schedule on this item, although the result of the comparison between the DA sample and the full CA sample only just reached the five per cent level of significance. This finding, however, may reflect differences in school policy regarding the use of counting or other computational aids. It may have been, for example, that the CA schools were less concerned to 'wean' the children from such aids during the final school year than the DA schools, although, in view of the general superiority of the CA children in mathematical achievement, one might think that the DA children showed a greater need of such aids.

On the teachers' ratings of the children's level of interest in mathematical activities, a curious pattern of results can be observed in the table in which the CA children show a steady decline in rated interest over the three successive schedules, in contrast to the consistent improvement of the DA children. The consequence of these opposing trends is that, whereas the CA sample received significantly higher ratings on this item at the end of the first school year, by the end of the final year, the DA children were rated as showing a (non-significantly) higher level of interest. It seems most unlikely that the level of interest shown by the CA children would, in reality, drop steadily over the two year period in question, so that one is inclined to regard this result as an artefact of differences in the standards of judgement adopted by the teachers completing the successive schedules, although such differences could be expected to lead to fluctuations in the ratings accorded to a group of children by successive teachers, rather than a consistent increase or decrease, as in this case.

Since the Basic Mathematics Test used was an experimental version, no standardization norms were available, so that it is not possible to relate the performance of the children in the present sample to that of their age-group in general. It is interesting to note, in passing, however, that the distribution of raw scores both for the CA and DA groups showed a good spread over the score range and was roughly 'normal' in shape.

Summary: mathematical skills

The CA children (and, to a lesser extent, the SWC area children considered separately) tended to receive higher ratings than the DA children on aspects of mathematical skills rated by the teachers over the infant school period, but the differences between the groups reached statistical significance in only about half of the comparisons made. There was no clear trend for the differences to become more pronounced over time but, by the end of the third year, the CA children were rated as significantly superior to the DA children in most aspects of mathematical skills and this result was supported by the fact that the former group obtained a significantly higher mean score on the Basic Mathematics Test given to the children at this time. (The SWC area children performed only marginally better than the DA children on this test, however.) These results, in the main, are in line with previous studies showing social class differences in mathematical achievement, and also with the findings of the intensive study of a sub-sample of culturally deprived children drawn from the present sample.

D. INTELLIGENCE

Included in the survey of basic attainments carried out on the sample during the children's final infant school term was the NFER Picture Test A which, as mentioned in Chapter 3, can be regarded as a test of general intelligence. Insofar as this test taps the children's fund of generalized intellectual skills and concepts it is appropriate to include a discussion of the results obtained from it in the present chapter.

Tables 65 and 66 present the results obtained on this test and the outcome of a 't' test analysis.

These tables show that both the CA sample as a whole and the SWC component of it taken by itself, achieved significantly higher mean scores than the DA sample, although the between-group difference in the latter comparison reached only the 2.5 per cent significance level. The fact of the superiority of the CA over the DA sample on a measure of what might be termed general intelligence, has, of course, some implications for the interpretation of the differences between the two groups in basic educational skills presented in this chapter. The obvious question that arises is to what extent are the differences between the two samples in intelligence related to their differences in educational achievement? This question will be considered more fully in Chapter 6.

Table 65

Raw scores of CA and DA samples on picture test during the children's final infant school term

CA group N=264		DA group N=276		difference between means (CA-DA)	standard error of difference	t	P (one-tail)
mean	s.d.	mean	s.d.				
32.84	10.91	27.24	11.33	5.60	0.96	5.84	< 0.1%

Table 66

Raw scores of SWC and DA samples on picture test during the children's final infant school term

SWC group N=142		DA group N=276		difference between means (SWC-DA)	standard error of difference	t	P (one-tail)
mean	s.d.	mean	s.d.				
29.54	11.06	27.24	11.33	2.30	1.16	1.97	< 2.5%

Table 67

Standardized scores of CA and DA samples on NFER Picture Test (with breakdown of CA sample)

CA group						DA group	
MC N=122		SWC N=142		MC+SWC N=264		N=276	
mean	s.d.	mean	s.d.	mean	s.d.	mean	s.d.
109.93	13.45	101.06	14.30	105.16	14.58	97.68	14.43

Figure 7

Distributions of standardized scores on Picture Test A: CA and DA samples

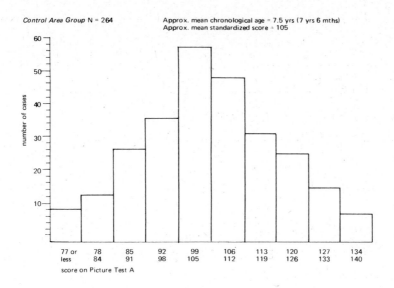

Note: First category includes 3 children falling below test norms

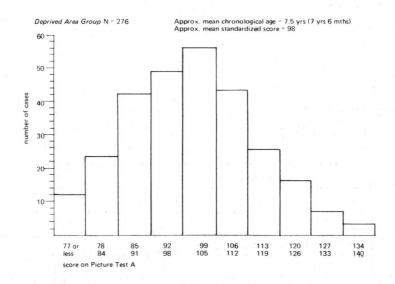

Note: First category includes 7 children falling below test norms

Table 68

Teachers' estimates of children's likely progress in the Junior school/department:

CA and DA samples (with breakdown of CA sample)

| Item | Rating | CA group | | | | | | DA group | |
| | | MC N=122 | | SWC N=143 | | MC+SWC N=265 | | N=279 | |
		n	%	n	%	n	%	n	%
1. How do you anticipate child's progress in Junior school?	no problems	72	59.0	85	59.4	157	59.2	146	52.3
	initial difficulty	35	23.7	45	31.5	80	30.2	80	28.7
	will certainly find difficulty	15	12.3	13	9.1	28	10.6	53	19.0
	Value of z CA vs DA = 2.12, p <2.5%								
	Value of z SWC vs DA = 1.90, p <5%								
2. Reason for anticipated difficulty (children rated 3 above)	immaturity	0	-*	3	-*	3	10.7	3	5.7
	behaviour difficulties	2	-	1	-	3	10.7	8	15.1
	low basic attainments	6	-	5	-	11	39.3	11	20.7
	combination of above	7	-	4	-	11	39.3	31	58.5

* Percentages not included due to small numbers.

136

The children's raw scores on the picture test were converted to standardized scores (mean 100, standard deviation 15) and Table 67 presents information on the performance of the two samples in terms of such scores.

It will be seen that the CA sample as a whole obtained a mean standardized score of just over 105, which is one third of a standard deviation above the test standardization mean of 100, whilst the mean DA score was approximately 98, slightly below that mean. Breakdown of the CA sample, however, shows that the MC sub-group mean was well above the standardization mean (by nearly two thirds of a standard deviation), whilst that of the SWC sub-group was very close to that mean. Thus, the mean score of the SWC sub-group was closer to that of the DA sample than that of the MC sub-group.

Figure 7 shows the distributions of the standardized scores for the two samples. This shows that the shape of distribution is roughly normal in appearance in either case, although that for the DA sample is slightly biased toward the lower end of the scale.

Taking the range of scores 85 to 112 as representing the broad average band of test performance (i.e. approximately one standard deviation above or below the mean of 100, which encloses roughly two thirds of the standardization population), approximately 63 per cent of the CA sample and 69 per cent of the DA sample, the bulk of either group, can be regarded as of average intelligence. Of the remaining children, approximately 7 per cent in the CA group and 13 per cent in the DA group fell below this range, and approximately 30 per cent and 18 per cent respectively fell above it. Thus, the great majority of children in either group (93 per cent of the CA sample and 87 per cent of the DA sample) performed at an average level or above on this test.

E. PREDICTED PROGRESS IN JUNIOR SCHOOL

In view of the overall superiority of the CA children over the DA children both on teachers' ratings and test measures of basic school attainment it is not surprising to find that there was a significant difference between the two groups, in favour of the former, in regard to the teachers' predictions of the children's likely progress in the junior school/department. The teachers were asked to make this prediction toward the end of the children's infant school careers (Schedule 6) and Table 68 presents the data obtained from this item, together with the results of a follow-up question concerning the children whom the teachers expected to experience difficulty at the junior school stage.

It will be seen that nearly 60 per cent of the CA group as compared with a little over 50 per cent of the DA group were expected to have no problems at the junior school stage, and, conversely, just over 10 per cent of the CA group as against 19 per cent of the DA group were definitely expected to experience difficulties. The separate figures for the MC and SWC components of the CA sample are roughly comparable.

The follow-up question gives the reasons for the anticipated difficulties. It will be seen that for approximately 20 per cent of the children in both groups expected to have problems, the reasons were immaturity or behaviour difficulties. The remaining reasons for predicting difficulty in adjusting to the junior school were low level of basic attainments or some combination of the three factors listed. It seems very likely that, in most cases, this combination included low basic attainments and, if this were the case, it means that the majority of the children (nearly 80 per cent of both groups) were expected to make poor progress in the junior school at least partly because of low basic attainments. No statistical analysis of the results from this item was carried out because the presence of the combined category made it impossible to differentiate clearly among the three reasons for expected difficulties.

6 Final Attainment Survey

(i) DIFFERENCES BETWEEN THE SCHOOL AREA GROUPS

Reference has been made in Chapter 5 to the results of the various school attainment and ability tests administered to the general study sample during the children's final school term. However, in that chapter, the results of each test or group of tests were presented in their own separate contexts in the discussion of basic skills. In the present chapter the results of the attainment survey will be presented and discussed as a whole. Moreover, comparisons will be made among the sub-groups comprising the full urban sample (MC, SWC and DA) to a fuller extent than in the previous chapter. Finally, the relative contribution of type of school area and intelligence to the variation in test scores will be looked at.

Table 69 presents the mean scores of the sub-groups comprising the whole urban sample on the survey tests and the results of 't' test analyses carried out between pairs of sub-groups as well as between the CA and DA groups. It will be seen, firstly, that on all of the tests, the CA sample as a whole obtained very significant higher mean scores on all of the tests than the DA sample. (All results were beyond the 0.1% level.) The same pattern of the clear overall superiority of the MC group held for the comparisons between the MC and SWC sub-groups of the CA sample and between the MC and DA groups. The results of the SWC vs DA group comparison reached rather lower levels of significance than in the other between-group comparisons on three of the tests (Neale Rate, WISC Vocabulary and Picture Test A) and, in the mathematics test, the difference between these two groups fell well below statistical significance. On the latter test the difference between the SWC and DA mean was only 0.43 points of raw score in favour of the SWC group (the standard error of the difference being 0.80).

With the exception of the latter, these results are all in the expected direction and, in general, accord with the results obtained from the school schedules reported in Chapter 5.

Thus, the MC group obtained the highest mean scores, followed by the SWC and DA groups in turn, although the disparities between the means of the pairs of groups (MC vs SWC and SWC vs DA) were not necessarily equal. The latter point is illustrated in Figures 8 to 15 which show the mean scores of each group on each test. It will be seen that, on all of the tests except WISC vocabulary, mathematics and the picture test, the score differences between the three groups look roughly equal, but on the latter three tests the disparity in means between the MC and SWC groups is appreciably greater than that between the SWC and DA groups. Such a pattern of results could arise if the SWC schools tended to emphasize the development of reading and related skills more strongly than the DA schools but gave the same weight as the DA schools to mathematical and vocabulary development, although other explanations are also possible. For example, it could be that parental interest in and encouragement of the child's reading and related skills tended to be higher in the SWC than in the DA group. With regard to the intelligence test results (Picture Test A), it is likely that these reflect the influence of schooling to a lesser extent than the school achievement measures (a point that will be amplified later in this chapter) and it was predictable that the mean scores of the SWC and DA groups in intelligence would be closer to each other, than to the mean of the MC group, since the former two groups fall into the same broad social class grouping (i.e. 'manual working-class').

The mean score for each school on each test was calculated and it was found that, with one exception, the mean scores of the MC area schools tended to be above those of the SWC and DA schools on most of the tests. The one exception was a school which obtained mean reading and spelling scores which not only were well below those of the remaining MC area schools and also of the SWC schools, but were comparable with the mean scores of the DA schools. The SWC schools tended to be fairly uniform in their mean scores but these overlapped with those of the DA schools on all tests, considerably so in some cases (e.g. mathematics and WISC vocabulary). The latter

Table 69

Raw scores of CA and DA samples (with breakdown of CA sample) on attainment survey test battery, showing result of t tests (for non-correlated samples)

Test	Mean				Result of t tests between groups (one-tailed probabilities)							
	MC	SWC	CA	DA	CA vs DA		SWC vs DA		MC vs DA		MC vs SWC	
	N=122	N=142	N=264	N=276	t	p	t	p	t	p	t	p
Burt Reading Test	44.40	35.88	39.10	26.24	8.45	<0.1%	5.24	<0.1%	8.68	<0.1%	3.07	<0.5%
Neale Reading Test												
Accuracy	36.43	28.43	32.38	19.80	7.78	<0.1%	4.58	<0.1%	8.47	<0.1%	3.37	<0.1%
Rate	49.27	41.62	45.40	36.76	4.41	<0.1%	2.08	<2.5%	5.28	<0.1%	2.68	<0.5%
Comprehension	12.28	9.34	10.79	6.82	6.66	<0.1%	3.70	<0.1%	7.58	<0.1%	3.25	<0.1%
WISC Vocabulary sub-test	24.42	20.42	27.27	19.23	6.30	<0.1%	2.14	<2.5%	9.06	<0.1%	5.65	<0.1%
Mathematics Test	26.38	19.80	22.83	19.37	4.97	<0.1%	0.53	N.S.	8.21	<0.1%	7.04	<0.1%
Spelling Test	24.43	20.04	22.21	14.05	9.14	<0.1%	5.32	<0.1%	9.54	<0.1%	3.81	<0.1%
Picture Test A (Intelligence)	36.69	29.53	32.84	27.24	5.84	<0.1%	1.97	<2.5%	8.05	<0.1%	5.60	<0.1%

Note 1. The number within each group for whom data was obtained on a particular test sometimes falls below the total number (N) given in the table.

Note 2. Strictly speaking, because of the large number of comparisons made and the fact that some of these comparisons were not independent, a more stringent test of significance of the results than the conventional one for t tests could have been used. However, in general, the direction of the between group differences for the various tests is so consistent and the t ratios so large that using a more stringent criterion of significance is unlikely to seriously change this pattern of results.

139

Figures 8−11

Mean raw scores of the MC, SWC and DA groups on the survey attainment tests

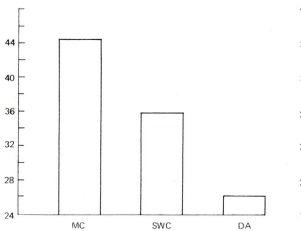

Fig. 8 Burt Reading Test

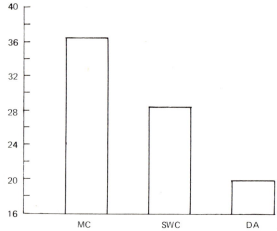

Fig. 9 Neale Reading Test: Accuracy

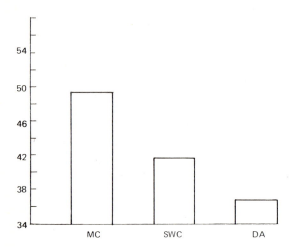

Fig. 10 Neale Reading Test: Rate

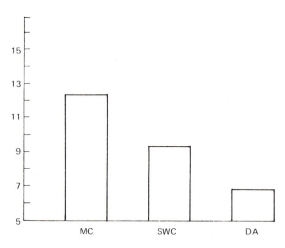

Fig. 11 Neale Reading Test: Comprehension

Figures 12—15

Mean raw scores of the MC, SWC and DA groups on the survey attainment tests

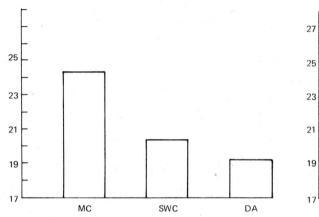

Fig. 12 WISC Vocabulary Test

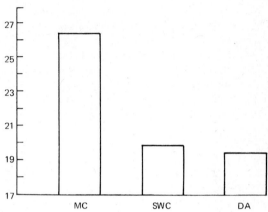

Fig. 13 Mathematics Test

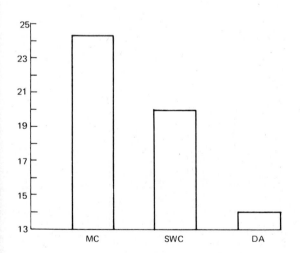

Fig. 14 Spelling Test

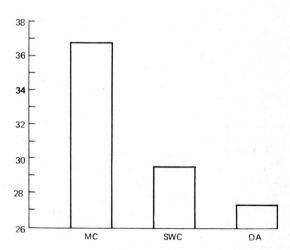

Fig 15 Picture Test A (intelligence)

schools showed a much greater degree of variation in their mean scores than the CA schools (excluding the one atypical MC school) on most of the reading and spelling tests. In one DA school the mean scores on the reading and spelling tests were consistently higher than those of the other schools in their group, and were in line with, or at least approached those of some MC schools. Another DA school had mean reading and spelling and mathematics test scores which were consistent with those obtained by most SWC schools. In contrast, one DA school showed mean reading test scores which were well below those of the remaining DA schools, and a relatively low mathematics test score, but this school also had the lowest mean picture test (intelligence) score. The greatest degree of between-schools variation appears to occur in the reading and spelling tests, although this may partly reflect differences between these and the other achievement tests in terms of the range and pattern of score distributions which they yield with children in the present age group. However, it seems probable that some of the sample schools concentrated more heavily on reading and related skills than others, which would tend to increase the range of variation in the mean school scores in the whole sample.

The correlations between each test in the battery and all of the remaining tests, in turn, were obtained and these are shown in Table 70. It will be seen from this that, with the exception of the Neale Rate measure, the reading and spelling tests all intercorrelate highly, the lowest correlation (between Neale Comprehension and spelling) being 0.75, and the highest 0.97 (between Neale Accuracy and the Burt Test). The latter figure is as high as that often obtained between test and re-test scores on the same measure. The correlations between the Neale Rate measure and the other reading tests and the spelling test ranged between 0.61 and 0.74. The other notable correlation in the table is that between the picture test and the mathematics test (0.74) which suggests a considerable degree of overlap between the skills tapped by these two tests. One common factor between them could well be reasoning ability. All of the correlations in the table, however, reached a high level of statistical significance. The table also shows that the correlations between the reading and spelling tests (excluding Neale Rate) and the WISC vocabulary test and the picture test respec-

tively, are very similar (ranging from 0.43 to 0.59 for the vocabulary test and between 0.47 and 0.54 for the spelling test), although the correlation between the vocabulary and picture tests themselves is only moderate (0.49). It would seem from this that the picture test is as good a predictor of the children's reading and spelling test scores as the vocabulary test, which is part of a verbal intelligence scale, and a better predictor of their mathematics test scores. The value of the picture test as a predictor or guide to a child's school achievement will be considered again in the following discussion.

Table 69 showed that there was a statistically significant difference between the CA and DA groups (and between the three sub-groups comprising the whole urban sample) on the picture test. As stated in Chapter 3, there appears to be no published evidence on the validity of this test or its correlations with other intelligence tests. Indeed, the publishers of the test (NFER) do not describe it as an intelligence test or give an indication of the purpose for which it was designed. Nevertheless, the three basic types of item incorporated in this test are typical of those found in so-called tests of general intelligence, so that, in terms of its content, it seems to qualify as such a test. Whether it should be described as a non-verbal test is arguable. It is non-verbal to the extent that no reading ability is required (the instructions are given orally and the items are composed entirely of pictures) but, it seems very likely that verbalisation may play a major part in the process by which children solve the items. For example, children will probably verbally identify the picture in each item prior to choosing the correct picture(s).

There is some controversy about the validity of distinguishing between ability or aptitude tests (including intelligence) from achievement tests (including basic educational skills). Some would argue that intelligence tests are just as much measures of achievement as, say, reading or arithmetic tests and, therefore, have no special status as predictors of school achievement. However, a strong case can be made out for a psychological distinction between ability and achievement tests and both Vernon (1960) and Jensen (1971) support such a distinction. Vernon regards intelligence measures (especially verbal ones) as giving an indication of a child's educational potentiality since,

Table 70

Correlations between attainment test scores:
Urban sample (N=540)

	Burt	Neale Accuracy	Neale Rate	Neale Comprehension	Vocabulary	Maths	Spelling	Picture Test A
Burt								
Neale Accuracy	0.97							
Neale Rate	0.73	0.74						
Neale Comprehension	0.86	0.87	0.61					
WISC Vocabulary	0.50	0.51	0.41	0.59				
Mathematics	0.58	0.58	0.46	0.61	0.54			
Spelling	0.89	0.88	0.69	0.75	0.43	0.59		
Picture Test A	0.47	0.47	0.34	0.54	0.49	0.74	0.47	

All correlations (product-moment) shown in this table are statistically highly significant (p <1%)

he argues, such tests measure a child's level of conceptual and generalized thinking skills, and these are rather less affected by schooling and other environmental factors than educational skills such as reading or spelling. Jensen makes a similar distinction, regarding achievement tests as sampling a relatively narrow range of skills specifically taught in school, whereas intelligence tests sample skills acquired in a child's general life experience within and outside school, which appear to be relatively less susceptible to teaching.

However, Vernon (1960) has warned against interpreting the results of pictorial and non-verbal intelligence tests as giving an index of a child's educational potentiality since, verbal rather than other abilities appear to play the major part in the development of educational skills. If it is true, however, that the picture test used in the present study is a valid measure of general intelligence and that, as discussed earlier, it entails verbal thinking, then it is of interest to relate the performance of children on this test to their school achievement, on the grounds that a child's score on the test may give an indication of his educational potentiality. The lack of published evidence here on the ability measured by this picture test is unfortunate in this respect. Nevertheless, it seems not unreasonable to regard the test as giving at least a very broad indication of the level of school achievement which a child should be capable of.

In the context of the present study it would be useful to know whether the difference between the CA and DA groups (and between the MC, SWC and DA groups considered seperately) in school achievement are largely attributable to the differences between these groups in the intelligence measure (Picture Test A) or whether a significant part of the between-group differences in school achievement reflect the school and home background factors which distinguish the groups. This question will now be considered.

In order to study the relative contribution of intelligence and home/school background factors to the variation in educational achievement, a two-way analysis of variance was carried out on the attainment survey data. For this purpose, each of the school area groups (MC, SWC and DA) was divided into three groups in terms of score on the picture test, i.e. 'high', 'medium' and 'low' intelligence, these groups being obtained by dividing the intelligence test scores of the total urban sample into approximate thirds, producing the design shown in Table 71.

This table shows that, as might be predicted on the basis of the known social class differences in intelligence, there is a difference among the school area groups in the pattern of their distribution over the three intelligence levels. The MC group, for example, has a relatively high proportion of children of high intelligence and a low proportion of children of low intelligence, whilst in the DA group the highest proportion of children fall into the low intelligence category. A 'Chi-Square' analysis of the data presented in the table showed a statistically highly significant association between level of intelligence and school area type (Chi-square (4 d.f.) = 45.53, p < 0.1%).

Since the numbers of children in each cell were unequal, a special method of analysis was used (see Appendix I for details). This uses the mean score of the children falling into each sub-category (cell) in the design rather than their individual scores, as in the normal method. These mean scores are probably not markedly different from those that

Table 71

Design for two-way analysis of variance (intelligence and school area type) of urban sample school achievement scores, showing numbers in each cell

	School area type			Total
Intelligence level	MC	SWC	DA	
Low	17	47	114	178
Medium	38	53	96	187
High	67	42	66	175
Total	122	142 *	276 *	540

* 1 child in both the SWC and DA groups did not take the Picture Test.

144

would be found if the sub-groups (cells) really were equal in number. For example, it will be seen from Table 71 that there are in fact, 114 DA children falling into the 'low intelligence' category, but only 17 MC children. By simply taking the mean achievement scores of these two sub-groups, this disparity in numbers is disregarded. The net effect of this procedure is to discount the inequality in numbers of children falling into the various cells and thus to enable the performance of the MC, SWC and DA groups in school achievement to be compared independently of their differences intelligence i.e. treating these groups as if they were 'matched' for intelligence.

It should be stressed that the above method gives only approximate results. Nevertheless, as will be seen, the pattern of results yielded by the analysis is so clear-cut that it seems unlikely that they are seriously in error. It must also be pointed out that the division of the three school groups into sub-groups according to the children's picture test scores was not entirely satisfactory since, for each level of this division (high, medium and low), the mean intelligence of the school groups varied. Table 72 shows the extent of this variation.

The table shows that, within the 'low' intelligence division, the mean picture test score drops steadily across the MC, SWC and DA groups, with nearly 4 points of raw score separating the MC and DA groups. The range of variation in the group means is less in the 'medium' and 'high' intelligence divisions, being under two points in each case. The net result of these discrepancies, as will be seen in the table, is that the three groups are not, in fact, 'matched' for intelligence (see the earlier discussion of the rationale of this method), for the overall mean intelligence score of the MC group is appreciably higher than that of the SWC group which, in turn, is a little higher than that of the DA group. The difference between these overall means was statistically significant ($F = 10.19$, $p < 0.1\%$).

The implication of these discrepancies is that some of the variation in school achievement scores which, according to the analyses carried out, is attributable to school area type could in fact,

Table 72

Mean Intelligence (Picture Test) scores

of Urban school groups

Intelligence level	School area type		
	MC (N=122)	SWC (N=142)	DA (N=276)
Low	19.94 (N = 17)	17.00 (N = 47)	16.09 (N=114)
Medium	31.76 (N = 38)	30.55 (N = 53)	30.40 (N = 96)
High	43.73 (N = 67)	42.29 (N = 42)	41.91 (N = 66)
Overall mean intelligence score (i.e. mean of cell means)	31.81	29.94	29.46

145

really be due to intelligence, due to the imperfect control of intelligence. However, it seems very unlikely that the amount of such variation accounted for by the imperfect 'matching' of the groups for intelligence is so great that it nullifies the findings, shortly to be presented, of highly significant differences in school achievement between the three school area groups. In other words, the amount of variation in school achievement scores attributable to school area type seems to be much greater than that attributable to the relatively small differences between the groups in overall mean intelligence indicated in Table 72.

The results of the analyses of variance are presented in Table 73. This shows that, on all of the school achievement measures, both intelligence and school area type made highly significant contributions to the variation in children's scores, or to put it another way, a child's performance on any of these tests was significantly related both to his level of intelligence and to his school area type. It will be seen from the table that the contribution of intelligence to the variation in children's scores is consistently higher than that for school area type over the range of tests, markedly so in the case of Neale Comprehension (F ratios of 62 and 9 respectively) and the mathematics test (F ratios of 152 and 19 respectively). (The latter result was not surprising in view of the relatively high correlation between the intelligence and mathematics tests reported earlier in this chapter.)

It will also be noted that in no case does the interaction between intelligence and school area type make a significant contribution to the variation in score, as might have been expected. For example, it seems quite possible that the influence of school area type, presumably a combination of home and school background factors, as already discussed, will vary according to the child's level of intelligence, having a greater influence on duller than brighter children. On this view, innately brighter children, regardless of their home/school background, will tend to show less variation among themselves in educational skills as compared with duller children, who will be more influenced by these background factors and thus show greater variation in achievement. In other words, bright children may be able to overcome the handicap of a poor cultural background. There is some support in the research literature for such a trend. Willerman et al. (1970), for example,

found that, among infants retarded in mental and motor tests at eight months, those from the lower social class groups were seven times more likely to be mentally retarded at age four than infants from higher social class groups. In contrast, among infants advanced in development at eight months, the incidence of mental retardation at age four was unrelated to social class. That is, retarded low social class infants seem highly vulnerable to the adverse effects of a 'poor' environment, whilst advanced infants from the same social class appear to overcome these adverse effects to some degree.

A similar analysis to that described above was carried out on the school achievement scores of the rural sample (see Section III). In that analysis, the relative contributions of intelligence and home background measures were studied and it was found that, whilst intelligence accounted for a significant part of the variation of the scores on all but one of the tests, home background (or its interaction with intelligence) did not make a significant contribution to such variation on any of the tests. Both analyses, therefore, agree in attributing relatively more of the variation in school achievement scores to intelligence than to environmental factors, but differ in their estimated weight of the contribution of the latter factors (home background or school area type respectively). However, this comparison of results can only be tentative since there were important differences between the two analyses. Firstly, home background and school area type are by no means equivalent 'factors' although there is probably considerable overlap between them, insofar as school area type is associated with a certain level or type of home background (for example, in terms of the socio-economic status of the families or their general level of cultural provision). However, as discussed in Chapter 3, school area type includes school factors in addition. Secondly, the analysis carried out on the rural sample was based on a two-level split of the background and intelligence factors whereas the present analysis is based on a three-level split, which is rather more sensitive to the influence of the factors studied. Thirdly, the present sample is far larger than the rural sample and more likely to show significant results.

Thus, the analyses of the school achievement data for both the urban and rural samples have shown that, relatively speaking, intelligence

Table 73

Results of Two-way analysis of variance (intelligence and school area type) of Urban sample school achievement scores

Dependent Variable (school achievement)	Independent Variable (intelligence, school area type)	between-groups variance	within-groups variance ($c MS_w$)	F	d.f.	p
Burt Reading Test	intelligence	186.36	5.55	33.60	2,485	<0.1%
	school area type	106.99		19.29	2,485	<0.1%
	interaction	10.35		1.87	4,485	N.S.
Neale Reading Test Accuracy	intelligence	221.65	6.23	35.55	2,485	<0.1%
	school area type	107.26		17.20	2,485	<0.1%
	interaction	9.46		1.52	4,485	N.S.
Neale Reading Test Rate	intelligence	196.68	9.94	19.78	2,485	<0.1%
	school area type	60.07		6.04	2,485	<1.0%
	interaction	12.08		1.22	4,485	N.S.
Neale Reading Test Comprehension	intelligence	49.51	0.79	62.60	2,485	<0.1%
	school area type	7.21		9.11	2,485	<0.1%
	interaction	0.08		1.0	4,485	N.S.
WISC Vocabulary Test	intelligence	20.71	0.55	37.38	2,526	<0.1%
	school area type	11.67		21.07	2,526	<0.1%
	interaction	0.14		1.0	4,526	N.S.
Mathematics Test	intelligence	115.97	0.76	152.99	2,529	<0.1%
	school area type	14.93		19.69	2,529	<0.1%
	interaction	1.55		2.04	4,529	N.S.
Spelling Test	intelligence	55.56	1.93	28.85	2,487	<0.1%
	school area type	51.20		26.59	2,487	<0.1%
	interaction	4.92		2.55	4,487	N.S.

Note: See Appendix Table A7 for cell numbers, means and variances.

147

appears to have a greater influence than home/school variables on children's school attainments. It should be stressed, however, that the results of both analyses should be regarded with some caution for reasons already stated and for additional statistical reasons given in Appendix I. Nevertheless, such a finding is not surprising for it has long been known that a measure of a child's general (especially verbal) intelligence is the best single predictor of his general level of school achievement. It must be borne in mind, of course, that intelligence is by no means independent of environmental factors such as the level of cultural and material provision in the home, so that the highly significant differences between the MC, and SWC and DA groups in the present sample in intelligence (picture test scores) may partly reflect such factors. As stated earlier in this section, however, it appears that the development of intelligence is *relatively* less influenced by environmental factors than that of basic educational skills, which are taught more directly. Therefore, although we no longer regard intelligence tests as measuring a child's 'innate intellectual potential' we can, as Vernon (1960) states, regard the results of a reliable and valid verbal intelligence test as giving a useful indication of a child's educational potential. For this reason, it is legitimate to regard intelligence, together with home and school environmental factors, as lying on the 'input' side of the educational process, the 'output' of which (among other things) is the child's level of achievement in oral language, reading and mathematical skills.

It should be remembered, however, that at least in the present analysis, the other 'variable' on the 'input' side, school area type, was also found to make a statistically highly significant contribution to such achievements. It will be recalled from Chapter 3 that, in general, the differences between the school area types appeared to be more pronounced in respect of factors in the children's home background than in factors relating specifically to the school. It seems probable, therefore, that the significant differences in school achievement associated with school area type in the present analysis reflect home background factors to a much greater extent than school factors. Moreover, research evidence such as that provided by a national survey of attainments carried out for the Plowden Committee (1967) suggests that

home background factors account for substantially more of the variation in measures of children's school achievement than do school variables. Nevertheless, it also seems likely that school factors account for part of the variation in the school achievement scores of the children in the present study. (It is hoped to explore systematically the contribution of such factors and report on them in a later publication.)

So far then, it has been established that both intelligence and school area type (although not these factors in interaction) make a significant contribution to the variation of children's scores in basic school achievement tests. The further question now arises as to whether the effects of intelligence and school area type are apparent at each level of these factors. More simply, knowing that there is a highly significant *overall* difference in school achievement among the three intelligence groups or the three school area groups, can one also say that each of these groups differs significantly from the other, and that the CA sample (MC and SWC groups together) differs significantly from the DA group? In order to answer this question, the difference between each pair or combination of group means on each measure was tested for statistical significance by the method of 'contrasts' (see Winer, 1962, Section 3.6 for details), and the results are presented in Tables 74 and 75.

Table 74 shows that the MC and SWC group (CA sample) obtained very significantly higher mean scores than the DA group on all of the achievement tests. When the MC group is compared with the SWC group the differences (all in favour of the MC group) are statistically significant on all but three measures; Burt reading, Neale Rate and Neale Comprehension. However, compared with the DA group, and with the SWC and DA groups combined (i.e. 'working-class children') the MC group was highly significantly superior on all test scores.

Finally, the table shows that only three of the SWC vs DA comparisons reached statistical significance; Burt, Neale Accuracy and Spelling test (which, interestingly, measure closely related skills), although, on all of the tests (except mathematics, where the DA mean was marginally higher) the SWC obtained higher means than the DA group. The most striking feature of these results is the marked superiority of the MC group over the

Table 74

Results of significance tests carried out on pairs of urban
sample group means on school achievement tests:
groups divided according to school area type

Groups compared	Test	between-groups variance	within-groups variance $(_c MS_w)$	F	p
1. (MC+SWC) vs DA	Burt Reading	184.00	5.55	33.15	<0.1%
	Neale Reading Test				
	Accuracy	166.28	6.23	26.69	<0.1%
	Rate	66.97	9.94	6.74	≤5.0%
	Comprehension	11.40	0.79	14.43	<0.1%
	WISC Vocabulary	10.61	0.55	19.29	<0.1%
	Mathematics	4.72	0.76	6.21	<5.0%
	Spelling	83.50	1.93	43.26	<0.1%
2. MC vs SWC	Burt Reading	29.97	5.55	5.40	N.S.
	Neale Reading Test				
	Accuracy	48.22	6.23	7.74	<5.0%
	Rate	53.16	9.94	5.35	N.S.
	Comprehension	3.01	0.79	3.81	N.S.
	WISC Vocabulary	12.73	0.55	23.14	<0.1%
	Mathematics	25.13	0.76	33.00	<0.1%
	Spelling	18.90	1.93	9.80	<1.0%
3. MC vs DA	Burt Reading	209.80	5.55	37.80	<0.1%
	Neale Reading Test				
	Accuracy	235.65	6.23	37.82	<0.1%
	Rate	115.19	9.94	11.59	<1.0%
	Comprehension	14.38	0.79	18.20	<0.1%
	WISC Vocabulary	21.20	0.55	38.54	<0.1%
	Mathematics	19.26	0.76	25.34	<0.1%
	Spelling	101.76	1.93	52.72	<0.1%
4. MC vs (SWC+DA)	Burt Reading	132.79	5.55	23.93	<0.1%
	Neale Reading Test				
	Accuracy	155.29	6.23	24.93	<0.1%
	Rate	108.29	9.94	10.89	<1.0%
	Comprehension	10.19	0.79	12,90	<1.0%
	WISC Vocabulary	22.27	0.55	40.49	<0.1%
	Mathematics	29.47	0.76	38.78	<0.1%
	Spelling	69.46	1.93	35.99	<0.1%
5. SWC vs DA	Burt Reading	81.18	5.55	14.63	<0.1%
	Neale Reading Test				
	Accuracy	59.22	6.23	9.50	<1.0%
	Rate	11.84	9.94	1.0	N.S.
	Comprehension	4.23	0.79	5.35	N.S.
	WISC Vocabulary	1.07	0.55	1.0	N.S.
	Mathematics	0.39	0.76	1.0	N.S.
	Spelling	32.94	1.93	17.07	<0.1%

Table 75

Results of significance tests carried out on pairs of urban sample group means on school achievement tests: groups divided according to intelligence (Picture Test score)

Groups compared	Test	between-groups variance	within-groups variance ($_c MS_w$)	F	p
1. High vs medium intelligence	Burt Reading	100.04	5.55	18.03	<0.1%
	Neale Reading Test				
	Accuracy	153.22	6.23	24.59	<0.1%
	Rate	100.70	9.94	10.13	<1.0%
	Comprehension	32.25	0.79	40.82	<0.1%
	WISC Vocabulary	12.79	0.55	23.26	<0.1%
	Mathematics	66.80	0.76	87.90	<0.1%
	Spelling	24.08	1.93	12.48	<1.0%
2. High vs low intelligence	Burt Reading	372.56	5.55	67.13	<0.1%
	Neale Reading Test				
	Accuracy	438.44	6.23	70.38	<0.1%
	Rate	393.34	9.94	39.57	<0.1%
	Comprehension	98.33	0.79	124.47	<0.1%
	WISC Vocabulary	41.24	0.55	74.98	<0.1%
	Mathematics	231.50	0.76	304.61	<0.1%
	Spelling	110.94	1.93	57.48	<0.1%
3. Medium vs low intelligence	Burt Reading	86.49	5.55	15.58	<0.1%
	Neale Reading Test				
	Accuracy	73.29	6.23	11.76	<1.0%
	Rate	96.00	9.94	9.66	<1.0%
	Comprehension	17.96	0.79	22.73	<0.1%
	WISC Vocabulary	8.10	0.55	14.73	<0.1%
	Mathematics	49.59	0.76	65.25	<0.1%
	Spelling	31.65	1.93	16.40	<0.1%

two 'working-class' groups, both separately and in combination. It should be remembered that all of the above results are independent of intelligence i.e. they represent the influence of school area type with intelligence averaged or 'partialled out' across the groups.

Table 75 shows that, in the comparisons between the three intelligence groups ('high', 'medium' and 'low'), all of the results reached statistical significance. As expected, the 'high' intelligence group obtained higher means on all tests than the 'medium' intelligence group, which, in turn, had higher means than the 'low' intelligence group. These results, it should be noted, are independent of school area type.

The results of the analyses of variance reported above can be presented graphically and this is done in Figures 16 to 22 and Figures 23 to 29, although the latter figures are not true graphs because the positioning of the school area type groups is quite arbitrary. Figures 16 to 22 show the performance of the three school area groups plotted over the three levels of intelligence, and Figures 23 to 29 show the converse of this i.e. performance of the three intelligence groups over the three school area types. The main impression given by a general comparison of the two sets of figures is that intelligence is a better predictor or discriminator of school achievement than school area type, for the range of differences in mean raw

Figures 16—19

Mean achievement scores of the three Urban school area groups at three levels of intelligence
(Picture Test A score)

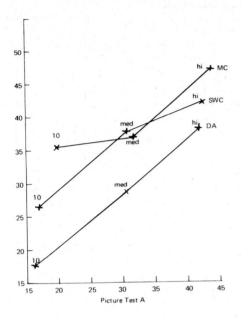

Fig. 16 Burt Reading Test

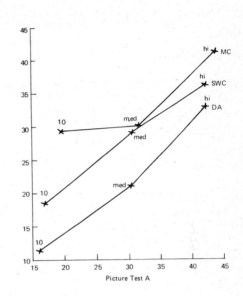

Fig. 17 Neale Reading Test: Accuracy

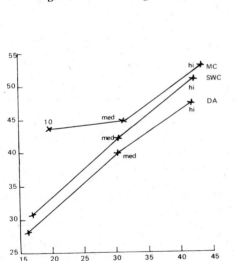

Fig. 18 Neale Reading Test: Rate

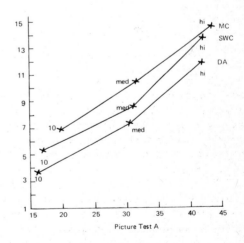

Fig. 19 Neale Reading Test: Comprehension

Note: attainment test scores are shown on the vertical axes

Mean achievement scores of the three urban school area groups at three levels of intelligence
(Picture Test A scores)

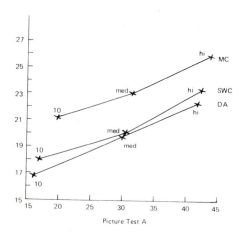

Fig. 20 *WISC Vocabulary Test*

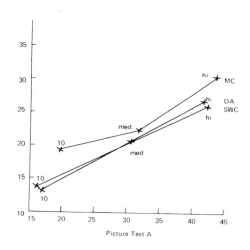

Fig. 21 *Mathematics Test*

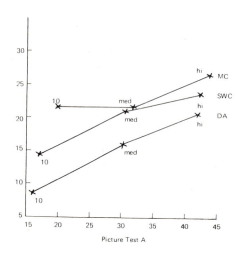

Fig. 22 *Spelling Test*

Note: attainment test scores are shown on the vertical axes

Mean achievement scores of the three intelligence groups in relation to school area type

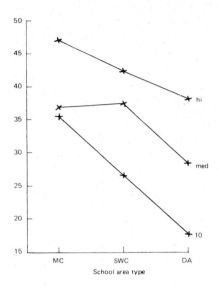

Fig. 23 Burt Reading Test

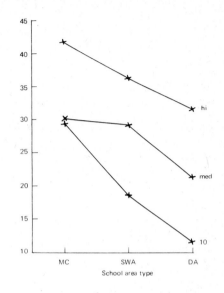

Fig. 24 Neale Reading Test: Accuracy

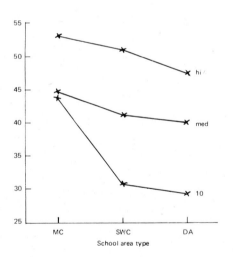

Fig. 25 Neale Reading Test: Rate

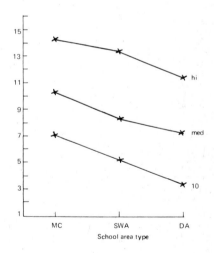

Fig. 26 Neale Reading Test: Comprehension

Notes: 1. In the above figures the positioning of the school area type groups is arbitrary. The figures give a pictorial representation of the contribution of intelligence to the variation in achievement test scores.
2. Attainment test scores are shown on the vertical axes.

Mean achievement scores of the three intelligence groups in relation to school area type

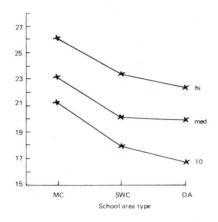

Fig. 27 WISC Vocabulary Test

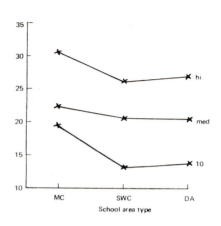

Fig. 28 Mathematics Test

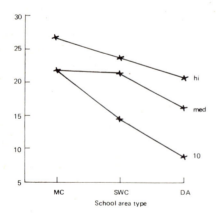

Fig. 29 Spelling Test

Note: 1. In the above figures the positioning of the school area type groups is arbitrary. The figures give a pictorial representation of the contribution of intelligence to the variation in achievement test scores.

2. Attainment test scores are shown on the vertical axes.

score between the three intelligence levels is greater than that between the three school area types on most of the tests. This, of course, is simply a reflection of the finding, reported earlier, that intelligence accounted for relatively more of the variation in school achievement than school area type.

As stated earlier, none of the interactions between intelligence and school area type were statistically significant, contrary to expectation. However, examination of the graphs in Figures 16 to 22 suggests that there may be a degree of interaction between the two factors, even though this does not reach statistical significance. There is a trend in some results, notably those for the Burt, Neale Accuracy and Rate measures (Figures 16 to 18), and the spelling test (Figure 22), for the differences between the group means to be greater at the low intelligence level than at the high intelligence level, in line with the prediction, stated earlier, that brighter children might overcome the adverse effects of a poor home background to a greater extent than duller children. However, this interpretation is not fully supported by the pattern of the results shown in these figures for it will be seen that, on most of the tests, the range of mean differences associated with school area type is least at the medium rather than the high intelligence level. The pattern of interaction between the two factors is probably therefore rather complex. The results depicted in these figures should be treated cautiously because of the disparity in mean intelligence score between the three school area groups at each level of intelligence (see page 145). Such disparity could at least partly account for the tendency for the school area groups to diverge more widely in achievement at the low intelligence level as compared with the high level.

Figures 23 to 29 show that, in general, the three intelligence groups are well separated in level of performance on the various tests and there is little indication of possible interaction effects, except that, on five of the tests (Burt, Neale Accuracy and Rate, mathematics and spelling) there is a tendency for the means of the 'medium' and 'low' intelligence groups of the MC children to converge. There seems no psychological reason why such a trend should occur but, again, it should be pointed out that this could be at least partly explained by the disparity in mean

intelligence score between the school area groups mentioned above.

(ii) SEX DIFFERENCES

Although the primary focus of this study was upon the association between school area type and school progress and adjustment, the school achievement survey data were also analysed for sex differences. This was done by means of a two-way analysis of variance (sex and school area type), using the same approximate method as for the study reported in the previous section of this chapter, since, again, there were unequal numbers in each cell. (The possibility of carrying out a more complex three-way analysis, based on sex, school area type and intelligence was explored but abandoned because of the very considerable variation in the cell variances.) Table 76 shows the numbers of children in each cell of the design. The table shows that there were slightly more girls than boys, this difference being concentrated in the MC group.

The results of the analysis of variance are presented in Table 77, and also, pictorially, in Figures 30 to 37 and Figures 38 to 45. It should be borne in mind that the spacing of the school area type groups in Figures 30 to 37 and of boys and girls in Figures 38 to 45 is quite arbitrary. The intention is to give a pictorial representation of the contribution of school area type and sex respectively to the variation in school achievement scores. Table 77 shows that the sex factor accounted for a statistically significant amount of the variation in test scores on the Neale Rate, WISC vocabulary and spelling tests only. In the case of Neale Rate and spelling test measures, the girls achieved higher means than the boys, but on the WISC vocabulary test it was the boys who were superior. As in the analysis based on intelligence and school area type reported earlier, school area type accounted for a very highly significant amount of the variation in test score on all of the survey tests, although it should be remembered that, in the present analysis, this result is partly attributable to differences in intelligence among the school area groups. None of the sex and school area type interactions reached statistical significance and indeed, there seems no reason to expect that sex differences in school achievement should

Table 76

Design for two-way analysis of variance (sex and
school area type) showing numbers in each cell

Sex	School area type			Total
	MC	SWC	DA	
Girls	48	74	139	261
Boys	74	68	137	279
Total	122	142	276	540

be related to school area type. There was a tendency on the Burt and Neale Accuracy tests, however, for the sex differences to be more marked in the MC and SWC groups than in the DA group (see Figures 30 and 31). In fact, if the girls had maintained their superiority in all three groups in these two tests, it seems very likely that overall sex differences would have reached statistical significance. However, since these interactions were not statistically significant and a similar pattern did not emerge on the remaining achievement measures, not much weight can be put upon them. The considerably greater importance of school area type over sex as a source of variation in school achievement scores is clearly revealed when Figures 30 to 37 and 38 to 45 are compared. School area type is a far better discriminator of children's school achievement than sex is.

The findings with regard to sex differences should be treated with some caution because the method of analysis used is only an approximate one and also for statistical reasons explained in Appendix I. A similar result was obtained, however, when 't' tests were carried out in the same data, comparing boys and girls, except that the difference in favour of the girls on the spelling test fell below statistical significance. The results of this analysis are shown in Table 78.

The finding that girls were superior to boys on most of the reading and spelling measures (signifi-

cantly in the case of Neale Rate and spelling) is supported by a similar result from the National Child Development Study (NCDS) of a very large national sample of children studied at age seven years and reported by Davie et al. (1972). This study showed that, on three criteria of reading ability (a standardized word recognition test, reading scheme level reached and teachers' ratings of reading skill on a five-point scale), girls were better readers than boys. However, it is not clear why, in the present study, significant sex differences did not also appear on the Burt reading test and the other Neale reading test measures. As already mentioned, the Neale Rate measure appears to be the least reliable and satisfactory of the three measures in this reading test.

However, the finding in the present study that the boys were significantly superior on the WISC vocabulary test was surprising, for it is not in line with the general finding that girls are ahead of boys in aspects of language development during the earlier school years. In the NCDS referred to previously, for example, girls showed better oral ability than boys, according to teachers' ratings. Moreover, that study produced other evidence of the slower language development of boys, such as the fact that mothers reported more often that boys were late in talking, and also that the incidence of speech difficulties at age seven was higher for boys than girls.

Table 77

Results of two-way analysis of variance (sex and school area type) of Urban sample school achievement scores

Dependent Variable (school achievement)	Independent Variable (sex, school area type)	between-groups variance	within-groups variance ($_cMS_w$)	F	d.f.	p
Burt Reading Test	sex	11.34		2.93	1,488	N.S.
	school area type	139.23	3.87	35.95	2,488	< 0.1%
	interaction	1.49		0.39	2,488	N.S.
Neale Reading Test Accuracy	sex	15.52		3.58	1,488	N.S.
	school area type	148.53	4.34	34.24	2,488	< 0.1%
	interaction	3.68		0.85	2,488	N.S.
Neale Reading Test Rate	sex	89.48		14.23	1,488	< 0.1%
	school area type	95.37	6.29	15.16	2,488	< 0.1%
	interaction	3.86		0.62	2,488	N.S.
Neale Reading Test Comprehension	sex	0.25		0.42	1,488	N.S.
	school area type	15.15	0.59	25.51	2,488	< 0.1%
	interaction	0.22		0.38	2,488	N.S.
WISC Vocabulary Test	sex	5.55		15.04	1,529	< 0.1%
	school area type	13.50	0.37	36.59	2,529	< 0.1%
	interaction	0.07		0.18	2,529	N.S.
Mathematics Test	sex	0.02		0.02	1,532	N.S.
	school area type	31.04	0.78	39.89	2,532	< 0.1%
	interaction	0.04		0.05	2,532	N.S.
Spelling Test	sex	8.43		6.39	1,490	< 2.5%
	school area type	56.85	1.32	43.14	2,490	< 0.1%
	interaction	0.30		0.23	2,490	N.S.

Mean achievement scores of boys and girls in relation to school area type

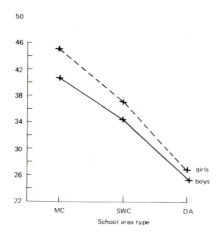

Fig. 30 Burt Reading Test

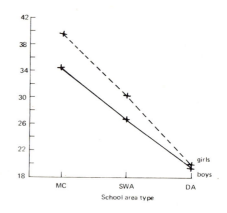

Fig. 31 Neale Reading Test: Accuracy

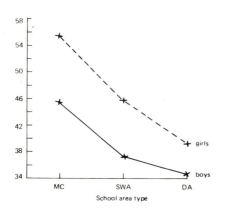

Fig. 32 Neale Reading Test: Rate

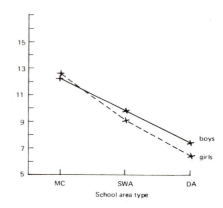

Fig. 33 Neale Reading Test: Comprehension

Note: 1. Attainment test scores are shown on the vertical axes.
2. In the above figures the spacing of the school area groups is arbitrary (see p. 153).

Mean achievement scores of boys and girls in relation to school area type

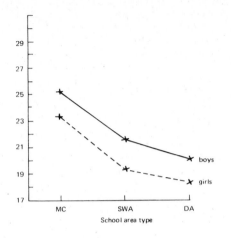

Fig. 34 *WISC Vocabulary Test*

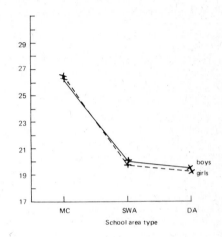

Fig. 35 *Mathematics Test*

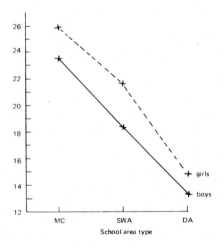

Fig. 36 *Spelling Test*

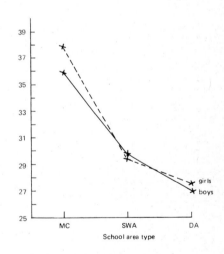

Fig. 37 Picture Test A

Note: 1. Attainment test scores are shown on the vertical axes.
2. In the above figures the spacing of the school area groups is arbitrary (see p. 153).

Figures 38–41

Mean achievement scores of school area groups in relation to sex

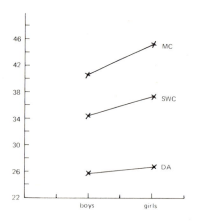

Fig. 38 Burt Reading Test

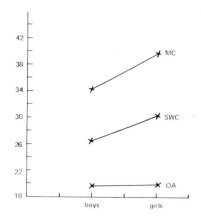

Fig. 39 Neale Reading Test: Accuracy

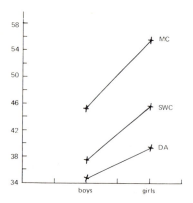

Fig. 40 Neale Reading Test: Rate

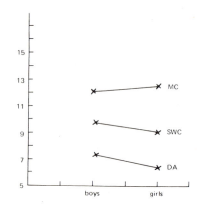

Fig. 41 Neale Reading Test: Comprehension

Note: 1. Attainment test scores are shown on the vertical axes.
2. In the above figures the spacing of the sex groups is arbitrary (see p. 153).

Figures 42—45

Mean achievement scores of boys and girls in relation to school area type

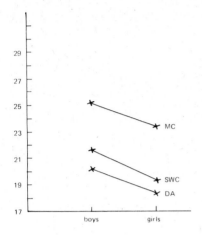

Fig. 42 WISC Vocabulary Test

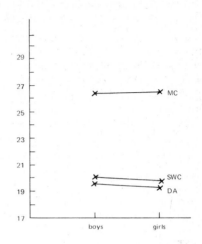

Fig. 43 Mathematics Test

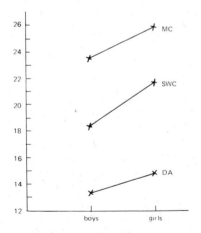

Fig. 44 Spelling Test

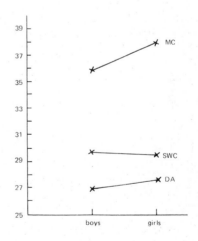

Fig. 45 Picture Test A

Note: 1. Attainment test scores are shown on vertical axes.
2. In the above figures the spacing of the school area groups is arbitrary (see p. 153).

The finding in the present study that the boys obtained a higher mean score than the girls in the mathematics test, although the difference was non-significant, was in line with the NCDS finding that, at age seven years, boys obtained higher scores in a short problem arithmetic test than girls.

It was found that, in all tests, the scores of the boys showed greater variability than those of the girls (see Table 78 and also Appendix Table A8) particularly in the case of the Burt and Neale readings tests (Accuracy and Comprehension measures).

It is not proposed to enter into the possible psychological, educational and other reasons for the differences between the sexes in school achievement measures reported above, but a good discussion of the factors which may underlie such differences can be found in the report on the NCDS by Davie et al. (1972).

Summary of Attainment Survey Results

On the battery of school achievement and ability tests given to the children in their final infant school term, the CA sample obtained very significantly higher mean scores than the DA sample on all of the tests. This result also applied to the SWC area children considered separately, but the between-group differences were less marked on some tests than in the main comparison and, on the mathematics test, the mean difference between these children and the DA children was negligible. The MC area children were clearly superior on all measures to both the SWC area and DA children. The mean score for each school on each test was calculated and it was found that the greatest degree of variation in means among the schools occurred in the reading and spelling tests. There was considerable overlap between the means of the SWC and DA schools on some tests but the MC area schools tended to have higher means than schools in both of these groups. A few schools in the sample were outstanding because their mean scores on some tests were very markedly above or below those of the other schools in their group. With the exception of Neale Rate, all of the reading and spelling tests intercorrelated highly. The picture test and mathematics test also showed a fairly high measure of correlation.

An analysis of variance showed that, whilst both intelligence (picture test score) and school area type contributed significantly to the variation in children's school achievement scores, intelligence accounted for more of this variation than school area type, although these results were only approximate. This outcome seems to accord with the fact that a measure of general intelligence is the best single predictor of a child's school performance. With intelligence held constant, the differences between the three school area types (MC, SWC and DA) were explored and it was found that the MC area children scored higher on all tests than the SWC area children who, in turn, did better on all but one of the tests than the DA children, although the differences between the school groups were not always statistically significant. The difference in mean test performance between the three intelligence groups ('high', 'medium' and 'low'), with school area type held constant, were much more pronounced, and all statistically significant. None of the interactions between intelligence and school area type reached significance.

The school achievement test data were also analysed for sex differences and it was found that on only three tests were such differences statistically significant. On two of these, Neale Rate and spelling, the girls were superior to the boys, in line with the findings of previous research, but surprisingly, the boys were better than the girls on the vocabulary test. None of the interactions between sex and school area type was significant.

SCHOOL PROGRESS AND ADJUSTMENT IN URBAN AREAS: SUMMARY AND CONCLUSIONS

Summary of the main findings

1. Compared with their controls, the 'deprived area' children were poorer in oral language, reading and related skills and mathematics. They were not so well adjusted, socially and emotionally, in the school setting and showed poorer concentration in some basic school activities. These findings still applied, although less strongly, when the 'deprived area' children were compared with the 'settled working-class' children, considered separately.

2. In general, these between-group differences remained when the disparity between the

162

Table 78

Raw scores of urban sample boys and girls in school attainment tests during the final infant school term

Test	N		Girls		Boys		difference between means (Girls-Boys)	standard error of difference	t	p (one-tail) %
	Girls	Boys	mean	s.d.	mean	s.d.				
Burt Reading	238	256	33.34	16.04	32.05	19.73	1.29	1.63	0.79	N.S.
Neale Reading Test										
Accuracy	238	256	26.80	16.90	25.43	20.76	1.37	1.71	0.80	N.S.
Rate	238	256	44.18	21.01	38.20	22.77	5.98	1.98	3.02	<1%
Comprehension	238	256	8.35	5.91	9.23	7.70	-0.88	0.62	-1.43	N.S.
WISC Vocabulary	259	276	19.58	5.48	21.80	5.85	-2.22	0.49	-4.52	<0.1%
Mathematics	259	279	20.69	8.18	21.41	8.27	-0.72	0.71	-1.02	N.S.
Spelling	238	258	18.90	10.25	17.39	11.10	1.51	0.96	1.57	N.S.
Picture Test A	261	279	29.97	11.23	29.98	11.70	-0.01	0.99	-0.01	N.S.

'deprived area' children and their controls on a measure of general intelligence was allowed for statistically, and they probably reflected differences in the children's home background to a greater extent than differences between the schools themselves.

3. These differences appeared quite early during the children's infant school careers and were maintained over the three year period under study. However, there was no evidence of a widening gap in achievement and adjustment between the two groups as they progressed through school, although the interpretation of trends in the ratings received by the children over the period under study was complicated by losses of children from the sample, which may have had the effect of reducing the differences between the two samples.

4. A substantial proportion of the 'deprived area' school children appeared to be seriously retarded in mechanical reading ability and spelling at the end of the infant school stage.

5. Intelligence accounted for more of the variation in the children's school achievement scores than school area type. There was no significant interaction between intelligence and school area type on any of the attainment tests.

Conclusions and implications

There is now well established research evidence in this country for a significant association between social class and children's educational achievement and, more specifically, between such achievement and the level of cultural provision in the child's home background and the level of parental interest in his education and development. However, as Davie et al. (1972) point out, few of these studies to date have been concerned with infant school children, and the National Child Development Study (NCDS), reported by these authors, has made a valuable contribution in showing that the earlier findings relating social class and associated factors to school achievement can be extended to seven-year-old children in the infant school. The finding of the present study that the CA children were significantly superior in basic educational achievement to the DA children is in accord with that of the NCDS, insofar as these between-group differences reflect, at least in part, differences in the social class composition of the two samples. In

general, the differences between the CA and DA samples were maintained, although at a reduced level, even when the 'middle-class' element was removed from the CA sample. This is supported by the finding of the NCDS that there were differences in school attainment between groups of children within the broad 'working-class' range (particularly between those in social class groups III and V) as well as between 'middle-class' and 'working-class' children.

An important feature of the present study, however, is that, unlike the NCDS, the progress of children *throughout* the infant school period was studied and it was shown that many of the differences between the CA and DA children appeared quite early in their infant school careers, so that the findings regarding differences in educational achievement between the CA and DA samples can be regarded as complementary to those of the NCDS.

The fact that differences in school adjustment and basic skills between the two groups in favour of the CA children appeared at a fairly early stage in their schooling no doubt reflects the more adequate preparation of these children for the demands of schooling by their parents. Moreover, the fact that the CA children maintained their superiority over the three year period under study was probably due, in part, to relatively greater parental support and interest in their educational achievement. Indeed, the CA children might have been expected to increase their superiority over the DA children during this period in the light of research evidence such as that produced by Deutsch (1965) in the USA, and Douglas (1964) in this country, for an increasing achievement gap over time between higher and lower social class groups. (However, in a recent large scale study in the USA, Jensen (1971) found no evidence of a 'progressive achievement gap' between white, Negro and Mexican children over the elementary school years.) Such a trend might also have been expected if, as discussed in Chapter 5 (page 108), there were differences between the CA and DA teachers in the present study in their levels of expectation of pupil performance. Contrary to expectation, there was no firm evidence in the present study for such a divergence between the two groups and this may be partly due to a 'compensatory' effect of infant schooling on the DA children's educational development. Indeed, there was some suggestion of a narrowing of the gap between the two groups in some skills (ability to concentrate, to understand stories and to follow oral instructions), according to the teachers' ratings. The evidence available suggests that the DA children who left their infant schools during the period under study tended to be below average for their group in some respects. It is possible, therefore, that this selective loss from the DA sample may have masked a tendency for the CA and DA children to draw apart in some aspects of their school achievement and adjustment over time. It could also account, to some extent, for the closing of the gap in achievement between the two groups which appeared to occur in items such as those mentioned above.

Despite the fact that the achievement gap between the CA and DA children did not appear to widen over time, a relatively high proportion of the latter children was found to be seriously backward in reading and spelling at the end of the infant school stage. (It was not possible to relate the children's performance on the mathematics test to that of a reference sample but the difference in performance between the two groups in mathematical skills tended to be less pronounced than that in reading.) A substantial number of these backward readers and spellers obtained scores on a 'non-verbal' intelligence test (Picture Test A) within the broad average band, so that their retardation did not seem attributable to low intelligence. These backward readers present a serious educational problem and, although the factors contributing to their poor progress may be many and complex, it seems likely that relatively poor oral language skills play an important part. According to the WISC vocabulary sub-test, a substantial proportion of both the CA and DA children, but particularly the latter, appeared to be retarded in vocabulary development, although the test norms are not strictly applicable to British children. Moreover, according to the teachers' ratings, the DA children were generally poorer in their development of oral language skills than the controls. It may be, therefore, that a more structured teaching approach to children's language skills in the 'deprived area' schools, might help to reduce the problem of backwardness in reading in such schools which was highlighted in the study, as well as generally raising the children's level of 'oracy'.

As already stated, the urban sample in the present sample cannot strictly be regarded as representative of the general population of children in social class terms, although it may not be markedly atypical. Similarly, the DA schools cannot be thought of as fully representative of schools serving 'deprived areas', especially since the definition of such areas is so variable and subjective. It seems probable, however, that the general degree of cultural or material deprivation characterizing the areas served by the DA schools in the present sample is not as severe as that which would be found among many depressed inner city or heavily industrialized areas in this country. It should be remembered, in this context, that a deliberately broad interpretation of the concept of deprivation was made in the present study and that school catchment areas containing relatively high proportions of immigrant children, which are among the most depressed areas in the country, were excluded from the sample. It could be argued, however, that if the DA children in the present study were shown to be significantly poorer than their controls in school progress and adjustment, then children from areas characterized by greater levels of cultural and material deprivation would probably show even more pronounced differences in this respect in comparison with children in more advantaged areas.

The analysis of variance carried out on the attainment test scores showed that intelligence made a larger contribution than school area type to children's school achievement. This raises the controversial question as to what extent a child's intelligence can be raised by environmental changes and underlines the important fact that a child's level of intelligence, itself a product of genetic and environmental factors, will set broad limits to his potential educational achievement. In other words, compensatory education can only succeed within these limits. However, there is very convincing and substantial evidence for the importance of environmental, particularly home background, influences on the early development of intelligence, so that the differences in school achievement between the higher and lower intelligence groups in the present study could be expected to reflect the operation of early environmental factors as well as genetic factors. A finding of equal importance from the point of view of the likely effectiveness of compensatory education is that school area type, a compound of home backgound and school factors, was found to account for a significant part of the variation in children's school achievement scores *independently* of intelligence. This finding was supported by the results of an intensive study, reported in Volume 2 (Part One) in this series, which showed that significant differences in cognitive, linguistic and basic educational skills appeared between a sub-sample of culturally deprived children and their controls even though the groups were matched for intelligence. This suggests that, within the broad limits set by his intelligence, there is considerable scope for raising a child's level of school achievement. Moreover, research supports the view that the contribution of environmental factors to the development of *educational* skills appears to be greater, and the influence of genetic factors smaller, than in the case of the development of general intelligence (cf. Jensen, 1971). It would seem, therefore, that, although it may be unrealistic to hope to raise the level of a child's general intelligence significantly by school-based educational intervention, the way lies clear for well planned compensatory education programmes designed to improve a disadvantaged child's school motivation and level of achievement in basic educational skills. Since, however, the present study showed that children from disadvantaged backgrounds lagged behind their more favoured peers in educational development at, or soon after school entry, it is clearly of great importance to introduce such 'compensation' as early as possible in the child's life, ideally at the pre-school stage, or some would argue, even the first years of life.

PART THREE — SCHOOL PROGRESS AND ADJUSTMENT IN A RURAL AREA

7 Context of Study and Selection of Sample

This study of rural children forms part of the general study of children and their schools described in this volume. As discussed in Chapter 3 the major part of the sample of children for the general study attended schools in urban areas and the findings relating to those children are reported in Chapters 4–6 of the present volume. The problems of 'deprivation' are, of course, not limited to urban areas, although the emphasis of most studies has been on urban problems. Teachers often feel that children from remote country areas start school with certain disadvantages, although these may be of a different kind from those associated with urban deprivation. It was, therefore, decided to include a small number of children from a rural area in the general study sample.

The county chosen for this study, although in Wales, had a very small proportion of its population Welsh-speaking. Only 4.5 per cent of the population were said to be Welsh-speaking at the time of the 1961 census, compared with 26.0 per cent for the country as a whole. The problems of deprived children in Welsh-speaking or bilingual areas were studied as a separate part of this research project and are discussed in a report entitled 'Deprivation and the Bilingual Child' (Lloyd, to be published).

In the urban area it was possible to classify each school catchment area as mainly 'middle-class', 'settled working class' or 'deprived', but no similar classification could be made of the rural schools' catchment areas. From the small Welsh county chosen for this part of the study, a representative sample of eleven schools was chosen to include both fairly large and very small schools, the numbers on the school roll varying from 29 to 200. Ten of these schools were combined junior and infant departments. From the eleven schools, those children were selected who had entered school in September 1968, and were born between September 1963 and March 1964 (inclusive). This gave a total sample of 62 children with numbers in the individual schools ranging from one to sixteen. During the period of three years over which the progress of these children was followed, four children left the area and were lost from the sample. Two more children changed schools but remained in the county and thus within the sample, as did a group of children who were transferred to a neighbouring primary school during the final year of the research. For much of the analysis, therefore, information was not available for all 62 children.

Much of the information collected for the schools and children in the rural areas was identical to that collected in the urban areas. Each school was visited and assessed on the basis of the Infant School Amenities Index and class and head-teachers in the schools were interviewed by members of the research team using the Head-teacher's and Class Teacher's Questionnaires during the early stages of the project. Information about the school catchment areas was also gathered from census and other relevant data. As in the case of the urban children, the rural sample class teachers were asked to complete, at intervals during the three years, the six specially designed school schedules concerning the child's social and emotional adjustment in school and his progress in school work. All of the above instruments can be found in Appendix III. During their final term in the infant school or department, the children were given the same battery of standardized tests as the urban children, giving information on their level of non-verbal intelligence, reading, spelling, vocabulary and number skills. In addition to this school based information, the project had access to the school medical records for all these children and, during the summer term of the second year of the project, the parent or parents of every child were visited and interviewed by the project social worker to seek relevant information on the home background of these children. The questionnaire used was similar to that used for parents in the deprived urban areas (First Home Interview

Schedule) with modifications to allow for the rural setting and some refinements which were felt to add precision to the ratings made.

The aim of this report will be to give a general picture of the home background and educational progress of this rural sample, to compare this information, where appropriate, with that available for the urban sample and to relate some of the factors in the children's home background to their educational attainment.

DESCRIPTION OF THE AREA

As the County Handbook informs its readers, 'The population of the county is very small and is decreasing, because of the nationwide drift to urban living'. To be more precise, the population is a little over 18,000 and the inhabitants are spread over the area with an average density of 37 people per square mile. It contains only three small urban districts, the largest of these having a population of about 3,250. According to the 1966 census data, the county has the highest number of cars per head of the population of any British county but, since public transport within the county is extremely infrequent (where it exists at all) this is not to be taken as a measure of affluence. It merely reflects the fact that, in an area with many isolated farmhouses and small villages, private transport is ranked high on the list of priorities for many people. Despite this fact, the traveller on the county's roads is more likely to be held up by wandering sheep than by traffic congestion.

For the most part, it is not an area of spectacular scenery like some other and more 'popular' areas of Wales, but it has a gentle scenic beauty, almost completely unspoiled and un-commercialized. On the memorial stone to a local artist in one parish church appears the phrase, 'although acquainted with the noblest scenes in Europe, he returned from foreign travel to love anew the charms of this valley'. There are few signs of prosperity, with the chief occupations of hill farming and forestry offering low wages and long hours of work. A little light industry is now to be found in the small towns. In an age when we are are constantly being made aware of the menace of pollution and over-population, this may not sound much like a description of 'deprivation', but the

process of 'socialization' for a young child may prove difficult if the nearest neighbour is over a mile away and an eight mile journey to school, picking up other children on the way, can mean a very long day for a five year old. Though they are rare today, there are still houses without electricity (and hence without television) and, for those without their own transport, a trip to a doctor, dentist, clinic or hospital can be an expensive, major expedition.

Four of the eleven schools in the sample lie within urban districts, though even these serve areas which include more isolated homes. Many children are collected from their homes (or as near as the road goes to their homes) by bus or car provided by the local authority. Road conditions during winter months can make transport difficult. One mother, when asked about this, said, 'Oh, it was quite a mild year. There were only two weeks when the children couldn't get to school'.

The Report on Primary Education in Wales (1967) states that 'the smaller and more rural the education authority, the more favourable is its pupil-teacher ratio'. Figures given in the report indicate that the county in which this study took place had the lowest pupil-teacher ratio and the highest cost per (primary) pupil. Smaller schools, as the report mentions, are more dependent on the quality of the staff for their success, since a child may have the same teacher for several years and facilities for activities such as sport or music, may be limited by the small number of pupils or lack of suitable teaching. However, these small, rural schools certainly have their advantages. To quote again from the Report, 'Environmental Studies and Science can begin at the doorstep of the school, in field, forest, or mountainside'. One headmaster described how the whole school had been able to watch a calf being born in the field adjoining the school playground.

In Table 79 details are given of the distance of each school from the nearest urban district and the facilities available in the school area. Where facilities are shown as 'not present in the area' it can be assumed that the nearest urban district will provide them. Those areas which do not have a library mostly have visits from a mobile library and in one area a 'voluntary' library was organized. Facilities such as clinics and dentists may only be available part-time, in some cases only for one day per week. For those school areas not in an urban

Table 79

Amenities of school areas in Rural sample

School No.	Distance from nearest U.D. Miles	Doctor	Dentist	Dispensing Chemist	Maternity and Child Welfare Clinics	General shop	Post Office	Library	Park with swings etc.	Youth Club	Cubs	Brownies	Scouts	Guides
1	11	✓	✓	✓	✓	✓	✓	✓	✓	✓	x	✓	x	x
2	6	x	x	x	x	✓	✓	x	x	x	x	x	x	x
3	2	x	x	x	x	✓	✓	x	✓	✓	x	✓	x	x
4	in UD	✓	✓	✓	✓	✓	✓	✓	✓	x	✓	✓	x	x
5	in UD	✓	✓	✓	✓	✓	✓	✓	✓	✓	✓	✓	✓	✓
6	in UD	✓	✓	✓	✓	✓	✓	✓	✓	✓	✓	✓	✓	✓
7	1	x	x	x	x	✓	x	x	x	x	x	x	x	x
8	8	✓	✓	x	x	✓	✓	x	x	x	✓	x	✓	x
9	4½	x	x	x	✓	✓	✓	x	✓	✓	✓	✓	✓	✓
10	in UD	✓	✓	✓	✓	✓	✓	✓	✓	✓	x	✓	x	✓
11	3	x	x	x	x	✓	✓	x	x	x	x	x	x	x

✓ = present   x = absent

district, *none* has even a daily bus service into the nearest town. In some cases there is no regular service and several have only one bus per week, on 'market day'. Only one urban district had a regular cinema (even this not opening *every* week day).

There are no facilities for nursery education nor any day nurseries provided by the local authority. Two privately organized playgroups provide the only opportunities for pre-school educational activities. No facilities for special education are provided and opportunities for further education at evening classes are very limited. Two quotations from parents will illustrate the difficulties. One parent said, 'If they don't pass the 11+ there's nothing for them — no night schools they can go to'. (The '11+' selection has since been aban-

doned.) Another parent described the difficulties of her teenage son who wanted to train as a motor mechanic. 'To go to classes he had to cycle six miles to the nearest small town to catch the 8 a.m. bus into town and if he had a late class he didn't get back until 8.30 p.m.'.

There are only two Youth Clubs in the county run by the local authority, but local churches or Young Farmers' Clubs organize groups in several other areas and there are also Guide and Scout groups in some areas. Table 79 includes voluntary Youth Clubs in addition to the two local authority clubs.

Census data for a school area generally give information which can be used for comparisons of the population and housing of these areas. For

Table 80

Population statistics for Rural sample area

	U.D.1	U.D.2	U.D.3	Rural Areas	County	England & Wales
% e.a. and ret. men in social class:						
I and II	24.3	31.7	27.9	45.5	39.6	20.2
III	48.6	41.6	37.2	24.7	31.1	50.3
IV and V	27.1	26.7	34.9	29.7	29.3	29.4
% people over 15, t.e.a. less than 16	84.4*	59.7	75.5**	77.1**	74.6**	78.6
Age composition %						
0 - 4 years	8.6	7.7	10.7	9.4	9.1	8.5
5 - 14	15.7	12.1	16.0	14.4	14.3	14.5
65+	11.7	17.8	13.0	15.7	15.4	12.4
No. of children under 15 per household	0.74	0.57	0.83	0.73	0.71	0.71
Females per 1,000 males	990	1152	1183	1028	1055	1064
% 15+ who are married						
Men	65.8	74.1	57.8	63.5	65.2	69.6
Women	69.9	59.5	52.9	63.8	62.8	63.6
% born outside U.K.	0.5	7.1	3.8	1.1	2.3	6.3[1]
% moving within L.A. during last year	8.1	9.8	4.6	2.3	4.4	N.A.
% moving into L.A. during last year	0	5.7	0	3.6	3.3	N.A.

KEY

e.a. and ret. - economically active and retired

t.e.a. - terminal education age

N.A. - not applicable

* - 'not stated' category over 10% of total

** - 'not stated' category over 5% of total

(1) - the figure for England and Wales is the percentage of economically active or retired persons only

rural areas this is more difficult since the areas for which census data are given are somewhat larger than the school catchment areas. Tables 80 and 81 show the information which is available for the three urban areas in which four schools are situated and overall figures for the rural areas in which the other seven schools are situated. For comparison, figures are given for the county as a whole and for England and Wales.

Looking first at the population statistics, the rather higher than average proportion in social classes I and II is largely due to the numbers of farm owners in the county. The county has fewer immigrants, but otherwise differs little from the characteristics of England and Wales as a whole. The figures in Table 81 show that, in some respects, housing conditions are less good, with fewer houses having exclusive use of all amenities,

Table 81

Housing statistics for Rural sample area

	U.D.1	U.D.2	U.D.3	Rural Areas	County	England & Wales
% with exclusive use of all amenities	67.7	91.4	61.9	76.9	77.2	82.4
% 6+ households	3.1	1.9	11.9	8.9	7.2	6.2
% single person households	13.8	22.3	23.8	13.7	16.0	15.1
% owner-occupied	46.1	50.5	64.3	50.8	51.2	48.4
% rented from Council	20.0	6.8	16.7	10.7	11.5	27.2
Average number of people per room	0.51	0.43	0.50	0.49	0.48	0.58
Densities:						
over $1\frac{1}{2}$	0	0	0	1.4	0.9	1.5
$1 - 1\frac{1}{2}$	3.1	2.0	4.8	3.3	3.1	5.4
$\frac{1}{2} - 1$	53.8	41.2	47.6	48.6	47.8	68.8
$< \frac{1}{2}$	43.1	56.9	47.6	46.7	48.2	24.3
% sharing households	0	16.5	0	1.9	4.1	3.0
Average rateable value per dwelling(£)	39.0	58.0	35.4	31-35[1]	N.R.A.	

KEY

N.R.A. - not readily available

(1) - a range is given here of the average values for the various rural rating areas making up the County

slightly more households sharing a dwelling, and lower rateable values but, on the other hand, there is less overcrowding and slightly more people own their own houses. The proportion of council housing is considerably lower in the rural than in the urban areas.

ORGANIZATION, STAFFING AND GENERAL INFORMATION

Information under this heading was obtained from the Headteachers' questionnaire (Part One) (see Appendix III for details), and also, where relevant, from the School Amenities Index discussed sub-sequently in this chapter. It is interesting to compare the rural and urban schools in the project in terms of their organization, staffing and general conditions. Differences between the two samples were tested for statistical significance and unless otherwise stated, these differences were not significant.

In nine of the eleven rural schools children entered school at the age of 4½, either individually (44 schools) or as a group once a term (5 schools). One headteacher said that there was considerable pressure from mothers to take children at this age. Children in the urban schools were, on average, 2.2 months older (the difference in age was statistically significant, $p < 0.1\%$) This difference was probably due to the fact that the majority of urban school children entered school when they were already five or 'rising five' (that is, they started school at the beginning of the term during which they attained the age of 5), and only in exceptional circumstances were individual children allowed to enter during the school term rather than at the beginning.

The majority of urban schools allocated children to infant classes on the basis of age, but the very small size of most infant departments in rural schools made this impractical. In six rural schools the age range within the classes was over a year and in some cases a child might remain in the same class for as long as four years. Of these schools five had only one infant class, covering the age range 4½ to 7 years, or in one school, 4½ to 8 years. One school had two classes, the first for 4½ – 5 year olds, and the second covering the age range 6 – 8 years. These arrangements meant that some grouping within the class was necessary; in three schools children were grouped according to age, in one school the class was grouped according to ability and a third school grouped children by a combination of age and ability. The remaining five rural schools arranged its classes in one year age groups.

All schools in the total sample (urban and rural) promoted children to the Junior School or department according to age, except for three rural schools which promoted children according to a combination of age and ability.

Although two headteachers mentioned staffing difficulties and said that younger teachers are unwilling to stay for long because of the isolation, the average turnover of teachers during the years 1968–71 was only 6.6 per cent in rural schools compared with 10.3 per cent in urban areas. However, over the three year period 1968–71, the situation fluctuated from year to year so that, at times, there was very little difference between the rural and urban areas.

The average teacher-pupil ratio was well below the national average of 28.2, with a teacher-pupil ratio of 22.8, compared with 31.4 in urban schools. In two rural schools the pupil-teacher ratio was a little above the national average of 28.2 (28.7 in one school and 32 in the other). No rural school had any staff other than full-time class teachers. For example, they did not have any part time specialist teachers or any infant helpers.

The rural school teachers had had longer teaching experience (15.6 years) than teachers in urban schools (11 years). Although 13 out of the 32 teachers (40.6 per cent) had received no infant training compared with 36 out of 147 urban teachers (24.5 per cent), rural infant teachers had had more experience of teaching infants (11.3 years) than infant teachers in urban schools (8.8 years).

In comparison with their urban counterparts, rural headteachers had had slightly less teaching experience (25.5 years compared with 28.4 years), although rural headteachers had been longer in their present post (9.9 years compared with 6.8 years). Whereas three quarters of urban heads had been trained for the nursery-infant, infant, or infant-junior age range, only two rural head teachers had had infant-junior training. Other rural head teachers had trained for the junior-secondary age range (6), secondary range (1), or for all ages (2). It must be remembered however, that ten of these eleven headteachers were heads of junior and infant schools, unlike the heads of urban schools who were predominantly heads of infant schools or departments. Seven headteachers were teaching fulltime and all but two rural heads were required to teach for at least half the week.

The only rural school to have any secretarial or ancillary help was one with a part time clerical assistant. Four rural schools were the only ones in the whole project sample not to have a school meals organizer. In six schools the percentage of children receiving free meals was above the national average, but the proportion of children in rural schools receiving free school meals (10.6 per cent) was lower than that of children in urban schools (14.8 per cent).

As would be expected the rural school population was a fairly stable one, at least during the years 1968–71. The average percentage pupil turnover was only 5.7 per cent compared with 11.1 per cent in the urban schools (statistically significant, $p < 5\%$).

SCHOOL AMENITIES

During the early stages of the research project all schools were visited and assessed on the basis of answers to 100 items on an Infant School Amenities Index (see Appendix III). These items, grouped under eight headings, covered features such as the

Table 82

Scores on Infant School Amenities Index :
Urban and Rural samples

	Urban schools (N=26)	Rural schools (N=11)
A. School Building		
Range	0-2	0-3
Mean	1.5	1.82
s.d.	1.25	1.19
Value of t = -0.70, N.S.		
B. Entrance and Circulation areas		
Range	0-5	0-4
Mean	1.8	1.09
s.d.	1.40	1.16
Value of t = 1.38, N.S.		
C. Provision of rooms		
Range	0-7	1-8
Mean	3.4	4.64
s.d.	1.82	1.87
Value of t = -1.90, N.S.		
D. Toilets and cloakrooms		
Range	0-6	0-6
Mean	2.6	2.09
s.d.	1.84	2.02
Value of t = 0.75, N.S.		
E. Classroom facilities		
Range	0-15	0-11
Mean	4.4	4.18
s.d.	3.78	3.83
Value of t = 0.12, N.S.		
F. Provision of materials		
Range	0-7	0-5
Mean	2.6	2.73
s.d.	1.71	1.54
Value of t = -0.18, N.S.		
G. School surrounds		
Range	1-9	1-8
Mean	4.4	3.82
s.d.	1.80	1.90
Value of t = 0.78, N.S.		

Continued overleaf

H. School conditions		
Range	2–10	3–7
Mean	5.9	5.18
s.d.	1.84	1.19
Value of t = 1.20, N.S.		
Total score on index		
Range	10–57	8–47
Mean	26.23	25.55
s.d.	10.85	11.15
Value of t = 0.17, N.S.		

school building, cloakroom and toilet facilities, classroom facilities, school surrounds and general items such as pupil-teacher ratio and proportion of untrained teachers. Table 82 presents the data from the Index for the rural schools and, for comparison, that for the urban schools, together with the results of 't' tests on the differences. It may be seen that neither on the total Index score, nor on any of the sectional scores did the difference between the rural and urban schools reach statistical significance. Examination of the information shown in this table together with that from the individual items making up the Index (not presented here) showed that, apart from the provision of rooms which becomes very costly on a 'per head' basis for small schools, the overall differences between the amenities provided in the urban and rural schools were very slight. Variations between the rural schools were quite marked, with recently built schools scoring few adverse points but, in general, this variation was comparable to that found in the urban schools. A description of some features of the rural schools, based on information provided within the Index now follows.

School buildings and facilities

Nine of the eleven schools were built before 1914, three of them having had no alterations made since 1930, and four had no central heating. Five schools had no entrance hall and seven had no hall for assembly. Four schools had no dining facilities in the infant department and three had to use classrooms for eating meals. Only four schools had a head-teacher's room and only one a medical room or waiting room. Four schools had no staff

room. In the general provision of rooms the rural schools fared rather worse than the urban area schools. Indoor sanitation was lacking in several schools and one school had no flush toilets at all. Several schools had classrooms lacking in space for play, storage or display, and lacking a sink, but provision of such classroom facilities was similar to that in the urban areas. Several schools mentioned lack of storage space for large equipment as a problem.

Provision of materials

Most of the schools in this sample had a capitation allowance below the national average, but only one school had an inadequate supply of apparatus or educational equipment in poor repair. All schools had an adequate supply of basic readers and library books. Two schools had neither a tape recorder nor record player, six had no piano in the reception classroom and one had no radio.

School surrounds

It might be expected that rural schools would be better provided with play space and better sited than urban schools. However, this does not seem to be the case. Traffic noise, industrial noise or pollution were not problems to any of the rural schools but three had direct access to a busy road. Four schools had inadequate playgrounds and in nine schools the playspace was shared by both infant and junior children. Eight schools lacked any covered play space, three had no climbing frame or slide, only four had a sandpit and two had over a quarter of the staff unqualified or temporary. All but two of the headteachers were required to teach for at least half of the week. Two schools specifically mentioned staffing difficulties and it was said that younger teachers are unwilling to stay for long because of the isolation.

Apart from the provision of rooms, which becomes very costly on a 'per head' basis for small schools, the overall differences between the amenities provided in the urban and rural schools were slight. Variations between schools in the rural area were however, considerable, with the recently built schools scoring very few adverse points.

8 Home Background

This chapter presents a general description of the characteristics of the home environment of the rural sample. Unfortunately the same background information was not available for the *total* urban sample, as similar interviews with parents had only been undertaken in the *deprived* urban areas. Comparisons with this relatively deprived urban sample are made in some cases as a matter of interest, but these cannot lead to generalizations about differences between rural children and urban children as a whole.

The parental interviews were undertaken during the summer term of the children's second year in school. Parents were very co-operative and interested on the whole and no parent refused or avoided an interview, only two 'second visits' being necessary to parents who were not at home on the first occasion. In the majority of cases the interviewee was the child's mother, but in eight cases the father was also present for at least part of the interview and in one case only the father was seen.

FAMILY COMPOSITION

Six children did not live with both of their own parents. One was adopted, the parents of one were separated, two mothers were widows and two children had their own mother and a step-father. From the whole sample only one parent was not British by birth and many of the parents had been born in or near the area in which they now lived. Eighteen parents had attended the same school as their child. The mean size of family was 3.03 and Table 83 shows the distribution of family size compared with that of the urban deprived sample. The rural sample contained no families with 7 or more children, whereas the urban sample had almost 10 per cent of families of this size. Using the 'Kendall's tau'(z) statistic to test the significance of the difference of the two distributions of family size, it was found that they do differ significantly (z = 2.00, p < 5%) with the rural families being generally smaller.

HOUSING CONDITIONS

All but one of the families interviewed lived in a house or bungalow, over half of these being 'detached', and almost half the sample owned their own homes. Only one family lived in a flat, this being over business premises. Seventeen families lived in homes rented from the council, six rented unfurnished accommodation and six had houses provided with the father's job. Two families shared their homes with relatives. A high proportion of the homes, fifty-one out of fifty-eight, had all amenities, but of those without, six lacked three or more of the usual facilities, one having no electricity. Eight families had an average of over one person per room but only one family had ever been 'homeless'. Ratings were made of the furnishings and general cleanliness of the home as observed during the interview, except in four cases when the interview did not take place in the home. Forty-two homes were rated as having good quality or adequate furniture, fourteen as having adequate but shabby furniture and no home fell into the lowest category. Thirty-three homes were given the highest rating on a four-point scale for cleanliness and again the lowest rating was not used. The results of these ratings and comparisons with those of the urban deprived sample are given in Table 84. As will be seen the rural sample fare considerably better on housing conditions and cleanliness.

HEALTH, WORK AND INCOME

Health problems affected only a small number of families in the rural sample. Four mothers and three fathers had minor ailments but only one mother felt that her illness affected the child in any way. One father was in poor health and was disabled. Eight children had had health trouble, some of these including long absences from school. The mother's mental stability was given a subjective rating by the interviewer, based in most cases only on a general impression gained during

Table 83

Distribution of family size:
Rural and Urban Deprived samples

No. of children in family	Number and % of families			
	Rural (N=58)		Urban Deprived (N=303)	
	n	%	n	%
1	6	10.3	20	6.6
2	18	31.0	77	25.4
3	14	24.1	73	24.1
4	12	20.7	51	16.8
5	4	6.9	33	10.9
6	4	6.9	19	6.3
7+	0	0	30	9.9

Note: In all tables percentages are 'corrected' usually to 1 decimal place and may not always total 100.

the interview. Forty-three mothers were rated as having a happy, stable personality and fourteen as showing slight signs of tension or depression (one mother was not seen). Comparisons with the results for the urban deprived sample again show that the rural sample has the advantage and differences are statistically significant in the case of the mother's health (see Table 85).

At the time of the interview, only one father was unemployed, this being the one who was disabled. Of the remainder, only two had been unemployed during the preceding year and these only for short periods. Asked about her husband's unemployment, one wife answered, 'Not since he got married. Once they knew we were getting married and they knew it was necessary they found him a job'. Only three mothers worked full-time away from home, thirteen worked part-time and nine did work, other than housework, in their own home, this last figure including several who helped their husbands with farm work. Table 86 shows the type of work done by the fathers

and it is perhaps surprising to find such a large proportion concerned with building or constructional work. The 'other' category includes a fairly wide range of occupations: teachers, clerical or administrative workers, postmen and policemen. One factor in the employment situation, which does not appear in the figures but was spontaneously mentioned by several parents, was the enjoyment that the men found in the agricultural work. It has been suggested by J. H. Goldthorpe (1969) and his colleagues that in modern industry men are 'taking on work of a particularly unrewarding or unpleasant kind' but this would certainly not be true of many of this rural sample. One wife of a farmer said, 'We get visitors here who work in the towns and have humdrum jobs. In farming you have to work very hard to get a decent living but you really get satisfaction out of it. We wouldn't do anything else'. Another said, 'When you're a farmer you live farming every minute of your life but that's better than having a job you can't wait to get away from'. One farm worker earning about

Table 84

Ratings of housing conditions and cleanliness
Rural and Urban Deprived samples

Ratings		Rural (N=58)		Urban Deprived (N=303)	
		n	%	n	%
Housing					
	1	32	55.2	74	24.4
	2	14	24.1	70	23.1
	3	9	15.5	121	39.9
	4	3	5.2	38	12.5
		z = 4.79, p < 0.1%			
Cleanliness *					
	1	33	56.9	125	41.4
	2	21	36.2	125	41.4
	3	4	6.9	40	13.2
	4	0	0.0	12	4.0
		z = 2.44, p < 1%			

* 4 rated on appearance of interviewee only in Rural
sample

1 not rated for Urban sample

Statistical note: two-tailed tests have been used
throughout since, except for a few items, there was
no prior expectation as to the direction of the
difference.

£15 per week said, 'I suppose we don't have much compared with some, but I wouldn't go to the steel works for £45 a week'.

There is little doubt that incomes in this area, particularly of agricultural workers, are lower than those in most industrial areas. One mother who helped her husband by keeping the accounts for their small farm said that they could only afford to take out a wage of £15 per week. However, expenses are also less in many ways. Many farmers and farm workers do not pay rents or rates out of their income and, for those who do, rents are generally low. Many families are able to grow their own fruit and vegetables and some can provide eggs, meat or dairy produce.

There is also considerably less temptation to spend money since, for many families, a trip to a large store would be quite a major expedition. In this area they are well insulated from 'impulse buying' or persuasive door-to-door salesmen. As one mother who had moved into the area said, 'If you can only use local shops you may have to pay a bit more but you only buy what you really need'. Another said, 'We don't get many callers here

Table 85

Health of parents: Rural and Urban Deprived samples

	Rural (N=58)		Urban Deprived (N=303)	
	n	%	n	%
Mother's Physical Health				
1. No ailment or handicap	53	91.4	225	75.2
2. Minor ailment or handicap not apparently affecting child	4	6.9	21	7.0
3. Minor ailment or handicap affecting child only little	1	1.7	44	14.7
4. Severe ailment or handicap affecting child considerably	0	0	9	3.0
	z = 2.81, p <1%			
Mother's Stability				
1. Happy, stable personality	43	75.4	135	48.0
2. Some signs of tension or depression	14	24.6	132	47.0
3. Definitely unstable mental state	0	0	14	5.0
	z = 3.77, p < 0.1%			
Father's Physical Health				
1.	51	92.7	235	85.1
2.	3	5.5	33	12.0
As for mother				
3.	1	1.8	7	2.5
4.	0	0	1	0.4
	z = 1.40, N.S.			

Notes: N.S. means that the value of z has a probability of more than 5% and the result is therefore regarded as not showing a 'significant' difference between the groups.

In the above tables some totals are lower because of the absence of one parent or inability to rate adequately. Percentages given are of the number rated.

Table 86

Occupations of fathers of Rural sample children

(N=58)

Type or Work	No.
Farmers or farm-workers	10
Other agricultural jobs: forestry, etc.	9
Industrial work	5
Building or constructional work	14
Other	16
Father unemployed or no father	4

Table 87

Rating of Income : Rural and Urban Deprived samples

	Rural (N=58)		Urban Deprived (N=303)	
	n	%	n	%
1. Over 40% above M.S.S. allowance	42	72.4	152	50.2
2. 20-40% above M.S.S. allowance	8	13.8	58	19.1
3. Less than 20% above M.S.S. allowance	3	5.2	35	11.6
4. Less than or equal to M.S.S. allowance	5	8.6	58	19.1
	z = 3.09, p < 1%			

when they have to walk across two open fields to get to our front door'. One expense which few families could avoid was that of running a car, since public transport covers so few areas and is so infrequent that it is not thought of by the local people as worthy of consideration as an alternative. Fifty of the fifty-eight families interviewed had their own car.

Families were asked about their income and many gave a figure for their weekly wage. However, some were unable to give such a figure and a small number were not happy to divulge their income. Information concerning income is not generally reliable. However, on what information was available, incomes were rated on a four-point scale and the results are shown in Table 87.

Table 87 may appear to conflict with the idea of low wage rates in the rural areas, but two factors should be borne in mind here. First, all except one of the rural sample were employed and earning a wage, whereas a number of the urban sample was not earning but drawing unemployment or sickness benefit or supplementary benefit. Second, in comparing incomes with Ministry of Social Security (M.S.S.) allowances, one is taking into account family size and this is greater in the urban areas. Each parent was asked to give a subjective rating of their income and thirty-eight said that they managed comfortably, seventeen that they 'just managed' and three that they found it difficult to manage. The interviewer also made a rating of probable level of income which put very slightly more of the families into the 'find it difficult to manage' category.

SOCIAL CLASS AND PARENTAL EDUCATION

The occupation of the father if present, or otherwise of the mother, was classified according to the Registrar-General's Classification of Occupations (1966). Table 88 shows the distribution of social class for the sample and that of the urban deprived sample. The only member of the rural sample falling into Class V was classified on the basis of the mother's occupation. The large proportion in the upper social classes includes a number of small farm owners. The differences between the rural and urban samples here are considerable, but are perhaps misleading in including all farm owners in Class II.

Exactly half of the mothers in the sample had received only the minimum education, going to a non-selective secondary school and leaving at the minimum leaving age. Of the remainder, five had O-level qualifications or equivalent and a further four had education beyond this level. The educational level of two of the fathers was not known, but of the remainder twenty-nine had the minimum education, three had O-level qualifications and eight had education beyond this level. Comparisons with the educational level of the parents in the urban deprived sample show that the rural sample parents had made more use of the available educational opportunities ($p < 0.1\%$ for both mothers and fathers).

PLAY SPACE

With just a few exceptions, the children in the rural sample have adequate play space both inside

Table 88

Social class distribution : Rural and Urban Deprived samples

		Rural (N=58)		Urban Deprived (N=303)	
		n	%	n	%
1.	Class I, II or III non-manual	25	43.1	32	10.6
2.	Class III manual	21	36.2	145	47.9
3.	Class IV	11	19.0	70	23.1
4.	Class V	1	1.7	56	18.5
		z = 5.16, p < 0.1%			

and outside the home. In over half the houses, the children have two or more rooms in which they can play and less than three other children with whom to share their play space. One home had a 'playroom' equipped as well as many a nursery or school room. For play space outside, as might be expected, the rural sample fared very much better than their urban fellows. No child was completely without space to play outside and only two parents felt that the children needed close supervision when playing outside. Many children had acres of farmland to roam, with all their natural facilities, and in addition, swings, slides or climbing frames were sometimes provided for their play. Table 89 shows the comparison between outside play space available for the rural and urban samples.

CULTURAL ENVIRONMENT IN THE HOME

One thing which became apparent during the course of interviewing in this area was that parents (and probably children too) spend more of their time in and around their own home. Hardly any second visits needed to be made because parents were not at home at the first call, and the interviewer rarely found neighbours or relatives in the home when she called. This state of affairs has two effects on the young children in the family; their mother spends more time at home with them but, on the other hand, the children have less contact with other adults (outside school) and thus are much more dependent on what their parents provide.

Some detail was obtained about the provision of books and toys and a 'composite' score was computed for each. Provision of comics was treated separately, since in the urban study it was found that they were often seen as substitutes for, rather than supplementary to, the use of books. Tables 90 and 91 give the distribution of categories for the provision of what might be termed 'cultural equipment' for the young child. Half of the children belonged to the public library and borrowed books at least occasionally. The information here is not strictly comparable with that obtained for the urban sample, since considerably more detail was asked for in the rural area. Comparisons are thus not really valid for the provision of books and play material.

Parents were asked about their involvement with the child in reading stories to him, joining in with his play, encouraging questions and conversa-

Table 89

Outside play space available : Rural and Urban Deprived samples

	Rural (N=58)		Urban Deprived (N=303)	
	n	%	n	%
1. Large, safe space with trees, swing, etc.	28	48.3	30	9.9
2. Reasonable-sized safe space	28	48.3	144	47.5
3. Very small space or needing close supervision	2	3.4	80	26.4
4. No safe space available	0	0	49	16.2
	z = 7.39, p< 0.1%			

Table 90

Provision of books and toys in the home
Rural sample (N=60)

	Books	Toys
1. Very wide provision	9	10
2. Good or adequate provision	38	39
3. Rather poor provision	10	10
4. Definitely lacking	3	1

Table 91

Provision of comics in the home
Rural sample (N=60)

1. Provided regularly	27
2. Provided occasionally	24
3. No comics provided	9

tion or using television programmes constructively. Forty parents read to their children regularly and only one child never had stories read to him. In only two families (both large ones) did the parents never join in with their child's play. Most children were allowed to talk freely at meal times, but fifteen were somewhat restricted and in three homes the children were expected to be silent at meal times. Parents were asked about the questions which their children asked and the sort of responses they gave. The replies were classified as 'truthful and adequate', 'inappropriate answers' or 'sometimes avoided', and 'sometimes untruthful'. Forty-two parents gave answers classified as truthful and adequate for the child's age and under-standing and only one gave some untruthful answers. Several parents commented on how naturally the subjects of birth and death came up when children had first-hand knowledge of farm animals being born and dying. Equivalent questions about reading stories and playing with the child were asked of the urban sample and Table 92 shows the results for both samples. The rural children more often have stories read to them, perhaps because parents have more time at home, but there is little difference in the extent parents join in with the children's play.

Television must have widened the horizons considerably for children and parents in these more remote areas. There is little opportunity

Table 92

Parental involvement in reading to and playing with child

Rural and Urban Deprived samples

	Rural (N=58)		Urban Deprived (N=303)	
	n	%	n	%
Reading				
1. Child read to frequently by parent	40	69.0	144	47.5
2. Child read to frequently by other adult	1	1.7	18	5.9
3. Child read to rarely or only by young sibling	16	27.6	106	35.0
4. Child never read to at all	1	1.7	35	11.6
	z = 3.00, p< 1%			
Play				
1. Both parents join in play often	16	27.6	90	29.7
2. One parent often, one occasionally	19	32.8	121	39.9
3. Only occasionally	21	36.2	86	28.4
4. Never	2	3.4	6	2.0
	z = 0.98, N.S.			

locally for attending theatres, cinemas, concerts or sporting events but only one family was without a television set. Thirty parents mentioned some degree of selectivity in the programmes which their children were encouraged, or allowed, to watch, twenty-four children watched non-selectively and three were said not to be able to settle to watch anything. These figures contrast sharply with those found in the urban sample where most children were allowed to watch indiscriminately, perhaps because there are fewer alternative ways of keeping the children 'out of mischief' (see Table 93).

Twenty-seven children had hobbies or particular interests in addition to those specifically mentioned in other questions. These included football, music (listening and playing), riding, fishing, cooking and collecting various things. At this age, of course, these are often parental activities in which the children join. Twenty children actually joined their parents at their work and were often encouraged to give real assistance. Farming particularly lends itself to this sort of participation by children but some parents doing other kinds of work also managed to involve the children. Thirty-eight children had pets (their own

Table 93

Use of television : Rural and Urban Deprived samples

	Rural (N=58)		Urban Deprived (N=303)	
	n	%	n	%
1. Constructive or selective use	30	51.7	37	12.2
2. Non-selective watching	24	41.4	224	73.9
3. Won't settle to watch much	3	5.2	37	12.2
4. Does not see T.V. at home	1	1.7	5	1.7
	$z = 5.82, \ p < 0.1\%$			

or shared with other children) ranging from goldfish to ponies, and twenty-eight of them did at least something to help look after their pets.

ISOLATION AND ITS EFFECTS

Children at this stage learn not only from the environmental and experiences in and around their own home, but also from their relationships with other children and adults and from outings to places of interest outside the home. It is this sort of learning situation which parents in isolated homes, or even in small rural towns, may find most difficult to provide for their children. Many families would have to travel considerable distances to visit shops, a park, cinema, zoo or theatre. Table 94 shows the degree of isolation of the homes of the sample children.

Table 94

Degree of isolation of homes : Rural sample (N=58)

Degree of isolation	n
1. In an urban district or small town	38
2. In a village less than 3 miles from an U.D.	5
3. In a village over 3 miles from an U.D. or isolated but less than 3 miles from an U.D.	7
4. Isolated and over 3 miles from an U.D.	8

Table 95

Provision of outings : Rural sample (N=58)

A. How often during the last month has the child been to the following places:	No. of children who have been:		
	3+ times	1-3 times	Never
a) local shops	50	6	2
b) nearest town	28	22	8
c) visiting friends or relatives	34	15	9
d) for a walk	45	5	8
e) park or playground	22	8	28
f) church or Sunday school	33	5	20

B. Has the child been to the following:	No. of children who have been:		
	More than once	Once	Never
a) seaside	55	3	0
b) cinema	22	10	26
c) theatre	14	16	28
d) library	32	5	21
e) zoo	23	15	20
f) circus	21	22	15
g) swimming bath	17	3	38
h) fairground	54	1	3

Table 95 shows the results of questions about the child's experiences outside his own home. Despite the difficulties, most parents did try to provide these 'widening' experiences for their children, even those parents who did not have their own transport. A 'total' score was computed for the child's outings, giving some measure of the frequency and variety of the child's experiences. From these 'totals' a four-point rating was made and so, although the original information is not the same, a comparison can be made with a similar four-point rating for the urban sample. This is one of the few items where a comparison shows that the urban sample fare rather better (although caution should be observed in interpreting comparisons of ratings based on different information here). Table 96 gives the distribution of ratings for both samples.

Opportunities to mix with other children are likely to be rather limited. As was mentioned earlier, the local authority ran no nursery classes (though some children were admitted early to

Table 96

Ratings of scores for outings
Rural and Urban Deprived samples

	Rural (N=58)		Urban Deprived (N=303)	
	n	%	n	%
1. Many and varied outings	5	8.6	74	24.4
2. Fairly wide range of outings	22	37.9	126	41.6
3. Some visits or outings	21	36.2	78	25.7
4. Few visits or outings	10	17.2	25	8.3
	z = 3.31, p< 0.1%			

infant schools) and only three children in the sample had attended a nursery class or play group. Ten children were said to have mixed with no children outside the home before they started school and a further ten had never mixed with other children of their own age. The parents of forty-two of the children found that their children got on very well with other children once they started school, but fourteen were said to be occasionally shy or quarrelsome and two to be definitely shy and still afraid of mixing. Most of the children in the sample were looking forward to school and had started before their fifth birthday, and most parents felt that this earlier start had been a help to the child. Several children had long journeys to school, fourteen being brought on a school bus or car and fourteen by their parents in a car. Thirty children were close enough to walk to their schools.

Parental contact with their child's school and teachers is likely to be difficult for those who live in isolated homes. Over half the parents, however, had been to the school with the child before admission and had spoken to either the head-teacher or the reception class teacher. In fifteen cases the child had not been to the school at all before admission and in five of these cases neither had the parent. This is another item where the urban sample fared better, but not quite to a statistically significant extent ($p < 10\%$). Forty-six parents had had the opportunity to attend at least one 'Open Day' at the school and forty-two had taken advantage of this opportunity. Of the four who did not go, three lived in very isolated homes and found transport difficult. Twenty-six parents felt that they had ample opportunity to discuss their child's progress with the teachers but over half the parents felt they had not had sufficient or adequate discussion. Thirty-four parents were completely happy about their child's schooling, eighteen had some reservations and six said they were not at all happy with the schooling. Some of the reasons for parents being unhappy were: overcrowding, classes too big, teacher having 'favourites', child frightened of the headteacher, and not enough 'work' at the school. The inter-viewer listed fourteen separate complaints from one mother.

Most parents said that they tried to help their child with school work, over half helping with all of the '3R's '. Only six parents never tried to help their children, some of these having been advised not to by the school. On the whole, parents were keen for the children to do well at school. As one parent, a newcomer to the district, said, 'Country people are different (about schooling). It's not easy to explain but they are *all* very keen for their children to do well even if they are not very bright themselves. The rich and poor live side by side and a little bit rubs off on each'.

Certainly the overall picture of the child's environment *within* the home is not one of deprivation, at least when compared with a sample of children living in deprived urban areas.

The main areas of deficit for the rural children are their comparative lack of experience of places of social and cultural interest outside the home, and the reduced opportunities for parents and children to make contact with the school before admission and for parents after admission. For the urban sample, ten final ratings of the home background were made, five being of mainly 'material' factors and five mainly 'cultural'. These ten factors were:

Material	*Cultural*
Income	Mother's education
Cleanliness	Social class
Housing conditions	Provision of play materials/books
Play space	Use of external stimuli (TV, outings)
Mother's health	Parental interest

Table 97

Comparison of total home background scores

Rural and Urban Deprived samples

	Rural (N=58)			Urban Deprived (N=303)		
	range	mean	s.d.	range	mean	s.d.
1. Material total (possible range 5-20)	5-15	7.29	2.30	5-19	10.10	3.14
	$t = 6.46$, $p < 0.1\%$					
2. Cultural total (possible range 5-20)	6-16	10.69	2.47	5-17	11.59	2.34
	$t = 2.66$, $p < 1\%$					
3. Overall total (possible range 10-40)	12-31	17.98	4.15	10-36	21.66	4.96
	$t = 5.29$, $p < 0.1\%$					

Note: The t-test requires certain assumptions about the data used, one being that the scores form a 'normal' distribution. The questionnaire was designed to give a 'good spread' of scores for deprived urban areas, and graphs showed the distribution of scores for the Urban sample to approximate to normality. However, for the Rural sample, the distribution of the total 'material' scores is definitely skew, with half the sample having the lowest scores of five or six (see Figures 46-48, p. 234). t-test results are quoted but should be treated with caution.

These same ratings were made for the rural sample and a total 'material', total 'cultural' and 'overall' total were computed and compared with those for the urban deprived sample. 't-tests' for the significance of the difference between the mean scores for the rural and urban samples show that all three totals are significantly lower (i.e. better) for the rural sample. Table 97 shows the results for the two samples. The difference in mean 'material' scores is greater than that between the 'cultural' scores. In other words, the rural sample children have more favourable home backgrounds, the differences being greater with regard to material than to cultural factors.

9 Teachers' Assessments of Children's Adjustment and School Progress

Information on the school progress and adjustment of the rural sample children was obtained by means of the same instruments used in the study of children in urban areas described in Part II of this volume. These instruments were the six school schedules, comprising teachers' assessments of the children's adjustment and progress, described in that section (see Appendix III for the actual schedules), and the battery of standardized tests administered during the final term of the children's infant school stage. A comparison between the rural and urban samples on the results of the teachers' assessments (school schedule data) is given in the present chapter and this is followed in Chapter 10 by the results of analyses of the school attainment test data, including a comparison between the rural and urban samples.

It will be recalled from Chapter 3 that the school schedules were completed at the following stages during the children's infant school careers: at the end of the first ten days in school and then at the end of the 1st, 2nd, 3rd, 6th and 9th terms.

Not all the items for each school schedule will be presented here. A selection has been made to include the initial 'settling-in' period, when the rural children may be at more of a disadvantage, having had less contact with the school and with other children prior to school entry. Items including the social and emotional aspects of the child's progress will also be discussed, together with the teachers' ratings of all aspects of the child's progress at the end of the three years.

A. THE 'SETTLING-IN' PERIOD

The early questions on the first school schedule asked about the contact that the child and parents had made with the school before the child's admission. As was mentioned previously, many families live several miles from the school and it is

not easy to 'pop in' to the school. Where transport is provided, parents do not have to take or collect older children so that opportunities for informal contact are limited. Information given by the teachers suggested even less contact than did that given by parents. Parents may well have taken a child to see the school *building* without teachers being aware of this.

Comparisons were made in the previous chapters with the urban deprived area children, since it was only for the *deprived* areas that comparable home background data were available. Information from the schools, however, is available for the *total* urban sample, including children from 'deprived', 'settled working-class' and 'middle-class' areas, so that in this and the following section any comparisons which are made will be between the rural sample and the *total* urban sample. This urban sample is not a 'random' sample, nor is it quite 'representative' of the general population with regard to social class distribution. Unfortunately full information on the parental occupations for the urban sample is not available, but the limited information suggests a slightly higher proportion of manual workers and a correspondingly lower proportion of white collar workers in the total urban sample than are found in the general population.

Table 98 shows the teachers' answers to questions about contact with school and pre-school experience in the rural sample and also in the total urban sample for comparison.

From the above results it would seem that the children in the rural sample had significantly less direct experience of the school setting before admission to the infant school and might thus be expected to have had more initial difficulty in adapting to the school routine.

Twenty-three of the sixty-two children in the rural sample were said by their teachers to have shown signs of distress at leaving their mothers on

Table 98

Contact with school prior to admission
Rural and Urban samples

Question	Answer	Rural (N=62)		Urban (N=670)	
		n	%	n	%
1. Did child visit school before admission?	On two or more occasions	12	19.4	219	32.7
	Once only	12	19.4	307	45.8
	Not at all	38	61.3	144	21.5
	z = 5.12, p < 0.1%				
2. Has child any siblings attending same infant school/department?	Yes	22	35.5	203	30.3
	No	40	64.5	467	69.7
	z = 0.70, N.S.				
3. Has parent contacted school prior to admission to register child?	Yes	41	66.1	488	72.8
	No	21	33.9	182	27.2
	z = 0.98, N.S.				
4. Has parent contacted school prior to admission for any other reason?	Yes	5	8.1	100	14.9
	No	57	91.9	570	85.0
	z = 1.28, N.S.				
5. Has child previously attended nursery school, day nursery or play group?	Yes	1	1.6	219	32.7
	No	61	98.4	451	67.3
	z = 4.96, p < 0.1%				

the first few days of school, but after ten days of schooling only six were *still* showing signs of distress. Both these figures represent a slightly higher percentage of the sample than was found in the urban sample, but the differences are not statistically significant.

The child's initial attitude to other children and to the teacher were also rated on this first schedule on a three point scale and the results are shown in Table 99. It can be seen here that the rural sample was rated somewhat more favourably in initial attitudes, though again the differences are not significant.

With long journeys to and from school, it might

Table 99

Initial attitude to other children and to teacher

Rural and Urban samples

	Rural (N = 62)		Urban (N=670)	
	n	%	n	%
Attitude to other children:				
1. Very positive (i.e. very friendly)	18	29.0	221	33.0
2. Positive on the whole (i.e. quite friendly)	37	59.7	329	49.1
3. Uncertain or negative (shy, withdrawn or actually hostile)	7	11.3	120	17.9
	z = 0.08, N.S.			
Attitude to class teacher:				
1. Very positive	30	48.4	272	40.6
2. Positive on the whole	28	45.2	305	45.5
3. Uncertain or negative	4	6.5	93	13.9
	z = 1.50, N.S.			

be expected that the rural sample would show more signs of tiredness in school. The teachers' ratings of the children's apparent tiredness by the end of the school day are given in Table 100 and here there is a statistically significant difference, with fewer of the urban sample showing any signs of tiredness. Teachers with fairly large numbers of new entrants may have had little opportunity to observe the behaviour of individual children, but certain problems of behaviour are likely to have become apparent even after only ten days of school. In the rural sample, seven children were said to have shown some form of unusual or difficult behaviour in school, four had wet themselves (on one or two occasions only) and two had soiled themselves. None had been sick in school. This pattern of early behaviour problems shows little difference between the rural and urban samples. Teachers were asked to rate the child's

initial overall adjustment to school on a three point scale and the results are given in Table 101 together with those of the urban sample who have slightly, but not significantly, lower ratings.

Teachers were also asked about the level of the children's interest in the material and experiences provided at school and about their ability to read, write and draw on entry, through here again opportunities for observation were limited at this stage and some children were rated as 'not observed'. No child in the rural sample was said to be able to read at all from a book, whereas twenty of the urban sample were so rated. Only four were said to be able to write their own name, as compared with ninety-three of the urban sample. Twenty of the fifty-four children (37%) rated were said to be able to draw simple recognizable objects, which again is a lower percentage than the 48% who were rated as able to do so in the

Table 100

Signs of tiredness in children: Rural and Urban samples

Rating	Rural (N = 62)		Urban (N=670)	
	n	%	n	%
1. No sign of tiredness at end of school day	27	43.5	444	66.3
2. Somewhat tired at end of school day	31	50.0	207	30.9
3. Definitely overtired at end of school day	4	6.5	19	2.8
$z = 3.54$, $p < 0.1\%$				

Table 101

Rating of children's initial overall adjustment to school Rural and Urban samples

Rating	Rural (N = 62)		Urban (N=670)	
	n	%	n	%
1. Very good (child seems very happy and settled)	33	53.2	291	43.4
2. Average (has settled quite well and seems quite happy on the whole)	24	38.7	347	51.8
3. Poor (seems definitely unhappy or unsettled)	5	8.1	32	4.8
$z = 1.00$, N.S.				

195

urban sample. This latter result is statistically significant (z = 2.85, p < 1%). It would seem then, that fewer children in the rural sample than in the urban sample enter school with any previous experience of the skills they will learn in school.

B. GENERAL CLASSROOM ACTIVITIES

Children are presented with a wide variety of activities in the reception class of the infant school. Some of these are specifically related to the two chief skills learned in the infant school, reading and number, but others are of a more general nature, and it is these which will be discussed in this section. On the second school schedule teachers were asked to give the children's preferred activities in the classroom. Not all children showed any particular preference, but Table 102 shows the preferences which teachers were able to observe for the rural and urban samples. It seems that teachers were able to specify the preferences of rather more of the rural sample, possibly because, in smaller classes, they had more chance to observe or even ask the children. For these children who did have an observed preference, the most frequent choice in both urban and rural samples was manipulative play. The rural sample showed a slightly higher percentage of those rated as choosing pre-reading or number activities (20% of those rated) than the urban sample (12.6% of those rated) but otherwise differences between the two samples were very slight.

After the first term in school teachers were asked to rate the child's interest in the materials and experiences provided in the school, his use of play materials and the quality of his creative activities. The results are given in Table 103.

A smaller proportion of the rural sample was reported as showing a very active interest in the materials and experiences provided but the use

Table 102

Preferred classroom activities : Rural and Urban samples

	Rural (N = 60)		Urban (N=689)	
	n	%	n	%
1. Vigorous physical play	6	10.0	34	4.9
2. Manipulative play (e.g. constructional, sand, water play)	19	31.7	152	22.1
3. Social/dramatic play	4	6.7	39	5.7
4. Painting/drawing/musical activities	7	11.7	70	10.2
5. Pre-reading, number activities	9	15.0	43	6.2
6. Other forms	0	0	4	0.6
7. No particular preference shown	12	20.0	211	30.6
8. Combination of activities 1-6	3	5.0	136	19.7

Table 103

Ratings of use of/interest in play materials

and quality of creative activities

Rural and Urban samples

	Rural (N = 60)		Urban (N=689)	
	n	%	n	%
Interest in materials/activities				
1. Very active interest	14	23.3	224	32.5
2. Quite active interest	41	68.3	403	58.5
3. Little active interest in anything provided	5	8.3	62	9.0
z = 1.06, N.S.				
Use of play materials				
1. Play usually leads to end product (e.g. model or painting) or successful completion of activity	22	36.7	232	33.7
2. Play sometimes leads to end product/successful completion of activity	33	55.0	337	48.9
3. Play rarely or never leads to end product/successful completion of activity (e.g. repetitive manipulative play)	5	8.3	120	17.4
z = 1.10, N.S.				
Quality of creative activities				
1. Often shows imagination/ originality in use of play materials	18	30.0	139	20.2
2. Sometimes	36	60.0	409	59.4
3. Rarely/never	6	10.0	141	20.5
z = 2.26, p < 5%				

Table 104

Ratings of use of materials and creative activities over a three-year period
Rural and Urban samples

Rating	End of first year				End of second year				End of third year			
	Rural (N=59)		Urban (N=655)		Rural (N=58)		Urban (N=589)		Rural (N=58)		Urban (N=557)	
	n	%	n	%	n	%	n	%	n	%	n	%
Use of Play Materials												
Play usually leads to end product or successful completion of activity	38	64.4	286	43.7	38	65.5	317	53.8	30	51.7	311	55.8
Play sometimes leads to end product or successful completion of activity	20	33.9	291	44.4	20	34.5	272	46.2	27	46.6	191	34.3
Play rarely or never leads to end product or successful completion of activity	1	1.7	78	11.9	not included		not included		1	1.7	55	9.9
	z = 3.28, p <1%				z = 1.57, N.S.				z = 0.08, N.S.			
Quality of Creative Activities												
Often shows imagination/originality in some or all of the following areas: free writing, story telling, handwork, painting, dramatic work	–		–		15	25.9	150	25.5	16	27.6	178	32.0
Sometimes shows imagination/originality in some or all of these areas	–		–		34	58.6	324	55.0	39	67.2	279	50.1
Rarely or never shows imagination/originality in any area	–		–		9	15.5	115	19.5	3	5.2	100	18.0
					z = 0.36, N.S.				z = 0.61, N.S.			

198

made of these materials was rated more highly, the differences in imaginativeness and originality being statistically significant. Ratings of the use of play materials and quality of creative activities were also made at the end of each year in school, and whereas the rural sample remained ahead of the urban sample in the quality of creative activities, the differences ceased to be statistically significant. Ratings of the use of play material at the end of the first year showed a highly significant difference between the groups, with the rural sample rated higher, but, by the end of the third year, the urban children were very slightly ahead. Details of these ratings are given in Table 104.

At the end of each year, teachers rated the child's usual level of concentration in activities of a more structured kind such as reading or pre-reading and number activities. At all these stages the rural sample were given slightly lower ratings on concentration than the urban sample, though none of the differences was statistically significant. Table 105 shows the ratings given at the end of the final year for both samples. Although rather more of the urban sample received the highest rating, there were also slightly more receiving the lowest rating.

C. SOCIAL AND EMOTIONAL ADJUSTMENT

It has been stated by some teachers that children who live in isolated homes find more difficulty in communicating with other children and with their class teacher. At several stages during the three years, teachers were asked to rate the child's relationship with other children in the class and with the teacher. Tables 106 to 109 show the results of these two ratings made at the end of the first term and the end of each year in school for both the rural and urban samples. The only differences between the two groups which are statistically significant are the levels of co-operation with other children at the end of the first and second years, but in all of these items the rural sample has somewhat higher ratings. Their lack of pre-school contact with other children and with the school does not seem to have inhibited their relationships once they entered school. No rural child was ever rated as hostile to the class teacher and only one child, at one stage, was rated as unco-operative with other children.

In the 'settling-in' period, the rural children were found to show slightly more signs of distress at 'leaving their parents', but after the first ten

Table 105

Child's level of concentration after three years' schooling
Rural and Urban samples

Rating	Rural (N = 58)		Urban (N=557)	
	n	%	n	%
1. Usually concentrates very well for quite long periods; ignores distractions	16	27.6	214	38.4
2. Varies, but can concentrate quite well if interested	33	56.9	236	42.4
3. Usually lacks concentration e.g. concentrates for a few minutes only, easily distracted	9	15.5	107	19.2
z = 0.79, N.S.				

199

Table 106

Child's relationship with other children and class teacher
after one term: Rural and Urban samples

	Rural (N=60)		Urban (N=689)	
	n	%	n	%
Relationship with other children				
1. Very positive (very friendly/ interested in other children)	26	43.3	238	34.5
2. Positive on the whole (quite friendly/interested in other children)	25	41.7	343	49.8
3. Uncertain or negative (shy/ withdrawn or actually hostile)	9	15.0	108	15.7
z = 1.01, N.S.				
Relationship with class teacher				
1. Very positive (very friendly/ responsive)	33	55.0	341	49.5
2. Positive (friendly or responsive on whole)	24	40.0	269	39.0
3. Uncertain or negative (shy, withdrawn, hostile)	3	5.0	79	11.5
z = 1.07, N.S.				

days of schooling only three rural children continued to show some signs of distress. It will be recalled from Section A that on School Schedule 1, completed after the first ten days of the children's schooling, the rural sample had a significantly higher proportion of children showing signs of tiredness at the end of the school day than the urban sample, At the end of the first term, the rural sample was still showing rather more signs of tiredness at the end of the day, though the difference between the rural and urban samples was not significant. Three rural children were showing definite signs of tiredness at this stage, although none had a long journey to and from school.

At the end of the first term in school, teachers rated the child's degree of self-dependence in dressing, his level of competence in managing school or class routines and his degree of self-reliance in classroom activities. Table 110 shows the results of these ratings.

The ratings in Table 110 show that the rural sample children were more dependent on adult help in dressing themselves and rather less self-reliant in carrying out classroom activities without much help from the teacher. The ratings of self-dependence in dressing show a significant difference between the rural and urban groups. In rating competence in school or class routine, however, the rural children fare better, possibly because in the smaller rural schools, the chances of getting lost or losing one's possessions are less. Very often, too, the new school entrants will be in a class with older children who help to 'look after' them.

Table 107

Child's level of co-operation with other children: Rural and Urban samples

Rating	At end of 1st year				At end of 2nd year				At end of 3rd year			
	Rural (N = 59)		Urban (N=655)		Rural (N = 58)		Urban (N=589)		Rural (N = 58)		Urban (N=557)	
	n	%	n	%	n	%	n	%	n	%	n	%
1. Very co-operative (usually willing and able to co-operate well, e.g. take roles in dramatic play, take share of responsibility in group activity)	36	61.0	295	45.0	31	53.4	229	38.9	30	51.7	258	46.3
2. Fairly co-operative (achieves simple forms of co-operation only, e.g. sharing materials, taking turns, taking part in simple class games, etc.)	23	39.0	330	50.4	26	44.8	329	55.9	28	48.3	276	49.6
3. Unco-operative (cannot or will not share materials, take turns in play, class games, etc. May disrupt activity of others or may be afraid of other children)	0	0	30	4.6	1	1.7	31	5.3	0	0	23	4.1
	z = 2.46,p< 5%				z = 2.18, p <5%				z = 0.95, N.S.			

Table 108

Child's relationship with class teacher : Rural and Urban samples

Rating	At end of 1st year				At end of 2nd year				At end of 3rd year			
	Rural (N = 59)		Urban (N=655)		Rural (N = 58)		Urban (N=589)		Rural (N = 58)		Urban (N=557)	
	n	%	n	%	n	%	n	%	n	%	n	%
1. Very positive (very friendly or responsive)	39	66.1	364	55.5	29	50.0	271	46.0	31	53.4	244	43.8
2. Positive (friendly or responsive on the whole)	18	30.5	237	36.2	24	41.4	255	43.3	26	44.8	252	45.2
3. Uncertain or negative (shy, withdrawn or hostile)	2	3.4	54	8.2	5	8.6	63	10.7	1	1.7	61	10.9
	z=1.62, N.S.				z = 0.56, N.S.				z = 1.82, N.S.			

Table 109

Descriptions of children rated as uncertain or negative

Rural and Urban samples

| Rating | At end of first year | | | | At end of second year | | | | At end of third year | | | |
| | Rural | | Urban | | Rural | | Urban | | Rural | | Urban | |
	n	%	n	%	n	%	n	%	n	%	n	%
1. Shy	2	3.4	32	4.9	1	1.7	27	4.6	1	1.7	28	5.0
2. Withdrawn	0	0	18	2.7	4	6.9	27	4.6	0	0	20	3.6
3. Hostile	0	0	4	0.6	0	0	9	1.5	0	0	13	2.3

Percentages in this table are of the total number in the samples.

Table 110

Children's social competence
Rural and Urban samples

Ratings after 1 term in school	Rural (N=60)		Urban (N=689)	
	n	%	n	%
A. Self-dependence in dressing				
1. Quite independent of adult help	4	6.7	165	23.9
2. Can dress self but may need help with buttons, laces, tie, bow, etc.	50	83.3	482	69.9
3. Very dependent on adult help in dressing	6	10.0	42	6.1
z = 2.98, p < 1%				
B. Competence in school/class routine				
1. Very competent and reliable	20	33.3	202	29.3
2. Quite competent and reliable	38	63.3	400	58.0
3. Not very competent or reliable (e.g. gets lost in school or loses/fails to recognize own possessions etc.)	2	3.3	87	12.6
z = 1.37, N.S.				
C. Self-reliance in class activities				
1. Very self reliant (often carries out activities without asking much help from teacher)	13	21.7	214	31.1
2. Fairly self reliant (can carry out activities on own, but quite ready to ask teacher to help)	37	61.7	367	53.3
3. Lacking in self reliance (cannot keep up activity for long without approaching teacher for help/reassurance)	10	16.7	108	15.7
z = 1.13, N.S.				

Behaviour and adjustment to school

Throughout the three years teachers were asked to rate the child's general level of adjustment to school and also certain specific aspects of the child's behaviour in the classroom. Not all of these results will be quoted here, but to give some idea of the prevalence of behaviour problems in the sample and to compare this with that in the urban sample, the ratings given in the schedules completed at the end of the first and third years are given in Tables 111, 112 and 113. The first six questions are referred to as the six 'Stott pointers', which are quoted in the Manual to the Bristol Social Adjustment Guides by Stott (1966). The seventh is an overall rating of adjustment drawn from a classroom behaviour inventory devised by Earl S. Schaefer (unpublished to date). A fuller reference to the incidence of behaviour problems in both the rural and urban sample can be found in Chazan and Jackson (1971, 1974). At the end of the third year, the rural sample had fewer adverse ratings on all six of the Stott pointers and no child was rated as 'aggressive' or 'not getting on well with other children' at this stage. At both stages none of the rural children was given the most adverse Schaefer rating of overall level of adjustment and slightly more of them were rated as 'well adjusted'. However, these differences between the rural and urban samples are not significant, except in the case of the total number of adverse items rated on the Stott pointers at the end of the third year, where the rural sample have fewer than the urban sample.

In the urban sample the tendency over the two year period is for the proportion of children rated adversely to increase. Though the size of the increase is comparatively small, the direction is the same for each behaviour item, whereas for the rural sample the reported incidence of these behaviour problems has decreased slightly. Not too much importance should be placed on this result, however, since the numbers in the urban sample had fallen considerably during the two year period and it could be that those who left the sample were not representative as far as behaviour problems were concerned.

The rural sample certainly seems to have had few children with really severe problems or multiple problems of behaviour. None received the lowest Schaefer rating at either stage and, at the later stage, none had four or more adverse ratings on the Stott pointers, only three children having more than one adverse rating (see Table 113). At the earlier stage it was found that almost half of the reported behaviour problems were concentrated in one school, though this was not the case at the later stage. (The test of significance used for these adjustment items was 'chi-square' as this was the test used in the earlier analysis of behaviour problems (Chazan and Jackson, 1971).)

D. ORAL LANGUAGE SKILLS

Patterns of speech and the ability to communicate verbally with other children and with the class teacher are important factors in the educative process. Many children in the rural sample may have had limited opportunity to learn or practise these skills outside their home. Ratings of three aspects of the child's oral skills were made after one term in school and again after two years in school, these aspects being clarity of speech, range of vocabulary in spoken language and power of oral expression. Table 114 gives the results of the teachers' ratings at the earlier stage, showing that the rural sample in fact received somewhat higher ratings on all three items. The same items were rated again after two and three years and the results of these later ratings are given in Table 115.

From Tables 114 and 115 it can be seen that the number of children in the rural sample whose speech was rated as 'very clear, precise and well-articulated', drops steadily during this period, giving a change-over in the relative positions of the rural and urban samples, the final difference being a significant one. This could suggest that, whereas mixing with other children in the school setting tends to improve the clarity of the urban children, it has the reverse effect on the rural sample. One possible explanation of this fact could be that, up to school entry, the speech patterns heard by the rural sample could have been primarily the adult pattern of their parents, whereas the urban children will have mixed much more with other children, thus picking up their immature speech patterns (particularly as most of the children free to play with the child ready for school entry will be *younger* children, the older ones being in school during the day). This, however, does not account for the urban children overtaking the rural after three

Table 111

Behaviour problems (Stott pointers) at end of first and third years

Rural and Urban samples

Question	Answer	At end of the first year Rural (N=60) n	%	Urban (N=664) n	%	At end of third year Rural (N=58) n	%	Urban (N=544) n	%
1. Is the child's behaviour such as you would expect of a normal alert child of his/her age?	Yes	53	88.3	597	89.9	54	93.1	481	88.4
	No	7	11.7	67	10.1	4	6.9	63	11.6
		$\chi^2 = 0.03$, N.S.				$\chi^2 = 0.74$, N.S.			
2. Is the child exceptionally quiet, timid or withdrawn	No	55	91.7	601	90.5	55	94.8	476	87.5
	Yes	5	8.3	63	9.5	3	5.2	68	12.5
		$\chi^2 = 0.004$, N.S.				$\chi^2 = 2.05$, N.S.			
3. Is the child restless in a way that seriously hinders his/her learning?	No	57	95.0	602	90.7	56	96.6	485	89.2
	Yes	3	5.0	62	9.3	2	3.4	59	10.8
		$\chi^2 = 0.79$, N.S.				$\chi^2 = 2.39$, N.S.			
4. Is the child very aggressive?	No	57	95.0	625	94.1	58	100.0	511	93.9
	Yes	3	5.9	39	5.9	0	0	33	6.1
		$\chi^2 = 0.0001$, N.S.				$\chi^2 = 2.64$, N.S.			
5. Does the child get on well with other children?	Yes	57	95.0	625	94.1	58	100.0	513	94.3
	No	3	5.0	39	5.9	0	0	31	5.7
		$\chi^2 = 0.0001$, N.S.				$\chi^2 = 2.42$, N.S.			
6. Is there anything in the child's behaviour to make you think that he might be unstable or suffer from nervous trouble?	No	53	88.3	595	89.6	55	94.8	476	87.5
	Yes	7	11.7	69	10.4	3	5.2	68	12.5
		$\chi^2 = 0.008$, N.S.				$\chi^2 = 2.05$, N.S.			

For each value of chi-square in this table there was one degree of freedom.

Table 112

Rating of overall level of adjustment (Schaefer rating) at end of first and third years

Rural and Urban samples

Rating	At end of the first year				At end of the third year			
	Rural (N = 60)		Urban (N=664)		Rural (N = 58)		Urban (N=544)	
	n	%	n	%	n	%	n	%
1. Well-adjusted: a child who is well-adjusted in his relationship with others and in his activities	25	41.7	229	34.5	26	44.8	211	38.8
2. No significant problems: a child who gets on reasonably well, and has little or no difficulty in adjusting to others or to classroom activities	28	46.7	338	50.9	24	41.4	266	48.9
3. Somewhat disturbed: a child who has moderate difficulties in adjusting, and to whom growing up represents something of a struggle	7	11.7	90	13.6	8	13.8	56	10.3
4. Very disturbed: a child who has, or at his present rate is likely to have, serious problems of adjustment and needs specialist help because of such problems.	0	0	7	1.1	0	0	11	2.0
	X^2 = 0.18, N.S.				X^2 = 0.01, N.S.			

For X^2 test, numbers in categories 1,2 and 3,4 are combined (1 d.f.)

Table 113

Number of adverse ratings on Stott pointers

Rural and Urban samples

| | At end of first year | | | | At end of third year | | | |
| | Rural (N=60) | | Urban (N=664) | | Rural (N=58) | | Urban (N=544) | |
	n	%	n	%	n	%	n	%
no adverse ratings	49	81.7	500	75.3	50	86.2	394	72.4
1 adverse rating	3	5.0	76	11.4	5	8.6	70	12.9
2 adverse ratings	2	3.3	33	5.0	2	3.4	29	5.3
3 adverse ratings	4	6.7	30	4.5	1	1.7	24	4.4
4+ adverse ratings	2	3.3	25	3.8	0	0	27	5.0
	χ^2 = 2.77, N.S.				χ^2 = 6.02, p <5%			

For χ^2 test (d.f.=2) the following three categories were used:

    those with no adverse ratings
    those with 1or 2 adverse ratings
    those with 3+ adverse ratings

Table 114

Patterns of speech at end of first term
Rural and Urban samples

Rating at end of first term	Rural (N = 60)		Urban (N=689)	
	n	%	n	%
a) Clarity of speech:				
1. very clear, precise and well articulated	35	58.3	310	45.0
2. quite clear on whole (some distortion e.g. 'wobin' for 'robin')	19	31.7	307	44.5
3. difficult to follow due to marked immaturity or defect	6	10.0	72	10.4
	z = 1.64, N.S.			
b) Range of vocabulary in spoken language				
1. wide range of vocabulary for age including variety of words	11	18.3	89	12.9
2. adequate vocabulary for age	42	70.0	491	71.2
3. very limited vocabulary for age-repetitive use of words	7	11.7	109	15.8
	z = 1.20, N.S.			
c) Power of oral expression				
1. very fluent and articulate	12	20.0	134	19.4
2. can express himself adequately	41	68.3	474	68.8
3. power of expression markedly poor - child cannot communicate adequately	7	11.7	81	11.8
	z = 0.03, N.S.			

Table 115

Patterns of speech after two and three years
Rural and Urban samples

Rating	End of second year				End of third year			
	Rural (N = 58)		Urban (N=589)		Rural (N = 58)		Urban (N=557)	
	n	%	n	%	n	%	n	%
a) Clarity of speech								
1. very clear, precise and well articulated	28	48.3	246	41.8	16	27.6	267	47.9
2. quite clear on whole (some distortion e.g. 'wobin' for 'robin')	22	37.9	287	48.7	40	69.0	257	46.1
3. difficult to follow due to marked immaturity or defect	8	13.8	56	9.5	2	3.4	33	5.9
	z = 0.38, N.S.				z = 2.42, p < 1%			
b) Range of vocabulary in spoken language								
1. wide vocabulary for age including variety of words	13	22.4	78	13.2	11	19.0	85	15.3
2. adequate vocabulary for age	37	63.8	435	73.9	41	70.7	407	73.1
3. very limited vocabulary for age - repetitive use of words	8	13.8	76	12.9	6	10.3	65	11.7
	z = 1.03, N.S.				z = 0.57, N.S.			
c) Power of oral expression								
1. very fluent and articulate	17	29.3	125	21.2	13	22.4	134	24.1
2. can express himself adequately	32	55.2	386	65.5	39	67.2	355	63.7
3. power of expression markedly poor - child cannot communicate adequately	9	15.5	78	13.2	6	10.3	68	12.2
	z = 0.67, N.S.				z = 0.11, N.S.			

years in school. In the Ministry of Education Report, 'Education in Rural Wales' (1960) it is stated that, in primary schools, training in the use of language is something of prime importance, since the rural child, in contrast with the urban child, is often reticent and slower in reaction and speech.

Listening and understanding skills are as important in the classroom as those of speech. Teachers rated two aspects of these: the child's understanding of stories he has heard and his ability to follow oral instructions. These ratings were made at the same three stages as those for speech patterns and are shown in Table 116. No significant differences between the groups emerge and there seems to be little change in the pattern of ratings over the three years.

E. READING AND RELATED ACTIVITIES

Many of the other ratings referred to earlier in this chapter are somewhat subjective, but the questions concerning pre-reading and reading activities and number concepts required more specific answers and should be more objective measures. On each of the six school schedules teachers were asked for some information on the children's progress in reading or related skills. As was reported earlier in the chapter, fewer children in the rural sample entered school already able to read or write their name than in the urban sample. By the end of the first term, some children in both samples had started on a reading scheme, but the majority were still engaged on pre-reading activities. Table 117 shows the pattern of the children's progress from pre-reading activities through the stages of the basic reading scheme. The categories marked with an * are the highest rating for that schedule and hence include anyone beyond that level. The category of 'beyond the basic reading scheme' was not introduced until Schedule 5, at the end of the second year.

From these figures, it appears that the urban sample was making significantly greater progress in reading at the earlier stages, but by the end of the first year the difference was only slight, and indeed a smaller percentage of the rural sample was still engaged in pre-reading activities only by then. Differences between the two groups remained slight at the end of the second and third years, by

which time *all* the children in the rural sample had begun a reading scheme.

In the early schedules, over two-thirds of the children had not started a reading scheme, so that in order to examine differences between the samples, it is necessary to record the children's progress in pre-reading skills. Table 118 shows the ratings on seven pre-reading activities for those children who were not reading at the end of the first term and little difference is shown between the two groups here. Pre-reading activities were rated again at later stages, but, since the numbers who had not embarked on a reading scheme became very small, no further results will be quoted here.

In addition to the actual level of reading reached, questions were asked about the children's interest in reading, comprehension and use of phonics. Some of these questions obviously can be answered only when the child has progressed to a reading scheme, so that the numbers rated for these questions will vary. The majority of children start learning to read using the 'look and say' method but by the later stages in the infant school most will also have been taught to build words phonically. Teachers were asked to rate the child's ability to do this at the end of the second and third years, at the earlier stage a 'not observed' category being included. The numbers 'not observed' are included in Table 119, but are *not* included in the calculation of z. Two urban children were not rated on the later schedule since they were still not reading at this stage.

At the final stage, when most children had progressed beyond the very simple reading books, teachers were asked to rate the child's comprehension of what he read. Again the two 'non-readers' could not be rated here. The results are given in Table 120.

Neither the ratings of phonics nor of comprehension show overall significant differences between rural and urban samples, though on both items the rural sample had a smaller proportion of children given the lowest of the three ratings. Only four rural children had little or no ability to build words phonically by the end of their third year and only one had *very* limited comprehension of what he read. In comparing the numbers in the *lowest* category with those in all other categories, the value of z is statistically significant in the case of the later rating of phonic ability and in the rating of comprehension.

Table 116

Children's understanding of stories and ability to follow oral instructions

Rural and Urban samples

Item	Rating	After one term Rural (N=60) n	%	After one term Urban (N=689) n	%	At end of second year Rural (N=58) n	%	At end of second year Urban (N=589) n	%	At end of third year Rural (N=58) n	%	At end of third year Urban (N=557) n	%
1. Understanding of stories	very well	22	36.7	327	47.5	26	46.4	261	46.0	27	47.4	263	50.1
	quite well	31	51.7	275	39.9	28	50.0	262	46.2	28	49.1	235	44.8
	poorly	7	11.7	87	12.6	2	3.6	44	7.8	2	3.5	27	5.1
	* not observed	0		0		2		22		1		32	
		z = 1.17, N.S.				z = 0.26, N.S.				z = 0.15, N.S.			
2. Ability to follow oral instructions	very well	23	38.3	265	38.5	21	36.2	213	36.2	24	41.4	256	46.0
	quite well	33	55.0	348	50.5	30	51.7	308	52.3	31	53.4	253	45.4
	poorly	4	6.7	76	11.0	7	12.1	68	11.5	3	5.2	48	8.6
		z = 0.27, N.S.				z = 0.06, N.S.				z = 0.23, N.S.			

* Number falling in not observed category not included in percentage figures or 'tau' analysis

212

Table 117

Reading levels at various stages throughout the three years

Rural and Urban samples

Level reached in reading scheme	After one term				After two terms				At end of 1st year				At end of 2nd year				At end of 3rd year			
	Rural (N=60)		Urban (N=689)		Rural (N=60)		Urban (N=664)		Rural (N=59)		Urban (N=655)		Rural (N=58)		Urban (N=589)		Rural (N=58)		Urban (N=557)	
	n	%	n	%	n	%	n	%	n	%	n	%	n	%	n	%	n	%	n	%
On pre-reading activities only	46	76.7	454	65.9	17	28.3	161	24.2	7	11.9	101	15.4	0	0	9	1.5	0	0	2	0.4
On introductory book	5	8.3	112	16.3	25	41.7	193	29.1	13	22.0	135	20.6	1	1.7	23	3.9	2	3.4	15	2.7
On book 1	9	15.0	74	10.7	10	16.7	152	22.9	20	33.9	143	21.8	9	15.5	67	11.4	3	5.2	19	3.4
On book 2	0	0	49	7.1	5	8.3	94	14.2	12	20.3	150	22.9	12	20.7	120	20.4	3	5.2	42	7.5
On book 3	-		-		3	5.0	41	6.2	4	6.8	61	9.3	21	36.2	105	17.8	8	13.8	88	15.8
On book 4 or beyond	-		-		0	0	23	3.5	3	5.1	65	9.9	12	20.7	234	39.7	28	48.3	247	44.3
Beyond basic reading scheme	-		-		-		-		-		-		3	5.2	31	5.3	14	24.1	144	25.9
	z = 1.62, N.S.				z = 2.07, p < 5%				z = 0.74, N.S.				z = 1.37, N.S.				z = 0.03, N.S.			

Table 118

Pre-reading abilities rated at end of first term
Rural and Urban samples

Item	Rating	Rural (N = 46)		Urban (N=454)	
		n	%	n	%
1. Matching shapes or pictures:	Easily and efficiently	22	47.8	190	41.9
	Quite efficiently on whole	14	30.4	217	47.8
	Unable to do so yet	10	21.7	47	10.4
	z = 0.05, N.S.				
2. Matching words to pictures:	Easily and efficiently	13	28.3	35	7.7
	Quite efficiently on whole	12	26.1	193	42.5
	Unable to do so yet	21	45.7	226	49.8
	z = 1.65, N.S.				
3. Matching words to words:	Easily and efficiently	13	28.3	94	20.7
	Quite efficiently on whole	13	28.3	180	39.6
	Unable to do so yet	20	43.5	180	39.6
	z = 0.08, N.S.				
4. Discriminating word/letter sounds:	Very well	5	10.9	52	11.5
	Quite well	19	41.3	206	45.4
	Poorly	22	47.8	196	43.2
	z = 0.44, N.S.				
5. Recognition of simple words/ phrases on flash cards:	7 words or more	13	28.3	86	18.9
	Between 1 and 6 words	26	56.5	272	59.9
	None	7	15.2	96	21.1
	z = 1.43, N.S.				
6. Interest in looking at picture/story books:	Very keen interest	9	19.6	93	20.5
	Quite keen interest	27	58.7	269	59.3
	Little/no interest	10	21.7	92	20.3
	z = 0.12, N.S.				
7. Overall level of reading readiness:	Ready for introduction to reading scheme	8	17.4	89	19.6
	Needs more pre-reading experience	28	60.9	237	52.2
	Unready	10	21.7	128	28.2
	z = 0.33, N.S.				

N.B. Children already 'reading' not rated on these items.

Table 119

Children's ability to build words phonically : Rural and Urban samples

| Level of proficiency | At end of second year | | | | At end of third year | | | |
| | Rural (N = 58) | | Urban (N=589) | | Rural (N = 58) | | Urban (N=557) | |
	n	%	n	%	n	%	n	%
1. very proficient – can build most phonically regular words	15	26.3	127	23.4	19	32.8	213	38.4
2. fairly proficient – can build easier words	26	45.6	235	43.3	35	60.3	247	44.5
3. little or no proficiency	16	28.0	180	33.2	4	6.9	95	17.1
4. *not observed	1		47		0		2	
	z = 0.69, N.S.				z = 0.13, N.S.			

* Number falling in not observed category not included in percentage figures or 'tau' analysis.

215

Table 120

Children's comprehension when reading
Rural and Urban samples

Level of comprehension	At end of third year			
	Rural (N = 58)		Urban (N=555)	
	n	%	n	%
1. comprehends very well	20	34.5	229	41.3
2. comprehends quite well	37	63.8	240	43.2
3. poor, very limited comprehension	1	1.7	86	15.5
	z = 0.23, N.S.			

Table 121 shows the ratings of the children's level of interest in reading at four stages. Again there are no significant differences between the groups, but smaller proportions of the rural sample fall in the lowest category. There appear to be some fluctuations of interest in reading over the period in both samples. Perhaps the most striking difference between the groups is in the numbers rated as having little or no interest, particularly at the final stage, when *no* rural children are rated in this category, whereas over 15 per cent of the urban children receive this rating. Comparing the numbers in this lowest category with the numbers in both the other categories, the differences between the two samples is statistically significant at the 0.5% level (z = 3.08).

In most schools writing skills are developed alongside those of reading, beginning with the children tracing or copying, writing their own name and leading on, at the later stages, to 'free writing'. The earliest rating in the area of mechanical writing skills was made by the teachers after one term, when they were asked whether the child could copy words correctly. Similar ratings were made after two terms and at the end of the first and second years. Some of these ratings are given

in Table 122. At each stage the rural sample has a smaller proportion of children in the lowest category ('unable to copy words') and, although at the earlier stage proportionately fewer rural children are given the highest rating, by the end of the second year they have overtaken the urban sample and the difference at this stage almost reaches the 5% level of statistical significance.

In free writing a rather similar picture emerges (see Table 123), with the rural sample initially given lower ratings but 'catching up' on the urban sample by the end of the second year (no differences being significant). Indeed, the overall picture of progress in reading and related skills is one of the rural sample consistently having fewer children given the lowest rating (at the later stages at least) and of the rural sample initially being behind the urban sample in these skills, but catching up during the period of this study. This picture of little difference between the groups at the final stage is supported by the results of the reading tests (see Table 131), which show no significant differences in reading skills.

On the sixth school schedule, completed during the children's final infant school year, the teachers were asked to rate the quality of the sentence

216

Table 121

Children's level of interest in reading

Rural and Urban samples

Rating	After two terms				At end of 1st year				At end of 2nd year				At end of 3rd year			
	Rural (N = 43)		Urban (N=503)		Rural (N = 52)		Urban (N=554)		Rural (N = 58)		Urban (N=580)		Rural (N = 58)		Urban (N=555)	
	n	%	n	%	n	%	n	%	n	%	n	%	n	%	n	%
1. Very keen interest	19	44.2	186	37.0	21	40.4	207	37.4	19	32.8	236	40.7	22	37.9	222	40.0
2. Fairly keen interest	24	55.8	260	51.7	27	51.9	289	52.2	33	56.9	280	48.3	36	62.1	245	44.1
3. Little /no interest	0	0	57	11.3	4	7.7	58	10.5	6	10.3	64	11.0	0	0	88	15.9
	z = 1.53, N.S.				z = 0.48, N.S.				z = 0.83, N.S.				z = 0.97, N.S.			

Note: Children on pre-reading activities only were not rated.

217

Table 122

Ratings of child's ability to copy words
Rural and Urban samples

Rating	At end of first term			
	Rural (N = 60)		Urban (N=689)	
	n	%	n	%
1. Easily, neatly and correctly	16	26.7	235	34.1
2. Fairly frequent reversals or omissions -positioning of letters rather hap-hazard	35	58.3	286	41.5
3. Scribbles or makes repetitive strokes, makes no effort to copy	9	15.0	168	24.4
z = 0.01, N.S.				

Rating	At end of first year				At end of second year			
	Rural (N = 59)		Urban (N=655)		Rural (N = 58)		Urban (N=589)	
	n	%	n	%	n	%	n	%
1. Easily and efficiently	32	54.2	348	53.1	41	70.7	350	59.4
2. Quite efficiently (may have some difficulties/ make some errors)	22	37.3	223	34.0	16	27.6	204	34.6
3. Poorly/unable to do so yet	5	8.5	84	12.8	1	1.7	35	5.9
z = 0.34, N.S.					z = 1.71, N.S.			

construction shown in each child's free (i.e. spontaneous) writing. This is a linguistic rating in contrast to the ratings of mechanical writing skills discussed above. Table 124 shows that there was no significant difference between the rural and urban samples on this rating, although the urban sample has higher proportions of children in the highest and lowest categories.

Γ. MATHEMATICAL ACTIVITIES

The variety of approaches to mathematics in the primary schools makes objective assessment of progress rather difficult. However, the acquisition of certain basic concepts and skills in number work is a vital task in the infant school. Even at a fairly early stage children start to learn the basic

Table 123

Rating of child's free writing : Rural and Urban samples

Item	Rating	After two terms				At end of first year				At end of second year			
		Rural (N = 60)		Urban (N=664)		Rural (N = 59)		Urban (N=655)		Rural (N = 58)		Urban (N=589)	
		n	%	n	%	n	%	n	%	n	%	n	%
Child can write words unaided (regardless of spelling)	1. Easily and efficiently	0	0	21	3.2	4	6.8	31	4.7	12	20.7	108	18.3
	2. Quite efficiently on the whole	6	10.0	84	12.6	10	16.9	170	26.0	25	43.1	270	45.8
	3. Poorly/unable to do so yet	54	90.0	559	84.2	45	76.3	454	69.3	21	36.2	211	35.8
		z = 1.15, N.S.				z = 0.86, N.S.				z = 0.07, N.S.			

219

Table 124

Rating of child's sentence construction in free writing

Rural and Urban samples

| Rating | At end of third year | | | |
| | Rural (N = 58) | | Urban (N=557) | |
	n	%	n	%
1. Very well-constructed sentences with good variety of sentence patterns	7	12.1	118	21.2
2. Adequately constructed sentences but with less variety of sentence patterns	26	44.8	193	34.6
3. Sentences generally complete and correctly constructed but very short, simple and repetitive in pattern	20	34.5	155	27.8
4. Sentences very poorly constructed or incomplete e.g. missing out subject or verb	5	8.6	91	16.3
	z = 0.07, N.S.			

counting skills and the number symbols. At the end of the first term, teachers rated three such number skills and, as will be seen from Table 125, the majority of children had at least made a start on counting and matching the written number symbols to the appropriate number of objects. The rural sample had slightly higher ratings at this stage, but none of the differences reached the level of statistical significance.

At later stages, a slightly wider variety of number activities were rated and the scope of the ratings in the basic skills was widened as children began to handle larger numbers, to do simple addition sums, to tell the time and to handle simple money transactions. Tables 126 and 127 show the results of teachers' ratings of such activities at the end of each year or for the final two years. An interesting pattern emerges in the differences between the rural and urban groups here. By the end of the first year, it seems that the rural sample children have made great strides forward in mathematical activities and are well ahead of their urban fellows. Differences between the groups on all of the items rated at the end of

the first year are statistically significant at the 5 per cent level or below. By the end of the second year, the rural group is still ahead of the urban group on most items, significantly so in the 'objective' measures of counting and sums. The only item where this trend is reversed is the children's ability to handle money, where the rural children show significantly less ability. By this stage, many of the urban children will have had practical experience of shopping, very often on their own, outside the school. Local shops are considerably less accessible to many of the rural children, so that they are not so likely to have had this experience out of school.

By the end of the third year, the urban children appear to have caught up the rural children and, apart from the use of counting aids which the rural sample needed less often, there is little difference between the ratings of the two samples, though again the urban sample has somewhat more of the highest and the lowest ratings, as was found with reading skills.

However, this situation of little difference between the groups in mathematical skills at the

Table 125

Ratings of number activities at end of first term
Rural and Urban samples

Item	Rating	Rural (N = 60)		Urban (N=689)	
		n	%	n	%
1. Child can count correctly the number of objects in a group presented to him of:	6 or more objects	37	61.7	370	53.7
	Between 2 and 5 objects	20	33.3	269	39.0
	Not at all	3	5.0	50	7.3
	$z = 1.14$, N.S.				
2. Child can give a specified number of objects from a larger number presented to him:	6 or more objects	29	48.3	330	47.9
	Between 2 and 5 objects	27	45.0	278	40.3
	Not at all	4	6.7	81	11.8
	$z = 0.34$, N.S.				
3. Child can match written number symbol to corresponding number of objects:	6 or more objects	22	36.7	242	35.1
	Between 2 and 5 objects	27	45.0	256	37.2
	Not at all	11	18.3	191	27.7
	$z = 0.90$, N.S.				

later stage is not borne out by the results of the mathematics test given at the end of the third year, when the rural sample had a significantly higher mean score than the urban sample (see Table 131).

Two possible explanations are suggested here for this apparent anomaly. First, it is possible that, since the rural sample would appear to have acquired their number skills at an earlier stage, the concepts were more deeply implanted and more easily applied in the relatively strange test situation (the test used did *not* include formal 'sums'). Second, the mathematics test was a group test and it is possible that the rural sample, who were mostly tested in somewhat smaller groups than the urban sample, had a slight advantage here (though this reasoning could also be applied to the spelling test, where the results show no significant difference).

G. GENERAL

At the end of the final year, teachers were asked for three additional items of information: their prediction of the child's likely progress in the junior school or department, the amount of contact they had had with the child's parents

Table 126

Ratings of number activities over the three years

Rural and Urban samples

Item	Rating	At end of first year Rural (N=59) n	%	Urban (N=655) n	%	At end of second year Rural (N=58) n	%	Urban (N=589) n	%	At end of third year Rural (N=58) n	%	Urban (N=557) n	%
1. Ability to match written number symbols to number of objects in a group	over 20 objects	} 33	55.9	161	24.6	43	74.1	296	50.3	43	74.1	427	76.7
	11 – 20 objects					11	19.0	180	30.6	13	22.4	101	18.1
	6 – 10 objects	20	33.9	319	48.7	} 3	5.2	103	17.5	} 2	3.4	28	5.0
	2 – 6 objects	4	6.8	134	20.5							1	0.2
	not at all	2	3.4	41	6.3	1	1.7	10	1.7	0		1	0.2
		z = 4.75, p < 0.1%				z = 3.42, p < 0.1%				z = 0.27, N.S.			
2. Ability to do simple addition sums with totals of:	over 20	} 32	59.2	156	28.6	32	55.2	226	38.8	40	69.0	396	71.1
	11–20					17	29.3	176	30.2	16	27.6	115	20.6
	up to 10	18	33.3	215	39.4	8	13.8	149	25.6	2	3.4	39	7.0
	unable	4	7.4	175	32.0	1	1.7	31	5.3	0		7	1.3
	*not observed	5		109		0		7		0		0	
		z = 4.87, p < 0.1%				z = 2.73, p < 1%				z = 0.02, N.S.			

Continued on next page

222

3. How much use does child make of counting aids?

Category	N	%	N	%	N	%	N	%	N	%	N	%
no longer/only occasionally uses	–				27	46.6	193	32.8	34	58.6	271	48.7
needs or uses them quite often	–				22	37.9	217	36.8	23	39.7	174	31.2
needs or uses them always/nearly always	–				9	15.5	179	30.4	1	1.7	112	20.1
					z = 2.53, p< 2.5%				z = 2.30, p< 2.5%			

4. How well child understands basic number concepts?

Category	N	%	N	%	N	%	N	%	N	%	N	%
good	–				23	39.7	216	36.7	18	31.0	216	38.8
adequate	–				29	50.0	281	47.7	33	56.9	270	48.5
poor – little or no grasp	–				6	10.3	92	15.6	7	12.1	71	12.7
					z = 0.71, N.S.				z = 0.78, N.S.			

5. Level of interest in mathematical activities

Category	N	%	N	%	N	%	N	%	N	%	N	%
very keen interest	18	30.5	146	22.3	14	24.1	142	24.1	10	17.2	133	23.9
fairly keen interest	36	61.0	373	56.9	35	60.3	333	56.5	46	79.3	324	58.2
little or no interest	5	8.5	136	20.8	9	15.5	114	19.4	2	3.4	100	17.9
	z = 2.19, p< 5%				z = 0.31, N.S.				z = 0.69, N.S.			

* Number falling in not observed category not included in percentage figures or 'tau' analysis

Table 127

Further number activities : Rural and Urban samples

Rating	At end of second year				At end of third year			
	Rural (N=58)		Urban (N=589)		Rural (N=58)		Urban (N=557)	
	n	%	n	%	n	%	n	%
1. Child's ability to tell time:								
to within 5 minutes	3	5.2	85	14.4	15	25.9	241	43.3
to within quarter of an hour	21	36.2	122	20.7	24	41.4	113	20.3
to within half an hour	15	25.9	126	21.4	12	20.7	87	15.6
knows hours only	13	22.4	168	28.5	6	10.3	84	15.1
not at all	6	10.3	88	14.9	1	1.7	32	5.7
	z = 0.81, N.S.				z = 0.77, N.S.			
2. Child's ability to handle money in simple classroom shopping activities:								
very proficient - can handle amounts over 2s. (10p)*	4	6.9	83	14.4	17	29.3	171	30.7
fairly proficient	16	27.6	246	42.7	34	58.6	280	50.3
can handle pennies only	35	60.3	221	38.4	7	12.1	98	17.6
no knowledge of money	3	5.2	26	4.5	0	0	8	1.4
* not observed	0		13		0		0	
	z = 3.03, p <1%				z = 0.46, N.S.			

* Number falling in not observed category not included in percentage figures or 'tau' analysis.

224

Table 128

Children's likely progress in junior school/department

Rural and Urban samples

Rating	Rural (N = 58)		Urban (N=557)	
	n	%	n	%
1. No problems anticipated, should make satisfactory or good progress	35	60.3	309	55.5
2. May have some initial difficulties but should make satisfactory progress on the whole	16	27.6	162	29.1
3. Will almost certainly find difficulty	7	12.1	86	15.4
	z = 0.70, N.S.			

Table 129

Parental contact with school : Rural and Urban samples

Frequency	Mothers' contact				Fathers' contact			
	Rural (N = 58)		Urban (N=557)		Rural (N = 58)		Urban (N=557)	
	n	%	n	%	n	%	n	%
Several times	32	55.2	369	66.2	15	25.9	58	10.4
Once or twice	20	34.5	151	27.1	14	24.1	142	25.5
Never (except possibly for admission)	6	10.3	36	6.5	26	44.8	314	56.4
Parent absent	0	0	1	0.2	3	5.2	43	7.7
	z = 1.67, N.S.				z = 2.49, p $<$ 2.5%			

Note: Parent absent category not included in calculation of z.

Table 130

Level of parental co-operation
Rural and Urban samples

Rating	Rural (N = 58)		Urban (N=557)	
	n	%	n	%
1. Over-keen interest i.e. over-anxious parent who pushes child in a way that may impede his progress	1	1.8	16	3.2
2. Keen interest in school activities, gives encouragement and constructive help to child	28	50.9	195	38.6
3. Interested but does not have much idea about the best way to help e.g. uses methods conflicting with those of school or simply lacks ideas	11	20.0	142	28.1
4. Passive attitude; no hostility but expects child to learn at school without any help or encouragement from home	13	23.6	148	29.3
5. Hostile, critical of school, may come only to complain	2	3.6	4	0.8
6. Not sufficient contact to assess *	3		52	

* Number falling in not observed category not included in percentage figures or 'tau' analysis.

during his infant school years, and their assessment of the help and co-operation given by the parents in their child's schooling.

Table 128 gives the teachers' ratings of likely progress in the junior school. Only seven rural children were expected to have lasting difficulties, five of these because of a low level of basic attainments and two because of a combination of either poor attainment, immaturity of personality or behaviour difficulties. Few of the rural children would have to change to either a new building or a new headteacher at the end of their three years as infants, so fewer difficulties might be expected in the change-over.

The isolation of many homes obviously makes frequent contact between parents and school difficult and it has already been stated that parents and children had less contact with the school prior to admission in the rural sample. Table 129 shows that the mothers of the rural sample continued to have less frequent contact with the school than did the mothers in the urban areas. However, this picture is reversed in the case of the fathers' contact, where the fathers of the rural sample had considerably *more* frequent contact with the school. The differences in ratings here are significant at the 2.5 per cent level.

As Table 130 indicates, almost half of the

parents of the rural sample were rated (by the headteachers) as showing a keen and constructive interest in their child's schooling. Only one was rated as over-anxious, two as hostile and it was felt impossible to assess three because of insufficient contact. The remaining parents were rated either as 'passive' or 'interested but not giving appropriate help'. Figures for the urban sample are also given but no statistical tests were made in this case for the complete distribution, though a comparison was made between the numbers rated in the second category with the numbers in all other categories combined. This comparison gives a value for z of 1.86, which is almost significant at the 5 per cent level (on a 'two-tail' test) with more of the rural sample receiving the second rating of 'keen interest'.

10 Background Factors Related to Children's School Attainment

A. RURAL AREA BACKGROUND FACTORS

During their final term in the infant school the sample children were given a battery of tests of reading, spelling, vocabulary, mathematics and 'intelligence'.* These tests were administered in the schools by members of the project team, the tests of mathematics, intelligence and spelling being given as group tests, the remainder being given individually. Table 131 gives a list of the tests given and the range, mean and standard deviation of the scores for this rural sample. Similar details are also given for the larger urban sample, together with the results of t-tests of significance of the differences between the mean scores for the two samples.

The rural sample had significantly higher mean

Table 131

Attainment test raw scores

Rural and Urban samples

Tests	Rural			Urban			Diff. of Means	t	p
	Range	Mean	s.d.	Range	Mean	s.d.			
1. Burt	2-77	31.8	15.3	0-93	32.7	18.1	0.9	-0.36	N.S.
2. Neale Accuracy	0-61	24.8	15.1	0-93	26.1	19.0	1.3	-0.49	N.S.
3. Neale Rate	6-110	40.0	21.6	0-113	41.1	22.1	1.1	-0.36	N.S.
4. Neale Comprehension	0-24	8.5	5.6	0-40	8.8	6.9	0.3	-0.36	N.S.
5. WISC Vocabulary	0-31	21.1	5.9	0-39	20.7	5.8	0.4	0.43	N.S.
6. Mathematics	6-36	25.0	7.0	3-38	21.1	8.2	3.9	3.53	<0.1%
7. Spelling	0-34	18.0	10.0	0-40	18.1	10.7	0.1	-0.08	N.S.
8. Picture Test A	9-51	33.3	11.0	0-54	30.0	11.5	3.3	2.10	<5%

*For convenience, 'intelligence' is used in this section somewhat loosely with reference to the NFER Picture Test A.

scores in 'intelligence' (Picture Test A) and mathematics, a slightly higher mean score on the WISC vocabulary test but slightly lower mean scores on all the reading and spelling measures. The range and standard deviation for nearly all tests was greater for the larger urban sample, and in the case of the Neale Accuracy and Comprehension scores the differences were significant at the 5% level.

The difference very nearly reached the 5% significance level in the case of the Burt reading score. In other words, the evidence suggests that the spread of reading ability is lower in the rural sample than in the urban sample. However, since the urban sample is not a random sample of the urban child population, no generalizations can be made here.

Table 132 shows the mean standardized test

Table 132

Mean Test Performance in terms of attainment age
or standardized score: Rural and Urban samples

	Rural (N = 58)	Urban			Total Urban Sample (N=542)
		Middle class	Settled working class	'Deprived'	
1. Mean chronological age (in years and months)	7.4	7.6	7.6	7.6	7.6
2. Burt reading age (in years and months)	7.2	8.2	7.7	6.7	7.4
3. Neale Accuracy (reading age: years and months)	7.10	8.7	8.0	7.4	7.11
4. Neale Rate	7.10	8.3	7.11	7.9	7.11
5. Neale Comprehension	7.4	8.5	7.6	7.3	7.6
6. WISC vocabulary	7.6	8.2	7.2	6.10	7.6
7. Mathematics * (mean raw scores only)	25	26	20	19	21.1
8. Spelling age (in years and months)	7.0	7.8	7.2	6.6	7.0
9. Picture Test A (standardized score)	105	109	99	97	100

* The mathematics test has not been standardized. The mean raw score
for the Urban and Rural sample combined is 21.4

Mean standardized scores have been converted from mean raw scores,
which gives a result which differs slightly from computing the mean
standardized score by standardizing each individual score.

scores of the rural sample and that of the three sections of the urban sample for comparison. While the Burt graded word reading score in the rural sample was a little below the children's chronological age, the score on the Neale Analysis of Reading (Accuracy and Rate) was somewhat higher. In comparison with the total urban population, the rural sample obtained mean scores equivalent to or a little below those of the total urban sample on most tests but above the mean of the latter group in the case of mathematics (raw score) and Picture Test A. Comparison between the rural sample and the three sub-sections of the urban sample shows that the rural children tended to perform consistently better than the 'deprived' area children and worse than the 'middle-class' area children, their mean scores being *relatively*

more in line with those of the 'settled working-class' area children.

Table 133 gives the correlations between the various test scores for the rural sample. All the intercorrelations are significant and the pattern of correlations is very similar to that found in the urban sample (see p. 143). It will be seen that the reading and spelling measures intercorrelate highly (correlations above 0.85) with the notable exception of the Neale Rate score which shows only a moderate correlation with the related measures. As discussed in Volume 2 of this series, it was felt that the Neale Rate measure was the least satisfactory of all the reading measures used in the test survey because it was liable to distortion, particularly at the extremes of performance in mechanical reading. For example, a child failing to read the

Table 133

Correlations between attainment test scores:
Rural sample (N=58)

	Burt	Neale Accuracy	Neale Rate	Neale Comprehension	WISC Vocabulary	Maths	Spelling	Picture Test A
Burt								
Neale Accuracy	0.97							
Neale Rate	0.59	0.62						
Neale Comprehension	0.86	0.91	0.54					
WISC Vocabulary	0.36	0.37	0.16	0.40				
Mathematics	0.56	0.55	0.33	0.54	0.58			
Spelling	0.88	0.90	0.66	0.80	0.29*	0.61		
Picture Test A	0.50	0.49	0.28*	0.49	0.61	0.66	0.45	

All correlations in the above table are significant at the 1% level except for the two marked with * which are significant at the 5% level.

first story could be credited with an artificially high Rate score.

It will also be noticed that the correlation between Picture Test A and the mathematics test, the two measures which significantly differentiated between the rural and urban samples, was moderately high (0.66).

The effects of isolation

One of the characteristics of the sparsely populated rural areas which might be termed a disadvantage is the degree of isolation of some of the homes. Over half the sample in fact lived in the three urban districts in the county, but the remainder lived in more remote areas and it was possible to classify these and to investigate the effects of isolation on the child's attainment at the end of the infant school years.

One factor which might have been related to isolation was felt to be the child's attendance at school. However, Table 134 shows that the rural sample as a whole had a higher mean percentage attendance than the urban sample and the dif-

ferences are statistically significant for both the first and third years. The figures in Table 135 also show that the degree of isolation within the rural sample had little effect on the child's attendance.

The sample was divided into four 'isolation' groups and the mean scores on the attainment tests were computed for each group. The results are given in Table 136.

From these figures it can be seen that the mean score on the tests given differ little between the four groups and follow no particular pattern in relation to the isolation categories. Standard deviations of the scores for the four groups differ considerably (significantly in several cases) with the most isolated group having the lowest s.d. in nearly all tests. In view of these results any further, more complex analysis of these scores seemed inappropriate. The deduction which can be made from these results is that in this sample of rural children the degree of isolation of the child's home appears to have had no direct effect on attainment in reading, number, spelling or vocabulary, nor is there any apparent relationship between isolation and intelligence test score. It

Table 134

Percentage attendance for first and third years in school

Rural and Urban samples

	Rural			Urban			Diff. of Means	t	p
	Range	Mean	s.d.	Range	Mean	s.d.			
Percentage attendance during first year	73-100	90.1	5.7	23-100	85.5	10.3	4.3	3.1	<0.5%*
Percentage attendance during third year	75-100	94.1	6.1	39-100	89.9	8.2	4.2	3.7	<0.1%*

* Standard deviations for the two groups are significantly different here. When a correction is made for this difference, in calculating t and the number of degrees of freedom, the probability level remains unchanged.

Table 135

Relationship between attendance and isolation in Rural sample

	Ratings of isolation			
	1	2	3	4
	In an urban district	In village under 3 miles from U.D.	In village over 3 miles from U.D. or isolated, under 3 miles from U.D.	Isolated and over 3 miles from U.D.
Number of children	38	5	7	8
Percentage attendance for first year	90.1	88.6	91.6	90.0
Percentage attendance for third year	93.2	94.4	97.1	95.3

should be borne in mind, however, that the numbers of children falling into the three 'more isolated' categories are very small.

t-tests of differences between the mean scores of groups 1 and 4, and between groups 1 and 2, 3, 4 combined showed no significant differences in any test, nor was there consistency in the direction of the differences observed.

B. HOME BACKGROUND FACTORS

As has previously been mentioned, the method of rating the home background of the children in this sample was basically the same as that used for the 'deprived' urban sample. This enabled a direct comparison of scores with those of the urban sample but, whereas the distribution of total scores for the 'deprived' urban sample was found to be approximately normal, the same cannot be said

for this smaller rural sample. Figures 46, 47 and 48 show that the distribution of total material scores is decidedly skewed, with a large proportion of the rural sample having either the minimum score of 5 or a score of 6. The total cultural scores, however, show a better spread, though they too have a slight skewness towards the lower scores. Figure 48, showing the distribution of total scores, in consequence also has a skewness towards the lower scores. This skewness in the distributions means that the assumptions necessary to use product-moment correlations or partial correlations cannot be made. It therefore seemed preferable to use home background scores to categorize the sample and to use an analysis of variance technique to investigate the relative effects of home background and intelligence on the attainment scores of the children.

First of all, however, it is worth looking at the scores of the children in the different categories of

Table 136

Relationship between isolation and attainment scores

	Ratings of isolation							
	1		2		3		4	
	In an urban district		In village under 3 miles from U.D.		In village over 3 miles from U.D., or isolated and under 3 miles from U.D.		Isolated and over 3 miles from U.D.	
Number of children	38		5		7		8	
Test	Mean	s.d.	Mean	s.d.	Mean	s.d.	Mean	s.d.
Picture Test A	33.4	10.6	31.6	9.6	32.9	14.1	34.4	10.3
Burt Reading	33.0	16.2	24.6	12.4	31.1	17.9	31.1	6.0
Neale Accuracy	25.8	16.0	20.6	15.5	24.0	16.6	23.5	4.4
Neale Rate	39.6	21.6	29.8	26.0	44.3	24.1	44.1	12.2
Neale Comprehension	8.7	5.7	8.2	7.6	9.0	5.5	7.0	2.8
WISC Vocabulary	20.8	6.1	23.0	4.6	20.3	7.5	21.6	3.2
Mathematics	25.9	6.5	20.2	3.8	24.4	10.4	24.5	5.9
Spelling	17.9	10.5	14.2	10.1	17.4	10.1	21.1	4.6

home background before any 'allowances' are made for differences in intelligence scores.

The upper portion of Table 137 shows the mean scores of three groups of children, the groups being determined by their total home background scores with group 1 having the lowest, or most favourable, home background scores and group 3 the highest, or least favourable, scores. The value of t and the probability are given for a test of significance of the difference between the mean scores of groups 1 and 3, using a one-tailed test since it would be reasonable to expect the more favoured group to have the higher scores. The lower portion of Table 137 gives the same results with the sample being split into three groups on the basis of their *cultural* home background score.

It can be seen from both portions of Table 137 that group 3, the children with the poorest home backgrounds, had the lowest scores on every test and in the case of the WISC vocabulary, mathematics, and Picture Test A (intelligence) measures, the differences between the mean scores of group 1 and group 3 are statistically significant. However, the differences between groups 1 and 2 are not always in the expected direction. The Picture Test A mean score of group 2 was a little higher

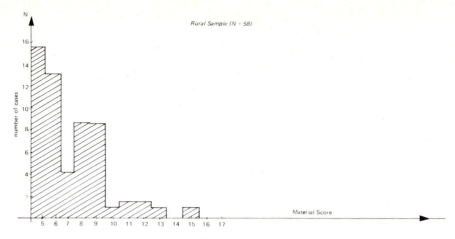

Figure 46

Histogram for material scores

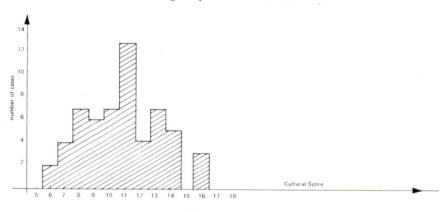

Figure 47

Histogram for cultural scores

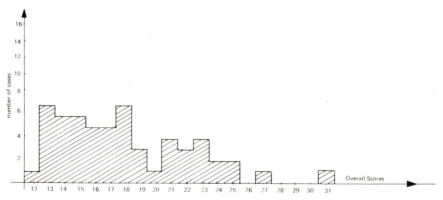

Figure 48

Histogram for total scores

234

Table 137

Home background and attainment scores : Rural sample (N=58)

Tests	Mean scores			t-tests (one-tail) between groups 1,3		
Group No.	1	2	3			
Total Home Background score	12 - 15	16 - 19	20+	t	d.f.	p
No. of children	20	20	18			
Burt graded word reading	33.8	34.2	26.8	1.41	36	N.S.
Neale Accuracy (story reading)	26.8	26.7	20.4	1.25	36	N.S.
Neale Rate	46.4	38.4	34.5	1.56	36	N.S.
Neale Comprehension	8.8	9.1	7.3	0.83	36	N.S.
WISC vocabulary	22.9	21.7	18.3	2.27	36	<2.5%
NFER mathematics	26.8	26.1	21.8	2.15	36	<2.5%
Daniels and Diack Spelling	20.1	17.0	16.8	0.94	36	N.S.
NFER Picture Test A	34.3	37.8	27.2	1.94	36	< 5%
Cultural Home Background score	5 — 9	10 - 11	12+			
No. of children	19	20	19			
Burt	31.7	36.9	26.5	1.09	36	N.S.
Neale Accuracy	25.4	28.9	20.0	1.10	36	N.S.
Neale Rate	46.2	39.7	33.9	1.55	36	N.S.
Neale Comprehension	9.1	9.3	7.0	1.13	36	N.S.
WISC vocabulary	22.9	22.1	18.2	2.30	36	<2.5%
Mathematics	27.6	26.1	21.3	2.84	36	<0.5%
Spelling	18.9	19.9	15.1	1.10	36	N.S.
Picture Test A	34.6	37.8	27.2	2.03	36	<2.5%

than that of group 1, so that the expected effects of home background and intelligence differences will act in opposite directions in those two groups, producing as can be seen, little to distinguish between the groups on the other test scores.

Since the third group had both poorer home backgrounds and lower Picture Test A scores, the two effects act in the same direction to give lower scores on every test, but significantly lower in only a few cases.

To try to compare the relative effects of home background and intelligence and to discover any interactions between these two factors, a two-way analysis of variance was undertaken. (This was by means of an approximate method of analysis for the case where the cell numbers are unequal, the rationale of which is described in Chapter 6, pages 144—145.) Unfortunately, it was not possible to split the two variables into three categories and keep a minimum of two observations per cell so both home background and intelligence were divided into two categories only. The analysis was performed three times, using material, cultural and total home background scores. The results of these analyses are given in brief in Table 138. (See Appendix II, Tables A9—A11 for fuller details of the results of this analysis.)

The picture gained from these results is remarkably clear cut. In no case is there a significant value for F due to any home background score or to the interaction between home background and intelligence. The values of F due to intelligence, on the other hand, are significant for every test score except the Neale Rate score (which is generally felt to be an unsatisfactory measure, particularly for relatively poor readers). For the scores on the WISC vocabulary (which is a sub-test of a general intelligence measure) and mathematics, both of which would be expected to be highly related to intelligence, the values of F are particularly great and are significant at the 0.1% level.

In other words, if one allows for the effects of the differences in intelligence which were found to exist between the different home background categories, the additional variance in test scores which can be accounted for by the category of home background is very small and in no case does it make a statistically significant contribution to the total variance.

It would seem, then, that in this rural sample the home environment appears to have had little effect on the child's attainment at school over and above that which is attributable to his intelligence test score. It is interesting to compare this result with that for the urban sample but, first, one or two reservations should be made. Firstly, because the sample was relatively small, only a two-way split of intelligence and home background was feasible and this is a rather crude categorization. Secondly, the analysis of variance technique involves an assumption of homogeneity of variances between the cells and F-tests on the ratios of the largest or smallest cell variances gave several significant values of F (see Appendix II, Tables A9 to A11).

The difficulties of satisfactorily separating out the effects of intelligence and home environment are many. To say that home background has little or no effect over and above that due to intelligence is begging the question of how far the intelligence test scores themselves are affected by home environment. However, given all these limitations, the picture which emerges is a surprisingly clear one for this sample.

Table 139 shows the results of a similar analysis of the results of the attainment tests for a larger sample of over 200 children living in relatively deprived urban areas. This sample had a wider spread of home background scores, with a higher proportion of children with high scores indicating more severely deprived backgrounds. Also, since the sample was considerably larger, a three way categorization of both home background and intelligence scores was possible. It will be seen from this summary of the results that here again the contribution of the interaction of home background and intelligence to the total variance is never significant. However, on all but one of the test measures (WISC vocabulary) the contribution of the home background categorization (after allowing for intelligence differences) is significant at least at the 5 per cent level.

To give a more graphic representation of the differences between the effects of intelligence and home background categories, Figures 49—54 show the mean scores for each 'cell' in the analysis of variance design. These diagrams show that the mean scores of both 'high intelligence' groups are consistently above those of both 'low intelligence' groups. However, although in the high intelligence groups the children from good homes score somewhat higher than those from the poor homes, the

Table 138

Two-factor analysis of variance
for home background and Picture Test A scores
(Summary Table) : Rural sample (N=58)

Dependent variables	Significant levels of contribution of independent variables					
	Picture Test A (intelligence)		Material home background		Interaction	
	F	p	F	p	F	p
Burt	5.871	< 5%	-		-	
Neale Accuracy	5.298	< 5%	-		-	
Neale Rate	1.124	N.S.	-		-	
Neale Comprehension	6.235	< 5%	-		-	
WISC vocabulary	22.531	<0.1%	-		-	
Mathematics	18.532	<0.1%	-		1.937	N.S.
Spelling	5.113	< 5%	-		1.643	N.S.
	Picture Test A (intelligence)		Cultural home background		Interaction	
	F	p	F	p	F	p
Burt	9.273	< 1%	-		-	
Neale Accuracy	9.026	< 1%	-		-	
Neale Rate	1.667	N.S.	-		-	
Neale Comprehension	8.987	< 1%	-		-	
WISC vocabulary	26.073	<0.1%	-		-	
Mathematics	28.342	<0.1%	2.878	N.S.	1.012	N.S.
Spelling	8.440	< 1%	-		-	
	Picture Test A (intelligence)		Total home background		Interaction	
	F	p	F	p	F	p
Burt	8.515	< 1%	-		-	
Neale Accuracy	8.174	< 1%	-		1.061	N.S.
Neale Rate	1.681	N.S.	-		-	
Neale Comprehension	9.342	< 1%	-		1.473	N.S.
WISC vocabulary	24.731	<0.1%	1.405	N.S.	-	
Mathematics	28.426	<0.1%	-		1.183	N.S.
Spelling	8.337	<1%	-		-	

Note: Values of F less than 1 are not quoted in the above tables.

Figures 49—52

Mean Test Scores for four analysis of variance 'cells'

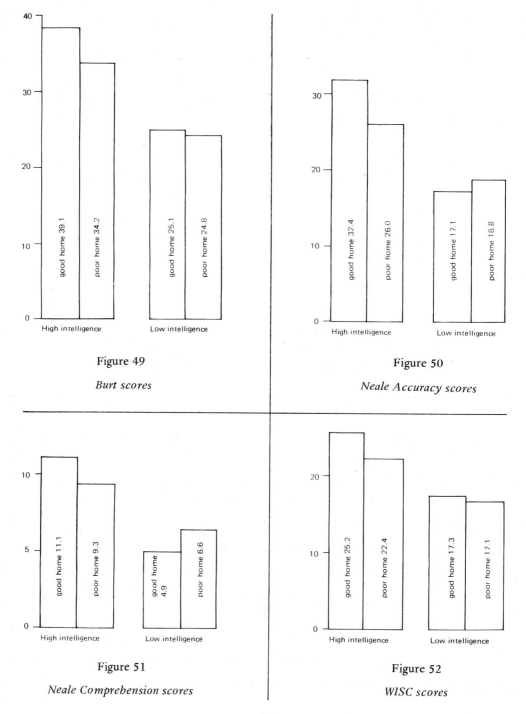

Figure 49

Burt scores

Figure 50

Neale Accuracy scores

Figure 51

Neale Comprehension scores

Figure 52

WISC scores

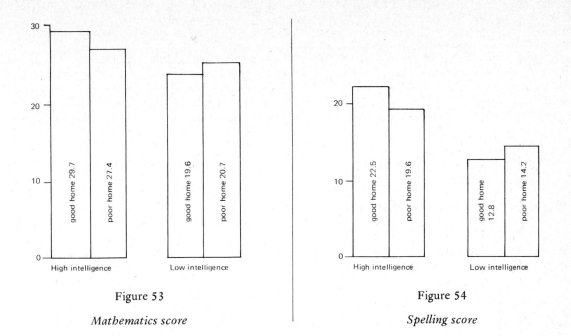

Figure 53

Mathematics score

Figure 54

Spelling score

Table 139

Two-factor analysis of variance

for total home background and Picture Test **A** scores

(Summary Table) : Deprived Urban sample (N=224)

Dependent variables	Significant levels of contribution of independent variables					
	Picture Test **A** (intelligence)		Total home background		Interaction	
	F	p	F	p	F	p
Burt	25.68	< 0.1%	4.20	< 5%	–	
Neale Accuracy	23.62	< 0.1%	5.03	< 1%	–	
Neale Rate	11.34	< 0.1%	3.41	< 5%	1.84	N.S.
Neale Comprehension	29.59	< 0.1%	3.09	< 5%	–	
WISC vocabulary	22.17	< 0.1%	2.48	N.S.	1.18	N.S.
Mathematics	48.59	< 0.1%	4.62	< 1%	–	
Spelling	17.86	< 0.1%	4.38	< 5%	1.15	N.S.

Note: Values of F less than 1 are not quoted in the above table.

two low intelligence groups differ little in their scores and, in over half the tests, the children from the poor homes score slightly higher. This illustrates the fact that differences in intelligence have more consistent effects than do differences in home background. (Home background categories here were based on *total* scores only.)

SUMMARY AND CONCLUSIONS (RURAL SAMPLE)

The children in this sample lived in an area described in the Ministry of Education Report, 'Education in Rural Wales' (1960), as 'the most exclusively rural county in Wales'. The eleven schools which they attended had varying provision, ranging from one with its own swimming pool to another without even flush toilets. Pupil-teacher ratios were relatively low on the whole, but no school had any ancillary help at the beginning of this project.

Parents were, without exception, co-operative in giving information about their child and the home environment. In comparing the material and cultural provision of the *homes* in this rural sample with that in a sample of urban children from relatively deprived areas, the rural sample appeared to fare better or at least as well on almost every item except outings to places of interest, most of which were much more easily accessible to urban families. In the rural sample physical home conditions were better, there was less ill health and unemployment among the parents and, possibly because there were fewer distractions, parents spent more time at home, read more to the children, had more hobbies in which their children could join and made more constructive use of television for their children. Though incomes were often low, families were smaller and there was considerable 'job-satisfaction' amongst the agricultural community. The children had much more outside play space and many were encouraged or allowed to help with their parents' work.

In considering *school-based* information, comparison was made with the total urban sample. The rural children and their parents had less contact with the child's school prior to entry and fewer children entered school with any ability to read or write. The rural sample children also exhibited more initial distress at leaving their mothers and more tiredness during the school day. They were more dependent on adult help for dressing and coping with classroom activities but they had fewer behaviour problems. Whereas in the urban sample the incidence of behaviour problems increased slightly over the three year period, in the rural sample the incidence decreased somewhat.

Despite their lack of opportunity to mix with other children or meet the teachers before starting school, the rural sample appeared to get on at least as well with their classmates and their teachers as the urban sample. Ratings of oral skills, of imagination and originality and of constructive use of play materials in the early stages were higher for the rural sample.

During the first year, the urban sample was significantly further ahead in reading skills, whereas the rural sample did better in number work. However, by the end of the three year period, teacher ratings showed little difference between the groups in either of these two fields, although the final test scores showed the rural sample to score significantly higher on the mathematics and intelligence tests, while being a little (but not significantly) behind in the reading tests. At the end of the three years, teachers rated the children's interest in reading activities and the rural sample had no child in the lowest category, whereas the urban sample had over 15 per cent in this category.

On most teacher ratings, in fact, the rural sample had few children falling into the lowest category, this applying to adjustment, interest and attainment. In some cases there were also fewer in the highest category, particularly in relation to reading attainment. This difference in spread of ability was also reflected in the lower standard deviations in the rural sample on nearly all test scores.

Teachers generally had less contact with the mothers of the rural sample but on the other hand they had more contact with fathers and rated more parents as having a keen interest in their child's schooling and giving constructive help at home.

The degree of isolation of the home appeared to have no effect on the child's attainment, and school attendance in the rural sample generally was considerably better than in the urban sample. The overall home background scores of the rural sample had lower (i.e. more favourable) means than those for the deprived urban sample, with many homes falling into the most favourable categories particularly on material provision. The group with the poorest home backgrounds had lower mean scores in attainment and intelligence tests, but an analysis of variance, with intelligence and home background as the independent variables, showed that, after allowing for the effects of differences in intelligence, the contribution to the variance of the test scores made by the home background categorization was never significant, nor was there a significant interaction between intelligence and home background for this sample.

In the school progress, adjustment and attainment of this sample of children, there is little to suggest that they are any more disadvantaged than the urban sample as a whole. They fare better in every respect, except outings to places of interest, than the children in relatively deprived urban areas. Indeed, the rural child of this age has many advantages over his urban fellows. The difficulties of isolation or lack of amenities seem to have little effect on most children of this age, while they are able to benefit readily from freedom and space for play, the greater attention and interest often shown by their parents and the smaller schools with greater opportunity for individual attention.

PART FOUR — TEACHERS AND PARENTS

11 Teaching Approaches

The general policy of the school and the methods used by the teachers are likely to have a considerable effect on the progress made by the children. It was therefore decided to investigate various aspects of teaching approaches in the project schools.

Separate questionnaires were produced for class teachers and headteachers, each consisting of two parts (Appendix III). A member of the project team completed the Class Teachers' Questionnaire (Part 1) during an interview with each teacher of project children during the summer term 1969. At this time the children's ages ranged from 5 years 2 months to 5 years 9 months, so that the majority interviewed were reception class teachers. However, in a few schools some children had already left the reception class, and in two schools classes were vertically grouped so that the project children were distributed among four classes. In these schools, therefore, more than one Class Teachers' Questionnaire was completed.

Schools were grouped according to the area in which they were situated i.e. 'deprived area' (DA), rural area (RA) and control area (CA), the last group being subdivided into 'settled working-class' (SWC) and 'middle-class' (MC). The total number of Class Teachers' Questionnaires completed (Part 1) was 48, consisting of 19 DA, 11 RA and 18 CA (11 SWC and 7 MC). The discussion which follows is, therefore, based on the replies of a small number of teachers and this should be borne in mind throughout.

At the same time Part II of the questionnaire was issued to the same class teachers for completion in their own time. The number completed was slightly different than for Part I, because in two schools only the reception class teacher had been interviewed for Part I but two teachers completed Part II, and in other cases not all the teachers who had been interviewed returned Part II. The total number of questionnaires (Part II) completed was 47, consisting of 17 DA, 13 RA and 17 CA (10 SWC and 7 MC).

The 37 headteachers of the project schools were given Part I of their questionnaire for completion during the same summer term 1969, and all were returned i.e. 14 DA, 11 RA and 12 CA (6 SWC and 6 MC). Finally, during the project children's second school year from September 1969 to July 1970, the headteachers were interviewed individually by a member of the project team in order to complete Part II of their questionnaire. It was not possible to interview one RA headteacher, so the total number of Head-teachers' Questionnaires (Part II) completed was 36 i.e. 17 DA, 10 RA and 12 CA (6 SWC and 6 MC).

Most of the information concerning teaching approaches was obtained from the Class Teachers' Questionnaire (Part I) and the Headteachers' Questionnaire (Part II), both of which were completed during an interview. Many of the questions were open-ended, and in others the schools were asked to make estimates of a somewhat global nature which some headteachers found difficulty in doing, e.g. 'What percentage of your children's parents show a desire for their children to make progress in reading?' *The data cannot therefore be regarded as very firm, and only a general picture and tentative conclusions can be drawn.*

(i) AIMS AND ORGANIZATION

Headteachers and class teachers were asked to rank four educational aims in order of importance i.e.

1. a basic grounding in the three Rs
2. development of adequate oral language skills
3. development of emotional and social maturity
4. development of each child's creative and expressive powers.

Several schools were very reluctant to differentiate between the aims because 'they are all equally important', while four DA schools found it difficult to place aims 2, 3 and 4 in order of importance because 'they are all prerequisites for learning the three Rs.' The ranking was therefore done under protest in many cases.

Results were averaged for each group and these are shown in Table 140. All groups placed the

Table 140

Headteachers' and class teachers'
average ranking of educational aims

	Grounding in the three Rs	Development of oral language skills	Development of emotional and social maturity	Development of creative and expressive powers
Head-teachers				
DA	4	3	1	2
RA	4	2	1	3
SWC	4	2	1	3
MC	2.5	2.5	1	4
CA (SWC+MC)	4	2	1	3
Teachers DA	4	3	1	2
RA	3	2	1	4
SWC	4	2	1	3
MC	4	2	1	3
CA (SWC+MC)	4	2	1	3

development of emotional and social maturity first, and a basic grounding in the three Rs seemed to be least important to all but MC headteachers and RA class teachers. Only DA schools ranked the development of creative and expressive powers above that of oral language skills, which might imply that DA children were more restricted in creative activities than those in other schools, and that their teachers felt that this aspect of their education should be emphasized.

There was considerable similarity in the ranking order of headteachers and class teachers, despite the fact that the latter, teaching mainly in the reception class, regarded the aims from the point of view of a child's early schooling, and several implied that they might have changed the order of positions if they were teaching older children. One DA teacher remarked that her ordering was the 'ideal pattern' for children with three years in the infant school, but that she would 'push the three Rs after the reception stage with two-year children'. Moreover, although so many teachers placed a grounding in the three Rs fourth, there was evidence in some remarks that they placed considerable emphasis on it.

'If a child can't read on leaving the infant school he won't learn to do so later' (DA)

'I hope to be able to concentrate on the three Rs in the third term' (MC)

'I wouldn't worry if children did not reach high proficiency in the three Rs in the *first year*, but I would concentrate on it afterwards, because there is a high level of parent expectation in this area' (MC)

'I put great stress on reading' (DA headteacher).

Other teachers added that their ranking order would vary according to individual and school differences.

'This order applies only to this school' (DA)

'The order would vary according to individuals e.g. for unstable children the developing of emotional and social maturity is most important' (DA teacher who marked 'a grounding in the three Rs' first)

'They already have a good grounding in oral language skills' (MC headteacher who ranked this item fourth).

Thus although the average ratings for each group were very similar, there seemed to be a general feeling that once a reasonable standard had been achieved in aims 2, 3 and 4, greater emphasis could be placed on the three Rs. The development of emotional and social maturity was regarded as most important because 'progress is more difficult to achieve without it', and 'it is basic to the other three aims'. However, there appeared to be a greater need to develop this maturity in some schools than in others. Two CA schools felt that the children were 'already fairly well developed emotionally and socially', but one DA headteacher said that 'half our children are most insecure'.

It would appear, therefore, that emphasis would be placed earlier on the three Rs in schools where the children had already developed adequate oral language skills and had reached a reasonable standard of emotional and social maturity at school entry. These schools were more likely to be in the CA than the DA group. As one DA class teacher observed, 'The main need in the first year is for love and attention. These children have social and emotional needs which have to be met. They have no power of concentration, unlike children in other areas who may be ready for disciplined educational activities sooner'.

The unanimity of the views of headteachers and class teachers on educational aims implied considerable co-operation between headteachers and staffs, though few schools held staff meetings regularly (Table 141). There was little difference between CA and DA groups in the frequency with which staff meetings were held, the majority holding them 'occasionally as the need arose'. In most RA schools staff meetings were never held, but this was probably explained by the fact that the staffs were usually smaller than in the other groups, two headteachers having only one member of staff, and meetings took place informally.

Most schools mentioned daily informal discussions during coffee or lunch breaks either instead of, or in addition to, formal staff meetings. One headteacher who held occasional meetings felt that the discussions were not very profitable, and another said that the staff preferred informal discussions. When staff meetings were regularly held they usually occurred once or twice a term,

Table 141

Frequency of formal staff meetings

| | DA | RA | CA | | Total |
			SWC	MC	
Regularly	4	–	3	1	8
Occasionally	7	4	2	5	18
Never	3	6	1	–	10
Total	14	10	6	6	36

though one school held them once a fortnight, and another held them once a week.

General school policy and organization were discussed in all but one project schools, and educational aims and materials in every school e.g. teachers reported on courses they had attended, discussed a new mathematics scheme etc. Other matters discussed included school events e.g. outings, and staff/parent concerns. Although most schools intimated that children were often discussed, eight headteachers felt strongly that individual children should only be discussed informally with the class teachers concerned, and not in the presence of all the staff.

Frequent discussion therefore took place in all schools, whether formally or informally, but this did not imply a unity of teaching approaches and classroom organization throughout the school. In the seven schools where more than one questionnaire was completed, teachers from the same school varied considerably in their organization of the children's activities.

The teachers were asked how they organized activities in the basic skills of reading or pre-reading, mathematics and language, and although the replies showed considerable variations, it was possible in most cases to classify them into one of three main types. The first type consisted of those who operated an integrated day, or a similar approach which one teacher described as 'an integrated day but not in the full sense of the word'. A typical class of this type would have six groups working on different activities at the same time. Three groups would be occupied with reading, writing and number, while the other groups would be doing creative work with paints, clay and 'junk', or playing freely with a choice of materials including sand and water, toys and the Wendy House.

In the second type of organization a period was set aside, generally in the morning, when the choice of activities was confined to the three Rs, and free choice took place during the afternoons or when assignments in the basic subjects had been completed. The third type of organization devoted separate periods of time to each of the basic skills, so that the children's activities in the three Rs were completely controlled by the teacher. In a typical class, all the children would be occupied with reading activities at the same time, generally until the mid-morning break, with mathematical activities after the break.

It appeared from the teachers' comments that the second type was slightly more formal in its approach than the first, and that the third type was the most formal of the three. Table 142 shows that the majority of DA teachers adopted the informal 'integrated day' approach, the CA schools favoured the slightly more formal type of organization which ensured that all children covered

Table 142

Classroom organization

	Type 1 Integrated Day approach	Type 2 Choice from three Rs	Type 3 Three Rs taken separately	Unclassified	Total
DA	12	1	5	1	19
RA	1	2	7	1	11
SWC	2 } CA=3	6 } CA=9	2 } CA=4	1 } CA=2	11 } CA=18
MC	1	3	2	1	7
Total	16	12	16	4	48

some aspects of the basic skills every day, while most RA schools belonged to the third type in which the choice of activities was far more restricted. As a rule there was a much wider age range in the rural than in the urban classes, resulting in a form of family grouping in some cases. Yet in the two urban schools which followed a policy of family grouping, most of the teachers adopted the 'integrated day' or the second type of approach.

Five teachers who had adopted the third type of approach and three who had adopted the second type, said that they did some class teaching in the basic subjects. These class activities included writing, work with flash cards and introductory phonics, and number games. One teacher spoke of 'starting off with class teaching in each of the basic subjects before forming the children into three groups for activities', while another teacher referred to language skills being taken on a class basis. This was one of only two references to language activities. All other teachers referred to the basic skills activities as consisting of pre-reading, reading, number and writing.

It often seemed as if teachers regarded the 'free play' groups as requiring little supervision, thus leaving the teacher free to concentrate on the groups working on the basic skills activities. One teacher with forty children in her class evidently shared this viewpoint. She had adopted the second type of classroom organization, setting aside a period in the morning for the basic skills, but she sometimes incorporated a 'free play' group because she could not cope with such a large number working on the three Rs at one time.

One SWC teacher had adopted an integrated day approach for the first two terms of the first year, but during the third term had adopted 'a more formal set-up i.e. separating the basic skills from the free play and other activities in order to have more work in the three Rs to show parents on Open Day'. This teacher seemed to feel that the children did less work in the basic skills during an integrated day than in the other two approaches. If this were so, then the replies to this question support the impression gained from the statements of educational aims, that DA schools placed less emphasis on the three Rs in the first year of schooling than the other schools.

One MC teacher stated that her children were taught individually in the basic skills, but all other schools divided the children into groups to a greater or lesser extent. The nature of the grouping varied throughout the sample, but the majority favoured grouping according to ability or progress in the basic skills, with free grouping for the free choice activities. A few teachers preferred mixed ability groups so that the more advanced children could help the slower ones, while seven DA and three CA teachers allowed free grouping in all activities. Most schools encouraged or arranged re-grouping at frequent intervals so as to develop social awareness among the children.

Rarely was the children's choice of activities entirely free during the whole day. Some form of teacher guidance or control was present in most schools, and similarly all schools allowed free choice of activity at certain periods, though the amount of time set aside for this varied considerably. In one school there was a period of free choice on only two afternoons in the week, while in another school which operated an 'integrated day', the school day was completely unstructured and the only teacher guidance consisted in asking a child to join an activity if the teacher found him inactive, 'though this is rarely necessary', she added.

However, teachers in other schools which adopted an integrated day approach found it necessary to guide children's choice of activities to a greater extent. 'This has to be so, or some children would just play all day and not do anything,' said one teacher. Another teacher tried to 'suggest a balance of activities, otherwise some children would just play', and a third tried to rotate the groups 'otherwise some children might be on the same activity all day'. Some schools changed their policy during the first year, either starting with strict teacher control and gradually allowing free choice of activities, or starting with a free choice and gradually introducing more teacher control and guidance, which mainly took the form of weaning children away from play activities in order to do some work in the three Rs.

During group activities, which generally took up the greater part of the school day, teachers in all schools were usually occupied in 'going round the groups', discussing, helping and directing activities, though they sometimes 'called out' certain groups for special tuition in reading or mathematical processes. Teachers who offered a wide range of activities at one time usually spent more time with groups occupied in the basic skills, and one teacher added, 'One tends to think of free play as "occupying" some children while one is dealing with the three Rs with the others'.

Even in an integrated day, some activities had to occupy set periods because the use of the hall or swimming pool was time-tabled, and because of the timing of radio and television broadcasts. Apart from these restrictions, the schools which adopted the first type of organization had a completely unstructured day during which the children moved around the classroom changing their activities spontaneously, and working at the basic skills at any time during the day, although eight schools put greater emphasis on these skills at certain times of the day. This free group activity was interspersed with some class activity such as radio and television programmes, music, PE, number games and rhymes, or a story. One teacher liked to 'do some class work in order to maintain the children's sense of class identity'.

Teachers who had adopted the second and third types of organization worked within a certain pattern of activities, though there was usually considerable flexibility within this framework. A typical school would start the day with class news or discussion, followed by group activities in the three Rs and some class work involving flash cards, number games or elementary phonics. The afternoon was usually devoted to more creative work such as music, drama and craft, and invariably ended with a story. Many teachers found it difficult to give adequate supervision to all groups, however systematically they 'tried to go round all the groups', though when the basic skills were thus allocated a specific time during the day, the teacher was able to ensure that all children did some work in the three Rs every day.

This was far more difficult to ensure when teachers adopted an integrated day approach. Several of these teachers were 'not concerned whether children did the basic skills each day', and two others were satisfied if a child did reading and writing every other day and mathematics on the intervening days, though even this was not always possible to achieve. Another teacher required the children to engage in a minimum amount of work in the basic skills every day. Each child kept a record of his work in an exercise book, and when he had completed his day's assignments, generally consisting of work cards made by the teacher, he showed his exercise book to her and was then free to move on to other activities. In another school, the teacher ensured that each child completed a basic minimum of work by setting tasks for each activity. When a child had completed the work in one group he moved on to the next, and so all children would have done most of the work in all groups during the day.

One DA teacher devised yet another method for ensuring that all children covered certain basic requirements every day. The class was divided into three main groups, described as 'top, average and slow groups', though the children worked individually. Members of the top group were given assignments for the day in reading and number e.g. two 'Colour Factor' cards and reading scheme work cards. The children could be relied upon to work on their own, said the teacher, and she allowed them to 'hear each other read'. When they had finished their set work they had a free choice of activity. Members of the average group were similarly given assignments, but the teacher spent more time with them and selected children for special help. Children in the slow group were given one assignment at a time, not, as in the other two groups, a battery to be completed in their own time. The teacher spent most of her time with the last two groups, and sometimes children in the top group spontaneously helped the slower ones. The teacher encouraged this. She also 'pulled out' groups for special tuition in reading or number processes occasionally.

Finally, one DA school which did not belong to any of the three types in Table 142, and was therefore unclassified, had a method of organization different from all the other schools. It adopted a team teaching approach, and the school day was fairly firmly structured. There were four activity rooms for mathematics, writing, house play and pre-reading/pre-number work, with one teacher in charge of each room. For two periods in the day, the children moved freely among the activity rooms with the rest of the school, but for the remainder of the time they stayed with their class teacher for free play, 'news', discussion, PE, music, painting, library, drama, poetry and story.

The children would probably be in the charge of the same teacher for the whole of their infant schooling, and she was responsible for recording their progress. After the second term of schooling, children were required to do a minimum of work in the basic skills in each activity room, and the teacher in charge of it made a record of each child's work. This she presumably handed to the class teacher, who had to keep a record of her children's progress. She also kept control of their activities, trying to see that they all had some number and reading experience each day if possible e.g. a child would have to ask her permission to go to another room. If a teacher saw a child playing for too long, she would 'encourage him to do some work'.

Since most DA schools followed a more unstructured, integrated day approach than the others, it is possible that some children who wished to do so could spend less time on the three Rs and more on 'play' activities than children in RA and CA schools, who had no choice at certain periods of the day but to do work in the basic skills. The comments of the DA teachers showed that they were aware of this possibility, and most of them took various steps to 'guide' children to activities in the three Rs. It might be that they were not completely successful in their attempts, in which case it could be an indication that the three Rs did not receive as much emphasis in DA schools as in the other project schools during the first year.

(ii) ACTIVITIES WITHIN THE SCHOOL

Play. Headteachers and class teachers were alike convinced of the value of 'free play' i.e. spontaneous activity with play materials. They felt that during this free activity the children learned to mix socially, to co-operate with others, to share their materials and experiences, and to organize themselves into groups, so that free play contributed greatly to their social development.

It also developed certain individual qualities. By the exercise of free choice, the children learned to be more responsible and self-reliant. They had to 'think for themselves and not accept what the teacher has to offer', and one DA headteacher added, 'They need the opportunity to discover and do things for themselves. They are used to parental direction at home — do this and do that'. She also thought that free play taught some children to be more child-like. They had been 'made to feel old at a very young age, as if they have missed out on the play period in their development'. Others felt that free play developed creative abilities and initiative, and stirred children's imagination. They gained confidence and developed qualities of leadership, they matured at their own rate and were able to develop their individual talents and interests.

When discussing their activities during free play, the children developed language skills, and they were able to express their thoughts and feelings not only through speech but by manipulating materials. Through manipulation of materials they increased their manual dexterity, and they were also able to explore the possibilities of various media by experimenting freely. This freedom was sometimes denied them in their homes. Many DA children lived in high-rise flats or in cramped living conditions with a restricted environment, while in CA schools, too, a minority had limited opportunities for play at home.

The value of free play in promoting emotional adjustment was stressed by all groups. It provided an outlet for frustration and aggression, got rid of inhibitions, and enabled children to 'act out' their worries in dramatic play. When playing in the home corner they resolved problems connected with their homes and families, and one headteacher also found that it relaxed DA children, 'who are often so tense'.

Some children had not developed strategies for learning and were not interested in school activities. Through free play they 'learned how to learn', and their interest was more readily aroused when they chose their own activity. They also enjoyed themselves, and this interest and enjoyment often led to a more positive attitude to school and to the basic skills. Several teachers from all groups felt that work in the three Rs benefited from free play because 'they are more ready for formal work after they have had their fling', 'they learn relationships and concepts, and exercise their powers of reasoning' and 'free play provides a basis for the three Rs'. As one headteacher observed, 'they get everything through play — physical, intellectual, emotional and social experiences'.

Finally, when observing the children in a free situation, the teacher gained an insight into their interests, their potential capabilities, their problems and their home backgrounds. By discussing their activities with them, she could also develop their linguistic skills. All this required her to devote some time to observing and participating in the children's free play activities, yet the majority of CA teachers, and almost half the DA and RA teachers, did not take a very active part in the children's play, because they used this time either to listen to children reading or to help the more backward ones. All but one MC teacher added that children could play quite purposefully alone. 'They have come from good homes and have a fund of experiences', they said. 'They don't need as much structuring of their experiences as less fortunate children'.

DA teachers were much less inclined to limit the children's choice of free play activities than the other two groups. The RA group controlled activities to the greatest extent in order, said the teachers, to ensure that children 'played with a purpose'. DA teachers, however, were more ready to take the initiative in the children's free play activities, while the other two groups were more inclined to wait until they were invited, or asked for help. The teachers' participation generally took the form of talking to the various groups, asking questions and making suggestions, and was gener-ally greatest in activities considered to be 'more educational'.

In four schools (2 DA, 1 RA and 1 MC) there was virtually no provision for free play during the children's first year in school because space was very limited. In a few other schools where there was also lack of space, teachers had to use the hall, corridors or playground for free play, and this considerably limited the time devoted to it. However, in most of the remaining schools, ample opportunity was given for free play during the first year. It was either available all day interspersed with activities in the basic skills, or confined mainly to the afternoons. During the free play period, most teachers allowed free choice of activities except for limiting numbers in certain cases.

Teachers were asked what materials were used during free play, and these were placed in descending order according to the number of times they were mentioned. As can be seen from Table 143, urban schools showed considerable similarity in

Table 143

'Free play' materials,
placed in order of frequency of use

	DA	CA	RA
Wendy House/house corner	1*	1*	2*
Paint/glue/clay etc.	2*	4*	5.5*
Large bricks/blocks	4*	2*	5.5*
Sand	4*	4*	8
Water	4*	4*	8
Dolls, prams etc.	6	8.5	3.5*
Dressing up	7.5	8.5	3.5*
Large toys e.g. see-saw, wheeled toys	7.5	7	8
Shop corner	9.5	11	1*
Constructional toys	9.5	6	10.5
Book corner	11	10	10.5

* The five activities occurring most frequently.

252

their responses, the five activities occurring most frequently being the house corner, creative and constructional activities, and sand and water play. The RA schools showed a pattern dissimilar in some respects, with the shop corner occurring most frequently, and 'dressing up' and play with dolls attaining greater prominence than sand and water. In all groups, the book corner seemed to be among the least used during free play activities.

When teachers were asked if they had any children who were very limited or inhibited in their free play, three DA, two CA and nine RA teachers said that they had no children of this description, the RA teachers adding that although some children were shy on entry, they soon became more communicative and sociable. The remaining teachers said that children who were limited or inhibited in their free play generally displayed two types of behaviour at entry. The first type was shy and reserved, happy to sit and watch until guided by the teacher to join a group. The second type, which was fewer in number, was destructive. Both were temporary stages through which many children passed before settling down to more social and constructive play.

Other forms of behaviour were described which occurred less frequently and generally persisted for a longer period. There were children who

'don't seem to know what to do, who wander around or stand about' (1 DA, 1 CA, 1 RA)

'prefer to play on their own' (1 DA, 1 CA)

'always do the same thing' (1 DA, 1 CA).

Finally, teachers described a few individuals who displayed various symptoms of emotional disturbance, such as 'a very withdrawn child who may be referred to the educational psychologist'.

The majority of teachers noted some development in free play behaviour during the first year. The children progressed from individual play to more co-operative group activity, they learned to share, and care for, their materials, they were able to sustain an activity for a longer period, and they became more controlled and organized in their behaviour. They made a more purposeful use of materials, were more constructive, and produced more recognizable end products. Their manual dexterity improved, and their art work became more realistic. A few teachers noticed that there

was some development in children's speech, they asked more questions, and their play became more varied.

Several teachers pointed out that not all children showed a development in their free play behaviour, and that some remained at an immature level. One DA teacher saw no obvious trend in development, and added that the children were not very resourceful in play, while two MC teachers noticed that children tended to move away from free play activities 'to do some work'. This tendency was also noted by a SWC headteacher, who said that after the first year the children 'did not really *want* free play, and would much rather get on with more formal activities'.

After the first year, less time was generally allocated to free play, but there was more opportunity for it in DA schools than in any other group. In schools which adopted an integrated day or a similar approach, free play was available throughout the day, except in two cases where it was confined to the afternoons, but there was more teacher control of activities than during the first year, in order to ensure that children carried out some activity in the basic skills. A few headteachers estimated that children spent an hour a day, on average, in free play.

Most RA schools, and half the CA schools, allocated a daily period, generally of half an hour's duration, to free play, and the remaining schools devoted a more lengthy period to it once or twice a week. There was also free choice of activities between the completion of one assignment and the commencement of the next.

Not all schools made the same provision for free play during the second and third years. One SWC school discontinued vertical grouping after the second year, and limited free play in the third year to half an hour a day. In two schools (DA and RA) all activities were teacher-directed in the third year, and opportunities for free play were very limited, while in a third school (MC) it was reduced to one afternoon a week. This trend to reduce free play in the top class was reversed in one RA school. There was no free play during the second year because of lack of space and the disinclination of the teacher, but during the third year there was a half-hour period every day.

After the first year, almost all schools gave children an opportunity to engage in modelling, art and craft during free play. Drama was also a free play activity in most schools, but this generally consisted of house play in the home corners. In a few schools, however, children were able to 'dress up' and sometimes a spare classroom was allocated for this activity. A DA headteacher observed that many children took about a year after entry to achieve a constructive level of play, and that when 'dressing up' at first they 'will put anything on, e.g. a boy would put on a wedding gown'.

A few schools, mainly urban, offered music as a free play activity, but it was usually only available to a limited extent because of practical considerations. Instruments available included the glockenspiel and chime bars, while in one school a class played instruments made by themselves or the class teacher. Children usually played with the instruments in the corridor or hall, and in one school they listened to recorded music in the classroom.

It seemed that during the second and third years differences between the schools in free play remained substantially the same as during the first year. DA schools generally allowed more time for it than the other two groups, but there was little difference between them in the variety of activities offered.

Some creative and expressive skills. In creative and expressive skills such as music, art, craft, drama and movement to music, a wide range of activities was offered in all schools during the first year, and there was little difference between them in this respect. Music, drama and movement to music were carried out mainly on a class basis, while art, modelling and craft were usually group or individual activities, though in RA schools there was slightly more class activity in art and craft than in the other two groups.

Art and craft were rarely differentiated, and the activities most often performed were painting, modelling with clay or plasticine, drawing and 'junk' modelling. Other activities included paper cutting, stick or potato printing and puppetry. The most common activity in drama was the acting of stories, rhymes or imaginary situations. Dramatic work also entered into the house corner and 'dressing up' activities, while RA schools performed mimes to a far greater extent than the other groups. Singing was the most common activity in music, and a close second was the

playing of percussion instruments. Children also listened to records, particularly in CA schools. Almost all schools followed 'Music and Movement' broadcasts, and in a few schools movement also accompanied music on the piano or on records.

During the first year, eighty per cent of teachers laid no particular stress on any one of these areas of activity, while the few remaining teachers devoted a little more time to one area, mainly art. However, in the school as a whole, more stress was generally laid on some areas of activity than on others. Art, craft, and to a lesser extent music, were given most attention in urban schools, one DA headteacher commenting that art gave children 'a release — a form of compensation for their lack of language'. Music was given equal stress with art and craft in CA schools but considerably less in DA schools. In RA schools movement to music was given most attention, and art, craft and music were given almost equal prominence.

Sometimes an area of activity was stressed because of the special interests of the headteacher, while in other cases it was the result of the enthusiasm or particular skill of the teacher. The effect of the latter was particularly noticeable in the replies of the class teachers. Few had any special qualifications or training for teaching any of the areas of activity mentioned, and those few teachers had qualified mainly in art and craft. The number of teachers with no special qualifications corresponded with the number which laid no particular stress on any activity.

In the second and third year classes, there were slightly more teachers with special qualifications in CA schools than in the other groups. In music, one teacher had received specialist training, two were 'gifted musicians' and others were 'able to play the piano'. Two teachers had special qualifications in art, and one speech and drama. In the RA group, a headteacher gave 'specialist teaching in music and drama for one term', but otherwise no special qualifications were mentioned apart from an ability to play the piano. In the DA group, one teacher had received special training in art, two schools had a 'visiting specialist' in music for certain periods in the week, and others were able to play the piano.

Few schools had any specialist teaching, and one DA headteacher felt that 'it would be inhibiting — we encourage self expression, not the teaching of technique'. However, although a teacher with special interests and qualifications did not usually teach other classes as well as her own, her influence was often felt outside her classroom, as she disseminated ideas and infected her colleagues with her enthusiasm. She was also more likely to arouse the interest and response of her own class in her particular field of activity, and several headteachers ascribed a high level of attainment or interest in an area of activity to 'enthusiastic teaching' or 'a reflection of the teacher's flair'.

Children's level of interest in, or response to, an activity also reflected the emphasis placed on it or the amount of time devoted to it. In the first year classes, where there was generally no emphasis on any area of activity, almost half the teachers thought that the children showed no marked interest or a particularly good level of response in any activity. Of the remaining teachers, the majority in DA schools felt that children showed the highest level of response in art, CA teachers thought that music aroused slightly more interest than art, and the replies of RA teachers showed no particular pattern of interest.

In the second and third year classes, art was most often mentioned in DA schools as arousing interest and a good response, with craft in second place. In RA schools the children were most enthusiastic about music and movement, and percussion bands were also popular. Music was most often mentioned by CA headteachers as arousing interest, enjoyment and a high level of response, with art and craft in second place. It seems, therefore, that the pattern of response shown by DA and CA children in their first year of schooling continued during their second and third years.

A high level of interest or response was not always accompanied by a similar level of attainment, and some headteachers in all groups followed the remark 'a good level of response and interest' with 'attainment average or varied'. In art, it would appear from the headteachers' comments that there was little difference between the attainment of the groups, and that a good level of attainment was sometimes reached. The children produced

colours' (1 DA)
'some very good art work – occasional competition success' (1 DA)
'a good standard of work in art' (1 MC)

'good art work – they are not afraid to express themselves/they can express themselves better in art and craft than in language' (1 DA, 1 RA).

Language skills. In order to develop oral language skills, most project schools used a general approach, encouraging the children to 'express themselves through every means available'. This was mainly through activities such as discussion, dramatization, reading and memorizing poetry, repeating nursery rhymes and jingles, and singing. A few schools mentioned the use of a tape recorder and a record player, and of television and radio programmes, in developing oral language skills, but others bemoaned the lack of audio-visual aids in general, and a tape recorder in particular, in their schools.

Discussions were organized on a class basis, or in small groups in which children discussed their activities and other topics with each other, their teacher, a part-time teacher or an aide. Several headteachers stressed the importance of children talking informally as much as possible, and they were encouraged to hold conversations with each other and with their teacher. One MC headmaster ensured that each member of his staff allowed a certain amount of time during the week for informal discussion, and it often took place in 'family group' situation with the children sitting around their teacher. He felt that this activity was valuable because it encouraged children to 'marshal their ideas'.

Some headteachers also felt it to be particularly important that children should converse with adults as much as possible. In one DA school which had some periods of team teaching during the day, there was a 'house room' which contained a fixed row of Wendy houses. The aim in setting up this room was language development, and the teacher in charge devoted her time to talking and listening to the children, and actively participating in their play.

During the first year of schooling, the same general approach was adopted as with the older children, and there was again an emphasis on discussion, mainly as a class activity. A large picture would be displayed, a story told or 'news' related, and then discussed. There was less discussion in small groups, one teacher thinking that the children were too young for group discussion, and groups generally carried out verbal activities such as 'making up a story', or held conversations with each other or with the teacher. A few teachers tried to structure these conversations by introducing suitable vocabulary into various situations, giving more attention to children with language difficulties, and encouraging withdrawn children to take part.

When group discussions did take place, the teacher was generally present, and topics were connected with the activity of the group e.g. 'laying a table' was discussed in the home corner. Several teachers stressed that language activities should arise out of the children's own experiences. One SWC teacher put greater emphasis on discussing pictures that children had drawn themselves rather than commercially produced pictures, while another SWC teacher took small groups of children on local visits e.g. to the park, church or shops, about twice a term. The help of a part-time teacher and an aide enabled her to carry out these visits, which then became topics for language activities.

All teachers spent considerable time telling stories to the children, and there was some dramatization of stories, nursery rhymes, films and events. A few schools used puppets for dramatic activities, and three schools mentioned miming as an activity 'which leads to speech'. Children also addressed the class or group by telling stories and relating their experiences, or singing and reciting, individually and in groups. Singing was thought to aid clarity of speech, and the reading and learning of poetry was felt to be particularly valuable in developing oral language skills.

Not much use was made of audio-visual aids. A few teachers mentioned television and radio programmes as an aid to language development, though one teacher felt that radio programmes were not very popular with the children. Four teachers played records such as the story 'Black Sambo', two teachers showed films, film strips and slides to stimulate discussion, and two others used a tape recorder to record children's voices and stories.

No one appeared to follow a definite language programme, a few teachers adding that 'the main aim is to get the children to talk freely', or that they preferred speech 'to develop naturally'. Many teachers constantly stressed the informality of their approach, but others felt that some structuring was necessary, and their approach was more

systematic. In one DA school, each child was expected to make a contribution to a conversation, discussion or 'news' period at least once in two days. Some children were shy and unable to make a spontaneous contribution, so that the teacher had to prompt them with questions. She also gave some oral language tuition and insisted on a certain standard of formal correctness in the children's responses.

In several schools, children repeated speech training rhymes and jingles to improve the clarity and rythm of their speech. This was done to a varying extent, in some schools once or twice a week for fifteen or twenty minute periods, and in other schools to a more limited extent, one teacher remarking that she did not 'use many speech ryhmes because they are too artificial and have no beauty'. However, one CA headteacher was particularly enthusiastic about speech training, adding that 'practice in correct enunciation has a definite effect on reading'. This more formal speech training was carried out to a far greater extent in CA schools than in the other schools, more than half the CA group carrying out this activity compared with less than a quarter of the DA and RA groups.

This was somewhat surprising in view of the fact that 'poor speech articulation' and 'limited vocabulary' were the two problems most often mentioned by DA headteachers when questioned regarding the difficulties they met in developing their children's oral language skills. One headteacher referred to the 'slovenly speech' of the children, and added that there was a definite need for speech training, although the reception class teacher in her school had not mentioned it as part of her oral language programme. Another headteacher spoke of children who did not know the words 'sheet' and 'blanket', and she referred to one child who, when asked to make the bed in the house corner, put coals on the fire!

This incident might be ascribed, however, to 'poor listening skills', which were mentioned by six schools. Some children 'did not seem to listen to spoken language', and at first 'even found difficulty in following stories'. Their lives were 'ruled by television', yet when they had seen a programme they were unable to talk about it or show evidence of having listened to it.

The same number of schools (six) mentioned children having

'a poor language background'
'lack of stimulation in the home'
'a low standard of language' and
'difficulty in expressing themselves'.

The children had poor parental speech models, and their knowledge of stories, fairy tales, nursery rhymes and jingles was very sparse. Parental conversation with the children was limited especially when both parents were working, so that headteachers found some difficulty in 'getting children to speak initially, and some were mono-syllabic on entry'. Their language was stilted, their sentence formation was poor, and it was difficult at first to establish rapport with them. There was 'a great lack of experience apart from language — they had never been anywhere and never done anything', said one headteacher, and another found that some children had never held a pencil before entering school.

Not one DA headteacher felt that she had 'no real problems in developing oral language skills', but three RA headteachers were in this happy position. Two RA headteachers who did mention problems added that their comments applied to only a few children, but not one DA headteacher qualified her remarks in this way. It seemed, therefore, that only half the RA schools had problems which applied to more than a few children.

Among these RA schools 'a poor language backgound' and 'a low standard of language' were most often mentioned. The children's cultural background was poor, and conversation with adults in the home was limited. Parental speech was sometimes ungrammatical, there was a tradi-tion of reserve and reticence in the community, and children in isolated homes lacked language experience outside it. Some children were shy, withdrawn and very sensitive to criticism. Half the RA headteachers commented on the shyness or 'traditional reserve and reticence' of the children, and one headteacher thought that their shyness explained why their language was stilted and lacking in fluency. How-ever, another headteacher felt that it was caused by reticence rather than shyness, and that they were conscious of the limitations in their vocabu-lary. He described them as 'having no conversation as such — they simply answer questions'.

Four MC and two SWC headteachers said that they had no real problems, and that the general

level of the children's oral language was good. The other six CA headteachers mentioned poor lan-guage background and lack of stimulation in the home, poor speech articulation, a limited vocabu-lary and inadequate listening skills. However, in all but two SWC schools, these remarks applied to only 'some' or a 'few' children.

In each DA school an average of four problems were mentioned, while in RA and CA schools the average number was only two. There was therefore a greater multiplicity of problems in DA schools than in the other two groups. Moreover, the problems usually applied to only a small minority in CA schools, but were more general in DA and some RA schools.

In the children's oral language activities, gram-matical correctness was least emphasized by all groups, two headteachers (RA and CA) adding that grammatical errors were rare. Greatest stress was placed almost equally on encouraging fluency, listening skills and vocabulary building, but RA and CA headteachers also emphasized good articu-lation to an equal extent, whereas DA head-teachers placed less emphasis on this. Some DA headteachers referred to the large number of children with speech defects, several of whom were receiving speech therapy. A MC headteacher also mentioned that some children received speech therapy, but added that she gave additional speech practice, and another MC headteacher remarked that 'unclear speech can usually be corrected in school'. It seemed as if, having recognized 'poor articulation' as one of their main oral language problems, few DA headteachers felt it necessary to organize formal speech training activities, but were usually content with referring the most serious cases to the speech therapist.

DA class teachers on the whole gave a less gloomy picture than their headteachers of the language deficiencies of the children on entry. Five schools met no special difficulties in developing the children's oral language skills, the children being able to 'express themselves quite well on the whole'. The remaining DA teachers mainly stressed limited vocabulary, but also referred to the other language deficiencies mentioned by their head-teachers. The children

'lacked adequate language experience. They haven't been anywhere or done anything'
'are not able to speak in properly constructed sentences at first. For instance, at news time a

257

child says "Tank". I tell him to say "I've got a tank at home", but he simply repeats "Tank" ' 'won't talk to, or even answer, the teacher on entry, and they usually take a few weeks to open up. Their speech is not clear, and sometimes incomprehensible, but speech therapy is regularly available'.

Half the RA teachers said that they had no particular problems, thus reflecting the views of their headteachers. The other RA teachers mentioned few difficulties apart from immaturity of speech (baby talk) and shyness. In the CA group, the majority of teachers had no real difficulties. One SWC teacher felt that the children lacked language experience, and that their parents did not encourage them to express themselves at home, but otherwise the problems were confined to a small minority and were mainly concerned with initial shyness.

During their language activities, teachers generally placed most stress on fluency, clarity of speech and increasing the range of vocabulary. A few CA teachers also emphasized correct sentence formation. No great attention was paid during the first year to grammatical errors in the children's speech or to variations from 'standard' English in their pronunciation of words. In some schools no correction at all was made, while in others the teacher repeated the child's statement with the errors corrected. In only a few schools did the teacher point out to the child that he had made an error, by saying, 'That is not quite right. You should say . . .'. The corrections were made without stress or criticism, in order to avoid inhibiting the children, and they were made individually and incidentally. Only one teacher sometimes pointed out common errors to the whole class or group.

Teachers were evenly divided in their opinion of the efficacy of their corrections. Some felt that there was an improvement in the children's grammar, while others said that errors persisted despite their efforts. One DA teacher added that children's speech showed most improvement after they had started reading.

In the children's written work, the main aim was fluency, and very few schools laid any stress on spelling, punctuation or grammar at first, 'because of the danger of inhibiting the children'. Later, generally after the age of six years, all schools corrected these incidentally and individually, with the main emphasis on spelling. In addition, usually during the final school year, three quarters of the CA schools, and almost as many RA schools, gave formal tuition in spelling, but only three DA schools did so. This tuition usually involved listing words needed for written work, teaching spelling rules, and using dictionaries and Schonell's 'Essential Spelling' books, and it was often linked with the teaching of phonics.

There was less emphasis on punctuation, which was usually confined to the full stop and linked with the use of the capital letter, and there was little tuition in grammar. Half the CA and RA schools, but only two DA schools, gave formal tuition in the use of capital letters and full stops. It seems, therefore, that there was more direct teaching of formal aspects of written English in CA and RA schools, than in DA schools.

Half the DA, and a few RA, teachers thought that their children were getting insufficient practice in speaking and listening, while only three DA and RA headteachers, compared with six CA headteachers, believed that the children needed more practice, especially in listening skills. Most schools, however, even when they thought that the children were given sufficient practice, suggested ways in which opportunities for oral language work could be extended.

They felt that class teachers needed more time to converse with the children, individually and in groups. This could be achieved by appointing more teachers and thereby reducing the size of classes, or by introducing aides into the existing classes to deal with the more menial tasks and thus freeing the teacher for language activities. A few schools suggested that more adults should enter the classroom to converse with the children. These could be NNEB trained helpers or suitable parents with a good command of language.

Two headteachers said that the difficulties were not in the school but in the home, and that parents should be educated in the importance of conversing with their children, viewing television selectively and widening their children's horizons. Some teachers wished to show films in school and pay visits to places of interest in order to enlarge the children's experience and vocabulary. Others thought that there should be more drama and movement work to enable children to express themselves, but they lacked the space for these activities.

Many teachers felt the need for more audio-visual aids, especially the tape recorder, which could be used to free the teacher for other duties. Tape-recorded stories could be used in conjunction with reading books in the book corner, or used by small groups, who could listen to the story and then discuss it. Two teachers also wanted more records or radio programmes produced which could train oral language and listening skills. However, a few teachers were wary of using mechanical aids. They felt such aids tended to encourage passive listening, and that more interaction was needed. The teacher/child relationship was built up by personal contact, and efforts should be made to increase this, not to replace it with mechanical aids.

Six headmasters, mainly in RA schools, complained that the infant teachers on their staff did not use the audio-visual aids available, and that 'they do not use the tape recorder *at all*'. They, and several other teachers, suggested that more courses should be organized to instruct the teachers not only in the mechanics of audio-visual media, but in a more imaginative use of them, so that maximum value could be obtained from these expensive pieces of equipment.

Reading. There was little difference between the groups in their approach to reading (Table 144). Most teachers used the whole word method, or the whole word combined with the sentence method, of introducing children to reading. This was followed by systematic phonic teaching, although initial letter sounds were taught incidentally from the beginning. A minority adopted a different approach. Seven urban teachers used a combination of the phonic, whole word and sentence method from the beginning, while four RA and two CA teachers used the phonic approach, either on its own, or combined with the whole word or sentence method. Two urban schools (DA and CA) used the i.t.a. approach, and were very enthusiastic about its results.

Teachers generally interpreted 'phonic teaching' as meaning word building, or the synthesis of sounds to form words, and distinguished between it and teaching initial letter sounds. A few teachers introduced systematic phonic teaching during the first year regardless of a child's reading ability. The majority, however, introduced it when a child had reached a certain fluency in reading, generally

Table 144

Class teachers' approaches to reading:
numbers using these methods

| Method used | DA | RA | CA | | Total |
			SWC	MC	
phonics only	–	1	–	–	1
whole word only	3	4	3	2	12
sentence only	–	–	3	–	3
i.t.a.	1	–	1	–	2
mixed methods:					
phonics and whole word	–	2	–	2	4
phonics and sentence	–	1	–	–	1
whole word and sentence	10	3	2	3	18
whole word and sentence and phonics	5	–	2	–	7
Total	19	11	11	7	48

judged by his having read Books 2, 3 or 4 in the reading scheme. This meant that many children were not considered ready for systematic word building during the first year, particularly in DA schools. On the whole, most phonic teaching during the first year took place in CA schools, and least in the DA group, which suggests that the CA children had gained the greatest fluency in reading during the first year.

In pre-reading work, the majority of teachers emphasized matching activities – of pictures, shapes, sentences and words – usually based on the vocabulary and pictures of the introductory book of the reading scheme used. These exercises were combined with frequent, often daily, activities with flash cards, which were also based mainly on the introductory reading primers. A few teachers systematically taught letter sounds at this early stage, and practised synthesizing them to form words.

Teachers used pre-reading apparatus produced with the reading schemes, such as large pictures and pre-reading books, as well as other published material including games and puzzles for teaching word recognition, film strips, materials for matching exercises and flash cards. In addition, teachers produced their own work cards, writing and tracing cards, games, matching materials and flash cards. In general, schools had a wide range of pre-reading apparatus.

Great importance was attached to language development as a preparation for reading, and activities included discussion of the characters and situations of the first reading primers, so that the children were familiar with them when they began reading. Children also discussed their own paintings, and dictated sentences which the teacher printed underneath them. This was felt to be valuable in enabling children to associate the printed with the spoken word, and labels were displayed around the classroom for the same purpose.

The children were invited to look at large picture books in the book corners, and their own paintings were sometimes collected into class books. The teacher read stories aloud, at the same time displaying the appropriate pictures in the book, and she emphasized the knowledge that could be obtained from books. In all these ways, she endeavoured to arouse children's interest in books and motivate them to learn to read.

Most teachers judged that a child was ready to start reading when he could recognize most of the words in the first book of the reading scheme without the aid of pictures. Many teachers relied on their observation of children's performance in pre-reading activities, but others tested the children's knowledge of vocabulary systematically, producing their own tests, using word lists supplied by the reading scheme, or testing with flash cards. The CA group had the highest proportion of teachers who tested the children in this way, and the DA group had the lowest proportion. Not one teacher used published tests of reading readiness, and very few teachers knew of their existence.

Several headteachers felt that no reading scheme was adequate in itself, and generally used books from another scheme to supplement the basic readers. One headteacher allowed children to choose freely from several parallel schemes, while another school which also used a variety of schemes preferred children to work systematically through the readers when they had chosen a scheme. Other teachers would begin with one scheme then switch to another, e.g. in one school children read the first four or five books of 'Key Words', then changed to the later books of 'Janet and John', and used 'Easy Reading' to supplement it.

The schemes most often used in RA and DA schools were 'Janet and John' and 'Happy Venture', with the 'Ladybird' series almost equally popular. In CA schools 'Janet and John' was also in the lead, with the 'Ladybird' series in second place, but 'Happy Venture' was used in only two schools. A few schools were dissatisfied with their schemes, and two (DA and RA) intended changing to the 'Ladybird' series.

The schools were asked to rate the suitability of the schemes they used, but when a scheme was only used as a supplement, it was sometimes not rated. As a result, final figures do not reflect the number of schools which used a particular scheme. Table 145 shows the ratings for the three main schemes, and it can be seen that class teachers generally found the 'Ladybird' series more satisfactory than the other two.

Headteachers rated only the main reading scheme used in the school, and schemes other than the three most often used are omitted in Table 146. It shows that the 'Happy Venture' scheme

Table 145

Class teachers' ratings of reading scheme

Rating	'Janet and John'	'Ladybird'	'Happy Venture'
very suitable	7	10	4
fairly suitable	9	5	4
not very suitable	4	-	4
Total	20	15	12

Table 146

Headteachers' ratings of reading schemes

Rating	'Janet and John'			'Ladybird'			'Happy Venture'		
	DA	RA	CA	DA	RA	CA	DA	RA	CA
highly suitable	1	2	6	2	2	1	1	2	-
quite suitable	5	-	2	1	1	1	3	1	-
not very suitable	-	-	-	-	-	-	1	-	-
Total	6	2	8	3	3	2	5	3	-

was deemed less suitable on the whole than the other two, and that DA headteachers gave fewer 'highly satisfactory' ratings than the other two groups.

There was some difference of opinion shown among the comments. One DA headteacher found the 'Ladybird' series 'too middle-class', while another, also in the DA group, found the subject matter 'within the experience of most children'. One DA headteacher felt that the content of the 'Happy Venture' books was 'not suitable. The story situations are unreal to these children, especially in the later books', while another DA headteacher liked the family theme because 'children can identify with this. The situations are realistic and there are interesting stories in the later books'. One DA headteacher thought that the 'Janet and John' scheme was the most successful of the ones she had tried, and two others (DA and SWC) commented that it was very well graded, adding succinctly, 'it works'. However, three DA head-teachers felt that although successful in teaching children to read, the background was foreign to the children because it was 'country based and did not show town life'. Four DA class teachers also felt that the scheme 'was not relevant to the lives of the children'. However, remarks stating the merits of the three schemes generally outnumbered the faults in all groups.

In addition to reading schemes, children's own productions were used as sources of reading material. They produced their own books and diaries, written at first by the teacher at their dictation, and contributed items to class books and wall charts. Almost all schools also had a class library or book corner, which included books other than the basic readers, in every classroom, and children were usually allowed free access to them apart from limiting the numbers when necessary.

Half the urban schools had an additional separate library in a central position such as a hall or entrance area, or in a spare classroom. RA schools generally had little room for a separate school library, but in addition to the book corners all classes had books kept separately, which were supplied by the country library service. The county library van called periodically at most schools to supply children with an even wider choice of books, and called termly at other schools to supply a new box of books and remove the old one. Many urban schools also had a school library service organized by the LEA or the local public library, as well as a special library book allowance from the LEA.

Only four schools, all urban, felt that their supply of library books was inadequate. Of these, one MC school had already bought books to the value of £400 and had an annual loan of 150 books from the County Hall library, but still thought the supply 'not yet adequate'. A MC school in the same area also received books on loan, but was not yet satisfied with its own collection. The other two schools, both DA, were in an area which did not have a school library service organized by the LEA, and they were still on the waiting list of the local public library to receive books on loan.

In all rural and several urban schools there was free access to the library books. In other urban schools, classes were given set times to use the library and limited free access to children who were fluent readers. More than half the urban schools were unwilling to allow children to take the books home, while the remaining schools usually allowed only fluent readers to do so. Most RA schools, however, allowed children to take library books home, though the younger ones were not encouraged to do so. Only half the RA schools, and very few urban schools, would allow children to take home books from the book corners. RA headteachers felt that this was not necessary because the county library books supplied all their needs, MC headteachers thought that the children had sufficient books at home, and a few DA and SWC headteachers feared that the books would become damaged or lost.

Class teachers were then asked what standard they hoped their children would have reached in reading by the end of the first year. This was difficult to answer in some cases because with the individual approach there was a wide range of achievement. However, teachers eventually gave the average standard they hoped would be achieved after three terms in school. The CA and RA groups generally had higher aspirations than the DA group, despite the fact that RA children usually started school earlier than the other two groups, and had a lower average age at the end of the first year. Almost all CA and RA teachers hoped that the children would have started on the reading scheme, and that most would be reading Book 2 or beyond. More than half the DA teachers hoped that their children would have reached the 'Approach' or introductory books of the scheme.

One DA teacher added that she expected most children to be still at the pre-reading level, because she 'didn't want to push the children in reading even though they wanted books'. When teachers estimated the percentage of children who would still be on pre-reading activities at the end of their first year in school, the average in DA schools was highest at 28.4 per cent, in the RA schools it was lower at 21.8 per cent, and it was least in the CA group at 6.1 per cent, the SWC schools (9.3 per cent) being considerably higher than the MC schools (1 per cent). This confirms the view that children in DA schools had, on the whole, made less progress in reading than the other groups by the end of the first year.

The difference in the aspirations of the schools had disappeared by the end of the children's infant school career. Headteachers were asked what standard they hoped most of their children would have reached before entry to the junior department. Replies varied from 'Book 3' to 'having completed the basic reading scheme'. Only one RA headteacher, compared with four DA and three CA headteachers, expected most children to have completed the reading scheme, the lower number in the RA group probably resulting from children being occasionally transferred to the junior classes at an earlier age than in the other two groups, which had few combined infant and junior departments. Results otherwise were very similar in all groups, yet when headteachers estimated the average percentage of children who were poor readers, i.e. needing special help at the end of their infant school course, the average for the DA group was highest at 18 per cent, the RA group being only 12 per cent and the CA group 11.5 per cent.

Several schools used standardized reading tests during the final school year, and sent the results to the junior department. Some headteachers also used tests at other times to help to group the children, to select those needing special help and to check their progress. Twenty one schools used attainment tests in reading and two used diagnostic tests as well. No standardized tests were used in eight DA, three RA and four CA schools, so that fewer DA children were systematically tested than in the other groups. The Schonell 'Graded Word Reading Test' was by far the most popular, being used in nineteen of the twenty one schools.

No class teacher used any standardized or diagnostic tests during the first year, but most teachers tested the children's knowledge of the vocabulary listed at the back of the primers, or compiled their own word lists. Apart from these lists, only one teacher (MC) devised her own tests, based on the reading scheme, in the form of work cards to test children's comprehension of what they had read.

Almost all teachers made a note of each child's progress in reading, generally by recording the page and book progress. Fewer than half the teachers, however, kept written records of specific pre-reading skills. In a few RA classes with a wide age range, and in two urban schools which were organized in family groups, teachers felt that the number of children involved in pre-reading activities was so small that they could 'keep track of progress quite easily without written records', and a SWC teacher kept no record because 'it gets very involved and takes up too much time'. Where records were kept of pre-reading skills, entries generally consisted of letter sounds known and words recognized, knowledge of these being tested periodically in some schools. A few teachers made additional notes of each child's performance in matching exercises, and of certain 'landmarks' in his progress e.g. the ability to write his name.

During the first year, a higher proportion of DA and RA teachers than of CA teachers heard each child reading every day. In RA schools they were able to do so because of the relatively small number in the class, while in some DA schools the number of children who had started on a reading scheme was fewer than in the CA group and it was therefore possible to hear them read oftener. In CA groups, the majority were heard reading twice or three times a week, but three SWC teachers hear; each child only once a week on average, and two of these taught in the same vertically grouped school.

Several teachers, more than half of whom taught in vertically grouped schools, felt that their main difficulty was insufficient time to give each child adequate attention. Children often had to wait to be heard reading, so that they became frustrated and liable to lose interest. Vertical grouping ceased after the first two years in one school, and the headteacher tended to concentrate on helping the children in the top class, so that teachers in the lower classes had a fairly wide age and ability range and had little additional help. One SWC teacher did not seem happy with family grouping because of the problems of noise, organization and different ability levels, and another teacher (DA) in a vertically grouped school which had an integrated day, also felt that her main problem was classroom organization. Three DA teachers whose classes had an integrated day found difficulty in persuading their children to move to reading activities from free play with toys. One teacher confessed that she was at a loss in dealing with some children who spent the whole year without showing any interest in reading, and would only carry out the reading activities if forced to do so.

Children's lack of interest in reading, which was often a reflection of parental indifference, was one of the two problems most often mentioned by DA teachers, the other being the low level of language development on entry. This prolonged the pre-reading period because it was necessary to develop the children's language skills before they were 'ready for reading'. Three DA teachers added, however, that once the children had started reading they were 'very keen'.

Only two DA teachers said that they had no real problems compared with seven RA and thirteen CA teachers. RA teachers who did have problems felt that the children's main difficulty was in learning and synthesizing letter sounds, while in a few RA schools the level of spoken language was low on entry, and the children needed a great deal of language experience before they were ready to commence on a reading scheme.

In CA schools the main problem was parental pressure, which was mentioned by five CA teachers. Parents bought the reading primers and taught the children to read parrot fashion and to memorize the pages, and occasionally parents expected too much of a child so that he became nervous and over-anxious. On the whole, however, CA teachers appreciated the parental support they received. The parents' interest was transferred to the children, whose motivation to read was very high. One teacher was surprised at the speed with which they learned to read, and another said that some children 'were already able to read on entry'.

Headteachers were also asked what difficulties they encountered in teaching reading, and their replies showed that the problems the first year class teachers had met generally persisted throughout the school. DA headteachers laid greatest stress on the children's low standard of oral language, their poor cultural background and, in some cases, their lack of interest in reading which resulted in poor concentration on it.

The majority of CA schools had no major difficulties, though one SWC headteacher found that her children needed a great deal of pre-reading work compared with the MC school in which she had previously taught, while another found that this was only necessary with children who entered school at the age of 4½ years. Only one RA headteacher felt that he had no general problems compared with seven of the RA class teachers. Some RA headteachers found that the level of reading readiness was low on entry, not only because the children started school earlier than in urban areas, but because of the poverty of their language experience and cultural background.

Another problem with the majority of RA headteachers was that they were full-time teachers, and were unable to assist their class teachers in giving extra help to backward children. Head-teachers from all groups mentioned a hard core of non-readers who needed constant individual attention and who 'didn't seem to respond to normal educational methods'. One headteacher (RA) felt the need for an advisory teacher, while others thought that additional teaching help for remedial reading was necessary.

In some schools the services of a part-time teacher, students, a teaching aide or a nursery assistant enabled class teachers to give additional help to slow learners, but otherwise many teachers were rarely able to do so because of lack of time and the large numbers in their classes. A few teachers in vertically grouped schools were torn between the needs of the older and younger children, and they found it difficult to give additional help in the pre-reading stage because of the demands of older children who had begun reading.

Some teachers attempted to give extra help during free play activities, the lunch period or when the rest of the school was being given hymn singing practice. Eight teachers organized their reading activities so that the slow learners were given more attention, one MC teacher placing the better readers in groups and then giving individual attention to the others. A few teachers, however, did not think that there was a need for extra help until after the age of six years, preferring to wait until the children showed more evidence of reading readiness, and one teacher added that the headteacher dealt with slow learners at a later stage.

In urban schools most headteachers gave extra tuition to slow learners, in groups or individually, but they usually concentrated their attention on the final school year. One DA headteacher placed the slow readers of the second and third year into one small class of twenty-five children so that they could be given more individual attention, while a SWC headteacher transferred backward readers to younger classes during reading sessions, or kept very slow-learning children in the same class for two years. One RA school had a part-time teacher, but otherwise, apart from occasional students, no RA school had any additional teaching help. Since most of the headteachers were also full-time teachers, there was no extra provision for slow learners apart from what the class teacher herself could give.

Most MC teachers felt that the additional help

the children received was adequate. One teacher had 'a good class and they could all read', and another felt that more emphasis would 'put children off reading'. Half the RA teachers thought that they were able to give sufficient help because of the favourable pupil/teacher ratio. However six teachers 'would like to give more help but time is limited; and they could do with some more help'. Since three of them had numbers on roll of only 18, 20 and 27, and some teachers in family grouped schools also had a wide age and ability range with 39 on roll, one wonders if the RA teachers were being altogether realistic. Most DA teachers felt that the extra help they were able to give was inadequate because they had insufficient time to give the individual guidance and attention that was needed, especially in language skills.

Mathematics. In mathematical activities, most headteachers in all groups stressed the 'understanding and application of the basic number concepts', while in the other schools no particular aspect of mathematical skills was emphasized. The Nuffield mathematics scheme, or a similar practical approach, had been adopted by the majority of urban schools. Six CA schools used traditional methods in addition, sometimes by arranging 'new mathematics' activities on three days of the week, and traditional work on the other two days. 'The general policy', remarked one MC headteacher, 'is to accept modern mathematical ideas without neglecting the basic four rules'. Only one DA headteacher mentioned that more formal work e.g. tables and counting activities, generally on a class basis, was carried out in addition to Nuffield mathematics. No RA school used the Nuffield scheme, but all used either what they described as a general approach i.e. a mixture of new and traditional mathematics, or in one case, traditional methods only.

During the first year, nearly all urban and half the RA teachers used published structural apparatus, mainly Unifix and Colour Factor, though the Cuisenaire and Sterne apparatus were also used, and a few schools made their own structural apparatus. Other counting aids, teaching charts, number games and puzzles, both commercially produced and teacher-made, were also used by almost all schools. Urban teachers either used no published children's books in mathematics, or used them only occasionally, while forty per cent of RA teachers used them 'for half the time or more'. Only two RA teachers used no children's mathematics books compared with eight CA and twelve DA teachers. The greater use of books by RA teachers was possibly the result of the wider age range in their classes, while most urban teachers who completed the schedules taught only the first year children, and the books might have been used only by the older RA children.

The main stress during the first year was usually on counting activities, in order to promote understanding of numbers and number bonds, and the recognition of figures. Other teachers emphasized sorting and matching activities, the language of number, time, money, measuring, weighing, and the recording of experiences. They did not generally use any one scheme or even one approach, but used aspects of several methods, the main aim being to give general experience with materials and practical situations.

During children's play experiences in mathematics, eighteen teachers carefully planned and structured the work, setting specific tasks so as to achieve progression. There was less structuring by seventeen teachers, who went from group to group, guiding the children by asking questions and making suggestions. Twelve teachers arranged no specific sequence of activities, the children being allowed to play by themselves until they discovered mathematical concepts for themselves. The teacher became involved in structuring or guiding only if 'the children are not getting anything out of their number play'.

Twelve teachers did not introduce formal arithmetic i.e. written sums in the four basic processes, during the first year, although some children were capable of doing it, because 'it is too early for children to get involved in formal work'. Others introduced it 'if the children are ready i.e. when they can count and have an understanding of number concepts'. Most teachers introduced formal work either individually, or in groups if several children were in the same band of ability, but it was introduced on a class basis by three teachers, and in two cases it was introduced both individually and as a class activity.

Most headteachers stressed that children should not be introduced to formal arithmetic 'until they are ready for it', or 'when they have achieved an understanding of number', and that written sums should be preceded by ample play activity. Head-teachers differed considerably, however, in their opinion of when children would be ready for formal arithmetic. Although children were usually introduced to it individually, headteachers could generally state at what time the majority had begun formal work, and this varied from 'at the end of the second term in the first year', to 'in the third year', and in one school, 'in the junior department'.

RA schools generally introduced formal arithmetic at an earlier stage than the other two groups. Seven RA schools introduced it during the first year, and the other three schools in the second year. The CA and DA groups showed considerable similarity in their approach to formal arithmetic. Several schools did not state a specific time for its introduction, but 'left it to the teacher's discretion to judge when the children are ready for it'. Four schools in each group introduced it in the first year, four CA and one DA in the second year, and three schools in each group in the third year. One SWC school did no formal arithmetic at all in the infant stage, and a DA headteacher 'wouldn't worry if the children were not introduced to it until they entered the junior school'.

Nineteen teachers kept records of children's mastery of specific skills, written at regular intervals, and five teachers kept a detailed record of progress in the Nuffield stages. Eighteen teachers wrote general observations of the children's progress, or kept a record of children's progress in formal work only, and six teachers kept no written records. When children were ready to move to another class, three teachers wrote a report for the next teacher, two schools kept cumulative record cards, and the majority discussed individual children informally with the other teachers. Two DA teachers gave Piagetian type tests, but no other tests were used. Several teachers said that most number activities were a series of tests, and that they were constantly checking to see if children had mastered specific rules.

A third of the teachers felt that they gave sufficient help to children finding difficulty in developing mathematical skills. Some teachers were able to do so because of the additional help they received from the nursery assistant or head-teacher, others spent most of their time with slower pupils, and the remainder did not wish to put undue pressure on children during their first year in school. The teachers who did not feel that they gave sufficient extra help, either had insufficient time to meet individual needs because of large classes, or thought that 'there can never be enough help'. Most children, however, found little difficulty in carrying out the various activities, and several teachers said that the Nuffield approach had improved the children's grasp of number concepts.

Almost half the teachers encountered no real problems in teaching mathematics, and found that they had far fewer difficulties than with the teaching of reading. Among the remaining teachers, the main problem mentioned was the lack of confidence they felt in their own ability to teach through the new approach to mathematics. Others spoke of lack of time to give adequate attention to the children and to ensure that they played constructively, of the need for more commercially produced apparatus, and of their difficulty in helping the children to record their findings.

Several DA headteachers commented that mathematics did not present the same degree of difficulty as reading. Motivation was not a problem because 'the everyday need for mathematical skill is more obvious to the children than is the case with reading', and 'the new approach arouses interest'. Eight DA headteachers felt that they had no difficulties in teaching mathematics, compared with only three RA and five CA headteachers.

The main problem mentioned by the other headteachers was the confusion and sense of inadequacy felt by some of the class teachers. They were still finding difficulty in adjusting to the new approach, and they felt the need for guidance, particularly on classroom organization. Many teachers had attended day and evening courses, but in some cases they felt that the lectures were not sufficiently practical. Four head-teachers (3MC and 1DA) complained of parental pressure on them to do more formal work, and that some parents were giving their children sums to do at home before they had reached an understanding of number. One DA headteacher spoke of the lack of commercially produced apparatus, so that teachers had to 'make a lot of apparatus for weighing and measuring activities'. Another DA headteacher, however, felt that this was no problem because 'there is an abundance of everyday material available, especially when using the Nuffield approach'.

A few headteachers from all groups said that children lacked mathematical experience before starting school. They were deficient in the vocabulary necessary for number, they could not count or say the numbers in sequence up to ten, and with the greater use of pre-packed foods they no longer had as much experience as formerly of weight, size and capacity. One SWC headteacher remarked that with the use of deep freezes her children did not go family shopping so often, and a RA headteacher said that the children lacked experience of money because so many parents paid their bills by cheque. Almost half the DA headteachers, however, mentioned that the children were adept in handling money because they did so much of the family shopping. It seems therefore that the DA children were not at a disadvantage in mathematics compared with those in the other groups.

Audio-visual aids. Of the three groups, the RA group was the most lavishly equipped with audio-visual aids in proportion to the number of schools, and the DA group had the least number of aids (Table 147). Two DA schools had formerly possessed tape recorders and a television set, but they had been stolen. In the CA group, one MC school had four tape recorders altogether, one large one and three small ones, and three record players,

while a SWC school had four tape recorders, two portable and two non-portable, as well as two record players. All schools had wireless sets.

Tape recorders were generally used to record radio broadcasts, music and children's voices. Music was taped for music appreciation, movement activities, accompanying percussion bands, and for accompanying singing when there was no pianist available. Children's voices were usually recorded during speech training and dramatic activities. A few teachers recorded a story so that groups or individuals could afterwards listen to it while following it in a reading book. Only urban schools used their tape recorders 'very frequently', and four RA schools used them 'rarely' or 'never' (Table 148). When teachers were reluctant to use these aids, it was generally because they were heavy to carry, 'children prefer their own classroom', they were difficult to use and there was no time to use them. The small tape recorders used in the one MC school would answer the first two objections, and a RA headmaster's suggestion that a course should be organized on the use of the tape recorder would answer the third.

Most teachers made good use of record players, mainly for music appreciation dance and movement to the music, and as an accompaniment to percussion bands. Records of songs, nursery rhymes and poetry were also played, and in urban

Table 147

Audio-visual aids available

| Audio-visual aid | DA | RA | CA | | Total |
			SWC	MC	
Tape recorder	2	7	4	4	17
Slide/film strip projector	4	9	3	2	18
Ciné projector	0	1	2	1	4
Record player	12	8	6	6	32
Television set	6	7	2	2	17
Total number of aids	24	32	17	15	88
Number of schools in group	14	10	6	6	36

Table 148

Frequency of use of audio-visual aids

(N, schools = 36)

Rating	tape recorder	slide projector	ciné projector	record player	television set	Total
very frequently	5	2	-	9	3	19
quite frequently	2	3	-	12	11	28
sometimes	6	9	-	8	2	25
rarely	2	2	4	2	-	10
never	2	2	-	1	1	6
Total	17	18	4	32	17	88

schools, records of stories were played extensively. A record player was used 'rarely or never' only when it was broken or in poor condition.

Slides and film strips were shown in connection with reading, religious education and environmental studies. They acted as a stimulus to discussion and were used to illustrate stories. Some teachers had taken transparencies of children at their activities, and in one DA school children had drawn their own slides, using felt tip pens. Where a projector was available, RA and DA schools used it more frequently than CA schools, though its use had lessened slightly with the arrival of a television set. Reasons for reluctance to use it included 'suitable film strips not available', takes too long to set it up and black out a room' and 'it is too heavy'. Two urban LEAs had a library of film strips and slides which the schools could borrow, while the rural LEA issued a supply of film strips to the schools, which it changed monthly. Schools under the third urban authority, which did not organize such a system of lending slides and film strips, generally made less use of their projectors.

One school could not use its television set because of technical difficulties, but most other schools welcomed it enthusiastically. The most popular programmes were 'Watch', and for younger children 'Watch with Mother'. A variety of other programmes was mentioned including some, like 'People of Many Lands,' intended for older children. One headmaster regarded the use of television in schools as a mixed blessing. He felt that its proper use entailed planning around a series, and that infant teachers were reluctant to do this. Their use tended to be haphazard, but since only one classroom had an electric point and viewing entailed disruption of classes, this was perhaps understandable. In other schools, however, an average of three programmes were viewed every week.

Radio programmes were also widely used, the most popular by far being 'Music and Movement', which was 'greatly enjoyed by the children'. It is well produced and provides a variety of good music'. Other programmes mentioned by several teachers included 'Music Box', 'Time and Tune', 'Let's Join in', 'Listen with Mother', 'Poetry Corner' and 'Story Time'. They were felt to be not only enjoyable and instructive, but also valuable in developing listening skills and enabling children to hear language well spoken. Schools sometimes taped the programmes so that they could be heard at a more convenient time or used in group activities. Some schools used 'all broadcasts relevant to infants' and one used a total of seven programmes per week. One headmaster, however, had limited the number to two per week because 'the teachers did not arrange follow-up activities'.

In schools where aids were not available, headteachers were most interested in having a slide/film strip projector, a tape recorder, and to a slightly lesser extent, a television set. They felt that slides and film strips would extend the children's knowledge of their environment and act as a stimulus for discussions and creative activities. One DA headteacher thought that showing a film strip while telling a story was valuable in focussing children's attention, and was a help in combating the distractibility of some children.

A tape recorder was felt to be valuable in developing language and listening skills. It would also be useful in enabling a teacher to concentrate on certain activities while other groups were listening to tape recordings. One DA headteacher thought that there should be a tape recorder in every classroom. It would be an incentive to children to talk, and in dramatic play they would give more thought to their responses.

Although the majority of headteachers were in favour of a television set, a few were doubtful about its value. They felt that there were too few programmes suitable for infants to justify the cost. One SWC headteacher also thought that her children already saw enough television at home, but a DA headteacher felt that this was an added reason for using it. The children were accustomed to seeing television at home and their interest in it was already aroused.

Of the thirty-two schools without a ciné projector only eleven would like to have one. The other headteachers felt that its cost would not justify its use, and that after the initial outlay there would be continuing expense in obtaining films. Slides and film strips were more suitable for infants because they liked to talk about what they had seen, and a ciné film moved too rapidly for this. There was no spare room available which could be blacked out for film shows and there was no one 'technically minded' on the staff who could operate it. One DA headteacher thought that a loop projector met the needs of young children better because they could use it themselves. Those headteachers who were in favour of a ciné projector believed that films would spark off discussion, increase the children's knowledge of their environment and provide enjoyment. One headmaster intended the children to make their own films, though he might have been thinking of junior age children, and another pointed out that the supply of films presented little difficulty because they could be borrowed from the LEA visual aids department.

In all four schools where a ciné projector was available, it was used only rarely, and one headteacher added that it was only used twice a term. These schools had all the five aids mentioned, and they made least use of the ciné projector. It seems therefore that it was of least value to infant schools.

(iii) SOME PROBLEMS ENCOUNTERED BY THE SCHOOLS

During the initial period after school entry, children found most difficulty in adjusting to noise and crowds, particularly in the school yard and dining hall. For this reason, some headteachers discouraged children from staying to school lunch during the first few weeks, and arranged for the reception class teacher to accompany her children during 'playtime' for the first few days. In addition, some younger children found the school day very long, particularly in RA schools, where the children were younger on entry than in the urban schools, and often lived too far from school to be able to go home for lunch.

These problems were generally transitory, however, and the majority of children found little difficulty in adjusting to the school situation after the initial period, particularly if they had previously attended a nursery class. Problems that persisted or recurred concerned only a few individuals who needed time to adjust to each new teacher, who were unable to co-operate with the rest of the group or who presented behaviour problems.

Headteachers' estimates of the incidence of children presenting emotional, social or behavioural problems, both mild and serious, varied widely, but the average percentage in the DA group was higher, and the range considerably wider, than in the other two groups (Table 149). The figures suggest that the average DA teacher would have one or two children in her class presenting serious problems of behaviour, whereas in the other groups there would only be this number on average in the whole school. The average DA class would also include four children presenting mild behavioural problems, compared with only 1 or 2 in the other groups. Children with behaviour difficulties, however few in number, can cause considerable disruption in a class, and interfere with the processes of learning of other children, so

Table 149

Incidence of social, emotional and behavioural problems –
headteachers' estimates

Type of school	N	Mild Problems		Serious Problems	
		Mean %	Range .%	Mean %	Range %
DA	13	12.2	1 – 30	5.2	0 – 18.2
RA	9	2.0	0 – 10	1.1	0 – 7.7
CA	11	4.5	0 – 10.7	0.9	0 – 4.4

that DA teachers would have had to spend more time dealing with problems of class control than teachers in the other groups, and have correspondingly less time to supervise group activities.

Class teachers ranked six types of problem behaviour in order of frequency of occurrence in their classes (Table 150). In all groups restlessness was placed first, but whereas urban schools placed aggressiveness next, RA teachers felt that shyness or withdrawal was second in frequency. DA teachers placed disruptive and unruly behaviour higher than nervousness, which was at the end of their list, while CA and RA teachers showed considerable similarity in their ratings, placing nervousness above unruly and anti-social behaviour.

Headteachers ranked the same problem types in order of frequency of occurrence in the whole school (Table 150). Their ratings were substantially the same as those of the class teachers in the DA and RA groups, but in the CA group restlessness and aggressiveness, which had been most apparent at school entry, had been replaced by nervousness and shyness as the behaviour types occurring most frequently. One wonders if this can be partly attributed to the excessive parental pressure for success in the basic skills, of which the CA schools had complained.

The majority of headteachers found most difficulty in coping with restlessness, aggressiveness and anti-social behaviour. Class teachers also selected these three as being the most difficult to

deal with, but aggressiveness topped their list and restlessness came third. It seemed therefore that not only did the DA class teachers have a slightly higher incidence of behaviour problems than the other groups, but the types of behaviour which occurred most frequently were the ones they found most difficult to deal with.

Headteachers named a variety of sources of help which was available to them in dealing with behaviour problems, including the educational psychologist, medical officer of health, welfare officer, child guidance clinic, school nurse or health visitor, the care committee and the child care officer, as well as the parents. A third of the headteachers (5 DA, 1 RA, 7 CA) were quite satisfied with this help. Of the remaining headteachers, the majority of the RA group said that they would like to be able to call upon the services of an educational psychologist, and three other RA headteachers felt that a child guidance clinic was needed, neither service being apparently available to them. Three headteachers thought that the existing services could be better operated, and two wanted the help of a social worker. However, not many schools appeared to make much use of outside services and the remaining headteachers wanted additional help within the school, including teachers' aides, peripatetic remedial teachers, special classes set up within the school and a lower pupil/teacher ratio.

Eighty per cent of the class teachers either did not need any help in dealing with behavioural

Table 150

Average rankings of problem types
in order of frequency of occurrence

Problem	Class teachers			Headteachers		
	DA	RA	CA	DA	RA	CA
	N=19	11	18	13	9	11
restlessness/distractibility/ poor concentration	1	1	1	1	1	3
aggressiveness to others	2	3	2	2	4	4
disruptiveness/unruly behaviour in class	3	5	5	3.5	5	5
shyness/withdrawal	4	2	3	3.5	2	2
anti-social behaviour (lying, stealing etc.)	5	6	6	5	6	6
nervousness (tearfulness, timidity etc.)	6	4	4	6	3	1

problems. or were satisfied with what was already available. When in difficulties they were able to contact parents, consult colleagues and, usually as a last resort, consult the educational psychologist. The remaining few teachers would like advice on how to cope with problems in the classroom, an aide in the classroom, more co-operation from parents, opportunities to take the children out of the classroom, and an earlier assessment of ESN children. As a means of dealing with disruptive behaviour, a more formal classroom setting was desired by one teacher, and better facilities for play by another.

It seemed that schools on the whole preferred to deal with children's behaviour problems themselves, and this applied in some cases to ESN children as well. Five headteachers (2 DA, 1 RA, 2 CA) remarked that they were 'not very keen on the segregation of infant children in an ESN school, and one added that she would not recommend children below the age of 7 years for special schooling. One DA headteacher, on the other hand, thought that there should be an assessment of the need for special ESN education at 6+ years, i.e. after one year in the infant school.

Most headteachers felt that only one or two children in their school at that time would benefit from a transfer to a special ESN school or class, and the remaining headteachers, mainly CA and RA, thought that no child came into this category. The percentage of children who might need to be transferred at the end of their infant school careers was then estimated by the headteachers. In the DA group the average was 5 per cent, compared with only 1 per cent in the other groups.

Provision for special ESN education at infant age varied in each area, and when headteachers were asked for details of transfers to special schools or units within the previous three years, responses varied according to the facilities available. In the DA group, the average number of transfers over the three years was one child per school, numbers ranging from 0 to 3. In eight CA schools no child had been transferred, and six was the total number in the other four schools. In the RA group no special provision was available for ESN children, so no referrals had been made. One SWC and three DA children had also been recommended for transfer, but the parents had refused to give their permission. The majority of schools seemed to consider the provision available to be adequate at the infant stage.

The DA group also had more problems with school attendance and lateness than the other groups. In two DA schools there were long absences for trivial reasons as well as a great deal of morning absence, especially on Mondays and Fridays, caused by late rising and parental indifference or fecklessness. Six other DA schools also mentioned persistently poor attenders, though only a few children were involved. In one DA school children from broken homes occasionally played truant, or, when families split up, the children were moved elsewhere temporarily, and sometimes missed their schooling for long periods. Another DA school also mentioned occasional truancy.

One RA school had one or two poor attenders, and in a SWC school two children were frequently absent for no apparent reason. Otherwise nine RA and eleven CA schools, but only four DA schools, had no problems with school attendance. No RA or MC schools had any serious problems of lateness either, a serious problem being defined as 'fifteen minutes late on average twice weekly or more'. In SWC schools only one per cent of the children presented such problems, but there was an average of five per cent in the DA group. This lateness was mainly attributed to oversleeping or similar minor reasons, and parental indifference or fecklessness.

Finally, DA children showed more signs of material and cultural deprivation than those in the other groups. Nineteen per cent of DA children on average were estimated by the headteachers to belong to 'needy' families compared with only two per cent in CA schools, one SWC and three MC schools having no children in this category. In several RA schools there was only one needy family, but since it usually contained a large number of children, and the schools were small, the mean estimate was raised to six per cent. One RA school had no needy children, in another the headmaster commented, 'Compared with town children, this family is good', and another felt that the family he had nominated 'was not really needy'.

Apart from referring children showing signs of neglect to various agencies, schools made direct, unofficial provision themselves if necessary. They paid for the children's school trips, distributed clothing, and in two schools, bathed the children.

In another two schools (1 RA, 1 SWC), the parents refused cast-off clothing, and in two RA schools offers to pay for the children's school trips were also refused by the parents. Help was given to one MC family, but in no other MC school was it necessary, because even 'free dinner' children were well clothed. Many headteachers in the other groups also commented that 'Even poor parents try to clothe their children well'.

Several DA headteachers, however, made particular reference to 'poorly clad, dirty and ill-fed children'. In one school an aide would take them to the clinic to bath them, issue clothes and visit the homes. In the majority of cases the cause of the children's neglect was 'not genuine poverty, but Bingo and drink'. Another headteacher would like the assistance of a social worker in dealing with cases of neglect because 'the NSPCC inspector is over-burdened, and the school nurse feels that it is not her job'.

Almost all schools had children who showed signs of coming from a culturally poor or limited home background. Only 2 per cent on average showed such signs in the MC group, but there was an average of 18 per cent in the SWC group, 27 per cent in the RA group and 47 per cent in the DA group, according to the headteachers' estimates. Almost half the DA children therefore showed such signs, compared with only 10 per cent in the CA group. When the class teachers' estimates were averaged for each group the results were surprisingly similar, being either identical or with a difference of only one per cent.

Several examples were given of indications of a culturally limited home background. All schools stressed the children's restricted language, which affected their performance of, and pleasure in, most activities, and which could cause an initial lack of rapport with their teacher. The children also lacked concentration and tended to flit from one activity to the other. They were undisciplined — 'I can't do nothing with him' was a typical remark from some of the mothers. There was a lack of social training, and examples were often given of poor table manners and inability to use a handkerchief. The children were not sent to bed in good time at night, and might have to sleep three or four to a bed, so that they appeared tired during the day. They were unable to use a pencil or crayon, and had to be taught to take good care of school equipment. They could not follow up school activities at home because there were so few educational materials there, and they tended to take school equipment home with them.

They showed little initiative, imagination or curiosity, and lacked general interest in school activities. They made little or no contribution to class discussions and brought few materials to school. They lacked knowledge of currents affairs outside their immediate environment, and their conversation revealed a poverty of general experience. In one MC school, rehousing of a slum area had brought some deprived children into the school. The headteacher described them as being 'overwhelmed by what the school had to offer. Their clothes were below the usual school standard, and they listened enviously during discussions to children with more advantageous backgrounds'. It seemed as if deprived children were more keenly aware of their disadvantage in CA schools, where they formed only a small minority, than in DA schools, and the way of life of their more fortunate classmates offered a greater contrast to their own.

A few teachers thought that infant educational methods i.e. stressing play and discovery methods of learning, and giving free choice of activities, were wholly suitable for deprived children, but that they would need more attention from the teacher and a greater variety of experiences than other children. There might be some disturbance in the classroom initially, but eventually deprived children would be helped to develop socially and linguistically, and they would learn what might not be normally taught in formal lessons. They would 'have to spend more time on the play stage than other children, but the three Rs are not so important in the first year'.

This tacit acceptance that the free play approach entailed a lower standard of achievement in the basic skills was apparent in many replies, and led to the majority of teachers giving only qualified support to this approch, and advocating more direction of activities by the teacher. One DA teacher was 'unhappy about the lowering of academic standards', and she felt that more formal methods were needed with deprived children. A fully integrated day presented big organizational problems in a deprived area, and the time-table should be more structured. Another DA teacher thought that unless the children were 'well-behaved and responsible — which in most cases

they are not — they need the security of a more formal system'. Both these teachers came from the same vertically grouped school, which had adopted an integrated day approach.

Several other teachers also felt that the integrated day was too unstructured, and that it was difficult for them to keep track of children's activities and give sufficient help. Deprived children had had too much freedom and unsupervised play, and were so unruly that free activity did not work smoothly with them, and they appreciated some organization. They did not need less free choice but more structuring of activities so that they learned to play with a purpose, and the teacher could ensure that the basic skills were covered.

Many schools stressed that discovery methods of learning needed to be supplemented by some direct teaching. Deprived children were unused to looking after equipment and much time was wasted in disruptive behaviour, 'fooling about, throwing bricks about the classroom etc'. They needed to be taught how to look after materials, and also how to use equipment such as the weighing scales. Two headteachers (1 DA, 1 SWC) summed up the views of the majority of teachers when they remarked that the free play approach 'was not sufficient in itself. There should be a very structured environment with a skilled teacher in charge who has specific aims and who understands the problems associated with cultural deprivation', and 'The teacher should not be simply a provider of a suitable environment'.

A final group of teachers was opposed to the modern approach. They felt that it was suitable only for small classes 'because in large classes deprived children cannot take advantage of the experiences and materials offered to them'. It was sometimes 'very uneconomical in time and effort and the children need more direct teaching'. They 'appreciate a good routine because they lack this at home', and 'more formal methods suit these culturally deprived children because it gives them a sense of security'.

Headteachers and class teachers were finally asked to suggest ways in which infant schools could help to 'compensate' children coming from poor or limited home backgrounds. The suggestions were as follows:

1. Teachers must be highly skilled, well trained and experienced for this work. Adequate

inducements should be offered to teachers to attract them to the area.

2. Colleges of education should prepare teachers more adequately for this work.

3. All DA children should have nursery schooling, and then have three full years in an infant school.

4. Deprived children require access to materials and experiences not available at home in order to widen their experiences.

5. More financial allowance should be available to enable schools to provide a good standard of materials, decoration and furnishing, and to obtain more audio-visual aids.

6. The development of oral language skills should be emphasized, and some schools felt the need for a language programme.

7. Dramatic activities are important to develop speech, and art activities are also needed because these children are usually allowed to play out-of-doors but are not encouraged to paint and model.

8. The children should be given more individual attention, perhaps in smaller classes.

9. More infant helpers could help to prepare apparatus, supervise small groups etc., so that the teacher would be able to give more individual attention to the children.

10. More adult/child contact is needed in the classroom.

11. Some teachers felt that there should be visits to places of interest, but these should be in the locality because long journeys were not appropriate for very young children. There should be monetary help available when parents could not or would not contribute to the cost.

12. People from outside the school should be brought in to talk about their experiences.

13. There should be parent guidance, and parents should be educated in ways in which they could help their children.

14. More discussion is needed between parents and teachers in small groups.

15. Headteachers should be relieved of some duties, especially teaching duties, so as to give them more time to talk to parents.

16. Parents often need help with social problems in deprived areas, and one headteacher suggested that a social worker be appointed to provide this help.

17. Communication between the school and social services should be improved.

18. Deprived children in particular need to be *cherished*, to feel that they matter. 'They are not upset by a reprimand, but they respond to praise'.

SUMMARY (TEACHING APPROACHES)

A. The School Programme

Although there was considerable similarity in the schools' ranking of educational aims, it appeared that when children entered school with a reasonable standard of emotional and social maturity, and of oral language skills, teachers felt able to emphasize the basic skills at an early stage in the children's school career. Since DA children generally entered school at a lower stage of emotional, social and linguistic development than those in CA schools, it is probable that DA teachers placed less emphasis on the three Rs than CA and RA teachers during the reception year.

Most DA schools adopted *the integrated day*, or a similar approach, while CA and RA schools set aside certain periods of the day during which all children had to do some activity in the basic skills. Although teachers who adopted the 'integrated day' approach tried to guide children to take part in activities in the basic skills, it is possible that they were not always successful. Moreover, some of the teachers were not concerned whether the children covered the three Rs every day. This substantiates the impression that less work in the basic skills was, on the whole, carried out in DA schools than in the rest of the project schools during the first year.

All schools stressed the value of *free play* in developing self-expression and social awareness, and in providing an emotional outlet. DA teachers were less inclined to limit the children's choice of free play activities than the other two groups, and were more ready to take the initiative in the activities. After the first year less time was generally allocated to free play, but there was more opportunity for it in DA schools than in the other groups.

Children's level of interest in, or response to, *a creative or expressive activity* generally reflected the emphasis placed on it and the amount of time

274

devoted to it. Music and Movement aroused most enthusiasm in RA children, and music in CA children. Art aroused most response in DA schools because, said one headteacher, 'it gives them a form of compensation for their lack of language'.

All DA headteachers felt that they had problems in *developing language skills*. The children had poor language development and listening skills, and their background of stories and rhymes was very limited. Fewer RA and CA schools encountered these problems. Moreover they applied to only a small minority in CA schools, but were more general in the RA and DA groups.

Although poor speech articulation was one of the two problems most often mentioned by DA headteachers, they were less inclined to carry out formal speech training exercises than CA schools. Apart from this, there was little difference between the groups in their approach to language skills despite the difference in the linguistic development of their children. All schools adopted a general approach, and not one appeared to follow a definite language programme. Greatest stress was placed almost equally on fluency, listening skills and vocabulary building, and correction of the children's speech was made individually.

In the children's *written work*, the main aim in all groups was fluency. There was, however, more direct teaching of formal aspects of written English, especially spelling, in CA and RA schools than in DA schools, particularly during the final year.

Suggestions for extending opportunities for *oral language work* included reducing the size of classes or appointing aides so that teachers would have more time to converse with the children. Some schools wanted more audio-visual aids, especially tape recorders, and the provision of courses to instruct teachers in their use.

Most schools started with the whole word and/or sentence method to introduce *reading*, and this was usually followed by systematic phonic teaching. A minority used the phonic approach to reading from the beginning, either on its own or combined with the whole-word and/or sentence method. On the whole, most phonic teaching during the first year took place in CA schools, and least in the DA group.

Schools generally had a wide range of *pre-reading apparatus*, both commercially produced and teacher-made. The CA group had the highest proportion of teachers who tested a child's knowledge of vocabulary systematically before starting him on a reading scheme, and the DA group was the most likely to rely on their observation of the child's performance in pre-reading activities, without formal testing.

A higher level of expectation of children's *performance in reading* at the end of the first year was shown by CA and RA teachers than by DA teachers. The DA group also had the highest percentage of children expected to be still on pre-reading activities at the end of the first year, and the CA group had the lowest percentage. Although there was little difference between the groups in headteachers' expectations of children's performance at the end of their infant school career, average estimates of the number of children who would be poor readers and needing special help in the junior school were one and a half times greater in DA schools than in the other two groups.

DA schools faced more difficulties than the other schools in teaching reading, e.g. the children's lack of interest, language experience and concentration. In urban schools, headteachers generally gave extra tuition to slow learners, usually during the final school year, but most RA headteachers were unable to do so because they were full-time teachers. Many teachers, mainly in the DA group, felt that they were unable to give adequate help to backward readers, and this was particularly the case in vertically grouped schools.

In *mathematics*, most urban schools used the Nuffield scheme or a similar practical approach. Six CA schools used traditional methods as well, but only one DA school did so. The majority of RA schools used a mixture of new and traditional methods, and not one used the Nuffield scheme. Structural apparatus was used in almost all the urban, and half the RA, schools. RA schools generally introduced formal arithmetic at an earlier age than urban schools, and they also made more use of published mathematics books for children.

The main difficulty in teaching mathematics was the lack of confidence felt by the teachers. They needed more guidance, particularly on classroom organization, and some felt that courses they had attended had not been sufficiently practical. A few headteachers also said that children lacked mathematical experience before starting school, but almost half the DA headteachers remarked that their children were adept in handling money because they did so much of the family shopping. It seems therefore that the DA children were not at a disadvantage in mathematics compared with the other project children.

The DA group, however, were less well equipped with *audio-visual aids* than the other two groups and they were particularly lacking in tape recorders. On the whole, schools made good use of all their aids except the ciné projector, which seemed to be of least value to infant schools. Each additional aid tended to lessen the use of the others, and if difficulties were associated with them, such as the necessity to darken a room or lack of technical expertise among the staff, their use might not justify their cost.

B. Problems encountered by the schools

Children found most difficulty in adjusting to noise and crowds on school entry, but problems of adjustment to the school situation were generally transitory, especially with children who had attended a nursery class.

DA schools had a slightly higher average percentage of children presenting *behavioural problems,* and the types of behaviour occurring most frequently i.e. restlessness and aggressiveness, were among those the teachers found most difficulty in dealing with. They also had a slightly higher incidence of ESN children. On the whole, schools preferred to deal with these children themselves, because 'the flexibility of infant school methods enables them to deal with most children'. However, some headteachers wanted additional help, such as teachers' aides, peripatetic remedial teachers, and in two cases, a social worker to enable them to deal with ESN children and those presenting behaviour problems. A few headteachers also thought that existing services could be better operated, and many RA schools, unable to call on the services of an educational psycholo-

gist and child guidance clinic, wished they could do so.

DA schools had more problems with *school attendance and lateness* than the other groups, though generally only a few children were involved, and the cause was mainly attributed to parental indifference and/or fecklessness. Almost a fifth of the DA children were estimated to belong to *needy families,* which the incidence was negligible in the other groups. Almost half the DA children showed signs of coming from a *culturally poor or limited home background,* which was nearly twice the incidence in RA schools and five times as many as in the CA group.

Some schools did not agree that modern infant educational methods, i.e. stressing play and discovery methods of learning, free choice activities etc., were wholly suitable for children from culturally or materially deprived home backgrounds. They felt that more formal treatment was needed, because the children were unruly and had already experienced too much freedom. Others thought that the modern approach was the only one which would succeed with these children, but that they would need more attention from the teacher and a greater variety of activities than more advantaged children. They would have to spend more time on free play, and formal work should be delayed even if this meant that academic achievements were lower.

The majority of teachers, while agreeing that the modern approach was suitable, felt that it should be modified for deprived children. They needed

1. more guidance and structuring of activities
2. more direct teaching e.g. on the care and use of equipment
3. more routine to give them a sense of security.

All schools, however, were agreed on the need for highly skilled and experienced teachers who could give the children the attention and consideration they needed.

12 Home-School Contact

INTRODUCTION

There have been many official recommendations in recent years for improving parent-teacher relationships. The report of the Plowden Committee (1967) emphasizes the importance of parental influence on a child's learning, and two reports of the Department of Education and Science, 'Teachers and Parents' (Report No. 4, 1967b) and 'Parent-Teacher Relations in Primary Schools' (Education Survey 5, 1968), and also a pamphlet issued by the Inner London Education Authority, 'Home and School', recommend closer links between teachers and parents and give examples of what can be done to achieve this.

Although there is still much controversy about how far parents can or should be involved in actually teaching children, the range of activities in which parents are invited to rake a part has been increasing in some schools beyond the traditional ones of helping with Christmas parties, school outings and money-raising. This has come about partly through an increasing realization on the part of teachers of the effects of parental interest and involvement on the young child's school progress, and also through pressure from many groups of parents to know more about the educational processes in a general sense, and about the progress and adjustment of their own child in particular. Parental initiative in this respect is more likely to come from the better educated parents, and parent-teacher associations have tended to flourish more in 'middle-class' areas or to cater for only the 'middle-class' element among the school population. Because less advantaged parents have not taken part to a great extent in this type of organization, it was often felt that they were apathetic or uninterested in their child's education. It was therefore decided to investigate various aspects of home-school contact in the project schools from the point of view of both teachers and parents.

A. LINKS WITH SCHOOL: THE TEACHERS' OPINIONS

The Headteachers' Questionnaire (Part II) (see Appendix III) devoted Section B and a few items in Section C to ascertaining the extent of parent-school contact in the project schools, and to obtaining the views of the headteachers on various aspects of the relationship between parents and schools. The point of view of class teachers was obtained from the final section of the Class Teachers' Questionnaire (Part I).

In the analysis of the data, schools were grouped according to the area in which they were situated, i.e. deprived area (DA) 14 schools, rural area (RA) 10 schools, and control area (CA) 12 schools, the last group being occasionally sub-divided into 'settled working-class' (SWC) and 'middle-class' (MC) with 6 schools in each sub-division. These figures refer only to the head-teachers' schedules (Part II). As already stated, more class teachers' schedules (Part I) were completed for each group (19 DA, 11 RA, 11 SWC and 7 MC, making a total of 18 in the CA group).

(i) General school contact with parents. Maintaining home-school contact on a formal basis by means of parent-teacher associations found most favour among rural headteachers. Three out of the ten RA schools had already established associations, and two more intended to start almost immediately, one having already made initial contact with the parents. However, the three existing PTAs had all been recently organized. One had been established the previous term and had held three meetings during that term, another was about to hold its first meeting, and the third was awaiting the completion of a building programme before holding its first meeting, although invitations to it had already been 'enthusiastically' accepted by the parents.

There was only one PTA in the DA group. In three other schools, one headteacher hoped to establish one shortly, another was considering it, and the third had formerly organized one but it had 'fizzled out – died a natural death'. The one existing PTA, which was run jointly with the junior school, had only recently been established, and it held general meetings consisting of talks and discussions twice a term. The headteacher was 'not very happy with it', as she felt that it tended to be 'run by the teachers', and she was more in favour of a parents' association. There was such an association in one MC school (but neither the headteacher nor the staff attended the meetings), and another in the junior department of a MC school to which the infant school staff was invited. Otherwise there was no PTA in any MC school.

There seemed to be little enthusiasm for PTAs on the whole among the urban schools. One DA headteacher 'wouldn't consider it. Some parents would rule the roost'. Another (MC) preferred the link with the school to be formed 'at the invitation of the headteacher rather than by right of the PTA. These associations tend to take over on many occasions – to impose themselves on a school'. He preferred informal contact, and this view was supported by several headteachers.

This informal contact generally took place when parents brought their children to school and then collected them, although this was far less prevalent in RA schools because of the large number of children who had to travel to school by 'bus. The majority of the project headteachers also encouraged parents to visit them at any time, stressing their informality with remarks such as 'free access to headteacher and school' (DA), 'open house' (SWC), and 'like a club – parents can enter at any time and do so' (SWC). Informal contact out of school hours was mentioned mainly by RA headteachers, more than half of whom referred to chance meetings between school staff and parents in the town or village streets, in church meetings or on 'special public occasions'.

A few headteachers, mainly in CA schools, attempted more systematic ways of ensuring contact between parents and school. One (SWC) invited all parents to attend school assembly once a month; another (also SWC) invited parents to see school activities such as 'Music and Movement' on average twice a term; while a third (MC) had recently issued a questionnaire to parents asking them in what ways they could help the school. Three-quarters of the questionnaires had been completed and returned, and the headteacher intended to act on the information received.

Already parents worked in the school library informally, some visiting the school for this purpose several times a week, and there were also weekly meetings when articles were made for sale. Finally, one DA school invited groups of parents regularly, two classes at a time, to talk to the class teacher, see the children working and have tea with the headteacher afterwards. In this way, every parent was invited to school at least once a term by letter.

A third of the urban, but nearly all the rural, headteachers mentioned that parents were contacted by letter regarding school activities, school closures etc., and one SWC school issued a termly newsletter. RA schools also appeared to make more use of the telephone as a means of communicating with parents, and one headteacher entered the home telephone number on the admission slips of the children. All but one of the RA schools, and a third of the CA schools, mentioned the telephone as a means of contact with parents, but only one DA school did so, probably because few parents in deprived areas possessed telephones in their homes. Finally, one RA headteacher not only circularized parents, but also placed notices in shop windows to advertise school meetings and activities.

A few urban schools (two DA and three CA) did not invite parents to any social occasions because of insufficient accommodation. Every RA school, on the other hand, invited parents to attend a variety of social functions despite lack of space e.g. no school hall, and in two schools this involved the use of the local church for the Harvest Thanksgiving and Ascension Day services.

In all the project schools, parents were most often invited to witness their children performing in plays and concerts, generally at Christmas time or on St. David's Day, or in carol or Harvest Thanksgiving services. Next in popularity in urban schools came Open Days, which were held in more than half the DA schools, while RA schools gave second place to Christmas and other parties, to which parents were invited, and only one school mentioned an Open Day. A very few schools in the whole sample invited parents to attend sports days or to accompany school outings, but otherwise the only other social activity consisted of various forms of fund-raising. Two DA and four CA schools mentioned jumble or bring-and-buy sales, while four RA schools showed considerable ingenuity in their fund-raising efforts. They held whist drives, garden fêtes, coffee evenings and bonfire night parties, as well as jumble sales. Several RA schools organized evening activities, but these were very rare among the urban schools.

Meetings on educational matters were far less frequent than the social occasions. Only five DA schools held such meetings, and these were usually very infrequent. One headteacher had called one meeting the previous year because she intended introducing reading by i.t.a. Another had held two meetings jointly with the junior school, during which a lecture had been given on the educational system of the LEA and a film had been shown on sex education. The third school called occasional meetings when, for instance, there was to be a change in the organization of family grouping, but did not discuss teaching methods. The other two schools held meetings more frequently. One, which was also the school which invited groups of parents at regular intervals, held classes to explain the methods used by the teachers. A series of talks was given over a period of a few weeks, mainly by the headteacher or her deputy, at 4.30 p.m. for the mothers and later in the evening for the fathers. The headteacher of the other school had given talks on reading, children's books and on the new mathematics scheme.

Only two RA headteachers had held any meetings on educational matters, but more would be arranged when the PTAs were fully operational. Of the two headteachers, one had arranged only one meeting, which he felt had not been succesful because the parents were only interested in the 11+ examination. The other headteacher had recently organized a PTA which had visited a comprehensive school and been addressed by an outside speaker on recent educational developments in the county. Other RA headteachers preferred to see parents individually, and felt that there was sufficient informal contact in and out of school, during which educational matters could be discussed.

The SWC schools were the most active in arranging meetings on educational matters. Three out of the six schools organized meetings fairly frequently. In one school, talks were given by outside speakers and by members of the staff, e.g. an account of school activities illustrated by slides. The second school held termly meetings, generally addressed by outside lecturers, while the third arranged a varied programme including a demonstration of a PE lesson 'because parents were worried about children undressing'.

Only in one MC school were meetings arranged on educational matters. The headteacher invited groups of mothers to the school to discuss reading, and she gave guidance to the parents on the making of 'books' on various topics. In two other schools, the parents' associations arranged meetings, and in a fourth school the headteacher had held one meeting when he was first appointed to explain his policy, but not one since. He felt doubtful if a short meeting could convey new ideas adequately, and he wondered if the parents would understand the underlying processes involved. It might be that a subject would be treated in a superficial way, and the meeting would do more harm than good.

Most schools testified to the overall helpfulness and co-operation of the parents, and only in a DA school was this statement qualified, when the headteacher remarked that 'the free dinner people make less contribution, and a third of them give very little help — they are mainly at the receiving end'. However, another DA headteacher referred to the strong community spirit in her area, adding that a group of parents soon gathered to offer help if a sick child was taken home from school.

The amount of help received depended on what was asked of the parents. They were far more ready to contribute money and materials than to give of their labour, and in one DA school, whereas more than 70 per cent would offer to help in the running of a jumble sale, very few would knit dolls' clothes etc. in preparation for it. When headteachers were asked to estimate the percentage of parents who were ready to help in any way, DA estimates ranged from 5 to 99 with an average of 74 per cent, RA estimates ranged from 75 to 100 with an average of 91 per cent, and CA estimates ranged from 33 to 100 with an average of 87 per cent.

This pool of available resources was rarely systematically tapped. Six DA, five RA and five CA schools did not ask parents to help in the way of labour, although more than half the headteachers added that it would be available if asked for. In the other schools, parents helped on social occasions, e.g. at parties, outings and sales. In addition, three headteachers enlisted the help of parents in undressing and dressing children for swimming, and in RA schools parents readily offered to transport children in their cars. On rare occasions fathers helped with carpentry, and they had once levelled ground for a swimming pool in one RA school, and cleared an overgrown school garden in another. In two DA schools, mothers made simple apparatus, and in two others a 'hard core of mothers' helped with sewing and covering books with cellograph. One MC school channelled the help available more systematically, by issuing the questionnaires already mentioned. From those returned, the headteacher had drawn up a list of volunteers to hear children read, to accompany children on school visits etc., and she intended to make use of this information in the future. Meanwhile parents helped in the school library, covered books and made articles for the sales at weekly meetings.

Parents contributed generously in kind with articles for classroom use and for sales, food for parties, items for Harvest Thanksgiving services and trade coupons. Many schools did not ask directly for money, apart from charity appeals, because the proceeds of school concerts and sales, the sale of photographs, crisps, biscuits and nuts, and Savings Bank interest appeared to supply sufficient funds. Moreover, one SWC headteacher refrained from asking parents for a financial contribution since, if forthcoming, it would weaken the school's case for a more liberal LEA allowance.

Thus, although headteachers' estimates had shown that there was more help available in the RA and CA schools, there seemed to be little difference between the groups in the amount of help actually given by the parents, because their assistance was only called upon to a limited extent.

(ii) Early school contact. Almost all CA parents registered their children prior to school entry, percentages estimated by the headteachers ranging from 95 to 100. Slightly fewer parents registered their children in DA schools, estimated percentages ranging from 40 to 100, with a mean of 91. In some infant and nursery schools, headteachers felt that this high rate of registration was due to the desire of the parents to obtain a place for their children in the nursery class, and in one DA infant school, a headteacher remarked that it was due to

the parents' anxiety to 'get the children into school out of their way'. The mean percentage in RA schools was also very high at 95, ranging from 75 to 100, but many parents registered their children informally, either when meeting the headteacher socially, or by visiting his home after school hours.

Of the whole sample, in only two schools (both DA) was it not considered necessary to introduce the parents and their children to the reception classroom and teacher before entry. Where there was a nursery class, it was generally felt that the children were already familiar with the school, and only the few entrants who were commencing their schooling in the infant department were introduced with their parents to the reception class teacher. In other DA schools, the introduction was made at the time of registration, although in many cases children did not accompany their parents on this occasion and therefore had no opportunity to have an introduction to the classroom situation prior to entry. Where the headteacher was also a full-time teacher, the introduction was necessarily brief because her time was limited.

Two DA headteachers made more systematic arrangements to introduce parents and children to the school before entry. One headteacher tried to ensure that each child visited the school on at least two occasions. If the mother arrived for registration unaccompanied, she was invited to return on a later occasion with the child. In addition, shortly before the end of the school term prior to entry, all parents were invited to visit the school with their children on any afternoon within a given week. The headteacher would talk to the children and show them around the school. Similar arrangements were made by the other headteacher, who set aside one afternoon for this purpose, and who also addressed the parents while the children joined a class.

Seven of the ten RA headteachers were also full-time teachers, and one pointed out that this left little time to introduce parents and children to the reception teacher and classroom at the time of registration. However, four headteachers arranged for the pre-school children to spend some time in the school before entry. The period varied from every afternoon for three weeks or a month, to one or two afternoons weekly for a period up to a term. This was done despite the transport problem (children below the statutory school age are not provided with transport by the LEA), and the fact that the children were not covered by insurance. In a fifth school, the children were invited to spend an afternoon playing with the reception class apparatus, which was displayed for their benefit.

Seven CA schools arranged for parents and children to have contact with the school prior to entry apart from the period of registration. Two headteachers invited parents to visit the school with their children during a given week or fortnight. No particular period was set aside in a third school for this purpose, because the majority of children attended the nursery class and few would need to avail themselves of the opportunity. The entire school entry (approximately 25 children per term) was invited by another headteacher to attend two school sessions during the previous term. Two vertically-grouped classes received the children and looked after them. Pre-school children spent half a day in the reception class in two other schools, and one SWC school arranged for the children to attend for a morning and an afternoon weekly throughout the term before entry, especially for children who, because of their birthday month, could have only two years' infant schooling. Although the headteacher had only introduced the arrangement the previous year, she already felt that as a preparation for schooling, and as some compensation for the shorter period in the infant school, it had been very successful. Finally, an eighth school invited parents to return with their children if the latter had not been present during registration.

Some headteachers were prevented by lack of space from allowing children to experience the classroom situation before entry. Others allowed pre-school children to attend occasionally if requested to do so, but it was not a regular part of school policy.

When the children finally entered school, few headteachers actively encouraged parents to stay with their children for part of the day during their first days at school, but some urban schools would allow it if the need arose. A few (three DA and one CA) felt quite strongly that the children settled down better when the parents had gone, and would only allow them to stay if absolutely necessary. In RA schools, all but one headteacher took this firm attitude of opposition to parents staying with their children. One pointed out that

the need did not arise because so many children travelled by bus unaccompanied by their parents and another remarked that with family grouping there was no problem in getting children to settle down in school.

A SWC headteacher noted that with prior introduction to the school situation (which she arranged systematically), children rarely found difficulty in settling down at entry. Some headteachers staggered the entry by accepting groups of children daily and varying the times of their arrival, thus allowing the reception teacher to attend to each child individually. Others made the children's entry to school a gradual process by allowing them to start later in the morning and leave early in the afternoon for a time.

In one DA school children commenced schooling on a Wednesday, and attended mornings only for the first three days, but this was the only school which arranged part-time attendance for initial period for all children. Other headteachers were prepared to arrange it for individuals who found difficulty in adjusting to the school situation, but had rarely done so because the situation had not arisen. Where it had been arranged, the children had sometimes attended for a part of the morning and afternoon so that they could be marked present for the whole day.

A few rural headteachers pointed out that the problem of transport made part-time attendance very difficult, and five urban headteachers (three DA and two SWC) were opposed to part-time attendance except on medical grounds because

'children should learn to adjust to the system. I do not regard the school as a stressful experience'

'If a child gets tired in school he should go to bed earlier'

'I haven't room for this'

'children accept the system – this practice would set up a bad habit'

'part-time attendance is not encouraged by the LEA – there is no insurance cover for these children'.

Most headteachers added that the problem of children finding great difficulty in settling down in school had never arisen.

(iii) Co-operation between school and home. All headteachers gave ample opportunity for parents to discuss their children's progress or other matters with them, and no school insisted on parents making an appointment. In DA schools the headteachers were available at any time to see parents although in practice parents consulted them when bringing and collecting their children, and on Open Days. One school organized at least one Open Week every year, during which the school operated normally and parents were encouraged to discuss any matter with the headteacher and staff.

Since most RA headteachers were also full-time teachers, they usually preferred parents not to call during lesson time, but otherwise they were available to be seen almost literally at any time, and seven of them specifically mentioned that parents, especially the fathers, came to see them at home during the evening. Although no headteacher insisted on an appointment being made, their teaching commitments made such a prior arrangement desirable, and some parents telephoned to arrange a convenient time for calling.

It seemed that to be sufficiently available to see parents without its interfering with the work of the school was a problem, and CA schools, particularly, had exercised considerable initiative in seeking to solve it. During the previous year, one headteacher, with 226 children on roll, had invited all parents to school on certain afternoons every week to discuss progress, but only four parents had arrived. She and another headteacher had also formerly arranged parental visits on an 'appointments only' basis, but they found that in practice it was not successful, partly because of official visitors calling unexpectedly during the day, so they had decided that an informal approach was preferable, and were available at any time to see parents, as were all but three schools.

These three schools seemed to have achieved a successful compromise. They set aside certain periods during the week for interviewing parents, and if these times were not convenient, appointments normally had to be made, though in practice they never refused to see a parent at any time. One headteacher filed a sample of each child's written work and reading scheme record every term, so that she could refer to these when discussing progress with his parents.

Open Days were also held in half the CA schools, and an Open Week in one school. During the Open Days, class teachers were freely available to discuss children's progress with the parents, and in two schools ancillary help was used to release the teacher when parents wished to speak to her. Another school held an Open Evening for parents unable to be present during the day, as well as an Open Week, during which parents were given an opportunity to make an appointment for a 15-minute interview with the class teacher and headteacher. About ten per cent of the parents had availed themselves of this opportunity.

In most urban schools class teachers were also available to be seen informally at any time, but in half the schools the headteachers wished to be consulted first. In practice, parents generally saw the class teachers when bringing or collecting their children, but on other occasions, during lesson time, a third of the headteachers were prepared to take charge of the class in order to release the teacher, while in four CA schools a part-time teacher or ancillary help was employed for this purpose. This was not always possible in RA schools where the headteachers were responsible for taking a class and there was no ancillary help, so parents were encouraged to arrive outside lesson time to see class teachers as well as headteachers. In all but one RA school, teachers could be seen directly without reference to the headteacher first, and in a few schools, the teachers lived locally and were available to be seen in the evenings.

It was difficult for headteachers to estimate the percentage of parents who consulted them concerning their children's progress. Moreover, attendance at Open Days was sometimes excluded, and some RA headteachers excluded parents who approached them out of school hours, so that only a general indication was obtained of the number of parents who consulted the school about their children's progress. The mean estimate for the CA schools was 35 per cent, 10 per cent above that for the RA and DA schools. Headteachers from all groups commented that parents showed little concern about their children's progress until the final year prior to entry into the junior department, and a RA headteacher had noted a marked diminution in inquiries since the announcement that the 11+ examination was being abandoned.

As might be expected, of the parents who visited the school, the majority were mothers. Fathers accounted for less than ten per cent of the total in DA schools, though this proportion was doubled in RA and CA schools. One SWC head-teacher mentioned that the fathers were mainly shift workers who were free to visit during the day, and one MC and several RA headteachers commented that fathers generally approached them out of school hours, because they were at work during the day. Fathers were also more likely to attend Open Days than to visit the school individually. Some parents appeared to feel diffident about consulting the school regarding their children's progress, especially in DA and SWC schools, and generally made their inquiries incidentally, while ostensibly visiting the school on another pretext.

Some urban class teachers had visited children's homes in an emergency such as an accident or illness in school, or during a child's prolonged illness, and one SWC teacher had visited homes at Christmas time to invite children (presumably absentees) to a school party. Another teacher (DA) had taken children to her own home, and on outings, and had written to them when she was on holiday.

Seven DA teachers had no objection to visiting the home if they were invited, or if a problem arose and the mother was unable to go to the school; two SWC teachers thought that it was 'part of the teacher's job to contact the home' and 'more liason between home and school was essential', but neither had actually visited homes except to take children home in an emergency or to invite children to a Christmas party; and three MC teachers felt that parents came to school so often that it was unnecessary to visit the homes, but they would be prepared to do so to discuss a child's problem if necessary, though such an occasion had never arisen.

All other urban teachers were either reluctant to visit or opposed to it except in an emergency. They felt that

'the headteacher knows the home background and we can refer to her' (6 teachers)

'it is not part of the teacher's work. The welfare officer/headteacher should visit the home, and parents can always come to school' (4 teachers)

'many parents would not welcome/be embarrassed by a visit' (2 teachers)

'I have not much time for this/I have enough to do in school' (2 teachers)

'one must be consistent. I have had invitations to tea but refused them because I should have to accept all or none' (1 teacher).

Three RA class teachers had visited homes occasionally, apart from emergencies, to attend birthday parties, inquire about a child's health, take work for a child to do if he had been absent for some time, and to return an article which had been left in school.

A quarter of the urban headteachers were opposed to visiting children's homes except in an emergency, such as children running out of school or having to be taken home due to illness or accident. DA headteachers gave a variety of reasons for their opposition. It was better for the headteacher to keep a little apart, the parents might not welcome the contact, parents tended to have many official visitors already, it was an invasion of privacy, it was not necessary if the school maintained good liaison with the home, and if parents were really interested they would come to school when invited. Even when invited to a child's party, one headteacher always refused because an acceptance could lead to a social round; and a CA headteacher made the same observation. Other CA headteachers felt that it was not part of their work to visit homes, it was an intrusion, and parents who were not prepared to visit the school might resent the visit.

The remaining urban headteachers had no objections to visiting the home if it was necessary, i.e. if parents were unco-operative or disinterested, but usually the need had never arisen. It was generally felt that a visit to the home was a last resort, after an invitation to the parent to come to the school to discuss a particular problem had been refused. Visits had been made on occasions of family bereavement, when a child was very ill, or to take clothing to needy families, while in one school a teachers' aide visited homes, mainly in cases of illness.

In only two urban schools (one DA and one SWC) had visits been made concerning educational matters. In the former, the headteacher had discussed children's progress, special problems e.g. concerning the placement of an ESN child, and matters on which the parents had proved unco-operative. In the latter school, the headteacher had on one occasion visited a home to discuss a behaviour problem and had also attended children's parties, while one of her staff had, on her own initiative, regularly visited the home of an ESN child, taken clothing there, and had also invited members of her class home to tea.

On the whole, there was little enthusiasm among urban schools for home visiting, contact being maintained mainly in the direction of home to school. In RA schools an outward movement, from school to home, was far more noticeable. Not one objection was raised to home visiting. Three headteachers had visited the homes of all, or nearly all, the children in the school (numbers on roll being 59, 61 and 30), and two others made constant visits. These were often social visits because the headteachers took a leading part in the community life e.g. in the church, and in organizations such as the Brownies and Cubs, but school matters were also discussed, and one headmaster mentioned visiting the homes of deprived children 'to see what can be done to help'.

When headteachers were asked to rate the general level of the parents co-operation with the school on a four-point scale (Table 151), the majority in RA and CA schools rated the overall level as 'very good', and the remainder as 'good'. Only four DA headteachers felt that the level was 'very good', and the majority was 'good', while in one school it was only 'satisfactory'.

The class teachers were asked to rate on a four-point scale the general level of interest shown by parents in their children's progress. A few teachers were unable to distinguish between the second and third points on the scale, 'quite positive' and 'fairly interested', so these results were combined in two groups. Although the wording of this question differed from that for the headteachers, the results showed a similar trend (Table 152). Almost 30 per cent of DA schools felt that in general the parents showed 'little evidence of interest'.

The parents showed their interest by inquiring regarding their children's progress, asking for books to take home so that they could hear their children read, buying the reading scheme books (though some teachers discouraged this), supplying materials when asked and supporting school activities. Two MC teachers felt that some parents were 'too positive' in their interest, and another noted that the parents had high ambitions for their children.

When asked to estimate the percentage of unco-operative or indifferent parents, some headteachers felt that it was difficult to define them, and two headteachers (SWC and RA) remarked that although some parents showed no apparent interest they might not be really indifferent. Generally, headteachers defined indifferent parents as those who did not attend school functions, never asked now the children were progressing, and did not help them with their work, e.g. by hearing them read or supplying materials for projects etc. On average 20 per cent of DA parents were placed in this category, 7 per cent in RA

Table 151

Headteachers' ratings of general parental co-operation

Rating	DA	RA	CA	
			SWC	MC
very good	4	7	5	5
good	9	3	1	1
satisfactory	1	-	-	-
poor	-	-	-	-
Totals	14	10	6	6

Table 152

Teachers' ratings of general parental interest in
children's progress

Rating	DA	RA	CA	
			SWC	MC
very positive	1	3	4	6
quite positive	13	8	4	1
fairly interested			3	-
little evidence of interest	5	-	-	-
Totals	19	11	11	7

schools and a negligible 3 per cent in CA schools.

Similarly the class teachers estimated the proportion of parents in the fourth category, i.e. showing little evidence of interest in their children's progress, and their results showed an even greater difference between the groups, with an average of 45 per cent DA, 20 per cent RA and 10 per cent CA parents in this category. Four RA and five CA teachers decided that no parents showed this lack of interest.

Parents showed their disinterest mainly by absenting themselves from the classroom or school. The teachers had 'never seen some parents. Even when the children started school they were brought by older children'. Other teachers had seen the parents on the child's first day at school, but not since. 'Some don't even know my name', said a DA teacher. Another DA teacher remarked that although they often showed interest at first (by attending Christmas parties etc.), it gradually waned as the year progressed. A teacher in the same DA school added that in the previous year only three or four parents had turned up at the Open Day. The school had tried every method to interest them, 'but to them, school is a place to get rid of the children'. Other DA teachers described disinterested parents as those who gave material things to the children but did not listen to them reading and talking.

Two RA class teachers placed nearly 90 per cent of their parents in this category, which considerably increased the mean percentage of rural parents showing 'little evidence of interest'. The teachers felt sure that most parents were interested in their own way, but there was little evidence of it, and one teacher added that because of the isolated position of most homes, children were brought to school by LEA transport and there was little home/school contact. A teacher in a third RA school also felt that most parents were fairly interested but there was little tangible evidence of it.

Several headteachers differentiated between unco-operative and indifferent parents, with very few of the former present in any school. Various reasons were given in DA schools for their unco-operative attitude. They were resentful or distrustful of authority, they themselves had had an unhappy school life so they were hostile and truculent, and in the case of immigrants there was sometimes a lack of co-operation due to cultural problems, e.g. a refusal to allow children to remove clothing for PE. In RA and CA schools, the few parents in this category were thought to be unco-operative because of unhappy home circumstances, or resentment because the children were 'not in the top flight' and were unlikely to succeed in the 11+ examination.

In all schools unco-operative parents were the exception, usually the fathers, and were described variously as 'work-shy and semi-alcoholic', 'unstable', 'at loggerheads with the community and in trouble with the police', and 'a very awkward customer'.

Indifference was far more prevalent than active hostility, and was ascribed to various causes. It was due to

'large families. Mothers have several small children and cannot cope' (4 DA, 1 RA, 1 SWC)

'lack of interest in education' (4 DA, 1 SWC)

'low mentality — parents not very intelligent' (3 DA)

'greater interest in having a good time — beer and bingo' (2 DA)

'their own background. They themselves are from poor homes and their standards are low' (1 DA)

'mothers thinking that once the children are in school, their responsibility for them ends' (3 DA)

'parents leaving everything to the school because they are satisfied with the child's progress' (2 RA, 1 SWC).

Nearly half the DA headteachers felt that they had problems concerning parents and their co-operation with school, and they instanced parental indifference or hostility e.g. refusal to hear children read, feckless families, chronic lateness or poor attendance of a small core of children (2 schools) and 'finding the time to get in touch with parents' (1 school).

The majority of RA and SWC, and all MC, headteachers said that they had no problems concerning parental co-operation. Two headteachers thought that their continuous informal contact with parents prevented problems arising, and one (MC) added that the parents were 'reasonably intelligent', could understand modern teaching methods and were 'easier to handle than uninformed parents'. The few problems in RA and SWC schools were concerned mainly with parental apathy. 'The parents I would most like to see don't come to Open Days even when specifically invited', said one SWC headteacher, and another referred to a falling off of interest, in that parents were not as ready to help as formerly. However,

since in that particular case they had been asked to do only menial tasks, this was understandable. Other headteachers referred to minor irritations, and the fact that a high proportion of working mothers lacked the time to co-operate fully with the school.

The headteachers named several sources of help on which they could call, including the care committee, the health visitor or school nurse (in cases of dirty or neglected children), family service units, the school welfare officer, the children's department, the social services, the infant school organiser and the director of education. Three DA headteachers preferred to deal with their problems themselves and had never called on this help, and most of the others in the DA group had done so only very occasionally. Only four RA schools had ever any occasion to use outside help, and those only very rarely, while CA schools had made even less use of it. As one SWC headteacher remarked, 'If parents are not interested there is not much that can be done — one can't make them so'.

Headteachers were then asked if there was any help not already available which they would like to have in dealing with problems concerning the co-operation of the parents with the school. All RA and CA headteachers felt that they 'knew most parents very well and could do a better job than an outsider', and that 'it would become very impersonal if dealt with by someone outside school'. However, four RA headteachers thought that they should have additional staff to free them from some of their teaching duties, and one SWC headteacher wanted more clerical assistance, so that they would have more time to deal with their problems themselves.

The majority of DA schools also thought that the present system was adequate, but three headteachers felt the need for a social worker to 'do home visits', another wanted 'full-time help to deal with teacher/parent relationships', and two others would like a return to the system of attaching a health visitor to a group of schools.

Most DA headteachers thought that parents should be more actively involved in their children's education, but the majority of CA headteachers felt that parents were already sufficiently involved and too competitive over school performance. These views were reflected by the class teachers, but in RA schools, whereas the headteachers were unanimous in thinking that parents should be more actively involved, half the teachers felt that this was not necessary.

Those who were in favour of more parental involvement in children's education were not always in agreement on the ways in which this might be achieved. While some schools wanted parents to 'count verbally and hear children read', others preferred parents to be involved in activities other than the three Rs, e.g. taking children on visits, giving them language experiences by holding conversations with them and reading to them, rather than repeating school activities. They should provide more opportunities for learning at home by making suitable books and toys available, and by extending their experiences. Children should also be given adequate rest and care, and be taught social competence prior to entry.

Several teachers wanted more extended parent/teacher contact, other than at the beginning and end of the school day when parents brought and collected their children. Parents should enter the classroom more often to exchange views with the teacher and to 'see what goes on so as to be more able to help the child at home'. Urban class teachers were less in favour of informal contact than headteachers, probably because their classroom duties made such contact inadequate, and nine teachers felt that parents should be enlightened on the modern approaches to education by means of formal meetings to explain teaching methods. One teacher stipulated that these should be held 'outside school hours, on a business-like basis, similar to evening classes', and not under the auspices of a PTA, which she felt tended to become more of a social gathering. In fact, urban class teachers were evenly divided on the subject of PTAs, those against them feeling there was already sufficient informal contact, or that parents

might 'take advantage', 'dictate school policy' and 'become aggressive'.

Although some schools felt that parents should not be involved in direct teaching at home, since reading particularly might then become a chore and burden to some children, this was more often the attitude taken by CA teachers, who felt that parents were already over-anxious. In the majority of schools, 'hearing children read' was most often quoted as a means of involving parents in their children's education.

Headteachers were therefore asked what percentage of parents showed a desire for their children to make progress in reading. The estimated percentage, on average, was lowest for the DA group, was increased for the RA and SWC, and was highest for MC schools (Table 153).

The interested parents asked advice on the books they should buy, bought books or asked to borrow them, inquired as to how they could help their children, and became anxious if their children could not read. This interest in reading was often accompanied by a competitive spirit which was transferred to the children, so it would appear that CA children were more highly motivated than other groups to increase their prowess in reading.

Headteachers were then asked if they encouraged parents to help their children with their reading. Only three headteachers did not do so, but others had certain reservations. One would only send books home with good readers 'because children dislike making mistakes in front of their parents', others stressed that there should be no active help and parents were told not to teach but only to listen. Schools complained that parents confused children by teaching the letter names instead of letter sounds, and by using capital letters. They bought the reading scheme books

Table 153

Headteachers' average estimates of parents showing interest in their children's progress in reading
(N, schools = 36)

	DA	RA	SWC	MC	CA
%	41.5	55	69	88	78.5

used by the school and taught their children to read by rote, and in some CA schools did more harm than good by putting pressure on their children. In view of these errors by parents, it seems strange that only three headteachers from all groups stated that they advised parents on the method of teaching reading.

When asked in what way they encouraged parents to help, the majority answered that they allowed parents to take reading books home, asked parents to listen to their children reading, and to read to them, advised them to join a library and 'to give the children plenty of encouragement'. This final remark illustrated a tendency among some headteachers to reply with vague generalities. 'I encourage the parents to take a general interest' (4 headteachers), and 'the operative word is "encourage" ' (2 headteachers).

Parents showed less interest in their children's progress in mathematics, and headteachers were far less likely to encourage them to help their children in this subject. The majority felt that there was a danger of parents confusing the children and of using an over-formal approach, parents were unfamiliar with recent changes in teaching number, they would stress the wrong things i.e. be more concerned with computational skills than number concepts, they would lack the necessary apparatus, and they would be unable to deal with the transition to decimalization and metrication. Only a third of all urban head-teachers, but half of those in rural schools, encouraged parents to help their children in mathematics, and even they hedged their answers with many reservations.

Two headteachers felt that only some parents were capable of helping their children, and one added that she 'told individual parents about the Nuffield scheme informally'. One wonders how many parents could grasp the principles underlying the modern method of teaching mathematics in an informal approach of this nature. Five head-teachers explained their methods to parents by organizing meetings, and two of these (both RA) remarked that it was the need for explaining their approach to mathematics that had provided the impetus to establish PTAs.

Other schools advised parents in more general terms by telling them to give their children mathematical experiences in connection with domestic activities, shopping, travelling etc., talk-ing about certain processes e.g. weighing, and allowing children to carry them out. One MC headteacher, who had previously taught in a slum clearance area, found that the children in her former school were more able to cope with money than those in her present school, because they had done so much shopping for their parents.

Several schools stressed that parents' involve-ment in their children's education should be confined to the home, and that they should be actively *interested*, not *involved*. One headteacher added that parents' activities should be *comple-mentary* to those of the school, and that parents should not interfere in the work of the school. The question as to whether parents could play a useful role in the day-to-day working of the school, therefore, aroused considerable opposition and the most fluent comments from both headteachers and staff.

Only four teachers (1 DA and 3 SWC) and three headteachers (one from each group except RA schools) gave an unreserved 'yes' as a reply. The others were all either firmly opposed to it or very dubious. A few teachers agreed to it in principle but felt it to be inapplicable in their area, because of the parents' poor education and low standard of speech in a DA school, and in a MC school, because the very strong spirit of competition would lead to parents comparing their children with others.

Other teachers felt that there would be diffi-culties involved in the selection of suitable parents, and that it would be unfair to children whose parents were not free to help or had not been chosen. There would be divided loyalties in the classroom, and children tended to behave less well when parents were present. Children needed a certain privacy in school, and with the separation from home they learned to be independent of their parents. Parents were unqualified and not competent to help effectively, and voluntary help was unreliable.

These were some of the many reasons given for the inadvisability of allowing parents to work in the classroom, but teachers were prepared to offer suggestions on ways in which parents could help. If their speech was of a reasonably high standard they could talk with children about their activities, help in creative work, supervise groups, listen to children reading, perform an ancillary role in the classroom e.g. by tidying up, dressing children, preparing materials and repairing apparatus, visit children's homes and help in social functions outside lesson time e.g. in fund-raising activities, stewarding in concerts and judging on sports day. Parents had come to one SWC school and talked to the children, e.g. a father showed how he made candy floss, and others had talked about their hobbies and shown their collections. The schools were adamant, however, that parents should not be concerned with actual teaching, and the majority were equally firmly opposed to their working in the classroom, although in several cases parents worked in spare classrooms or other areas not occupied by a teacher and her class. Even the few who felt that parents could play a role in the day-to-day working of the school, generally stipulated that this help should be given outside the classroom.

One junior and infant SWC school, however, took a different attitude and already had parents working in the classroom. In addition, the school made considerable efforts to maintain contact with the home. It published a termly newsletter, issued circulars, and invited parents to attend jumble sales, Christmas plays and morning assemblies. Parents helped to run the sales, made costumes for the plays and generally made themselves useful behind the scenes. Children attended school for two sessions a week before entry, and parents stayed with new entrants for as long as they wished. The headteacher gave the parents an introductory talk and occasionally arranged other educational meetings. She and her staff were available at any time to see parents, a part-time teacher relieving the class teacher for this purpose. Parents entered the classroom to feed pets and help with needlework and other activities, mainly creative, though they also heard children read. The class teacher approached selected parents to help in this way, and they usually arrived twice weekly, one or two at a time. The teacher was in favour of bringing outside people into the classroom and felt that it created 'fresh situations'. She put forward several considerations and suggested ways in which parent participation in classroom activities could be extended.

It would have to be well organized and parents should meet the teacher beforehand so that they could plan the procedure together. Only a few parents should be admitted at a time and there would need to be a rapid changeover, perhaps on a termly or half-termly basis, when the parent groups would be changed. Care would have to be taken to invite the 'right parents', usually those who were well-spoken, though she would not debar mothers with a lower standard of speech 'if they had something to offer'. Parents would help mainly in creative work, helping, encourage and talking to the children. They might also 'bring something fresh to talk about' e.g. they could bring a baby and bath it. Finally, they could take out small groups of children on short outings e.g. on 'bus or train rides.'

SUMMARY (LINKS WITH SCHOOL: THE TEACHERS' OPINIONS)

General school contact with parents. Rural schools organized a greater variety of social occasions than the other groups, and were more ready to make use of other buildings e.g. the local church, when the school building was inadequate. The staffs were also generally more available to parents out of school hours, they were more inclined to organize evening activities so that parents who were at work during the day were able to attend, and more schools were in the process of establishing PTAs. This may be due to the fact that the schools were almost all junior and infant, and as a rule infant schools felt less need for PTAs because informal contact was made when parents brought and collected their children. Fewer parents did this in the rural than in the urban schools, because of the number of children travelling to school by bus.

Meetings of an educational nature took place less often in rural than in urban schools. Open Days were held most often in DA schools, and were very rare in rural schools.

Early school contact. On average the CA group made the greatest efforts to ensure that parents and children were introduced to the reception classroom and teacher before school entry. Not only did almost all parents arrive for registration, but additional meetings were arranged in most cases. Rural schools made most effort to enable children to spend some time in school before entry. The DA group not only had a slightly lower mean percentage of parents registering their children before entry than the other groups, but also fewer schools arranged additional meetings between parents, children and teachers than in the CA group, so that if a parent arrived for registration unaccompanied by the child, the latter would in most cases have no other opportunity of making contact with the school situation prior to the day of entry.

There was little difference between the groups in arrangements made to help children who found difficulty in settling down during their first days at school, except that RA schools were more firmly opposed than the others to allowing parents to stay with their children.

Co-operation between school and home. Head-teachers were available at any time to be consulted by parents, though the CA schools were more systematic than the DA schools in trying to ensure that this did not interfere with school routines. RA headteachers encouraged parents to visit them and the class teachers out of school hours because of their teaching commitments.

Urban teachers were generally consulted when parents brought or collected their children, and during Open Days, and several CA headteachers made systematic arrangements to relieve teachers of their classroom duties when parents wished to speak to them. A higher proportion of fathers consulted the headteachers in CA and RA schools than in DA schools, and more RA school staffs visited children's homes.

The level of parental co-operation was higher in CA and RA than in DA schools. The DA group had made more use of outside sources of help, such as the care committee and health visitor, in dealing with problems concerning parents' co-operation, while CA and RA headteachers preferred to deal with such problems themselves, though some wanted additional assistance in order to have time to do so. A few DA headteachers felt the need of a social worker or similar help to deal with parent/teacher relationships.

CA parents showed most interest in their children's progress, especially in reading, so that the children in this group were probably more highly motivated than in the DA group to persevere in their school activities.

Several class teachers felt that there should be more meetings arranged to explain teaching methods, and that the informal approach was inadequate. There was an occasional tendency for

headteachers to lean too heavily on the words 'encourage' and 'informal', and to reply with vague generalities instead of concrete examples. It seemed in a few cases that too great a reliance on informality could develop on occasion into an unsystematic approach.

The majority of schools encouraged parents to help their children at home, but few were prepared to allow parents to assist in the work of the classroom.

B. LINKS WITH SCHOOL: THE PARENTS' OPINIONS

To complement the views of the teachers on the question of home-school relations reported in the previous section, it was felt important to seek the parents' views on the opportunities they had had for contact with the teachers and their impression of their child's schooling. Parents were also asked for their views on some suggested ways of increased involvement with the school and on some more general aspects of parent guidance. The sample involved consisted of 120 parents living in urban areas. It was structured so as to include 30 parents from 'middle-class' areas (MC), 30 from 'settled working-class' areas (SWC), 30 from relatively advantaged homes in 'deprived' areas (LD) and 30 from relatively disadvantaged homes in 'deprived' areas (MD). Because of losses from the sample, the actual number of homes visited was reduced to 29 MC, 28 SWC, 30 LD and 29 MD, a total of 116 parents. Further details of the sample and the reasons for the losses are to be found in Chapter 13. A structured questionnaire (see Appendix III) was completed as a result of a home visit to each of the above families, part of this questionnaire dealing with links with school from the parental viewpoint. The questions related in the main to the school which the child concerned attended and were intended, as has been said, to investigate the contact the parents had had with the child's infant school teachers, the parents' views on the child's education and progress and any further links they would like to see between home and school.

Analysis of parental interview data (presented in present chapter and Chapter 13)

In several tables questions asked and responses given are abbreviated. For details of the questions and coding of the responses, reference should be made to the interview schedule in Appendix III.

In order to keep tables as simple as possible, no percentages have been quoted. Since the numbers in each of the four groups are similar, direct comparisons can be quite easily made.

With four different groups to compare on a substantial number of items, a very large number of statistical tests of the significance of the differences between the groups could have been made. In most cases, it was obvious from the figures in the tables either that differences were very slight, in which case no statistical tests were carried out, or that one group stood out as different from the other three, in which case the only statistical test made was between that one group and the remainder of the sample. Where more than two categories of answer were possible, the categories were sometimes combined if this seemed logical, to give larger cell sizes, before calculating the value of 'chi-square.'

Significant values of 'chi-square' are quoted below the tables or referred to in the text. These are not calculated from the full information given in these tables but only after combining the figures for certain groups or categories. Table A12 (Appendix II) gives the actual figures from which the values of 'chi-square' were computed. In some cases groups or categories have been combined in two or more different ways, as indicated in Table A12. The comparisons between the LD and MD group are particularly relevant since this gives essentially a 'within-schools' rather than a 'between-schools' comparison.

Opportunities for Parent-Teacher Contacts

This section of the questionnaire commenced with a fairly general question asking whether parents felt they would like to know more about what their child did at school or how he was taught. The answers were classified in one of four ways: showing very keen interest, showing mild interest, showing no interest or feeling that they already knew sufficient. Table 154 shows the distribution of the answers for each of the four groups and it

can be seen that the MD group have a lower number showing a keen interest and rather more showing no interest. The difference in distributions of these answers is significant if one compares the MD group with either the whole of the rest of the sample ($p < 1\%$) or with the LD group ($p < 2\%$). The latter comparison is in some respects more relevant, since the LD and MD groups of children were selected from the same schools, so that their opportunities for contact with the school would have been the same. The interviewer felt that in several cases an expression of 'no interest' reflected a complete faith that the teachers knew what they were doing and would get on better without any interference from parents, or occasionally a feeling that the new methods used in the school would be completely beyond their comprehension anyway. Parents were asked what they felt were or would be the most helpful ways of letting parents know about what was going on in the school. The following is a list of the experiences parents mentioned which they had found most helpful:

1. opportunity for informal chats with child's teacher (4 MC, 13 SWC, 6 LD, 7 MD)
2. open days (5 MC, 7 SWC, 12 LD, 5 MD)
3. talking with the child (3 MC, 1 SWC, 6 LD, 4 MD)
4. seeing child's work books (at home or in school) (2 MC, 4 SWC, 5 LD, 1 MD)
5. parent-teacher association (3 MC, 1 LD, 2 MD)
6. meetings for parents in the evenings (4 MC, 1 LD)
7. watching lessons in progress (4 MC)
8. notes or letters from school (1 MC, 1 LD, 1 MD)
9. seeing a 'merit list' on classroom wall (1 MC)
10. working part-time in the school (1 MD)

Obviously the experiences actually offered by the child's school affected directly the choice available to the parents and a few parents could give no answer to this question.

When asked what they thought *would* be helpful ways of letting parents know more, parents had a wider scope, though here again the answers were probably limited to some extent by their own experiences or those of friends or relatives.

Many parents replied that they would just like *more* opportunity to talk to teachers or more frequent Open Days. Many felt that they would

Table 154

	Total Sample	MC	SWC	LD	MD
	116	29	28	30	29
No. who show 'very keen' interest	37	10	9	13	5
No. who show 'mild' interest	17	4	3	4	6
No. who show no interest	8	0	2	0	6
No. who feel they already know enough	54	15	14	13	12

Chi-square test of differences between MD and rest of sample gives $\chi^2 = 7.27$, p < 1%

Chi-square test of differences between MD and LD groups gives $\chi^2 = 5.78$, p < 2%

like a *definite invitation* to go, such as they received on Open Days, as they felt they were making themselves a nuisance if they went at other times. Others mentioned the need for opportunities to see teachers in the evening, so that fathers could also attend, or in private rather than with the child present or with other parents waiting their turn. Some felt they would like to be able to discuss the child's work in more detail and a few felt that teachers were 'glossing over' difficulties in behaviour or progress. Several parents felt that ample opportunities already existed and that it was their own fault that they had not found out more. A number of parents in each group felt that regular reports on the child's progress should be sent home, two mentioning that they would then like the chance to discuss these with the child's teacher. Two parents said that they would like the chance to see an ordinary lesson in progress, rather than work specially prepared and selected for Open Days or concerts. Three parents said that they would like to discuss

with the teachers how they could help the child at home with subjects in which they were behind other children.

Just a small number of parents (all in the MC and SWC areas) felt that they were actually made to feel unwelcome in their child's school. These were a small minority but the number who felt reticent about 'bothering' teachers was much larger and can be illustrated by quoting a few of the parents' own comments:

'We are asked once a year to Open Day. You *can* go at other times but the teachers are so busy; you don't like to bother them'

'I felt I haven't really *needed* to go because she is getting on so well'

'I know I *can* go but I feel I am worrying them unless there is a very good reason'

'I don't like to go at other times because it upsets the child if she thinks I'm making a fuss'

To put into perspective the suggestions for improved information from the school, it should be noted that almost half the parents felt that they already knew as much as they wanted or needed to about their child's education. The numbers of parents in this category varied very little between the four groups, as can be seen from Table 154 and are similar to those found in the survey for the Plowden Committee (1967).

Although the initial question had been framed in a general sense, parental responses seemed more concerned about knowing how their own child was getting on than about school activities in general. Thus, to some extent, a further question asking about the chances they had had to discuss their own child's progress was superfluous. However, the answers to later questions did add some information by giving a picture of how satisfied parents were generally with existing opportunities. The vast majority of parents were quite satisfied in this respect and differences between the four groups were slight. The results of the further questions on parent-teacher contacts are given in Table 155. It is interesting to note that exactly half the parents had never discussed their child's behaviour with the teachers because they felt there was no need. The majority of talks with teachers had been arranged or initiated by the parents and, apart from general invitations to Open Days, only four parents had been asked by the teacher to discuss their child. Most parents preferred to talk to the child's own teacher, saying that they felt that she knew the child better. The MD group appeared to have a greater preference for seeing the headteacher and, combining the 'headteacher' and 'both' categories, the difference between the MD group and the rest of the sample is statistically significant (χ^2 = 4.35, p < 5%). The reason for this difference is not obvious and was not stated by the respondents. One possible explanation is that the MD group parents go to the school to discuss problems of a more general type rather than just the progress of their child and feel that the headteacher, who is often older than class teachers, would be more able to help them and have more time to devote to such problems.

Within the MC group, the parents showed a slight preference for making definite appointments to see teachers. In all other groups the majority of parents preferred to be able to go to the school at any time, as particular needs arose. There were significant differences between the MC group and the rest of the sample (more MC parents preferring appointments) and between the MD group and the rest of the sample (less MD parents preferring appointments). These results are probably somewhat influenced by the fact that only a small number of parents, mostly in the MC group, had any experience of making appointments to speak to teachers.

When the interview was with the mother, as it was in most cases, the mother was asked whether she thought her husband would like the opportunity to meet the child's teachers. Some fathers already had and took the opportunity, but over a third of those replying said that they thought their husbands would like to go if there was an opportunity after normal working hours. Thirty-seven mothers (over a third of the sample) said that they did not think their husbands would go, not necessarily because of a lack of interest, but often because they felt that it was the mother's function to talk to teachers and report back to them. This tendency appears to be particularly strong at the infant level, as several mothers said that fathers attended meetings at junior or secondary schools, but not at the infant stage.

In almost every school there is a group of parents who do not attend any school function or come to talk to the child's teacher even though ample opportunity is given. The reasons for such non-attendance might be many. Mothers who work, are on their own with several young children, are physically or mentally ill, or have difficulty in speaking or understanding English, may find severe practical difficulties in visiting the school. Parents who have unhappy memories of their own school days, or who feel that their own child is particularly backward or difficult, or who feel markedly socially inferior to other parents in the area, may have psychological barriers to contact with teachers. In such cases initiative for home and school links can come only from the teachers, possibly through visits to the child's home.

Such a suggestion raises alarm among some teachers who feel that they would not be welcome in the homes. In order to discover how justified such a fear was, parents were asked about their views on teachers visiting them at home. The question was put in the context of parents who find it difficult to get to school (see

293

Table 155

Parent-teacher contacts

Questions	Responses	Total Sample	MC	SWC	LD	MD
		116	29	28	30	29
1. Have you been satis-fied with opportun-ities to discuss N's progress with teachers?	Quite satisfied	92	22	22	23	25
	Reservations	18	6	5	4	3
	Unsatisfied	6	1	1	3	1
2. Have you ever discussed N's behav-iour with teacher ?	Yes satisfactory	49	14	12	13	10
	Yes reservations	8	2	3	2	1
	Yes unsatisfactory	1	0	1	0	0
	No need	58	13	12	15	18
3. Do you prefer to see head teacher or child's class teacher?	Head teacher	19	3	1	5	10
	class teacher	80	23	22	20	15
	both	16	2	5	5	4
	either	1	1	0	0	0
4. Do you prefer to have a definite appointment?	Yes	31	15	4	8	4
	No	75	12	20	18	25
	Don't mind	10	2	4	4	0
5.* Would N's father like opportunity to meet teachers?	Yes in evening	35	11	8	13	3
	Can go now	29	12	7	7	3
	Not interested	37	5	10	9	13

* Numbers for this question are lower because of 12 families where there was no father and three where there was no mother, so that the father had answered the earlier questions.

Chi-square test of difference between MC and rest of sample on question 4 gives $\chi^2 = 7.86$, p $< 1\%$

Chi-square test of difference between MD and rest of sample on question 4 gives $\chi^2 = 6.65$, p $< 1\%$

Qu. E6), and thus in several cases gave rise to a response criticising parents who did not go and saying that teachers should not be expected to undertake this in addition to teaching the children in school. If parents gave this response, they were then asked to say whether they would actually *mind* a teacher visiting them. The vast majority of parents (104 out of 116) said they would be quite happy to welcome a teacher to their home. Only two parents said they would definitely not want a teacher to visit them, both of these being in the MD group. A further four MD parents had certain reservations about teachers visiting them, as did five parents from the other three groups. Those who were not happy about teachers visiting them were asked if they would be more or less happy about that, than about the project's interviewer, who was to them a fairly neutral outsider, visiting them. Seven said they would feel less happy about teachers visiting them and four said that they would feel the same.

Though there was little variation in the parent's willingness to accept teachers into their homes, there was a considerable difference of opinion as to whether they saw such visits as of value in a general sense, or whether home visits should be used only as a 'last resort' or in an emergency situation. Again some of the comments of the parents themselves illustrate their attitudes, and the comments quoted have been divided into the four area groups, since there were differences in the emphasis of the groups.

Comments on teachers visiting the home: From parents in MC areas

'I wouldn't mind myself, but I think it might upset the child'

'You shouldn't expect teachers to do this except in very special circumstances'

'I'd love to have the teacher here and be able to talk in private'

'I would be very grateful to a teacher for coming here'

'Parents can always make time to go to school. The teachers are too busy to do this'

From parents in SWC areas

'It would be a good idea, particularly if you live a long way from the school — it would save bus fares'

'I would be quite happy, but I would make the effort to stop off work to go to school because teachers shouldn't have to do this'

'I'd feel embarrassed because I was imposing on them. You can always *make* time to go to school'

From parents in 'deprived' areas, LD group

'You should only expect teachers to do this if a serious problem arose'

'It would be a good thing for teachers to see the sort of environment the children live in'

From parents in 'deprived' areas, MD group

'It should not be expected of the teachers. It is wrong for mothers to work while children are in school'

'I would be only too pleased for a teacher to call in the evening. I can't go to school because of my work' (from a father on his own)

'I'm not very keen. It wouldn't be necessary because I could always go to school'

'I am not keen, I'd rather go there to see them'

Parent-Teacher Associations

Some of the schools were known to have parent-teacher associations and parents were asked about this. There seemed to be some confusion in the minds of parents about exactly what constituted such an association. This was so particularly in schools where occasional parents' meetings were arranged, but no organized association existed. From the sample of 116, only 31 parents said that there was a PTA at their child's school and, of these, only 19 parents belonged to such an association. It might have been expected that there would be a greater number of associations and members in the MC areas, but differences between the four groups were in fact found to be slight, both in the numbers of such associations and the proportion of parents belonging to them. There was a slight tendency for more *fathers* to belong in the MC areas, but numbers are so small that

Table 156

Parents' experiences of parent-teacher associations

Questions	Responses	Total Sample	MC	SWC	LD	MD
		116	29	28	30	29
1. Is there a PTA at the child's infant school?	Yes	31	11	6	6	8
	No	85	18	22	24	21
2. If there is a PTA, do you (mother) belong?	Yes	19	6	3	4	6
	No	12	5	3	2	2
3. If there is a PTA, does child's father belong?	Yes	8	5	2	0	1
	No	19	6	3	6	4
4. If there is no PTA at child's school, have you ever belonged to a PTA?	Yes	12	3	1	6	2
	No	73	15	21	18	19
5. Would you like a PTA at child's school?	Yes very keen	33	4	13	11	5
	Yes keen	25	4	5	8	8
	No	27	10	4	5	8
6. If so, would you join yourselves?	Yes both parents	31	6	7	14	4
	Yes one parent	23	1	11	4	7
	No	4	1	0	1	2

Note: numbers for items 3 and 6 are reduced because of the one-parent families

generalizations would not be justified. Table 156 gives the results of some of the questions concerning PTAs.

In areas where there was no PTA in the infant school, parents were asked whether they had ever belonged to a PTA at another school, whether they would like to have one at the local infant school and whether they would join it themselves. Seventy-three parents had no experience of a PTA and several of those asked the interviewer what sort of activities such an association usually

arranged. Thirty-three parents showed a keen interest in having such an association, twenty-five had a mild interest and twenty-six felt quite definitely that they would not want one locally. Most of those who would like a PTA said they would be able to join it themselves and also thought their husbands would like to join, though here again there was a difference between the groups, with rather fewer of the MD group believing that their husband would join, though numbers are again rather small here.

On a more 'qualitative' level, parents were asked what benefit they thought a PTA had been to them if they had belonged or, if not, what sort of things they thought a PTA could (or should) do. Some of the benefits experienced or expected by parents from membership of a PTA are listed below:

1. learning more about teaching methods used in the school (particularly the 'modern' methods)
2. discussing ways of improving school and recreational facilities and raising money for this
3. learning about what happens to children at the '11+' stage
4. meeting other parents and discussing mutual problems
5. more chance to meet teachers
6. discussing proposed new ideas and finding out the school's problems
7. organizing parents' help with 'functions' (e.g. sports days, outings, parties)
8. helping with school library, escorting children who go out for visits or 'nature walks', supervising playtimes, running clubs
9. a chance for the parents to air *their* views
10. discussing what parents could do to help child at home

A few parents also mentioned that they enjoyed PTA meetings as social functions, and one parent felt that the school should have a PTA 'so that we can be like America.'

Some more general comments made by parents about PTAs are listed below, as they give an interesting insight into parents' interpretation of their functions:

Comments on Parent-Teacher Associations: From MC area parents

'The schools do very well now. They can do better *without* parents pushing them'

'There is too much emphasis on older children rather than infants'

'You don't need it for the infants. They're only babies then'

'Teachers know what they are doing and parents shouldn't interfere'

'I'm not pro PTAs — it just becomes a social clique'

'It's not necessary here. They do things so well and we get to know a lot'

From SWC area parents

'I'm not keen . They don't serve much use'

'We've been wanting one for a long while and we have just persuaded the school to form one'.

From 'deprived' area parents in LD group

'There is one but it's mainly run for the juniors'

'Only a few teachers attend. You don't get to know anything about individual children — only about the toilets'

From 'deprived' area parents in MD group

'It's enjoyable and it gives you a lot of information'

'It would pass the time away'

'I've never thought about it. I don't know anything about them'

'I've thought of lots of things I'd like to tell the committee, but I don't go because my hearing isn't good enough'

'I wouldn't go. You've got to be like the Bingo people to go out like that'

Parents helping in the classroom

The idea of parents going into the classroom to help the teacher was a novel one to most parents in this sample (apart from the parents who were paid nursery assistants or infant helpers). As far as is known to the writers, only one school in the project's sample had tried using parent help in the classroom on a voluntary basis. There are schools which have experimented with this sort of help on a wide scale and believe that the children's progress has benefited from such help. Parents in this sample were asked about their views on this and how they themselves would feel about giving help in this way. The answers were classified into four categories: those who would be keen to help in this way, those who would be willing to help if anyone asked them, those who did not feel happy about the idea and, finally, those who would be definitely unwilling or unable to help. Table 157 shows the results of this classification for the four

Table 157

Parents' views on helping in infant school classroom

	Total Sample	MC	SWC	LD	MD
	116	29	28	30	29
1. Keen to help	25	7	8	8	2
2. Willing to help if asked	35	9	6	11	9
3. Reservations	27	6	6	7	8
4. Unwilling or unable	29	7	8	4	10

groups. Most of the parents in the fourth category were unable to help for purely practical reasons, such as their own work or having several younger children at home who could not be left, but a few felt either that it was not a good idea anyway or that they were not 'clever' or 'patient' enough to undertake the work. The most common reservation mentioned was that it was undesirable for parents to be in the same classroom as their own child. The MD group had rather fewer parents who were keen to help and a rather larger number who were unwilling or unable, mainly because of having more young children at home. Again some of the comments made by the parents are very interesting.

Comments on parents helping in the classroom: From parents in MC areas

'Children might have less respect for parents they know well'

'I feel I'm needed at home'

'My child would cling to me – she's better away from me'

'They do need help and I'd love to go. My husband would help too'

'I could look after the others while the teacher helped the slower ones'

'I have already offered to help in any way any time I'm needed'

From parents in SWC area

'I wanted to be a teacher. I'd love to help in any way'

'Some parents did go in and help when the bus strike was on and teachers arrived late'

'I have no patience with other people's children'

'It's not a good idea. They need people with qualifications – not just any mother'

'It's a good idea. You understand children better when you're a mother'

'I could listen to children reading. The teacher only has time to hear them once a week now'

From 'deprived' area parents in LD group

'I could help keep law and order'

'It's not my cup of tea, but it's a good idea'

'It needs somebody with a lot of understanding and patience and lots of children of their own'

'It's a very good idea. I'd do anything they asked'

'I'd love to help; reading stories or helping in the nursery'

'It would give the teacher more time to give individual attention'

From 'deprived' area parents in MD group

'I enjoy it. I've helped at Christmas, with swimming, and done paid work in the nursery'

'I'm not clever enough for that'

(From a father) 'I'm willing. I could help put up shelves like they have in the nursery classes'

'A splendid idea. I would help if asked'

'As long as they only ask you to do *simple* things'

'I've got enough on my plate at home'

'I would like to help if I could take the younger children with me'

'Only if it was desperate and there were no teachers'

Parental knowledge of teaching methods

In most infant schools the methods used to teach the basic skills of reading and number have changed considerably during the last few years. In two of the project schools the initial teaching alphabet (i.t.a.) had been introduced, and the differing notation of the 'new maths' was being used in several schools. Parents were asked whether the methods used in the school were similar to those they remembered being used when they were at school themselves. The aim of this question was not to investigate the actual methods used, since this information was more accurately obtained from the schools, but rather, to discover how familiar parents were with the methods used in their child's school. The answers and comments were classified on the basis of the knowledge shown by parents as 'adequate', 'sketchy' or 'none'.

In fact, remarkably few parents in any of the four groups gave replies which indicated an adequate knowledge, though the majority had at least some idea of the methods used. Table 158 shows the classifications for each of the four groups and it will be seen that the numbers having *no* knowledge of the teaching methods used is considerably larger in MD group, while only one parent in MC group was so rated. The difference between the distribution of answers in the MD group and the other groups is highly significant, when compared with the whole of the rest of the sample or with the LD group, which attended the same schools. The difference between the MC group and the rest of the sample is also significant, the difference being mainly in the number who have *no* knowledge of teaching methods. The differences between MD and LD groups cannot be attributed to the differing policies of the schools, since these two groups of children attended the same schools. The difference probably reflects a lesser interest shown by the MD group parents in the details of the educational process and, perhaps, less ability to comprehend the methods used. However, it must also reflect to some extent the lack of communication between the child and the parent about what the child does in school.

Parents were also asked whether they would have liked more opportunity to learn about modern teaching methods or whether they thought this was something that should be left to the school. Those who were interested to know more were asked a few practical details about when they would like instruction to be given and whether *both* parents would like to attend. Presenting parents with an alternative of leaving teaching methods to the school probably decreased the numbers who expressed interest in knowing more, as otherwise most parents would have felt that they *ought* to express at least some interest. Table 158 shows the answers given to these further questions. Considerably more parents in the deprived areas were content to leave teaching methods entirely to the school, particularly those in the MD group.

In some schools children are encouraged to take their reading books home. This can enable the parents to help their child by listening to him read, a task which teachers of large classes are not able to undertake as often as they would like to, and also shows the parents what sort of progress the child is making in reading. Against this practice, some teachers feel that, particularly in the early stages, children can learn a book 'off by heart' at home and it is then hard to tell whether the child can 'read' it. Also, they fear that parents may attempt to 'teach reading' rather than just listen to the child, and may use methods conflicting with those used by the school. Parents were asked for their views on this practice and it was found that well over half the sample *did* bring reading books home, the numbers in the MC group being rather less than in the other groups, possibly because teachers felt that the need was less, or alternatively, because teachers feared that more pressure would be put upon children in this way by 'middle-class' parents.

Most parents were in fact in favour of children bringing reading books home. Only 15 were not in favour, 10 of these being in the MC group. Table 159 shows the results of these two questions. The difference between the distribution of answers for

Table 158

Parental knowledge of teaching methods in infant school

Question	Reasons	Total Sample	MC	SWC	LD	MD
		116	29	28	30	29
1. Rating of knowledge of teaching methods	Adequate	10	2	1	7	0
	Sketchy	85	26	23	19	17
	None	21	1	4	4	12
2. Would you like to know more about teaching methods or is this something which should be left to the school?	Keen interest	55	16	19	16	4
	Mild interest	22	5	3	4	10
	Leave to school	39	8	6	10	15
3. If talks or demonstrations had been arranged, would you have attended? (those interested only)	Yes	75	21	22	20	12
	No	2	0	0	0	2
4. What sort of time would be best? (those who would attend only)	Day	11	2	4	1	4
	Evening	29	11	6	7	5
	Any time	35	8	12	12	3
5. Do you think your husband would be interested too? (fatherless families excluded)	Yes	55	17	14	18	6
	No	12	2	5	1	4
	Don't know	1	1	0	0	0

Chi-square tests for item 1 show significant differences between:-

MD group and rest of sample (χ^2 = 12.11, p < 0.1%)

MD group and LD group (χ^2 = 4.54, p < 5%)

MC group and rest of sample (χ^2 = 4.36, p < 5%)

Chi-square test for item 2 shows significant difference between

MD group and rest of sample (χ^2 = 4.65, p < 5%)

300

Table 159

Parents' views on children bringing reading books home from school

	Total Sample	MC	SWC	LD	MD
	116	29	28	30	29
1. No. of children who take reading books home	76	9	19	25	23
2. No. of parents who think this is/would be a good idea	101	19	27	29	26

the MC group and the rest of the sample is significant in both cases. In some of the schools where reading books were not sent home, parents were encouraged to buy 'parallel' readers for the children to use at home. Several parents bought their own copies of reading schemes for use at home, so that if teachers have a deliberate policy in not sending books home, it very often fails since most schemes are fairly readily available.

Parents' views on organization and discipline

Not only have teaching methods changed over the past few years, but also the general organization, layout and discipline have changed in many schools. Parents were asked if they were aware of a difference between their child's school and their own school in this respect and if so, whether they felt this was a change for the better. It is rather surprising to find that as many as 43 parents felt that there had been no general change, these being fairly evenly spread among the four groups. However, well over half of the parents were aware of changes and the majority, but by no means all, felt that these were changes for the better. Table 160 shows the answers to these questions. A somewhat higher proportion of the MC group felt that there had been changes for the better and a slightly larger proportion of the MD group saw changes for the worse, but the differences were not statistically significant.

Again some of the parents' own comments on modern trends of organization and discipline in the infant school are of interest, but it should be remembered that the parents who were dissatisfied were also more vocal, so that the following comments should not be interpreted as representative of the whole sample, but as interesting individual observations.

Parents' comments on organization/discipline: From parents in SWC areas

'There are lots of advantages now like trips and outings'

'The schools are much brighter places and the teachers are less frightening'

'They learn through play — it's much better for them'

'They are more lenient now. I would like to see firmer discipline, particularly as they grow older'

From parents in SWC areas

'They think of the children more as individuals now'

'It's much easier to talk to the teachers now — for children and parents'

'There's less wallopping now'

Table 160

Parents' views on changes in organization/discipline

	Total Sample	MC	SWC	LD	MD
	116	29	28	30	29
1. No. of parents who feel there has been no change	43	9	14	11	9
2. No. who feel there has been a change : better	41	15	9	9	8
3. No. who feel there has been a change : worse	18	2	3	5	8
4. No. who feel there has been a change : neutral	14	3	2	5	4

'There are too many holidays. Children need as much education as they can get. They should bring books home for the holiday'

'They should all have homework. It keeps them off the streets'

'I think the teacher doesn't like boys'

From parents in 'deprived' areas: LD group

'There are many more things like concerts that involve the parents now'

'There are better buildings; warmer, more colourful and cheery'

'They have more freedom — it's much better'

'The teachers are younger and more pleasant now'

'The teachers are afraid to check the children now. I would like them to be stricter'

'They used to line up to go into school. There's no discipline now'

'Children need firmer discipline or they disrupt the class'

From parents in 'deprived' areas: MD group

'More variety now. Every day we had religion and sums in the morning and composition in the afternoon'

'There's no discipline. Authority is authority. If they were stricter at school the children would behave at home'

'They don't bother now about things like punctuality, and that is important later on'

Training for parenthood

Some parents undoubtedly embark on marriage and parenthood with very little preparation or training for either role. Many parents seek advice on how to bring up their children or how to prepare them for school from friends and relatives, from magazines or from books such as those by Dr. Spock and others. A selection of questions was included in the interview to try to find out what parents of infant school children felt they needed to know in this area and to investigate their likely response to any programme of help. More specifically, they were asked if they would have liked more advice on the sort of things they could do with their children before school, their need for

Table 161

Parents' views on aspects of training for parenthood

Question	Response	Total Sample	MC	SWC	LD	MD
		116	29	28	30	29
1. Parental interest in advice on pre-school activities	very interested	53	16	17	14	6
	mildly interested	22	6	4	6	6
	not interested	41	7	7	10	17
2. Has parent felt need for general advice in bringing up children?	Yes	23	6	4	7	6
	No	93	23	24	23	23
3. Should more be taught about needs of young children in secondary schools? (1 not classifiable)	Yes	94	23	23	21	27
	No	21	5	5	9	2
4. If 'Yes', should this be for both boys and girls?	girls only	20	3	6	5	6
	both	74	20	17	16	21

Chi-square test on differences between MD group and the rest of sample for item 1 gives $\chi^2 = 7.86$, $p < 1\%$

general advice in bringing up children, whether any secondary school courses had been helpful in preparing them for parenthood and whether they thought that secondary schools should teach more about the needs and development of young children. The results of these questions are shown in Table 161. From the first item it will be seen that significantly fewer parents in the MD group felt any need for advice on pre-school activities, and yet by the nature of the selection of this group they were almost certain to be the group which provided less preparation for school. Some of the reasons given by parents in this group for their lack of interest are listed below:

'She learned by playing school with the older children'

'The child is better off if this is all left to the teachers'

'I don't bother learning her anything — she picks it up from the older ones'

'They all went to the nursery class'

'They'll learn soon enough in school'

'If they're quick they'll learn anyway'

'We did a lot anyway — they all learned to dress and use the toilet'

Some of the reasons for lack of interest given by parents from the other three groups are given below:

'You can prepare them yourself without help. It's only common sense you need'

'If they do too much before school, they might be bored when they get there'

'I'd like her to be a child until she starts school. I don't like parents "showing off" what their child can do'

'I would have liked to have started him reading but I was told not to'

'We did try to help him but it confused him. It would have been better to leave it to the teachers'

Just a few mentioned the importance of learning the most *appropriate* way of helping the child, so as not to conflict with methods used in the school, and several parents felt the need for help in keeping four-year-olds occupied at home.

The other items in this section showed very little difference between the four groups. Only a fairly small number of parents had felt the need for general advice in bringing up children since the majority had already sought advice from relatives, their doctor or the health visitor and found this satisfactory. Few parents had received any more than cookery or housecraft lessons at school, and while many had found these very helpful, others felt that they had learned much more from their own parents at home. Most parents agreed that it would be a good thing for secondary schools to widen their scope to include child development courses, and most mothers said that such courses should be for both boys and girls.

Apart from instruction on child development, which was specifically mentioned in the question, some parents mentioned the need for children to be taught to budget carefully, while others mentioned the thorny problem of sex education. The comment of one father present at an interview (in the LD group) was, 'There is no need for anything *special*; all education helps you to be a better parent'. A small number felt that while at school children would not be sufficiently interested, or felt that they would 'find out for themselves soon enough'.

General level of interest in schooling

Two questions were added at the end of the interview to try to give some assessment of the general level of interest in school or educational aspirations of the parents. The first of these two questions asked whether parents would like their child to stay at school beyond the minimum leaving age and possibly progess to some form of further education or training. The second question asked for a comparison of the degree of interest shown by the child's father as compared with that of the mother, who was the interviewee in most cases. The answers to these questions are shown in Table 162. On all three items the MD group have significantly different distributions of answers, showing lower aspirations for their child and less parental interest in the child's schooling. The differences between the other three groups are only slight. To a limited extent the answers given for the first two items were dependent on the child's sex. Few parents would be unwilling to allow girls to pursue further education, but some parents did say that they thought it was much more important for a boy. Many parents were aware of an increasing need for training or qualifications even in the manual occupations.

Taking the sample as a whole, in 79 families out of 101 (i.e. in 78% of families) where comparisons were possible, the father took at least as much interest in the child's schooling as did the mother. Thus, although fathers are less likely to visit the infant school, they probably exert considerable influence on the child's education in the background. Several mothers attributed to their husbands greater patience over school work and said that they had more free time to devote to the children in the evenings and at weekends.

Likely response to a programme of help

Finally, an interviewer's assessment was made of the parents' likely response to any programme of help or advice in educational or related matters which might be provided before or during a child's infant school career. The following five categories were used:

1) keen, no obvious practical difficulties
2) provision already good, parent sees no need for further help.
3) keen to learn, practical difficulties at home
4) probably could help more, but would need convincing that it was necessary or desirable
5) probably incapable of giving any help

The ratings were inevitably subjective. The type of 'practical difficulties' included in the third

Table 162

Parental aspirations and interest

Question	Response	Total Sample	MC	SWC	LD	MD
		116	29	28	30	29
1. Parents' views on child staying at school after minimum leaving age	Keen	68	20	17	19	12
	Willing	39	9	9	11	10
	Unwilling	9	0	2	0	7
2. Parents' views on child having further education or training	Keen	87	26	23	24	14
	Willing	23	3	5	6	9
	Unwilling	6	0	0	0	6
3. Comparison of father's and mother's interest in schooling (for families with both parents)	Equal/Father more	79	24	21	23	11
	Father less	16	3	4	5	4
	No difference	6	1	0	1	4

Chi-square test for item 1 on difference between MD group and rest of sample gives $\chi^2 = 11.60$, $p < 0.1\%$ (combining 'keen' and 'willing' categories)

Chi-square test for item 2 on difference between MD group and rest of sample gives $\chi^2 = 12.89$, $p < 0.1\%$ (combining 'willing' and 'unwilling' categories)

Chi-square test for item 3 on difference between MD group and rest of sample gives $\chi^2 = 4.30$, $p < 5\%$

category were overcrowding in the home, a number of younger children at home or both parents working during the day. The reasons for making the final classification of 'incapable of giving help' were ill health of the parent, low intelligence or instability of one or both parents, or a complete lack of order in the home. Table 163 shows the ratings to each group and here again the MD group have more of the lower ratings. No statistical test was made here since the numbers in some cells are small and combining categories would be meaningless. However, the differences are quite obvious from the table.

SUMMARY (LINKS WITH SCHOOL: THE PARENTS' OPINIONS)

The questions in this section of the interview provoked a great deal of interest on the part of the parents and some interesting and revealing comments, some of which have been quoted in the text. The overall impression gained was that there is a great deal of goodwill towards the infant schools on the part of parents, a faith in the capability and effectiveness of the teachers and a willingness to help the school or their own child in any way possible. While some parents, it is true,

305

Table 163

Likely parental response to programme of help

Rating	Total Sample	MC	SWC	LD	MD
	116	29	28	30	29
1. Keen; no obvious practical difficulties	55	15	17	20	3
2. Provision already good, parent sees no need for further help	12	8	0	4	0
3. Keen to learn; practical difficulties at home	12	2	3	0	7
4. Probably could help more but would need convincing that it was necessary or desirable	29	4	7	6	12
5. Probably incapable of giving any help	8	0	1	0	7

are happy to leave the whole task of education to the school, many are keen both to learn more about the school's methods and to help and co-operate more than they do at present. Naturally the parents' emphasis is on knowing more about their own child's individual progress.

In several ways the responses of the 'most deprived' group were different from those of the other three groups. They were more inclined to feel that they could or should leave the child's education entirely to the school, they more often favoured informal contact with teachers with no appointment system, feeling that they would not know what to say in a rather 'artificial' arranged interview, and the child's father was less likely to take as much interest in the child's schooling, particularly at this early stage. This group of parents also had somewhat lower aspirations for their child's later education, though this should not be taken to imply that they were not keen for their child to do well in learning the more basic skills.

The Plowden Report (1967) states that '. . . . one of the essentials for educational advance is a closer partnership between the two parties to

every child's education'. It would seem that there are some parents and, regretfully, still a small number of teachers who need to be convinced that there *are* 'two parties to every child's education'. In some sense any and every sort of contact between parents and teachers should increase the awareness of this partnership. Little evaluation has been undertaken of the feasibility or effectiveness of different methods of improving home-school contacts, but the results of this survey suggest what parents find most helpful and what further opportunities they would like for contact or involvement.

Parents, on the whole, prefer informal contact with the child's class teacher, and, in this enquiry, while only a small number felt unwelcome in the school, many were hesitant about approaching teachers except at times when some problem had arisen. This was particularly true in connection with discussing the child's behaviour in school. Many fathers would like the opportunity to visit the school and meet the teachers, and parents would value an *honest* assessment of their child's behaviour and progress, which they feel they do not always receive. They enjoyed the chance to see the child's work, and the few who had had the chance to observe ordinary lessons in progress had found this particularly instructive. Mothers also enjoyed the opportunity to meet other parents and discuss problems which they might have in common.

On the whole parents are willing to contribute much more to the school than they are generally asked to do. In most cases, however, they wait for the school to take the initiative in asking for help. In the deprived area schools, while there are parents who are keen and free to help, there are many who would be reticent about helping or whose commitments at home or work would make it difficult for them to offer much assistance.

The purpose of closer relationships between home and school as recommended by the Plowden Committee was to attempt to alter and improve the parents' attitude to education, since this was shown by the research undertaken for this committee to account for more of the variation in school achievement than either home circumstances or factors in the school. The process of attitude changing is by no means clearly understood, so that it is hardly surprising that the purposes of extending home-school contract are rarely clearly spelled out. However, most parents and teachers agree that closer links are 'a good thing,' and feel that getting to know more about the environment in which the other lives or works gives a greater understanding of the other's difficulties and also of the child's reactions to school (D.E.S., 1968; Young and McGeeney, 1968).

The greatest difficulties in forging closer links between the home and the school probably exist at the extremes of the social class spectrum. Teachers may well feel threatened by the more articulate and educated professional parent who has very high scholastic aspirations for his or her child and knows, sometimes almost too well, his rights as a parent. At the other end of the scale the teacher can be discouraged by the apparent apathy and lack of understanding of the purposes of modern education of parents whose own educational level was low, and who are sometimes overwhelmed by the problems of coping with large families, low income, overcrowded conditions in the home and other social or emotional problems. Any bridging of the gap between home and school in this latter case will depend largely on the initiative being taken by the school, since these are parents who are shown by this study to see less need for advice and help, and to have more practical difficulties in attending functions at school. On the whole, the survey suggests that home visits by teachers would be welcome, particularly if these were known *not* to be restricted only to instances of problem behaviour or backwardness.

Undoubtedly there are a few parents who are so completely overwhelmed by the problems of coping at a minimal level with a home and family that they can offer little to the child or the school to ease the burden on the teacher. However, even in the 'deprived' areas of this study, there are large numbers of parents who are keen to do anything to help their own child or the school, and it would seem a pity if some effort were not made to utilize this voluntary help to the full.

13 Parents' Use of Services

INTRODUCTION

Teachers can seldom attempt to tackle the problems in the home which lead to or are associated with material, emotional or cultural deprivation. Indeed, the enquiries of the Plowden Committee (1967) suggest that a number of teachers have very little knowledge of their pupils' home circumstances. The social, medical and welfare services, however, do go some way to provide expert help, material and financial aid, and social support for those families who are in need.

The present study would have been incomplete if it had not investigated the use made of these services by the children or parents in the sample. A major survey of the use of all social services would not have been possible, so the enquiry was limited to those services which it was felt were most likely to benefit young children, directly or indirectly. These included the school medical services, financial benefits, free meals, clothing grants, guidance services, nursery and library facilities.

SELECTION OF THE SAMPLE

It was expected that there would be differences in the parents' use of services between the three types of area included in the survey ('middle-class,' 'settled working-class' and 'deprived') since, on the whole, families in 'deprived' areas have greater needs and fewer resources within the family. It was thus decided to select a sample of parents from all three types of area for this investigation, so that contrasts between the groups could emerge. However, it was also felt to be important to look at differences within the 'deprived' areas, so that two groups were chosen, one relatively 'advantaged' and one relatively 'deprived'.

The planned sample for this survey consisted of 120 parents selected from all the urban schools; 30 from 'middle-class' areas, 30 from 'settled working-class' areas, 30 from relatively advantaged homes situated in 'deprived' areas and 30 from relatively disadvantaged homes in 'deprived' areas. In the 'middle-class' and 'settled working-class' areas five children were chosen at random from each of the six schools taking part in the research project. One parent in each of these groups was not willing to be interviewed and it further proved impossible to contact one parent in a 'settled working-class' area. In the 'deprived' areas information about the home backgrounds of over 300 of the children had been collected in connection with the more intensive study of two small samples. Full details of the procedure for making assessments of the homes will be found in "Deprivation and Development' (Chazan et al., to be published). It was on the basis of this assessment of the home that the children in the deprived area schools were allocated to the 'least deprived' or 'most deprived' groups for this sample.

It was decided to exclude from this sample children whose parents had already been interviewed on three occasions in connection with an intensive study of children with problems of adjustment to school (reported in Volume 2, "Deprivation and Development", Chazan et al., to be published). This means that the present sample excludes parents of children who showed the most or least problems of initial adjustment to school. One parent in the 'most deprived' category left the area before being interviewed. The sample actually interviewed consisted, then, of 29 parents in 'middle-class' areas (MC), 28 parents in 'settled working-class' areas (SWC), 30 parents living in 'deprived' areas, but relatively least deprived (LD) and 29 parents living in 'deprived' areas and relatively most deprived (MD), making a total sample of 116 parents. The questionnaire used was piloted on a small group containing each of the four 'types' listed above but in only one of the three urban areas. In investigating the parents' use or knowledge of social services, emphasis was laid on those services which might either directly or indirectly affect the infant school child. Most questions, however, were worded in a general manner so that parents' views could be gathered even if services had been used for other children in the family or were of benefit to the family as a whole.

The questionnaire was divided into two parts, the first containing four sections as follows:

Part I — Use of Services

Section A concerned medical and related services.
Section B concerned material and financial benefits.
Section C concerned help given for social or emotional problems.
Section D concerned nursery, library and other services.

Part II — Links with School

The information from this part of the questionnaire has already been presented and discussed in Chapter 12.

Interviews were undertaken during the child's final year in the infant school. All parents were visited by the same interviewer and in the majority of cases the child's mother answered the questions, though in a small number of cases the father was also present or was the sole interviewee.

The results of the interviews will be given section by section, wherever possible giving both the overall picture for the whole sample and any interesting contrasts between the four groups making up this sample. Many of the comments and suggestions made by parents will be given, though the wording is not necessarily identical to that used in the interview, since only brief notes were made at the time. A note on the statistical analysis of the data from this questionnaire will be found in Chapter 12.

RESULTS, SECTION A: MEDICAL AND RELATED SERVICES

At the time of the interview only one parent said that her child had not had a medical examination at school and two parents were unsure about this. Eleven parents (3 SWC, 1 LD, 7 MD) had not attended the child's medical examination themselves.

Thirty children in the study (26% of the sample) had received treatment through the school medical services and seven more had had further tests following the usual medical examination but had not been found to need treatment. A further sixteen parents said that other school-age children had received treatment through the school medical services. Only seven parents (2 MC, 1 LD, 3 MD) were not aware that treatment could be arranged by the school medical services if it was found to be necessary at the medical examination. The types of treatment most frequently given were for teeth, eyes and hearing. Most parents felt that the medical check on school children was helpful and had been satisfied with any treatment which had been given. Although there were a few isolated cases of dissatisfaction, and some parents preferred to use the services of their own dentist or G.P., several parents commented that the school doctors or dentists were particularly patient and understanding with young children. The only item mentioned above which showed a significant difference between the groups was in the number of parents who did not attend their child's medical examination, this being higher in the MD group than for the remainder of the sample.

Parents were asked specifically about any difficulties their children had had in their speech. Although this item might have arisen from discussion of the medical examination, no parent had already mentioned this. Nine parents replied that the child being studied had experienced some difficulty (4 MC, 2 SWC, 1 LD, 2 MD). Only three parents had sought treatment for their children, though some others had asked for advice and been told that treatment was not necessary. Two MC children had received treatment, one privately and one with the Local Authority speech therapist. One MD child had attended the child guidance clinic for help. Fifteen parents mentioned other children in the family who had had speech difficulties, ten of whom had received treatment (8 MD, 2 SWC). Thirty parents, almost evenly distributed between the four groups, did not know that it was possible to obtain speech therapy for children who had difficulties.

More of the MD group parents had at least one child who had had some speech difficulty but this difference might well be attributable to the larger size of family in this group. Apart from this, differences between the groups were very slight. Speech therapists are in short supply in some areas and two children who needed help could not be given this help locally.

RESULTS, SECTION B: FINANCIAL AND MATERIAL BENEFITS

By far the most widely used of the benefits provided by the social services asked about in this survey, were financial assistance given by the Ministry of Social Security and free school meals. Thirty-two parents (28% of the sample) said that they had experienced one or more periods of financial difficulty due mainly to sickness or unemployment or, in a few cases, to parental separation. The provision of this financial or material help was also more widely known than most other services. Only fourteen parents could not mention any kind of help which was available for school children or their parents in cases of financial hardship. As might be expected, there were significant differences between the four groups in the use made of such services. Table 164 shows the numbers in each group who had experienced financial difficulty and the numbers who had received help from the Ministry of Social Security. It is interesting to note that a small number of parents who had received such help did not regard themselves as having been in financial difficulties. It is possible that more people had received help since, in general, details of help given were not asked of those people who had answered 'No' to the first question in this section. Table 165 shows the number of families who had received free school meals or clothing grants and also who had initiated or suggested this form of help. As is clear from these tables, the most deprived group received significantly more help in all these forms

than any other group. (A chi-square test of significance gives $p < 0.1\%$ for the difference between the MD group and the remainder of the sample.)

Many parents were unaware that clothing grants for school children (as opposed to grants for special uniform) could be given and provision appeared to vary considerably from area to area. No parent had received a maintenance grant for a child at school, but few families had children who would have been eligible. Again this was a benefit of which very few parents seemed to be aware.

This section gave rise to a considerable number of comments and criticisms. All the comments made by the 'middle-class' and 'settled working-class' parents who had received help were favourable. Their reasons for needing help were 'respectable' and easily identifiable such as being separated or divorced wives, widows, cases of severe sickness or disability. Parents found the officers helpful, suggesting other benefits such as free meals and clothing grants, and were visited only rarely by the officers (a point which they obviously appreciated). In the MD group, opinions of the help given varied considerably. Again, the majority of parents had been quite satisfied with the help given, but a small number complained of a lack of 'special grants' for specific items over and above the weekly allowance, particularly if they

Table 164

Numbers receiving financial help
from Ministry of Social Security

	Total Sample	MC	SWC	LD	MD
	116	29	28	30	29
No. who said they had experienced period(s) of financial difficulty	32	1	8	1	22
No. who had received help from Ministry of Social Security	29	2	4	2	21

Table 165

Numbers receiving free school meals or clothing grants

	Total Sample	MC	SWC	LD	MD
	116	29	28	30	29
No. receiving free meals for child in survey	31	1	7	1	22
No. receiving free meals for other child in family, but not child in survey	2	0	0	0	2
No. receiving clothing grant for child in survey	15	1	0	0	14
No. receiving clothing grant for other child in family but not child in survey	6	0	3	1	2
No. who initiated help themselves	7	1	2	0	4
No. where help initiated by school or school welfare officer	12	1	3	0	8
No. where help initiated by other person or agency	15	0	4	1	10

had been without any other income for a long period. Others said that they had asked for help and been refused, and as one parent said, 'When you've asked for something and been refused, you don't like to ask again.' Other complaints concerned the operation of a 'wage stop' and the fact that no allowance was given for a child who had just left school at fifteen.

A small number of families had received help from various voluntary organizations. The scope and nature of such help again seemed to vary from area to area. Six families, all in the MD group, had one or more of their children provided with a free holiday, ten (9 MD, 1 SWC) had received help with toys or food at Christmas time and several had been given toys or clothing by the W.R.V.S. or by health visitors.

RESULTS, SECTION C: SOCIAL AND EMOTIONAL PROBLEMS

Most families go through some period of disturbance or crisis through occurrences such as the death or illness of a member of the family or even the birth of a new baby. Usually neighbours, friends or relatives are able to give whatever help is needed, but this is not invariably true.

Parents were asked whether there had been any period of family crisis or breakdown when they had needed outside help with looking after the home or children. Only three parents had been in such a situation, one in the MC group who had been helped by the 'Home Help' service, and two in the MD group, both of whom had received help through the local authority 'Care of Children'

Table 166

Parental knowledge of agencies able to help
at time of family crisis

	Total Sample	MC	SWC	LD	MD
	116	29	28	30	29
No. giving 'correct' answer, e.g. Home Help or Children's Dept.	25	14	2	6	3
No. giving 'indirect' answer e.g. Citizen's Advice Bureau, health visitor, G.P.	18	5	8	3	2
No. unable to give any answer	73	10	18	21	24

department. When asked what agencies might be able to provide help to a family who found themselves in such plight, a considerable number of parents could suggest none at all. The MC group seemed to know most about these services (particularly the Home Help service) and the MD group knew least. Several parents suggested agencies who, though not able to help directly, would undoubtedly have been able to advise where they could go to get help. Table 166 gives the distribution of answers to this question.

Child behaviour or development can present problems to many parents and, when asked about this, 45 of the parents interviewed (39% of the sample) said they had been worried about this at some stage. For 25 of these parents, the worries had concerned the child included in this study. Differences between the four groups were slight and not significant on a chi-square test. Of the 45 parents who had been worried, 31 had sought help or advice often from doctors, teachers or health visitors. Two of these parents had attended the child clinic for advice in connection with the child in this study. The types of problems mentioned varied considerably but the ones which recurred were enuresis, timidness, difficulty in getting children to bed or to sleep, or poor progress in school work. A selection of parents' descriptions of the problems, and advice or treatment given, follows, to give the reader a more detailed picture.

Problem	Help or advice
Child very highly strung — lives in a world of fantasy and can't tell it from the truth.	None — mother treated it almost as a joke.
Child anti-social, wouldn't mix with other children.	Saw G.P. who said this was nothing to worry about.
Nervous habit of squinting and rolling eyes.	Teacher suggested mother consult health visitor, who said he would grow out of it.
Child frequently wets bed.	Saw G.P. No tests or treatment given but G.P. reassured her by saying this was quite common.
Child very boisterous — still awake at midnight.	Saw G.P. who gave both child and mother tranquillizers.
Child inclined to be nervous of school.	Saw teacher, who advised mother not to help child at home.
Child sulks a lot and hits his parents when upset.	Mother talked to teacher, who said behaved well in school.

Table 167

Parents' knowledge of help given by Child Guidance Clinic

	Total Sample	MC	SWC	LD	MD
	116	29	28	30	29
No. giving fairly accurate description	14	9	3	1	1
No. giving only sketchy description	23	8	3	9	3
No. completely unaware of its function	79	12	22	20	25

Chi-square test of difference between MD and rest of sample
gives $\chi^2 = 4.78$, p < 5%

Chi-square test of difference between MC and rest of sample
gives $\chi^2 = 11.13$, p < 0.1%

Five parents (1 MC and 4 MD) had attended the child guidance clinic for advice, treatment or tests, not necessarily in connection with the child in the study. The comments of those parents who had attended and others showed little understanding of the function of such a service. Only 14 parents had any adequate idea about what sort of help the child guidance clinic offered and over half the sample had no idea at all. There was a significant difference between the groups in their knowledge of this service, with more of the MC group of parents being aware of its function than the remainder of the group and the MD having least knowledge. Table 167 shows these results in full.

RESULTS, SECTION D: NURSERY CLASSES, LIBRARIES AND OTHER SERVICES

Nursery Schools or Classes

It is a well-publicized fact that nursery classes are very unevenly provided in different parts of the country and that, in most areas, the demand for places in a nursery class greatly exceeds the supply. Methods of selection for those who occupy the limited number of places available also vary considerably, emphasis being put either on children of 'working mothers' or children from 'problem families' or large families, or even on the only child who otherwise lacks company. Very often the policies of the local authority are not made clear and certainly parents seemed confused about their child's 'eligiblity' for nursery schooling. The picture of local authority provision is further complicated by the fact that, in some areas, children are admitted to school well before they are five.

The questions concerning nursery class provision for the children included in the study were being asked 'in retrospect' and in a few cases parents had lived in a different area prior to the child's admission to school. This accounts for apparent discrepancies in the numbers in Table 168, which gives the figures for availability of and attendance at nursery classes. From this limited sample (which, taken from a relatively small

Table 168

Provision and use of nursery class facilities

		Total Sample	MC	SWC	LD	MD
		116	29	28	30	29
1. Is there an L.A. nursery class within easy reach? (or was there when child was pre-school age?)	Yes	54	11	12	16	15
	No	62	18	16	14	14
2. If Yes, did child in study attend?	Yes	32	7	6	10	9
	No	22	4	6	6	6
3. If child in study did not attend, has any other child?	Yes	5	0	2	2	1
	No	18	4	5	3	6
4. If there was no L.A. nursery class, was there a private nursery class or playgroups?	Yes	26	17	8	0	1
	No	36	1	8	14	13
5. If Yes, did child in study attend?	Yes	10	9	1	0	0
	No	16	8	7	0	1
6. No. whose child did not attend any nursery class and who would have liked him to do so.		40	3	9	14	14
7. No. of these for whom payment would have made any difference	Yes	12	1	3	0	8
	Possibly	13	0	3	5	5
	No	15	2	3	9	1

number of areas, may not be at all typical in this respect), it appears that the local authority provision of nursery classes is evenly spread over the three types of areas (MC, SWC and 'deprived'). However, two factors here may be disguising the objective situation. One is that the provision of nursery places *per head of the pre-school population* of the area may be very different, and the second is that the phrase 'within reasonable walking distance' which was used in the initial question was interpreted rather widely. A few middle-class parents in fact took their children some distance by car to attend a nursery class or play group. The proportion of children in this sample who had attended a nursery class is 27%, which is higher than that found in the National

Survey undertaken for the Plowden Committee (1967) where it was found that 16 per cent had attended nursery classes. This is due, at least in part, to the fact that in one area concerned *all* the infant schools had a nursery class of their own and hence a very high proportion of the infant pupils had attended the attached nursery class.

Combining the figures in Table 168 for local authority and private nursery classes, it appears that only one parent in the MC areas felt that there was no provision of either a local authority or a private nursery class, while 8 SWC, 14 LD and 13 MD said that neither was available in their area. These differences are reflected in the number of parents whose children did not go to a nursery class or playgroup, either because there was no provision or because places were insufficient, and who would have liked their children to attend. Almost half the 'deprived' area children were in this category, as compared with about a third of the SWC children and only 10 per cent of the MC children. It would appear, then, that the 'unmet need' for nursery class provision is far from equally distributed. The provision of private nursery classes or playgroups is limited almost entirely to SWC and MC areas in this sample. If such provision were made in other areas, the need for payment would certainly exclude some children, according to their parents' answers, though by no means all. Of those children who had been given places in a nursery class only a small number, six in all, did not attend regularly once they had started.

Opinions of parents on whether a child should or should not have some sort of pre-school education varied considerably. Some saw it as a definite educational advantage to the child, some as a social advantage, particularly for only children or the youngest child in a family. Very few felt that its chief purpose was to free mothers to go to work (and in families where incomes were low and rents high, this could have become a major consideration). Other parents felt that children should be at home with their parents until school age, or even regretted having to send them to school as early as five years old.

Again, perhaps a selection of the comments made by the parents themselves will give a more vivid picture.

From parents whose children attended a nursery class or play school:

'It helped her to learn to talk'

'It helped her when she came to settle into school and it gives the parents a few hours free'

'He was in a shell before' — the nursery class brought him out a lot'

'Every area should have one. They get used to mixing with other children there before they have to start learning'

'Before she went she was overpowered by the two older children at home and wouldn't try anything on her own'

'Children can start learning things before they are five'

From parents who would have liked their child to attend nursery class:

'I couldn't afford the private one — I would have liked her to go if there had been a free one' (from a MC parent on MSS allowance)

'He was the only one at home — he needed company'

'It would give them a better start in school'

'He could have played with sand and water there, which I won't allow in the house'

'She was on the waiting list for a long time but there were no vacancies. She was very lonely after her older brother started school'

'She needed company and stimulation by four'

'It would have benefited her. You can't keep children occupied or take them out much on an MSS allowance'

'Children get bored at home, particularly if there is nowhere for them to play outside'

'I would have liked him to go but the health visitor told me nursery classes were only for problem families'

'I think every mother would like the children out of the way sometimes'

'It keeps the children off the streets'

'It would have been a big help to me. I had the two younger children very quickly'

'He was the last one at home. I liked having him around me'

'It wasn't necessary because he was able to start school before five'

'You would miss the best years of their lives — why should somebody else have the benefit? At that age they are saying new words, doing new things. I wouldn't miss that for worlds'

'I don't agree with it — they learn enough in school'

(From a father) 'My wife could look after him — there was no need'

'He wouldn't have left me at that age'

'It wasn't worth the journey for just half a day'

'They go to school soon enough — they're only babies once'

The most common reason given by parents for wanting the child to go to a nursery class were: mixing with other children, preparation for school routine, keeping children occupied, starting to learn (speech, reading etc.), 'bringing out' children who are shy, and giving parents some free time.

The rather smaller number who did not want their child to attend a nursery class or playgroup gave as the most common reasons, their own enjoyment of the child at home or the feeling that it was not *necessary* and therefore they should not take up scarce nursery class places.

Surprisingly, perhaps, only two parents mentioned the chance for mothers to go out to work when their children attended nursery class, one of these being a mother separated from her husband. In many cases children attended nursery class for only half the day, which would scarcely allow time for even part-time work. Two fathers who were coping with a family on their own both mentioned the need to give the parents some time to themselves.

Libraries

Only five parents in this sample said that there was not a library within reach of their home, even if the parents took the child. Of the remainder, one parent did not know where the nearest library was.

Seventy-eight said the child in the study would need to be taken to the nearest library, and 32 had libraries near enough for the children to go on their own. The five who had no library nearby were in 'deprived' areas, otherwise there was little difference between the areas in library provision. However, there was a significant difference between the groups in the use made of the library by the children in the study. In the MD group only seven children (24%) in the study had ever used library books, whereas 57—72 per cent of the other three groups had used this service. Table 169 shows the distribution of answers to the questions about the use of public libraries.

Both the findings of Jean Jones (1966) and the report of the survey undertaken for the Plowden Committee (1967) show similar overall class differences in the use made by primary school children of public libraries. The figures in Table 169 emphasize the differences which exist *within* working class areas (i.e. between the MD and LD groups).

In addition to *public* libraries, several schools or local authorities run their own libraries, so that some of the children who did not use public libraries did bring library books home from school. On the whole, those parents whose children used a public library felt that there was a good selection of suitable books available. Several parents were under the impression that children were not able to join a library until they were seven years old. According to official information, children were eligible for library membership in all the areas involved from the age of five, but in a few school areas the belief that the necessary age was seven was so widespread that one wondered whether individual librarians were discouraging younger children, particularly if not accompanied by an adult.

A few parents had themselves discouraged children from having library books because of the fear that they would be damaged or lost either by the infant school child or by younger siblings.

Other services

As a final question in this section, parents were asked if, apart from the services that had already been mentioned, there was any service or facility they would particularly like to see provided in their area which would benefit young children or

Table 169

Provision and use of public libraries

	Total Sample	MC	SWC	LD	MD
	116	29	28	30	29
1. Library near enough for child to go on own	32	5	10	5	12
Library near enough to take child	78	24	18	22	14
No library nearby	5	0	0	3	2
Parent did not know	1	0	0	0	1
2. If library nearby: a)No. of families in which child in study belongs	65	21	20	17	7
b)No. of families in which other member of family belongs but not child in study	17	3	4	3	7

Chi-square test of difference for item 2(a) between MD and rest of sampl gives $\chi^2 = 14.29$, $p < 0.1\%$

their parents. Despite the intended exclusion of services mentioned specifically, several parents reiterated the need for local nursery classes at this stage, suggesting that this is a particularly strongly felt need. The other answers given reflect a wide variety of individual or community needs.

Undoubtedly the most pressing need for parents as a whole is for further play facilities and spare-time activities for children. Playgrounds were often not near enough for children between the ages of five and seven to attend unaccompanied and they were sometimes 'monopolized' by teen-age children. The school holidays are times when facilities are particularly needed and many parents emphasized the need for indoor provision and definite supervised activities. Parents made general comments about the lack of children's play facil-ities such as, 'They soon put a "pub" up (on a new

estate), but nowhere for the children to go,' or 'People assume that because you live near the sea the children need nothing else,' or 'It seems unfair that because you struggle to afford to live in "better" area you get nothing provided and yet council estates get playgrounds and community halls provided'.

A summary of the suggestions made is given below, with the numbers who mentioned each item and any special comments made about the needs.

1. playground (3 MC, 5 SWC, 12 LD, 12 MD). Comments: supervised, nearer to estates, enclosed, separate one for *young* children.
2. clubs, cubs, brownies or similar (3 MC, 1 SWC, 10 LD, 3 MD). Comments: especially for *young* children, with definite activities or instruction.

3. play centre for evenings and for holidays (4 MC, 2 SWC, 3 MD). Comments: indoor, could open school building for this.
4. swimming pool (beginners) (2 MC, 2 SWC, 1 LD, 1 MD)
5. better sports or coaching facilities (4 MC, 1 SWC)
6. better clinic facilities (1 MC, 2 SWC, 1 LD)
7. pedestrian crossings (1 SWC, 1 MD)
8. parent-teacher association (1 SWC)
9. film shows for young children (1 SWC)
10. ice rink (1 SWC)
11. classes for dancing and singing (1 MD)
12. a rota of mothers to look after pre-school children to give others a break for a day (1 MD)
13. chemist (1 MD)
14. another school to ease the overcrowding in this one (1 MC)

The suggestions made by the parents in this sample are very similar to those reported by the Plowden Committee in the survey of a national sample of parents of primary school children, with the major emphasis on playgrounds or indoor play facilities. Not all parents had any suggestions to make here and some appeared to be quite satisfied with the services and facilities already provided locally.

SUMMARY AND CONCLUSIONS (PARENTS' USE OF SERVICES)

The services mentioned in this section differ considerably in both the general extent of the problems for which they cater and in the range of the population which they expect to serve.

The school medical examination is given to *all* children and the follow-up services which are offered were used by a similar proportion of each of the four groups studied. The majority of parents were quite satisfied with this service, though not one parent mentioned that she had used the medical examination as an opportunity to discuss any problems of health, behaviour or development.

The remaining services might conveniently be divided into those providing for financial and material needs and those providing for social and cultural needs. For the former, the need will obviously not be evenly distributed, and it was found that financial aid, free meals and clothing grants were received much more frequently by families in the 'most deprived' group than by any other group. Of the total 32 families in the sample who had experienced financial difficulty, 29 had received financial help from the MSS, 31 had received free school meals for the child in the survey and 15 had received a clothing grant. Not all parents were aware of the help available or how eligibility for help was assessed. In the majority of cases where free meals or clothing grants were given, this help had been initiated by the school, the educational welfare officer or some other agency rather than by the parents themselves.

Only very small numbers of families had made use of services such as speech therapy, child guidance, home helps or child care. The knowledge of these less common services was much less wide than that of financial and material aid, and the 'middle-class' group had the greatest knowledge of the existence and purposes of such services.

The two services which might be thought of as catering for the cultural or social needs of young children are the children's sections of the public libraries and the provision of nursery class education. Library facilities were readily available to almost all the children in the sample, but the use made of this service showed a considerable difference between the groups, with fewer of the 'most deprived' children borrowing library books. The largest number of children whose parents would have liked them to go to a nursery class but for whom no place was available were in the two 'deprived' area groups. The provision of privately-run nursery classes and playgroups was confined almost entirely to the 'middle-class' and 'settled working-class' areas. Almost all the parents whose children had attended nursery classes felt that the child had benefited socially or educationally from this experience. It seems unfortunate that these two services cannot be used more widely by those who would appear to need them most. The need for nursery education is most certainly perceived by the parents as a 'priority'. On the other hand, parents in the 'deprived' areas were not so aware of the need for, or relevance of, greater use of the public libraries by young children. Some were apprehensive of damage to, or loss of, books, some were unaware that children of five were eligible for membership and some felt the fact that their child was not yet a fluent reader made the use of library books pointless.

There is little doubt that, in all types of area, the chief unmet need according to parents is that for adequate play facilities for young children. This need is particularly great in families where there is overcrowding in the home, or no garden or yard for the children to use for play. The need, however, is not just for space but also for equipment, for indoor activities in poor weather, for extra activities during school holidays, and in some cases for separate spaces for young children or for some kind of supervision.

Two more general points emerge from this study. The first of these is the extent to which the provision of some statutory and also voluntary services vary from area to area. Provision of clothing grants was one example of this and free holidays for disadvantaged children was another. The second point is that health visitors, general practitioners and school teachers were being asked by parents to give advice on quite a wide range of social and emotional problems, often in areas for which their training may not have equipped them.

This investigation was carried out before the implementation of the recommendation of the Seebohm Committee (1968) for closer co-ordination of welfare services, and also before the Government's recommendations for extended nursery provision (D.E.S., 1972).

While it seems that, on the whole, the most deprived group make wider use of financial and material aid, their use of other services is no greater and in some cases less than that of other groups of the population. This could be due to a genuine lack of need for help, a lack of *perceived* need of help or a lack of knowledge that such help is available. A greater awareness of services available on the part of teachers and a more co-ordinated approach from the reorganized social service departments could perhaps extend the use of some of these services where this seems appropriate.

PART FIVE — SUMMARY AND CONCLUSIONS

14 Summary and Conclusions

A. SUMMARY

I Background to the study

The Schools Council Research and Development Project in Compensatory Education had three major aims:

1. to provide screening techniques so that children in need of compensatory education may be identified as soon as possible after entry to the infant school;
2. to make longitudinal studies of infant school children in deprived areas, with particular reference to their response to schooling and their emotional development;
3. to develop teaching programmes, involving materials in a variety of media, which may be used to help culturally deprived children at the infant school stage.

The present volume is one of two dealing with the second of these three aims. Its companion volume (Deprivation and Development, Chazan et al., to be published) presents a detailed comparison of the cognitive and emotional development of one sub-sample of children considered to be high in deprivation, and another sub-sample of children having many emotional problems, with a matched group of children considered to be low in deprivation, or relatively free of emotional problems. In the present volume, the information is of a more general nature and covers the educational progress and emotional adjustment of children in three urban areas and one rural area over their three years in the infant school. Information was obtained from the children's teachers and headteachers, and from some of the children's parents. At the end of the three years, the children's performance on a number of objective tests was measured so that attainments in the different school area types included in the sample could be examined.

The summary will be presented section by section and then some general conclusions will be drawn.

In Part One, the complex concept of deprivation, as it affects children, is discussed. It is stressed that there are many different kinds and degrees of deprivation, which may result from conditions at home, at school, or in the neighbourhood. The wide range of individual differences in children's reactions to adverse circumstances should not be overlooked, nor the interaction between varous kinds of deficit, often found in combination.

In the studies of urban children reported in this volume, the main aim was to highlight the problems of schools serving catchment areas where conditions of both 'material' deprivation (especially low income and poor housing) and 'cultural' deprivation (especially a lack of sensory and linguistic stimulation) were prevalent. In the case of the rural children, particular attention was given to the effects of isolation.

II School progress and adjustment in urban areas

The study reported in Part Two of this volume was aimed at examining the effects of material and cultural deprivation on the educational progress and school adjustment of infant school children living in *urban* areas. Deprivation was given a fairly wide interpretation so that schools serving housing estates were studied as well as those in inner-city areas. The response to schooling made by the children in the DA ('deprived' area) schools was compared with that made by children living in the same urban area but coming from MC ('middle-class') or SWC ('settled working-class') backgrounds, these two sub-samples combining to form the CA (control area) schools. A variety of measures was used to estimate the conditions in the schools to which the children went and background information on the areas was collated from the 1966 Census data. Most of the findings are, however, based on a series of six school schedules completed by the schools at intervals throughout the three years the children spent in the infant department.

1. The nature of the study
(a) The sample. Twenty-six schools (14 DA, 6 SWC and 6 MC) were involved in three different

cities. All the children born between 1 September, 1963 and 31 March, 1964 were included, a total of 689 children, although not every measure was completed for this number. The DA children were significantly older than the CA children (Tables 14 and 15) and attended school less regularly than the CA group (Table 17), although it was felt that neither of these facts had a marked effect on their educational progress. Rather more DA children had some minor physical defect, such as impaired hearing, defective eyesight, bad teeth or poor speech, but the number of children affected was small.

(b) The children's home background. A larger proportion of the DA children than the CA children came from 'lower working-class' families (Table 7), were members of large (3+) families (Table 8) and were later born rather than first born (Table 9), although the differences in family size and birth order were not statistically significant. The percentage of DA children receiving free school meals was above the national average and considerably above that of the CA group (Table 10). The DA children also changed schools more often than the CA children, an indication that some of the families did not settle anywhere for long or were moved to other housing by the authorities.

In all but two cases, the census and other background data on the school areas supported their designation as deprived (DA), 'settled working-class' (SWC) and 'middle-class' (MC) respectively. The exceptions were two schools, selected as serving 'deprived' areas, which were found to be serving areas similar to the SWC schools. All of the areas were found to be much the same in the availability within them of social, cultural and other amenities (Table 4 and pages 28–30).

(c) The schools. The majority of the schools favoured horizontal grouping, admitting children in the term in which they were five, although in a few schools children were admitted at a younger age and two schools used some form of vertical grouping.

A higher proportion of DA teachers than CA teachers were untrained or had been trained for other age ranges, and the CA teachers had rather longer teaching experience and more of it in infant schools. Class size, however, was smaller in the DA

schools and the pupil-teacher ratio lower. There were few staffing problems in the CA schools but the DA schools reported more difficulties in this aspect with regard to training, supply and turnover. No trend was apparent in the training and experience of the headteachers and all spent approximately the same amount of time weekly in teaching activities.

In terms of school buildings, amenities and general school conditions, the DA schools showed more adverse features than the CA schools but the differences between the schools were not significant. Much more marked were the differences between the policies of the various LEAs, one area in particular being well provided with secretarial assistance, ancillary help and medical rooms in comparison with other two. Only in the DA schools was any mention made of vandalism on school premises.

In general, the DA and CA groups appeared to differ less on the factors relating specifically to school than they did on the home background factors.

(d) Sample losses. A number of children were lost to the sample in the course of the three years of the survey. Approximately 25 per cent of the DA group left the sample schools, as compared with approximately 17 per cent of the CA group. From the data available for these children, it appears that the losses from the CA schools were fairly random and the sample remained representative. The children who were lost from the DA group, however, received rather low ratings on the available schedules and it is possible that they represented a proportion of the children who were thought to be poor in progress and adjustment. Their loss must, therefore, be borne in mind when examining the information from the schedules over the years.

2. Starting school
(a) Preparation for school entry. More of the SWC than the DA children had been in their school prior to entry and were acquainted with the reception class teacher and classroom (Tables 22 and 23). The CA parents had made more contact with the school than the DA parents. However, largely because of differing LEA policy, more DA children had attended nursery classes than CA, and

more of them had siblings or relatives in the infant school (Tables 26, 27).

(b) Settling into school The DA children appeared to make a less happy start in school in some respects. A significantly higher proportion of the DA children showed signs of distress on leaving their mother during the first two weeks at school (Table 29) and were inclined to cling to adults (Table 31). Although not hostile to their teachers or their peers, the DA children were less often rated as showing highly positive attitudes to them (Table 33). A few children in both groups showed unusual or difficult behaviour during the first ten days in school (pp. 63—67). The MC children in particular made a good start and were frequently rated considerably higher on the items than the SWC as well as the DA children, so that the differences which appeared were at times the result of their superior ratings rather than of any particular difficulties on the part of the DA children.

(c) Response to the infant school programme. The MC children showed a significantly more active interest in the materials and experiences provided in the first term (Table 41) and their play was more likely to lead to a definite end product or a successful conclusion, as well as being rated rather more often as imaginative or original (Table 43). There was little difference in the children's preferences for the activities offered (Table 42).

It had been anticipated that the DA children would show less concentrated application to structured activities but in fact no real differences appeared between them and the CA group except at the end of the first year. Indeed, the DA children seemed to improve in concentration over the years but this may reflect the change brought about in the DA sample through the selective bias of the sample losses.

3. Social and emotional adjustment
Although a roughly similar proportion of DA and CA children were rated as showing no signs of behavioural difficulties, the DA children who were noted by their teachers as showing some symptoms of maladjustment (on the Stott six pointers) were more often given three or more adverse ratings than the CA children. Aggressive behaviour

was most frequently noted for these DA children (Table 39) in their first year. By the end of the third year the differences between the DA and CA groups had become more pronounced on some of the ratings (Tables 38—40), with 'abnormal behaviour' being noted significantly more often for the DA group.

The difference between the groups in adjustment was not so marked as might have been expected but it appeared to present a real problem in the schools, inasmuch as the DA headteachers felt that their pupils were more restless and aggressive than children in other schools, although this view was not always supported by the class teachers.

4. Educational progress
(a) Language skills. On the *productive language ratings* (for speech articulation, range of spoken vocabulary and fluency in oral expression) the CA children were clearly and consistently superior to the DA children throughout. This superiority was marked in the case of the MC children and sustained by the SWC children, although with the latter the differences did not always reach the necessary level of significance (Table 44). The ratings on these language items did not, however, show a trend over time which might have indicated that the gap between the CA and the DA groups progressively widened. The absence of a 'cumulative deficit', which might have been expected from findings on other deprived populations, may have been produced by the nature of the losses from the sample or, in the case of the teachers' ratings, by variations in the standards on which the judgements were based. In the final test battery, the results of the WISC vocabulary sub-test (standardized on American children) showed the CA children's mean score to be in line with their mean chronological age (the MC children's mean vocabulary score was a year above that of the SWC children), with the DA children's mean falling over six months below their mean chronological age (Table 48).

In the *receptive language skills* (understanding stories and following oral instructions) differences again appeared, largely because of the MC group's superiority. However, the differences were not consistent (Table 44) and failed to reach statistical significance on the final school schedule. The DA children appeared to some extent to catch up on the CA children, although similar difficulties exist in the interpretation of these results as in the final ratings on the other language skills.

The findings on the receptive and the productive language skills of the urban sample are in agreement with those presented in Deprivation and Development (Chazan et al., to be published), the companion volume to the present study, which reports a more extensive inquiry into the cognitive development of deprived children. This study showed that the deprived children were significantly poorer than their controls on the whole range of language skills, both receptive and productive.

(b) Reading and related skills. As with progress and attainment in the language skills, the CA children were more highly rated throughout in reading skills than the DA children. Some of this superiority was attributable to the performance of the MC children but the DA children's poorer response in a number of aspects was still evident when compared with the SWC children (Tables 51—53). The CA children required less time to be spent on pre-reading skills and moved more rapidly on to the reading schemes in use, although by the end of the second year virtually all of the children in both groups had transferred to the reading scheme. In the test battery given at the end of the third year of their schooling, the CA group as a whole, and the SWC component considered separately, achieved significantly higher scores than the DA group on all of the reading tests and the spelling test, thus confirming the superior progress which had been evident in every schedule (Tables 54, 55).

In terms of attainment ages, the MC children's mean ages in reading and spelling were above their mean chronological age (Table 58), the SWC children's mean attainment ages approximated to their mean chronological age and the DA children obtained reading (except for Neale Rate) and spelling ages ranging from one month to eleven months below their chronological age. In both the CA and the DA groups, the distribution of scores on these standardized measures was skewed towards the lower end of the score range (Figures 2-6), but at least twice as many DA children as CA children were retarded by one year or more on the word recognition test and the spelling test, the extent of retardation being more

difficult to estimate at this age on the Neale tests. Children with severe reading retardation (i.e. of eighteen months or more) were, with few exceptions, in the DA schools.

The development of mechanical writing skills conformed to the pattern noted for linguistic and reading skills, with the CA children being rated in the early schedules as more advanced and retaining this superiority throughout the later schedules.

(c) Mathematical skills. The superiority of the CA children was not so marked in mathematical skills as in the other aspects of the educational programme which have been discussed. By the third year, however, the CA children were rated significantly higher in computational skills and in their grasp of time and money concepts (Table 62). They were also rather better than the DA children in their understanding of basic number concepts (although the between-groups difference was non-significant), a finding which was supported by their performance on the mathematics test in their third year when they obtained significantly higher scores. The performance of the SWC group on this test was marginally better than that of the DA group (Table 64), the difference between the CA and DA groups, therefore, being largely produced by the scores of the MC children.

(d) Predicted progress in the junior school. As the DA children's progress in the areas vital to their educational success was seen by the teachers as being poorer than that of the CA children and their attainments at the end of the infant school were correspondingly lower, it is not surprising that difficulties at the next stage of education were anticipated for a higher proportion of them. Nineteen per cent of DA children were estimated by their teachers as definitely likely to experience difficulties in the junior school as compared with just over ten per cent of the CA children (Table 68). It is probable that the teachers were not basing their judgements solely on low school attainment but this must have played a considerable part in their prognosis.

5. The final school attainment survey
On the battery of school attainment and ability tests given to the children in their final infant school term, the CA group obtained higher mean scores than the DA group on all of the tests (Table

69). In the CA group, the MC children were significantly superior in performance to the SWC children. In their turn, the SWC children did better than the DA children in the various tests but the differences were not always statistically significant.

The superior performance of the CA children on the final battery included their performance on the NFER Picture Test A, a non-verbal test of intelligence. It, therefore, became necessary to look at the effect which intelligence had had on performance and to attempt to isolate this effect from that of school area factors (i.e. the child's home background and the school which he attended). It also seemed advisable to look at the performance of boys separately from that of girls.

Statistical analysis (Tables 71—77) showed that both intelligence and school area type made highly significant contributions to the variations in the children's scores but the child's sex affected only three measures (Neale rate and spelling in favour of the girls; WISC vocabulary in favour of the boys). The contribution of intelligence was consistently higher than that of school area type and, in the latter, the factors relating to the children's home background appeared more important than the factors specifically concerned with school.

Interaction, of course, exists between home background factors and intelligence test scores, but the home background may have relatively less effect on intelligence than it has on educational attainment. It was, therefore, decided to look at the mean attainment scores in the school area groups, controlling for the effect of intelligence, and at the performance of the high, medium and low scorers on the intelligence test, controlling for the effect of the school area type. With intelligence held constant, the CA group obtained very significantly higher mean scores on all the attainment tests than the DA group (Table 74). It is of interest, also, to note that when the performance of the MC group was compared with that of the SWC and DA groups combined, the MC children were superior on all tests. When the SWC and DA groups' mean scores were compared, the SWC children were consistently above the DA children in performance but the differences were not always significant. With school area type held constant, the expected differences in the attainment scores of the three intelligence groups appeared (Table 75) and a graphical presentation (Figures 16—29) showed

that intelligence level differentiated the children's performance more clearly than grouping by school area type. There was some indication that school area type had a greater effect at the low than at the high intelligence level but this was not consistent across all tests nor was it sustained at the medium intelligence level. In any case, none of the interactions between intelligence and school area type reached statistical significance. It does, however, hint at what has been revealed in other studies, for example Garner's (1972) finding that infant school children who were above the median in intelligence were unaffected in their 'task attention' by teacher behaviour or home background factors whereas low intelligence and 'low class parental background' (p. 40) produced a high level of task avoidance.

III Children's school progress and adjustment in a rural area

Rural areas present special problems with regard to the education of young children and deprivation in this setting is very different from the deprivation to be found in areas of inner urban decay or bleak housing estates. The county which was studied in this research is one of considerable scenic beauty and attracts visitors at all times of the year. Yet it is the least densely populated of any of the Welsh counties and, therefore, its schools are most likely to be exposed to the twin dangers of social and professional isolation described in the Gittins Report (1967).

Because of the limitations imposed by the small numbers of children of the appropriate age available in the representative sample of schools selected, the research design for the rural schools differed from that of the urban schools. Eleven schools were involved with a total of 62 children initially, dropping to 58 in the course of the study. As for the urban sample, information was collected by means of six school schedules, a final test battery and a number of questionnaires. In addition, the parents, or parent, of all the children in the sample were interviewed. The progress of the rural children in the first three years in school was compared with that of the urban children and home background factors were described and related, as seemed relevant, to that progress.

The general findings from the rural study were:

1. There was some evidence of the professional isolation which the Gittins Report mentioned. Some schools had no school meal organizer, only one had any form of part-time clerical help, practically all of the head teachers were teaching full-time for part of the week and young teachers were reluctant to stay for any length of time in the more remote schools.

2. There was also evidence of some degree of social isolation in the age range on which this study was centred. Provision of pre-school education was minimal, regular bus services to the nearest small town for those living in other than urban districts were non-existent, visitors were few and the children were seldom taken to places of interest (Tables 95 and 96), presumably partly through lack of time on the part of the parents and partly through the distances involved.

3. Some of the schools were lacking in fairly basic amenities (e.g. indoor sanitation, dining facilities, staff room, storage space) but the overall differences between the facilities in the rural schools and those in the urban schools were slight, largely because some of the rural schools were well-equipped, new buildings and these helped to raise the average ratings considerably.

4. Most of the sample lived in houses or bungalows, almost half of which were owned, not rented, and most of which had all amenities. The majority of the houses were well kept and clean (Table 84) and the health of the parents (Table 85) compared favourably with that of parents in *deprived* urban areas. Although incomes were lower than in industrial areas (pp. 182–183), expenditure also appeared lower and the farm workers in particular seemed to enjoy considerable job satisfaction.

5. The rural parents were, on the whole, completely happy about their children's schooling (34 parents; 59 per cent), and most (52 parents; 90 per cent) tried to help their children at home and were keen for them to do well (p. 189).

6. There was significantly less deprivation in the rural area than in the deprived urban areas studied (Table 97), especially with regard to material factors.

The major findings on the school progress and adjustment of the rural children, as compared with those for the *total* urban sample, were:

1. Despite the fact that the children in the rural sample appeared to have had significantly less direct contact with the school before entry (Table 98), there was no real difference between them and the urban sample children in initial 'settling in' difficulties (Table 101). Early signs of distress were on the whole quickly forgotten and the majority of the entrants showed very positive or positive attitudes to their teachers and their fellow pupils (Tables 99 and 106–108). More of them, however, found the school day tiring, presumably mainly because of the amount of travelling involved.

2. The rural children made good use of the creative activities offered to them (Tables 103, 104), especially in the first year, being highly rated by their teachers in imaginativeness and originality. Throughout the three years of the study, fewer of them were placed in the lowest category of the ratings for these characteristics than the urban children.

3. The urban children were more independent of adult help in matters such as dressing than the rural children (Table 110) but rather more of the urban children got lost in school or showed other signs of inability to cope with the school routine, problems which seldom arose in the small rural schools. With regard to overall adjustment in the school setting, the rural children were consistently rated as better adjusted than the urban children, although the differences are only significant at the end of the third year for the total Stott rating (Tables 112, 113).

4. The teachers' ratings of the children's speech patterns showed an interesting change, from the rural children being rated rather higher than the urban children in clarity and range of vocabulary at the end of the first term in school to the rural children being rated significantly lower in clarity, although still a little higher in range of vocabulary, at the end of the third year (Tables 114, 115). Why this should be so, is not easily determined. Both groups showed similar competence in listening activities (Table 116).

5. No rural child was said to be able to read on entry to school and only four were said to be

able to write their own name. The ability to draw simple, recognisable shapes was significantly lower in the rural sample than in the urban sample (p. 196). In early pre-reading activities, however, there were no real differences between the two samples (Table 118). Progress through the reading scheme was a little slower at first (Table 117) but by the end of the third year the pattern was practically identical for both samples, with approximately 70 per cent of the children being said by their teachers to be on Book IV of the reading scheme or beyond. With regard to reading comprehension and to knowledge of phonics, there were no differences between the two samples in ability (Tables 119, 120) and significantly fewer of the rural children were said to have little or no ability in these aspects. The same pattern is found in the distribution of the children for interest in reading (Table 121), no child in the rural sample being rated as having little or no interest at the end of the third year.

6. In writing skills, the rural children at first tended to cluster in the middle rating categories (Table 122), pulling away from the urban children at the end of the second year (Table 122), when 71 per cent of them were said to be copying words easily and efficiently as compared with 59 per cent of the total urban sample, a difference which just fails to reach statistical significance.

7. At the end of the first year, the rural children were rated significantly higher than their urban counterparts in mathematical activities, a position which they maintained in several of the items at the end of the second year (Tables 126, 127). By the end of the third year, the urban children appeared to have caught up with them (Tables 126, 127), a finding which was not, however, confirmed by the children's performance in the final mathematics test (Table 131) where the RA children had a higher mean score.

8. As with the urban sample, only a few of the rural sample were thought likely to have any adjustment problems on entering the junior stage of their education (Table 128) but, with most of the rural children remaining in the same school as previously, this could be expected.

The rural children's performance on the final battery of attainment tests was compared with that of the total urban sample and then related to factors in their home background, an analysis which was possible only for the rural sample as every child's home was visited.

1. The test battery (Table 131) showed that the rural children made a significantly higher mean raw score on the NFER Picture Test A ($p < 5\%$) and on the NFER Basic Mathematics Test ($p < 0.1\%$). In the other tests, of reading and spelling, the differences in mean raw scores between the two populations were not significant. In nearly all of the tests, the range of scores tended to be narrower for the rural than the urban children. The standardized attainment scores (Table 132) show that on the Burt Word Recognition test and the Daniels and Diack Spelling test the rural children were a little below their chronological age but in all other measures they were at or above it.

2. When the rural children were grouped into four categories (Table 94) according to the degree of isolation of their homes, it was found (Table 136) that no consistent pattern emerged in relation to their performance on any of the tests. The number of children placed in the 'most isolated' category (8 out of 58) was, however, too small for any firm conclusions to be drawn.

3. The home backgrounds of the children in the rural sample showed less evidence of material deprivation and signs of cultural deprivation were fewer than in the urban sample as a whole. The rural children rated as having the poorest home backgrounds (Group 3: Table 137) consistently made the lowest scores in the final test battery and, in the tests of vocabulary, mathematics and intelligence, these were significantly lower than the scores made by the rural children with the most advantageous home backgrounds.

4. When the effects of the difference in intelligence in the rural children were controlled, it was found that differences in home background, whether material or cultural, had little effect on performance in the final test battery, the differences in scores noted previously being almost entirely accounted for by differences in intelligence (Table 138). This finding must, of course, be treated with caution as it is not possible to separate home background com-

pletely from intelligence test scores. Nevertheless, graphic representations of the data (Figures 49—54) support the finding that differences in intelligence appear to have more consistent effects on attainment than do differences in home background, as far as the rural children are concerned.

IV A. Teaching Approaches

The views presented in Chapter 11 on the teaching situation within the project schools were representative of head teachers and teachers in schools serving a variety of local conditions. Thirty-six head teachers (14 DA; 10 RA; 6 SWC and 6 MC, i.e. 12 CA) and forty-eight class teachers (19 DA; 11 RA; 11 SWC and 7 MC, i.e. 18 CA) were interviewed (for questionnairies used see Appendix III).

1. Educational aims
On the whole most schools agreed on the order of importance of the various aims presented (Table 140). All placed first the development of social and emotional maturity, although several thought all of the aims presented were of equal importance. Specific circumstances did, however, have an effect. In DA schools, the development of creative and expressive powers were more stressed in the first year than in CA schools and 3R skills were postponed until the teachers felt confident that the children were sufficiently prepared to be able to cope with them. The CA and RA schools ranked the development of oral language skills second, although the MC schools thought a grounding in the 3Rs to be of equal importance. The other groups placed the latter aim in the fourth (final) place, although their remarks showed that they considered it of vital importance.

2. Co-operation between head teacher and staff
In all schools this appeared to be good. As staff numbers were small, discussions were usually informal. Formal staff meetings were arranged in most schools but these were mainly occasional meetings. Problems involving individual children were frequently discussed, usually with all the staff who were present, but eight head teachers preferred to confine such discussion to the staff member immediately concerned.

3. Classroom organization
The integrated day approach, with the teaching of the basic skills incorporated in the on-going activities, was most favoured in the DA schools (Table 142). The CA schools preferred a concentration on three R activities in the morning sessions and a free choice of activities in the afternoons. In the RA schools the allocation of certain topics to specific periods of time was typical. The organization adopted by the various schools was, therefore, in keeping with their ordering of educational aims. Several teachers, however, remarked that the organization, and the aims, changed as the children moved through the school.

4. Classroom activities
(a) Free play. All schools were convinced of the value of allowing children to make active use and independent choice of a variety of creative materials and situations. Children's choice of activity seemed to be influenced by their out of school experience, with the urban children turning most frequently to the Wendy house or house corner and rather less often to the book or shop corner, while the rural children favoured the shop corner and made less use of the book corner, large toys and sand and water.

(b) Language skills. Although no school would underestimate the importance of language, the amount of time given to this aspect and the nature of the help required by the children varied from area to area. On the whole, the CA schools had few problems with regard to the children's linguistic abilities. The RA schools found their major problem to be the child's reluctance to speak, because of shyness and lack of experience of being in a large group of children. Most work had to be done with the DA children, teachers commenting on their poor articulation and inability to listen, as well as their limited language background. Teachers facing difficulties in this aspect felt the solution lay in expanding linguistic opportunities for the children either by increasing the number of available adults in the classroom or by the use of tape recorders or other audio-visual aids. In this respect it should be noted that only two DA schools had tape recorders, the RA and CA schools having much better provision (Table 147).

(c) Reading. In the DA schools, progress in reading was rather slower than in the other areas, presumably because the teachers had first to establish some basic linguistic competence. Introduction to phonic skills was later for the DA children, more were expected to be still on pre-reading activities at the end of the first year and teachers expected less of them in reading than in CA or RA schools. The estimated number of DA children who would require considerable help with reading in the junior school was half as much again as that of the CA or RA children.

Most schools used some form of a 'look and say' approach in beginning reading, phonics being introduced later, either systematically or incidentally. All made use of one or more of the established reading schemes, Janet and John (DA, CA and RA), Ladybird (DA, CA and RA) and Happy Venture (DA and RA) being the most frequently mentioned. Some teachers made critical comments on the presentation, content and gradient of difficulty in the schemes but more were favourable towards them. Only four (2 DA, 2 CA) out of twenty-six urban schools felt the supply of library books to be less than adequate and all ten RA schools were satisfied, their supply being, of course, often augmented by visits from the County mobile library.

(d) Mathematics. No real differences appeared between the groups in their response to the mathematical opportunities presented although these varied between the areas with the DA schools favouring a practical, experimental approach to basic principles, the CA schools mixing this with more formal, traditional methods and the RA schools using a general approach, although none of the latter schools used the Nuffield scheme. RA schools most frequently mentioned the use of published books.

Again, out of school experiences affected the children's competence, with the DA children having few problems in understanding the handling of money and some RA children finding this difficult.

Some of the teachers expressed a lack of confidence in their own ability to implement the new approaches to mathematics teaching and some MC teachers felt the parents lacked confidence in the effectiveness of the new approaches. The RA teachers were, at the time of the interview, particularly worried about decimalisation and metrication, these changes also being a matter of concern for some of the urban teachers.

5. Problems mentioned by the head teachers and teachers

The familiar problems associated with children coming from homes in which there are low educational aspirations were already in evidence. Eight out of fourteen DA schools had problems connected with attendance and a few children were persistent absentees. Only two RA and two CA schools mentioned any attendance difficulties. Five per cent of DA children were consistently late, again a problem which was negligible in CA and RA schools. Twenty per cent of DA children came from 'needy' families and the estimation of cultural deprivation was five times higher in the DA than the CA group. In the RA group, little mention was made of 'needy' families but where these existed, they constituted quite a problem in the school as the families were also large in number.

IV B. Links with School: the Teachers' Opinions

The information presented in Chapter 12 was taken from questionnaires completed at interview by 36 head teachers (14 DA; 10 RA 6 SWC and 6 MC, i.e 12 CA) and 48 class teachers (19 DA; 11 RA; 11 SWC and 7 MC, i.e. 18 CA). Many of the questions were open-ended in order to allow all of the teachers to express their opinions freely and, consequently, it has proved difficult to formalize objectively what were highly subjective data. However, the views expressed are probably more accurate representations of what the teachers actually felt than they would have been had a structured format been employed.

1. General school contact with the parents

(a) Parent teacher associations. Urban schools (DA and CA) showed little enthusiasm for PTAs but in the rural schools three out of the ten schools had established them and a further two schools were intending to start them. Teachers, for a variety of reasons, preferred informal contact with the parents, when children were collected (DA and CA) or in out-of-school hours (RA).

(b) Invitations to school. Systematic invitations to attend a variety of school functions (school assembly; music and movement sessions; plays and concerts; special services; open days) were given by all schools, some more regularly and more enthusiastically than others. In RA schools many of the functions were social rather than educational and evening activities were arranged more frequently than in the urban schools. The SWC schools were most active in arranging meetings on educational topics (school activities; demonstration lessons) but some MC schools seemed a little wary of the value and success of these. In more than half of the DA schools, open days were regular features and, in some, fund-raising activities, such as jumble sales, were also held. The support of the DA parents was, however, qualified.

No clear pattern emerged as to ways of establishing and maintaining contact with parents. Schools devised their own arrangements to suit their premises, the nature of the neighbourhood from which the children came, parental pressures and their own inclinations. Some schools were more successful than others in the type of activities arranged, their methods of informing the parents and the response they received. Practically all schools considered the parents to be co-operative and willing to help if asked but sixteen schools (6 DA, 5 RA, 5 CA) had never asked for help.

(c) Letting the parents know. Letters giving information on school activities or organization were sent in all rural areas and in a third of the urban areas. Where telephones were installed, they also proved a frequent means of contact, although of little use in the DA schools as few parents had a telephone. Only one SWC school mentioned a termly newsletter and one RA head teacher displayed notices of school functions in the local shop windows.

2. Early school contact

(a) Registration. In the CA and RA schools, practically every child was registered prior to entry, although in the rural areas this was sometimes done informally in out of school situations. In the DA schools, the pattern varied according to whether a nursery class was attached to the school or not. If it were, parents were more inclined to register their children in the hope of getting them into school before five. If there were no nursery facilities, the percentage of children registered prior to entry was low, being estimated at 40 per cent in one school.

(b) Children's introduction to the reception class. This was usually done at registration if the child accompanied the parent. The DA and RA children were, therefore, most likely to miss out on this opportunity. In some DA schools, the lack of contact was accepted, in others systematic arrangements were made to encourage the parent to bring the child along, even on more than one occasion, and two DA head teachers invited all the new entrants and their parents to the school, talking to the parents themselves while the children joined a class. The RA teachers also tried to arrange for extended sessions of time to be spent in school in the term before entry, despite transport difficulties. Whether or not, of course, RA or DA children were able to take advantage of the opportunities offered, depended on the amount of effort the parents were able, or willing, to make. The CA children were much more fortunate in this respect. Parents had more time to bring them and the schools responded in various ways, helpful to both parents and children, dependent on the space available.

(c) Entry to school. Parents were seldom encouraged to remain with their children on actual entry. Indeed, this was usually seen as unhelpful. In one DA school, part-time attendance was arranged to begin with but this was virtually impossible in RA schools and thought to be unsettling in five urban schools.

3. Co-operation between home and school
(a) Interviewing parents. All schools said that parents could discuss their child's progress without making an appointment. In the DA schools, parents usually confined their contact with the staff to incidental interviews on the occasion of visits to school for open days and so on. In the RA and CA schools, the main problem was how to make the head teacher or teacher available to see the parents, especially when the head was engaged in full-time teaching for most of the week. RA teachers solved the problem in many cases by seeing the parents out of school hours. In the CA schools, three set aside certain periods

during the week for interviews, one arranged an 'open evening' as well as an 'open week', two brought in ancillary help to release the teachers during open days and another had invited parents on certain afternoons in the week to discuss progress. The response from the parents was mixed. About 35 per cent of CA parents were thought to avail themselves of the opportunities offered but only about 25 per cent of DA and RA parents, although a much higher number of the RA parents was seen informally. Parents were most likely to be concerned about progress in the final year of their child's infant schooling and, especially in DA and SWC schools, seemed diffident about approaching members of staff at all. Very few DA fathers were seen (less than 10 per cent) but rather more RA and CA fathers (about 20 per cent), more often at set functions than at individual interview.

(b) Home visits. All schools were prepared to take a child home in an emergency but opinions on other forms of home visiting were divided. RA teachers were less opposed to this form of contact than CA teachers but several DA teachers were strongly against it. Where home visiting was supported by the urban teachers it was seen as an opportunity to discuss problems which had arisen in school (7 DA teachers), an essential part of the teacher's job (2 SWC), to invite absentees to school functions (1 SWC), to discuss the placement of an ESN child (1 DA and 1 SWC) or to deal with specific difficulties such as bereavement, giving help to families in need or as a last resort if parents would not attend school. Where home visiting was opposed it was considered to be an intrusion into the parents' privacy and to be unnecessary if the school was succeeding in maintaining liaison with the parents, in which case they would be quite willing to come to the school. Some teachers accepted invitations to visit the home but more often these were refused in case it would look like favouritism. RA teachers, on the other hand, with small numbers on the roll and themselves resident in the area, raised no objections to home visiting and three head teachers had visited the homes of nearly all of their pupils, there being no formality about this, as the teachers were involved in the community in a number of ways and the visits were frequently social or over matters other than the school in the first instance.

(c) Level of parents' co-operation with the school. The co-operation of the RA and the CA parents was mostly very good (Table 151) but the DA parents were rated rather less highly. Parental interest in their child's progress (Table 152) was high in the MC areas and showed a steady decline through the SWC and rural areas to the 'deprived' area. Twenty-seven per cent of teachers in the DA schools thought that the parents showed 'little evidence of interest' in their child's progress in school and only one DA teacher found the parents' attitude 'very positive'. Teachers rated parents as interested to the extent to which they came to school and supported the school either in its activities or in providing educational stimulation at home. As DA parents were less likely to visit school than the other parents and the home background may have been culturally arid, they were judged as lacking in interest by the teachers. In rural schools serving the remote areas, teachers had little contact with parents and felt, therefore, that they were receiving little support from the home and that the parents showed few signs of interest. Two headteachers (1 SWC; 1 RA) were willing to allow that parents might be interested but still not come to school and two MC teachers felt that some of their parents were over-anxious for their child to succeed.

The major problems mentioned in respect to parental co-operation were apathy, a waning of interest in the school (sometimes parents found the links with school offered them unrewarding and gave up coming), diffidence and, in a very few instances, active hostility.

(d) Improving contact with parents. Few constructive suggestions were made by the school staffs. Some were, of course, content with the situation as it existed and felt (especially in RA schools) that there was good and easy contact already. Some MC schools almost seemed to be defending themselves against parental help and interest. The DA schools did, on the whole, feel the need for improvement. Three DA headteachers would have welcomed the attachment of social workers to the schools, another wanted someone available full-time to help with home-school contact and two others would have liked the health visitor to be linked to a number of schools as formerly.

(e) The parents as teachers. CA teachers felt that parents were already providing sufficient, if not too many, learning experiences in the home. They appreciated a reasonable level of parental encouragement but were not always in support of parents' purchasing reading books and being involved in other three R activities. They were very much in favour of educational visits, of parents' conversing with their children and of the purchasing of suitable story books and toys. The DA schools hoped for more parental involvement and were willing that the parents hear their child read although dubious over how often this actually happened. Little in the way of specific practical advice seemed to be given to parents in most areas and it is not surprising, therefore, that the DA parents were unsure as to how to 'encourage' their child and so did very little that would be of real use to the school.

Only four teachers (1 DA and 3 SWC) and three head teachers (1 DA, 1 SWC and 1 MC) were in favour of parents working in the classroom. Others felt that parents were unsuitable (DA school), over-ambitious for their own child (MC school) or, in general, over-involved, unreliable and unqualified. However, occasional parental assistance was welcomed in tidying up, repairing, dressing and undressing and stewarding, activities which could usefully be carried on outside the classroom. On the whole, teachers would very much have preferred additional professional help, such as clerical assistants or social workers or relief teachers, and more classroom aides, rather than parents.

IV C. Links with School: the Parents' Opinions

The sample of parents interviewed was drawn from the urban areas only, 116 parents in all (30 LD (least deprived DA); 29 MD (most deprived DA); 28 SWC and 29 MC) being involved. Their views will be summarized, as far as possible, under the same headings as given for the head teachers and teachers.

1. General parental contact with the school
(a) Parent teacher associations. Parents were not always clear exactly what constituted a PTA, especially when the school organized meetings regularly for the parents. Thirty-one parents said there was a PTA in the school to which their child went and, of these, nineteen mothers (6 MC, 3 SWC,

4 LD and 6 MD) and eight fathers (5 MC, 2 SWC, 0 LD and 1 MD) belonged (Table 156). Fifty-eight per cent of those who said the school had no PTA professed themselves to be 'very keen' or 'keen' to have such an organization and had a number of suggestions as to what they expected from it, not always quite in keeping with what the schools might have been aiming for.

(b) Invitations to school. A number of parents said that they had found the opportunities offered them to visit the school for informal chats or for organized functions useful. Many would have welcomed more opportunities to visit, especially with a definite invitation extended to them, as otherwise they felt they might be interfering with the work of the school. A number mentioned that they were to blame for not going to the school and only a few (in MC and SWC areas) felt unwelcome. There was some desire to know more about educational topics (Table 154), significantly less interest being shown in this respect in the MD group.

(c) Letting the parents know. No parent mentioned that an opportunity to contact the school had been missed through lack of communication but it is obviously impossible to say whether or not this had happened. A number of parents in each group would have welcomed regular reports on their child's progress but no reference was made to termly news letters. Only four parents said they had been asked by the teachers to visit the school to discuss particular behaviour problems. Half of the sample said they had in fact done so but at their own instigation.

2. Early school contact
No questions were asked at the home interview about this aspect but no parent made any comment, favourable or unfavourable, about the child's first experiences of school, although there was opportunity to do so. It must be assumed that the parents accepted the situation as it existed and that any initial difficulties had been smoothed over by the time of the interview (i.e. the child's final year in the infant school). The views of some of the parents whose children were in the project sample can be found in 'Just Before School' (Chazan et al., 1971).

3. Co-operation between home and school

(a) *Interviewing parents.* Most parents were appreciative of the efforts which the schools made to see them but indicated that they would welcome more discussions and opportunities for evening visits when fathers might attend. Over a third of the sample, however, thought that while the child was in the infant school, his schooling was the concern of the mother. Except for the MC parents, the feeling was against definite appointments being made (Table 155). Parents were less interested in seeing or hearing about general school activities and more concerned with their own child's progress. Almost half of the parents felt that they already knew enough about how their children were taught (Table 154). Significantly more of the MD parents preferred to see the head teacher to the class teacher, possibly because their problems were of a more general nature, but in the other groups the preference was for talking to the class teacher as being most knowledgeable about the child.

(b) *Home visits.* The majority of the parents (90 per cent) said they would be happy to welcome teachers to their home. Eleven parents would not have liked such a visit (6 of these living in MD areas). Parents were more divided on the purpose of the visit, some seeing it as an opportunity to chat freely to the teacher, others feeling that it should only take place in special circumstances, if a serious problem arose. Some thought that visiting was expecting too much of the teacher, others thought it would be economical of time, and money, for the parents. There was, therefore, little evidence that the parents felt visits by a member of the school staff to be an invasion of their privacy.

(c) *Parents' interest in and co-operation with the school.* Parents in the MD group were felt to show significantly less interest in the school than the rest of the sample and also significantly less than the LD parents (Table 154). Where little interest appeared to be shown it was sometimes felt to reflect lack of concern, but sometimes a belief that the school was doing all it could for the child anyway or a reluctance on the part of the parent to intervene in a system which was probably beyond her comprehension. In the MD group in particular, parental knowledge of the teaching methods used in the infant school appeared very inadequate and the parents were content to leave these entirely to the school (Table 158).

(d) *Improving contact with parents.* Again, no new suggestions were made. The initiative for making contact was felt to lie with the school and parents contented themselves with commenting on the approaches they, or their neighbours or relatives, had experienced.

(e) *Parents as teachers.* Twenty-five out of the 116 parents expressed keen interest in helping in the classroom on a voluntary basis and a further 35 were willing to help in this way if asked to do so (Table 157). Twenty-seven, evenly spread out through all the groups, had reservations, mainly a reluctance to be in the same classroom as their own child. Their comments reveal an interesting agreement with the views expressed, both for and against, by the teachers, except that the parents did not see themselves as unreliable.

Well over half of the children in the sample brought home reading books, rather fewer in the MC group than in the others, presumably because teachers were afraid of parents exerting undue pressure. Most parents favoured this practice (Table 159) and presumably, in varying degrees, attempted to co-operate. Several parents had, in fact, bought their own copies of the reading scheme in use in the school.

The parents were asked a number of additional questions on discipline, school organization, training for parenthood and on their educational aspirations for their children.

Discipline and school organization. Forty-three of the parents felt that there had been no changes in these aspects since they had been at school themselves (Table 160). Of those who felt things had changed, most, but not all, felt the changes were for the better (especially the MC parents).

Training for parenthood. Significantly fewer MD parents felt any need for advice on pre-school activities (Table 161). In all groups general advice on bringing up children was sought from relatives, doctors and health visitors and most found this satisfactory. Many of the parents did feel, however, that more information and advice could be given at the secondary stage to boys and girls, especially in the field of child development (Table 161).

Educational aspirations. Again the answers of the MD parents were significantly different from the other parents. Their aspirations for their children were lower than the other groups, including the LD parents (Table 162), and six of them would be unwilling for their child to have any further education or training beyond the necessary minimum. The other groups showed little difference between them, practically all of the parents being keen or willing for their children to stay in school or in some form of further eduction or training, for as long as would be of benefit to them.

IV D. Parents' Use of Services

The services discussed in Chapter 13 of this volume were those which seemed to have most direct relevance to the well-being of young children. One hundred and sixteen parents in all were interviewed (29 MC; 28 SWC; 30 LD (least deprived DA) and 29 MD (most deprived DA)).

Section A: Medical and related services.
With only one definite exception, all the children in the selected sample had been medically examined at school, although eleven parents had not attended on that occasion, seven of these being in the MD group, a difference from the other groups which was statistically significant. Twenty-six per cent of the sample had received further treatment following the examination. Most of the parents were satisfied with the examination as given but none saw it as an opportunity to ask for advice on aspects of the child's development which were not routinely covered.

Nine parents said their child had had some speech difficulty but only three children had received treatment because of this. Almost a quarter of the parents interviewed did not know that speech therapy could be obtained for their children but presumably the need to seek for help had never arisen in many of these cases.

Section B: Financial and material benefits.
The majority of the parents were aware of possible sources of financial and material help and of the

32 parents who had experienced financial difficulties, 29 had received assistance from the Ministry of Social Security (Table 164). In the MD group, significantly more help had been given in the way of free school meals and clothing grants (Table 165) than in any other group yet these parents were not always satisfied with the system of granting allowances and mentioned a number of anomalies in it.

Section C: Social and emotional problems.
Very few parents were knowledgeable about agencies which might provide help in the event of extreme domestic crises (Table 166) or about the nature and purpose of child guidance services. Yet 39 per cent of the sample (45 parents) had faced some behavioural or developmental problem in their children. The MC parents were most aware of the function of child guidance clinics and the MD parents least (Table 167).

Section D: Nursery schools or classes, library and other services.
The distribution of nursery places appeared to be fairly even over the different types of social areas studied here (Table 168), but this does not necessarily mean that these places were equally available within each area or that the provision made was equally accessible to all the parents and children. Twenty-seven per cent of the sample had attended a nursery school or class, an above average figure largely caused by the fact that in one of the major areas studied a nursery class had been attached to many of the infant schools. The unmet need for nursery places seemed greatest in some of the 'deprived' areas perhaps because in the MC and SWC areas recourse could be had to private nursery classes or to playgroups. Not all parents were completely in favour of the idea of universal pre-school education, some feeling that children under five years of age fare better at home and others being reluctant to lose the pleasure they gained from having the child with them in these early years. Those who favoured nursery school attendance stressed the educational and social advantages which accrued.

On the whole, libraries were within reach of the parents in the sample and 32 said that the library was near enough for the child to go on his own. The MD group, however, made significantly less use of the facilities available to them (Table 169) with only 24 per cent of the MD children ever having used library books, compared with 57 per cent of the LD children and 72 per cent of the MC and SWC children. Although children in all of the districts studied were officially eligible to join the library at the age of five, some parents in certain districts appeared to have been persuaded that the age was seven.

Other services which the parents would have found useful.

A wide variety of suggestions was made, the most frequent being the need for increased provision of play space for young children, especially during school holidays when indoor facilities and supervised activities would be particularly welcomed.

B. CONCLUSIONS

The information presented in this volume requires detailed reading as a superficial overview is only too likely to distort the picture and lead to facile or inaccurate statements. However, some of the main findings will now be discussed across the sections in order to integrate the results where possible.

1. The children's home background

Although over 600 children were studied, the sample was not, nor was it intended to be, representative of all urban, or all rural areas. The main focus was on children considered to be living in deprived areas but the definition of deprivation was deliberately wide. As far as possible, immigrant children, who often predominate in poor and inadequate areas and whose cultural background may differ markedly from the school's expectations, were excluded. Some of the most deprived children were lost to the sample in the course of the study. Despite these reservations, there did seem to be justification from the background data for considering the DA children as a deprived group and certainly their performance at school compared unfavourably with that of the other groups. If this conclusion can be reached about the DA children in this study, it is reasonable to suggest that the performance of children who are yet more deprived will be even poorer.

Despite the fact that some of the children in the rural sample lived in remote areas and attended small schools of the type described in the Gittins Report (1967, Chapter 7), their comparative isolation did not seem unduly disadvantageous. Indeed, in some respects they appeared favoured in comparison with some of the urban children, inasmuch as their parents were eager that they should do well and their environment, although somewhat restricted, was full of opportunities to observe and learn.

It was noticeable that the provision of services concerned with the welfare of families, and of the younger members in particular, varied considerably from area to area. Some parents had fairly easy access to nursery school places if they wished to send their child; others who were eager for their child to go could find no place available. The provision of material benefits was often at the instigation of someone other than the parent or parents in need, and help over behavioural problems was often not sought through ignorance of the services available. Despite the efforts being made to inform parents more fully of the various services, much remains to be done, in particular with regard to help other than financial or material assistance.

2. The children's schools

The CA schools were not without their problems and it would be wrong to think that poor amenities, inadequate facilities and difficulties in staffing were solely confined to the DA schools. The latter, however, did have rather a higher proportion of adverse factors in comparison with the CA schools but in their favour was the finding that DA classes tended to be smaller, and where additional help was provided for the teacher, it was likely to be in the DA schools. The problems of organization and staffing are quite different in rural areas and the Gittins Report saw a danger of educational stagnation which might particularly affect the young child. There is little indication of this in the present study either in the children's educational progress or in their adjustment to school.

In the RA schools, the organization of the school day was more formal and compartmentalized than in the other areas. Where a wider age range than usual has to be coped with, it is probably inevitable that the young children cannot be allowed complete freedom in the classroom and they may begin their school careers in a setting which is more comparable to that found in the other schools in the third year of schooling. The DA schools showed the least formality of organization. They made the most use of free play activities in the first year, considering these invaluable in promoting linguistic development and in encouraging choice, independence and self control. Half of the DA teachers joined in with the children in their activities, often guiding them unobtrusively as they considered necessary. In the CA schools, the teaching of the basic skills was safeguarded by devoting the morning sessions to them, creative activities taking place in the afternoon or being used as a means of occupying some of the classroom groups while the teacher worked on reading or mathematics with individual children or small groups. No criticism is implied of these different forms of organization. The teachers obviously arranged their day in the way that seemed best suited to the children, themselves and the parents. It is worth noting, however, that the DA teachers felt compelled to make not a different, but a slower start than the others and this may have contributed to the fact that their children had not advanced so much in the basic skills at the end of three years. The suggestion is not they they should begin work in the basic skills sooner in the present circumstances but that a more extensive provision of early educational facilities might give the DA children a more equal start in the infant school.

Perhaps because the DA teachers were anxious to promote communication as well as observation and concentration, considerable emphasis was placed on art activities in their schools. The CA schools mentioned musical activities more often and the RA schools favoured music and movement. In the teaching of the basic skills, the approach to reading was roughly similar in all schools but in mathematics the DA schools used experimental approaches more often than the CA or RA schools. In the MC schools in particular, where parents were anxious to see their children's progress, there was a greater emphasis on accepted methods, and experimental approaches were often implemented in addition to more formal approaches.

The questionnaires from which this information is extracted were completed outside of the class-room and there was no observation of the actual teaching situation. It is, therefore, very difficult to generalize from the data available as the classifications made may not accurately represent reality. The number of schools and teachers involved was small and the questionnaires fairly unstructured. The findings need to be treated with caution.

3. Progress and adjustment

The differences between the CA and the DA urban children in attainment were in evidence from the first schedule onwards. The lower level of intelligence and the poorer home background of the DA children both appear to have contributed to their relative lack of success in school despite their teachers' efforts. The differences between the schools were neither so marked nor so important as the differences between the children's home background and their differences in intelligence.

The CA children were not only better prepared for school, in the sense that their early upbringing fostered the skills which were useful to them in school, but throughout their infant school career they were, on the whole, more sustained by their parents' interest in them and more encouraged at home by their parents' better understanding of school activities and the benefits to be gained from education. In the RA homes, too, encouragement and interest were usually high. Differences in attainment according to school area type were found to exist independently of intelligence. The latter, however, accounted for more of the variation in performance. This was especially so in the rural sample where material deprivation was little in evidence, although some of the children were very isolated. In the RA sample, the differences in the scores on the final battery were almost completely accounted for by differences in intelligence.

The issue is a complicated one as home background exercises an effect on the development of intelligence, and genetic endowment imposes limitations on the extent to which the environment may promote intellectual development. The combination of poor endowment and poor environment is particularly inhibiting for school progress, as it is the low ability children who need all the encouragement they can get if they are to have any measure of success in school.

By the end of their infant schooling, a substantial proportion of the DA children appeared to be quite seriously retarded in mechanical reading ability and some of the related skills. A number of these children scored within the average range on the intelligence test which would seem to indicate that they were underfunctioning. It has already been mentioned that DA teachers have to delay the teaching of reading in order to increase the children's competence in language in particular, but there would seem to be reason for looking at the DA children's subsequent experience of reading skills very carefully. There is little place in their case for a chance encounter with these skills. They must meet them in a meaningful sequence and must be given the opportunity to attend to them and practise them in an uncluttered setting so that they build up an understanding of the essentials. Formal teaching is not necessary but rather structured learning. When this can be incorporated in other activities the learning opportunities are increased. At the same time so are the dangers that the child may gloss over some aspect too quickly or be faced with a step which is too big for him.

Perhaps because of their relative lack of success in school, the proportion of DA children rated as showing some signs of unsettled behaviour tended to increase over the three years in comparison with the CA and RA children. Although difficulties in social and emotional adjustment were to be found in all groups, rather more DA children were noted as displaying them and their difficulties were rated as more severe. The schools did not seem to feel that more clinical help was required but suggestions were made that teachers needed more time to give individual children the attention and the affection they were demanding. There was also a feeling that some of the parents would benefit from guidance as to how they might best help their children.

4. Home-school contact

The overall impression gained from the investigation into this area is of a considerable amount of untapped potential on both sides. Most schools were making efforts to reach the parents and to interest them in what was going on in school. They did not always succeed and, unfortunately, the parents they failed to contact were often those they most wanted to meet. Most parents, on the other hand, professed their interest in their own child's school progress but frequently saw no need to contact the school if no serious problems arose. Again, many parents were willing to help the school but some were never asked, others were asked but could not cope (in the DA schools) or become bored with repetitive chores (in an SWC school). The greatest difficulties lay at the extremes of the social class spectrum. Some teachers felt under too much pressure from articulate, educated parents and some parents felt under too much pressure from articulate, educated teachers.

Each school has, of course, its own particular problems but all should remember that the underlying concern in every parent is for his own child and that arrangements of a general nature or those where the individual child may be overlooked or shown in a bad light will not be successful. Open days will not appeal to the parent whose child's work is not displayed or is obviously of poorer quality than the rest and the 'most deprived' parents revealed this by their infrequent attendance. Specific invitations to parents encourage them to come, although the domestic circumstances of the 'most deprived' parents militate against the school's efforts. Teachers must be able to give time to parents, knowing that their classes are being looked after by someone else.

Informal gatherings in the evening where teachers can unobtrusively make contact over a cup of tea, and parents can meet one another, might open the way to further meetings. Home visits on a rota basis may not be as difficult as some teachers fear, once it becomes known that the teacher is not there to pry or to complain. No one solution can be suggested. It is probably best for schools to try a variety of approaches, so that parents, and teachers, may find some situation in which they feel confident and accepted.

5. Compensatory education

Teachers were asked specifically for their views on compensatory education, in particular whether they thought special programmes were required for 'deprived' children and what form any additional help should take. A variety of opinions was expressed.

Some teachers felt that the informal approach of the typical infant school was too permissive and that the children would benefit from a more formal approach in which there would be fewer opportunities to move at will from one activity to another and more concentration by the whole class or group on the matter in hand. Others felt that the informal approach was the correct one but the teacher might have to exercise some control by guiding the children towards certain activities or taking time to establish a clear routine in using apparatus and in other aspects of classroom behaviour.

It was stressed that teachers need to be highly skilled to encourage learning in 'deprived' children and that help should be given in this respect in initial teacher training, and presumably also in in-service training. Lack of cognitive stimulation in the home could be alleviated by nursery school attendance, by the use of language programmes in school and by the school providing opportunities for enrichment of the children's limited experiences. It was felt that 'deprived' children needed more attention and more affection from adults and, therefore, either smaller classes or more aides or infant helpers were required. Parents should be helped more, either in small groups or in individual discussion with the head teacher or a social worker. Finally, schools should present as attractive a learning environment as possible with a good standard of furnishing and equipment and ample facilities for expressive activities so that children, and parents, could take pleasure in coming and in the programme provided.

It is fitting that the last word should be given to the headteachers and teachers for without their help, and the co-operation of the parents, this book could never have been written.

References

ABEL-SMITH, B. and TOWNSEND, P. (1965). *The Poor and the Poorest*. Occasional Papers in Social Administration, No. 17. London: Bell and Sons.

AINSWORTH, M. D. (1962). The effects of maternal deprivation: a review of findings in the context of research strategy. In *Deprivation of Maternal Care* (A Reassessment of its Effects). Geneva: World Health Organisation Paper.

ASHER, P. (1967). One thousand school children. *The Medical Officer*, 16 June, 1967.

AUSUBEL, D. P. (1966). A teaching strategy for culturally deprived pupils: cognitive and motivational considerations. In WEBSTER, S.W. (ed.), *The Disadvantaged Learner*. California: Chandler Publishing Co.

AUSUBEL, D. P. (1967). How reversible are the cognitive and motivational effects of cultural deprivation? Implications for teaching the culturally deprived child. In PASSOW, A. H. et al. (eds.), *Education of the Disadvantaged*. New York: Holt, Rinehart and Winston.

BANKS, O. (1968). *The Sociology of Education* (2nd edition, 1971). London: Batsford.

BEREITER, C. and ENGELMANN, S. (1966). *Teaching Disadvantaged Children in the Preschool*. Englewood Cliffs, New Jersey: Prentice-Hall.

BERNSTEIN, B. (1960). Language and social class. *Brit. J. Sociol.*, 11, 271–276.

BERNSTEIN, B. (1961). Social class and linguistic development. In HALSEY, A. H., FLOUD, J. and ANDERSON, C. A. (eds.), *Education and Society*. New York: Free Press of Glencoe.

BERNSTEIN, B. (1965). A socio-linguistic approach to social learning in GOULD, J. (ed.), *Penguin Survey of the Social Sciences*. Harmondsworth: Penguin Books.

BERNSTEIN, B. (1970). Education cannot compensate for society. *New Society*, 26 February, 1970.

BERNSTEIN, B. and HENDERSON, D. (1969). Social class differences in the relevance of language to socialisation. *Sociology*, 3, 1–20.

BLACKSTONE, T. (1971). *A Fair Start*. London: Allen Lane, the Penguin Press.

BLALOCK, H. M. (1960). *Social Statistics*. New York: McGraw-Hill.

BLANK, M. and SOLOMON, F. (1969). How shall the disadvantaged child be taught? *Child Dev.*, 40, 48–60.

BLOOM, B. J., DAVIS, A. and HESS, R. (1965). *Compensatory Education for Cultural Deprivation*. New York: Holt, Rinehart and Winston.

BOWLBY, J. (1952). *Maternal Care and Mental Health* (2nd ed.). Geneva: World Health Organisation Monograph Series, No. 2.

BOWLBY, J., AINSWORTH, M. D., BOSTON, M. and ROSENBLUTH, D. (1956). The effects of mother-child separation: a follow-up study. *Brit. J. Med. Psychol.*, 29, 211–247.

BRANDIS, B. and HENDERSON, D. (1970). *Social Class, Language and Communication*. London: Routledge and Kegan Paul.

CARROLL, J. B. (1964). *Language and Thought*. Englewood Cliffs, New Jersey: Prentice-Hall.

CENTRAL ADVISORY COUNCIL FOR EDUCATION (ENGLAND) (1959). *Fifteen to Eighteen* (The Crowther Report), Vol. 1. 1960, Vol. II. London: HMSO.

CENTRAL ADVISORY COUNCIL FOR EDUCATION (ENGLAND) (1954). *Early Leaving*. London: HMSO.

CENTRAL ADVISORY COUNCIL FOR EDUCATION (ENGLAND) (1963). *Half Our Future* (The Newsom Report). London: HMSO.

CENTRAL ADVISORY COUNCIL FOR EDUCATION (ENGLAND) (1967). *Children and their Primary Schools* (The Plowden Report). Vol. I, Report. Vol. II, Research and Surveys. London: HMSO.

CENTRAL ADVISORY COUNCIL FOR EDUCATION (WALES) (1967). *Primary Education in Wales* (The Gittins Report). London: HMSO.

CERVANTES, L. F. (1965). Family background, primary relationships and the high school dropout. *J. Marr. and Fam.*, 27, 218–229.

CHAZAN, M. (1964). The incidence and nature of maladjustment among children in schools for the educationally subnormal. *Brit. J. Educ. Psychol.*, 34, 292–304.

CHAZAN, M., LAING, A. F., and JACKSON, S. (1971). *Just before School.* Oxford: Basil Blackwell.

CHAZAN, M., COX, T., JACKSON, S. and LAING, A. F. (to be published) *Studies of Infant School Children 2—Deprivation and Development.* Oxford: Basil Blackwell (for Schools Council).

CHAZAN, M. and JACKSON, S. (1971). Behaviour problems in the infant school. *J. Child Psychol. Psychiat.*, 12, 191–210.

CHAZAN, M. and JACKSON, S. (1974). Behaviour problems in the infant school: changes over two years. *J. Child Psychol. Psychiat.*, 15, 33–46.

COATES, K. and SILBURN, S. (1967). *St. Ann's: Poverty, Deprivation and Morale in a Nottingham Community.* Nottingham University, Department of Adult Education.

COLEMAN, J. S. et al. (1966). *Equality of Educational Opportunity.* Washington, D. C.: U.S. Government Printing Office.

COMMITTEE ON HIGHER EDUCATION (1963 and 1964). *Higher Education* (The Robbins Report). London: HMSO.

COX, T. and WAITE, C. A. (eds.) (1970). *Teaching Disadvantaged Children in the Infant School.* University College of Swansea Faculty of Education and Schools Council Research and Development Project in Compensatory Education.

CRELLIN, E., PRINGLE, M. L. K., and WEST, P. (1971). *Born Illegitimate: Social and Educational Implications.* Slough: National Foundation for Educational Research.

CROWTHER REPORT. See CENTRAL ADVISORY COUNCIL FOR EDUCATION (ENGLAND) (1959).

CURRY, R. L. (1962). The effect of socioeconomic status on the scholastic achievement of sixth grade children. *Brit. J. Educ. Psychol.*, 32, 46–49.

DANIELS, J. C. and DIACK, H. (1958). *The Standard Reading Tests.* London: Chatto and Windus.

DAVIE, R., BUTLER, N. and GOLDSTEIN, H. (1972). *From Birth to Seven.* London: Longman and National Children's Bureau.

DAVIS, K. (1964). Legitimacy and illegitimacy. In GOODE, W. J. (ed.), *Readings on the Family and Society.* Englewood Cliffs, New Jersey: Prentice–Hall.

DENENBERG, V. H. (1966). Animal studies on developmental determinants of behavioural adaptability. In HARVEY, O. J. (ed.), *Experience, Structure and Adaptability.* New York: Springer Publication Co.

DEPARTMENT OF EDUCATION AND SCIENCE (1967a). *Statistics of Education*, 1966, Vol. I – Schools. London: HMSO.

DEPARTMENT OF EDUCATION AND SCIENCE (1967b). Report No. 41 – *Teachers and Parents.* London: HMSO.

DEPARTMENT OF EDUCATION AND SCIENCE (1968). *Education Survey 5: Parent-Teacher Relations in Primary Schools.* London: HMSO.

DEPARTMENT OF EDUCATION AND SCIENCE (1972). *Education: A Framework for Expansion* (Cmnd. 5174). London: HMSO.

DEUTSCH, C. (1964). Auditory discrimination and learning. Selected papers from the Institute for Developmental Studies, Arden House Conference on Pre-school Enrichment of Social Disadvantaged Children. *Merrill-Palmer Quarterly*, 10, 277–295.

DEUTSCH, M. (1963). The disadvantaged child in the learning process. In PASSOW, A. H. (ed.), *Education in the Depressed Areas.* New York: Teachers College Press.

DEUTSCH, M. (1964). Early social environment: its influence on school adaptation. In SCHREIBER, D. (ed.), *The School Dropout.* Washington, D.C.: National Education Association.

DEUTSCH, M. (1965). The role of social class in language development and cognition. *Amer. J. Orthopsychiat.*, 25, 78–88.

DOUGLAS, J. W. B. (1964). *The Home and the School.* London: MacGibbon and Kee.

DOUGLAS, J. W. B. (1970). The influence of parents. In MacARTHUR, B. (ed.), *New Horizons for Education.* London: Council for Educational Advance.

DOWNING, J. A. (1964). The Initial Teaching Alphabet (2nd ed.) London: Cassell.

EDWARDS, A. L. (1968). *Experimental Design in*

Psychological Research. New York: Holt, Rinehart and Winston.

EVANS, K. M. (1962). *Sociometry and Education.* London: Routledge and Kegan Paul.

EVANS, R. (to be published). *Swansea Evaluation Profiles: Infant Schools.*

FERGUSON, G. A. (1965). *Nonparametric Trend Analysis.* Montreal: McGill University Press.

FERGUSON, N., DAVIES, P., EVANS, R. and WILLIAMS, P. (1971). The Plowden Report's recommendations for identifying children in need of extra help. *Educ. Res.,* 13, 210–213.

FLOUD, J. E., HALSEY, A. H. and MARTIN, F. M. (eds.) (1957). *Social Class and Educational Opportunity.* London: Heinemann.

FRASER, E. D. (1959). *Home Environment and the School.* London: University of London Press.

GARNER, J. (1972). Some aspects of behaviour in infant school classrooms. *Research in Education,* 7, 28–47.

GITTINS REPORT – See CENTRAL ADVISORY COUNCIL FOR EDUCATION (WALES) (1967).

GOLDTHORPE, J. H., LOCKWOOD, D., BECHOFER, F. and PLATT, J. (1969). *The Affluent Worker in the Class Structure.* Cambridge University Press.

GOODACRE, J. (1968). *Teachers and their Pupils' Home Background.* Slough: National Foundation for Educational Research.

GREVE, J. (1970). Housing policies and prospects. In ROBSON, W. A. and CRICK, B. (eds.), *The Future of the Social Services.* Harmondsworth: Penguin Books.

HALSEY, A. H. (ed.) (1972). *Educational Priority. Vol. I: E.P.A. Problems and Policies.* London: HMSO.

HARRINGTON, M. (1966). The invisible land. In WEBSTER, S. W. (ed.), *The Disadvantaged Learner.* California: Chandler Publishing Co.

HARVARD EDUCATIONAL REVIEW (1969). Reprint Series No. 2: *Environment, Heredity and Intelligence.* Cambridge, Mass.

HARVEY, O. J. (1966). System structure, flexibility and creativity. In HARVEY, O. J. (ed.), *Experience, Structure and Adaptability.* New York: Springer Publication Co.

HEBB, D. O. (1949). *Organisation of Behaviour.* New York: John Wiley and Sons.

HEBB, D. O. (1966). *A Textbook of Psychology* (2nd edition). Philadelphia: W. B. Saunders Co.

HESS, D. and BEAR, R. M. (eds.) (1968). *Early Education.* Chicago: Aldine Press.

HIMMELWEIT, H. T. and SWIFT, B. (1969). A model for the understanding of school as a socialising agent. In MUSSEN, P., LANGER, J. and COVINGTON, M. (eds.), *Trends and Issues in Developmental Psychology.* New York: Holt, Rinehart and Winston.

HOME OFFICE (1968). *Report on Local Authority and Allied Personal Social Services* (The Seebohm Report). Cmnd. 3703. London: HMSO.

HOLMAN, R. (ed.) (1970). *Socially Deprived Families in Britain.* London: National Council of Social Service.

HUNT, J. McV. (1966). The psychological basis for using preschool enrichment as an antidote for cultural deprivation. In GOWAN, J. C. and DEMOS, G. D. (eds.), *The Disadvantaged and Potential Dropout.* Springfield, Illinois: Charles C. Thomas.

INNER LONDON EDUCATION AUTHORITY (1968). *Home and School.* London: ILEA.

JENSEN, A. R. (1966). Social class and perceptual learning. *Mental Hygiene,* 50, 226–239.

JENSEN, A. R. (1967). The culturally disadvantaged: psychological and educational aspects. *Educ. Res.,* 10, 4–20.

JENSEN, A. R. (1971). Do schools cheat minority children? *Educ. Res.* 14, 3–28.

JONES, J. (1966). Social class and the under fives. *New Society,* No. 221, 21 Dec., 935–936.

KELSALL, R. K. and KELSALL, H. M. (1971). *Social Disadvantage and Educational Opportunity.* London: Holt, Rinehart and Winston.

KENDALL, M. G. (1970). *Rank Correlation Methods.* London: Griffin.

KIRK, S. A. (1958). *Early Education of the Mentally Retarded.* University of Illinois Press.

LENZ, T. (1927). Relation of IQ and size of family. *J. Educ. Psychol.,* 18, 486–496.

LEWIS, H. (1962). *Deprived Children.* London: Oxford University Press.

LLOYD, G. (to be published). *Studies of Infant School Children 3 – Deprivation and the Bilingual Child.* Oxford: Basil Blackwell (for Schools Council).

LOBAN, W. (1963). *The Language of Elementary*

School Children. Champaign, Illinois: National Council of Teachers of English.

LOBAN, W. (1965). *Problems in Oral English.* Champaign, Illinois: National Council of Teachers of English.

MARSDEN, D. (1969). *Mothers Alone — Poverty and the Fatherless Family.* London: Allen Lane, the Penguin Press.

MAYS, J. B. (1962). *Education and the Urban Child.* Liverpool University Press.

MILLER, G. W. (1972). *Educational Opportunity and the Home.* London: Longman.

MILLER, W. B. (1966). Lower-class culture as a generating milieu of gang delinquency. In WEBSTER, S. W. (ed.), *The Disadvantaged Learner.* California: Chandler Publishing Co.

MINISTRY OF EDUCATION (1950). *Reading Ability: Some Suggestions for Helping the Backward.* Pamphlet No. 18. London: HMSO.

MINISTRY OF EDUCATION (1960). *Education in Rural Wales.* London: HMSO.

MINISTRY OF SOCIAL SECURITY (1967). *Circumstances of Families.* London: HMSO.

MOORE, T. (1968). Language and intelligence: a longitudinal study of the first eight years. Part II: environmental correlates of mental growth. *Hum. Dev.,* 2, 1—24.

MORRIS, J. M. (1959). *Reading in the Primary School.* London: National Foundation for Educational Research.

MORRIS, J. M. (1966). *Standards and Progress in Reading.* Slough: National Foundation for Educational Research.

MORRIS, T. P. (1957). *The Criminal Area.* London: Routledge and Kegan Paul.

MORRISON, A. and McINTYRE, D. (1971). *Schools and Socialization.* Harmondsworth: Penguin Books.

NATIONAL FOUNDATION FOR EDUCATIONAL RESEARCH (undated). *Manual of Instructions for Picture Test A:* Slough: NFER.

NEALE, M. D. (1966). *Neale Analysis of Reading Ability: Manual of Directions and Norms.* London: Macmillan.

NEWSOM REPORT — see CENTRAL ADVISORY COUNCIL FOR EDUCATION (ENGLAND) (1963).

NISBET, J. D. (1953). Family environment: a direct effect of family size on intelligence.

Occasional Paper on Eugenics, No. 8. London: Eugenics Society.

PASSOW, A. H. (ed.) (1972). *Opening Opportunities for Disadvantaged Learners.* New York: Teachers College, Columbia University.

PHILLIPS, C. J., WILSON, H. and HERBERT, G. W. (1972). *Child Development Study* (Birmingham 1968—71), Part I. School of Education, University of Birmingham.

PHILP, A. F. (1963). *Family Failure.* London: Faber and Faber.

PIDGEON, D. (1965). Date of birth and scholastic performance. *Educ. Res.,* 8, 1, 3—7.

PLOWDEN REPORT — see CENTRAL ADVISORY COUNCIL FOR EDUCATION (ENGLAND) (1967).

PRINGLE, M. L. K., BUTLER, N. R. and DAVIE, R. (1966). *11,000 Seven Year-Olds.* London: Longman.

REGISTRAR-GENERAL (1966). *Classification of Occupations.* London: HMSO.

REX, J. and MOORE, R. (1966). *Race, Community and Conflict: A Study of Sparkbrook.* London: Oxford University Press.

RIESSMAN, F. (1962). *The Culturally Deprived Child.* New York: Harper and Bros.

ROBBINS, J. E. (1948). The home and family background of Ottawa public school children in relation to their IQs. *Can. J. Psychol.,* 2, 35—41.

ROBISON, H. F. (1972). Early childhood education for the disadvantaged: what research says. In PASSOW, A. H. (ed.), *Opening Opportunities for Disadvantaged Learners.* New York: Teachers College Press.

ROSENTHAL, R. and JACOBSON, L. (1968). Self-fulfilling prophecies in the classroom: teachers' expectations as unintended determinants of pupils' intellectual competence. In DEUTSCH, M., KATZ, I., and JENSEN, A. R. (eds.), *Social Class, Race and Psychological Development.* New York: Holt, Rinehart & Winston.

RUTTER, M. (1972). *Maternal Deprivation Reassessed.* Harmondsworth: Penguin Books.

SARASON, S. B. and GLADWIN, T. (1958). *Psychological and Cultural Problems in Mental Subnormality: A Review of Research.* Genet. Psychol. Monog., 57, 3—290.

SCHOOLS COUNCIL (1970). *Working Paper 27:*

Cross'd with Adversity – the Education of Socially Disadvantaged Children in Secondary Schools. London: Evans/Methuen Educational.

SCOTTISH COUNCIL FOR RESEARCH IN EDUCATION (1949). *The Trend of Scottish Intelligence.* London: University of London Press.

SEEBOHM REPORT (1968) – see HOME OFFICE.

SEXTON, P. C. (1961). *Education and Income.* New York: The Viking Press.

SHAW, R. C. and McKAY, H. D. (1942). *Juvenile Delinquency and Urban Areas.* Chicago University Press.

SKEELS, N. R. (1942). A study of the effects of differential stimulation on mentally retarded children: a follow-up report. *Amer. J. Ment. Def.,* 46, 340–350.

STEIN, Z. and SUSSER, N. (1960). Families of dull children. Part 2: identifying family types and subcultures. *J. Ment. Sci.,* 106, 1296–1303.

STOTT, D. H. (1966). *The Social Adjustment of Children* (Manual to the Bristol Social Adjustment Guides). London: University of London Press.

TANNER, J. M. (1961). *Education and Physical Growth.* London: University of London Press.

TAYLOR, G. and AYRES, H. (1969). *Born and Bred Unequal.* London: Longman.

TELFORD, C. W. and SAWREY, J. M. (1967). *The Exceptional Individual.* Englewood Cliffs, New Jersey: Prentice-Hall.

TEMPLIN, M. C. (1957). *Certain Language Skills in Children.* Minneapolis: Institute of Child Welfare.

TOWNSEND, P. (ed.) (1970). *The Concept of Poverty.* London: Heinemann.

TYERMAN, M. J. (1968). *Truancy.* London: University of London Press.

VERNON, P. E. (1938). *The Standardisation of a Graded Word Reading Test.* London: University of London Press.

VERNON, P. E. (1960). *Intelligence and Attainment Tests.* London: University of London Press.

VYGOTSKY, L. S. (1939). *Thought and Language.* New York: John Wiley.

WECHSLER, D. (1949). *Manual: Wechsler Intelligence Scale for Children.* New York: The Psychological Corporation.

WILKERSON, D. A. (1970). Compensatory programs across the nation. In PASSOW, A. H. (ed.), *Reaching the Disadvantaged Learner.* New York: Teachers College Press.

WILLERMAN, L., BROMAN, S. H. and FIEDLER, M. (1970). Infant development, preschool IQ, and social class. *Child Develop.,* 41, 69–77.

WILSON, H. (1962). *Delinquency and Child Neglect.* London: George Allen and Unwin.

WILSON, H. (1970). The socialisation of children. In HOLMAN, R. (ed.), *Socially Deprived Families in Britain.* London: National Council of Social Service.

WIMPERIS, V. (1960). *The Unmarried Mother and Her Child.* London: Allen and Unwin.

WINER, B. J. (1962). *Statistical Principles in Experimental Design.* New York: McGraw-Hill.

WISEMAN, S. (1964). *Education and Environment.* Manchester: Manchester University Press.

WISEMAN, S. (1968). Educational deprivation and disadvantage. In BUTCHER, H. J. (ed.), *Educational Research in Britain,* Vol. I. London: University of London Press.

WYNN, M. (1964). *Fatherless Families.* London: Michael Joseph.

YOUNG, M. and WILLMOTT, P. (1957). *Family and Kinship in East London.* London: Routledge and Kegan Paul.

YOUNG, M. and McGEENEY, P. (1968). *Learning Begins at Home.* London: Routledge and Kegan Paul.

YUDKIN, S. (1967). *0–5: A Report on the Care of Pre-School Children.* London: National Society of Children's Nurseries.

APPENDICES

Appendix I
Notes on Statistical Techniques Used

For the data derived from simple ordered rating scales, such as the teachers' ratings on the school schedules and the items in the home interview schedule presented in Chapter 8, it was decided to use a method of analysis making use of the statistic 'S' as described by Kendall (1970) in the definition of the coefficient of rank correlation 'tau'. This technique was chosen in preference to the more widely used 'chi-square' method since, unlike the latter, it is sensitive to the *pattern* of the distribution of frequencies in a table, i.e. it provides an index of any directional trend in the data. In order to establish whether there was a significant correlation between the rank ordering of the groups of children being compared (e.g. CA and DA children in Part Two) and the rankings received by the children within each of the variables under consideration, the ratio of 'S' to its standard error was computed (expressed as a z value) and referred to the normal distribution table. The values of z and the appropriate levels of significance are quoted in the tables of results presented in this report but it was not considered necessary to quote the values of the statistic 'tau' since these are derived directly from 'S'. Also, the sign of z is not given since the direction of the association will be clear from inspection of the tables.

For the analysis of data derived from non-ordered (i.e. unranked) categorizations, as, for example, in the case of many of the items in the school medical records, the 'chi-square' test was used. (Some of the medical record data could, in fact, have been analysed by the 'tau' technique but, for the sake of consistency, the 'chi-square' method of analysis was used for all of these data.)

The analyses of variance reported in Chapters 6 and 10 were based on a method using treatment means as single observations put forward by Edwards (1968) for the case where cell numbers in the design are unequal. The author points out that this method gives approximate results, the more accurate and powerful method being that of 'least squares' described in Winer (1962). Strictly speak-

ing, the Edwards method, which uses unweighted means, is appropriate for those situations where the uneveness in cell numbers reflects random factors rather than systematic trends in the populations from which the samples are drawn. As discussed in Chapter 6 (page 144), the inequality of numbers in the design for the two-way analysis (intelligence x school area type) probably reflects the pattern of distribution of intelligence in the general population according to social class, i.e. a systematic trend. (The same point applies to the distribution of intelligence over the cells of the two-way analysis, level of home background x intelligence, presented in Chapter 10.) In such a case, the 'least squares' method which weights the cell means according to the cell frequencies is appropriate. Since, however, the total frequencies for each level of intelligence (i.e. row totals) in this design are fairly equal (see Table 71), it was considered justifiable to use the Edwards method in order to examine the data for main effects. From this point of view the method is unlikely to give distorted results because of the unequal cell frequencies, but the interactions between the two variables should be treated very cautiously on that account. In the event, however, none of the interactions reached the significance level. An additional source of error in the interaction results is the fact noted in Chapter 6 (page 145) that the mean intelligence scores of the three school area types differ *within* the categories of 'high', 'medium' and 'low' intelligence, which reflects the social class distribution of intelligence already mentioned. (This does not apply to the analysis of variance design presented in Chapter 10.) This source of error affecting the interactions between the variables would still have been present even if the more accurate 'least squares' method had been used.

The main assumptions underlying the use of the analysis of variance are as follows:

(i) that the scoring system constitutes an equal interval scale of measurement;

(ii) that the scores are normally distributed in the

populations from which the samples are drawn;

(iii) that the treatment population variances are equal or homogeneous;

(iv) that the samples are independent and randomly selected from the general population.

With regard to the attainment test data of the present study the first two assumptions appear quite reasonable. Assumption (iv) does not strictly apply since the present samples were not randomly selected but could be regarded as 'judgement samples'.

In respect of the third assumption, Appendix Tables A7 and A8 show the cell variances for the analyses reported in Chapter 6, together with the ratio for each test, of the maximum to the minimum cell variance ('F max'). Since the cell frequencies are unequal it is not, strictly speaking, appropriate to use Hartley's 'F max' statistic to test the cell variances. However, Winer (1962, p. 94) suggests that this statistic can be used in an approximate fashion by using the greatest cell frequency instead of 'n' in obtaining the degrees of freedom required for use in the Hartley tables. In the data presented in these tables, the largest cell frequency is always greater than 60, which is the highest number given in the table of distribution of the 'F max' statistic (Winer, 1962, p. 653). This means that for the case of 9 cell variances, 'F max' will be significant at the 5 per cent level if it lies somewhere between 2.26 (d.f. of cell variance = 60) and 1.00 (d.f. of cell variance = infinity). Using this method with the above data, therefore, it is not possible to specify exactly the critical F ratio and thus to identify the cases where the assumption of homogeneity of variances is not tenable. It will be seen from these tables that 'F max' ranges from 1.26 (Mathematics, Table A8) to 4.72 (Neale Comprehension, Table A7). It seems likely that the majority of these 'F max' values would reach statistical significance if it were possibly to specify the critical F ratio but, on the other hand, in absolute terms, the disparities between the cell variances, in general, do not seem so marked as to invalidate the findings of the analyses. In any case, as Winer (1962) points out, the F test has been shown to be quite robust with respect to departures from the assumption of homogeneity of variance.

In the data given in Appendix Tables A9 to A11 for the analyses reported in Chapter 10, because the cell numbers are relatively small, it is possible to specify the critical F ratio and, where the 'F max' statistic exceeds this ratio for any particular set of data, this is indicated in the table. It will be seen that whereas, for all of the achievement tests, 'F max' reaches statistical significance in the case of the analysis of variance based upon material home background scores (Table A10), in the analysis based on the cultural home background scores there is no significant difference among the cell means on any of the tests (Table A9). In the analysis using the total home background scores (Table A11) 'F max' is significant for only two tests. From this it would seem that the results of the analyses based on the material background scores should be viewed with some caution, although here too the 'robustness' of the F test can be invoked.

LEVELS OF SIGNIFICANCE

The levels of significance quoted in the tables range from the 5 per cent to the 0.1 per cent levels, and probabilities greater than 5 per cent are stated to be 'not significant' (NS). However, a large number of statistical tests were carried out because of the volume of the data and this, in consequence, enhanced the possibility that some of the results presented as significant might represent the 5 per cent of cases which could, in theory, arise by chance. The adoption of a more stringent level of probability as the criterion of significance (say the 1 per cent level) was considered, but rejected on the grounds that differences of psychological and educational interest might thus be overlooked. It was decided, therefore, to adopt the 5 per cent level and to refer to other evidence supporting a given result where this was available.

ONE-TAILED TESTS VERSUS TWO-TAILED TESTS OF SIGNIFICANCE

(i) Study of urban children

In the case of all of the dependent variables i.e. all ratings or measures of the children's development, achievement and school adjustment, one-tailed tests were used because the direction of the difference between the CA and DA groups was predicted on the basis of previous research into the effects of disadvantage on development, summarized in Chapter 1.

For the assessment of some aspects of the children's emotional adjustment in Chapter 4, however, two-tailed significance levels are quoted because the research evidence justifying a prediction of the direction of the between-group differences is rather less firm. In cases where the direction of difference was predicted but the result obtained was in the opposite direction to that prediction, then, of course, two-tailed tests were used.

For the background data presented in Chapter 3 and the first part of Chapter 4, two-tailed tests of significance were used since the comparisons between the two groups were more explanatory in nature and intended to define certain characteristics of the samples.

(ii) Study of rural children

In all of the rural versus urban children comparisons reported in Part Three, two-tailed significance tests were used since there was no firm prediction of the direction of difference. In the case of some comparisons within the rural sample, e.g. between groups divided according to home background score, where there were stronger grounds for such a prediction, then one-tailed tests were used, as indicated in the appropriate tables.

NOTES ON COMPUTATION

Virtually all of the statistical tests were carried out on the College computer and most of the programmes used were specially written by a member of the College Computation Department staff. All results presented are corrected to two decimal places (or the first significant figure if this is not within the first two decimal places).

(i) 't' test for non-correlated samples

The standard formula for this test was used, but where the variances of the two groups were significantly different, a correction was made for this. (See Blalock (1960), pp. 170–176.)

(ii) Correlations

All correlations quoted in the two studies are product moment correlations, unless otherwise stated, and these were calculated on the College computer using a 'package' programme, the 'ICL Statistical Analysis Mark II'.

(iii) Kendall's 'tau'

The method of calculating the statistic 'S' was one described by Kendall (1970, pp. 45–46) for the case where both sets of ranks contain numerous ties and the data can be cast in the form of a contingency table. The formula for calculating the variance of 'S' (var S) was the one given by Kendall (1970, p. 55) for the case where ties are present in both rankings.

In the case of 2 x 2 tables where both variates are dichotomies, the correction for continuity given by Kendall (1970, p. 56) was used. In the case where one variate is dichotomized and the other contains ties of varying extents (this was the most common case in the present data), the following correction for continuity given by Ferguson (1965) was used:

$$\frac{1}{m-1}\left[k - \frac{t_l + t_m}{2} \right]$$

where m = number of groups in the
non-dichotomous ranking,
k = the total number of cases,
t_l and t_m are the numbers of tied values
in the first and last groups.

(iv) 'Chi-square' tests

The 'chi-square' calculations were performed on the College computer using a programme which includes the Yates correction for continuity for 2 x 2 tables. Not observed' or 'don't know' categories were excluded from these calculations unless specifically stated otherwise in the table.

NOTES ON CENSUS DATA TABLES

Most of the figures quoted in Tables 80, A4 and A5 are based on information from the 1966 census data sheets. This was a census of 10 per cent of the population so that small figures, such as those for percentage born outside U.K. and percentage with densities over 1½ people per room, are subject to considerable error, with the result that differences between areas may not be as significant as they appear.

Enumeration districts are the smallest areas for which figures are quoted and these areas are somewhat smaller than a school catchment area, but their boundaries do not, in most cases, correspond with the boundaries of the school areas, so the following procedure was adopted for obtaining the figures quoted for school areas in the tables.

Figures were recorded for all the enumeration districts which lay wholly or partly within the school catchment area, these figures were totalled and a percentage then calculated for the school area. It should be remembered that this means that the figures quoted describe an area in most cases larger than the school area, but one which completely contains it.

Several of the items in the table are not independent. For example, a relatively high proportion of single-person households will lead to a smaller number of children per household. This could mean that the figure quoted in Tables 80, A4 and A5 for the number of children under 15 per household could be considerably lower than the average number of children per *family*. In the housing table a high percentage of Council housing will usually give a high percentage with exclusive use of all amenities.

The figures for terminal education age are based on the 1961 census, as no information was asked for on this item in the 1966 census. 'Amenities' and 'rooms' are as defined for the purposes of the 1966 census.

The one figure in the tables which was not taken from census data is that for the average rateable value of private dwellings. This was obtained by using the records in the Rates Department and totalling the individual rateable values of private dwellings in the area. The bulk of the records of rateable values are kept in alphabetical order but recent alterations or additions are not, so it is impossible to be certain that we have included *all* of these, but the proportion omitted should be very low, and in any case is unlikely to affect the average value very much. As demolition and new building is going on all the time in some of these areas, no figure quoted will be accurate for very long.

Appendix II Additional Tables

Table A1

Comparison of leavers with the full CA and DA samples on level of reading

	CA group				DA group			
Rating	Full sample (N=317)		Leavers (N=9)		Full sample (N=372)		Leavers (N=26)	
	n	%	n	%	n	%	n	%
Child's level of reading								
Schedule 2								
First book of scheme/beyond	126	39.7	1	11	109	29.3	6	23
Pre-reading activities	147	46.4	6	67	209	56.2	15	58
Little interest in pre-reading activities	44	13.9	2	22	54	14.5	5	19
	z = 1.47, N.S.				z = 0.67, N.S.			
Schedule 4	(N=308)		(N=28)		(N=347)		(N=38)	
Pre-reading/Introductory book	62	20.1	4	14	174	50.1	21	55
Books 2 and 3	184	59.7	16	57	109	31.4	12	32
Books 3 and 4 or beyond	62	20.1	8	29	64	18.4	5	13
	z = 0.98, N.S.				z = 0.65, N.S.			
Schedule 5	(N=280)		(N=16)		(N=309)		(N=31)	
Pre-reading to book 1	24	8.6	1	6	75	24.3	10	32
Books 2 and 3	118	42.1	8	50	107	34.6	8	26
Book 4 or beyond	138	49.3	7	44	127	41.1	13	42
	z = 0.36, N.S.				z = 0.28, N.S.			

Notes: 1. All probabilities given in this table are two-tailed.

2. In Tables A1 to A4 percentages have been rounded to the nearest whole number where the sample size drops below 100.

Table A2

Comparison of leavers with the full CA and DA samples on power of oral expression

Rating	CA group				DA group			
	Full sample (N=317)		Leavers (N=9)		Full sample (N=372)		Leavers (N=26)	
	n	%	n	%	n	%	n	%
Child's power of oral expression								
Schedule 2								
Very fluent and articulate	83	26.2	4	44	51	13.7	5	19
Adequate	207	65.3	4	44	267	71.8	19	73
Markedly poor	27	8.5	1	11	54	14.5	2	8
	z = 0.61, N.S.				0.95, N.S.			
Schedule 4	(N=308)		(N=28)		(N=347)		(N=38)	
Very fluent and articulate	77	25.0	7	25	50	14.4	6	16
Adequate	190	61.7	17	61	206	59.4	17	45
Poor	41	13.3	4	14	91	26.2	15	39
	z = 0.08, N.S.				1.05, N.S.			
Schedule 5	(N=280)		(N=16)		(N=309)		(N=31)	
Very fluent and articulate	59	21.1	2	12	66	21.4	5	16
Adequate	191	68.2	14	87	195	63.1	20	64
Poor	30	10.7	0	0	48	15.3	6	19
	z = 0.16, N.S.				0.64, N.S.			

Note: 1. All probabilities given in this table are two-tailed.
        2. See note 2 to Table A1.

354

Table A3

Comparison of leavers with the full CA and DA samples
on ability to match number symbol to objects

Rating	CA group				DA group			
	Full sample (N=317)		Leavers (N=9)		Full sample (N=372)		Leavers (N=26)	
	n	%	n	%	n	%	n	%
Child's ability to match written number symbol to corresponding number of objects								
Schedule 2								
6 or more objects	120	37.8	3	33	122	32.8	6	23
2 to 5 objects	108	34.1	1	11	148	39.8	11	42
not at all	89	28.1	5	55	102	27.4	9	35
	z = 0.90, N.S.				z = 0.95, N.S.			
Schedule 4	(N=308)		(N=28)		(N=347)		(N=38)	
beyond 10 objects	59	19.2	5	18	102	29.4	9	24
6 to 10 objects	190	61.7	17	61	129	37.2	12	32
2 to 5 objects	52	16.9	6	21	82	23.6	8	21
not at all	7	2.3	0	0	34	9.8	9	24
	z = 0.12, N.S.				z = 1.54, N.S.			
Schedule 5	(N=280)		(N=16)		(N=309)		(N=31)	
more than 20 objects	153	54.6	7	44	143	46.3	13	42
11 to 20 objects	93	33.2	7	44	87	28.2	9	29
2 to 10 objects	34	12.1	2	12	69	22.3	8	26
not at all	0	0.0	0	0	10	3.2	1	3
	z = 0.61, N.S.				z = 0.40, N.S.			

Notes: 1. All probabilities given in this table are two-tailed.
        2. See note 2. to Table A1.

Table A4

Comparison of leavers with the full CA and DA samples on relationship with class teacher

	CA group				DA group			
Rating	Full sample (N=317)		Leavers (N=9)		Full sample (N=372)		Leavers (N=26)	
	n	%	n	%	n	%	N	%
Child's relationship with class teacher								
Schedule 2								
very positive	171	53.9	6	67	170	45.7	10	38
positive	123	38.8	3	33	146	39.2	12	46
uncertain/negative	23	7.3	0	0	56	15.0	4	15
	z = 0.65, N.S.				z = 0.45, N.S.			
Schedule 4	(N=318)		(N=28)		(N=247)		(N=38)	
very positive	193	62.7	13	46	171	49.3	16	42
positive	104	33.8	14	50	133	38.3	17	45
uncertain/negative	11	3.6	1	4	43	12.4	5	13
	z = 1.47, N.S.				z = 0.63, N.S.			
Schedule 6	(N=280)		(N=16)		(N=309)		(N=31)	
very positive	143	51.1	9	56	128	41.4	14	56
positive	121	43.2	7	44	134	43.4	10	44
uncertain/negative	16	5.7	0	0	47	15.2	7	0
	z = 0.40, N.S.				z = 0.01, N.S.			

Notes: 1. All probabilities given in this table are two-tailed.
2. See note 2 to Table A1.

Table A5(a)

Population characteristics of the school areas: CARDIFF

	Middle class areas		Settled working class areas		Deprived areas				Cardiff County Borough	England and Wales
	A	B	C	D	E	F	G	H		
% economically active and retired men in social class:										
I and II	15.6	62.1	9.5	13.2	7.0	6.4	6.9	20.5	18.0	20.2
III	62.9	32.8	61.8	59.4	56.5	61.4	52.6	62.7	54.1	50.3
IV and V	21.5	5.1	28.7	27.4	36.5	32.2	40.4	16.8	27.9	29.4
% people over 15, with terminal education age less than 16 (1)	70.6	34.5	88.6	78.5	89.9	86.9	90.5	80.2	76.8	78.6
Age composition:										
% 0 – 4 years	8.6	8.1	9.5	7.4	9.6	9.0	11.1	12.7	8.8	8.5
5–14 years	12.7	15.1	27.5	18.6	19.4	20.9	17.0	22.3	15.3	14.5
65+	15.3	14.2	6.6	9.8	7.4	10.6	9.4	9.1	12.3	12.4
Number of children under 15 per household	0.67	0.75	1.4	0.95	1.1	1.0	0.97	1.31	0.77	0.71
% born outside U.K.	1.1	4.0	1.7	1.7	1.3	0.9	2.7	1.7	3.0	6.3 (2)
% moving within Local Authority during last year	3.6	5.4	5.6	5.2	4.3	7.8	7.2	36.7	7.1	–
% moving into Local Authority during last year	1.3	4.2	2.0	2.8	2.3	1.5	1.1	0.7	2.4	–

Notes: 1. For several areas the % 'not stated' was 5% or more of the population.
2. This figure is the percentage of economically active and retired persons only.

For information about the nature of the census data presented in this and subsequent tables
see Appendix 1, page 351.

Table **A5**(b)

Population characteristics of the school areas: LONDON

	Middle class areas		Settled working class areas		Deprived areas					England and Wales
	A	B	C	D	E	F	G	H	I	
% economically active and retired men in social class:										
I and II	28.5	25.9	18.7	22.4	7.2	9.5	9.5	9.3	11.2	20.2
III	61.8	57.7	65.6	62.1	48.1	38.9	49.6	52.5	55.6	50.3
IV and V	9.7	16.4	15.6	15.5	44.6	51.4	40.9	38.2	33.2	29.4
% people over 15, with terminal[1] education age less than 16	63.0	62.7	-(2)	69.9	91.5	90.0	92.7	92.7	91.7	78.6
Age composition:										
% 0 - 4 years	7.0	6.1	8.2	4.9	8.9	8.9	10.8	10.2	9.5	8.5
5 - 14 years	12.6	14.8	13.7	14.1	20.2	17.3	17.0	15.5	16.2	14.5
65+	13.3	9.5	9.4	8.3	8.0	7.3	9.5	9.9	13.4	12.4
Number of children under 15 per household	0.54	0.69	0.64	0.63	0.95	0.72	0.91	0.80	0.85	0.71
% born outside U.K.	2.8	3.2	3.9	2.2	4.8	29.6	6.0	13.8	11.0	6.3 (3)
% moving within Local Authority during last year	3.3	0.5	2.3	1.2	8.0	5.4	5.9	4.4	4.3	-
% moving into Local Authority during last year	7.3	3.7	5.9	3.2	2.8	4.2	2.0	2.7	2.7	-

Notes: 1. For several areas the % 'not stated' was 5% or more of the population.

      2. The greater part of the catchment areas for this school was in a borough for which 1961 census figures were not readily available.

      3. This figure is the percentage of economically active and retired persons only.

Table A5(c)

Population characteristics of the school areas: SWANSEA

	Middle class areas		Settled working class areas		Deprived areas					Swansea County Borough	England and Wales
	A	B	C	D	E	F	G	H	I		
% economically active and retired men in social class:											
I and II	41.6	40.3	11.5	11.6	12.9	5.9	5.8	6.0	7.7	17.7	20.2
III	39.6	45.8	54.4	57.1	55.5	47.4	47.4	47.0	53.6	50.5	50.3
IV and V	18.8	13.9	34.1	31.3	31.6	46.6	46.8	47.0	38.6	31.8	29.4
% people over 15, with terminal education age less than 16 [1]	71.2	55.5	85.8	83.1	83.0	90.2	90.1	94.1	91.3	83.2	78.6
Age composition: %											
0 to 4 years	5.0	4.9	9.6	6.3	10.0	15.1	7.2	17.6	8.0	8.3	8.5
5 to 14 years	11.4	13.1	12.7	15.0	19.1	20.2	14.5	20.6	14.1	14.6	14.5
65+	17.7	17.7	16.0	8.3	7.8	6.3	10.7	5.1	14.7	12.4	12.4
Number of children under 15 per household	0.46	0.56	0.68	0.69	0.92	1.25	0.71	1.37	0.64	0.72	0.71
% born outside U.K.	3.2	2.1	2.1	0.8	2.0	0.6	1.6	0.6	2.5	2.2	6.3(2)
% moving within Local Authority during last year	5.9	5.8	9.4	3.4	9.5	16.7	5.4	23.7	7.0	7.7	-
% moving into Local Authority during last year	5.7	3.7	0.8	0.4	1.2	2.7	0.7	2.7	1.2	2.5	-

Notes: 1. For several areas the % 'not stated' was 5% or more of the population.
2. This figure is the percentage of economically active and retired persons only.

Table A6(a)

Housing characteristics of the school areas: CARDIFF

	Middle class areas		Settled working class areas			Deprived areas			Cardiff County Borough	England and Wales
	A	B	C	D	E	F	G	H		
% with exclusive use of all amenities	95.7	96.7	97.4	92.6	76.7	63.8	20.2	94.2	64.4	82.4
% 6+ households	5.4	7.0	18.6	14.5	18.3	14.1	16.4	12.8	9.0	6.2
% single person households	10.3	12.0	9.5	7.0	7.7	12.2	11.8	9.6	13.5	15.1
% owner occupied	54.5	82.4	10.4	41.3	12.6	9.5	46.8	36.5	51.3	48.4
% rented from council	34.5	0	85.9	48.8	80.2	84.7	8.8	55.8	28.5	27.2
Average number of people per room	0.55	0.53	0.77	0.66	0.71	0.66	0.59	0.67	0.57	0.58
densities										
% over 1½ persons per room	0	0	2.3	2.1	3.9	2.7	0.7	1.3	1.0	1.5
1 – 1½ persons per room	5.5	1.1	8.5	7.5	7.3	7.4	6.6	5.2	4.0	5.4
½ – 1 person per room	59.9	58.5	75.8	63.5	62.9	62.5	53.2	72.1	58.8	68.8
< ½ person per room	34.6	40.4	13.4	27.0	25.9	27.3	39.4	21.4	36.3	24.3
% sharing households	2.4	4.2	0	0	1.0	1.5	13.5	0	2.8	3.0
Average rateable value of private dwellings (in £)	75.5	119.9	61.6	75.7	65.0	59.3	48.7	56.9	72.1	73

Table A6(b)

Housing characteristics of the school areas: LONDON

	Middle class areas		Settled working class areas		Deprived areas					England and Wales
	A	B	C	D	E	F	G	H	I	
% with exclusive use of all amenities	89.7	97.6	93.2	99.0	62.0	36.0	53.4	63.8	40.1	82.4
% 6+ households	3.7	8.3	3.8	5.6	13.0	9.7	8.0	7.4	7.3	6.2
% single person households	22.9	7.1	7.5	7.6	15.6	28.0	17.1	16.1	22.6	15.1
% owner occupied	82.6	59.8	75.3	40.6	0.7	2.3	1.7	3.1	1.2	48.4
% rented from council	0.9	34.3	10.9	54.8	61.0	29.2	46.3	52.7	64.1	27.2
Average number of people per room	0.50	0.59	0.56	0.59	0.75	0.84	0.72	0.75	0.78	0.58
densities										
% over $1\frac{1}{2}$ persons per room	0	0.6	0	0.5	4.1	13.9	4.9	5.6	4.7	1.5
$1 - 1\frac{1}{2}$ persons per room	1.4	1.8	0.4	1.0	11.5	13.3	8.0	12.3	11.8	5.4
$\frac{1}{2} - 1$ person per room	54.6	71.6	65.4	75.1	65.0	54.0	65.8	63.7	63.8	68.8
$< \frac{1}{2}$ person per room	44.0	26.0	34.2	23.3	19.3	18.9	21.2	18.4	19.7	24.3
% sharing households	15.6	0	4.2	0	21.6	24.2	20.2	18.9	4.1	3.0
Average rateable value of private dwellings (in £)	98.4	105.2	97.9	93.3	85.5	53.0	77.8	86.6	70.4	73

Table A6(c)

Housing characteristics of the school areas: SWANSEA

	Middle class areas		Settled working class areas			Deprived areas				Swansea County Borough	England and Wales
	A	B	C	D	E	F	G	H	I		
% with exclusive use of all amenities	80.3	87.4	49.0	80.9	89.3	81.2	70.8	81.8	38.5	70.5	82.4
% 6+ households	5.4	6.0	5.8	7.4	7.5	11.8	7.3	11.9	5.5	7.1	6.2
% single person households	19.4	15.1	11.2	9.8	15.7	11.3	8.8	9.8	13.3	13.8	15.1
% owner occupied	77.0	78.9	61.9	50.2	36.5	39.6	16.1	44.9	59.2	52.6	48.4
% rented from council	0	5.9	2.9	36.7	56.7	52.0	78.2	42.9	18.3	31.3	27.2
Average number of people per room	0.47	0.52	0.58	0.58	0.63	0.69	0.67	0.70	0.58	0.58	0.58
densities % over 1½ persons per room	0	0.3	0.3	0	0.3	2.6	1.2	2.8	0	0.8	1.5
1 - 1½ persons per room	1.8	1.6	4.4	2.7	8.2	7.9	7.3	6.3	4.1	4.6	5.4
½ - 1 person per room	44.8	51.4	58.5	64.5	62.9	69.0	65.4	75.5	61.5	59.5	68.8
< ½ person per room	53.4	46.7	36.7	32.8	28.6	20.5	26.2	15.4	34.4	35.1	24.3
% sharing households	5.8	5.2	1.4	0.8	0.4	1.7	0.8	0	5.5	5.9	3.0
Average rateable value of private dwellings (in £)	89.7	103.8	44.9	58.6	54.9	51.1	57.2	46.4	39.3	67.5	73

Table A7(a)

Cell numbers, means and variances for two-way analysis of variance
(intelligence and school area type) of Urban sample school achievement scores

| Cell | Burt Reading Test | | | Neale Reading Test | | | | | | | | |
| | | | | Accuracy | | | Rate | | | Comprehension | | |
	N	mean	variance	N	mean	variance	N	mean	variance	N	mean	variance
MC Low Intelligence	17	35.80	211.36	17	29.47	225.26	17	43.82	414.28	17	7.00	18.75
SWC "	37	26.70	182.83	37	18.62	174.08	37	30.92	427.47	37	5.38	15.63
DA "	102	17.77	183.76	102	11.59	132.90	102	28.19	256.96	102	3.68	13.05
MC Medium Intelligence	38	37.00	241.95	38	30.16	339.27	38	44.87	546.55	38	10.50	43.45
SWC "	48	37.62	271.69	48	29.31	320.35	48	42.06	388.57	48	8.65	24.49
DA "	90	28.51	236.81	90	21.18	230.33	90	40.00	440.76	90	7.29	26.61
MC High Intelligence	67	47.12	280.26	67	41.76	388.00	67	53.15	494.52	67	14.63	59.15
SWC "	40	42.27	253.38	40	36.45	307.69	40	51.00	506.82	44	13.85	61.62
DA "	55	38.24	268.04	55	32.76	358.33	55	47.36	492.49	55	11.87	49.41
F max (largest ÷ smallest variance)			1.53			2.92			2.13			4.72

Table A7(b)

Cell numbers, means and variances for two-way analysis of variance
(intelligence and school area type) of Urban sample school achievement scores

Cell	Spelling Test			WISC Vocabulary Test			Mathematics Test		
	N	mean	variance	N	mean	variance	N	mean	variance
MC Low Intelligence	17	21.82	68.90	17	21.29	29.60	17	19.41	34.13
SWC " "	37	14.46	97.37	47	18.02	31.33	47	13.13	23.71
DA " "	104	8.93	79.31	111	16.79	21.58	113	13.82	39.27
MC Medium Intelligence	38	21.74	75.82	38	23.08	26.62	38	22.34	50.23
SWC " "	49	21.16	78.39	52	20.13	25.18	53	20.66	34.19
DA " "	91	16.09	99.90	95	19.86	14.44	96	20.65	35.22
MC High Intelligence	67	26.63	56.27	67	25.97	29.09	66	30.50	30.28
SWC " "	39	23.92	71.65	42	23.45	33.62	42	26.14	31.59
DA " "	54	20.46	94.44	66	22.41	30.21	66	27.03	29.17
F max (largest ÷ smallest variance)			1.78			2.33			2.12

Cell numbers, means and variances for two-way analysis of variance (sex and school area type) of Urban sample school achievement scores

Cell		Burt Reading Test			Neale Reading Test								
					Accuracy			Rate			Comprehension		
		N	mean	variance	N	mean	variance	N	mean	variance	N	mean	variance
MC	Female	48	45.08	198.63	48	39.85	286.81	48	55.35	389.13	48	12.50	51.62
SWC	Female	66	37.23	206.67	66	30.20	226.50	66	45.64	411.65	66	9.00	27.45
DA	Female	124	26.73	206.72	124	19.94	203.02	124	39.07	411.69	124	6.39	22.43
MC	Male	74	40.66	332.17	74	34.22	432.64	74	45.32	555.07	74	12.14	59.52
SWC	Male	59	34.37	352.48	59	26.46	419.56	59	37.14	554.74	59	9.73	64.37
DA	Male	123	25.76	363.24	123	19.66	365.47	123	34.43	446.18	123	7.25	49.03
F max (largest ÷ smallest variance)				1.83			2.03			1.43			2.87

Cell		WISC Vocabulary			Mathematics			Spelling			Picture Intelligence		
		N	mean	variance	N	mean	variance	N	mean	variance	N	mean	variance
MC	Female	48	23.33	32.57	47	26.51	62.65	48	25.87	52.66	48	37.90	58.61
SWC	Female	74	19.31	35.07	74	19.66	60.42	65	21.55	85.03	74	29.43	130.63
DA	Female	137	18.41	20.73	138	19.25	59.04	125	14.84	98.51	139	27.53	121.31
MC	Male	74	25.12	29.45	74	26.30	55.55	74	23.50	78.03	74	35.91	106.85
SWC	Male	67	21.64	30.51	68	19.96	52.91	60	18.40	102.38	68	29.65	116.92
DA	Male	135	20.06	30.27	137	19.50	66.58	124	13.25	122.89	137	26.95	137.31
F max (largest ÷ smallest variance)				1.69			1.26			2.33			2.34

365

Table A9

Two way analysis of variance; intelligence and cultural home background: Rural sample

Cell sizes: $n_{11}=18$, $n_{12}=14$, $n_{21}=8$, $n_{22}=18$

Dependent variable		Cell means		Independent variable	Variance	cMS_w	F	d. of f.	p
		Good home	Poor home						
Burt	High int.	38.1	36.4	Intelligence	150.1	16.182	9.273	1,54	< 1%
	Low int.	25.4	24.7	Home background	1.4		<1	-	-
				Interaction	0.2		<1	-	-
Neale Accuracy	High int.	31.4	28.6	Intelligence	141.8	15.716	9.026	1,54	< 1%
	Low int.	17.7	18.4	Home background	1.2		<1	-	-
				Interaction	3.2		<1	-	-
Neale Rate	High int.	45.8	41.9	Intelligence	60.8	36.45	1.667	1,54	NS
	Low int.	39.1	33.0	Home background	24.9		<1	-	-
				Interaction	1.3		<1	-	-
Neale Comprehension	High int.	10.7	10.2	Intelligence	19.4	2.164	8.987	1,54	< 1%
	Low int.	6.1	5.9	Home background	0.1		<1	-	-
				Interaction	0.01		<1	-	-

Continued on next page

366

WISC	High int.	25.1	23.1	Intelligence	46.9	1.797	26.073	1,54	<0.1%
	Low int.	17.6	16.9	Home background	1.75		<1	-	-
				Interaction	0.4		<1	-	-
Mathematics	High int.	30.7	26.6	Intelligence	66.8	2.358	28.342	1,54	<0.1%
	Low int.	21.0	19.9	Home background	6.8		2.878	1,54	NS
				Interaction	2.4		1.012	1,54	NS
Spelling	High int.	22.6	20.1	Intelligence	58.2	6.898	8.440	1,54	<1%
	Low int.	13.7	13.7	Home background	1.7		<1	-	-
				Interaction	1.5		<1	-	-

Table A10

Two-way analysis of variance; intelligence and material home background: Rural sample

Cell sizes: $n_{11}=27$, $n_{12}=5$, $n_{21}=15$, $n_{22}=11$

Dependent variable		Cell means		Independent variable	Variance	$c\,MS_w$	F	d.f.	p
		Good home	Poor home						
*Burt	High int.	38.0	34.0	Intelligence	121.3	20.666	5.871	1,54	< 5%
	Low int.	24.3	25.6	Home background	1.8		<1	-	-
				Interaction	7.0		<1	-	-
*Neale Accuracy	High int.	30.7	27.2	Intelligence	106.0	20.005	5.298	1,54	< 5%
	Low int.	16.5	20.6	Home background	0.1		<1	-	-
				Interaction	13.3		<1	-	-
*Neale Rate	High int.	45.0	39.2	Intelligence	52.9	47.101	1.124	1,54	N.S.
	Low int.	35.2	34.5	Home background	10.7		<1	-	-
				Interaction	6.4		<1	-	-
*Neale Comprehension	High int.	10.6	10.0	Intelligence	17.0	2.729	6.235	1,54	< 5%
	Low int.	5.1	7.2	Home background	0.6		<1	-	-
				Interaction	1.7		<1	-	-
*WISC	High int.	24.3	24.2	Intelligence	52.3	2.320	22.531	1,54	< 0.1%
	Low int.	18.0	16.0	Home background	1.1		<1	-	-
				Interaction	0.9		<1	-	-
*Mathematics	High int.	29.3	27.0	Intelligence	58.6	3.162	18.532	1,54	< 0.1%
	Low int.	19.1	21.8	Home background	0.04		<1	-	-
				Interaction	6.1		1.937	1,54	N.S.
*Spelling	High int.	21.9	19.6	Intelligence	43.9	8.584	5.113	1,54	< 5%
	Low int.	11.5	16.7	Home background	2.3		<1	1,54	-
				Interaction	14.1		1.643	1,54	N.S.

Table **A11**

Two-way analysis of variance; intelligence and total home background: Rural sample

Cell sizes: $n_{11}=21$, $n_{12}=11$, $n_{21}=9$, $n_{22}=17$

Dependent variable		Cell means		Independent variable	Variance	$_c MS_w$	F	D.F.	p
		Good home	Poor home						
Burt	High int.	39.1	34.2	Intelligence	136.4	16.021	8.515	1,54	< 1%
	Low int.	25.1	24.8	Home background	6.8		<1	-	-
				Interaction	5.1		<1	-	-
Neale Accuracy	High int.	32.4	26.0	Intelligence	126.0	15.415	8.174	1,54	< 1%
	Low int.	17.1	18.8	Home background	5.5		<1	1,54	-
				Interaction	16.4		1.061	1,54	N.S.
*Neale Rate	High int.	45.8	40.9	Intelligence	61.6	36.654	1.681	1,54	N.S.
	Low int.	37.4	33.5	Home background	19.2		<1	-	-
				Interaction	0.2		<1	-	-
Neale Comprehension	High int.	11.1	9.3	Intelligence	19.8	2.115	9.342	1,54	< 1%
	Low int.	4.9	6.6	Home background	0.004		<1	1,54	N.S.
				Interaction	3.1		1.473	1,54	-
*WISC	High int.	25.2	22.4	Intelligence	43.6	1.764	24.731	1,54	< 0.1%
	Low int.	17.3	17.1	Home background	2.5		1.405	1,54	N.S.
				Interaction	1.7		<1	-	-
Mathematics	High int.	29.7	27.4	Intelligence	71.1	2.500	28.426	1,54	< 0.1%
	Low int.	19.6	20.7	Home background	0.4		<1	-	-
				Interaction	3.0		1.183	1,54	N.S.
Spelling	High int.	22.5	19.6	Intelligence	57.5	6.892	8.337	1,54	< 1%
	Low int.	12.8	14.2	Home background	0.5		<1	-	-
				Interaction	4.5		<1	-	-

Note: In table **A9**, **A10** and **A11**: 1. * indicates that the 'F max' statistic (see Appendix 1, page 350)
is significant at the 5 per cent level or beyond.

2. n_{11} - good home background, high intelligence
   n_{12} - poor home background, high intelligence
   n_{21} - good home background, low intelligence
   n_{22} - poor home background, low intelligence

Table of Results, Values of χ^2 and Probabilities
(Chapters 12 and 13)

(Number of degrees of freedom is 1 for all cases)

Item	Table No.	Classification	Groups		χ^2	p
1. Nos. who had experienced financial difficulty	164	Yes No	MD 22 7	Rest 10 77	41.95	< 0.1%
2. No. who had help from M.S.S.	164	Yes No	MD 21 8	Rest 8 79	43.05	< 0.1%
3. No. receiving free meals for child in survey	165	Yes No	MD 22 7	Rest 9 78	44.39	< 0.1%
4. No. receiving clothing grant for child in survey	165	Yes No	MD 14 15	Rest 1 86	38.82	< 0.1%
5. Knowledge of service given by child guidance clinic	167	Any knowledge None	MD 4 25	Rest 33 54	4.78	< 5%
		Any knowledge None	MC 17 12	Rest 20 67	11.13	< 0.1%
6. Use of public library by child in survey	169	Uses/has used Never used	MD 7 22	Rest 58 29	14.29	<0.1%
7. Parents' wish to know more about school	154	Very keen Mild or no interest	MD 5 12	Rest 32 13	7.27	<1%
		Very keen Mild or no interest	MD 5 12	LD 13 4	5.78	<2%
8. Parents who prefer appointment to see teachers	155	Yes/don't mind No	MD 4 25	Rest 37 50	6.65	<1%
		Yes/dont' mind No	MC 17 12	Rest 24 63	7.86	<1%

Continued on next page

	N		MD	Rest		
9. Parents' knowledge of teaching methods	158	Adequate or sketchy None	17 12	78 9	12.11	<0.1%
			MD	LD		
		Adequate or sketchy None	17 12	26 4	4.54	< 5%
			MC	Rest		
		Adequate or sketchy None	28 1	67 20	4.36	< 5%
			MD	Rest		
10. No. of parents who would like to know more about teaching methods	158	Leave it to school Like to know more	15 14	24 63	4.65	< 5%
			MC	Rest		
11. No. of children bringing reading books home	159	Yes No	9 20	67 20	18.37	<0.1%
			MC	Rest		
12. No. of parents who like/would like child to bring books home	159	Yes No	19 10	82 5	13.50	<0.1%
			MD	Rest		
13. Parents' interest in advice on pre-school activities	161	Keen or mild interest No interest	12 17	63 24	7.86	< 1%
			MD	Rest		
14. No. of parents wanting child to stay at school beyond 16	162	Keen Less keen or unwilling	12 17	56 31	3.84	N.S.
			MD	Rest		
		Keen or willing Actually unwilling	22 7	85 2	11.60	< 0.1%
			MD	Rest		
15. Parental interest in further education or training	162	Keen Less keen or unwilling	14 15	73 14	12.89	<0.1%
			MD	Rest		
		Keen or willing Actually unwilling	23 6	87 0	15.00	<0.1%
			MD	Rest		
16. Father's interest in child's schooling (compared with mother's)	163	Equal or more Less or none	11 8	68 14	4.30	< 5%

Appendix III
Questionnaires and School Schedules

STRICTLY CONFIDENTIAL

SCHOOLS COUNCIL RESEARCH AND DEVELOPMENT PROJECT IN COMPENSATORY EDUCATION

Units for Emotional Development and Response to Schooling
SCHOOL INDEX

Name of School: _____ School Code No: _____

Name of Headteacher:
(State whether Mr.
Mrs. or Miss)   _____

Question Number	Criterion	Description applies	Description does *not* apply	Column Number
	A. School Building			
1	Pre-1914 building	1	0	1
2	Pre-1914 building which has not had any major structural alterations since 1930	1	0	2
3	Converted premises not wholly suited to children aged 5 to 7 years	1	0	3
*4	Mostly hutted accommodation with no covered ways	1	0	4
5	Building has not been painted internally within the last 7 years	1	0	5
6	Building in poor state of repair e.g. leaking roof, rising damp, leaking guttering and down pipes	1	0	6
7	Alterations to structural fabric of building now under way and children in temporary accommodation	1	0	7
8	Poor drainage	1	0	8
9	Ratio of number of pupils on roll at beginning of spring term in current year to number of children for whom the building was designed greater than 1	1	0	9
10	No central heating	1	0	10
	TOTAL			

Question Number	Criterion	Description applies	Description does *not* apply	Column Number
	B. Entrance and Circulation Areas			
*1	No entrance hall	1	0	11
*2	Entrance hall dark and narrow	1	0	12
*3	Electric switchgear and/or protruding radiators fixed to walls presenting hazard to children	1	0	13
*4	Access to most classrooms by open verandahs only	1	0	14
5	Half or more classrooms used for access to other parts of school	1	0	15
6	Frequent congestion in circulation areas	1	0	16
*7	Uneven surfaces in corridors (e.g. awkward steps)	1	0	17
8	Infants' accommodation not completely on ground floor level	1	0	18
	TOTAL			
	C. Provision of Rooms			
1	No hall	1	0	19
2	Hall used as dining area	1	0	20
3	Hall used as classroom for 1 term or more during current school year	1	0	21
4	One or more classrooms shared or partitioned	1	0	22
*5	Hall too small for normal P.E. lessons with whole class	1	0	23
6	Meals eaten in classrooms or converted classrooms	1	0	24
7	No dining provision within infant-school building	1	0	25
8	No headteacher's room	1	0	26
9	No staff room	1	0	27
10	No medical inspection room	1	0	28
11	No waiting room for visitors	1	0	29
12	No school kitchen	1	0	30
	TOTAL			
	D. Cloakrooms and Toilets			
1	Indoor sanitation lacking or in poor repair	1	0	31
2	Outdoor sanitation in poor repair	1	0	32

374

Question Number	Criterion	Description applies	Description does *not* apply	Column Number
3	No hot water in toilets or cloakrooms	1	0	33
4	Toilets unheated	1	0	34
5	Cloakrooms unheated	1	0	35
6	Two or more broken hand-basins in infant cloakroom	1	0	36
7	Drinking fountain lacking or unusable for a term or more within current school year	1	0	37
8	No special room or area for hanging coats	1	0	38
9	Fewer pegs than children in cloakrooms serving reception and other first year classes	1	0	39
10	Fewer lockers than children or no lockers in reception or other first year classes	1	0	40
11	Cloakrooms not immediately accessible to infant children in one or more classrooms	1	0	41
	TOTAL			

E. *Classroom Facilities*
(N.B. To be scored if description applies in *half or more* infant classrooms *unless otherwise stated*)

Question Number	Criterion	Description applies	Description does *not* apply	Column Number
1	No sinks in reception class/classes	1	0	42
2	Classroom furniture unsuited to size of children	1	0	43
3	Children's furniture heavy and difficult to move (e.g. iron desks)	1	0	44
4	Blackboard and easel only	1	0	45
5	Wall blackboard less than 4ft wide	1	0	46
6	Poor natural lighting/enjoying no southern light	1	0	47
7	Poor artificial lighting	1	0	48
8	Poor heating	1	0	49
9	Poor ventilation	1	0	50
10	Poor sound insulation or poor acoustics	1	0	51
11	No built-in storage space e.g. cupboards or adjacent stockroom	1	0	52
12	Play space very small or lacking in reception class/classes	1	0	53

Question Number	Criterion	Description applies	Description does *not* apply	Column Number
13	Sand tray and/or water tray lacking in reception class/classes	1	0	54
14	Wall display space very small or lacking in reception class/classes	1	0	55
15	Table display space for models etc. lacking or inadequate	1	0	56
16	Classroom display space for books lacking or inadequate	1	0	57
17	Size and/or layout of classroom unsuitable for group infant activities	1	0	58
18	Classroom lacks adequate storage space for educational equipment	1	0	59
19	Rough, unpolished wooden floors	1	0	60
20	No power point	1	0	61
	TOTAL			

	F. Provision of Materials			
1	Capitation allowance *below* national average	1	0	62
2	Capitation allowance not fully spent in previous year	1	0	63
3	No special allowances (e.g. library)	1	0	64
4	Provision of educational equipment and apparatus (including books) insufficient for number of children in *half or more* classrooms	1	0	65
5	Educational equipment and apparatus (other than books) in poor state of repair in *half or more* classrooms	1	0	66
6	Children's basic readers in poor state of repair in *half or more* classrooms	1	0	67
7	Library book provision insufficient for number of infants	1	0	68
8	Tape recorder lacking or unusable for a month or more within current school year	1	0	69
9	Record player lacking or unusable for a month or more within current school year	1	0	70

Question Number	Criterion	Description applies	Description does *not* apply	Column Number
10	Children's musical instruments (e.g. percussion) lacking or unusable for a month or more within current school year	1	0	71
11	No piano in reception class	1	0	72
12	Wireless lacking or unusable for a month or more within current school year	1	0	73
13	Small games apparatus inadequate e.g. balls, quoits, bean bags, skipping ropes	1	0	74
	TOTAL			

G. School Surrounds

Question Number	Criterion	Description applies	Description does *not* apply	Column Number
*1	Incessant traffic noise	1	0	75
*2	School in area of industrial noise and pollution	1	0	76
*3	School has direct access to busy main road	1	0	77
*4	Playground inadequate (e.g. too small, unpaved, too sloping)	1	0	78
5	No immediate access to grassed areas	1	0	79
*6	No covered play space in school yard	1	0	80
*7	Changes in elevation in yard or playground	1	0	81
*8	Dangerous steps from one level to another	1	0	82
*9	No climbing frame or slide	1	0	83
*10	No sandpit	1	0	84
11	Playground shared with other departments	1	0	85
	TOTAL			

H. School Conditions

Question Number	Criterion	Description applies	Description does *not* apply	Column Number
**1	No secretarial assistance	1	0	86
**2	No ancillary staff e.g. teachers' aides	1	0	87
**3	No school meals supervisor/s	1	0	88
**4	Percentage of children eligible for free meals during spring term of current school year *above* national average (8.34%)	1	0	89

Question Number	Criterion	Description applies	Description does *not* apply	Column Number
5	Percentage of attendances made by children during Autumn term of current year *below* national average (90.6%)	1	0	90
**6	Number of children per class *exceeds 34* in half or more classes	1	0	91
*7	Amount of space per child in reception class *less than* D.E.S. recommendation	1	0	92
*8	Amount of space per child in top infants' class *less than* D.E.S. recommendations	1	0	93
9	No telephone or extension in infant school building	1	0	94
**10	Pupil/teacher ratio in infant classes taking into account the full-time equivalent of part-time teachers *above* national average (28.2)	1	0	95
**11	Ratio of teachers in infant classes *not* infant trained *1 in 4 or higher*	1	0	96
**12	Ratio of temporary and/or unqualified teachers (excluding supply teachers) in infant classes *1 in 4 or higher*	1	0	97
13	Part-time teachers sharing the teaching in one or more infant classes	1	0	98
**14	Reception class teacher in probationary year	1	0	99
**15	Headteacher teaching for half the week or more	1	0	100

TOTAL

```
ACTUAL SCORE.      ____
POSSIBLE SCORE.    100
```

KEY
* Item can be scored on basis of observation.
** Item can be scored from information in Headteachers' Questionnaire.

References

The figures of national averages, etc., quoted in Section H were obtained from the following sources:

Item 4 Education and Science (1967), Report of the Department of Education and Science: Cmnd. 3564 HMSO
Item 5 Survey of county boroughs in England and Wales (1969). Figures for Autumn term, 1968.
Item 6 Statistics of Education (1967) Vol. 1. Schools. HMSO

Items 7 For recommendations see Statutory Instruments (1959) No. 890. (Education, England and Wales).
 and 8   Standards for School Premises Regulations. HMSO
Item 10 Statistics of Education (1967) Vol. 1. Schools. HMSO

Capitation allowance (Section F, 1) calculated from information supplied by a sample of local authorities in England and Wales (1969).

Note. Further information on the construction and use of the index can be found in Laing, A. F. (1971), The construction of an infant school amenities index. *Brit. J. Educ. Psychol.*, 41, 1, 94—95.

SCHOOLS COUNCIL RESEARCH AND DEVELOPMENT PROJECT IN COMPENSATORY EDUCATION

Headteachers' Questionnaire

PART I

SECTION A.   SCHOOL ORGANIZATION

Name of Headteacher_____

Date of completing this Schedule_____

1. *Type of School:*

	tick as appropriate
Infants	_____
Infants with nursery class	_____
Junior mixed and infants	_____

N.B. Unless otherwise stated the following items apply to the *infants department* only in the case of Junior Mixed and Infant Schools and to the *whole school* in the case of primary schools without an infant department (e.g. small rural schools).

2. *If a Junior Mixed and Infant School please state:*

(a) the number of children on roll in whole school on first day of summer term, 1969   _____

(b) the number of junior classes   _____

3. (a) *How are children allocated to classes in the infant school/infant department?*   tick as appropriate

(i) Parallel cross-sections by age/ability of more than one year group (family or vertical grouping)   _____

(ii) by age in one or more year groups   _____

(iii) by age within year groups (e.g. by term of entry)   _____

(iv) by age combined with achievement (streaming)   _____

379

(v) combination of above

please give details_____

_____

(vi) other arrangements

please give details_____

_____

(b) *If the children starting school in September, 1968 were allocated to more than one reception class, please give details of how they were allocated (i.e. to which classes) and on what basis (e.g. age, random allocation etc.).*

4. *Present composition of infant school/dept. in terms of class organization at beginning of Summer term 1969.*

Name/No. of Class	If applicable, whether recep., 1st, 2nd, or 3rd year class	Total No. of children in class	No. of project children in class	Age range of children in class at begin. of summer term, 1969	Normal length of stay in this class

Total No
of classes_____

Total No.
of children_____

5. *Was a new class formed to accommodate your intake of children into school during the summer term 1969?*

Yes_____

No_____

6. *What is the normal promotion procedure for your infant children?*

7. (a) *Usual date of children's entry to school:*

    (i)   all children enter at beginning of appropriate term (i.e. term in which they reach age 5 yrs.) _____

    (ii)   individual children enter on attainment of school age _____

    (iii) children admitted before the term in which they attain school age. Please give details _____

    (iv) other arrangements — please specify _____

(b) *Do all the children in a given intake start school on the same day?*

    Yes_____

    No_____

(c) *If 'No', how is their entry staggered?*

    over a few days_____

    over 1/2 weeks_____

    longer period please specify _____

8. *Allocation of teaching staff:*

    (i)   classes/groups have same teacher for all activities _____

    (ii)   classes/groups have same teacher for most activities (i.e. some specialization) _____

    (iii) classes/groups shared by several teachers (team teaching) _____

    (iv) other arrangements — please specify: _____

9. *Pupil Turnover: Autumn term 1968 & Spring term 1969*

    (a)   total number of children on roll on first day of Autumn term, 1968 _____

    (b)   number of children who left school during Autumn term, 1968 and Spring term, 1969 _____

    (c)   total number of children on roll on last day of Spring term, 1969 _____

Please leave blank

$$\% \text{ turnover} = \frac{b}{a} \times 100 = \underline{\hspace{2cm}}$$

10. *Free School Meals.*

Please enter the numbers of children receiving free meals during the following weeks:

	1st week Autumn term, 1968	1st week Spring term, 1969	1st week Summer term, 1969
Mon.			
Tues.			
Wed.			
Thurs.			
Fri.			
Total No. of children on school roll during each week			

Please leave blank

Av. % free meals:

1st week_____

2nd week_____

3rd week_____

Av. %   _____

SECTION B.   STAFFING

11. *Headteacher*

(a)   Teaching qualifications:_____

(b)   Age-range trained for:_____

(c)   Length and type of teaching experience:

No. of years experience in:

as:	Nursery Schools	Infants Schools	Junior Schools	Secondary Schools	Other, e.g. Special Schools	Total Years
Assistant Teacher						
Deputy Head Teacher						
Head Teacher						

Total teaching experience   _____

382

(d)   Length of time in present appointment (years)   _____

tick as
appropriate

(e)   Do you spend any time teaching in your present post?   Yes_____

No_____

(f)   If 'Yes', please give details:

No. of hours per week spent in   (i) class teaching   _____hrs.

(ii) small groups or individual children   _____hrs.

(g)   Do you have a school secretary?   Yes_____

No_____

(h)   If 'Yes', is she: full-time_____

part-time_____

shared with
another dept._____

Note 1
Please indicate temporary teachers (excluding supply teachers) with an asterisk in the first column.

Note 2
In case of schools *without* infant departments please indicate, by circling the teacher's number in the first column, those teachers now engaged on teaching infant children.

12.   *Assistant Teachers on School Staff on first day of Summer term, 1969*

Please give details of teachers as follows:

	Miss Mrs. Mr.	Country of birth	Age range trained for	Teaching qualifications	Years of teaching experience				
					Nursery Schls.	Infant Schls.	Jun. Schls.	Other Schls.	Total Yrs.
A. Full-time teachers									
No. 1									
No. 2									
No. 3									
No. 4									

	Miss Mrs. Mr.	Country of birth	Age range trained for	Teaching Qualifications	Years of teaching experience				
					Nursery Schls.	Infant Schls.	Jun. Schls.	Other Schls.	Total Yrs.
No. 5									
No. 6									
No. 7									
No. 8									
No. 9									
No. 10									
No. 11									
No. 12									
No. 13									
No. 14									
B. Part-time class teachers 1. 2. 3. 4.									
C. Part-time non-class teachers 1. 2.									

	Miss Mrs. Mr.	Country of birth	Age range trained for	Teaching Qualifications	Years of teaching experience				
					Nursery Schls.	Infant Schls.	Jun. Schls.	Other Schls.	Total Yrs.
3.									
4.									

Total No.
Full-time
teachers

Part-time
class
teachers

Part-time
non-class
teachers

13. *Weekly teaching hours of Part-time Staff.*

        Hours teaching weekly

    (a)   Part-time class teachers:

                1.   ———————

                2.   ———————

                3.   ———————

                4.   ———————

        Total hours   ———————

        Hours teaching weekly

    (b)   Part-time non-class teachers:

                1.   ———————

                2.   ———————

                3.   ———————

                4.   ———————

        Total hours   ———————

        Total hours
    (all part-time teachers)   ———————

14. *Please leave blank*

   (a)   No. of teachers on roll (taking into account full-time equivalent of part-time
         teachers)   _____

   (b)   No. of children on school roll   _____

   (c)   teacher-pupil ratio   _____

15. *Turnover of teaching staff* (including part-time and temporary teachers but not supply
    teachers).

Autumn 1968 & Spring term, 1969

School Year 1968/69	No. still on staff at end Spring term '69	No. leaving staff during Autumn term 68 & Spring '69	Total No.
No. of teachers on staff at start of Autumn term, 1968			
*No. of teachers joining staff since start of Autumn term, 1968			
Total no.			

*If this number includes temporary teachers appointed specially for a new intake of children, please
indicate here how many such teachers are included.

   Please leave blank
   % turnover =
   % turnover for teachers joining staff since start of Autumn term 1968 =

16. *How many class teachers (excluding supply teachers) have the Project children in your school had
    during the two terms Autumn, 1968 and Spring, 1969?* Please give separate figures for each class
    now containing Project children if several classes are involved.

Name/No. of Class now containing Project Children.	No. of teachers since 1st Sept., 1968

17. (a)   *Do you have any infant helpers/nursery assistants?*

tick as appropriate

Yes_____

No_____

386

(b)   *If 'Yes' please give details as follows:—*

    (i)   number of nursery assistants   _____

    (ii)   number of infant helpers   _____

    (iii) brief details of their qualifications and training _____

          _____

    (iv) which classes (nursery, reception, first year etc.) are they allocated to? _____

SCHOOLS COUNCIL RESEARCH AND DEVELOPMENT PROJECT IN COMPENSATORY EDUCATION
Headteachers' Questionnaire
PART II

Section A.   General Aims and Problems

1.   Ask Headteacher to rank following educational aims in order of importance:

    1. a basic grounding in '3 Rs'
    2. development of adequate oral language skills
    3. development of emotional and social maturity
    4. development of each child's creative and expressive powers

1A.   (a)   Do you hold staff meetings?
           regularly/occasionally as need arises/rarely/never

     (b)   If yes, what do you discuss at such meetings?

           general school policy and organization
           educational aims/materials
           individual children
           other matters

2.   Do you have any special problems or difficulties concerning the

    (a)   school building?

    (b)   school equipment?

    (c)   school amenities?

3.   Do you have any special problems or difficulties concerning staffing?

    (a)   teachers

    (b)   other staff aides/canteen helpers etc.

4.   If school has infant aides/helpers, details of how used:

    (i)   general care of children, dressing, toilet etc.

    (ii)   general help in classroom (preparing materials etc.)

    (iii) involvement in educational activities — brief details

5. Are you in favour of the employment of aides/helpers in infant classes? If so, what training or qualifications do you think they should have and how do you see their role?

       qualifications/training

       role

6. What percentage of your infant children do you estimate present

   (i)   mild

   (ii) serious emotional, social or behavioural problems in school?

mild_____

serious_____

7. Rank following problem types in order of frequency of occurrence in school:

aggressiveness to others
shyness/withdrawal
nervousness (tearfulness, timidity etc.)
restlessness/distractibility/poor concentration
anti-social behaviour (lying, stealing, destruction of property)
disruptiveness/unruly behaviour in class

8. (a) Which of the above problems do you find most difficulty in coping with?

   (b)   Have you had to exclude any children for behaviour problems within the last 5 years?

   (c)   What help is available to you in dealing with these problems and to what extent do you call upon it?

   (d)   What help not at present available would you like to have?

9. What aspects of the school situation do your children find the most difficulty in adjusting to:

   (i)   during their first year in school?

   (ii) subsequently?

10. What percentage of your children do you estimate would benefit from transfer to a special E.S.N. school/class:

   (i)   now during their infant school careers? (i.e. immediate transfer)

   (ii) the end of their infant school careers? (i.e. might need transfer later on)

   (iii) within the last 3 years have any children been transferred to special schools/units whilst attending your school?

      details_____

11. (a) Do you have any problems concerning your children's school attendance?

   (b)   Rank in order of frequency the type of reasons which you think underlie the children's absence:
sickness/indisposition of child
genuinely difficult family circumstances (illness, overburdened mother etc.)
overprotectiveness of parents
parental indifference/fecklessness
difficulties within school

12. (a) What percentage of your children present serious problems of lateness (say 15' late on average twice weekly or more)?

  (b) Rank in order of frequency the type of reasons which you think underlie the children's lateness:
  oversleeping and similar minor reasons
  genuinely difficult family circumstances
  parental indifference/fecklessness

13. Any other problems not mentioned above?

Section B. School Contact with Parents

1. (a) Is there a parent-teacher association?

  (b) If yes, how often does it meet?

  (c) If no, how are parents associated with the school?

2. Are there any school social occasions to which parents are invited?

3. Are meetings arranged by the school/PTA on educational matters?

4. (a) Do parents provide substantial help for the school in money, kind, or labour?

  (b) If yes, what percentage do and details of help?   percentage _____
  details:

  _____

5. Initial School Contact

  (a) What percentage of parents usually come to register their children before entry?

  (b) Do you encourage parents to come with their children before entry in order to see the reception class teacher/classroom?
  If yes, what percentage actually do come?

  (c) Do you arrange for pre-school children to spend some time in school (other than for above reason) before they start regularly?

  (d) Do you encourage parents to stay with their children for part of the day during their first days at school?
  If yes, for how long each day and over what period of time?

6. (a) Following the child's entry into school are you able to arrange for him to attend on a part-time basis for a period if this seems desirable for the child?

  (b) If yes, is this on an ad hoc basis or with official approval?

7. (a) What opportunities do individual parents have to discuss their children's progress or other matters with you?

  (b) Do you ask parents to make an appointment to see you?

8. What opportunities do individual parents have to discuss their children's progress or other matters with the class teacher?

9. (a) What percentage of parents come to see you concerning their children's progress?

  (b) of these what percentage are

    (i) mothers
    (ii) fathers

10. (a) Do parents enter school during the normal school day?
    (b) If so, when and under what circumstances?

11. (a) Do you or your class teachers ever visit the homes of your children?
    (b) If so, under what circumstances?

12. (a) About what percentage of children from 'needy' families do you have?
    (b) Does the school make any provision for them (apart from free meals)?

13. (a) How would you rate, in general, the level of co-operation of your parents with the school:
    very good
    good
    satisfactory
    poor?

    (b) What percentage of unco-operative or indifferent parents (rated poor above) do you estimate you have? _____

    (c) Why do you think they are unco-operative?

14. (a) Do you have any problems concerning parents and their co-operation with the school?

    (b) If so, is there any help you can call on in dealing with such problems and to what extent do you call on this help?

    (c) If so, is there any help not already available which you would like to have in dealing with such problems?

15. (a) Do you think that the parents of your children should be more actively involved in their children's education? If so, in what ways do you think this might be achieved?

    (b) Do you think that parents could play a useful role in the day to day working of the school?

    (c) If yes, what do you think they could do to help?

Section C. Basic Skills

(i) *Reading*

1. (a) What standard in reading (primer level) do you hope most of the children will have reached at the end of their infant school course?

   (b) What percentage of your children, on average, are poor readers (needing special help) at the end of their infant school course?

2. (a) Which of the following methods are used in the introduction of children to reading? Phonic/whole word/sentence/ita etc.

   (b) At what stage, if at all, are your children introduced to the systematic teaching of phonics?

   (c) In the teaching of reading in your infant school/dept. does a change of emphasis take place at any stage?

3. What provision is made for children experiencing difficulty in learning to read in your school?

4. Are any reading tests (attainment or diagnostic) used in your school?
   Details of tests and reasons for use:

5. (a) What percentage of your children's parents show a desire for their children to make progress in reading?

   (b) In what ways?

6. What problems/difficulties do you encounter in teaching your children to read?

7. (a) What basic reading scheme/schemes do you use?

    (b) (If a basic reading scheme/s is in use in school) How suitable for your children do you consider the scheme/s to be?
highly suitable
quite suitable
not very suitable

    main merits   *main faults*

8. Do you encourage your parents to help their children with reading? If so, how?

9. (a) Is there an infant school/dept. library?

    (b) If yes, where is it sited?

    (c) How is the children's use of the library organized?

    (d) Do you have an adequate supply of library books?

    (e) Do you obtain books from sources other than L.E.A. allowance (e.g. public library, parents)?

    (f) Are children allowed to take library books home?

10. (a) Are there book corners (i.e. including books other than basic readers) in the classrooms?

    (b) Are children allowed to take these books home?

(ii) *Mathematics*

1. (a) Do you use any particular approach/scheme (e.g. Nuffield) in maths throughout the school?

    (b) Which particular aspects of maths skills do you stress?

    (c) At what stage are your children introduced to 'formal arithmetic' (written sums)?

2. What provision is made for children experiencing difficulty in learning maths skills in your school?

3. What problems or difficulties do you meet in teaching your children mathematical skills?

4. Do you encourage parents to help their children in learning maths? If so how?

(iii) *Language Skills*

1. Do you use any particular approach/scheme for the development of oral language skills in your children (e.g. through drama, audio-visual aids)?

2. Do you lay stress on any particular aspects of *oral* language skills in the language activities for your children (good articulation, grammatical correctness, vocabulary building, listening skills, fluency/accuracy of expression)?

3. (a) How much emphasis do you place on teaching the more formal aspects of *written* language (spelling, punctuation and grammar)?

    (b) How are these aspects taught and at what age?
spelling
punctuation
grammar

4. What problems or difficulties do you meet in developing language skills in your children?

5. (a) Do you think that all your children are getting sufficient practice for their needs in speaking and listening in school?

   (b) If not, in what way would you like to see the children's opportunities extended?

(iv) *Other Creative and Expressive Skills and Play*
(music, art, craft, drama, music & movement etc.)

1. Do you lay particular stress on or devote a relatively large amount of time to any of these particular areas of activity?

2. Is there any specialist teaching of these activities for your children?

3. Do your children show a marked interest or a particularly good level of response in any of these areas of activity?

4. (a) What opportunities do your children have for 'free play' (i.e. spontaneous activity with play materials) after their first year?

   (b) Which of these areas of activity do the children have an opportunity to engage in during 'free play' after their first year?

   music
   art
   drama
   modelling
   craft

5. What do you think is the main value of 'free play' to your children?

(v) *Use of Modern Media*

1. How much use is made of

   (a) school radio broadcasts in your school?
   (b) television

2. How much use is made of audio-visual media in your school?

	Whether available	Frequency of use v. freq./quite freq./ sometimes/rarely/ never	Brief details of use
tape recorder			
slide/film strip projector			
ciné projector			
record player			
T.V.			

3.   Which of these aids not at present available would you like to have in your school?

                                                           Brief details of how you would use them

   tape recorder

   slide/film strip projector

   ciné projector

   record player

   T.V.

(vi)   *Compensatory Education*

1.   (a)   Do any of your children show signs of coming from culturally poor or limited home
            backgrounds?
     (b)   If yes, what are these signs?

     (c)   What percentage of your children show such signs?

2.   Do you think that infant educational methods (stressing play and discovery methods of learning, free
     choice activities etc.) are wholly suitable for children from culturally/materially deprived home
     backgrounds? If not, please elaborate:

3.   (a)   In what main ways do you think that infants schools can help to 'compensate' children coming
            from such backgrounds?

     (b)   What resources (staffing or money) would such compensatory education need?

SCHOOLS COUNCIL RESEARCH AND DEVELOPMENT PROJECT IN COMPENSATORY EDUCATION

Class Teachers' Questionnaire

PART I

*Information can be drawn from Headteachers' Questionnaire.

A.   *BACKGROUND INFORMATION*

   1.   Teacher's name (Miss, Mrs)

   *2.   Qualifications, training and length of teaching experience:

3.   Number of children in class: 4.   Age range in class
     (including number of Project
     children)

*5. Method of allocation of children to class:

6.   Details of any additional help available to teacher:

     (a)   from part-time teachers   (e.g. taking reading groups)
           or visiting specialists   (e.g. in music)

     (b)   from infant helpers/nursery assistants: details of amount of help available (in time) and
           nature of help:

           (i)   general care of children (dressing, toilet etc.)
           (ii)   general help in classroom (preparing materials etc.)
           (iii) direct involvement in educational activities (e.g. telling stories)

           amount of help:

           full-time / half-time / less than half-time

     (c)   Are you in favour of the employment of aides/helpers in infant classes? If so, what
           qualifications do you think they should have and how do you see their role?

           qualifications / training:

           role:

B.   *CLASSROOM EQUIPMENT*

Question Number	Criterion	Description applies	Description does *not* apply
1.	No sinks in reception class/classes	1	0
2.	Classroom furniture unsuited to size of children	1	0
3.	Children's furniture heavy and difficult to move (e.g. iron desks)	1	0
4.	Blackboard and easel only	1	0
5.	Wall blackboard less than 4ft wide	1	0
6.	Poor natural lighting/enjoying no southern light	1	0
7.	Poor artificial lighting	1	0
8.	Poor heating	1	0
9.	Poor ventilation	1	0
10.	Poor sound insulation or poor acoustics	1	0
11.	No built-in storage space e.g. cupboards or adjacent stockroom	1	0

Question Number	Criterion	Description applies	Description does *not* apply
12.	Play space very small or lacking in reception class/classes	1	0
13.	Sand tray and/or water tray lacking in reception class/classes	1	0
14.	Wall display space very small or lacking in reception class/classes	1	0
15.	Table display space for models etc. lacking or inadequate	1	0
16.	Classroom display space for books lacking or inadequate	1	0
17.	Size and/or layout of classroom unsuitable for group infant activities	1	0
18.	Classroom lacks adequate storage space for educational equipment	1	0
19.	Rough, unpolished wooden floors	1	0
20.	No power point	1	0
21.	Provision of educational equipment and apparatus (including books) insufficient for number of children	1	0
22.	Educational equipment and apparatus (other than books) in poor state of repair	1	0
23.	Children's basic readers in poor state of repair	1	0
24.	Library book provision insufficient for number of infants in class	1	0
	TOTAL		

25. Availability of special equipment: tick as applicable

	Permanently available in recep. class	Not kept in recep. class but available for class teacher's use	Not available for class teacher at all
a. piano			
b. tape-recorder			
c. television set			
d. wireless			
e. record player			
f. flannelgraph board or similar item			
g. filmstrip projector			
h. ciné projector			

C. GENERAL METHODS AND AIMS

  1. How do you organize the children's activities in the 'basic skills' of reading/pre-reading, maths and language (details of method of classroom organization, e.g. nature of grouping and extent of teacher's control over children's choice of activities)?

  range of activities at one time:

  nature of grouping: by ability/progress/free grouping/other:

  children's choice of activities: entirely free
                                    teacher guided
                                    teacher controlled

  nature and extent of teacher's guidance of children's activities:

  2. (a) Do you have a regular organization of children's activities during the day?

        degree of organization (time-tabling):

     (b) Do you always follow this pattern of organization?

        flexibility of organization:

  3. Ask teacher to rank following aims in order of importance:
        1. a basic grounding in '3 Rs'
        2. development of adequate oral language skills
        3. development of emotional and social maturity
        4. development of each child's creative and expressive powers

D. PLAY

  1. What opportunities do your children have for 'free play'?

  how organized: (details of time-tabling, grouping etc.)

  materials: (large toys, structured play corners etc.)

2. Do you take any part in these free play activities?

nature and extent of teacher's structuring and development of play experiences:

3. During the year do you see any progression or development in your children's free play patterns?

4. Do you have any children who are very limited or inhibited in their free play?

5. What do you think is the main value of free play to your children?

E. *READING*

1. (a) What standard in reading (primer level) do you hope most of your children will reach by the end of this term?

in terms of completed work:

(b) What proportion of the children do you estimate will still be on pre-reading activities by this time?

(c) Is this about the usual proportion?

2. Are there any activities which you particularly emphasize in *preparing* children for reading?

3. How do you judge when a child is ready to start reading systematically?

4. Do you use any reading readiness tests? Give details.

published tests:

teacher-produced tests:

5.   (a)   Which method do you use in the *introduction* of children to reading?

               Classify as follows:

               phonic / whole word / sentence / i.t.a. etc.

    (b)   Do you introduce your children to any (i) systematic (ii) incidental phonics teaching during their first year in school?

               systematic:

               incidental:

    (c)   If yes, with which children and when?

               all children:

               individual children:

6.   (a)   Do you make any record of each child's progress in reading/pre-reading skills? If yes, what sort of record and how often are entries made?

               record of page and book progress:

               record of mastery of specific skills:
               (e.g. letter sounds, sight vocab.
               of first book)

               free report:

    (b)   Do you use any tests in connection with the children's reading progress?

               published tests:

               teacher-produced tests:

7.   What are the main problems/difficulties you encounter in teaching your children to read?

8.   Is any use made of the children's own productions (oral or written), e.g. stories or diaries, as a source of reading material? If so, please give details:

9.   (a)   Is there a class library?

    (b)   If yes, how do you control the children's access to the books?

    (c)   What opportunities do the children have for looking at/reading these books?

10. (a) How often, on average, are you able to hear each child read?

    (b) How much extra help are you able to give?

    (c) Do you feel this is enough help?

F. *MATHS*

1. (a) Do you use any particular approach/scheme (e.g. Nuffield) in maths?

    (b) How do you organize your children's play experiences in maths?

    (nature and extent of teacher's guidance and structuring of children's play):

    (c) Are any particular aspects of mathematical skills stressed in your maths programme?

2. (a) At what stage, if at all, do you introduce your children to 'formal arithmetic', i.e. written sums in the four basic processes?

    (b) If 'formal arithmetic' is introduced, is this done for class as a whole or for individual children?

3. (a) How much extra help are you able to give to children showing difficulty in developing math. skills/understanding?

    (b) Do you feel this is enough help?

4. Do you keep a record of each child's progress in maths? Give details:

   record of mastery of
   specific skills:

   free report:

5. Do you use any tests in connection with children's progress in mathematics? Give details:

6. What are the main problems or difficulties you find in teaching your children mathematical skills/understanding?

G.   *LANGUAGE*

1.   Do you use any particular approach to the development of oral language skills in your children (e.g. thro' drama, audiovisual aids)? (Answer to this question should give indication of whether there is a definite language programme.)

2.   Do you lay stress on any particular aspects of oral language skills in the language activities for your children?

3.   What problems/difficulties do you meet in developing oral language skills in your children?

4.   How much attention do you pay to:

(a)   grammatical errors in your children's speech?

(b)   variations from 'standard' English in your children's pronunciation of words, e.g. due to local dialect, immaturity or slackness of speech?

5.   Do you think that all your children are getting sufficient practice for their needs in speaking and listening in school? If not, in what ways would you like to see the children's opportunities extended (e.g. use of infant aides, tape recorder)?

H.   *PROBLEMS CONCERNING CHILDREN AND THEIR HOME BACKGROUNDS*

1.   (a)   Please rank the following categories of 'problem' behaviour in order of their frequency in your class:

aggressiveness to others
shyness/withdrawal
nervousness (marked fearfulness, timidity etc.)
restlessness/distractibility/poor concentration
'anti-social behaviour' (lying, stealing, destruction of property)
disruptiveness/unruly behaviour in class

(b)   Which of the above problems do you find most difficulty in coping with?

(c)   What help, if any, would you like in dealing with such problems?

2. What aspects of the school situation, if any, do your children tend to find most difficulty in adjusting to after their initial settling-in period?

3. How would you rate, in general, the level of interest shown by the parents in your children's progress? Classify as follows:

      (a)   very positive
      (b)   quite positive
      (c)   fairly interested
      (d)   little evidence of interest

4. How many of these parents do you estimate show little evidence of interest?

express as proportion:

5. Do you ever visit the homes of your children? If so, under what circumstances?

6. (a) Do you think that the parents of your children should be more actively involved in their children's education? If so, in what ways do you think this might be achieved?

    (b) Do you think that parents could play a useful role in the day to day working of the school (e.g. help in classroom)?

7. Do any of your children show signs of cultural or material 'deprivation'? If so, how many of the children do and what are the indications?

cultural deprivation only	cultural and material deprivation

8. Do you think that 'normal' infant educational methods are wholly suitable for children from culturally/materially deprived home backgrounds? If not, please elaborate:

9. In what ways do you think infant schools can help to 'compensate' children coming from such backgrounds, given unlimited resources of staffing and equipment?

Class Teachers' Questionnaire

PART II

I. *OTHER CREATIVE AND EXPRESSIVE SKILLS*

    1.   (a)   Please indicate briefly the range of activities which your children have the opportunity to engage in within the following areas:

        1. Art _____

        _____

        2. Modelling _____

        _____

        3. Craft _____

        _____

        4. Drama _____

        _____

        5. Music _____

        _____

        6. Music and movement or movement _____

        _____

      (b)   Please indicate whether these activities are carried out *mainly* on:

        1. a class basis, i.e. all children engaged on this area of activity at the same time, or
        2. a group basis, i.e. one group engaged on this area of activity whilst others are on different activities, or
        3. an individual basis, i.e. individual children may be engaged on this area of activity whilst others are on different activities.

	tick as appropriate				
	mainly on class basis	mainly on group basis	mainly on indiv. basis	about equal proportion of all 3 arrangements	Comment
1. Art					
2. Modelling					
3. Craft					
4. Drama					
5. Music					
6. Music and movement or movement					

tick as appropriate

2.   (a)   Do you lay particular stress on or devote a relatively large amount of time to any of the above areas of activity?

Yes _____

No _____

     (b)   If yes, please give details _____

_____

3.   (a)   Have you any special qualifications or training for teaching any of the above areas of activity?

Yes _____

No _____

     (b)   If yes, please give details _____

_____

4.   (a)   Do your children show a marked interest or particularly good level of response in any of the above areas of activity?

Yes _____

No _____

(b)   If yes, please give details _____

_____

General Comments

J.   *USE OF MODERN MEDIA*

   1.   Please give details of any school broadcasts which you make regular or occasional use of, with brief comments on why you use them, and their main merits:

       Radio

       Television

   2.   (a)   Do you make use of any of the following audio-visual aids   tick as appropriate

tape recorder	_____
slide/film strip projector	_____
ciné projector	_____
record player	_____

       (b)   Please give brief details of how you use them, i.e. in connection with what activities:

           Tape recorder _____

           Slide/film strip projector _____

           Ciné projector _____

           Record player _____

   3.   If some aids are available but you do not use them, please state:

       (a)   which aids _____

_____

       (b)   any particular reason for not using them _____

_____

(c) in what circumstances you might use them _____

_____

4. Which of the following aids not at present available would
    you like to have available in school?

                              tape recorder   _____

                              slide/film strip projector _____

                              ciné projector   _____

                              record player   _____

Please give brief details of how you might use them:

Tape recorder _____

Slide/film strip projector _____

Ciné projector _____

Record player _____

General Comments

K. *BASIC SKILLS*

1. (a) Which, if any, published basic reading schemes do you use?

    (b) If two or more schemes are used, please indicate briefly how they are combined, e.g. one
         basic scheme supplemented by a selection from others used as alternative schemes, etc.

N.B. In the following questions, if more than one basic reading scheme is used please answer separately for each scheme.

2. (a) How suitable do you consider the reading scheme/schemes to be for your children?

tick as appropriate

	Scheme 1 (Title)	Scheme 2 (Title)	Scheme 3 (Title)
very suitable	_____	_____	_____
fairly suitable	_____	_____	_____
not very suitable	_____	_____	_____
definitely unsuitable	_____	_____	_____

(b) What do you consider the main faults of the scheme are?

(c) What do you consider the main merits of the scheme are?

(d) Do you think the scheme (schemes) has sufficient supplementary material (games and puzzle apparatus, supplementary readers etc.) attached?

Yes _____

No _____

(e) If no, what type of supplementary material would you like to see included in it?

3. *Reading/pre-reading apparatus used in class.*

tick as appropriate

	Published apparatus	Teacher made apparatus
1. Games and puzzles (including matching materials)	_____	_____
2. Teaching charts (large pictures and wall charts)	_____	_____
3. Flash cards	_____	_____
4. Film strips	_____	_____
5. Other apparatus — please specify	_____	_____

406

4. *Mathematics apparatus used in class.*

Please record here brief details of apparatus used:

		Published apparatus	Teacher made apparatus
1.	'Structural apparatus' (e.g. Stern, Cuisenaire, Colour Factor, etc.)	_____	_____
2.	Other counting aids	_____	_____
3.	Number games and puzzles	_____	_____
4.	Teaching charts	_____	_____

5. (a) How much use do you make of published children's mathematics books in your class?

tick as appropriate

none	_____
a little	_____
half the time	_____
more than half the time	_____

(b) Brief details of published books used, if any.

General Comments

SCHOOLS COUNCIL RESEARCH AND DEVELOPMENT PROJECT IN COMPENSATORY EDUCATION

Units for Emotional Development and Response to Schooling

School Schedule No. 1

Leave Blank	Data Block No.		School and Area No.			Child's No. and sex						
	1	0	1									

Girls — 1
Boys — 2

Cols. 1   2 3 4   5   6   7   8   9   10   11   12   13   14

*Name of Class Teacher*_____

A.   *Particulars of Child:*

1.   *Surname:* _____

       Christian name(s):_____

2.   *Address:* _____

       _____

       _____

3.   *Date of Birth*
       (Please enter actual day, month and year in boxes,
       e.g. a child born on the 6th Dec. 1963 would be
       entered thus: ⬚0⬚6⬚1⬚2⬚6⬚3⬚ and a child
       born on the 25th Feb. 1964 would be entered as
       ⬚2⬚5⬚0⬚2⬚6⬚4⬚)

Cols. 15, 16, 17, 18, 19, 20

⬚ ⬚ ⬚ ⬚ ⬚ ⬚

4.   *Date child started present school*
       (Please enter actual day, month and year in boxes
       as before e.g. a child starting school on the 4th
       Sept., 1968 would be entered thus:
       ⬚0⬚4⬚0⬚9⬚6⬚8⬚)

Cols. 21, 22, 23, 24, 25, 26

⬚ ⬚ ⬚ ⬚ ⬚ ⬚

B.   *Preparation for School* (to be completed by *Headteacher*)

Please ring appropriate number

5.   Did this child visit the school before admission?

	Col. 27
on 2 or more occasions	1
once only	2
not at all	3

		Please ring appropriate number
		Col. 28
6. If the child visited the school before admission, did he also visit his present classroom and/or teacher?	on 2 or more occasions	1
	once only	2
	not at all	3
		Col. 29
7. Has the child any brothers and sisters attending the same infant school/department?	Yes	1
	No	2

Please give details: _____

_____

_____

		Col. 30
8. Has either parent made any contact with the school concerning the child prior to admission to register him?	Yes	1
	No	2
		Col. 31
9. Has either parent made any contact with the school concerning the child prior to admission for any other reason?	Yes	1
	No	2

Please give details if applicable:

		Col. 32
10. Has the child previously attended a nursery school, a day nursery or a play group?	Yes	1
	No	2

C.   *Settling into School* (to be completed by *class teacher*)

		Col. 33
11. Did the child show signs of distress at leaving his mother when he came to school on the first few days?	Yes	1
	No	2
		Col. 34
12. If Yes, is child still showing signs of distress?	Yes	1
	No	2

Please comment if desired:_____

_____

_____

Cols 35, 36

13.   How many of the 20 sessions in the first 10 days of schooling has the child attended?
(Please enter actual number of sessions in box as before, e.g. for 7 sessions enter 0 7 and for 20 sessions enter 2 0)

409

		Please ring appropriate number

14. To what extent is the child over-tired at the end of the school day?

		Col. 37
no sign of tiredness		1
somewhat tired		2
definitely over-tired		3

15. Has the child shown any unusual or especially difficult behaviour in school so far?

		Col. 38
Yes		1
No		2

If Yes, please give details: _____

_____

_____

_____

16. Has child wet himself/herself during the school day?

		Col. 39
not at all		1
once or twice		2
3 times or more		3

17. Has the child soiled himself/herself during the school day?

		Col. 40
not at all		1
once or twice		2
3 times or more		3

18. Has the child been sick during the school day?

		Col. 41
not at all		1
once or twice		2
3 times or more		3

19. Does the child show an active interest in the materials/experiences provided in school?

		Col. 42
very active interest		1
quite active interest		2
little interest or response to anything provided		3

410

	Please ring appropriate number

		Col. 43
20.	How would you rate the child's initial attitude to you, the class teacher?	very positive, (i.e. very friendly)	1
		positive on the whole (i.e. quite friendly)	2
		uncertain or negative (shy/ withdrawn or actually hostile)	3

		Col. 44
21.	If uncertain or negative in Question 20, please state whether shy/withdrawn or hostile	shy or withdrawn	1
		hostile	2

		Col. 45
22.	How would you rate the child's initial attitude to other children in the class?	very positive (i.e. very friendly)	1
		positive (i.e. friendly on the whole)	2
		uncertain or negative (i.e. shy/withdrawn or actually hostile)	3

		Col. 46
23.	If uncertain or negative in Question 22, please state whether shy/withdrawn or hostile	shy or withdrawn	1
		hostile	2

		Col. 47
24.	How would you rate the child's initial overall adjustment to school?	very good (i.e. child seems very happy and settled)	1
	Please comment if desired (e.g. if there has been a marked change in the child's adjustment during the period).	average (i.e. has settled quite well and seems quite happy on the whole)	2
		poor (i.e. seems definitely unhappy or unsettled)	3

25. On entry to school, could the child read from a book? (N.B. We do not wish teachers to make a special effort to find out whether, or to what extent, each child can read but merely to record any information on this point which may have been gained through incidental observation in the normal course of events)	Yes No not observed	**Col. 48** 1 2 3
26. If yes in Question 25, how well can he/she read? (based on teacher's general impression)	can recognize only odd words here and there correctly can read whole sentences but with some mistakes/omissions can read whole sections fluently and with few errors	**Col. 49** 1 2 3
27. On entry to school could the child write his name legibly?	Yes No not observed	**Col. 50** 1 2 3
28. On entry to school could the child draw simple recognizable objects?	Yes No not observed	**Col. 51** 1 2 3
29. Does the child tend to 'cling' to the teacher on playground duty or to an older brother or sister at playtimes? Please comment if desired:_____	Yes No not observed	**Col. 52** 1 2 3

_____

_____

_____

_____

_____

30. Please comment on any features concerning the child not recorded above:—

_____

_____

_____

_____

_____

STRICTLY CONFIDENTIAL

SCHOOLS COUNCIL RESEARCH AND DEVELOPMENT PROJECT IN COMPENSATORY EDUCATION
Units for Emotional Development and Response to Schooling

School Schedule No. 2

To be completed by the child's class teacher

Leave Blank	Data No.			School and Area No.			Child's No. and sex						
	1	0	2										

Cols. 1   2   3   4   5   6   7   8   9   10   11   12   13   14

*Name of Class Teacher*_____

*Date of completing this schedule*_____

A. *Particulars of Child and his/her Parents*
1. Child's name   Surname_____

                 Christian name(s)_____

	Please ring appropriate numbers
	Col. 15
2. Child's sex Girl	1
Boy	2

413

3. (a) Country of birth of mother

U.K.   Col. 16

U.K.   1
Other   2
Not known   3

If 'other' please specify _____

_____

(b) Country of birth of father

Col. 17

U.K.   1
Other   2
Not known   3

If 'other' please specify_____

_____

B. *Adjustment to School*

4. (a) Does the child show signs of distress on leaving the mother, excluding first 10 days of child's schooling?

Col. 18

Yes   1
No   2
Not applicable   3

(b) If yes, for how long has the child been showing these signs of distress?
(Excluding first 10 days of child's schooling)

Col. 19

few days only   1
1–2 weeks   2
3 weeks or more   3

(c) If yes, please specify nature of signs of distress, their frequency and severity of occurrence.

_____

_____

_____

5. To what aspects of the school situation has the child made relatively the *most* successful adjustment? e.g. personal relationships with other children/teacher

Col. 20

school/classroom routines

educational activities

_____

_____

_____

	Please ring appropriate number
	Col. 21

6. To what aspects of the school situation has the child made relatively the *least* successful adjustment? e.g. personal relationships with other children/teacher

_____

school/classroom routines

_____

educational activities

_____

		Col. 22
7. To what extent is the child over-tired at the end of the school day?	no sign of tiredness	1
	somewhat tired	2
	definitely overtired	3

		Col. 23
8. How would you rate the child's overall adjustment to school this term?	very good (child seems very happy and settled)	1
	quite good (has settled in quite well and seems happy on whole)	2
	poor (seems unhappy, unsettled or otherwise ill-adjusted to school)	3

C. *Classroom Activities: General*

		Col. 24
9. (a) What classroom activities does child seem to show a preference for?	vigorous physical play	1
	manipulative play (e.g. constructional, sand water play)	2
	social/dramatic play	3
	painting/drawing/ musical activities	4
	pre-reading/ number activities	5
	other forms	6
	no particular preference shown	7

(b) If 'other forms', please specify: _____

415

	Please ring appropriate number

10. In general does the child show an active interest in the materials/experience provided in school?

very active interest	1
quite active interest	2
little active interest in anything provided	3

11. Please rate the child's use of play materials as follows:

	Col. 26
play usually leads to end product (e.g. model or painting) or successful completion of activity	1
play sometimes leads to end product/successful completion of activity	2
play rarely or never leads to end product/successful completion of activity (e.g. repetitive manipulative play)	3

12. Please rate the quality of the child's creative activities:

	Col. 27
often shows imagination/originality in use of play materials	1
sometimes shows imagination/originality in use of play materials	2
rarely/never shows imagination/originality in use of play materials	3

416

13. Any other comment on child's play activities:

_____

_____

_____

_____

		Please ring appropriate number
D. *Classroom Activities: prereading, number and related activities*		**Col. 28**
14. Can the child copy words written for him/her by the teacher?	easily and neatly and correctly	1
	fairly frequent reversals or omissions/ positioning of letters rather haphazard	2
	scribbles or makes repetitive strokes/ makes no effort to copy	3
		Col. 29
15. (a) Please rate the child's pre-reading or reading level as follows:	on first book of reading scheme or beyond	1
	on pre-reading activities	2
	shows little interest in pre-reading activities	3
		Col. 30
(b) If child has started on a reading scheme, what book in the series is he/she at present engaged on?	Book 2 or beyond	1
	Book 1	2
	Introductory book or 'pre-primer'	3

		Please ring appropriate number
16. If child is engaged in pre-reading activities, can he/she: (a) match shapes or pictures?	easily and efficiently	Col. 31 1
	quite efficiently on whole (may have some difficulty/makes some errors)	2
	unable to do so yet	3
(b) match words to pictures?	easily and efficiently	Col. 32 1
	quite efficiently on whole (may have some difficulty/ makes some errors)	2
	unable to do so yet	3
(c) match words to words?	easily and efficiently	Col. 33 1
	quite efficiently on whole (may have some difficulty/ makes some errors)	2
	unable to do so yet	3
(d) discriminate word/letter sounds, e.g. in rhyming/ speech games?	very well quite well poorly	Col. 34 1 2 3
(e) recognize single words/phases, e.g. on flash cards around classroom? (including child's name)	7 words or more between 1 and 6 words none	Col. 35 1 2 3
(f) does he/she show an interest in looking at picture/ story books?	very keen interest quite keen interest little/no interest	Col. 36 1 2 3

418

	Please ring appropriate number

		Col. 37
(g) please rate child's overall level of reading readiness:	ready for intro-duction to reading scheme	1
	needs more pre-reading experience	2
	unready — needs great deal more pre-reading experience	3

		Col. 38
17. Can child count correctly the number of objects in a group presented to him?	6 or more objects	1
	between 2 and 5 objects	2
	not at all	3

		Col. 39
18. Can child give you a specified number of objects correctly from a larger number presented to him?	6 or more objects	1
	between 2 and 5 objects	2
	not at all	3

		Col. 40
19. Can child match the written number symbol to the corresponding number of objects?	6 or more objects	1
	between 2 and 5 objects	2
	not at all	3

E.   *Language Skills*

		Col. 41
20. (a) How would you rate the child's clarity of speech, discounting possible lack of clarity due to dialect?	very clear, precise and well articulated	1
	quite clear on whole — may be some distortion/substitution of sounds due to immaturity e.g. 'wobbin' for 'robin'	2
	difficult to follow due to marked immaturity, slovenliness or defect of speech	3

(b)   If speech defect, please give details:

_____

_____

_____

		Please ring appropriate number
		Col. 42
21. Please rate the range of vocabulary shown in the child's spoken language	wide vocabulary for age (rich variety of words)	1
	adequate vocabulary for age	2
	very limited vocabulary for age — repetitive use of words	3
		Col. 43
22. Please rate the child's power of oral expression	very fluent and articulate	1
	can express him/herself adequately	2
	power of expression markedly poor — child cannot communicate adequately	3
		Col. 44
23. How attentively does the child usually follow stories told/read to him/her?	follows most stories very attentively and with obvious interest	1
	quite attentive on whole	2
	generally inattentive — e.g. fidgets, easily distracted, etc.	3

	Please ring appropriate number

	Col. 45
24. How well can the child follow simple oral directions?	very well (directions carried out promptly and accurately) — 1
	quite well (may sometimes make errors/need directions repeated) — 2
	poorly (frequently fails to understand, gets confused etc. even when directions repeated) — 3

F. *Social Competence*

	Col. 46
25. Please rate child on self-dependence in dressing as follows:	quite independent of adult help in dressing/undressing — 1
	can dress/undress him/herself but may need help with buttons, laces, tie bow etc. — 2
	very dependent on adult help in dressing/undressing — 3

	Col. 47
26. Please rate the level of child's competence in managing school/class routines, e.g., finding way about classroom/ school, looking after materials assigned to him, recognizing and looking after his/her own possessions	very competent and reliable — 1
	quite competent and reliable — 2
	not very competent or reliable (e.g. gets lost in school, loses/fails to recognize possessions etc.) — 3

G. *Social Adjustment*

27. (a) How would you rate child's relationship with other children in class?

	Col. 48
very positive (very friendly/interested in other children)	1
positive on whole (quite friendly/interested in other children)	2
uncertain or negative (shy/withdrawn or actually hostile)	3

(b) If uncertain or negative, please state whether child is:

Comment:_____

_____

_____

_____

	Col. 49
shy (but would like to be friendly)	1
withdrawn or indifferent (cut off from others)	2
hostile (seems antagonistic or resentful to other children)	3

28. (a) How would you rate the child's relationship with you, the class teacher?

	Col. 50
very positive (very friendly or responsive	1
positive (friendly or responsive on whole)	2
uncertain or negative (shy, withdrawn/hostile)	3

(b) If uncertain or negative, please state whether child is:

Comment:_____

_____

_____

	Col. 51
shy (but would like to be friendly)	1
withdrawn or indifferent (difficult to make contact with)	2
hostile (aggressive, truculent)	3

	Please ring appropriate number
29. Please rate the child's general level of co-operation with other children:	**Col. 52** very co-operative (usually quite willing and able to co-operate well, e.g. take on roles in dramatic play, take share of responsibility in group activity) — 1 fairly co-operative (achieves simpler form of co-operation only, e.g. sharing materials, taking turns, taking part in simple class games etc.) — 2 unco-operative (cannot or will not share materials, take turns in play, class games etc. May disrupt activity of others or may be afraid of other children) — 3
30. Please rate the child's general degree of self-reliance in class activities as follows:	**Col. 53** very self-reliant (often carries out activities without asking much help from teacher) — 1 fairly self-reliant (can carry out activities on own, but quite ready to ask teacher to help) — 2 lacking in self-reliance (cannot keep up activity for long without approaching teacher for help/reassurance) — 3

		Please ring appropriate number

H. *Emotional Adjustment*

31. Is the child:

		Col. 54
(a) aggressive toward other children?	not at all	1
	sometimes	2
	usually	3

Please give details if applicable:_____

_____

_____

		Col. 55
(b) nervous or fearful?	not at all	1
	sometimes	2
Please give details if applicable:_____	usually	3

_____

_____

		Col. 56
(c) restless or overactive?	not at all	1
Please give details if applicable:_____	sometimes	2
	usually	3

_____

_____

		Col. 57
32. Has child wet him/herself during the school day, *excluding the first ten days of schooling?*	not at all	1
	on one or two separate days	2
	on three or more separate days	3

		Col. 58
33. Has child soiled him/herself during the school day, *excluding the first ten days of schooling?*	not at all	1
	on one or two separate days	2
	on three or more separate days	3

		Col. 59
34. Has child been sick during school day, *excluding the first ten days of schooling?*	not at all	1
	on one or two separate days	2
	on three or more separate days	3

		Please ring appropriate number

		Col. 60
35. What is child's normal state of alertness during school day?	very wide awake and alert	1
	fairly wide awake and alert	2
	tired or rather apathetic, listless or dreamy	3

		Col. 61
36. Has the child shown any signs of unusual or difficult behaviour not mentioned above?	Yes	1
	No	2

If Yes, please give details:_____

_____

_____

_____

I. *Miscellaneous*

		Col. 62
37. Does the child:	Yes	1
(a) wear glasses?	No	2

		Col. 63
(b) wear a hearing aid?	Yes	1
	No	2

		Col. 64
38. Does child suffer from frequent heavy colds/catarrh?	Yes	1
	No	2

		Col. 65
39. (a) Have you suspected that child may have an uncorrected physical handicap or defect? (e.g. of vision or hearing)	Yes	1
	No	2

(b)   If Yes, please give details:_____

_____

_____

_____

			Col. 66

40. Does the child suffer from poor general health?

      Yes   1
      No   2

    If Yes, please give details:_____

_____

_____

Col. 67

41. (a) Have you suspected any intellectual handicap in the child?

      Yes   1
      No   2

  (b) If Yes, please give details:_____

_____

_____

42. Please comment on any features concerning child not recorded in above Schedule:

_____

_____

_____

STRICTLY CONFIDENTIAL

SCHOOLS COUNCIL RESEARCH AND DEVELOPMENT PROJECT IN COMPENSATORY EDUCATION

Units for Emotional Development and Response to Schooling

School Schedule No. 3

To be completed by the child's class teacher

Leave Blank	Data Block No.			School and Area No.			Child's No.			Sub-categories			
	1	0	3										

Cols. 1   2 3 4   5 6 7   8 9 10   11 12 13 14

Name of class teacher: _____

Date of completing this schedule _____

Child's Name: *Surname*_____

                 *Christian name(s)*_____

Note to Class Teacher

Please ring the number on the extreme right hand column opposite the appropriate answer in each question, unless you are requested to do otherwise. *Only one* number per question should be circled.

  We would like to stress that the items of behaviour or achievement included in this and other schedules in no way represent standards or levels to be expected of children of this age. We are simply trying to build up an objective picture of each child in his school setting at given stages in his career, and the items in these schedules are intended to do this.

  In question 11 you may not at this stage be looking for indications of the children's knowledge of letter sounds and, for this situation, we have provided a 'not observed' category.

  In question 12 you may not have had the opportunity to observe evidence of understanding of stories in each of your children and so, again, a 'not observed' category is provided.

SECTION A.   SOCIAL AND EMOTIONAL ADJUSTMENT

<table>
<tr><td></td><td></td><td></td><td>Please ring appropriate No.</td></tr>
<tr><td></td><td></td><td></td><td>Col. 15</td></tr>
<tr><td>1.</td><td>Is the child's behaviour such as you would expect of a normal alert child of his/her age?

Please comment if desired:_____</td><td>Yes
No</td><td>1
2</td></tr>
<tr><td></td><td></td><td></td><td>Col. 16</td></tr>
<tr><td>2.</td><td>Is the child exceptionally quiet, timid or withdrawn?

Please comment if desired:_____</td><td>Yes
No</td><td>1
2</td></tr>
<tr><td></td><td></td><td></td><td>Col. 17</td></tr>
<tr><td>3.</td><td>Is the child restless in a way that seriously hinders his/her learning?

Please comment if desired:_____</td><td>Yes
No</td><td>1
2</td></tr>
</table>

		Please ring appropriate number
		Col. 18
4. Is the child very aggressive?	Yes	1
	No	2
Please comment if desired:_____		
		Col. 19
5. Does the child get on well with other children?	Yes	1
	No	2
Please comment if desired:_____		
		Col. 20
6. Is there anything in the child's behaviour to make you think that he might be emotionally unstable or suffer from nervous trouble?	Yes	1
	No	2
Please comment if desired:_____		

7. Below are descriptions of four levels of adjustment, numbered 1, 2, 3 and 4. Please classify the child you are assessing by circling the number which best describes the child's adjustment:

Col. 21

1. *Well adjusted:* a child who is well adjusted in his relationship with others and in his activities   1
2. *No significant problems:* a child who gets on reasonably well, and has little or no difficulty in adjusting to others or to classroom activities   2
3. *Somewhat disturbed:* a child who has moderate difficulties in adjusting, and to whom growing up represents something of a struggle   3
4. *Very disturbed:* a child who has, or at his present rate is likely to have, serious problems of adjustment and needs specialist help *because of such problems*   4

		Col. 22
8. Now please indicate the degree of confidence you feel in your assessment of the child's level of adjustment by circling one of the following:	very confident	1
	fairly confident	2
	not very confident	3

		Col. 23
9. (a) Please rate the child's level of pre-reading/reading as follows:	on pre-reading activities only	1
	on introductory book of reading scheme	2
	on Book 1 of reading scheme	3
	on Book 2 of reading scheme	4
	on Book 3 of reading scheme	5
	on Book 4 of reading scheme, or beyond	6
	not applicable, i.e. no basic reading scheme used	7
(b) If *no* basic reading scheme is used in the class, please tick the word which best describes the child's progress in reading activities and comment if desired. _____ _____	good average slow	
		Col. 24
10. How well can the child: (a) match words to words?	easily and efficiently	1
	quite efficiently on whole (may have some difficulties/ make some errors)	2
	poorly/unable to do so yet	3
		Col. 25
(b) match words to pictures?	easily and efficiently	1
	quite efficiently etc.	2
	poorly/unable to do so yet	3

	Please ring appropriate number

	Col. 26
(c) trace words written by the teacher?	
easily and efficiently	1
quite efficiently etc.	2
poorly/unable to do so yet	3

	Col. 27
(d) copy words written by the teacher?	
easily and efficiently	1
quite efficiently etc.	2
poorly/unable to do so yet	3

	Col. 28
(e) write his name?	
easily and efficiently	1
quite efficiently on whole (may have some difficulties/ make some errors	2
poorly/unable to do so yet	3

	Col. 29
(f) write words unaided (regardless of spelling), i.e. in attempts at 'free writing'?	
easily and efficiently	1
quite efficiently on whole etc.	2
poorly/unable to do so yet	3

	Col. 30
11. How well does the child know the letter *sounds*?	
very well (knows all or most)	1
quite well	2
very little or no knowledge	3
not observed	4

	Col. 31
12. How well does the child understand stories he has heard?	
very well	1
quite well	2
poorly	3
not observed	4

430

		Please ring appropriate number

PLEASE ANSWER *EITHER* QUESTION 13 *OR* QUESTION 14 AS APPLICABLE:

13. If the child is now *'reading'*

(a) What is the range of his/her sight vocabulary?

	Col. 32
wide; recognizes many words at sight	1
adequate; has working sight vocabulary	2
limited; recognizes rather few words at sight	3

(b) What is his/her general level of interest in reading?

	Col. 33
very keen interest	1
fairly keen interest	2
little/no interest	3

14. If the child is *engaged wholly on pre-reading activities* (i.e. rated 1 in Question 9):

(a) Can he/she recognize his/her own name?

	Col. 34
Yes	1
No	2

(b) Can he/she recognize single words/phrases, e.g. classroom labels, captions to pictures etc.?

	Col. 35
ten words or more	1
up to ten words	2
none	3

(c) How well can he/she match shapes or pictures?

	Col. 36
easily and efficiently	1
quite efficiently on whole (may have some difficulty/make some errors)	2
poorly/unable to do so yet	3

(d) What is his/her level of interest in looking at picture/story books?

	Col. 37
very keen interest	1
quite keen interest	2
little/no interest	3

431

		Please ring appropriate number
		Col. 38
(e) Please rate the child's overall level of reading readiness:	ready for introduction to reading scheme	1
	needs more pre-reading experience	2
	unready — needs great deal more pre-reading experience	3

Any special comment on child's progress or adjustment this term:

_____

_____

_____

STRICTLY CONFIDENTIAL

SCHOOLS COUNCIL RESEARCH AND DEVELOPMENT PROJECT IN COMPENSATORY EDUCATION

Units for Emotional Development and Response to Schooling

School Schedule No. 4

To be completed by the child's class teacher

Leave Blank	Data Block No.			School and Area No.			Child's No.		Sub-categories				
	1	0	4										

Cols. 1   2   3   4   5   6   7   8   9   10   11   12   13   14

Name of class teacher: _____

Date of completing this schedule: _____

Child's Name: *Surname*_____

                      *Christian name(s)*_____

Note to Class Teacher
Please ring the number on the extreme right hand column opposite the appropriate answer in each question, unless you are requested to do otherwise. *Only one* number per question should be circled.

We would like to stress that the items of behaviour or achievement included in this and other schedules in no way represent standards or levels to be expected of children of this age. We are simply trying to build up an objective picture of each child in his school setting at given stages in his career, and the items in these schedules are intended to do this.

In question 8 you may not at this stage be looking for indications of the children's knowledge of letter sounds and, for this situation, we have provided a 'not observed' category.

In question 9 you may not have the opportunity to observe evidence of understanding of stories in each of your children and so, again, a 'not observed' category is provided.

In question 16 the children may not yet be engaged on written 'sums', so we have provided a 'not observed/no opportunity' category.

SECTION A. — GENERAL

		Please ring appropriate number
1. How would you rate the child's overall adjustment to school this term?	very good (child seems very happy and settled)	Col. 15 1
	quite good (has settled in quite well and seems happy on whole)	2
	poor (seems unhappy, unsettled or otherwise ill-adjusted to school)	3
2. Please rate the child's general level of co-operation with other children:	very co-operative (usually quite willing and able to co-operate well, e.g. take on roles in dramatic play, take share of responsibility in group activity)	Col. 16 1
	fairly co-operative (achieves simpler form of co-operation only, e.g. sharing materials, taking turns, taking part in simple class games etc.)	2
	unco-operative (cannot or will not share materials, take turns in play, class games etc. May disrupt activity of others or may be afraid of other children)	3

433

	Please ring appropriate number

3. (a) How would you rate the child's relationship with you, the class teacher?

	Col. 17
very positive (very friendly or responsive)	1
positive (friendly or responsive on whole)	2
uncertain or negative (shy, withdrawn/ hostile)	3

(b) If uncertain or negative, please state whether child is:

Comment:_____

_____

_____

	Col. 18
shy (but would like to be friendly)	1
withdrawn or indifferent (difficult to make contact with)	2
hostile (aggressive, truculent)	3

4. Please rate the child's usual level of concentration in activities of a more structured kind (reading and number etc.)

	Col. 19
usually concentrates very well for quite long periods; ignores distractions	1
varies, but can concentrate quite well if interested	2
usually lacks concentration, e.g. concentrates for few minutes only, easily distracted etc.	3

5. Please rate the child's use of play materials as follows:

	Col. 20
play usually leads to end product (e.g. model or painting) or successful completion of activity	1
play sometimes leads to end product/ successful completion of activity	2
play rarely or never leads to end product/ successful completion of activity (e.g. repetitive manipulative play)	3

SECTION B. – PRE-READING, READING, AND LANGUAGE
        ACTIVITIES

			Col. 21
6.	(a)	Please rate the child's level of pre-reading/reading as follows:	on pre-reading activities only	1
			on introductory book of reading scheme	2
			on Book 1 of reading scheme	3
			on Book 2 of reading scheme	4
			on Book 3 of reading scheme	5
			on Book 4 of reading scheme or beyond	6
			not applicable, i.e. no basic reading scheme used	7

				Col. 22
	(b)	*If no basic reading scheme is used* in the class, please rate the child's progress in reading activities and comment if desired	Good	1
			Average	2
			Slow	3

_____

_____

				Col. 23
7.		How well can the child:	easily and efficiently	1
	(a)	match words to words?	quite efficiently on whole (may have some difficulties/ make some errors)	2
			poorly/unable to do so yet	3

				Col. 24
	(b)	match words to pictures?	easily and efficiently	1
			quite efficiently on whole etc.	2
			poorly/unable to do so yet	3

				Col. 25
	(c)	trace words written by the teacher?	easily and efficiently	1
			quite efficiently on whole etc.	2
			poorly/unable to do so yet	3

(d) copy words written by the teacher?	easily and efficiently	Col. 26
	quite efficiently on whole etc.	1 2
	poorly/unable to do so yet	3
(e) write his name?	easily and efficiently	Col. 27 1
	quite efficiently on whole etc.	2
	poorly/unable to do so yet	3
(f) write words unaided (regardless of spelling), i.e. in attempts at 'free writing'?	easily and efficiently	Col. 28 1
	quite efficiently on whole (may have some difficulties/ make some errors)	2
	poorly/unable to do so yet	3
8. How well does the child know the letter *sounds*?	very well (knows all or most)	Col. 29 1
	quite well	2
	very little or no knowledge	3
	not observed	4
9. How well does the child understand stories he has heard?	very well	Col. 30 1
	quite well	2
	poorly	3
	not observed	4
PLEASE ANSWER *EITHER* QUESTION 10 *OR* QUESTION 11 AS APPLICABLE. THEN GO ON TO QUESTION 12.		Col. 31
10. If the child is now '*reading*':		
(a) what is the range of his/her sight vocabulary?	wide; recognizes many words at sight	1
	adequate; has working sight vocabulary	2
	limited; recognizes rather few words at sight	3

		Please ring appropriate number
		Col. 32
(b) what is his/her general level of interest in reading?	very keen interest fairly keen interest little/no interest	1 2 3
11. If the child is *engaged wholly on pre-reading activities* (i.e. rated 1 in Question 6):		Col. 33
(a) can he/she recognize his/her own name?	Yes No	1 2
		Col. 34
(b) Can he/she recognize single words/phrases, e.g. classroom labels, captions to pictures etc.?	ten words or more up to ten words none	1 2 3
		Col. 35
(c) how well can he/she match shapes or pictures?	easily and efficiently quite efficiently on whole (may have some difficulty/make some errors) poorly/unable to do so yet	1 2 3
		Col. 36
(d) what is his/her level of interest in looking at picture/ story books?	very keen interest quite keen interest little/no interest	1 2 3
		Col. 37
(e) please rate the child's overall level of reading readiness:	ready for introduction to reading scheme needs more pre-reading experience unready — needs great deal more pre-reading experience	1 2 3
		Col. 38
12. Please rate the child's power of oral expression, e.g. in re-telling stories, relating experiences etc.	very fluent and articulate — easy command of language can express him/ herself adequately power of expression poor — child cannot communicate adequately	1 2 3

SECTION C. — MATHEMATICAL ACTIVITIES

		Col. 39
13. Can the child count correctly the number of objects in a group presented to him?	beyond 10 objects	1
	6 to 10 objects	2
	2 to 5 objects	3
	not at all	4

		Col. 40
14. Can the child give you a specified number of objects correctly from a larger group presented to him?	beyond 10 objects	1
	6 to 10 objects	2
	2 to 5 objects	3
	not at all	4

		Col. 41
15. Can the child match the written number symbol to the corresponding number of objects?	beyond 10 objects	1
	6 to 10 objects	2
	2 to 5 objects	3
	not at all	4

		Col. 42
16. Can the child carry out simple addition sums, i.e. involving the written number symbol (with help of counting aids if needed)?	adds numbers totalling 10 or more	1
	adds numbers with total up to 9	2
	unable to do so yet	3
	not observed/no opportunity yet	4

		Col. 43
17. What is the child's general level of interest in mathematical activities?	very keen interest	1
	fairly keen interest	2
	little/no interest	3

18. Any special comment on child's school progress this term?

_____

_____

_____

_____

19. Any special comment on child's school adjustment this term?

_____

_____

_____

_____

STRICTLY CONFIDENTIAL

SCHOOLS COUNCIL RESEARCH AND DEVELOPMENT PROJECT IN COMPENSATORY EDUCATION

Units for Emotional Development and Response to Schooling

School Schedule No. 5

To be completed by the child's class teacher

Leave Blank	Data Block No.			School and Area No.			Child's No.		Sub-categories				
	1	0	5										

Cols. 1   2   3   4   5   6   7   8   9   10   11   12   13   14

Name of class teacher: _____

Date of completing this schedule _____

Child's Name: *Surname* _____

                   Christian name(s) _____

Note to Class Teacher
Please ring the number on the extreme right hand column opposite the appropriate answer in each question, unless you are requested to do otherwise. *Only one* number per question should be circled.

We would like to stress that the items of behaviour or achievement included in this and other schedules in no way represent standards or levels to be expected of children of this age. We are simply trying to build up an objective picture of each child in his school setting at given stages in his career, and the items in these schedules are intended to do this.

In question 10 you may not have had the opportunity to observe evidence of understanding of stories in each of your children and so, a 'not observed' category is provided.

In question 15(c) you may not at this stage be looking for indications of the child en's ability to build words phonically and, for this situation, we have provided a 'not observed'/'no opportunity' category.

In question 19 the children may not yet be engaged on written 'sums', so we have provided a 'not observed'/'no opportunity' category.

	Please ring appropriate No.

SECTION A — GENERAL

		Col. 15
1.	Below are descriptions of four levels of adjustment, numbered 1, 2, 3 and 4. Please classify the child you are assessing by circling the number which best describes the child's adjustment:	
	1. *Well adjusted:* a child who is well adjusted in his relationship with others and in his activities	1
	2. *No significant problems:* a child who gets on reasonably well, and has little or no difficulty in adjusting to others or to classroom activities	2
	3. *Somewhat disturbed:* a child who has moderate difficulties in adjusting, and to whom growing up represents something of a struggle	3
	4. *Very disturbed:* a child who has, or at his present rate is likely to have, serious problems of adjustment and needs specialist help *because of such problems*	4

			Col. 16
2.	Please rate the child's general level of co-operation with other children:	very co-operative (usually willing and able to co-operate well, e.g. take on roles in dramatic play, take share of responsibility in group activity)	1
		fairly co-operative (achieves simpler form of co-operation only, e.g. sharing materials, taking turns, taking part in simple class games etc.)	2
		unco-operative (cannot or will not share materials, take turns in play, class games etc. May disrupt activity of others or may be afraid of other children)	3

440

		Please ring appropriate No.
3. (a) How would you rate the child's relationship with you, the class teacher?	very positive (very friendly or responsive) positive (friendly or responsive on whole) uncertain or negative (shy, withdrawn/ hostile)	Col. 17 1 2 3
(b) If uncertain or negative, please state whether child is: Comment_____ _____ _____	shy (but would like to be friendly) withdrawn or indifferent (difficult to make contact with) hostile (aggressive, truculent)	Col. 18 1 2 3
4. Please rate the child's usual level of concentration in activities of a more structured kind (reading and number etc.):	usually concentrates very well for quite long periods; ignores distractions varies, but can concentrate quite well if interested usually lacks concentration, e.g., concentrates for few minutes only, easily distracted etc.	Col. 19 1 2 3
5. Please rate the child's use of play materials as follows:	play usually leads to end product (e.g. model or painting) or successful completion of activity play sometimes leads to end product or successful completion of activity	Col. 20 1 2

	Please ring appropriate number

6. Please rate the quality of the child's creative activities e.g. free writing, story telling, handwork, painting, dramatic work:

		Col. 21
	often shows imagination/originality in some or all of these areas	1
	sometimes shows imagination/orig. in some or all of these areas	2
	rarely/never shows imag./orig. in any area	3

SECTION B — ORAL LANGUAGE SKILLS

7. Please rate the child's power of oral expression, e.g. in re-telling stories, relating experiences etc.:

		Col. 22
	very fluent and articulate — easy command of language	1
	can express him/herself adequately	2
	power of expression poor — child cannot communicate adequately	3

8. Please rate the quality of the child's speech articulation:

		Col. 23
	very clear, precise and well articulated	1
	quite clear on whole but may show some faulty enunciation	2
	difficult to understand because of marked immaturity, poor enunciation or over-rapid speech	3

9. Please rate the range of the child's vocabulary in oral language:

		Col. 24
	wide vocabulary for age — rich variety of words	1
	adequate vocabulary for age	2
	poor, very restricted vocabulary — repetitive use of words	3

		Please ring appropriate number
		Col. 25
10. How well does the child understand stories he has heard?	very well	1
	quite well	2
	poorly	3
	not observed	4

		Col. 26
11. How well does the child follow oral instructions?	very well—instructions carried out accurately and efficiently	1
	quite well — may make some errors or need instructions repeated sometimes	2
	poorly — frequently makes errors or gets confused or often needs instructions repeated	3

SECTION C — PRE-READING, READING AND WRITTEN LANGUAGE ACTIVITIES

		Col. 27
12. (a) Please rate the child's level of pre-reading/reading as follows:	on pre-reading activities only	1
	on introductory book of reading scheme	2
	on Book 1 of reading scheme	3
	on Book 2 of reading scheme	4
	on Book 3 of reading scheme	5
	on Book 4 of reading scheme or beyond	6
	beyond basic reading scheme	7
	not applicable, i.e. no basic reading scheme used	8

		Please ring appropriate number

<table>
<tbody>
<tr><td>(b) If no basic reading scheme is used in the class, please rate the child's progress in reading activities and comment if desired:</td><td>Good
Average
Slow</td><td>Col. 28
1
2
3</td></tr>
<tr><td>_____
_____</td><td></td><td></td></tr>
<tr><td>13. How well can the child copy words written by the teacher?</td><td>easily and efficiently
quite efficiently on whole; may have some difficulties/make some errors
poorly/unable to do so yet</td><td>Col. 29
1
2

3</td></tr>
<tr><td>14. How well can the child write words unaided in 'free writing,' regardless of spelling?</td><td>easily and efficiently
quite efficiently on whole; may have some difficulties/make some errors
poorly/unable to do so yet</td><td>Col. 30
1
2

3</td></tr>
<tr><td>PLEASE ANSWER *EITHER* QUESTION 15 *OR* QUESTION 16 AS APPLICABLE
15. If the child is now '*reading*' (i.e. rated 2 or beyond in Question 12a)

(a) what is the range of his/her sight vocabulary?</td><td>

wide; recognizes many words at sight
adequate; has working sight vocabulary
limited; recognizes rather few words at sight</td><td>Col. 31

1

2

3</td></tr>
<tr><td>(b) How well does the child comprehend when he reads?</td><td>comprehends very well
comprehends quite well
poor, very limited comprehension</td><td>Col. 32
1
2

3</td></tr>
</tbody>
</table>

		Please ring appropriate number
		Col. 33
(c) Please rate the child's ability to build up words	very proficient — can build most phonically regular words	1
	fairly proficient — can build easier words	2
	little or no proficiency	3
	not observed/no opportunity yet	4
		Col. 34
(d) What is his/her general level of interest in reading?	very keen interest	1
	fairly keen interest	2
	little/no interest	3
		Col. 35
16. If the child is engaged wholly on pre-reading activities (i.e. rated 1 in Question 12a)	Yes	1
	No	2
(a) Can he/she recognize his/her own name?		
		Col. 36
(b) Can he/she recognize single words/phrases, e.g. classroom labels, captions to pictures etc.?	ten words or more	1
	up to ten words	2
	none	3
		Col. 37
(c) How well can he/she match shapes, pictures or words?	easily and efficiently	1
	quite efficiently on whole (may have some difficulty/make some errors)	2
	poorly/unable to do so yet	3
		Col. 38
(d) What is his/her level of interest in looking at picture/ story books?	very keen interest	1
	quite keen interest	2
	little/no interest	3
		Col. 39
(e) Please rate the child's overall level of reading readiness:	ready for introduction to reading scheme	1
	needs more pre-reading experience	2
	unready — needs great deal more pre-reading experience	3

17. Can the child count correctly the number of objects in a group presented to him?

	Col. 40
beyond 20 objects	1
11 to 20 objects	2
2 to 10 objects	3
not at all	4

18. Can the child match the written number symbol to the corresponding number of objects?

	Col. 41
beyond 20 objects	1
11 to 20 objects	2
2 to 10 objects	3
not at all	4

19. Can the child carry out simple addition sums, i.e. involving the written number symbol (with help of counting aids if needed)?

	Col. 42
adds numbers totalling more than 20	1
adds numbers totalling up to 20	2
adds numbers totalling up to 10	3
unable to do so yet	4
no opportunity yet	5

20. How much use does the child make of counting aids (e.g. counters) in computational work?

	Col. 43
no longer/only occasionally needs or uses them	1
needs or uses them quite often	2
needs or uses them nearly always/always	3

21. How well can the child tell the time?

	Col. 44
tells time to within 5 minutes	1
tells time to within quarter of an hour	2
tells time to within half-an-hour	3
knows hours only	4
not at all	5

	Please ring appropriate number

		Col. 45
22. Please rate the child's ability to handle money in simple classroom shopping activities:	very proficient — can handle amounts over 2/- (10p)	1
	fairly proficient	2
	can handle pennies only	3
	no knowledge of money	4

		Col. 46
23. Please rate the level of the child's general understanding of basic number concepts:	good	1
	adequate	2
	poor — little or no grasp	3

		Col. 47
24. What is the child's general level of interest in mathematical activities?	very keen interest	1
	fairly keen interest	2
	little/no interest	3

25. Any special comment on child's school progress this term?

_____

_____

_____

_____

26. Any special comment on child's school adjustment this term?

_____

_____

_____

_____

SCHOOLS COUNCIL RESEARCH AND DEVELOPMENT PROJECT IN COMPENSATORY EDUCATION

Units for Emotional Development and Response to Schooling

School Schedule No. 6

To be completed by the child's class teacher

Leave Blank	Data Block No.			School and Area No.			Child's No.		Sub-categories				
	1	0	6										

Cols. 1   2   3   4   5   6   7   8   9   10   11   12   13   14

Name of class teacher: _____

Date of completing this schedule _____

Child's Name: *Surname* _____

Christian name(s) _____

Note to Class Teacher

Please ring the number on the extreme right hand column opposite the appropriate answer in each question, unless you are requested to do otherwise. *Only one* number per question should be circled.

We would like to stress that the items of behaviour or achievement included in this and other schedules in no way represent standards or levels to be expected of children of this age. We are simply trying to build up an objective picture of each child in his school setting at given stages in his career, and the items in these schedules are intended to do this.

In question 16 you may have had no opportunity to observe evidence of understanding of stories in each of your children and so a 'not observed' category is provided

Question 31 (parental contact with school) is intended for the Headteacher in consultation if necessary with the class teacher.

		Please ring appropriate number
SECTION A – GENERAL		Col. 15
1. Is the child's behaviour such as you would expect of a normal alert child of his/her age?	Yes No	1 2
Please comment if desired:_____		

448

		Please ring appropriate number
2. Is the child exceptionally quiet, timid or withdrawn? Please comment if desired:_____ _____	Yes No	**Col. 16** 1 2
3. Is the child restless in a way that seriously hinders his/her learning? Please comment if desired:_____ _____	Yes No	**Col. 17** 1 2
4. Is the child very aggressive? Please comment if desired:_____ _____	Yes No	**Col. 18** 1 2
5. Does the child get on well with other children? Please comment if desired:_____ _____	Yes No	**Col. 19** 1 2
6. Is there anything in the child's behaviour to make you think that he might be emotionally unstable or suffer from nervous troubles? Please comment if desired:_____ _____	Yes No	**Col. 20** 1 2

	Please ring appropriate number
	Col. 21

7. Below are descriptions of four levels of adjustment, numbered 1, 2, 3, and 4. Please classify the child you are assessing by circling the number which best describes the child's adjustment:

1. *Well adjusted:* a child who is well adjusted in his relationship with others and in his activities

2. *No significant problems:* a child who gets on reasonably well, and has little or no difficulty in adjusting to others or to classroom activities

3. *Somewhat disturbed:* a child who has moderate difficulties in adjusting, and to whom growing up represents something of a struggle

4. *Very disturbed:* a child who has, or at his present rate is likely to have, serious problems of adjustment and needs specialist help *because of such problems*

Level	Number
1	1
2	2
3	3
4	4

8. Please rate the child's general level of co-operation with other children:

Description	Col. 22
very co-operative (usually willing and able to co-operate well, e.g. take on roles in dramatic play, take share of responsibility in group activity)	1
fairly co-operative (achieves simpler form of co-operation only, e.g., sharing materials, taking turns, taking part in simple class games etc.)	2
unco-operative (cannot or will not share materials, take turns in play, class games etc. May disrupt activity of others or may be afraid of other children)	3

450

	Please ring appropriate number

	Col. 23
9. (a) How would you rate the child's relationship with you, the class teacher?	very positive (very friendly or responsive) — 1
	positive (friendly or responsive on whole) — 2
	uncertain or negative (shy, withdrawn/ hostile) — 3

	Col. 24
(b) If uncertain or negative, please state whether child is: Comment_____ _____ _____	shy (but would like to be friendly) — 1
	withdrawn or indifferent (difficult to make contact with) — 2
	hostile (aggressive, truculent) — 3

	Col. 25
10. Please rate the child's usual level of concentration in activities of a more structured kind (reading and number etc.)	usually concentrates very well for quite long periods; ignores distractions — 1
	varies, but can concentrate quite well if interested — 2
	usually lacks concentration, e.g. concentrates for a few minutes only, easily distracted etc. — 3

	Col. 26
11. Please rate the child's use of play materials as follows:	play usually leads to end product (e.g. model or painting) or successful completion of activity — 1
	play sometimes leads to end product/ successful completion of activity — 2
	play rarely or never leads to end product/ successful completion of activity — 3

		Please ring appropriate number

12. Please rate the quality of the child's creative activities e.g. free writing, story telling, handwork, painting, dramatic work:

	Col. 27
often shows imag-ination/originality in some or all of these areas	1
sometimes shows imagination/orig. in some or all of these areas	2
rarely/never shows imag./orig. in any area	3

SECTION B — ORAL LANGUAGE SKILLS

13. Please rate the child's power of oral expression, e.g. in re-telling stories, relating experiences etc.:

	Col. 28
very fluent and articulate — easy command of language	1
can express him/herself adequately	2
power of expression poor — child cannot communicate adequately	3

14. Please rate the quality of the child's speech articulation:

	Col. 29
very clear, precise and well articulated	1
quite clear on whole but may show some faulty enunciation	2
difficult to under-stand because of marked immaturity, poor enunciation or over-rapid speech	3

15. Please rate the range of the child's vocabulary in oral language:

	Col. 30
wide vocabulary for age — rich variety of words	1
adequate vocabulary for age	2
poor, very restricted vocabulary — repetit-ive use of words	3

		Please ring appropriate number
		Col. 31
16. How well does the child understand stories he has heard?	very well	1
	quite well	2
	poorly	3
	not observed	4
		Col. 32
17. How well does the child follow oral instructions?	very well — instructions carried out accurately and efficiently	1
	quite well — may make some errors or need instructions repeated sometimes	2
	poorly — frequently makes errors or gets confused or often needs instructions repeated	3

SECTION C — PRE-READING, READING AND WRITTEN LANGUAGE ACTIVITIES

			Col. 33
18.	(a)	Please rate the child's level of pre-reading/reading as follows:	
		on pre-reading activities only	1
		on introductory book of reading scheme	2
		on book 1 of reading scheme	3
		on book 2 of reading scheme	4
		on book 3 of reading scheme	5
		on book 4 of reading scheme or beyond	6
		beyond basic reading scheme	7
		not applicable, i.e. no basic reading scheme used	8

(b) If no basic reading scheme is used in the class, please rate the child's progress in reading activities and comment if desired:

		Col. 34
	Good	1
	Average	2
	Slow	3

_____

_____

19. Please rate the quality of the child's sentence construction in his/her free writing:

		Col. 35
	very well constructed sentences with good variety of sentence patterns	1
	adequately constructed sentences but with less variety of sentence patterns	2
	sentences generally complete and correctly constructed but very short, simple and repetitive in pattern	3
	sentences very poorly constructed or incomplete, e.g. missing out subject or verb	4

20. If the child is now 'reading' (i.e. rated 2 or beyond in Question 18a)

(a) What is the range of his/her sight vocabulary?

		Col. 36
	wide; recognizes many words at sight	1
	adequate; has working sight vocabulary	2
	limited; recognizes rather few words at sight	3

(b) How well does the child comprehend when he reads?

		Col. 37
	comprehends very well	1
	comprehends quite well	2
	poor, very limited comprehension	3

		Col. 38
(c)	Please rate the child's ability to build up words phonically:	very proficient — can build most phonically regular words — 1 fairly proficient — can build easier words — 2 little or no proficiency — 3
		Col. 39
(d)	What is his/her general level of interest in reading?	very keen interest — 1 fairly keen interest — 2 little/no interest — 3

N.B. If the child is still on pre-reading activities (i.e. rated 1 only in Qu. 18a) omit the above question.

SECTION D — MATHEMATICS

		Col. 40
21.	Can the child match the written number symbol to the corresponding number of objects?	beyond 20 objects — 1 11 to 20 objects — 2 2 to 10 objects — 3 not at all — 4
		Col. 41
22.	Can the child carry out simple addition sums, i.e. involving the written number symbol (with help of counting aids if needed)?	adds numbers totalling more than 20 — 1 adds numbers totalling up to 20 — 2 adds numbers totalling up to 10 — 3 unable to do so yet — 4
		Col. 42
23.	How much use does the child make of counting aids (e.g. counters) in computational work?	no longer/only occasionally needs or uses them — 1 needs or uses them quite often — 2 needs or uses them nearly always/always — 3

		Please ring appropriate number

24. How well can the child tell the time?

	Col. 43
tells time to within 5 minutes	1
tells time to within quarter of an hour	2
tells time to within half-an-hour	3
knows hours only	4
not at all	5

25. Please note the child's ability to handle money in simple classroom shopping activities:

	Col. 44
very proficient — can handle amounts over 50 pence	1
fairly proficient	2
can handle one pence coins only	3
no knowledge of money	4

26. Please rate the level of the child's general understanding of basic number concepts:

	Col. 45
good	1
adequate	2
poor — little or no grasp	3

27. What is the child's general level of interest in mathematical activities?

	Col. 46
very keen interest	1
fairly keen interest	2
little/no interest	3

28. (a) How well do you anticipate that the child will progress in the Junior school/department?

	Col. 47
no problems anticipated, should make satisfactory or good progress	1
may have some initial difficulties but should make satisfactory progress on whole	2
will almost certainly find difficulty	3

456

	Please ring appropriate number
	Col. 48
(b) If child will find difficulty (rated 3 above) please indicate the reason as follows:	immaturity of personality — 1
	behaviour difficulties — 2
Please comment if desired:_____	low level of basic attainments — 3
_____	some combination of above — 4

29. Any special comment on child's school progress this term?

_____

_____

_____

_____

30. Any special comment on child's school adjustment this term?

_____

_____

_____

_____

FOR COMPLETION BY HEADTEACHER

	Col. 49
31. Please rate the school contact with and co-operation of the child's parents as follows:	
(a) *Frequency of contact* (Contact includes speaking to teacher, attending concerts, Open Days, etc. but *not* just bringing or collecting child.) mother (or mother substitute)	several times — 1
	once or twice — 2
	never (except for admission) — 3
	no mother/mother substitute — 4

		Please ring appropriate number
		Col. 50
father (or father substitute)	several times	1
	once or twice	2
	never (except for admission)	3
	no father/father substitute	4
		Col. 51
(b) Level of co-operation of parent(s):	keen interest in school activities; gives encouragement and constructive help to child	1
	over-keen interest, i.e. over-anxious parent who pushes child in way that may impair his progress	2
Please comment if desired: _____	interested, but does not have much idea about the best way to help, e.g. uses methods conflicting with those of school, or simply lacks ideas	3
_____	passive attitude; no hostility but expects child to learn at school without any help or encouragement from home	4
_____	hostile, critical of school, may come only to complain	5
	not sufficient contact to assess	6

SCHOOLS COUNCIL RESEARCH AND DEVELOPMENT PROJECT IN COMPENSATORY EDUCATION

Home Interview — Rural Areas

Leave Blank	Data block No.	School and Area No.	Child's No.	Sex	Pre-School	Blank

A.

       Christian name   Surname   Sex

1. Name of child _____ _____ _____

2. Address_____

3. School child attends_____

4. Ordinal position of child_____

5. (a) No. of children in family_____ (b) No. dependent_____

      1   2   3   4   5
6. Is he: your own child / adopted / foster / grandchild / other

                        1   2   3   4   5
7. (a) Is child's father alive and living with family? Yes / dead / divorced / separated / other
    (b) Is child's mother alive and living with family? Yes / dead / divorced / separated / other

               1   2   3
8. Nationality of mother: British / Other, Eng. speaking / Other, non-Eng. speaking

               1   2   3
9. Nationality of father: British / Other, Eng. speaking / Other, non-Eng. speaking

                            1   2
10. If not English: Normal tongue of mother _____ Always / mixed with English

                            1   2
11. If not English: Normal tongue of father _____ Always / mixed with English

12. If child not with own parents is child:

    1   2   3   4
  British / Other / Other / D.K. _____
        white coloured

B. HOME

13. Type of house:
    1. detached house
    2. bungalow
    3. semi-detached house
    4. terrace
    5. pre-fab
    6. s. cont. flat in block
    7. s. cont. flat in house
    8. cottage
    9. hut
    10. rooms
    11. caravan
    12. other

14. Tenure:
    1. owner occupier
    2. rented from Council
    3. rented unfurnished
    4. rented furnished
    5. provided with job (details)_____

    _____

    6. Other (details)_____

    _____

15.   No. of rooms_____

| | 1 | 2 | 3 | 4 |
16. State of repair of home: good/fair/poor/bad

| | 1 | 2 | 3 |
17. Do you have: separate kitchen: own/shared/none

| | 1 | 2 | 3 |
18.   bathroom   own/shared/none

| | 1 | 2 | 3 |
19.   WC inside   own/shared/none

| | 1 | 2 | 3 |
20.   WC outside   own/shared/none

| | 1 | 2 | 3 |
21.   hot water tap   own/shared/none

| | 1 | 2 |
22.   mains gas   Yes/No

| | 1 | 2 |
23.   mains electricity   Yes/No

| | 1 | 2 |
24. Is there a yard or garden for play?   Yes/No

| | 1 | 2 | 3 |
25. Is it safe?   Yes/Yes, if supervised/No

26. Does child have his own bedroom?   1 2
                                        Yes/No

27. Does child have his own bed?   1 2
                                    Yes/No

28. Does anyone else besides mother, father and children live here?   1 2
                                                                       Yes/No

    Specify_____

29. Total number living at home_____

30. Number of people per room_____   1   2 3   4
                                                Over 1/1/½—1/under ½

31. Have you ever been homeless?   1 2
                                    Yes/No

    If so, give reason._____

C. *HEALTH*

32. Is mother's health good?   1   2   3   4
                                Good/fair/poor/very poor ·

    Give details, if not good_____

33. If not good, do you find this affects your ability to cope with the home or children?
                                                        1   2   3
                                                        Yes, considerably/only a little/No

34. Is father's health good?   1   2   3   4
                                Good/fair/poor/v. poor

    Give details if not good _____

35. (a)   Is child's health generally good?   1   2   3   4
                                                Good/fair/poor/v. poor

    Give details if not good _____

    (b)   Has child had any long periods of absence from school through illness?   1 2
                                                                                     Yes/No

    If yes, give details _____

    _____

    _____

461

D. EDUCATION

Father   Mother

36. Type of Sec. School:
    1. Grammar
    2. Sec. Mod.
    3. Comp.
    4. Tech.
    5. All-age
    6. Special
    7. Other

37. Age of leaving   Father_____

                    Mother_____

38. Was this min. leaving age?   Father Yes/No (1 2)

                                  Mother Yes/No (1 2)

39. If not, how long after?   Father: less than yr./1—2yrs/over 2yrs (1 2 3)
                                 Mother: less than yr./1—2yrs/over 2yrs (1 2 3)

40. Did you enjoy school yourself?   Mother: Mostly/partly/No (1 2 3)
                                   Father: Mostly/partly/No (1 2 3)

41. Did you have any education or training after leaving school?   Father: Yes/No (1 2)
                                                     Mother: Yes/No (1 2)

    Give details: Father_____

                      Mother_____

E. WORK

42. Father's work: Occupation_____

                          _____

43. Other wage-earners: Mother's occupation_____

44. Are there any other wage-earners? Yes/No (1 2)

    Details_____

| | | 1 | 2 | 3 | 4 |
| 45. | Does father work shifts? | Yes/sometimes/No/not employed. |

45. Does father work shifts?   1   2   3   4   Yes/sometimes/No/not employed.

46. Does father work overtime?   1   2   3   4   Yes/sometimes/No/not employed.

47. Is breadwinner unemployed?   1   2   Yes/No

48. If yes, for how long?   1   2   3   4   5   less than mo./1—3 mo./3—6 mo./6 mo.—1 yr./over 1 yr.

49. Has breadwinner been unemployed during last year?   1   2   Yes/No

50. If yes, for how long?   1   2   3   4   5   less than mo./1—3 mo./3—6 mo./6 mo.—1 yr./over 1 yr.

F.   INCOME

51. Father's take-home wage_____ / DK/refusal.

52. Any other income_____

_____

53. Do you find that you
       1. manage quite comfortably
       2. just manage
       3. find it very difficult to manage

54. Has income changed considerably during last year?   Yes/No

55. If yes, give details _____

56. If mother works:
     (a)   Is she here when child leaves school?   1   2   3   Yes/No/not working

     (b)   If not what does child do?   1   2   3   goes to relative/goes to friend/other

G.   CHILD

57. Does child like looking at books?   1   2   3   4   often/occ./never/has none

58. (a)   How many books does he have?   1   2   3   over 5/1—5/none

     (b)   If yes, does he have   (a)   annuals or comic books?   1   2   3   over 3/1—3/none

                              (b)   story/picture books?   1   2   3   over 3/1—3/none

$$\begin{array}{ccc} & 1 & 2 & 3 \end{array}$$

(c)   drawing/colouring books?   over 3/1—3/none

$$\begin{array}{ccc} 1 & 2 & 3 \end{array}$$

(d)   school reading scheme books? over 3/1—3/none

$$\begin{array}{cc} 1 & 2 \end{array}$$

(e)   reference books? Yes/No

$$\begin{array}{cc} 1 & \qquad 2 \end{array}$$

59. Are these books his own?   Yes (some)/No, shared

60. Does child bring school reading books home at all?_____

61. Does child have library books?_____

$$\begin{array}{ccc} 1 & 2 & 3 \end{array}$$

62. Does child have comics?   reg./occ./not at all

$$\begin{array}{cc} 1 & 2 \end{array}$$

63. (a)   Does child like listening to stories at home?   Yes/No

$$\begin{array}{ccc} 1 & 2 & 3 \end{array}$$

    (b)   If yes, do you *read* to child yourself?   Mother/Parent/Other

        Specify_____

$$\begin{array}{ccc} 1 & 2 & 3 \end{array}$$

    (c)   If yes, do you *tell* child stories yourself?   Mother/Parent/Other

        Specify_____

$$\begin{array}{ccc} 1 & 2 & 3 \end{array}$$

64. How often have you read to N, say during last week?   3+/1 or 2/none

$$\begin{array}{cc} 1 & 2 \end{array}$$

65. If 'No' to 63(a) did you read to N or tell him stories when he was younger?   Yes/No

66. What are child's favourite toys or games?_____

_____

67. Does he ever play with

$$\begin{array}{ccc} 1 & 2 & 3 \end{array}$$

    (a)   building/constructional toys   often/occ./has none

$$\begin{array}{ccc} 1 & 2 & 3 \end{array}$$

    (b)   jig/saw puzzles   often/occ./has none

$$\begin{array}{ccc} 1 & 2 & 3 \end{array}$$

    (c)   dolls, soft toys   often/occ./has none

$$\begin{array}{ccc} 1 & 2 & 3 \end{array}$$

    (d)   cars, trains, etc.   often/occ./has none

$$\begin{array}{ccc} 1 & 2 & 3 \end{array}$$

    (e)   pencil and paper   often/occ./has none

                                          1   2   3
(f)   paints   often/occ./has none

                                                1   2   3
(g)   plasticine or clay   often/occ./has none

                                   1   2   3
(h)   sand   often/occ./has none

                                           1   2   3
(i)   dressing-up outfits   often/occ./has none

                                                              1   2   3
68. (a)   How often does mother join in and play with child?   often/occ./never

                                                              1   2   3
    (b)   How often does father join in and play with child?   often/occ./never

                                                              1   2
69. If child is playing inside, whereabouts is he allowed to play?   allowed anywhere/limited

70. How many living rooms can child use for play?_____

                                                                      1   2   3
71. Does child look after toys/books well or is he inclined to be destructive?   well/average/destructive

72. (a)   Had child mixed with children outside the home before going to school?
                                               1   2   3   4
                              Yes, 3 or more/one or two/no/none to play with

                                                      1   2
    (b)   If yes, were these children of a similar age?   Yes/No

73. How does child get on with other children?
                        1   2   3
            very well/mostly well, occ. quarrels or sometimes shy/shy, afraid, or never mixes

74. Does child ask you a lot of questions?_____

75. Has he ever asked about
                                                      1   2   3
    (a)   every day items (e.g. why can't I go out to play?)   often/occ./never

                                         1   2   3
    (b)   what new words mean   often/occ./never

                                                1   2   3
    (c)   how things work or nat. phenomena   often/occ./never

                                     1   2   3
    (d)   birth, death, God etc.   often/occ./never

76. Suppose child asked you these questions what would you say to him?

    (a)   Why can't we go to the park today?_____

(b)   Why does it get dark at night?_____

(c)   Where do babies come from?_____

$$$$

                                                           1   2   3

77. Do you sit down together for the main meal?   frequently/sometimes/never

                                             1   2   3

78. Do you allow children to talk at meal times?   freely/limited/hardly at all

                            1 2

79. Do you have a T.V. set?   Yes/No

                          1   2   3   4

80. Does child watch?   regularly/occ./never/no T.V.

81. Favourite programmes_____

82. Are there any programmes you encourage child to watch?_____

_____

83. Are there any programmes you do not allow child to watch?_____

_____

84. Does child listen to radio or records?_____

85. If yes, does he hear

(i)   music only

(ii)   some stories etc.

                                    1   2   3   4

86. What time does child normally go to bed?   6–6.30/6.31–8/8.01–9.30/9.31+

                        1   2   3

87. Does he sleep well?   very well/quite well usually/not very well

If not well give details:_____

H.   *OUTINGS*

88. Do you have your own transport?

                   1   2   3   4

    Yes, can use anytime/Yes, but father uses it for work/occ. borrowing or lifts/none

89. How far away is the nearest bus route?_____

90. How frequent is bus service?_____

91. How often during the last month has the child been:

                                         1   2   3
(a)   to local shops   3 or more times/1—3/none

                                      1   2   3
(b)   to nearest town   3 or more times/1—3/none

                                            1   2   3
(c)   visiting friends or relatives   3 or more times/1—3/none

                                1   2   3
(d)   out for a walk   3 or more times/1—3/none

                                  1   2   3
(e)   to park or playground   3 or more times/1—3/none

                                      1   2   3
(f)   to Sunday School or Church   3 or more times/1—3/none

92. Has child been to:

                          1   2   3
(a)   seaside   more than once/once/never

                          1   2   3
(b)   cinema   more than once/once/never

                          1   2   3
(c)   theatre   more than once/once/never

                          1   2   3
(d)   library   more than once/once/never

                      1   2   3
(e)   zoo   more than once/once/never

                      1   2   3
(f)   circus   more than once/once/never

                          1   2   3
(g)   swimming bath   more than once/once/never

                      1   2   3
(h)   fairground   more than once/once/never

93. Does child have any particular interest of his own or join in with parents? e.g. music, riding,

fishing etc._____

94. (If applicable) Does child join in any farm work or similar at home? _____

_____

95. Does child have any pets *of his own*? (i.e. that he helps to look after)

I. SCHOOL

96. Had child been to Nursery School, or similar, before infants' school?   1   2   Yes/No

97. Was child looking forward to school?   Definitely/mixed feelings/apprehensive

98. What do you think was the reason for this?_____

_____

99. Before entry, had you been to the school?   1   2   3   Parent and child/parent only/neither

100. Before entry, had you met child's class teacher?   1   2   3   4   Parent and child/parent only/neither/new teacher

101. When did child start school?_____

102. How old was child when he first started school?_____

103. If before 5, do you feel child has benefited from starting earlier than at 5 yrs. of age?_____

_____

104. Did either parent attend the same school?_____

105. Is child taken to school (all or part way) by parent/sibling/other/no?

106. Is child brought home from school?_____

107. How does child travel to/from school?_____

108. How long does the journey take?_____

109. Do you feel happy about the transport arrangements for the child's journey to and from school?

Comments_____

_____

110. Since child started school has either parent spoken to

(a)   headteacher_____

(b)   class teacher_____

111. Was this contact (a)   at open-day, concert etc.

(b)   for private discussion

112. If yes, have you discussed

    (a)   child's progress in school work

    (b)   any other problems

113. If yes to 112(b), was this

    (a)   at your own suggestion

    (b)   at teacher's suggestion

114. Does child bring home any work done in school?_____

_____

115. Do you ever help child with school work at all?

    (a)   listening to child read

    (b)   helping with writing

    (c)   helping with sums

116. (a)   Do you feel that child has settled in well at school now?_____

    (b)   Did child take a long while to settle?_____

117. Do you feel happy about the schooling and the progress your child is making?_____

_____

J.   *OBSERVATIONS*

                          1   2   3   4

1.   Who answered questions?   Mother/Father/M and F/other

                          1   2

2.   Were any children present?   Yes/No

                           1   2   3   4

3.   Appearance of interviewee(s):   Clean/average/slightly grubby/dirty

                                1   2   3   4

                                Well dressed/average/slightly shabby/very shabby

                                1   2   3   4   5

4.   Appearance of other children: Clean/average/slightly grubby/dirty/not seen

                                1   2   3   4   5

                                Well dressed/average/slightly shabby/very shabby/not seen

                             1   2   3   4

5.   Co-operation of interviewee(s):   Co-op. and interested/willing, little interest/apathetic/hostile

6.   Speech of interviewee(s):

    Comment_____

7. State of home and district_____

   _____

| | 1 | 2 | 3 | 4 |
8. Interior decoration: good state, tasteful/adequate/patches need redec./whole needs redec. badly

| | 1 | 2 | 3 | 4 |
9. Furniture: good quality, good repair/adequate and fair repair/adequate, shabby/v. poor condition
                                                                              or noticeably lacking

| | 1 | 2 | 3 | 4 |
10. Cleanliness: v. clean and tidy/only dirt or clutter 'of the day'/needs a thorough clean/permanent dirt
                                                                              beyond cleaning

11. Any toys or books seen:_____

12. Interviewer's estimate of financial situation:

    1. manage quite comfortably
    2. just manage
    3. find it difficult to manage

13. Classification of answers to child's questions:

    1. truthful answers, adequate to child's age
    2. sometimes avoids answering, or answers not appropriate
    3. sometimes untruthful

14. Time taken_____

15. Comments_____

    _____

    _____

RATINGS

Home Interview Rural Areas

Name_____   School_____

1. *Income*

   1. Family income exceeds M.S.S. rate by more than 40%
   2. Family income exceeds M.S.S. rate by 20–40%
   3. Family income exceeds M.S.S. rate by less than 20%
   4. Family income less than or equal to current M.S.S. rate

470

2. *Cleanliness*
Total score for questions J3, 8, 10_____

    1. Total score 4–6
    2. Total score 7–9
    3. Total score 10–12
    4. Total score 13–16

3. *Housing*

    1. Less than 1 person per room and no amenities lacking
    2. Exactly 1 person per room and not more than 1 amenity lacking
    3. Either more than 1 p.p.r. or 2 or more amenities lacking
    4. More than 1 p.p.r. and 2 or more amenities lacking, or over 2 p.p.r.

4. *Playspace Inside*

    1. 2 or more playrooms, less than 4 children
    2. 2 or more playrooms, and 4 or more children
    3. Only 1 playroom, less than 4 children
    4. Only 1 playroom, less than 4 or more children

Outside

    1. Large safe space with swing, trees or similar
    2. Reasonably-sized safe space
    3. Very small space or needing close supervision
    4. No safe space available

Total score_____

Ratings

    1. Total score 2 or 3
    2. Total score 4 or 5
    3. Total score 6 or 7
    4. Total score 8

5. *Mother's Health and Stability*
Physical health

    1. No ailment or handicap
    2. Minor ailment or handicap not apparently affecting child
    3. Minor ailment or handicap affecting child only a little
    4. Severe ailment or handicap affecting child considerably

Stability

    1. Happy, stable personality
    2. Some signs of tension or depression
    3. Definitely unstable mental state

Activity

1. Lively, active
2. A little lethargic
3. Considerably lethargic

Total score_____

    Ratings

      1. Total score 3, 4
      2. Total score 5, 6
      3. Total score 7, 8
      4. Total score 9, 10

6.   *Mother's Education*

    1. Any further education beyond O-level
    2. O-level qualifications
    3. Any education above min. age or attended Grammar school
    4. Sec. Mod or all-age school, min. leaving age

7.   *Social Class*

    1. Social class I, II or III w.c.
    2. Social class, III man.
    3. Social class IV
    4. Social class V

8.   *Play material and books*

    Books   Total score for questions 57–59 and 62_____

    Ratings

      1. Score 9, 10
      2. Score 11–13
      3. Score 14–16
      4. Score 17+

    Comics   Rating_____

    Toys   from question 67

    Ratings

      1. All 9 items available
      2. 7 or 8 items available
      3. 5 or 6 items available
      4. Less than 5 items available

Total score for books, comics, toys_____

Ratings

1. Total score 3 or 4
2. Total score 5, 6
3. Total score 7, 8
4. Total score 9—11

9. *External Stimuli*

T.V.

1. Constructive, selective use
2. Non-selective watching
3. Won't settle to watch much — rather play out
4. Does not see T.V.

Outings

1. Scores less than 19 for Questions 91, 92
2. Scores 19—23 for Questions 91, 92
3. Scores 24—28 for Questions 91, 92
4. Scores 29+ for Questions 91, 92

Total Score_____

Ratings

1. Total score 2 or 3
2. Total score 4, 5
3. Total score 6, 7
4. Total score 8

10. *Parents' Interest*

Stories

1. Read to frequently by parent
2. Read to frequently by adult (15+)
3. Read to rarely by adult or only by young sibling
4. Never read to at all

Play

1. Both parents play often
2. One often, one occasionally
3. Only occasionally
4. Never

Questions   As for Qu. J13 or 4 for none asked.

School Contact

1. Parent and child visited, saw head or rec. class teacher
2. Parent and child visited, not spoken to teachers
3. Parent only visited
4. No contact

School Interest

1. Positive answers to Qu. 111(a), 112 and 2 or 115
2. Positive answers to 3 of above
3. Positive answers to 2 of above
4. Positive answers to 1 or 0 of above

Total score_____

   Ratings
   1. Total score 5—8
   2. Total score 9—12
   3. Total score 13—16
   4. Total score 17—20

11. *Isolation*

   Ratings

   1. In urban district
   2. In village, less than 3 miles from U.D.
   3. In village, over 3 miles from U.D. or isolated less than 3 miles from U.D.
   4. Isolated, over 3 miles from U.D.

Total Material Score (Ratings 1—5)_____

Total Cultural Score (Ratings 6—10)_____

Overall total score (Ratings 1—10)_____

SCHOOLS COUNCIL RESEARCH AND DEVELOPMENT PROJECT IN COMPENSATORY EDUCATION

First Home Interview

SECTION I

Leave blank	Data block No.			School and area No.			Child's No.		Sex	Pre-School	Blank		
	1	9	9										
1	2	3	4	5	6	7	8	9	10	11	12	13	14

A.   Christian name_____ Surname_____ Sex_____

  1. Name of child:_____   _____   _____

  2. Address_____ _____

3. School child attends_____

4. Ordinal position of child_____ 15, 16

5. No. of children in family_____ 17, 18

                          1   2   3   4   5

6. Is he: your own child/adopted/foster/grandchild/other   19

                                                       1   2   3   4

7. Is child's father alive and living with you?   Yes/dead/divorced/separated/   20
                                                                            5
                                                                      other

8. Nationality of   1   2   3
    mother: British/Other, Eng. speaking/Other, non-Eng. speaking   21

9. Nationality of   1   2   3
    father: British/Other, Eng. speaking/Other, non-Eng. speaking   22

10. If not   1   2
    English: Normal tongue of mother_____ Always/mixed with Eng.   23

11. If not   1   2
    English: Normal tongue of father_____ Always/mixed with Eng.   24

12. If child not with own   1   2   3   4
    parents, is child: British/other white/other coloured/DK _____ 25

B.   *HOME*

13. Type of house: 1. detached house   7. s. cont. flat in house
                      2. bungalow   8. cottage
                      3. semi-detached house   9. hut
                      4. terrace   10. rooms
                      5. pre-fab   11. caravan
                      6. s. cont. flat in block   12. other   26, 27

14. Tenure: 1. owner-occupier
                2. rented from Council
                3. rented unfurnished
                4. rented furnished
                5. other_____   28

15. No. of rooms_____ 29, 30

                                    1   2   3   4

16. State of repair of home: good/fair/poor/bad   31

17. Do you have: separate kitchen
$$1 \quad 2 \quad 3$$
own/shared/none

18. bathroom
$$1 \quad 2 \quad 3$$
own/shared/none

19. WC inside
$$1 \quad 2 \quad 3$$
own/shared/none

20. WC outside
$$1 \quad 2 \quad 3$$
own/shared/none

21. hot water tap
$$1 \quad 2 \quad 3$$
own/shared/none

22. Mains gas
$$1 \quad 2$$
Yes/No

23. Mains electricity
$$1 \quad 2$$
Yes/No

24. Is there a yard or garden for play?
$$1 \quad 2$$
Yes/No

25. Is it safe?
$$1 \qquad 2 \qquad 3$$
Yes/Yes, if supervised/No

26. Does child have his own bedroom?
$$1 \quad 2$$
Yes/No

27. Does child have his own bed?
$$1 \quad 2$$
Yes/No

28. Does anyone else besides mother, father and children live here?
$$1 \quad 2$$
Yes/No

Specify_____

_____

_____

29. Total number living at home_____

30. Number of people per room_____
$$1 \quad 2 \quad 3 \qquad 4$$
Over 1/1/½—1/under ½

31. Have you ever been homeless?
$$1 \quad 2$$
Yes/No

If so, give reason _____

C. HEALTH

           1   2   3   4

32. Is mother's health good?   Good/fair/poor/v. poor   48

      Give details, if not good_____

33. If not good, do you find this affects your ability to cope with the home or
      children?   1   2 3   49
                       Yes, considerably/only a little/No

              1   2   3   4

34. Is father's health good?   Good/fair/poor/v. poor   50

      Give details, if not good _____

              1   2   3   4

35. Is child's health good?   Good/fair/poor/v. poor   51

      Give details, if not good _____

SECTION 2

Leave blank	Data block No.			School and area No.			Child's No.		Sex	Pre-School	Blank		
	1	9	8										
1	2	3	4	5	6	7	8	9	10	11	12	13	14

D. EDUCATION

                                Father   *Mother*   Col.
                                                    Nos.

36. Type of Sec. School: 1. Grammar   Father   15
                            2. Sec. Mod.   Mother   16
                            3. Comp.
                            4. Tech.
                            5. All-age
                            6. Special
                            7. Other

37. Age of leaving   Father_____   Father   17, 18

                      Mother_____   Mother   19, 20

                           1   2

38. Was this min. leaving age? Father   Yes/No   21
                              1   2
                    Mother   Yes/No   22

39. If not, how long after? Father: $\begin{matrix}1 & 2 & 3\end{matrix}$ less than yr./1—2 yrs/over 2 yrs

Mother: $\begin{matrix}1 & 2 & 3\end{matrix}$ less than yr./1—2 yrs/over 2 yrs

40. Did you enjoy school up to 11? Father $\begin{matrix}1 & 2\end{matrix}$ Yes/No

Mother $\begin{matrix}1 & 2\end{matrix}$ Yes/No

41. Did you enjoy school after 11? Father $\begin{matrix}1 & 2\end{matrix}$ Yes/No

Mother $\begin{matrix}1 & 2\end{matrix}$ Yes/No

42. Did you have any education after leaving school? Father $\begin{matrix}1 & 2\end{matrix}$ Yes/No

Mother $\begin{matrix}1 & 2\end{matrix}$ Yes/No

Give details: Father_____

Mother_____

E. WORK

43. Father's work: Occupation_____

_____

Social Class_____

44. Other wage-earners: Mother's occ.
Social Class

45. Are there any other wage-earners? $\begin{matrix}1 & 2\end{matrix}$ Yes/No

Details_____

_____

46. Does father work shifts? $\begin{matrix}1 & 2 & 3 & 4\end{matrix}$ Yes/sometimes/No/not employed

47. Does father work overtime? $\begin{matrix}1 & 2 & 3 & 4\end{matrix}$ Yes/sometimes/No/not employed

48. Is breadwinner unemployed? $\begin{matrix}1 & 2\end{matrix}$ Yes/No

Col Nos.

23
24
25
26
27
28
29
30

31
32
33
34
35
36

478

					Col. Nos.

49. If yes, for how long?
　　　　　　　　1　　　2　　　3　　　4　　　5
　　　　less than mo./1—3 mo./3—6 mo./6 mo.—1 yr./over 1 yr.　　　37

　　　　　　　　　　　　　　　　　　　　　1　2
50. Has breadwinner been unemployed during last year?　Yes/No　　　38

51. If yes, for how long?
　　　　　　　　1　　　2　　　3　　　4　　　5
　　　　less than mo./1—3 mo./3—6 mo./6 mo.—1 yr./over 1 yr.　　　39

F.　INCOME

52. Father's take-home wage_____/DK/refusal

53. If 52 not answered, Mother's housekeeping allowance_____ /DK/refusal

54. Family allowance_____

55. Any other regular income_____

　　　　　　　　　Total_____

Coding　1. M.S.S. rate or less
　　　　2. M.S.S. rate + less than 20%
　　　　3. M.S.S. rate + 20—40%
　　　　4. M.S.S. rate + over 40%
　　　　5. No figures given　　　　　　　　　　　　　　　　40

　　　　　　　　　　　　　　　　　　　　1　2
56. Has income changed considerably over last year?　Yes/No　　41

57. If yes, code previous income as for Qu. 55 _____　42

　　　　_____

58. If mother works:
　　　　　　　　　　　　　　　　1　2　　　3
　　(a) Is she here when child leaves school?　Yes/No/not working　　43

　　　　　　　　　　　　　　　1　　　　2　　　　3
　　(b) If not, what does child do?　Goes to relative/goes to friend/other　　44

SECTION 3

Leave blank	Data block No.			School and area No.			Child's No.		Sex	Pre-School	Blank		
	1	9	7										
1	2	3	4	5	6	7	8	9	10	11	12	13	14

G.   CHILD

               1   2   3
59. Does child have comics?   Yes, new/Yes, passed on/No   15

           1   2   3   4
60. How often?   Weekly/monthly/rarely/has none   16

                    1   2   3
61. Does child have books to look at?   Yes, many/a few/none   17

              1   2
62. Are they his own?   Yes/No, shared   18

                       1   2   3   4
63. Does he like looking at books?   Often/occasionally/never/has none   19

                    1   2   3   4
64. Does child play with pencil and paper?   Often/occasionally/never/has none   20

                 1   2   3   4
65. Does child play with paints?   Often/occasionally/never/has none   21

                          1 2
66. Does mother ever read to him or tell him stories?   Yes/No   22

                    1   2   3   4
67. If Yes, how many times last week?   Daily/more than one/one/none   23

                     1 2
68. Do others ever read to him or tell stories?   Yes/No   24

              1   2   3   4
69. If Yes, who reads to him?   Father/grandparent/sibling/other   25

                    1   2   3   4
70. If Yes, how many times last week?   6 or 7/3—5/1 or 2/none   26

71. Has child a favourite story?_____

                  1   2   3
72. Is he read to mainly at bedtime?   Anytime/bedtime/never read to   27

                       1   2
73. If the weather is bad, where does child play?   Allowed anywhere/limited   28

74. How many rooms can children use for play?_____   29

75. What are his favourite toys?_____

                  1   2   3
76. Is mother able to play with him?   Often/occasionally/never   30

77. Does father play with him?   ¹ ² ³
    Often/occasionally/never

78. Had child mixed with   Yes, many/yes, selected/No/none to play with
    children before school?

79. How does he get on with other children?
    Very well/mostly well, occ. quarrels/shy, afraid or not allowed to mix

80. Does child ask a lot of questions, of all sorts?   Yes/a few/No

81. Do you find you   Always/sometimes/No/no questions asked
    have time to answer and help?

82. Do you sit down together for the main   Frequently/sometimes/never
    meal?

83. Do you allow children to talk at meal times?   Freely/limited/hardly at all

84. Do you have a T.V. set?   Yes/No

85. Does child watch?   Regularly/occasionally/never/no T.V.

86. Favourite programmes:_____

87. Are there any programmes you encourage child to watch?_____

    _____

88. Are there any programmes you do not allow child to watch?_____

    _____

89. Does child listen to radio?   Regularly/occasionally/never/no radio

90. Favourite programmes_____

91. What time does child normally go   6—6.30/6.31—8/8.01—9.30/9.31+
    to bed?

92. Does he sleep well?   Very well/quite well usually/not very well

    If not well, give details_____

481

H.   OUTINGS

93. Do you (or other person) take child:

(a)   shopping
     1   2   3   4
     Frequently/occasionally/never/no facilties available   43

(b)   visiting friend relatives
     1   2   3   4
     Frequently/occasionally/never/no facilities available   44

(c)   park or playground
     1   2   3   4
     Frequently/occasionally/never/no facilities available   45

(d)   beach
     1   2   3   4
     Frequently/occasionally/never/no facilities available   46

(e)   library
     1   2   3   4
     Frequently/occasionally/never/no facilities available   47

(f)   cinema/theatre
     1   2   3
     More than once/once/never   48

(g)   zoo/circus
     1   2   3
     More than once/once/never   49

(h)   swimming pool
     1   2   3
     More than once/once/never   50

94. Is there any outing above, or any other, child particularly enjoys?   51   52

Specify_____

95. Do you have any particular interests or hobbies which child is involved in?
                                                          1   2
                                                         Yes/No   53

Specify_____

I.   SCHOOL

                                                          1   2
96. Had child been to Nursery School, or similar, before infants' school?   Yes/No   54

97. Was child looking forward to school?
          1   2   3
     Definitely/mixed feelings/apprehensive

98. What do you think was the reason for this?_____

_____

99. Before entry, had you been to the school?
          1   2   3
     Parent and child/parent only/neither   56

482

100. Before entry, had you met child's   Parent and child/parent only/neither
      class teacher?

                              1   2   3   57

101. When did child start school?_____

                       1   2   3   4

102. How has child settled   V. well/fairly well/not v. happy/v. unhappy   58
      in school?

                      1   2   3   4

103. Has child been absent   Not at all/up to 5 days/1–2 weeks/over 2 weeks   59
      much?

      Give reason_____

                            1   2

104. Does anyone fetch child home from school?   Yes/No   60

105. Does child come straight home from school?
             1   2   3
            Yes/plays on way home (less than ½ hour)/plays away for longer time   61

J.   OBSERVATIONS

                    1   2   3   4

106. Who answered questions?   Mother/Father/M and F/other   62

                 1   2

107. Were any children present?   Yes/No   63

                       1   2   3   4

108. Appearance of interviewee(s):   Clean/average/slightly grubby/dirty   64
                    1   2   3   4
                Well dressed/average/slightly shabby/very shabby   65

                    1   2   3   4   5

109. Appearance of other children: Clean/average/sl. grubby/dirty/not seen   66
                   1   2   3   4   5
                Well dressed/average/sl. shabby/v. shabby/not seen   67

110. Co-operation of interviewee(s):
                  1   2   3   4
             Co-op. and interested/willing, little interest/apathetic/hostile   68

111. Speech of interviewee(s)

      Comment:_____

112. State of home and district_____

113. Interior decoration:

        1   2   3   4

Good state, tasteful/adequate/patches need redec./whole needs redec. badly

114. Furniture:

        1   2   3

Good quality, good repair/adequate and fair repair/adequate, shabby/

        4

v. poor condition or noticeably lacking

115. Cleanliness:

        1   2   3

V. clean and tidy/only dirt or clutter 'of the day'/needs a thorough clean/

        4

permanent dirt beyond cleaning

116. Any toys or books seen?_____

117. Time taken _____

118. Comments:_____

_____

_____

		Col. Nos.
		69
		70
		71

SECTION IV

Leave Blank	Data block No.			School and Area No.			Child's No.		Sex	Pre-School	Blank		
	1	9	6										
1	2	3	4	5	6	7	8	9	10	11	12	13	14

RATING SHEET
MATERIAL

1. *Income*   4. Family income less than or equal to current M.S.S. rate (ignoring rent allowance)
                3. Family income exceeds M.S.S. rate by less than 20%
                2. Family income exceeds M.S.S. rate between 20—40%
                1. Family income exceeds M.S.S. rate more than 40%

2. *Cleanliness*   Total score for Qu. 98(a) (b), 103, 105 _____

                        Rating on 4-pt scale

	Col. Nos.
	15
	16

3. *Housing*   No. of amenities lacking_____

        4. More than 1 person per room and 2 or more amenities
           lacking (? gross overcrowding or lack of amenities)
        3. Either more than 1 person per room or 2 or more amenities
           lacking
        2. Exactly 1 person per room, and not more than 1 amenity
           lacking
        1. Less than 1 person per room and no amenities lacking

                                                                17

4. *Playspace*
  Inside   4. Only 1 playroom, 4 or more children
        3. Only 1 playroom, less than 4 children
        2. 2 or more playrooms (or 1 very large) and 4 or more children
        1. 2 or more playrooms, less than 4 children

  Outside 4. No safe space available
        3. V. small space, or needing close supervision
        2. Reasonably-sized, safe space
        1. Large safe space with swing, trees or similar

                        Total score_____

                   Rating on 4-pt scale_____   18

5. *Mother's Health and Child Care*

  Health   4. Severe ailment or handicap, affecting child care considerably
        3. Minor ailment or handicap, affecting child care only a little
        2. Minor ailment or handicap, not apparently affecting child
        1. No ailment or handicap

  Care   4. Child plays anywhere, mother does not mind
        3. Child stays out, mother knows where usually
        2. Child plays for short time on way home
        1. Child is fetched from school, or comes straight home

                        Total Score_____

                   Rating on 4-pt scale_____   19

                   Total material score_____   20, 21

CULTURAL
6. *Mother's Education*

        1. Any further education beyond O-level
        2. O-level qualifications
        3. Any education above min. age or attended Grammar School   22
        4. Sec. Mod. or all-age school, minimum leaving age

7. *Social Class*

       4. Social class V
       3. Social class IV
       2. Social class III man.
       1. Social class I, II, or III w.c.

8. *Availability and suitability of play material/books*

Comics
4. Never sees comics
3. Only has comics rarely
2. Has shared or handed on comics regularly
1. Has own comics regularly

Books
4. Has no books
3. Has few books, looks rarely
2. Has shared books, uses often
1. Has own books, uses often

Pencil and Paper
4. Has none
3. Has them, never uses
2. Uses occasionally
1. Uses often

Paints   as above: 1. 2. 3. 4.

Other toys
4. Poor, toys broken, nothing 'constructive'
3. Not much provided, not 'imaginative'
2. Plenty of toys, not very 'imaginative'
1. Good provision, good condition, and some 'constructive' toys

Total_____

Rating on 4-pt scale _____

9. *External Stimuli*

T.V.
1. Constructive, selective use
2. Non-selective watching
3. Won't settle to watch much—rather play out
4. Does not see T.V.

Outings
1. Scores less than 12
2. Scores 12–14
3. Scores 15–17
4. Scores over 17

Total_____

Rating on 4-pt scale_____

Col. Nos.

23

24

25

486

10. *Parents' Interest*

Stories	1. Read to frequently by parent
	2. Read to frequently by adult or 15+ sibling
	3. Read to rarely by adult or only by young sibling
	4. Never read to at all

Play	1. Both parents play often
	2. One often, one occ.
	3. Only occasionally
	4. Never

Questions	1. Many, answered 'sensibly'
	2. Few asked, or some avoided
	3. Usually avoided
	4. None asked or answered

School Contact	1. Parent and child visited, seen head or rec. class teacher
	2. Parent and child visited, not spoken to teachers
	3. Parent only visited
	4. No contact

Comments	1. Helpful, constructive attitude
	2. Tries to help, doesn't really know how
	3. Not much interest
	4. Hostile to school

Col. Nos.

Total_____

Rating on 4-pt scale_____ 26
Total Cultural _____ 27, 28

Total overall score_____ 29, 30

Notes on Coding of Questionnaires

First Home Interview

Question 31. 'Homeless' was interpreted as meaning either that the family have been in Local Authority Accommodation for homeless families, or that the family has been split up because of a lack of accommodation.

Observation 110. The 'co-operative and interested' category was used when the parent interviewed showed some interest in the nature and purpose of the research.

Ratings

1. *Income:*   If no figure was given for income an estimate was made on the basis of the father's occupation (and hence likely wage) and any other information available. If a figure was given, the M.S.S. allowance for the family was computed and compared with the income stated. In many cases this was an approximation, since rents were not always known exactly nor the ages of the dependent children. The income of non-dependent children or lodgers was not included.

2. *Cleanliness:*   Total score of   4—6   rated 1
    Total score of   7—9   rated 2
    Total score of   10—12   rated 3
    Total score of   13—16   rated 4

3. *Housing:*   No amenities were considered lacking if the family had their own separate kitchen (however small), their own inside toilet, bathroom, hot water from a tap and electricity. 'Gross overcrowding' described families living with over 2 persons per room.

4. *Playspace:*   'Playrooms' did not include bedrooms, but included sitting rooms or any rooms with no other purpose.

    Total score of   2—3   rated 1
    Total score of   4—5   rated 2
    Total score of   6—7   rated 3
    Total score of   8   rated 4

5. *Mother's Health and Child Care:*   Ratings of 'stability' and 'activity' were made on the basis of the interviewer's judgement.

    Total score of   3—4   rated 1
    Total score of   5—6   rated 2
    Total score of   7—8   rated 3
    Total score of   9—10   rated 4

6. *Mother's Education:*   School Certificate or Matriculation were taken to be the equivalent of O-level qualifications.

7. *Social Class:*   This was based on the father's present occupation in most cases. If the father had been unemployed for over 3 months the rating was one point lower than his last or usual job. If the father was not present in the family the rating was based on the mother's occupation if she worked, or was otherwise given the lowest rating.

8. *Availability and suitability of play materials and books*

    Total score of   5—8   rated 1
    Total score of   9—12   rated 2
    Total score of   13—16   rated 3
    Total score of   17—20   rated 4

9. *External Stimuli:*   The rating of 'constructive, selective use' was given if *any* form of selection was mentioned in answer to questions 87, 88. The 'score' for outings refers to the total of the scores for question 93.

    Total score of   2, 3   rated 1
    Total score of   4, 5   rated 2
    Total score of   6, 7   rated 3
    Total score of   8   rated 4

10. *Parents' Interest:*

Total score of	5—8	rated 1
Total score of	9—12	rated 2
Total score of	13—16	rated 3
Total score of	17—20	rated 4

SCHOOLS COUNCIL RESEARCH AND DEVELOPMENT PROJECT IN COMPENSATORY EDUCATION

Use of Services — Links with School

Leave Blank	Data Block No.			School and Area No.			Child's No.		Sex	Pre-School	Blank		
	1	9	5										
1	2	3	4	5	6	7	8	9	10	11	12	13	14

Name of child_____

Address_____

School attended _____

As you remember, one of the aims of our research was to suggest improvements in the facilities available both in and out of school for young children and their parents. I would like to ask you about the facilities which are available in your area, what use you have made of them, and what other services you would like to see provided.

Section A — Child's Physical Health

As I expect you know there are certain services concerned with the health of young children.

1. Do you know whether N has had a medical examination at school?   Yes/No/DK

2. *If Yes*, were you able to attend?   Yes/No/NA

3. Has any medical treatment been provided for N through the school e.g., dental treatment, glasses etc.?   Yes/No

   If Yes, specify_____

   If No, have any other children received treatment?   Yes/No/NA

   If No to both, did you know that treatment of this kind could be provided by the school health services?   Yes/No/NA

489

4.   Has N had any sort of speech difficulty which has worried you?   Yes/No

   Specify _____

   If Yes, have you tried to obtain any treatment?   Yes/No/NA

   Specify _____

   Did someone suggest this to you, or was this your own idea?_____

   _____

   If No, has any other child had any speech difficulty?   Yes/No/NA
   If No, did you know that such treatment was available?   Yes/No/NA
   If Yes, has any treatment been given?   Yes/No/NA

   If Yes, who suggested this?_____

   Comments_____

   _____

   If any service used, did you find the service helpful?_____

   Is there any way you think it could be improved?_____

   _____

Section B — Welfare

1.   Have you had any period of financial difficulty, when you have needed help?   Yes/No

   If Yes,
   (a)   Have you had help from the Min. of Soc. Security?   Yes/No/NA

      Who initiated?_____

   (b)   For how long was help given?_____

   (c)   Have you ever had

      (i)   free meals   Yes, for N/Yes, for other/No
      (ii)   clothing grant   Yes, for N/Yes, for other/No
      (iii) maintenance grant   Yes, for N/Yes, for other/No

      If help received, who initiated?_____

      How often has help been given?_____

   (d)   Have you had help from a voluntary organization such as W.R.V.S.?   Yes/No; For N/for other

      Specify_____

      Who initiated?_____

(e) Has a free holiday ever been arranged?   Yes, for No/ for other/No

Specify_____

Who initiated?_____

(f) Has any help with food or toys at Christmas been given?   Yes, for N/for other/No

Specify_____

Who initiated?_____

(g) Has any other help been given?   Yes/No

Specify_____

Who initiated?_____

If No, do you know what help is available for school children or their parents in cases of

hardship?_____

2. *If any service used*, did you find the service helpful?_____

_____

3. Is there any way you think the service(s) could be improved?_____

_____

Section C − Emotional Difficulties
1. Has there been any period of family crisis or breakdown when you have needed help with looking after the children?   Yes/No

If Yes, specify_____

(a) *If Yes*, what help did you receive at that time?_____

(b) Have you received help from
    (i)   Children's Dept.   Yes, for N/for other/No
    (ii) probation officer   Yes, for N/for other/No
    (iii) other   Yes, for N/for other/No

Who initiated?_____

(c) *If No*, do you know what agencies would be able to provide help in these circumstances?

_____

2. Have you ever been worried about the behaviour or development of any of your children?   Yes/No
    If Yes

    (a)   Was this N or another child?   for N/another child

    (b)   Have you been given any help or advice about this?_____

    _____

          Who initiated?_____

3. Do you know whether there is a child guidance clinic in your area?   Yes/No/DK

4. Do you know in what way a child guidance clinic helps people and how to go about getting this help?

                                     Accurate knowledge/sketchy knowledge/no knowledge

5. *If any service used*, did you find the service helpful?

6. Is there any way you think the service(s) could be improved?

Section D — Children's Amenities
1. Is there a nursery school or class within reasonable walking distance?   Yes/No
    If Yes

    (a)   Did N go?   Yes/No
    (b)   Has any other child been?   Yes/No
    (c)   If not,

          (i)   Is there any particular reason why N did not go?_____
          (ii)   Do you know at what age they take children?   Yes, accurate/Yes, wrong/No
          (iii)   Do you know whether you have to pay?   Yes, accurate/Yes, wrong/No

    If No

    (d)   Is there a playgroup or anything similar?   Yes/No
    (e)   Has N ever been?   Yes/No
    (f)   *If N went to nursery or playgroup*, did he attend regularly once he had started?   Yes/No

          If not, ask reason_____
    (g)   *If no nursery or playgroup available*, would you have liked N to attend if one had been
          available?   Yes/No

    (h)   What benefit do you think this would have been?_____
    (i)   Would the need for payment have made any difference?   Yes/perhaps/No

2. Is there a public library near to you?   Can go on own/if taken/No/DK
    If Yes

    (a)   Does N belong?   Yes/No

    If No

    (b)   Do you know whether N is old enough to belong?   Yes, accurate/Yes, wrong/No
    (c)   Do any other members of the family belong?   Yes/No

    If no library, would you like N to belong if there was one nearer to you?   Yes/No

3. Apart from the services already mentioned, is there anything you would like to see provided in this area which would help young children or their parents?

Section E — Links with School
Now I would like to ask you about N's school.

1. Have you ever felt that you would like to know more about what children do at N's school or how they are taught?   Yes, very keen/mild interest/no interest/already know

2. *If satisfied,*
What do you feel has been the most helpful way of letting parents know about what is going on in

the school?_____

If Not,
What do you think would be the most helpful way of letting parents know about what is going on in

the school?_____

3. Have you felt satisfied with the opportunities you have had for discussing N's progress with his teachers?   Quite satisfied/reservations/unsatisfied

4. How about N's behaviour — have you been able to discuss this with the teachers?
Yes, satisfied/reservations/unsatisfied/no need
If Yes to 3 and 4, did the teachers arrange this or did you ask for the discussion?   Teacher/Parent

5. (a) Do/would you prefer to discuss N's progress and behaviour with the headteacher or class teacher?   Head/Class
   (b) Would you prefer to be able to make a definite appointment?   Yes/No/don't mind
   (c) If yes, would you prefer this during or after school?   During/after
   (d) Would your husband like the chance to see the teachers?   Yes, evening/can go now/No/NA

6. Some parents find it difficult to go to school themselves: how would you feel about N's teacher coming to visit you at home?   Quite happy/reservations/against

7. Would you feel more or less happy about a teacher visiting than you do about someone like myself calling here?   More/same/less

8. Is there a parent-teacher association or parents' association at N's school?   Yes/No
   If Yes

   (a) Do you belong?   Yes/No
   (b) Does N's father belong?   Yes/No/NA
   (c) Do you attend most meetings?   Yes/No
   (d) What benefit do you think this has been to you? _____

   If No

   (e) Have you ever belonged to one at another school?   Yes/No
   (f) Would you like to have one at N's school?   Yes, keen/yes, mild/No
   (g) Would you join yourself?   Yes/No
   (h) Do you think your husband would join?   Yes/No/DK/NA
   (i) What sort of things do you think a P.T.A. or P.A. can do?

9. In a few areas parents have actually helped in the infant school classroom; how would you feel about doing this yourself?   Keen/willing/reservations/unwilling

   In what ways do you think you could help?_____

10. Do you know whether the methods used in N's school are similar to those used when you were at school yourself?   Adequate knowledge/sketchy knowledge/no knowledge

    (a)   in reading
    (b)   in number

11. Is N's school very different from what you remember of your own schooling as far as general organization and discipline goes?_____

    _____

12. Would you have liked the opportunity to learn more about modern teaching methods or do you feel that this is something which should be left to the school?   Yes, keen/yes, mild/No

    _____

    If Yes

    (a)   Suppose that talks or demonstrations had been arranged at N's school, do you think you would have attended these?   Yes/No
    (b)   Would daytime, evening or week-end be the best time?   Day/evening/weekend
    (c)   Do you think your husband would like to attend too?   Yes/No/DK/NA

    If No, perhaps you could tell me why you feel this way?_____

    _____

13. Some schools encourage children to take reading books home so that parents can hear them read.

    (a)   Does N's school do this?   Yes/No
    (b)   Do you think it is/would be a good idea?   Yes/No

14. Some parents feel they would like more advice on the sort of things they could do with their children before they start school. If some instruction was given, say a year before the child started school, would you be/have been interested?   Very interested/mildly interested/not interested

15. Have you ever felt the need for someone who could give you general advice in bringing up children (further than that given by friends and relatives)?   Yes/No

    If Yes, specify_____

16. Did you have any courses in your own secondary school which helped you in the tasks of being a parent?_____

    _____

    If Yes, specify_____

17. Do you think it would have helped you to have been taught more about the needs and development of young children during your last years in the Secondary school?   Yes/No

    If Yes, do you think this should be for both boys and girls?   Girls only/both

18. By the time N is in the secondary school, the leaving age will probably be 16; do you hope that N will

    (a)   stay on at school after this?   Keen/willing/No
    (b)   have any further education after leaving school?   Keen/willing/No

19. In some questions I have asked whether N's father would be interested. In general, would you say that your husband leaves dealing with N's schooling to you or does he take an equally active interest?   Equal interest/husband's interest less/husband has no interest/no father

*Comments*_____

_____

_____

Index